**FIELDBOOK
FOR AUSTRALIAN
SCOUTING**

REVISED EDITION

THE SCOUT ASSOCIATION OF AUSTRALIA
FIELDBOOK FOR AUSTRALIAN SCOUTING

McGRAW-HILL BOOK COMPANY Sydney
New York   San Francisco   Auckland   Bogotá
Caracas   Lisbon   London   Madrid   Mexico City
Milan   New Delhi   San Juan   Singapore
Toronto   Kuala Lumpur

REVISED EDITION

First published 1994

Revised edition 1996

Text © 1994 The Scout Association of Australia
Illustrations and design © 1994 McGraw-Hill Book Company Australia Pty Limited
Additional owners of copyright material are credited on the Acknowledgments page.

Apart from any fair dealing for the purposes of study, research, criticism or review, as permitted under the *Copyright Act*, no part may be reproduced by any process without written permission. Enquiries should be made to the publisher, marked for the attention of the Permissions Editor, at the address below.

Copying for educational purposes
Under the copying provisions of the *Copyright Act*, copies of parts of this book may be made by an educational institution. An agreement exists between the Copyright Agency Limited (CAL) and the relevant educational authority (Department of Education, university, TAFE, etc.) to pay a licence fee for such copying. It is not necessary to keep records of copying except where the relevant educational authority has undertaken to do so by arrangement with the Copyright Agency Limited.

For further information on the CAL licence agreements with educational institutions, contact the Copyright Agency Limited, Level 19, 157 Liverpool Street, Sydney NSW 2000. Where no such agreement exists, the copyright owner is entitled to claim payment in respect of any copies made.

Enquiries concerning copyright in McGraw-Hill publications should be directed to the Permissions Editor at the address below.

National Library of Australia Cataloguing-in-Publication data:

Fieldbook for Australian scouting.

Rev. ed.
ISBN 0 07 470365 X.

1. Boy Scouts—Australia—Handbooks, manuals, etc. 2. Girl Scouts—Australia—Handbooks, manuals, etc. I. Scout Association of Australia.

369.40994

NSC 50199

Produced in Australia by Book Generation Pty Ltd, North Melbourne, Victoria for
McGraw-Hill Book Company Australia Pty Limited
4 Barcoo Street, Roseville NSW 2069, Australia
Typeset in Australia by Bookset Pty Ltd, North Melbourne, Victoria
Printed in Australia by Star Printery Pty Limited, New South Wales

Your fieldbook

You will need to use this book for all your Scouting career. The requirements for the Scout Badges will be found in the *Australian Scoutbook* and the *Scout's Book of Challenges*.

Your Leader will find reference material and resource advisers to help you with further information on the various subjects.

Good luck and good Scouting!

FOREWORD

The *Fieldbook for Australian Scouting* is a guide to preparedness, a resource that will help you develop the necessary skills to be of service to others and to take care of yourself. Two phrases have been linked with Scouting since 1910: *Be prepared* and *Outdoor adventure*.

This fieldbook is based on the initiatives found in the fieldbooks published by the Boy Scouts of America and the Boy Scouts of Canada. Using the fieldbook will help you develop confidence and self-reliance in the great outdoors. Many challenges and unlimited adventures await you in Scouting's exciting program.

The fieldbook has been developed to carry the Scout and Scout Section Leaders into the skills not detailed in the *Australian Scoutbook*, the *Scout's Book of Challenges* and the *Scout Leader's Handbook*. It is hoped that this fieldbook will also become a valuable resource for the Cub Scout, Venturer and Rover Sections.

KIRSTY M. BROWN,
August 1993

ACKNOWLEDGMENTS

The Scout Association of Australia expresses its thanks to Chris Silagy and Paul Thomas (Victorian Branch), Marcus Higgs and Ray Christie (Tasmanian Branch), Lyle Bird and Bryan Brown (Queensland Branch), and Roy Belshaw and Andy Walker (New South Wales Branch), for their contributions and input of specialist material. A special thanks is owing to Kenn Gardner for his writing input and research of material and to Kirsty Brown for her work in the writing, preparation and compilation of this new publication as a result of the 1989 National Scout Section Review.

The following resources were used: *Fieldbook for Canadian Scouting*; *Australian Scout Handbook*, *Help to Save the World* (World Scout Bureau); *The Scout Handbook* (United Kingdom); *Fieldbook for Scouts* (United States); *Veld Lore* (South Africa); *NZ Scout Handbook*; *The Pathfinder Awards* (New Zealand); the PH Projects (World Bureau).

The extract on p. 376 is from Kenneth Grahame, *The Wind in the Willows*, Victor Gollancz, London, 1988.

Photographs for the Air Activities chapter were kindly contributed by the Civil Aviation Authority (CAA), the Federal Airports Corporation, Qantas Airways Limited, the Royal Australian Air Force (RAAF) and Australian Picture Library/Brian Maginnity.

The Scout Association of Australia also wishes to thank the following people and organisations for their help in supplying illustrations and photographs for inclusion in this Fieldbook: Air New Zealand; Artstaff Pty Limited; The Australian Museum, Sydney; Douglass Baglin Pty Limited; British Aircraft Corporation Limited; John Carnemolla; Civil Aviation Authority; Arthur E. Cooper; Department of the Prime Minister and Cabinet, Canberra; Detroit Diesel Allison Division of General Motors Corp., Indianapolis, Indiana, United States; Federal Airports Corporation; Gernsheim Collection, University of Texas; Hawker Siddeley Aviation Ltd, Kingston-on-Thames, United Kingdom; Robert Klippel; Colin Lancely; Modern Boating; NSW Department of Lands; Piper Aircraft Corporation; Reg Preston; Qantas Airways Limited; RAAF Public Relations Department; Rex Aviation Sales (NSW) Pty Ltd, Cessna Aircraft Distributions; United States Embassy, Canberra; Bruce Wakeling; Wormald International (Aust.) Pty Limited.

Finally, The Scout Association of Australia wishes to thank the following Scouting organisations for their help in supplying illustrations and material: Boy Scouts of America; Boy Scouts of Canada; Boy Scouts of South Africa; The Scout Association (New Zealand); The Scout Association (United Kingdom); World Scout Bureau.

Every care has been taken to trace and acknowledge copyright. The publisher apologises for any accidental infringement where copyright has proved untraceable and would be pleased to come to a suitable arrangement with the rightful owner in each case.

CONTENTS

✈ 1 AIR ACTIVITIES *1*

Scouting and air activities *1*
Australian aviation—1910 till when? *2*
The role of the Civil Aviation Authority *6*
Modern airports *8*
Air-traffic control *10*
Meteorology *11*
  Weather *11*
  Clouds *12*
  Forecasting *16*
  Effect on aircraft *19*
Aircraft types and uses *21*
  Light aircraft *22*
  Commercial aircraft *22*
  Military aircraft *24*
Principles of flight *25*
Light-aircraft engines *33*
  Piston engine *34*
Jet engine *35*
  Gas turbine engine *35*
  Prop jet engine *35*
Navigation *35*
Gliding and soaring *39*
Kite flying *43*
Aeromodelling *43*
Radio control *48*
Aeromodelling clubs *48*

↓ 2 BUSHCRAFT *49*

Hiking and journeys *49*
  Planning *50*
  Predicting walking time *50*
  Mini first-aid kit *51*
The Country Code *52*
Care of your feet *53*
  Footwear *53*

  Feet *55*
Clothing *55*
  Shirt *55*
  Trousers *56*
  Hat *56*
  Jumper *56*
  Showerproof jacket *56*
  Waterproofing *56*
  Outdoor clothing *56*
Safety and survival *58*
  Hot, dry desert conditions *58*
  Winter conditions *59*
Navigation *60*
  Scale *60*
  Ground features *61*
  Date of map *63*
  Grid references *63*
  Care of maps *63*
  Compass *64*
Nature's compasses *67*
  Direction from the sun *68*
  Direction by the stars *68*
  Time from the stars *69*
Making a map *69*
  Base point *70*
  Base line *70*
  Double base line *72*
  Plane table *74*
  Traverse *78*
Bushcraft skills *79*
  Weather *79*
  Estimation *79*
  Hygiene *83*
  Tracking and trails *84*
  Lightweight food *91*
  Backwoods cooking *92*
  Hike tents *97*
  Tent poles *98*
  Emergency shelter *99*
  How to make tents *100*

xi

Contents

Fire making *102*
Other methods *104*

3 CAMPCRAFT *105*

What is camping? *105*
Where should you begin? *106*
When should you go camping? *106*
Where should you go camping? *107*
With whom can you camp? *107*
What gear will you require? *108*
Patrol camping gear *108*
  Equipment for a standing camp *109*
  Equipment for bike camping *109*
  Equipment for water camping *110*
  Equipment for hiking camps *110*
Tents *114*
  Selecting a tent *115*
  Transporting *117*
  In camp *117*
  Storing *118*
  Maintaining *118*
  Pitching a tent *118*
Cooking gear *119*
  Plastic *119*
  Cooking tools *120*
  Patrol box *120*
Camp ovens *121*
  Drum oven *121*
  Reflector oven *121*
  Dixie oven *121*
  Hay box *121*
  Dutch oven *123*
  Cooking on charcoal fires *125*
Hot water *125*
Camp gadgets *126*
  Camp loom *128*
Fires and fuel *130*
  Commonsense routine *131*
  How to build and light a fire *132*

Fireplaces *132*
Firewood *133*
Fire lighting *134*
Stoves and lanterns *134*
Fuels *135*
Camp tools *136*
  Rake *136*
  Post-hole borer *136*
  Digger *136*
  Saws *137*
  Hand axes *138*
  Knives *142*
Camp cleanliness *143*
  Waste disposal *143*
  Personal cleanliness *146*
Sleeping gear *147*
  Sleeping bags *147*
Personal gear *151*
Food storage *153*
Cooking *154*
  How to begin before you start *155*
  Menu *155*
  Have a cooking plan *156*
  Cooking timetable *156*
  Food allowances: rationing and packaging *157*
  Meals *160*
Cooking methods *161*
  Cooking with a Dutch oven *162*
  Recipes to try *163*
  Novel cooking ideas *164*
  Dutch oven camp recipes *164*
Water *167*
Insects *169*
Your campsite *169*
Look and listen *171*
Camp adventures *172*
Campfires *173*
Breaking camp *174*

4 CITIZENSHIP *175*

Aim of the Association *175*
Scouting *176*
Australian heritage *176*
  United Nations *176*
  Commonwealth of Nations *177*

Contents

Parliament *177*
  Federal Parliament *177*
  Judicial system *177*
  State Parliament *178*
  Local government *178*
You as a citizen *178*
  Your future *179*
Religion in your life *181*
The Australian flag *181*
Australian national anthem *183*
Aborigines *184*
Good turns and service to others *184*
  What type of service? *185*
Preparing a talk *188*
Take part in meetings *189*
  Patrol Programs *189*
  Self-discipline *189*
Fitness *191*
  What is fitness? *191*
  Your health *191*
  Your body *192*
Substance abuse *193*
Scouts against smoking *195*
The body—how it works *196*
  The value of exercise *199*
  Components of fitness *199*
  Training *201*
Living in a community *201*

5 CONSTRUCTION *203*

Construction through the ages *203*
How strong are materials? *206*
  Tension members *207*
  Compression members *208*
  Beams *209*
  Concrete and bricks *209*
  Bricklaying made easy *210*
Joining materials *211*
  Permanent and temporary joints *211*
Rope *212*
  What is rope? *212*
  How is rope made? *212*
  Rope making *213*
  Rope-making machine *213*
  How is rope measured? *214*
  Care of rope *215*
  Coiling rope *215*
Knotting *216*
  Terms *216*
  Bends *218*
  Knots *222*
  Hitches *231*
  Whippings *237*
  Splices *239*
Lashings *242*
  Standard lashings *242*
  Instant lashings *247*
Anchorages *250*
Tackle *252*
Trimming a tree *254*
Logging up *255*
Pioneering *256*
  Ideas for projects *256*
  Camp projects *256*
  Ropeways *256*
  Towers *260*
  Bridges *263*
  Some ideas for crossing the creek *264*
  Flagpoles *269*
  Shear legs and balistas *270*
  Hyperbolic-paraboloids *271*
  Rafting *275*

6 EMERGENCIES *279*

Emergency *279*
  Report *280*
  Rescue *280*
  Principles and practice of first aid *281*
Circulation of blood *281*
Treatments *282*
  Unconsciousness *282*
  Concussion or stunning *282*
  Fainting *282*
  Seizures *284*
  Bleeding *284*
  Shock *285*
  Burns *286*
  Bandages *287*
  Fractures *292*
  Carrying a patient *295*
  Methods of carrying *295*
  Bites *298*

Bee and wasp stings *302*
Mosquito and sandfly bites *302*
Stings caused by marine creatures *302*
Sunburn *304*
Cramps *305*
Heat exhaustion *305*
Heat stroke *305*
Electric shock *305*
How to make a mock emergency *306*
First-aid kit *308*
Fire *308*
Road safety *310*
Bicycle safety *311*
Explosives *312*
Walking along a road *313*
Personal stereos *314*
Home safety *314*
Childproofing *315*
Poisoning *315*
Water safety *317*
  Self-rescue *317*
  The 'HELP' position *317*
  The 'huddle' position *318*
  Treading water *318*
  Slow swimming and floating *319*
  Swimming with a personal flotation device *319*
  The surface dive and underwater swim *319*
Rescue of others *319*
  Rescue *319*
  Throwing a rescue line *321*
  Undressing in the water *322*
  Tows *322*
  Methods of landing *324*
Safety knowledge *325*
  At the beach *325*
  At the river *325*
  At the pool *326*
  Dams and lakes *326*
Expired Air Resuscitation *326*
  Mouth-to-mouth resuscitation *327*
Survival *329*
  Bushfires *329*
  Safety and survival in a bushfire area *329*

How to survive in a bushfire *330*
If you are lost *332*
Signals *332*
Survival kit *333*
Winter first aid *336*
  Frostbite and freezing *336*
  Snowblindness *336*
  Carbon monoxide *337*
  Hypothermia *338*
Winter survival *339*

7 ENVIRONMENT *340*

Natural and human environments *340*
Heavens — stars and planets *341*
Two precious life cycles *342*
  Oxygen–carbon *342*
  Water *344*
Pure water *346*
  Water is scarce and important *346*
  Conservation of water *349*
  Water quality *350*
  Water harvesting *351*
Clean air *352*
  The thin layer of air on which all life depends *352*
  Photosynthesis *354*
  Conservation of air *355*
Fertile soil *356*
  How soil is formed *356*
  Soil fertility *357*
  Physical fertility *358*
  Soil structure *358*
  Tilth *358*
  Soil texture *358*
  Chemical fertility *359*
Conserving soil fertility *360*
  Reducing soil erosion by wind and water *361*
  Erosion: how soil is destroyed *362*
The conservation balance sheet *363*
Conservation of vegetation *364*
  Bushfires *364*

Native vegetation *365*
Australian-flora
conservation *366*
  Plant communities *366*
  Parks, gardens and
  reserves *366*
Fauna conservation *367*
  Where to start? *367*
Become a naturalist *367*
  Birds *367*
  Shells *370*
Conservation of human
history *370*
Litter-free land *370*
  No littering! *370*
  Recycling has many
  benefits *372*
Protect our world *373*
The Australian Scout
Environment Charter *374*
Conservation *374*

8 WATER ACTIVITIES *376*

Safety in boats *376*
Weather *377*
  Signs *379*
Tides *380*
  Ebb and flow *380*
  Tides and currents *382*
Personal Flotation
Devices *383*
Rescue and resuscitation *384*
  Safety rules and
  precautions *384*
  Distress signals *385*
  Reserve buoyancy *386*
Canoeing *386*
  Hulls *386*
  Parts of a canoe *388*
  Paddles *388*
  Paddling a canoe *390*
  Strokes *391*
  Types of canoeable
  waters *396*
  Balance and paddle
  support *398*
  Capsized canoe *399*
  Boarding and alighting from a
  canoe *401*

Putting a canoe or kayak into
the water *402*
Loading and trimming a
boat *403*
Canoe signals *404*
Portaging *404*
Towing *405*
Journey equipment *406*
Clothing and camp gear *406*
Making a canoe *407*
Repair kit *408*
Rowboats and rowing *408*
  Rowing terms *408*
  Types of rowing boats *409*
  Oars and rowlocks *410*
  Entering a boat *411*
  Rowing *412*
  Terms *413*
Sailing *414*
  Types of sailboats *422*
  Parts of a sailboat *426*
  Types of sails *427*
  Parts of a sail *430*
  Rule of the road *431*
  Returning to shore *432*
  Capsize and recovery *432*
  Unrigging and storing *434*
  Maintenance *434*
  Racing *435*
Sailboarding *437*
Power boating *439*
  Safety equipment *440*
  Care of motors *443*
  Submerged motors *443*
  Anchoring and mooring *444*
  Sea anchor *446*
  Charts *447*
  Storing power boats *450*
  Rafting *450*
Learn the language *452*
  Glossary *452*
Learning to swim *454*

9 WINTER FUN *463*

Winter camping *463*
What to wear *464*
  Footwear *465*
  Clothing *466*
  Headwear *467*

What to take *468*
  To wear *468*
  To pack *468*
How to get there *470*
Transporting gear *472*
  Toboggan *472*
Snowshoes *474*
Making camp *477*
  Camp setup *477*
    Putting up shelters *478*
    Pitching your tent *478*
    Snow shelters *480*
Bedding *481*
Night wear *482*
Fires for cooking and warmth *482*
Food and menus *483*
Water for cooking *484*
Sanitation and hygiene *484*
Camp hints *485*
Let us make a sleigh *486*

1

AIR ACTIVITIES

Scouting and air activities

When Scouting first started, aeroplanes remained in a very early stage of development. At that time, many learned people declared that these 'new-fangled' flying machines, although interesting, would not have any practical value. How wrong this has proved to be in the short space of a lifetime!

Air activities add an interesting and exciting field for today's Scout. Had our founder B.P. foreseen the advances aviation was to make, we would certainly have seen this type of activity much sooner.

To undertake the air-activities target you do not have to spend a great amount of money, but, as in anything you do, you must be prepared to spend time to achieve your target. By using your time to best advantage you will discover interesting and exciting things that have happened and are happening in air activities.

Try, with other members of your Patrol, to visit an air-activities centre. If this is not possible, visit your local airport, flying or gliding club. Research through libraries, and aeromodelling, will help you in the knowledge and skill required to complete your target. Start your target at the bottom: very few successful people have ever started anything in life at the top!

A good idea when starting is to find out how many in your Patrol and Troop are interested in working with you towards the target. When you have a group interested, approach an experienced aeromodeller or the aeromodelling association in your state. You will find that experts in this field will be pleased to help and guide you in building your models. Do not think that a hand-launched glider is simple; although they appear simple and very cheap to make, they take a lot of skill to fly properly.

If you know a pilot (commercial or private) in your district, they will possibly be pleased to help you and your Patrol with some items of the target. The following pages are intended to help you with basic information, but you will have to follow up with outside practical help. If you think you would like to undertake Air Activities, give it a go, and you will find your interest increasing with each stage. You will find the more you learn, the more you will want to learn and find out.

Happy landings!

Australian aviation — 1910 till when?

No Australian, regardless of age or sex, who has the slightest interest in aeroplanes, can fail to pause and wonder at what has taken place in this country's aviation era. We can go back as far as the year 1851 where we find an Australian, Dr William Bland, designing an 'atmotic ship', comprising a long balloon with suspended cabin and steam-driven engines.

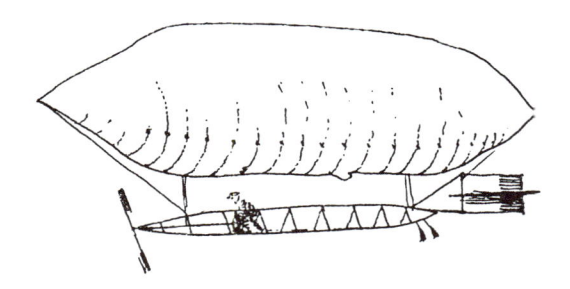

An early airship, 1904

This was followed by some forty years of balloon flights and experiments in various states, by men such as Harry L'Estrange, Pierre Maigré, Thomas Gale and John Allen. However, serious Australian-aviation history truly started with the now famous Lawrence Hargrave and his experiments using box kites to lift himself into the air.

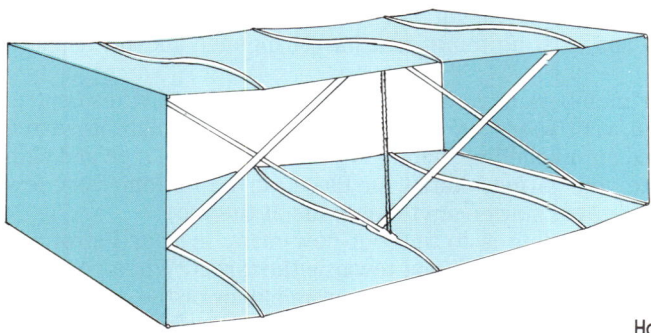

Hargrave's box kite, 1890

It is interesting to note that he achieved an ascent in 1894 using four kites weighing only a little over 15 kilograms, some 76 kilograms less than the weight they lifted to an altitude of 5 metres. Many people today build and fly kites, different in size and design but still ably demonstrating many of the properties that helped get aviation started in the world.

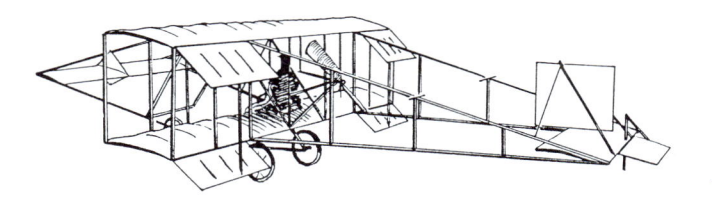

J. R. Duigan, 1911

We come to the first powered flight in Australia, and with it much controversy about who is entitled to the honour. We leave it to you to decide for yourself, based on what has been recorded. On 9 December 1909, Colin Defries took off in a Wright biplane from Sydney's Victoria Park Racecourse, resulting in a flight of five and a half seconds, covering 104 metres, at a height of from 1 to 5 metres.

The next challenge to the title came on 17 March 1910, at Bolivar, just north of Adelaide, when Fred Custance in a Bleriot Monoplane recorded a flight of some five and a half minutes, the first flight in Australia by an Australian.

Next day, 18 March 1910, Harry Houdini, the famous escapologist, took off from Digger's Rest near Melbourne in a French-built Voisin biplane and flew some three and a half minutes in what has been described as perfectly controlled flight. It would appear that the controversy centres around what can truly be called flight. Is it the time airborne, the amount of control displayed, the height reached, or the distance covered? Argue on, but all three were great pioneers of Australian aviation.

Powered flight in Australia was on its way, and with the advent of World War I came the chance for many Australians to enter the field of military aviation through their enlistment in the Royal Flying Corps. From the ranks of the RFC and the Australian Flying Corps came our first military 'aces' before there was ever an official Royal Australian Air Force (RAAF).

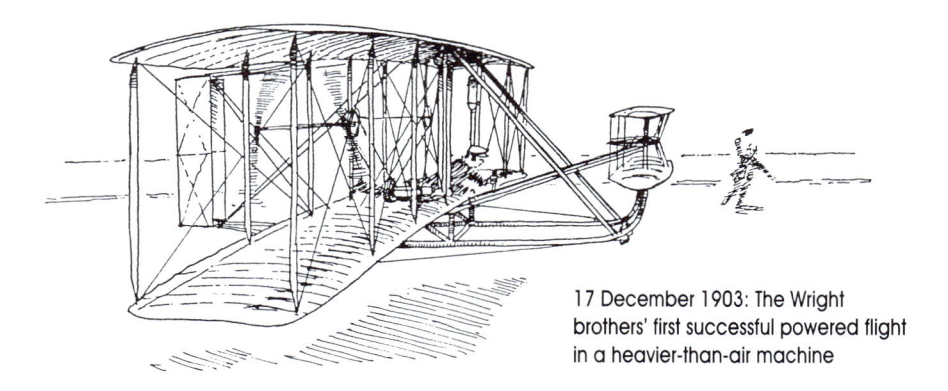

17 December 1903: The Wright brothers' first successful powered flight in a heavier-than-air machine

Melbourne pilot Lt A.H. Cobby shot down a total of thirty-two enemy aircraft, and won the DSC and three DFCs to become Australia's leading ace of the war. The combat record of the three AFC Squadrons serving in Europe was indeed impressive: 284 enemy aircraft were shot down, and a further 163 were forced down, for a total Australian loss of sixty aircraft.

A Bristol Bulldog

Source: RAAF

Some famous Australian aviation names to come out of the services after World War I were Bert Hinkler, Charles Kingsford-Smith, Oswald Watt, Sir Lawrence Wackett, Sir Hudson Fysh, Sir Ross and Sir Keith Smith, Sir Richard Williams and many others whose wartime experience both on the ground and in the air contributed greatly to Australia's aviation progress.

The years that followed the Armistice brought a gradual progression in commercial aviation in this country, from barnstorming all over the country to the formation of the Aero Club movement and to the first England-to-Australia air race including a $10 000 prize offered by Prime Minister W. M. Hughes for the first Australian crew to reach Australia within 720 hours before the end of 1919. On 10 December 1919 the Smith Brothers, Ross and Keith, arrived in Darwin in their famous Vickers Vimy Bomber, to claim the prize and bring to the Australian public the reality of international air travel.

The years 1920 and 1921 saw the evolution of some control over the aviation scene in Australia when a Controller of Civil Aviation was appointed and a system of licences for pilots and engineers was formulated. When Parliament passed the Air Navigation Bill, the 'anything goes' and 'aerial circus' atmosphere surrounding the industry began to disappear.

The next fifteen years saw fantastic development in the domestic air services, the formation of the RAAF and record-breaking flights to and from the Australian continent.

The birth of the internal airline system saw the making and breaking of many companies, the names of most of which are rarely heard. They included West Australian Airways, Guinea Airways, New England Airways, Airlines of Australia, ANA, Butler Air Transport and many others. However, two names from the formative years live on, although their operations have changed

Air activities

An early passenger aircraft DH86

Source: Qantas Airways Limited

considerably since those early years. One is MacRobertson Miller Airlines (MMA—Mickey Mouse Airlines as it was affectionately referred to), which first formed in South Australia and then shifted to Western Australia and became part of the Ansett Group. The other is the mighty Queensland and Northern Territory Air Services, now known as Qantas Airways Limited, which is a real success story, from spanning the bush to spanning the world.

On the military side, 1 April 1921 heralded the birth of the RAAF with a collection of aircraft consisting of Avro 504Ks for training, DH9s, and some SE5As. About 140 officers and airmen operated from its one and only station, Point Cook, in Victoria. Gradually the airforce was expanded, more stations were opened, more people were recruited, and more modern aircraft, such as the Bristol Bulldog and Hawker Demons, were added to strength.

Meanwhile record breakers were speeding over the new air lanes between Australia and the rest of the world. In 1924 the round-Australia record was established by a Department of Civil Aviation crew, only to be broken less than three years later by the famous team of Kingsford-Smith (Smithy) and Charles Ulm. In 1928, Bert Hinkler from Bundaberg knocked six hours off the England-to-Darwin record of the Smith brothers. The same year Smith and Ulm were at it again, to set a California-to-Brisbane record of 83 hours 43 minutes. These feats were followed by Sir Francis Chichester, Amy Johnson and Jean Batten, to name but a few. Scott and Black won yet another England-to-Australia air race in 1934.

Many books could be written, and indeed have been written, on Australian aviation during the period 1939–45. The exploits of the RAAF in action deserve much more space than is available here. The RAAF saw service in Europe, the Pacific, the Middle East, India–Burma, the Far East and other areas, and rose in strength to a peak of over 182 000 men and women. Within Australia, great expansion was seen in the fields of aircraft servicing and manufacture, while little expansion was possible in commercial aviation because most civil aircraft were put into military service.

The years following World War II have shown great strides in the Australian aviation scene in almost all fields. The notable exception is that of aircraft manufacture which has had many ups and downs over recent years. The light aircraft registered in this country have grown enormously in numbers, variety and sophistication. We now have small jets operating in the general aviation field and helicopters operating from the heart of our cities to the remotest areas of this continent. International airline services are almost entirely jet operated and competition is closely controlled by government policy. Qantas continues to compete at the highest level of international air travel, with its fleets of Boeing 747s and 767s.

Military aviation continually expanded in all three services, the RAAF having sent squadrons to war in Korea and Vietnam. Keeping pace with all this progress, the Civil Aviation Authority is expanding its services with radar installations, modern radio aids, longer runways, new aerodromes and everything required to service this vast industry.

All this happened in a very short time. What can we expect in the next fifty years?

Civil Aviation Authority
AUSTRALIA

The CAA logo

The role of the Civil Aviation Authority

Because of the vast areas of land and water in Australia and its territories, transport has become an integral part of the country's way of life and has been essential to national development, particularly over the past two decades.

The need for some form of control over civil flying was apparent in 1920, and following a Bill passed by Federal Parliament, the Civil Aviation Branch was established within the Department of Defence. In 1938 the Department of Civil Aviation (DCA) was established.

In 1946 the Air Traffic Control section of the DCA came into being. Several changes in name followed: the Department of Air Transport Group in 1973, the Department of Aviation in 1982, and, finally, the Civil Aviation Authority (CAA) came into being on 1 July 1988. At the beginning of 1988 a separate government body, the Federal Airports Corporation, was formed to cover the commercial and administration identity, and to collect fees at major airports.

The CAA headquarters are in Canberra and a Flying Unit is at Essendon Airport in Melbourne. Australia is divided into five *regions* of control: New South Wales, Victoria/Tasmania, Queensland, Western Australia, and South Australia/Northern Territory.

As well as flying operations, the CAA is involved with policy and ground facilities. It provides, operates and maintains the entire Australian Air Traffic Control, the air-navigation network, and aeronautical-information service. It is also responsible for the provision of a national weather-information service for aircraft, and has a section that involves the design and maintenance of airports and their facilities.

Among its other activities are the licensing of pilots, engineers and technicians and the control and supervision of standards associated with the maintenance of aircraft by qualified personnel. One of the Flying Unit's functions is to regularly check the accuracy and operation of the many navigation aids that the Authority has installed throughout Australia.

Air activities

Source: Qantas Airways Limited

Source: Qantas Airways Limited

A pilot testing in a simulator

A Qantas cockpit

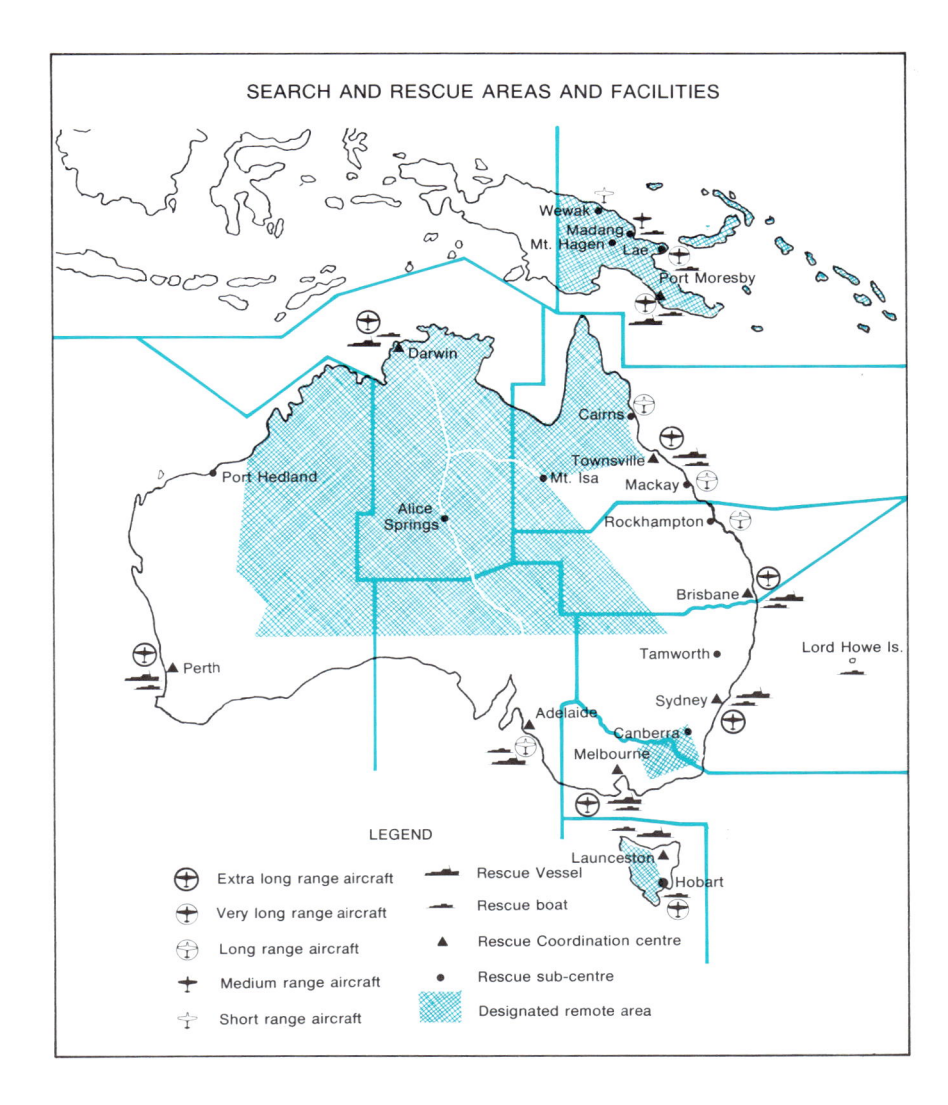

SEARCH AND RESCUE AREAS AND FACILITIES

LEGEND

- ⊕ Extra long range aircraft
- ⊕ Very long range aircraft
- ⊕ Long range aircraft
- ✈ Medium range aircraft
- ⊤ Short range aircraft
- ━ Rescue Vessel
- ━ Rescue boat
- ▲ Rescue Coordination centre
- • Rescue sub-centre
- ▨ Designated remote area

7

To ensure that high standards of safety are maintained, close attention must be given to the Authority's operations, to airworthiness, and to communicating new ideas in technology. The Authority is also responsible for maintaining air search-and-rescue facilities. It virtually monitors all flights and swings into action when doubt exists about the safety of an aircraft.

When an aircraft is lost, a trained team co-ordinates ground, air and sea rescue teams to locate the missing aircraft. This is a most important function of the CAA.

Modern airports

The modern airport is a far cry from the original 'airports' that were used during the early days of aviation in this country. These early aerodromes were no more than the most suitable and readily available paddocks. The surface was usually rough and there were certainly no facilities for the people eager to go on a joy flight with the early aviators. Nor was there anything to help the pilot, who had to rely solely on skill, judgment and observation. If it was necessary to refuel the aircraft, the pilot had to have a supply of aviation fuel and be prepared to hand pump it from drums into the aeroplane.

No longer are paddocks or streets used for commercial airlines, although light aircraft still operate from these places in remote areas. In their place we have massive areas of bitumen and concrete pavement and runways.

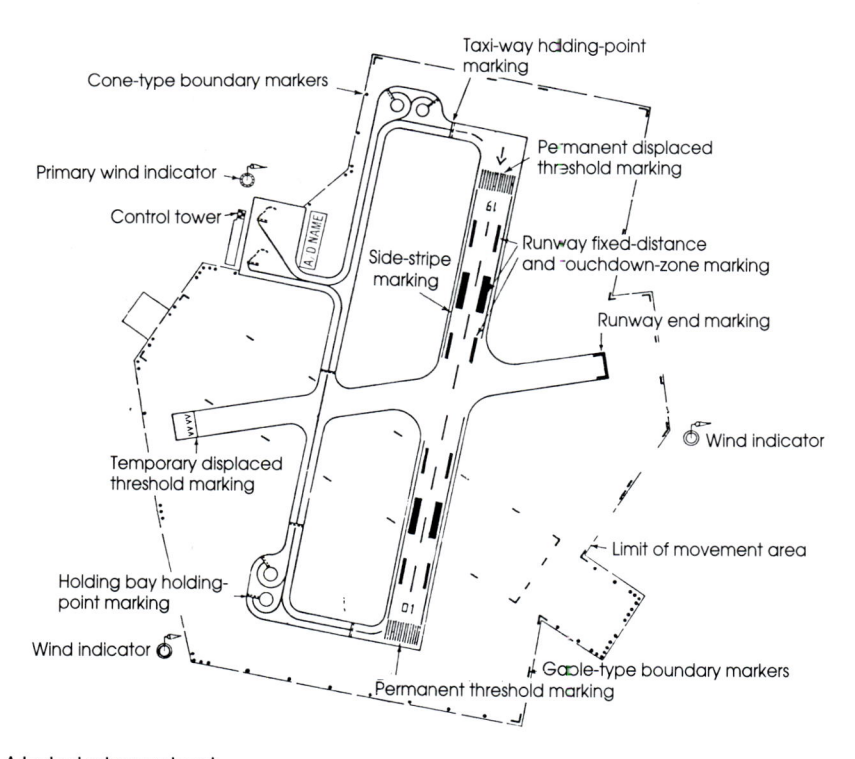

A typical primary airport

Air activities

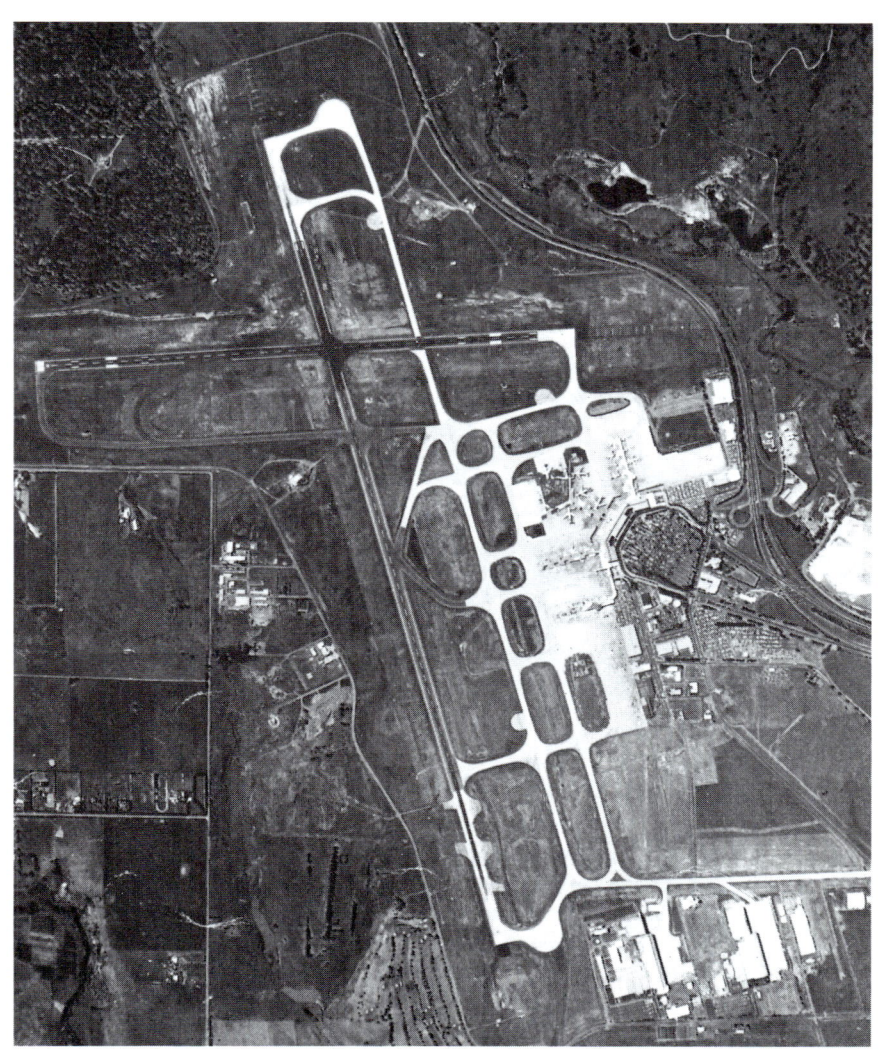

Melbourne airport at Tullamarine
Source: Federal Airports Corporation

These runways have been designed by civil engineers who have to take into their calculations not only the enormous weights of the present civil and military aircraft but the probable requirements of the future. Melbourne's airport at Tullamarine was the first completely new major aerodrome built in Australia since Adelaide airport was opened in 1954. Tullamarine boasts two runways, each 145 cm thick and capable of handling the largest aircraft now flying—the 327-tonne Boeing 747. As well as the runways there are taxiways 22 m wide that run parallel for the full length of these strips and lead into the main terminal area. Considerable thought has also been given to these taxiways, and they feature high-speed turnouts to increase the runway efficiency and capacity during peak traffic periods.

Sydney airport at Mascot

Source: Australian Picture Library/Brian Maginnity

The actual terminal area was designed to handle thirty-two of the large modern airline aircraft—eight international and twenty-four domestic. Further development is under way to increase the capacity to sixteen international and sixty domestic aircraft. Aero bridges are used to allow passengers to board and disembark from aircraft completely sheltered in all weathers. Consideration is being given to the introduction of a metropolitan rail service to the airport.

Air-traffic control

Air-traffic control is divided into various sections, each of which has a specific function. The section most familiar to the public is the aerodrome control which is directed from the equally familiar control tower. The aerodrome controllers are responsible for the safe operation of aircraft within a specified area (the circuit area) surrounding the airport and also while they are on the ground manoeuvring area. The controller directs this traffic on the ground and in the air and has to ensure that local weather conditions are known by the pilots of incoming and outgoing aircraft. The controller also has the responsibility of closing the aerodrome when weather conditions, such as cloud, rain and turbulence, do not permit safe operation of aircraft.

Air activities

A radar operations room   Source: CAA

Not as well known are the officers who co-ordinate with the other sections and have the task of ensuring safe separation of aircraft as they approach and depart from aerodromes. Radar is continuing to be used at an ever increasing rate to ensure that this separation occurs even in adverse weather, when the pilots fly solely on instruments.

Another section of control has similar functions to those mentioned but its area of responsibility is situated between major aerodromes. The service that these controllers give applies not only to airline aircraft but to any aircraft the pilot of which is qualified to use the facilities.

Meteorology

Weather

The science of weather—meteorology—is used to make our lives safer and better. Modern forecasting is 95% accurate. Storms and tornados are tracked and warnings given in plenty of time for people to take precautions or to evacuate. Clouds are now being seeded to cause rainfall where it is needed. A vast network of weather stations allows planes to fly safely and boats to navigate without danger.

What in the world makes the weather? There are four elements that basically give us the kind of weather we have, and they are as follows:
1. The air, carrying clouds, bringing heat waves or cold spells.
2. Heat, making sunny days warmer than days that are cloudy, and summer warmer than winter. Heat makes the winds blow and sends water into the air.
3. Water, which we often call moisture. Water goes into the air, or evaporates from bodies of water or from the ground. This water soon forms clouds from which rain or snow may fall.
4. Our own earth, helping air and heat produce winds, and causing the difference between summer and winter.

Winds and clouds are two of the best ways of forecasting weather.

Clouds are formed when air is cooled below its saturation point and the water vapour in the air condenses to form clouds. The clouds that cover the sky almost every day are all formed from the same general process, but because of other aspects, they may appear in several forms.

Clouds are described by the use of Latin words. There are three general types: *cirrus*—featherlike, *stratus*—in a layer, *cumulus*—in big heaps. *Nimbus* is the name given to any cloud from which rain falls. If the word *alto* is put in front of the name, it indicates a formation of clouds of medium height in the atmosphere.

Weather forecasters use symbols to show cloud types, and some of these are shown in the illustration.

Clouds

High clouds

High clouds are entirely made up of tiny ice crystals. Their bottoms average about 6100 metres above the earth.

Cirrus, cirrostratus and *cirrocumulus* clouds are all high-level clouds and will not affect a light aircraft which normally flies well below 3050 metres.

1. Cirrus Cirrus clouds are thin, wispy and feathery. They are frequently blown by high winds into feathery strands called 'mare's tails'.

1. Cirrus

H4

High ice-crystal clouds. Indicates strong upper level winds. With N to NW winds—precipitation likely 20 to 30 hours. With SW winds improving weather

2. Cirrostratus Cirrostratus clouds form at about 7600 metres and are thin sheets that look like white veils. Both the sun and moon shine through them, making rings of hazy light called halos.

2. Cirrostratus

H7

Prismatic effect of sun or moon on ice crystals causes halo. With N to NW winds precipitation within 10 to 20 hours

Air activities

3. Cirrocumulus

3. Cirrocumulus

H9

High ice-crystal clouds, not often seen over Australia. In summer they may precede afternoon thunderstorms

Middle clouds

Middle clouds are basically stratus or cumulus. Their bases average about 3050 metres above the earth.

Altocumulus varies in the base height from 750 to 6100 metres and is usually about 750 metres thick. Light aircraft usually fly safely below this.

4. Altocumulus Altocumulus are patches or layers of puffy or roll-like clouds, grey or whitish in colour. The sun often shines through as a disc usually pale blue or yellow inside and reddish outside.

4. Altocumulus

M3

Water and ice-crystal cloud. In summer mornings it can mean possible afternoon thunderstorms. Often referred to as 'mackerel sky'

5. Altostratus Altostratus are dense veils or sheets of grey that often appear fibrous or lightly striped. The sun or moon does not form a halo but appears as if seen through frosted glass.

5. Altostratus

M1

13

6. Nimbostratus Nimbostratus are true rain clouds and form thick layers that have no special shape. They look grey because they cut off the sunlight and often cover the sky for many kilometres.

6. Nimbostratus

M2 ---

Sky has grey leaden appearance. Rain likely to continue for long periods. Heavy falls likely. Light winds usually mean long period of rain

Low clouds

These have bases that range in height from near the earth's surface to 1980 metres.

Cumulus is a dense cloud with a fairly flat base from 455 metres upwards, and its thickness can be as high as 4575 metres. It has the appearance of a cauliflower top which can develop into a cumulonimbus cloud. Aircraft should avoid flying in cumulus clouds because they are very turbulent and icing may occur within the cloud.

Cumulonimbus is a high mountainous cloud with tops shaped like an anvil. These clouds are extremely turbulent inside and very dangerous to fly in. The base may be 455 metres with tops as high as 12200 metres. Aircraft have been broken up in a cumnim cloud.

Stratus is a stable but darkish cloud. The sun may be seen through it as a clear disc. It is a nuisance because it is very low to the ground and extends up to 610 to 1220 metres. It is a fog-like cloud, and may prevent aircraft from landing or taking off.

7. Cumulus Cumulus clouds are puffy, cauliflower like. The shapes constantly change. Over land, cumulus clouds usually form by day in rising warm air, and disappear at night. They usually mean fair weather, unless they pile up into cumulonimbus clouds.

7. Cumulus

L2

Fine-weather cumulus usually develops in afternoon over the land. Can cause light brief showers, if over ocean at night.
When cumulus clouds grow rapidly, they often develop into shower clouds or afternoon thunderstorms

Air activities

8. Stratus Stratus clouds are a low, quite uniform sheet, like fog. They may bring a light drizzle but almost never heavy rain because there is very little movement in them. Dull-grey stratus clouds make a heavy, dark sky.

8. Stratus

9. Fractostratus

9. Fractostratus

L7 — — —

This cloud, which is often very dark and ragged looking, is associated with bad weather. Often found under nimbostratus or cumulonimbus clouds

10. Cumulonimbus Cumulonimbus clouds are the familiar thunder heads. Bases may almost touch the ground, but updraughts carry the tops sometimes to 22 875 metres. Winds often shape the tops into a flat anvil-like form.

10. Cumulonimbus

L9

Bring moderate to heavy precipitation including snowfalls over the ranges during the winter. Often develop over mountainous regions on summer afternoons

11. Stratocumulus Stratocumulus clouds are irregular masses of clouds spread out in a rolling or puffy layer. Grey with darker shading, they do not give rain but sometimes develop into nimbostratus, which does.

11. Stratocumulus

L5

Forecasting

You can become a true weather prophet at camp or on hikes by simply knowing a few weather signs. If you use these signs often and study the weather conditions in your locality, you should be able to forecast your local weather with reasonable accuracy. We have all heard weather sayings such as 'Red sky at night, sailor's delight' or 'Red sky in the morning, sailors take warning'. Most weather lore comes from farmers, hunters, and sailors—the people who are most concerned about the weather. Many of these weather proverbs have some truth in them because they are based on some experience. However, by observing wind direction, barometer readings and cloud formations, you can be right in your weather forecasting about 75% of the time.

Following are some general rules of thumb that will be of use to you.

1. Red sky at sunset: fair day tomorrow.
2. Check the moon—if there is a ring around it it means there is probably a storm or rain on the way.
3. Winds: observe type and direction of cloud movement.
4. Clouds: the appearance of large heavy banks of increasing heaped cumulus warns you of the danger of severe squalls and suction winds, thunder and lightning in summer, hail and snow in winter.

Weather conditions are very important when you are flying, especially for light aircraft. Various parts of Australia have different weather patterns, so you should have an understanding of your local weather. One way is to make a chart like the one on p. 17.

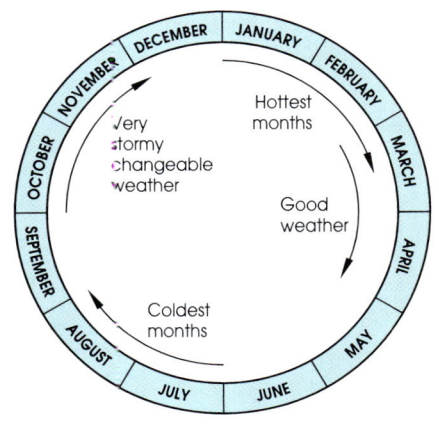

Weather chart

Air activities

Fill in the seasons: summer, winter, spring, monsoon, dry season, and so on—whatever your region has. Some places have four seasons, others have two.

Fill in the hottest months, the coldest, the wettest, the driest, the windiest, snow time, cyclone season, frost times, fogs, the calmest times.

Keep a log for four weeks to see how the weather actually follows the pattern. Prepare a chart like the one following. We have put one entry in, for a hot summer's day, with a northerly wind but with a cold change coming in the afternoon.

The basis of all weather forecasting is the weather map or chart on which is plotted the meteorological observations made at weather stations throughout the country and sent into the various meteorological offices at

Date	Cloud			Rain			Wind				Temperature (°C)			
	Most of day	About 1/2 day	Very little	None	Some	A lot	Calm day	Some	A lot	Direction	Cold below 10	Med. 11–20	Warm 21–30	Hot 30
Jan. 1														
Jan. 2														
Jan. 3														
Jan. 4														
Jan. 5														
Jan. 6														
Jan. 7														
Jan. 8														
Jan. 9														
Jan. 10														
Jan. 11														
Jan. 12														
Jan. 13														
Jan. 14														
Jan. 15														
Jan. 16														
Jan. 17														
Jan. 18														
Jan. 19														
Jan. 20														
Jan. 21														
Jan. 22														
Jan. 23														
Jan. 24														
Jan. 25														
Jan. 26														
Jan. 27														
Jan. 28														
Jan. 29														
Jan. 30														
Jan. 31														

Weather chart

regular time intervals. The observations show the weather conditions existing at places over the entire continent of Australia.

Each weather station reports on the following sorts of observations:

1. dry-bulb temperature
2. dew point
3. types of cloud overhead in the sky
4. amount of cloud covering in the sky
5. height of cloud
6. surface-wind direction
7. surface-wind speed
8. horizontal visibility
9. barometric pressure
10. change in barometric pressure over the past four hours
11. weather at the time of observation
12. time of observations.

When the meteorological offices receive this information from weather stations throughout the country, they plot the weather on to their charts and produce a weather map and forecast.

The following is a typical weather map during the winter months. The 'highs' give fine clear weather over most of Australia, with cold, frosty nights inland. In Victoria, light scattered rain may be expected in the western and coastal areas. Winds are light, because the isobars (pressure lines) are not spaced closely together. The arrows show the wind directions.

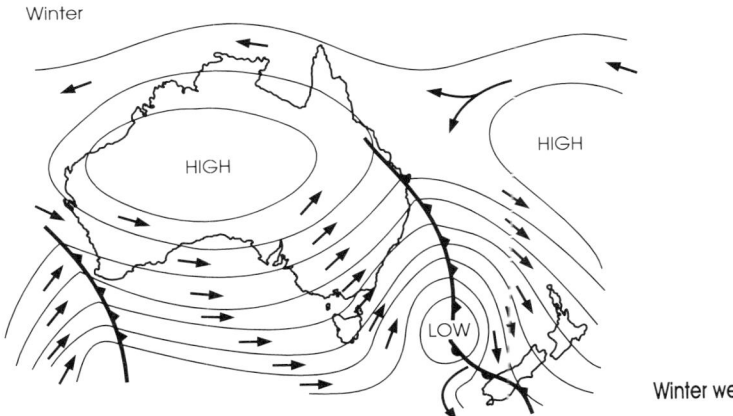

Winter weather map

The following is another chart—for summer. On the day this chart was drawn, Melbourne's highest temperature was 20°C, but Perth's was 36°C. Why? Look at wind directions!

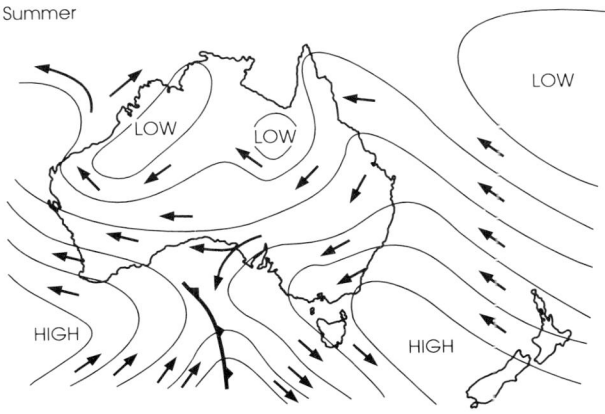

Summer weather map

Air activities

Weather instruments

Barometer Measures the pressure of the air.
Thermometer Gives temperature readings.
Hygrometer Measures the moisture (humidity) in the air.
Rain gauge Measures the amount of rain or snow that falls in a given time.
Wind vane Indicates wind direction.
Anemometer Measures the speed of the wind.

You can set up your own weather station and make some of these instruments yourself.

Effect on aircraft

Wind

Head-winds will slow the speed of an aircraft relative to the ground. It is as if it is pushing the aircraft back.
Tail-winds have the opposite effect. They push the plane forward so that it takes less time to go a certain distance.
Cross-winds can also affect the speed of an aircraft more or less, depending on the angle.

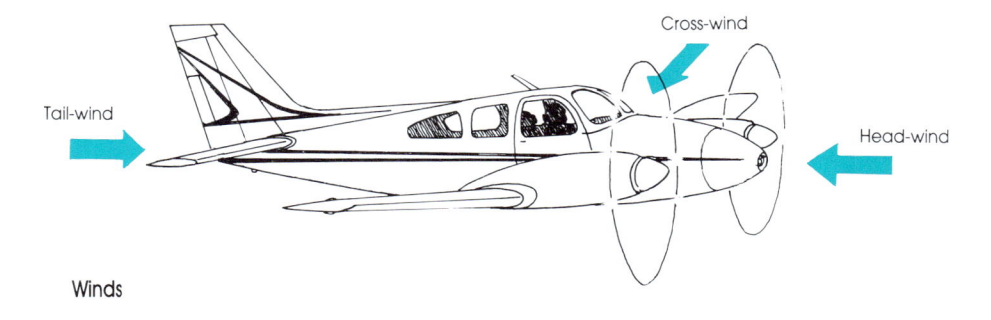

Winds

Head-wind

19

An aircraft should take off or land into the wind. This helps the aircraft obtain lift, at a lower ground speed.

Visibility

In poor visibility a pilot cannot see a safe distance. The control tower would tell the pilot to 'hold' and wait for further takeoff instructions. Should the pilot wish to land, they may be instructed to circle or go to another airfield.

Rain, fog, duststorm and snow can all reduce visibility. If the pilot cannot see clearly it is dangerous to fly, so the control tower may stop the flight. Light aircraft would then have to wait for clearer conditions.

Cloud

Some types of cloud can cause ice to form on the aircraft's wings. This would make the aircraft overweight and unsafe to fly.

Temperature

Car engines run better on cold days, and so do aircraft engines. Air is more dense on a cold day, so the engine doesn't have to work as hard to build up enough power for takeoff. This means the aircraft does not require as much runway on a cold day as it does on a hot one.

As mentioned earlier in this chapter, the CAA provides a national weather-information service. This service is available to all pilots on request and deals with cloud, wind velocities, visibility and general weather conditions covering all flights throughout Australia. Pilots travelling from one city to another may have to use two or three 'area forecasts' to help them in planning and conducting their flight. They are able to gauge the conditions likely to be encountered at their destination from the terminal forecasts available. They are also able to request the latest forecast while en route to their destination when weather conditions may be doubtful for their flight.

Aircraft types and uses

Nowadays we have a variety of aircraft types performing, in some cases, very specialised work. For our purposes we can divide these aircraft into three basic categories which will be described in fairly general terms:
1. light aircraft
2. commercial-airline aircraft
3. military aircraft.

It is possible to subdivide these further.

(a) Cessna 421 Golden Eagle

(b) Cessna 152

(c) Cessna Pressurised Centurion

Light aircraft

Fieldbook for Australian Scouting

Light aircraft

Light aircraft include single-seat ultra-light aircraft, through two- and four-seat training aircraft, up to eight- and ten-place light twin-engined aircraft used for charter work by the smaller commercial operators. Most of these aeroplanes are designed to be utility aircraft in that they can be adapted to perform several tasks from training and carriage of passengers to carriage of freight.

Some light aircraft are built mainly for training purposes while others are designed to be used solely for crop spraying and fertiliser spreading in agricultural work. Some are now pressurised.

At this point, mention should be made of the small two- and three-place helicopters that have shown their versatility in performing an amazing number of jobs. They are even used for cattle mustering in the outback areas of Australia, where inaccessible terrain makes normal methods impossible.

Commercial aircraft

Over the past forty-five years, tremendous advances have been made in commercial aircraft. A comparison of the faithful DC3, with its two engines, 130-knot speed and its 20-plus passenger capability, with today's modern jets, will soon make this evident.

(a) Concorde

(b) Fokker F27 (background)
Boeing 737-200 (foreground)

Commercial aircraft

(c) Boeing 727-300 Long Range

Air activities

Jet aircraft today range from small two-jet engines up to the largest, the 747 with four massive engines and a passenger capacity of approximately 450 people. Also we have a variety of the prop. jet aircraft designed about three decades ago still being used. Some are now superseded for passenger work and are being refitted for the important task of quick freight transport between the cities of the world.

Future trends indicate that while the aircraft may not get smaller, more emphasis may be placed on their ability to become airborne in very small areas. Therefore we have designers now concentrating on STOL and Vertical Take Off type aircraft.

Boeing 767-300   Source: Qantas Airways Limited

Airbus A300   Source: CAA

23

Boeing 747-400

Source: Qantas Airways Limited

There is no doubt, however, that the advent of the jet passenger aircraft has been responsible for the tremendous growth of airline transport. The first of these was the De Havilland Comet which first went into service in 1952. Builders from other countries soon followed this lead and we saw aircraft such as the Boeing 707, 727, Douglas DC8 and DC9, BAC111 and VC10 aircraft.

We have now moved to the B737 and wide-bodied DC10, B747, B767 and the airbus A300 and have seen the move into the supersonic transport era with aircraft such as the Concorde and the Russian Tupolev TU144.

Military aircraft

This is the field in which we have seen enormous advances in technology which stimulated the development of civil aircraft. Military aircraft today are extremely sophisticated pieces of machinery. They range from single-seat supersonic jet fighters capable of fantastic performance, such as the Mirage, F111 and F18, massive heavy bombers that can remain airborne for twenty-four hours or more — such as the B52, and to intermediate fighter-bomber types that will eventually supersede the bombers. Another variation to suit a special purpose is the Harrier, a fighter-type aircraft that can take off vertically and then reach supersonic speeds.

In the middle of these are numerous light, medium and heavy transport aircraft, such as the Caribou and B707, and the Hercules, each of which has been designed to do a specialised job. Also in the military aircraft range we have a multitude of helicopters used for an equally large number of purposes such as spotting, gun platforms in war zones, evacuation work, and transport of important arms and equipment to normally inaccessible areas.

Air activities

Bell Iroquois

Military aircraft

Caribou transport

C130 Hercules

Mirage fighter

Development of new aircraft has required the development of new materials, and it appears at present that the scope for future military aircraft is enormous and restricted only by the time taken to devise and produce new metallic alloys and electronic equipment.

Parts of an aircraft

The basic components that will concern us are shown in the following illustrations.

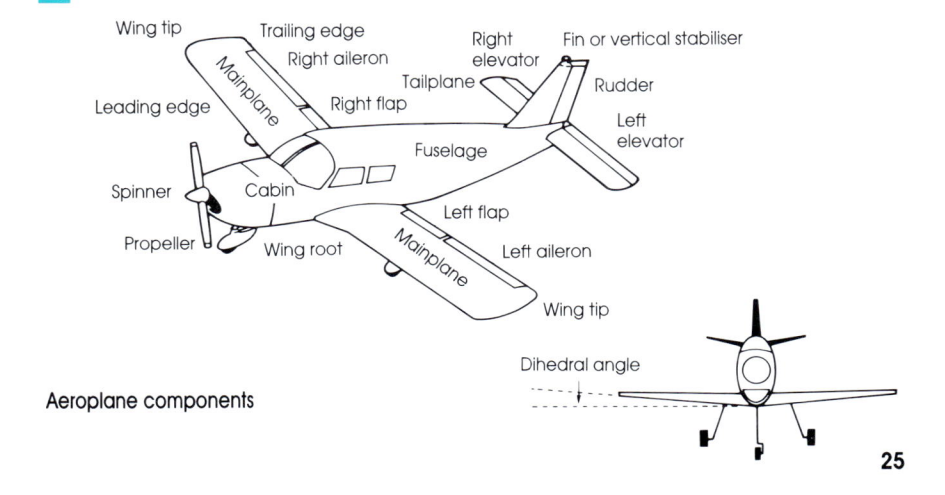

Wing tip, Trailing edge, Right aileron, Right elevator, Fin or vertical stabiliser, Mainplane, Tailplane, Rudder, Leading edge, Right flap, Left elevator, Fuselage, Spinner, Cabin, Left flap, Propeller, Wing root, Mainplane, Left aileron, Wing tip, Dihedral angle

Aeroplane components

25

A biplane

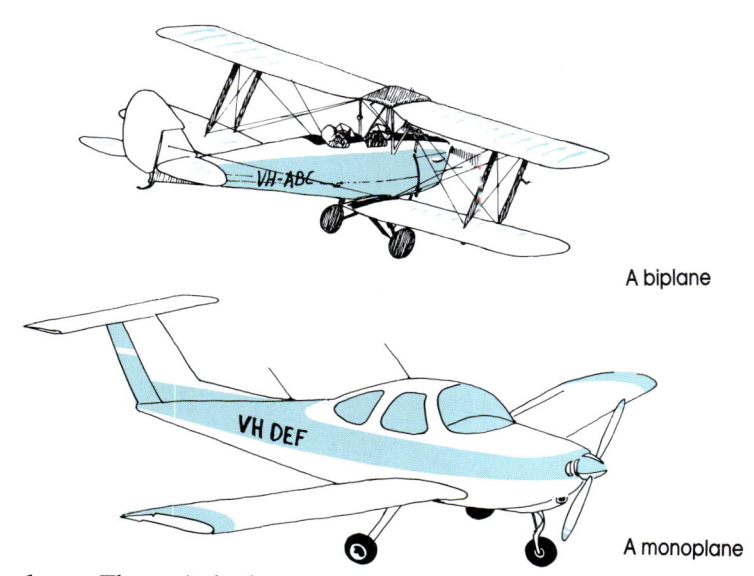

A monoplane

Fuselage The main body.
Mainplane The larger front wing (supports the weight of the aircraft).
Tailplane The smaller wing at the rear (controls the angle of the main plane to the airflow).
Leading edge The front edge of any part or surface, including mainplane, tailplane, struts, propellor blade, fins etc.
Trailing edge The back edge of any part or surface, including mainplane, tailplane, struts, propellor blade, fins etc.

Rudder

This is the movable vertical panel at the rear of the fin. When the pilot pushes on a rudder pedal in the cabin it turns the rudder in the direction of the pedal (left pedal or right pedal). The airflow (or slipstream) passing along the fuselage strikes the rudder and causes the aircraft to turn left or right. This is called yawing.

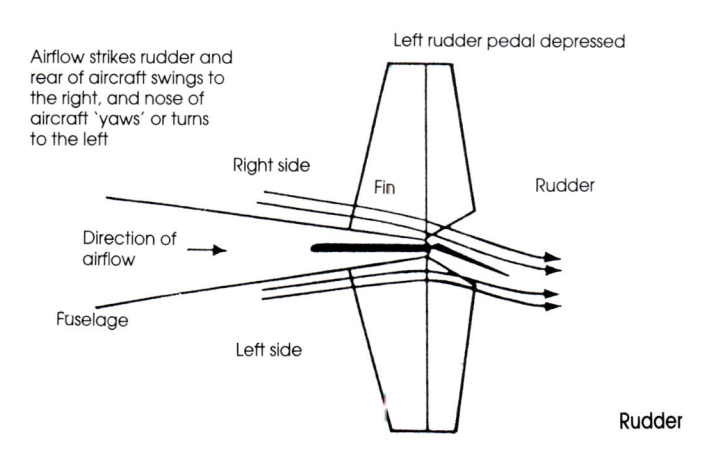

Left rudder pedal depressed

Airflow strikes rudder and rear of aircraft swings to the right, and nose of aircraft 'yaws' or turns to the left

Right side

Fin   Rudder

Direction of airflow

Fuselage

Left side

Rudder

Air activities

Elevators

These are horizontal panels attached to the tailplane. They are moved by the control column in the cabin. If the control column is pushed forward, the elevator will go down, causing the aircraft to descend. If the control column is pulled back, the aircraft ascends, or goes up.

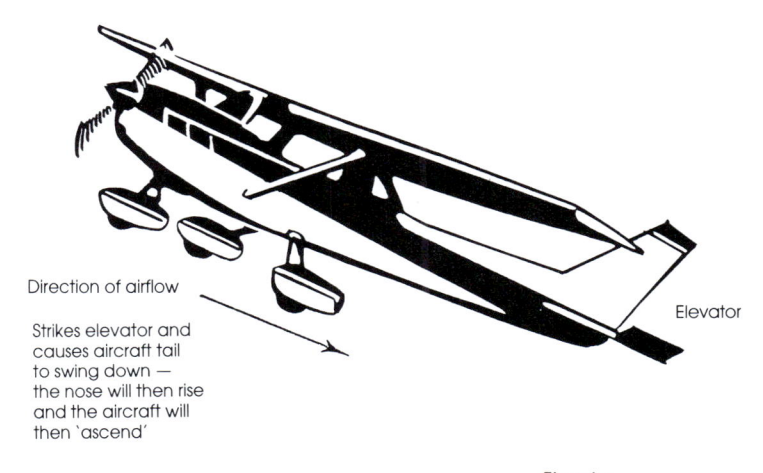

Direction of airflow

Strikes elevator and causes aircraft tail to swing down — the nose will then rise and the aircraft will then 'ascend'

Elevator

Elevator

Ailerons

These two panels, on each side of the aircraft, are attached to the trailing edge of the wings. They cause the aircraft to bank or tip to one side or the other. This is made possible by turning the control wheel. If the wheel is turned to the left, the left aileron will go up and force the wing down. At the same time the other aileron, on the right wing, will go down and the airflow will lift the wing up. If you turn the wheel to the right the opposite will happen.

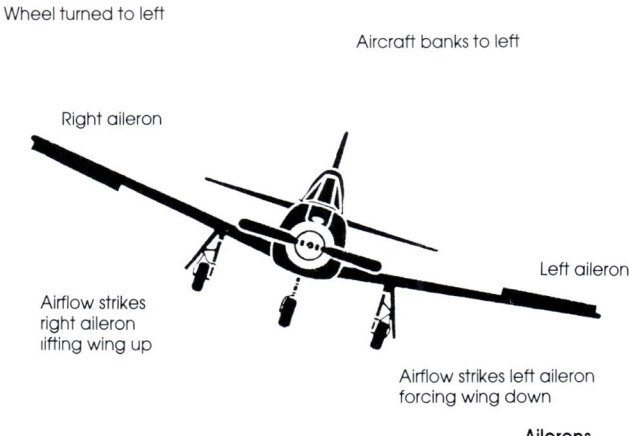

Wheel turned to left

Aircraft banks to left

Right aileron

Left aileron

Airflow strikes right aileron lifting wing up

Airflow strikes left aileron forcing wing down

Ailerons

27

Flaps (or air brakes)

These are attached one to each wing on the trailing edge between the ailerons and the fuselage. They both operate in the same direction and may be partly lowered before takeoff to provide extra lift. On landing they are lowered and act as a barrier to the airflow, or an air brake, as well as providing extra lift at lower airspeed.

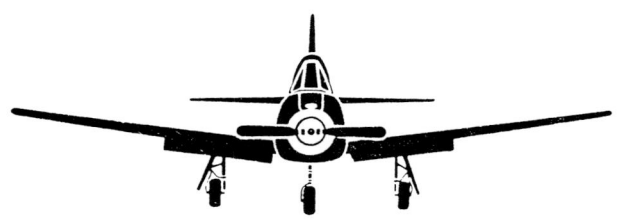

Partial flaps down on takeoff traps airflow and assists with lift.
Partial flaps down on landing traps airflow and acts as a brake.

Flaps (or air brakes)

Undercarriage

This is the underneath part of the aircraft which enables the aircraft to move about, or taxi on the ground. Most aircraft these days have three sets of wheels. Two sets of wheels are under the mainplane, and a set of wheels or one wheel is under the nose. This is a tricycle undercarriage. Other aircraft have a set of wheels under each wing and a very small wheel at the rear of the aircraft.

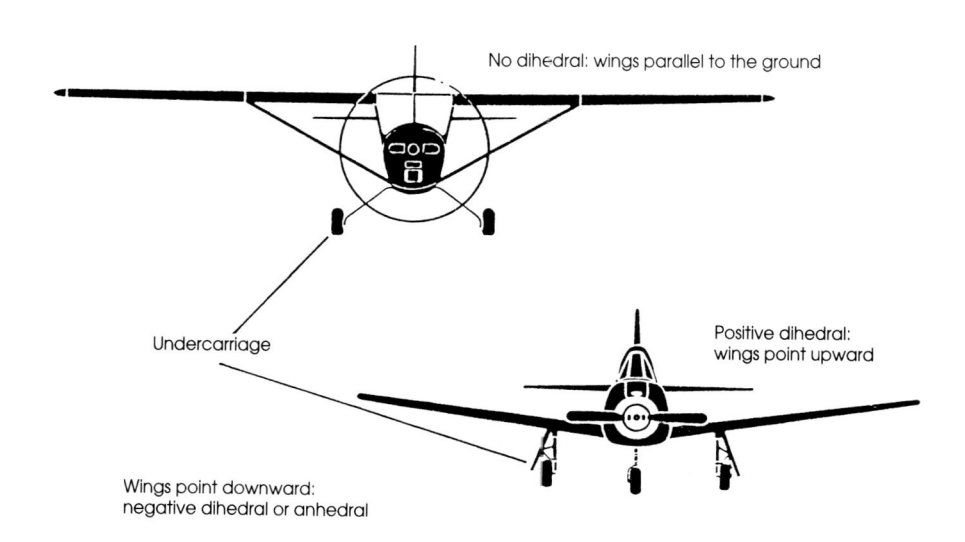

No dihedral: wings parallel to the ground

Undercarriage

Wings point downward: negative dihedral or anhedral

Positive dihedral: wings point upward

Undercarriage and dihedral

Air activities

Dihedral

This is the angle the wing makes where it joins the fuselage.

Sweepback or sweep forward

These are the shapes of the leading and trailing edges of the wing.

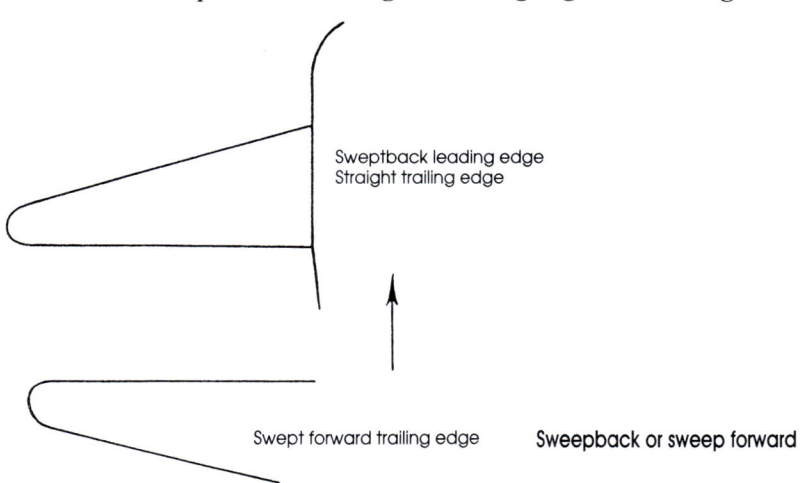

Sweptback leading edge
Straight trailing edge

Swept forward trailing edge

Sweepback or sweep forward

Principles of flight

The atmosphere

The atmosphere is divided basically into two layers; the lower in which we live is the troposphere. The upper is called the stratosphere. We are mainly interested in the former. We need air to produce power in a combustion engine and also to enable an aircraft, be it glider or powered, to be supported and manoeuvred by the pilot.

Lift

A heavier-than-air aircraft requires a lifting force at least equal to its weight in order that it may fly. This force can be demonstrated as follows. Hold a stiff piece of cardboard at a slight angle to the horizontal (*see* diagram) and walk quickly across the room. You will notice that this produces an upward force by deflection of air. If you release the card while walking you should notice that the card will rise slightly before falling. Note that the cardboard stops rising as it loses its horizontal movement. In a crude form our piece of cardboard acts like the wings of an aeroplane. However, an aeroplane wing is shaped in cross-section; this is called an aerofoil section.

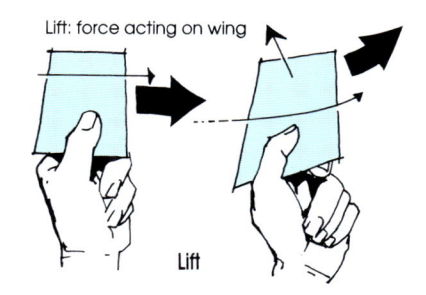

Lift: force acting on wing

Lift

29

These sections are designed to give a larger amount of lift than a flat surface and provide sufficient thickness to make it strong enough.

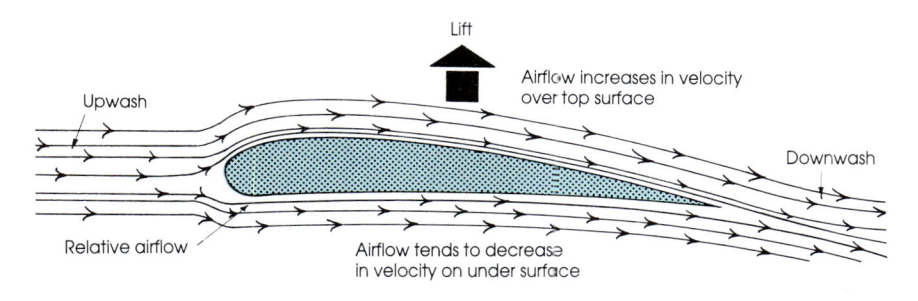

Aerofoil section

Drag

This is a force on an aeroplane which opposes the forward motion and acts in the opposite direction.

There are two kinds of drag:
1. drag caused by the wing while producing lift, called 'induced drag'
2. 'parasite, or form drag' caused by all the parts of the aeroplane that do not produce lift.

Induced drag is greatest at low speed, while parasite drag is greatest at high speed.

Angle of attack

A wing must be at an angle to the relative airflow to produce lift (our experiment with the piece of cardboard). This angle varies with speed, but for every speed above stall speed in straight and level flight there is an angle of attack that produces the amount of lift to counter the aircraft's weight.

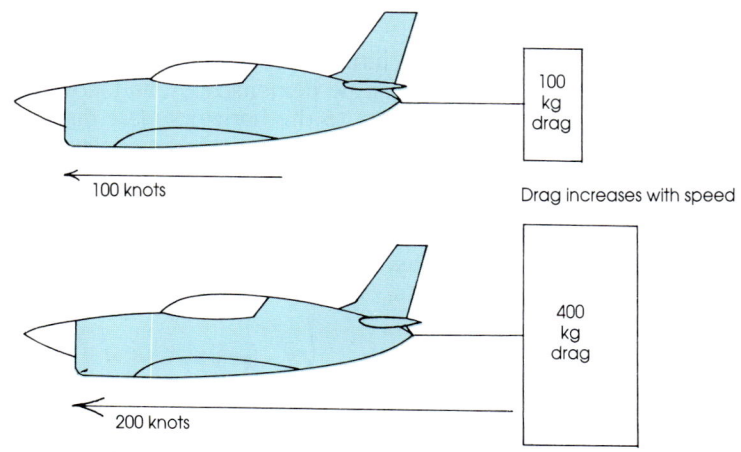

Drag increases with speed

To help overcome parasite drag, modern aircraft are streamlined

Air activities

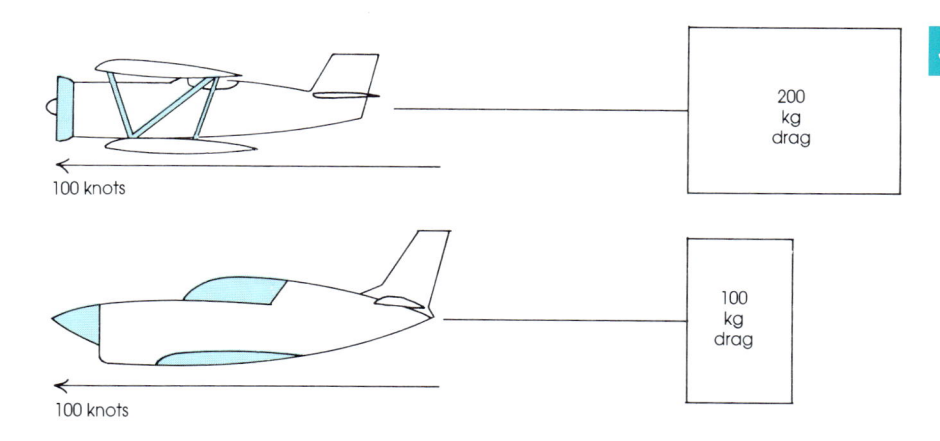

Effect of shape and smoothness on drag

Thrust

This is the forward force produced by the propeller which moves the aircraft through the air and produces the relative airflow over the wings.

Mass

This is the downward force of the aeroplane which lift must equal.

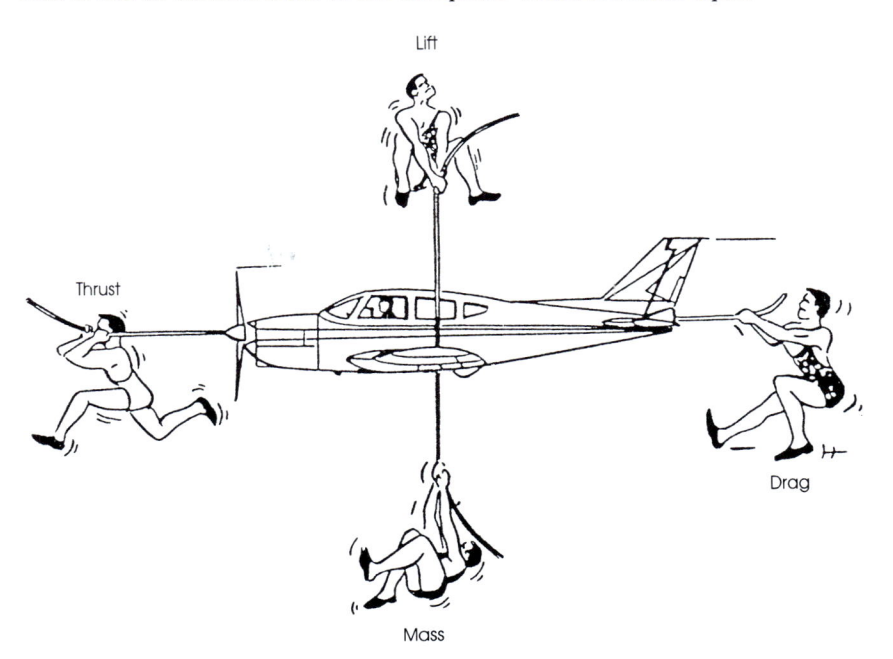

The flow forces acting on an aircraft are shown in the diagrams: as you can see, these forces do not act through one point. Find out why.

31

Tailplane

This is, in effect, another 'wing' and is used to balance the aircraft. Its primary job is to control the angle of attack of the main plane.

Axes

An aircraft manoeuvres through three axes, as shown in the diagram, which in turn all go through the centre of gravity of the aircraft.

Stability

The designer of the aircraft tries to build it as stable as possible about each axis. When this is achieved, the aircraft, after a disturbance, returns to its original attitude.

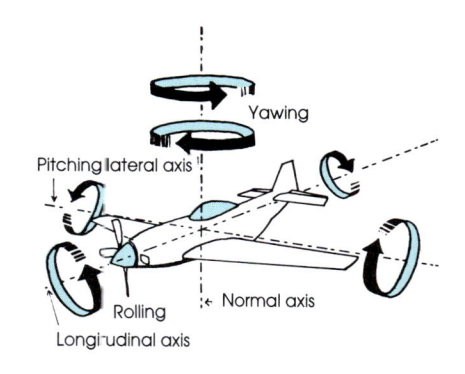

Dihedral angle

This is the angle at which the wings are set to help the aircraft regain level flight should one wing drop because of a disturbance or after a bank.

Controls

An aircraft can be manoeuvred by the pilot about the three axes as follows.

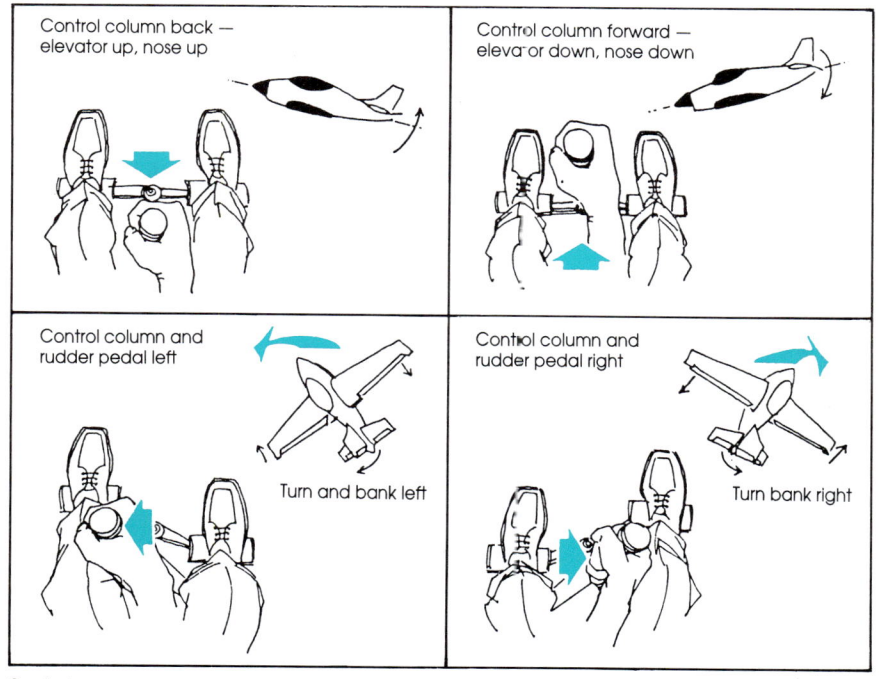

Control column back — elevator up, nose up

Control column forward — elevator down, nose down

Control column and rudder pedal left — Turn and bank left

Control column and rudder pedal right — Turn bank right

Controls

Air activities

Flaps

Another control in universal use on aircraft today is the flap. Flaps are aerofoil-shaped surfaces that are attached to the wings. Their main purpose is to allow an aircraft to approach to land at a lower but safer speed that would be possible without them. When lowered they increase the lift produced by the wing at a given speed, while increasing drag at the same time. This latter effect usually results in a lower nose position, which, apart from improving the pilot's visibility, allows the aircraft to make a steeper approach.

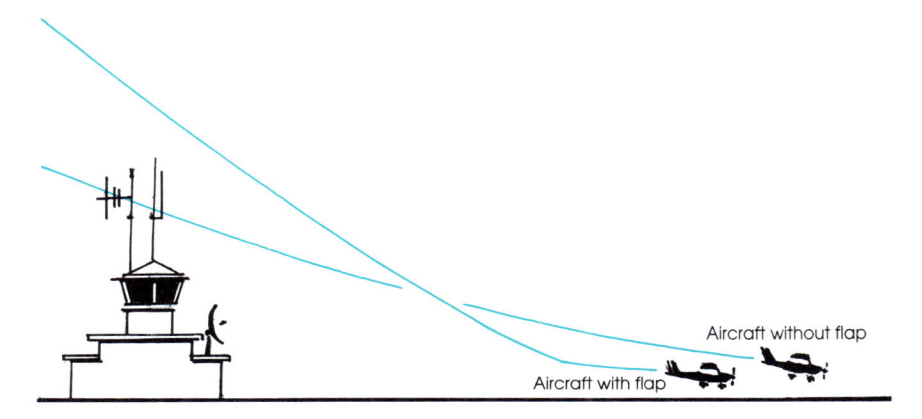

Flaps (or air brakes)

Light-aircraft engines

The modern light-aircraft engine is a far cry from early aircraft engines which were usually quite heavy, bulky in size for the power output, uneconomical with reference to fuel consumption and, worst of all from the aviator's point of view, unreliable. The light-aircraft engine today is the result of many years' work by designers striving to overcome, if not eliminate entirely, some of these unacceptable features that were commonplace in the early engines.

No longer do we have to worry about unreliable engines. They are proved, by extensive testing during development, to be able to operate efficiently and without fear of damage at high-power settings. We have only to look back a few years to the London–Australia air race when we had a large number of *single*-engine light aircraft operating at relatively high power settings for long periods over some of the most inhospitable terrain and oceans in the world. This race commenced at an RAF (Royal Air Force) base at Mildenhall in Suffolk.

Gone are the old bulky and unwieldy engines, and in their place are light compact units that are remarkably economical for their power output. These came into being as aircraft designers became more aware of the need to streamline aircraft. One of the major requirements was a need to reduce the frontal area (and therefore the engine size) to achieve comparable performance from a smaller capacity engine. A look around at today's range of light aircraft, in which the horizontally opposed cylinder concept is predominant, will soon make you aware of the advances made in this field. If we take off the engine cowls we will find a small well-designed and extremely well-finished piece of machinery, making extensive use of light-alloy materials, the operation of which is relatively foolproof. The engine has a dual-magneto ignition system (mainly for safety); a simple electric starting procedure, which eliminates the old method of hand starting; a simple-mixture control to improve performance and economy at higher altitudes, and even a simple-to-operate hot-air device to offset the carburettor icing problems that plagued the early aviators.

With all its refinement, the reliability of the modern engine is further improved by regulations that require progressive inspections and overhauls at regular specified intervals.

Piston engine

When a person stands near an engine that is running it is possible to feel the heat being given off.

These engines are 'heat' engines, which means they get their power from the energy given out when fuel is burnt making a gas.

The fuel used is petrol. It is first vapourised and mixed with air. The carburettor delivers the correct mixture of petrol and air.

The fuel is delivered into a chamber where it is compressed by a piston. When fully compressed it is ignited by a flash of flame from a spark plug. This causes the gas to explode. It becomes heated and expands. The piston is forced down and a rod attached to the piston head turns a shaft that is linked to the propeller shaft. As it rotates it will make the propeller spin thousands of times per minute.

The propeller will bite into the air causing it to pull the aircraft forward through the air. A four-stroke cycle engine is the type used and the following diagram shows how it works.

Engines

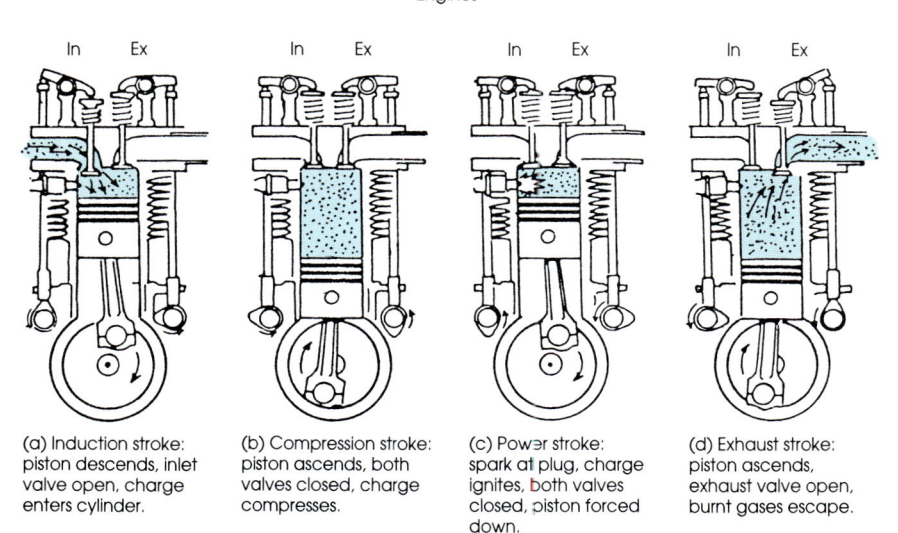

(a) Induction stroke: piston descends, inlet valve open, charge enters cylinder.

(b) Compression stroke: piston ascends, both valves closed, charge compresses.

(c) Power stroke: spark at plug, charge ignites, both valves closed, piston forced down.

(d) Exhaust stroke: piston ascends, exhaust valve open, burnt gases escape.

The four-stroke cycle

Air activities

Jet engine
Gas turbine engine

When a rifle is fired, the bullet is forced out of the barrel and the rifle jerks backwards into the shooter's shoulder. A machinegun fires rapidly with much jerking backwards or recoiling. If the machinegun is mounted on to the back of a dinghy or small boat, the continuous recoiling of the machinegun will push the boat through the water. The jet engine works the same way.

Air is dragged into a chamber by means of a turbine or fan; it is ignited in a chamber, and the exploding gas is forced out the back of the engine by a rear turbine. This provides the same reaction as the machinegun and forces the aircraft forward. Naturally, the turbines rotate at a fantastic speed causing a continuous thrust of exploding gas out of the engine, and this provides sufficient power to move the aircraft through the air. The following diagram of the gas turbine will show you in detail how it works.

The jet engine was developed mainly by a British engineer, Frank (later Sir Frank) Whittle. He made his first engine in 1937. The Germans made the first successful jet aircraft. It flew in August 1939 and was named Heinkel 179. The first British aircraft, a Gloster E28/29, flew in May 1941. The second aircraft was the famed Gloster Meteor.

Prop jet engine

As pure jet engines are best suited to high speed, high altitude aircraft, light aircraft normally use an adaption of the turbine engine in which the turbine shaft is extended forward to a speed reduction gearbox which then drives a propeller, which provides most of the thrust, although the jet exhaust still does provide some thrust also. For lower speed and lower altitude aircraft, the propeller provides thrust more efficiently than a pure jet, which is very important for aircraft used mainly for relatively short, low altitude journeys. Many helicopters also use prop jet engines.

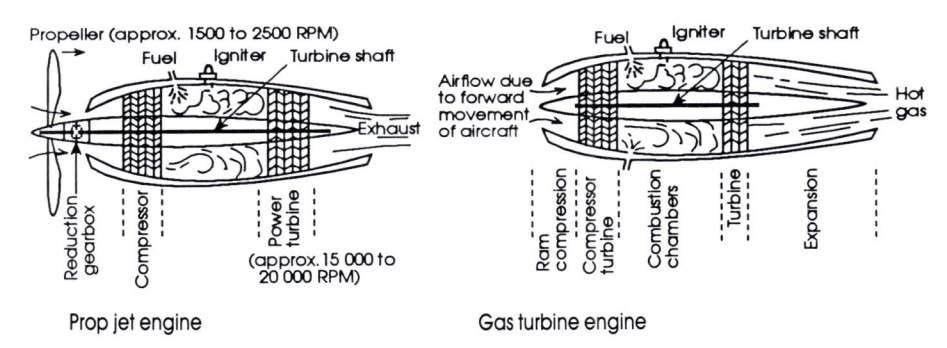

Prop jet engine

Gas turbine engine

Navigation

The first task confronting pilots is to draw a line on an aeronautical map joining two places. They then measure the track (bearing) with a protractor and the distance by comparing with the nautical-miles scale. They also check other CAA charts to make sure they will not be going through restricted areas (for example military flying areas), and from them they will also learn things such as radio frequencies en route. A most important part in planning is to obtain a weather forecast, which, if adverse, may mean the cancellation of their flight. A forecast will tell them of wind speed and directions at various heights from which they can compute their heading, ground speed, fuel consumption and time for the flight.

Once in the air, pilots have to check their planned course constantly. The airline pilots have many radio and navigation aids at their disposal, but the light-aircraft pilot must rely on visual ground checks and calculations on their computer to keep check on their progress.

Speed in the aircraft is usually measured in *knots*; 66 knots equal 122 kilometres per hour. The *knot* or nautical mile per hour is used because on all navigation maps a degree of latitude equals 60 nautical miles.

Ground speed

This is the actual speed of an aircraft relative to the ground below it. The speed will be affected by the wind that is blowing. Examples follow.

There is always some wind, so that the first example of No Wind never occurs. If the wind is blowing on the aircraft at an angle, it will increase or decrease the airspeed to a lesser degree.

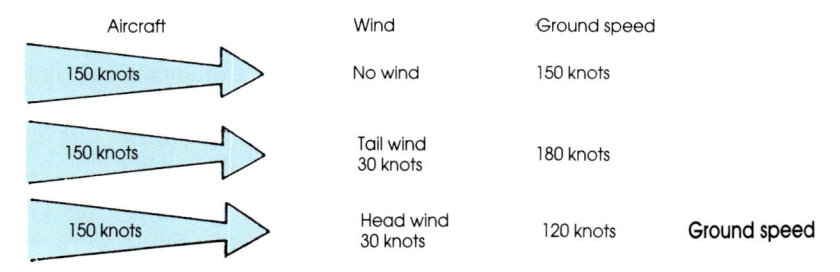

Aircraft	Wind	Ground speed
150 knots	No wind	150 knots
150 knots	Tail wind 30 knots	180 knots
150 knots	Head wind 30 knots	120 knots

Ground speed

Airspeed

This is the speed of an aircraft in relation to the surrounding air. It is measured by air flowing into an instrument called a Pitot (pronounced 'peetoe') tube which leads to the airspeed indicator.

However, as an aircraft increases its height the air becomes thinner, therefore there is less pressure, and because of this the indicated air speed has to be amended. This is done with a small hand-held instrument called a navigation computer or dead reckoning computer. All pilots have one in their kit. When you next go to an airport or airfield, ask the pilot to show you his/her computer and how it works.

Airspeed indicator (ASI) Cars have a speedometer to show speed. In an aircraft, this is called an airspeed indicator.

The basic principle of the ASI is the measurement of pressure differences in the air. A probe called a pitot head is attached to the outside of the aircraft. It has a hole in it facing the airflow. Pressure differences are measured that give a reading on the airspeed indicator in knots. This speed is called indicated airspeed, and by using the pilot's navigation computer a correction is made for the density of the air based on outside-air temperature and height of the aircraft. This new speed is called true airspeed, TAS.

Air activities

Altimeter This is an instrument that measures the aircraft height above a reference point, usually sea-level. With this information the pilot knows the height above the ground. Maps show the height of mountains and other objects such as radio towers.

Magnetic Compass A magnetic needle that can swing freely always points in a north–south direction. The magnetic needle is mounted on a card, divided into 360°. This card is called a compass rose. Also marked on the instrument is the front or heading of the aircraft. From this the direction the aircraft is heading can be decided. As the aircraft changes direction the compass needle will always point to the magnetic north. To find the heading of the aircraft you read the direction (in degrees) against the heading point or mark.

Because magnetic north is slightly different to true-north an allowance must be made and this compass variation added on.

Estimate time of flight

Some of the factors required to estimate the time it would take to cover a particular distance in the air are described as follows.

First, you would require the following items:
1. a navigational map; that is, one that has a nautical-mile scale
2. a navigational computer. This is an instrument like a circular slide rule. The pilot uses it to make navigational calculations, and it is also used to work out wind vectors
3. the true compass bearing from point A to point B, that is, your departure point and your destination
4. the weather conditions, particularly wind force and direction; this will be given to you in knots and degrees (T)
5. the cruising speed of the aircraft in which you are to fly
6. an accurate watch
7. a geometrical protractor
8. the variation applicable.

Now take your map, and with a sharp pencil, draw a line from point A to point B. This is your intended track along which you want to fly.

From point A, draw in the wind direction and speed for one hour. We will call this AC.

From the end of the wind vector (point C), with a pair of compasses measure off an arc equal in length to the true airspeed for one hour. For this exercise the TAS can be equal to the cruising speed of the aircraft. This arc is to cut the track line AB, and let us call this point D.

Join CD. The distance AD is now the ground speed of the aircraft for one hour.

Measure AB and calculate that distance at the ground speed just found and you will have the flight time to go from A to B.

If you know the time you intend to leave for your flight, this is expected time of departure (ETD), and if you add the flight time to it you will have the expected time of arrival (ETA).

One final point to remember: the ETD is the time you intend to leave on your takeoff run, and your ETA is your time of arrival on the ground at your destination. It does *not* include the time you spend starting up your aircraft, taxiing and waiting for a clearance to take off. You will also have to allow time on arrival to taxi in at the new airfield.

Draw in a line AE such that AE is parallel to CD. AE is then the heading to fly so that you will track along AB. You will see that there is a drift of 14° to the right of your track (angle EAB), therefore your heading must be 066° (T) to fly a track of 080° (T). Your ground speed is 110 knots, giving you a flight time of 88 minutes. If you start your takeoff run from A at 0916 hours, your ETA at B will be 0916 + 88 mins = 10.44 hours.

The following sketch will show how it is plotted on a map.

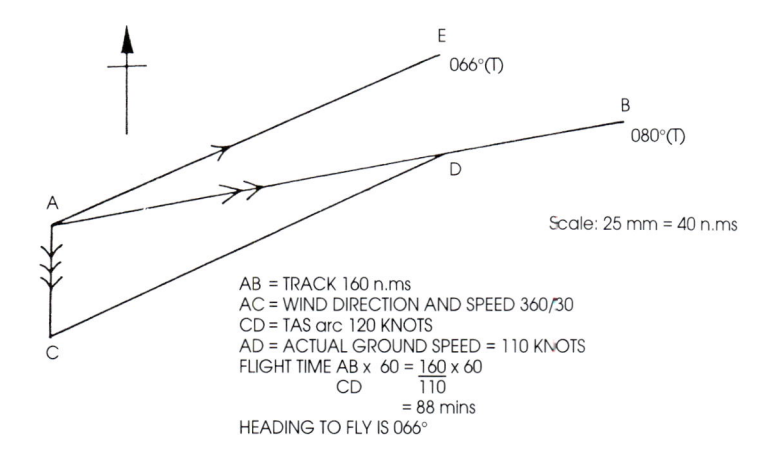

AB = TRACK 160 n.ms
AC = WIND DIRECTION AND SPEED 360/30
CD = TAS arc 120 KNOTS
AD = ACTUAL GROUND SPEED = 110 KNOTS
FLIGHT TIME AB x 60 = 160 x 60
              CD   110
              = 88 mins
HEADING TO FLY IS 066°

Scale: 25 mm = 40 n.ms

How to read and apply the 24-hour clock

Because there are 24 hours in one day, the hour hand has to go around the clockface twice and you have to know whether it is a.m. or p.m. If you spent several days in a sealed room you would soon lose track of day and night.

Because aircraft travel so fast, and at all hours of the day and night, this could cause misunderstandings. If a pilot were told to depart from an airport at 6.30, does this mean in the morning or the evening?

To overcome this, airlines use the '24-hour clock'. This is simply a clock that tells the time by having 24 hour marks on it instead of the usual 12 hours.

After 12 noon you simply add an extra hour to the time. In other words, 1 p.m. becomes 12 noon plus one hour, which is 13 hours. The time on the 24-hour clock is always measured with four numbers, two for the hour and two for the minutes. Some examples are as follows:

- 10 mins past midnight is 0010.
- 1.00 a.m. is 0100.
- 6.30 a.m. is 0630.
- 10.05 a.m. is 1005.
- 12.55 p.m. is 1255.
- 1.00 p.m. is 1300.
- 4.15 p.m. is 1615.
- 9.45 p.m. is 2145.
- 11.50 p.m. is 2350.
- 11.59 p.m. is 2359, the last minute of the day.

When we are speaking, 1 p.m. is called 'thirteen hundred hours'.

Correct procedure for communication

To communicate with the control tower while on the ground or in the air, you will have to

1. have a serviceable radio and know the frequency of the tower you are calling
2. know how to correctly use the radio set and microphone
3. know the phonetic alphabet
4. speak clearly and precisely
5. wait your turn to speak and *never* interrupt into another call
6. always identify yourself and name the tower you are calling, for example 'Tango Delta Xray calling Melbourne Tower'. Your answer should be 'Melbourne Tower to Tango Delta Xray'. You should then acknowledge—'Tango Delta Xray, landing instructions'; or whatever your message is. When your conversation/s is/are finished and you have received the last of the information from the Melbourne Tower, you end this way: 'Tango Delta Xray'. Always, when calling, use the three letters of your aircraft registration.

The phonetic alphabet is as follows:

A	ALPHA	N	NOVEMBER	1	WUN
B	BRAVO	O	OSCAR	2	TOO
C	CHARLIE	P	PAPA	3	THREE
D	DELTA	Q	QUEBEC	4	FOWER
E	ECHO	R	ROMEO	5	FIFE
F	FOXTROT	S	SIERRA	6	SIX
G	GOLF	T	TANGO	7	SEV-EN
H	HOTEL	U	UNIFORM	8	AIT
I	INDIA	V	VICTOR	9	NINER
J	JULIETTE	W	WHISKY	0	ZERO
K	KILO	X	XRAY		
L	LIMA	Y	YANKEE		
M	MIKE	Z	ZULU		

Gliding and soaring

Gliding and soaring are for the flying enthusiast or flying sportsperson. A fascinating hobby for many pilots, and a highly competitive sport for many other people, gliding offers membership of a flying fraternity that is worldwide. This sport is international. World championships are held every two years and most countries hold annual national contests.

There are many types of sailplanes used by clubs today. There are four groups:

1. trainers, which are two-seater aircraft in which the student usually sits in front of the instructor
2. advanced aircraft, which may be single seaters
3. high-performance sailplanes, which can be single or twin seaters and are used for competitions
4. powered or self-launch sailplanes, which are mainly used for initial training, although, as they become more common, competitions will no doubt be organised.

Early in the history of gliding, trainers were pure gliders that did not have the ability to soar like the trainers available today. Most of the above-mentioned types can be seen at the larger soaring clubs throughout Australia.

A sailplane may be launched with any of the following four methods:
1. from a hilltop into the updraught of the rising airstream created by the hill
2. by an automobile or winch pulling it into the air at a speed of around 40 knots
3. by an aeroplane towing it to a suitable height
4. self-launching.

Each of these methods is widely used. Although using aeroplanes as tugs is the most expensive, it is also considered the most practical by the larger training clubs. It has the advantage of pilots being able to remain on tow until they have reached their desired area or lift, or they may decide to continue to search a wider field before releasing from tow.

Self-launching gliders are becoming increasingly popular especially as training aircraft. These powered gliders use the motor for initial climb only, and then after switching off the motor have all the characteristics of a sailplane and perform very well without the motor.

Soaring is the art of using the energy of the atmosphere in such a way that the aircraft is able to climb and travel cross-country, remaining airborne for a considerable period of time.

This energy is derived from vertical currents of warm air rising from the ground and perhaps forming clouds, or from waves caused by layers of air of different density in the prevailing airstream or from mountain ranges.

We usually make most use of these thermal air currents up to about 3000m, but if we are experienced enough and equipped with warm clothing and oxygen we may venture up into wave conditions where height in excess of 10 000m are possible.

Ferdinand Schultz flew for eight hours in this glider in the early 1920s

Air activities

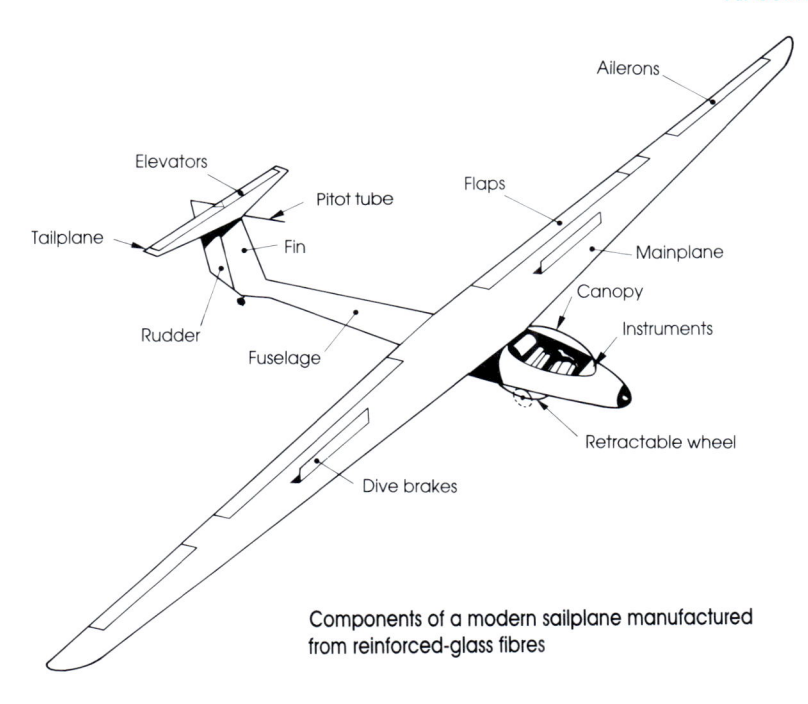

Components of a modern sailplane manufactured from reinforced-glass fibres

Gliding clubs are spread fairly widely throughout Australia and function under the Gliding Federation of Australia as the controlling body responsible for air-safety standards and general administration within the requirements of the CAA.

In 1981–82, 70 000 hours were flown, made up of instructional flying, training, cross-country flying and general flying among private owners. We have now in Australia some 600 gliders in 103 clubs with a total of around 3500 members. Privately owned aircraft amount to about 50% of this total.

Full-time gliding training and flying is carried out by at least one club in each state, so that this now means that people wishing to learn to glide may attend full-time courses for periods of approximately two weeks and thereby speed up the time necessary for solo flight. It may usually be assumed that about ten hours under instruction is necessary to graduate to solo standard. Once having gone solo there is still much to learn, such as cross-country flight, aerobatics, meteorology and navigation. In fact, for those who would make the sky their domain there are always things to be learned and skills to be acquired.

The modern competition sailplane is a beautiful machine to see on the ground or in the air. It depends on its aerodynamic efficiency to give glide ratios of almost 50:1, with considerable speed ranges, and carrying a pilot and equipment such as radio and oxygen, enabling him/her to fly courses in any direction of several hundred kilometres out and return or of up to ten hours duration. A record distance of over 1450 kilometres has been flown. These sailplanes were mainly constructed of timber and fabric in the past, but today all-metal and all-fibreglass machines are common. Resin-bonded reinforced-fibre construction appears likely to make better sailplanes in the future.

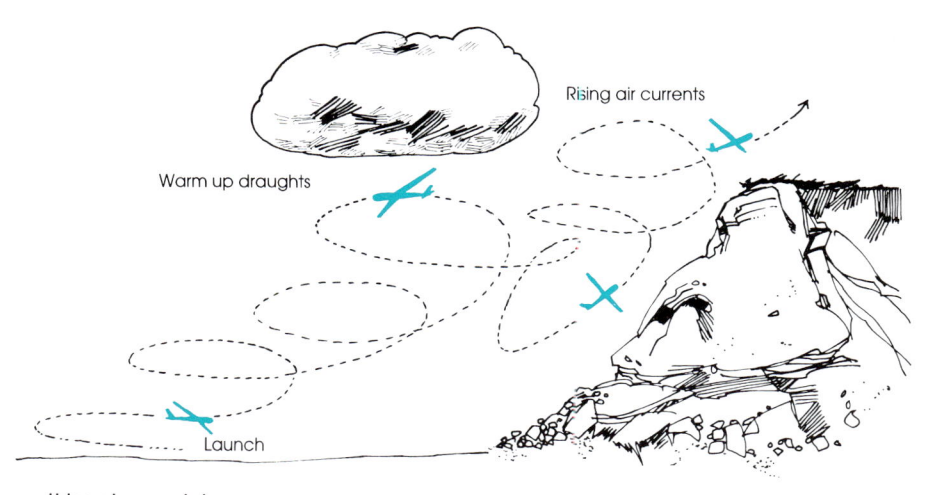

Using air currents to soar

Learning to glide requires only the ability to apply yourself to learning new skills. Naturally, it is necessary to be healthy and capable of adapting to a new environment. Instruction is given in two-seat aircraft and only qualified instructors are permitted to give flight instruction. Certificates of qualifications are issued and are recognised throughout the world by the Federation Aeronautique Internationale (FAI). However, students are not permitted to fly solo until they are fifteen years of age.

Basic instrumentation of a sailplane consists of airspeed indicator, a compass, turn and bank indicator, altimeter and variometer. It is the variometer that indicates when the aircraft is entering rising or descending air currents. The pilot circles the aircraft within rising currents to gain height, or when passing through descending colder air the pilot will increase air speed to pass through it more quickly. Other instruments not normally required may be carried for specialised purposes such as cloud flying or high-altitude flight.

Some knowledge of meteorology is essential because it is often by the clouds that we are able to recognise the thermal conditions necessary for soaring flight. Although convection may be present in a clear atmosphere, it is always present when clouds are forming, and may be dangerously powerful in well-developed cumulonimbus clouds which are associated with thunderstorms.

Wave clouds are high-altitude clouds capable of lifting a sailplane to great heights, enabling it to cover ground rapidly in a straight line with little or no apparent loss of height. Therefore, we must recognise the clouds from day to day, to use their forces to the best advantage.

These paragraphs are intended only as an introduction to the art of gliding and soaring, and we would stress that the actual technique can be acquired only by constant practice under skilled supervision, while an understanding of the atmosphere and its relation to flight is necessary through theory-of-flight studies. All these things are given to the student in correct order by competent instructors who make learning to fly a pleasure.

Most pilots recollect with pride their first 'solo', and the memory of it is a very personal experience.

Air activities

Kite flying

Kite flying was one of the earliest forms of air activities and it has developed over the centuries into an interesting outdoor activity for all ages. During its history, the kite has been used as a fun toy, a military weapon, scientific equipment and, today, a very sophisticated outdoor activity.

Have you ever built a kite? Do you know how to build one? How many different types of kites are there? It is fun to find out what type of kite flies best in your location. You can experiment by building the same model using different materials or altering the dimensions. Try shortening the tail or altering the guy line in relation to the balance point and, to make your experiment more useful, you will need to measure the wind speed. For ideas on kites, refer to the air activities chapter in the book *Program Ideas for Scouts* (S.A.A. resource book).

Aeromodelling

Aeromodelling is a hobby that can be enjoyed by the young and the young at heart. Scouts can start off with the simplest of hand-launch gliders and through their growing-up years move on to the many more complicated and intriguing models. Like any other interests, this hobby requires work and money, but because of the wide variety of model aeroplanes that can be built, there is something to fill everybody's ambitions at a reasonable cost.

Aeromodelling virtually started in the early 1900s when most aircraft being built were rubber-powered models. The hobby passed through a period of depression when it ranked as little more than the curious pursuit of adults who should have known better and youngsters to whom it could do no harm. In 1928 the Wakefield Trophy, an international competition for rubber-power models, started to give aeromodelling some prestige. In 1929 came the first of the petrol engines, the Brown Junior, which opened a whole new field to model-aeroplane builders.

Where do I start?

The beginner has a few choices when starting as an aeromodeller, as follows.

Plastic models These are excellent injection-moulded scale models of real aircraft, and although all the parts are of the highest quality detail, they are usually small and an amount of skill is required to put them together. Care and patience are rewarded by a model to decorate your home or Patrol corner.

Hand-launch gliders This is usually the first type of flying model a beginner tries. Here we are introduced to some of the common modelling materials: balsa, glue, lacquer, and tissue. The tools required are not very unusual and a good job can be done with a 'Stanley' knife (razorblades are dangerous), a steel rule, fine sandpaper and sanding block, and pins. An important item is a building and cutting board, which saves the tabletops, and when dinner is ready, the board and the plane under construction can be shifted without any trouble. A plan of a typical beginner's hand-launch glider (chuckie) with many helpful hints is shown a little further on to get you started.

Materials These are available from local model shops and consist of
- 1 of 1 metre $\times$ 6.5 mm hard balsa (will make several fuselages)
- 1 of 1 metre $\times$ 6.5 mm medium balsa (will make two sets of wings)
- 1 of 1 metre $\times$ 1.5 mm medium balsa (will make several tailplanes).

Building With carbon paper between the plan and the balsa, trace directly over the outline of the wing, fuselage and tailplane, then cut carefully around the outline on the balsa. Next the wing (still in one piece) can be sandpapered to the aerofoil shape shown on the plan; this is important if the model is to fly well. The wing can now be cut and re-glued to give the polyhedral shown. The fuselage can be shaped with sandpaper to round off the edges with the exception of the wing platform, which is left flat. The tailplane is rounded off at the edges and sanded flat. The finished components can now be assembled using glue and steel pins. At this stage make sure that your model is squared off as in the front view shown on the plan. Once again this is critical, or the model won't fly. One or more coats of clear lacquer will help to toughen the glider and reduce the drag.

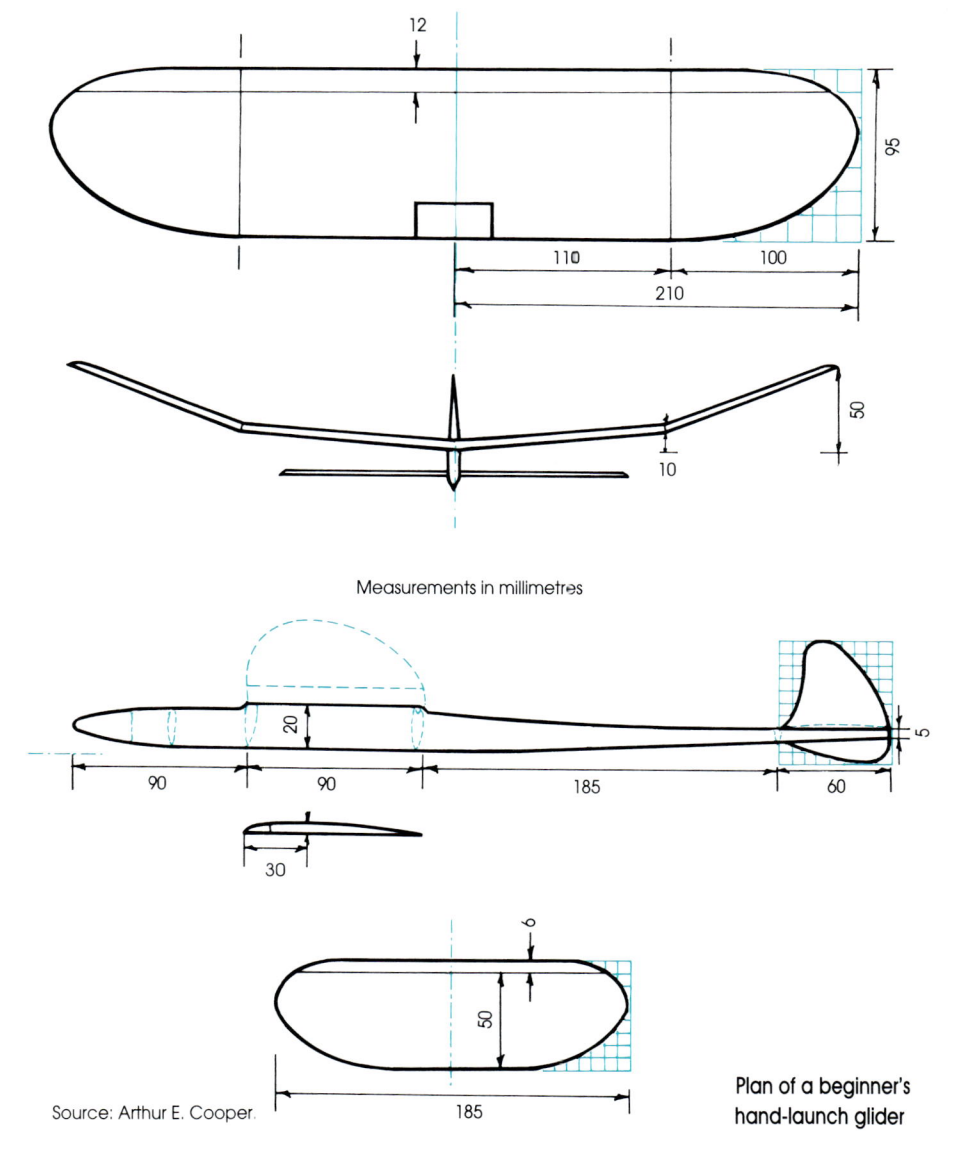

Measurements in millimetres

Source: Arthur E. Cooper.

Plan of a beginner's hand-launch glider

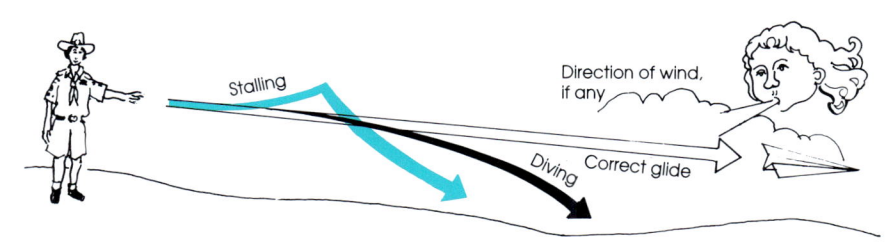

Flying The model will almost certainly have to have a small quantity of lead sheet glued to its nose to achieve a balance at a point about one-third of the distance between the leading and trailing edges of the wing (centre of gravity shown on plan). With a *gentle* hand launch, the glider should descend in a gentle slope to the ground (*see* illustration on facing page). Stalling is corrected by increasing the nose weight; diving is corrected by reducing the nose weight.

If at all possible, enlist the aid of an experienced aeromodeller to help your group through all the stages of building to flying—there is no substitute for experience.

Sailplane or glider This is often the next step, and a model of 60 to 100cm wing span should be built from either a plan or a commercial kit available from your nearest hobby or model shop. As the modeller gains experience, larger models can be built and these invariably fly better and for longer times than the smaller ones. A sailplane is usually towed on a towline like a kite, and when it is well overhead the tow ring on the end of the line slips off, leaving the glider in free flight.

Rubber models This type of model is also frequently built by the beginner, but a considerable amount of know-how is required to trim the model so that it will fly successfully. A small commercial kit is certainly the best way to get started in rubber models.

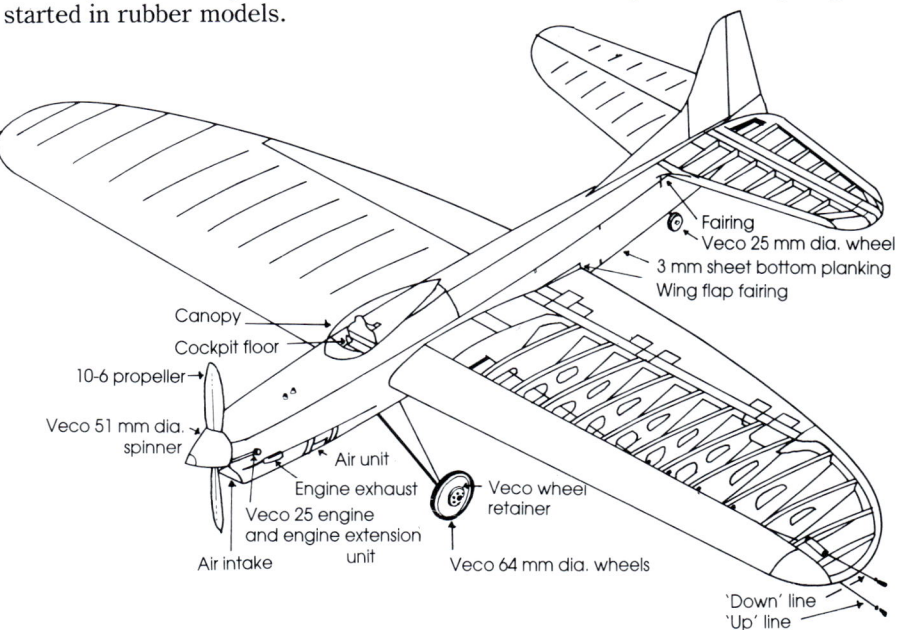

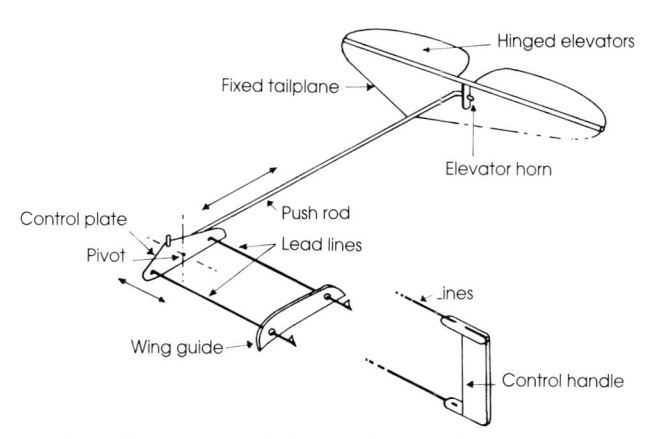

Figure: Control-line model aeroplane showing hinged elevators, fixed tailplane, elevator horn, push rod, control plate, pivot, lead lines, wing guide, and control handle.

Power models The advent of the small model-aeroplane motor, which is now a very powerful and reliable power unit, paves the way to both free-flight power models and control-line flying.

Free-flight power This is a plane for the modeller with a reasonable amount of experience and is not recommended for the beginner.

Control line After a few months of building and flying gliders, a simple control-line model is well within your scope. Control liners of 60 to 90 cm wing span powered by a 1.49 cc–2.5 cc diesel or glow-plug motor, are usually of built-up construction, but sometimes sheet-balsa model kits are available.

A control-line model is, as the name suggests, a model that flies in a circle tethered to two control wires held by the pilot at one end and connected to the elevator of the aeroplane, via a control plate, at the other end.

By moving the control handle, the pilot gives corresponding elevator movement causing the model to respond accordingly.

That is to say, backward movement of the control handle is the natural action for climb. Pushing the handle forward is the natural action for a dive.

With this relatively simple system of elevator control, almost any manoeuvre in the pitching plane, such as climbing, diving, looping and flying inverted, can be accomplished. Practical limits are, first, the design of the model itself, and, second, the ability of the pilot. While it is relatively simple to produce a sports-type control-line model that will fly satisfactorily, climb and dive and, possibly, loop, the design of models capable of a full aerobatic range is much more specialised.

Control-line flying lends itself to many variations. All in all, this is a very enjoyable part of model flying which does not require a big area to fly in. It is certainly advisable, however, to get the help of an experienced modeller to help you build and fly your first model and to advise you where you can fly, as many town councils now have by-laws limiting where you can fly engine-powered

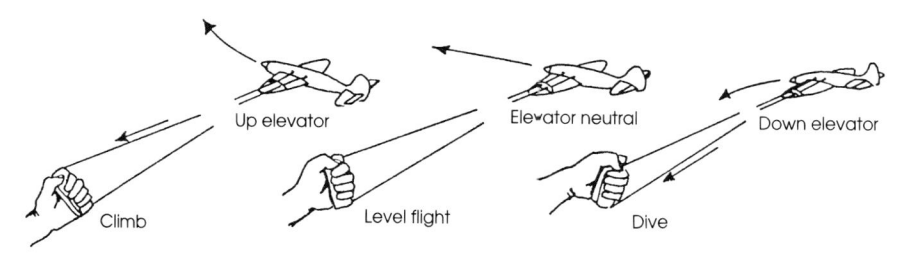

Figure: Control handle positions — Up elevator (Climb), Elevator neutral (Level flight), Down elevator (Dive).

Air activities

models due to the noise they make. Even models with silencers may still be prohibited. The types of models described here are the types of models to be built and flown to the requirements set down in the rules.

From this point onwards, the scope of types of models to fly is endless, even reaching to remote control by radio.

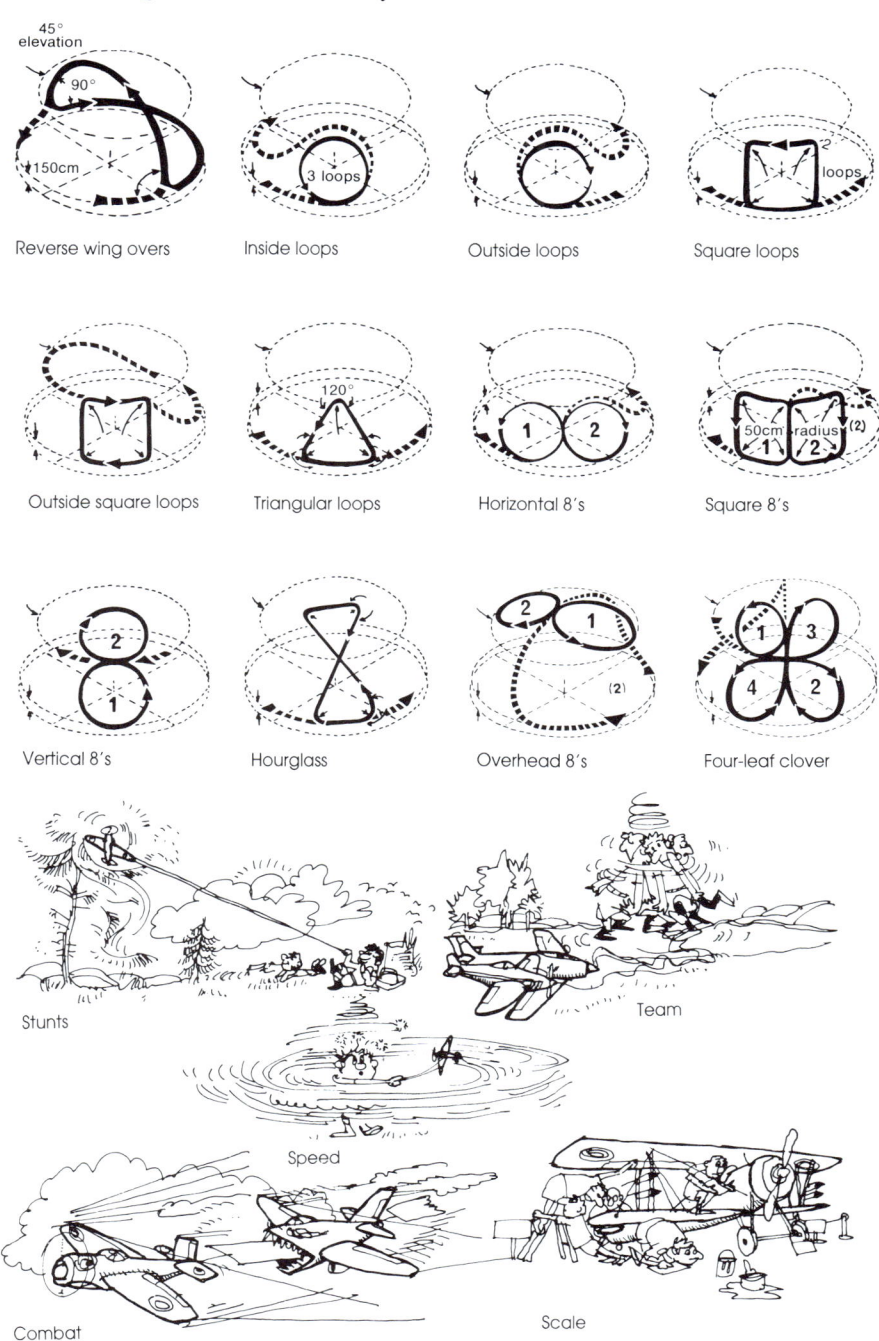

Reverse wing overs

Inside loops

Outside loops

Square loops

Outside square loops

Triangular loops

Horizontal 8's

Square 8's

Vertical 8's

Hourglass

Overhead 8's

Four-leaf clover

Stunts

Team

Speed

Combat

Scale

47

Radio control

A transmitter operated by the pilot sends a radio signal to a small receiver tuned to a given frequency inside the model. The signal is decoded within the radio receiver and the pulse then operates a small electric motor which in turn is connected to the various control surfaces of the aircraft.

This type of equipment is used to fly both sport and competition power models and gliders. With this equipment trained pilots can fly their model in exactly the same way as a pilot inside a real aeroplane.

Model flying is a worldwide activity, and many national and international competitions in all phases of the sport are conducted each year.

Aeromodelling is a hobby that can be enjoyed by anyone from six to sixty-six. It is a perfect training ground for any ambitious young person who perhaps wants to go on to full-size glider or power flying or even to making commercial aviation a lifetime career.

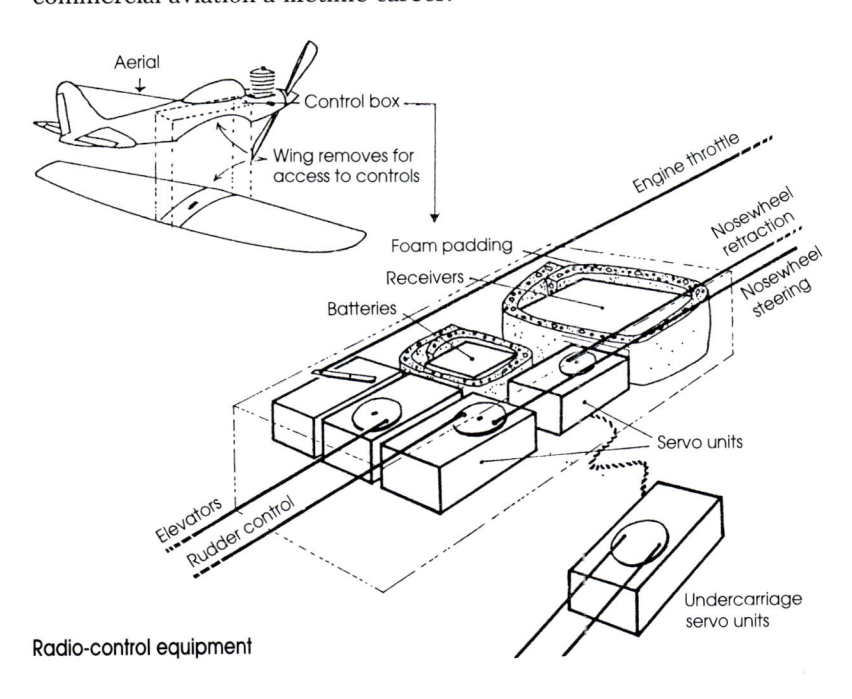

Radio-control equipment

Aeromodelling clubs

By this time you will no doubt be a very enthusiastic aeromodeller looking to build and fly even bigger and better models.

Joining a model-aeroplane club is the best way to progress because you will get the help of many other modellers who will be only too pleased to help you.

It is advisable to join a club affiliated with the Model Aeronautical Association of Australia, the controlling body responsible to the FAI in France, the organisation controlling all aeroplane-glider and parachuting competition throughout the world.

2
BUSHCRAFT

Hiking and journeys

People have always been explorers and today we are still looking into the unknown. Although journeys of exploration into space are often in the news these days, here in Australia much exploration remains to be done.

Since Australia was first colonised, explorers have tackled the challenges of the unknown wide spaces. Explorers such as Blaxland, Wentworth, Lawson, Oxley, Hume and Hovell were among the first to explore the Blue Mountains and the lands beyond. These early explorers were bushcraft experts.

Even today, people are finding out more about areas seldom seen before. They are crossing the Simpson Desert, travelling through the wilds of Cape York and setting off to explore the Antarctic.

Today's Scouts continue to find adventure by exploring areas unknown to them and to others of their age, as they meet the challenge of venturing into mountains, forests and national parks.

They find the inner joy that comes from being free, from having accomplished a hard climb to the top of a mountain, from camping alongside a clear pool or a waterfall in a little-known creek, from finding the nest of a bowerbird or from seeing a platypus in its natural habitat. People who live with only the roar of traffic, the blare of radios, who get square eyes from watching television, may never know the vivid colouring of finches, the call of the kookaburra or cockatoo. Nor will they know the joy that comes from sitting around the cooking fire at night with their friends reliving the adventures of the past day.

Hiking is a year-round activity. Scouts will want to hike because hiking is how they are able to probe deep into forest areas, to climb the highest summits and to seek out the most interesting facets of nature. The Scout 'bush person' enjoys finding little-used tracks, observing birds and animals in their natural surroundings, discovering secluded camping places, climbing the peak that he/she has not seen before, and seeing the sun rise and set with the noises and calls of the bushland all around.

Planning

What is the difference between 'just a walk' and a 'hike'? A hike is a walk with a purpose, and lasts more than an hour; it will often last all day.

When you plan a hike, with a friend or with your Patrol, you have to think about where you are going, when you intend to leave and return, equipment, food, parental permission, and what you will be doing on the way.

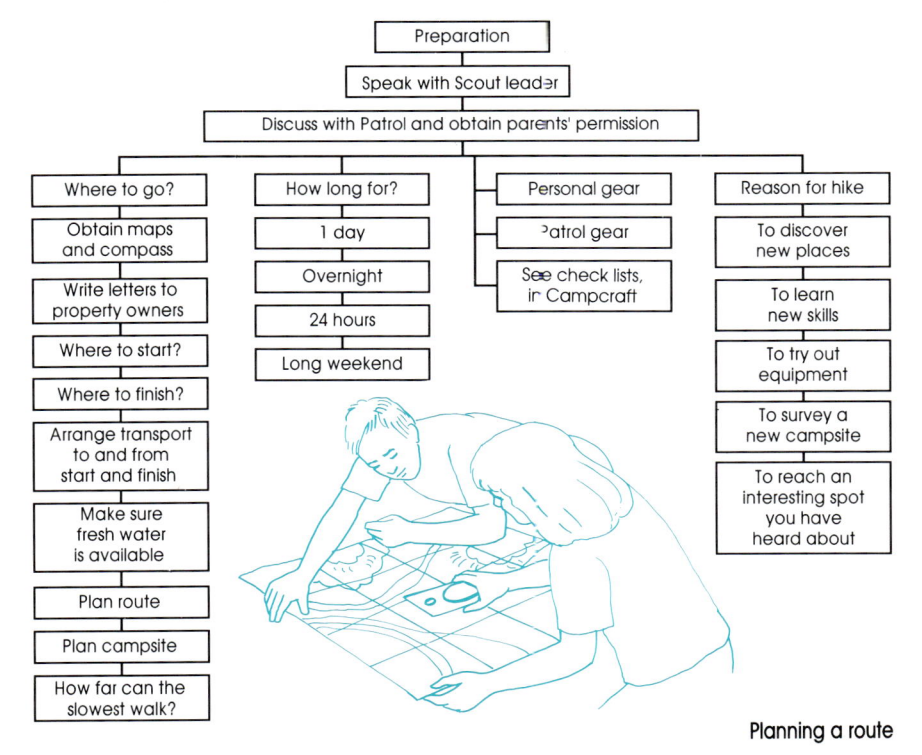

```
                    Preparation
                         |
              Speak with Scout leader
                         |
     Discuss with Patrol and obtain parents' permission
```

Where to go?	How long for?	Personal gear	Reason for hike
Obtain maps and compass	1 day	Patrol gear	To discover new places
Write letters to property owners	Overnight	See check lists, in Campcraft	To learn new skills
Where to start?	24 hours		To try out equipment
Where to finish?	Long weekend		To survey a new campsite
Arrange transport to and from start and finish			To reach an interesting spot you have heard about
Make sure fresh water is available			
Plan route			
Plan campsite			
How far can the slowest walk?			

Planning a route

Predicting walking time

Naismith's 'rule'

For an average walker with a medium pack, allow 1 hour for every 5 kilometres of easy going, every 3 kilometres of easy scrambling, and every 1.5

kilometres of extremely rough country, deep sand, soft snow or thick bush, plus 1 hour for every 500 metres up and 1 hour for every 1000 metres down. For every hour over 5 hours, include up to 1 hour to allow for fatigue. For very fit and experienced walkers, reduce the total time by one-third. Always work out your time on your slowest, smallest or most tired member.

These estimates are satisfactory for groups walking in Australian conditions.

Table 2.1 Naismith's 'rule' for an average walker with a medium pack

Allow 1 hour for
- 5 km easy going
- 3 km easy scrambling
- 1.5 km of extremely rough country, deep sand, soft snow or thick bush.

Add 1 hour for
- every 500 m up
- every 1000 m down.

For every hour (after 5 hours) add an extra hour for fatigue.

Very experienced and very fit walkers can reduce the total by one-third.

Mini first-aid kit

Part of your equipment for a hike or a journey is your personal first-aid kit. It might contain the following items:

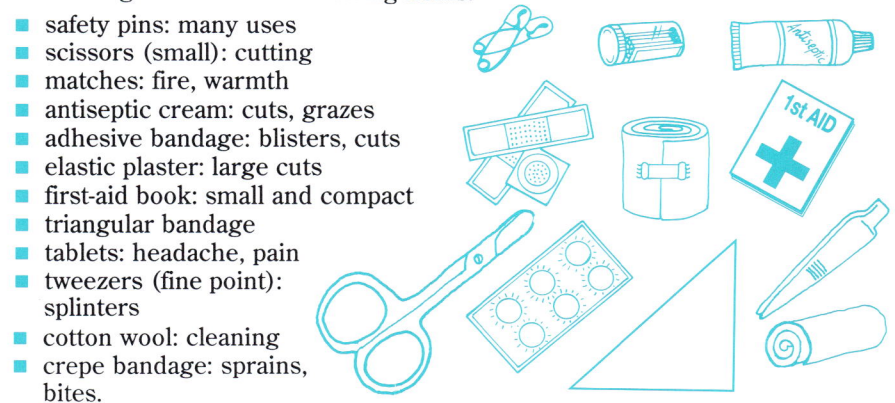

- safety pins: many uses
- scissors (small): cutting
- matches: fire, warmth
- antiseptic cream: cuts, grazes
- adhesive bandage: blisters, cuts
- elastic plaster: large cuts
- first-aid book: small and compact
- triangular bandage
- tablets: headache, pain
- tweezers (fine point): splinters
- cotton wool: cleaning
- crepe bandage: sprains, bites.

Have competitions

Components of a first-aid kit

See which Scout in your Patrol can produce:
(a) the lightest
(b) the smallest
(c) the most comprehensive
(d) the most economical
(e) the most practical kit.

Combine with another Patrol. One Patrol prepares a series of incidents involving the type of accident a Scout could meet on a hike.

Each Scout from the other Patrol visits an incident individually and has to produce the equipment he would need and say how the accident would be managed.

When you and your Patrol are going on a hike, follow a simple plan of preparation so nothing is forgotten or left to chance. Two things should be watched carefully during preparation. First, do not take too much gear: keep your pack as light as possible. The other point is to make sure you have shelter and a warm sleeping bag because if you do not have a good night's sleep you will find the going pretty tough on the next day.

The wise hike leader is one who delegates duties to each Patrol member early in planning so that everyone has a responsibility both during the hike and in collecting equipment beforehand.

The Country Code

Just as the knights in armour we read about in history books had a special code of behaviour, so do hikers. There is good reason for this because when hiking we are almost always walking on land owned by other people. Although they belong to us as members of the community, even national parks are the property of others. We have to show we have respect for others by adhering to the 'Country Code', as follows.

- When possible, ask permission before going on to private land. It is always best to go to the homestead and speak to the owner and let him know what you would like to do. A courteous request will almost always be granted and it is surprising how much interesting local information, such as where good swimming spots or campsites are, the local person may be able to give you.
- Be sure to leave gates exactly as found—usually closed.
- Use gates rather than climb over fences and thereby run the risk of straining or breaking them. If it is necessary to climb fences, cross by a large sturdy post.
- Leave no litter—either bury it or carry it away with you.
- Do not disturb grazing sheep or cattle—especially bulls!
- Walk around crops and not through them.
- Obey the fire regulations; they vary from place to place. Find out what they are.

Curious emus can suffocate if you leave litter behind

- If it is necessary to walk on the road, walk in single file on the right-hand side of the road, that is, facing the oncoming traffic. At night, carry a torch at the front and back of the party.

Remember: To behave in a way contrary to the Country Code is to make yourself and any other Scouts most unwelcome in the future.

Care of your feet

Hiking is certainly a great experience, but it can also really test you out. If you think about it, which part of your body do you think might crack first? These days when we travel mostly by car or by bicycle, our feet really get very easy treatment. On a hike, they will have to carry all the load—not only you; your rucksack. Therefore your feet will require particular attention both before and during your hiking trip.

Your feet are not alone—they have shoes, or boots, and socks to protect them, and it is at this point that you should start your preparation.

Footwear

Why wear boots? Why not joggers or sandshoes? In many cases joggers are all you will need, but when the going gets rougher and your pack gets heavier, good boots start to make sense. They keep your feet dry. They give ankle and knee support (important when carrying a heavy backpack on rough terrain) and many of the new models have shock absorption built into the boot to make for easy walking.

Your boots may not be your most expensive piece of equipment. They are, however, one of the most important items for your comfort, so put a lot of time and thought into buying them.

The shoes or boots you wear must have good thick soles and heels so sharp stones cannot push into your foot when you walk over them. The soles should also have a tread pattern so they can get a grip on grass-covered hillsides. Smooth soles are useless on a steep grassy slope, no matter whether the grass is green or dry; in either case you are likely to slip three paces back for every one pace forward.

If the ground you plan to hike over is not particularly rocky or steep, stout-soled shoes will be quite adequate and you need not invest in a pair of boots. Boots, rather than shoes, are heavier for you to lift at every step; on the other hand, they give your ankles much more support. If you are prone to ankle injuries, lightweight boots are the thing for you.

If you are buying boots or shoes especially for hiking, it is a good idea to get a half-size larger than usual. This allows you to wear two pairs of socks, which provide extra cushioning for your feet, and also allow for your feet to swell a little, which they will do under the unaccustomed load.

Synthetic or leather boots

Synthetic are much lighter and do not require as much looking after as leather and are probably more suited to the first-time buyer because they require much less breaking-in time. Their disadvantages are that they will not last as long as a leather boot and usually cannot be made waterproof without stopping their ability to 'breathe'. While waterproof synthetic boots are available, unless they are made of Gore-tex they are usually unsuited for Australia's hot conditions.

Leather boots that are made from a natural material 'breathe' much better than synthetic, resulting in more comfortable feet. Leather boots will also form themselves to the shape of your feet, and unlike synthetic boots, will retain this shape for the life of the boots. With proper care and use of preservative/waterproofing products, a good pair of leather boots will outlast two or three pairs of synthetic boots. Leather boots can also be made stiffer than synthetics, thereby giving more support to the feet and ankles.

Boot care

Good boots are expensive, but with proper care they will give many years of service. Our suggestions for general maintenance are as follows.

1. After each trip, clean off any dirt or caked mud with a wet rag or water and a soft nylon brush.
2. Excessive exposure to water and heat can be very damaging, so wet boots should be dried as soon as practicable but never near a direct source of heat such as heaters, open fires, or on the back shelf of a car. Dry in a dry, shady, well-ventilated position, and, if boots are thoroughly saturated, stuff with crumpled newspaper which should be changed regularly until the boots are dry.
3. When boots are dry, treat leather with a light coat of appropriate preservative/waterproofing product.
4. When not in use, store your boots in a cool dry place that allows air circulation around the boots.

Feet

Woollen socks are best because they are resilient; that is, after you tread on them they tend to spring back rather than stay compressed. Wool is also absorbent, so that if your feet perspire you will not notice it. Mending socks by darning is good Scouting, but darned socks are not very good to hike in because the mended area can rub the skin and cause a blister.

Blisters are one thing you should avoid, and you can do so by always stopping at the first sign of a sore spot and covering the spot with an adhesive bandage or similar dressing to prevent any further rubbing.

Some more points to note in looking after your feet are as follows.

1. Each night, take off your socks and fluff them up by hitting them against a stick.
2. When you stop for lunch on a long day's hike, change each sock to the other foot; the pressure comes in different places, and further helps to prevent blisters.
3. Avoid swimming for long periods before hiking because it softens the feet too much.
4. Keep your feet clean by washing and drying carefully, especially between the toes.

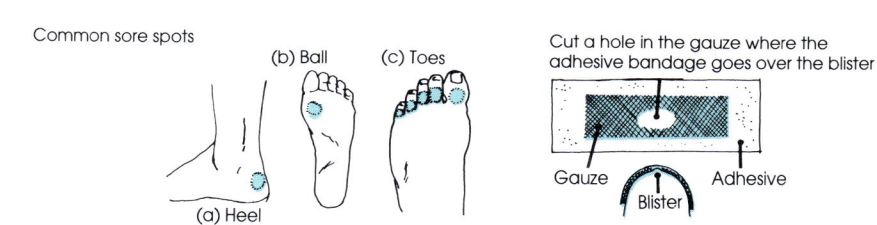

Common sore spots
(a) Heel
(b) Ball
(c) Toes

Cut a hole in the gauze where the adhesive bandage goes over the blister

Gauze Blister Adhesive

Clothing

For bushwalking, as for every other outdoor sport, you need suitable clothes and these can be quite inexpensive. Any old clothes that are comfortable and strong will do.

The most comfortable garb is shirt and shorts. Some bush is so thick, however, that it is advisable to have long trousers available. Any garments worn should be light, yet strong and not easily snagged by thorns and bushes.

Wind and rain may be kept out by a lightweight impervious jacket whereas the body heat is conserved by several layers of insulating clothing. It is impossible to keep completely dry in steady rain, so choose clothing that remains warm even when wet. Wool is ideal.

Shirt

Roominess is essential. Your shirt should be long enough to protect the stomach and kidneys, and long-sleeved for protection against cold, sunburn and scrub. The pockets should have buttoned flaps. Wool is the best material because it provides some warmth when wet.

Trousers

Your Scout shorts are usually adequate. Long trousers are worn when the wearer needs extra protection against cold, scrub, insects and sun. Long trousers should be light and roomy. Perhaps the best are wool and synthetic mixtures.

Hat

Scout hats shed water well and keep the wearer warm in winter and cool in summer. In cold conditions a woollen balaclava reaching below the collar is best for warmth. A towelling 'floppy' hat or the army-style 'giggle hat' is also ideal.

Jumper

At least one woollen jumper is essential, but do not pin your faith on a single heavy garment in extreme cold. Two light fluffy jumpers of equal weight are much warmer.

Showerproof jacket (parka)

Jackets that have a hood with drawcords and reach to the knees give best protection from wind and rain. Parkas made of PFTE, Z-cote oil and dry-proofed japara and proofed nylon are recommended.
    Condensation readily forms inside nylon jackets, and lightweight nylon materials quickly lose their waterproofing.

Waterproofing

Woollen items can be made water repellent by having the lanolin restored. This is done by immersing them in a solution of 100 grams of anhydrous lanolin in 7 litres of white spirit (Shellite). Then hang them up to dry over the bath or basin overnight. *Do not wring out.*

Outdoor clothing

Outdoor clothing may be separated into three divisions: outer or shell garments, warmth or insulating garments, and underwear or wicking garments.

Shell garments

These are the most important piece of outdoor clothing you can buy, because they are designed to keep out the wind and rain. Wind disturbs and displaces the still air entrapped in the insulating garments, causing higher convective and conductive heat loss. If you prevent wind from reaching your body and clothing, you will feel warmer. Many materials are windproof, the only criteria being that the fabric is made of small tightly woven threads, that is nylon, Gore-tex, closely woven cotton, and so on. Wool, fleece and other coarsely woven materials are not completely windproof unless they are covered with one of these fabrics.

While keeping the wind off you is perhaps all you will require in order to keep warm on many occasions, it is also important at all times to keep dry. Water conducts heat away about fifteen times faster than dry air. In addition, the process of drying (evaporation) is always accompanied by a cooling effect. Rain wetting your insulating garments displaces the still air, causing greater heat loss, and, in some garments, wetting of the insulation may cause it to collapse. As well as rain, perspiration is a source of moisture and should be kept to a minimum. A shell garment, therefore, must be windproof and waterproof, yet not be so hermetic as to leave you drenched in sweat. Materials that stop rain getting in, but allow sweat vapour out, are said to 'breathe'.

Insulating garments

No piece of clothing creates warmth. It only insulates your body so the heat your body produces is not sapped by the cold air outside.

The best insulator is a layer of still air, and while it is easy to provide a layer of air around the body, keeping it still is more of a problem. Your body heat warms the layer next to you, while the cold environment outside cools part of the layer next to it. Hot air rises and cold air falls, causing convection currents within the layer. Therefore, insulating garments have two functions—to create a layer of air and to eliminate convection currents within this layer. While insulating garments may be made of synthetic or natural materials, the most efficient insulators are those with millions of fine interwoven fibres with air spaces between them. They provide a lot of loft (thickness) for their weight because only a small proportion of their volume is actually insulating material; the rest is air, and they keep the air still because their millions of fibres intercept the convection currents and break them up. For many years, the best insulation materials available were down, fur and wool. Today there is also a wide range of synthetics to choose from to suit every need.

Underwear

Made from polypropylene or chlorofibre, these are the so-called 'thermal' underwear, a misname, because they do not produce heat; they work by keeping your skin dry and minimising heat loss by evaporation. Your skin measures comfort by the temperature and humidity of the air right next to it. If it is wet (from perspiration or wet clothes), you feel clammy and uncomfortable, and because of the cooling effect of evaporation, you will soon feel cold. These skin-tight garments transfer moisture from your skin to the next layer of clothing, enabling you to stay dry and warm. Polypropylene and chlorofibre do not absorb moisture, unlike wool which can absorb 17% of its weight in water, so they feel much warmer. They also transfer moisture away six times faster than wool, and so dry much quicker if wet. Very lightweight, they require no special care. Simply rinse or wash to remove body oils and salts, and, if necessary, wear straight away. They will dry with body heat in about 10 to 15 minutes. Because they dry so quickly at room temperature, they should not be dried in commercial dryers or drying rooms because they may overheat and shrink.

Discuss your needs with the staff at your Scout Outdoor Centre.

Safety and survival

Hot, dry desert conditions

You may have to spend longer periods than you planned in desert country. Food will be much harder to find under these conditions, but water will be much more important to you than food. Animal tracks will usually lead you to water. Birds flying quickly and straight in one direction in the early morning or late afternoon are probably heading for water.

Around a waterhole is where you are likely to find wildlife—and this means food. So, if you are held up in this kind of country, stay put with the water supply until help arrives.

However, do not wait until you find yourself in these conditions to try to collect water. Practise it as a Patrol project until you become expert.

If you have any water with you, conserve it carefully. If you are running short of water and have some plastic bags or sheeting, the simple process of evaporation and condensation can be used to get you enough water to keep you alive.

An apparently dry creek bed may have running water a little way below the surface. Dig down, looking for moisture. If you find damp earth only, place a cup or billy in the bottom of the hole and spread a sheet of plastic over the hole. Seal the edges with sand or dirt so the hole is completely air tight. Place a small weight on the plastic, to make the lowest point straight above the cup. The sun will draw moisture up to the plastic, and during the cool night the moisture will condense, run down to the lowest point, and drip off into the cup.

Vegetation can be cut and placed in the hole, and this will yield water. Foul water can be turned into pure water by the same method. Plastic bags tied tightly around a leafy branch will yield drinkable water. Be careful not to puncture the bag!

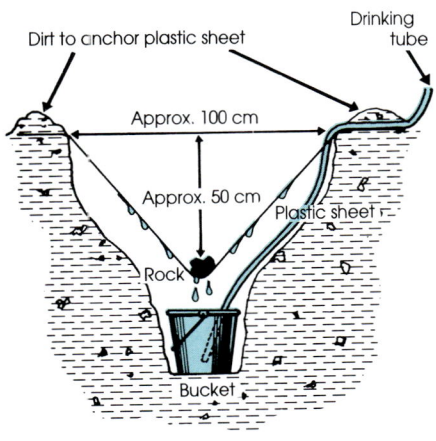

Fresh vegetation under the plastic will help

Winter conditions

In Australia, winter camping can be anything from camping under ideal conditions, as in the north; a slightly modified program and camping style in the temperate coastal regions; through to extreme winter conditions, including snow and blizzards, as in the southern highlands.

The highlands are fascinating and exciting country to camp and hike in, but special training and planning is essential before you venture into them. Extreme cold, and blizzard conditions, may be encountered even during the summer months. Unless you are properly prepared, you may find yourself in danger, even to the extent of losing your life.

If you are caught in a blizzard, there are two dangers to watch out for.

Becoming lost

You can become lost through wandering off the trail. If it is obvious the weather will turn very bad and you have no hope of reaching your destination, look for the most sheltered spot nearby and make your camp as quickly as possible.

Hypothermia

The second danger is hypothermia or loss of body heat. The cause is simply a drop in body temperature through wearing clothing that is inadequate for the wet, cold and windy conditions that blizzards bring. Fatigue will bring on this condition much more quickly, and the symptoms are a tendency to stagger and stumble, lagging behind the party, and a reluctance to carry on. It is difficult to recognise, and the affected person does not know there is something wrong.

Treatment involves getting the victim to immediate shelter, into dry and warm clothes, and preferably into a sleeping bag. A warm drink and some hot food will help to restore body warmth, but external heat, such as from a fire, may be very harmful.

If you plan going into this type of country, make sure you are wearing woollen clothes, have spare clothes and a waterproof garment, and that everyone else in the party is properly prepared in the same way.

Precautions

Be prepared for bad conditions. Act promptly if they occur.
1. Whatever the time of year, or length of the trip, prepare for it carefully. Listen to, and take heed of, weather forecasts.
2. Take a waterproof, windproof parka even for a day or half-day walk.
3. Have a good meal before setting out, and have frequent snacks during the day.
4. Plan your day so as to reach your destination, with time to spare, before nightfall. If the weather deteriorates, turn back, or take a safe alternative route that provides shelter.
5. Remember: there is always the chance of having to spend the night in the open, in which case an emergency groundsheet can save your life.
6. For safety, four is the minimum number for a party.

Cold + fatigue + low morale = high probability of hypothermia.

Fieldbook for Australian Scouting

Navigation

The most useful item a traveller carries on any trip is probably a map. A map is a way of illustrating the many features of the earth's surface, and it illustrates the many features that lie in the area in which you are travelling. By using a map you virtually have a 'bird's eye view' of the countryside. You can tell whether the road or waterhole for which you are headed is just over the hill, to the east of you, or to the west. It is certainly quicker than climbing both hills simply to find out.

Scale

A map used by a person planning a world cruise or by an astronaut circling the earth would show many countries on the one sheet of paper, whereas a map of your Troop's Easter campsite would show fine details such as tents and trees.

To reduce the whole world on to a single sheet requires a very small scale by which 1 centimetre on paper may represent 60 million centimetres on the earth's surface. By comparison, the map of your campsite has a large scale, and on it, 1 centimetre may represent 10 metres. Between these two examples are many types of scales—a motorist, for example, would probably use a map on which 1 centimetre represents 4 kilometres. This means that, on a single piece of paper, which is easy to handle in the car, the motorist would have a 'picture' of about 300 kilometres of roadway that has enough road details to enable the correct turns to be made.

Walkers, on the other hand, will usually wish to go only 15 to 25 kilometres in a day. In order to select the most direct or enjoyable route, walkers will want a map that represents an area smaller than that of the motorist's map but that gives much more information about the nature of the ground. For example, walkers will usually want to know in advance about tracks and footpaths, hills and valleys, scrub patches and hostels. This kind of information is shown on the *Australian Army Ordnance Survey Map Series* with the scale of 1:50 000, that is, 1 centimetre on the map represents 50 000 centimetres or 0.5 kilometre on ground.

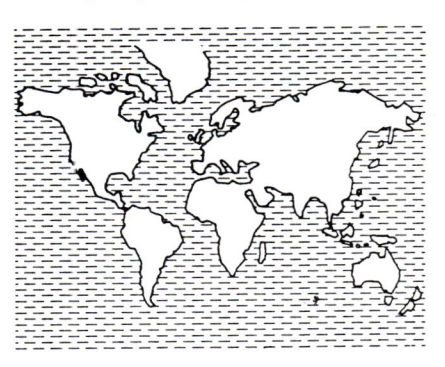

The world — a small-scale map

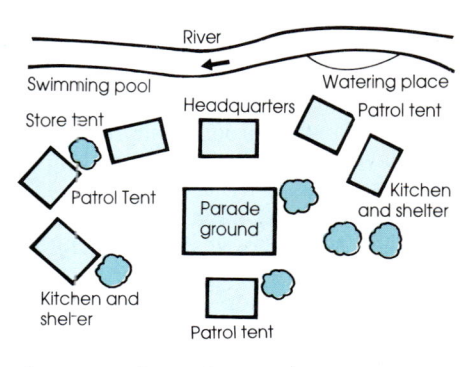

Troop campsite — a large-scale map

60

Bushcraft

Ground features

Symbols

Very early maps were pictorial even to the extent that bridges were drawn as bridges, churches as churches, and so on. These days, however, maps use *symbols* rather than pictures, which means more information can be given on one page. Even fine details such as whether a road has a fence alongside it, or whether a creek dries up in summer, can be shown by the use of symbols.

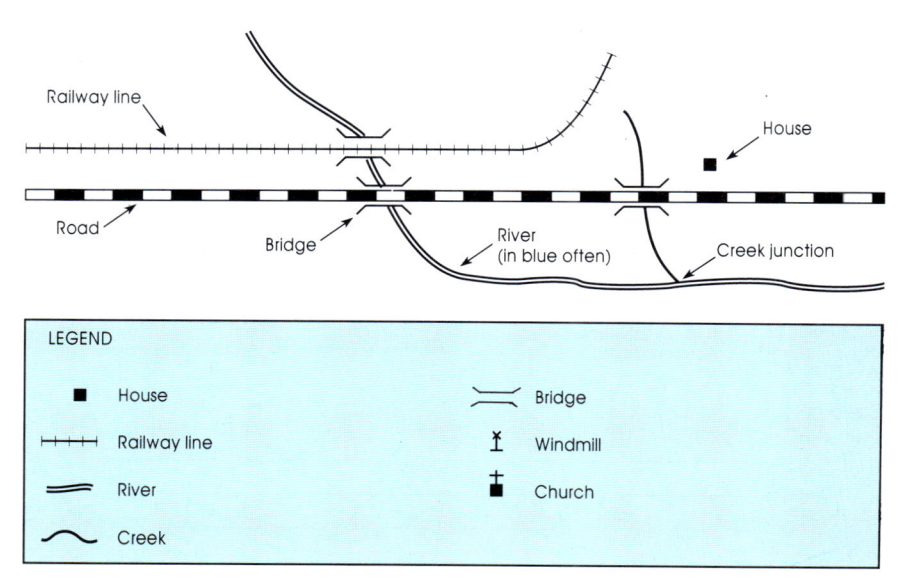

Most maps have a legend at the bottom

Contours

The shape of hills and valleys is indicated by brown lines called *contour lines*. Every point on one contour line has the same altitude above sea level. Follow a heavy brown line on the map and you will find a number, for example, 100;

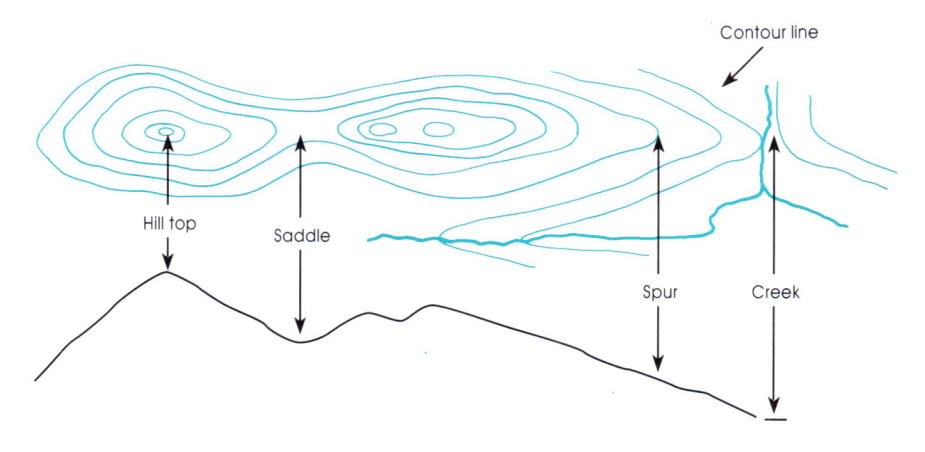

Fieldbook for Australian Scouting

everything on that line lies 100 metres above sea level. The *interval* of height between lines is stated on the map, usually 20 metres. Where lines are far apart, the ground slopes gently. Where they are close together, the hill is steep. Where lines are crowded, they show a cliff.

The top of a prominent hill may be indicated by a number called a *spot location* which shows the altitude of the crest.

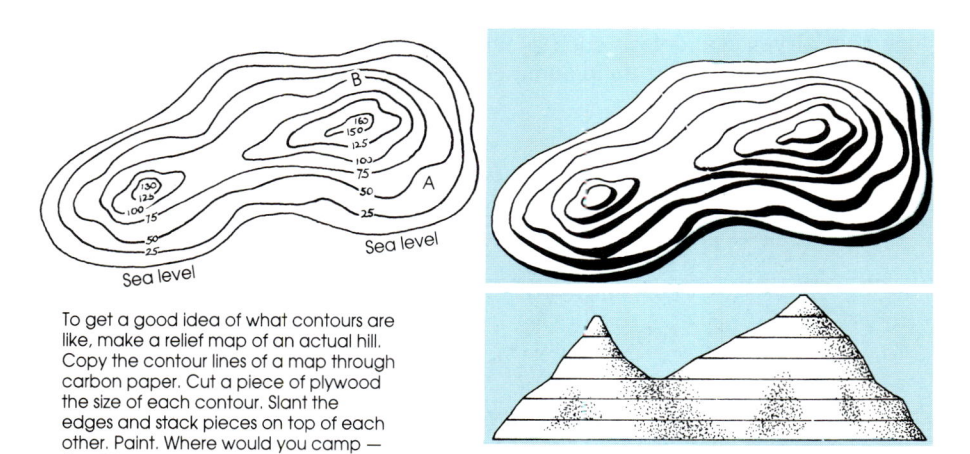

To get a good idea of what contours are like, make a relief map of an actual hill. Copy the contour lines of a map through carbon paper. Cut a piece of plywood the size of each contour. Slant the edges and stack pieces on top of each other. Paint. Where would you camp — A or B?

Contours

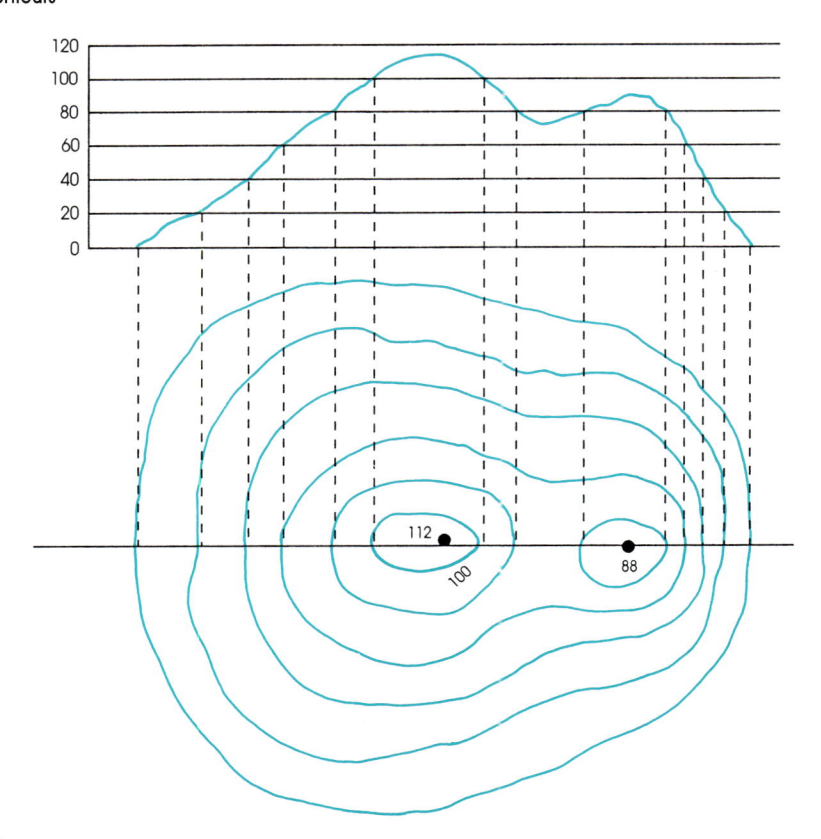

Date of map

It is important to note the *date* on which the map was made. This is usually printed in the margin. New roads and buildings may have been built since, and these may confuse you when not shown on the map. It is much better to use as landmarks natural features such as creeks, creek junctions and hill-tops, which do not change very much with time.

Grid references

Maps are covered with a network of lines forming a *grid*. The grid lines are parallel and make it easy to give the *exact* position of a point on the map. Each grid line is identified by a number on the map border.

The position of a point is indicated by a six-figure map reference. The first three digits identify its position from west to east (the *easting*) and the second three locate it from south to north (the *northing*). Find the number of the vertical grid line lying immediately to the left (or west) of the point, then estimate how many tenths of the way the point is to the next vertical line. In the example, the point X is just beyond the vertical line 30 and is about seven-tenths of the way to the next line.

The first three figures are, then, 307. The second three figures are obtained in a similar way by working from south to north. In the example, the second three figures are 758. The final reference would be 307758.

You can remember that the easting is given before the northing, because 'E' comes before 'N' in the alphabet, or remember that you read as for a book—across, then down. The name of the map sheet must always be included in the reference.

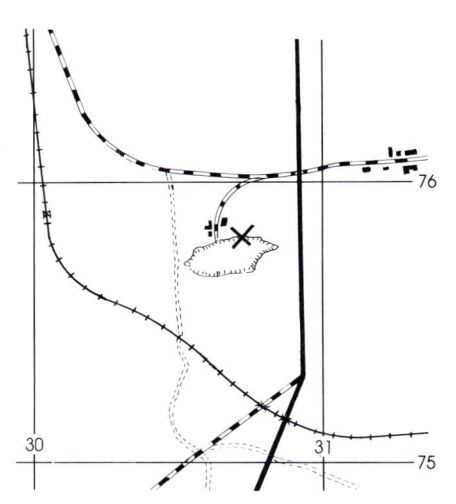

Care of maps

Maps that are frequently folded in windy, wet weather soon become torn and ragged. To mount a map on backing material, use unbleached calico or a similar material. Wash and iron the calico before use. Lay the backing material on a flat surface and spread paste all over the surface of the calico. Carefully place the map on to the material and press or roll firmly to squeeze out excess paste. Carefully lift the material and hang it on the clothesline to dry. When dry, trim the edges.

Fieldbook for Australian Scouting

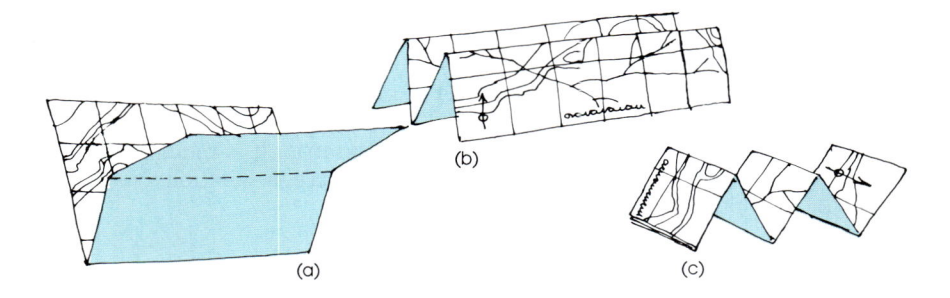

Steps in folding a map

Compass

The magnetic compass has been used for centuries by mariners and explorers on their journeys of discovery. Scouts use them in conjuction with maps when on ventures and hikes and activities such as orienteering. As its name implies, the compass needle is magnetised and aligns itself with the earth's magnetic field so it always points to the magnetic north. This is actually not always true, because the magnetic compass needle can be deflected by the close proximity of any electrical or metallic objects, for example, power lines, steel fences, and even your belt buckles or watches.

Hand compasses come in many varieties, and you should look for one on which the needle does not move too freely when it is used. If the needle swings too freely after the compass is brought to rest, it is hard to take an accurate reading. Some compasses are filled with liquid, and you will note that the needle swings slowly into place and is very steady. This liquid-dampened compass is available in makes used by Scouts.

Compass construction

The leaflet with your compass will give you details about it, and you should read the instructions carefully. There are basically three main parts: the needle, the housing and the base.

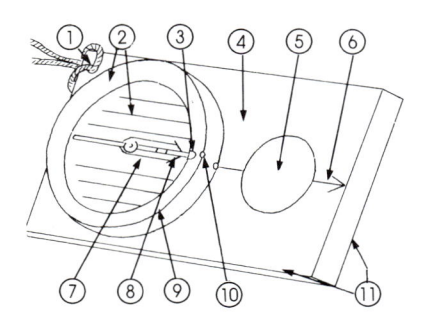

1. Hole for safety cord and the cord
2. Compass housing with dial and orienting lines
3. North of dial (luminous)
4. Base plate (transparent)
5. Magnifying lens
6. Direction of travel arrow
7. Orienting arrow
8. Magnetic needle (liquid dampened with north end red and luminous)
9. Dial graduation (standard 360° with 2° graduations
10. Index pointer (for setting or reading bearing)
11. Scales in inches, in centimetres and millimetres

Note: On Slva Type 5 the orienting lines are on the dial

The parts of the Silva orienteering compass

Points of a compass

Between the cardinal points of the compass (north, east, south and west) are many others, but the most commonly used are those shown in the diagram. These are used in sailing and for indicating the wind direction, but are used less nowadays than 360° bearings which are more easily understood: 'NE' becomes 45°, 'E' 90° and 'W' 270°, as in our diagram.

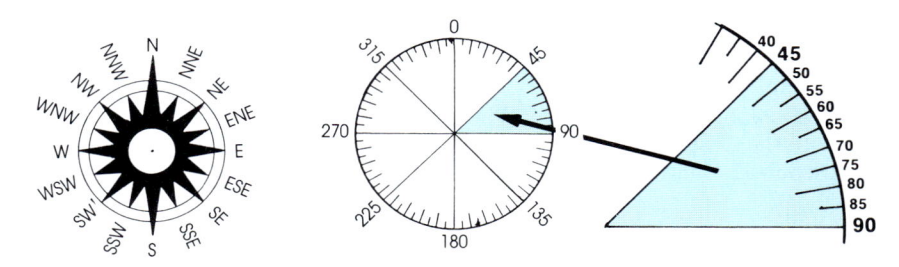

Relationship of true to magnetic north

Maps are made in relation to true north, and this can vary from magnetic north by a varying number of degrees from place to place. Ordnance maps, charts and maps of similar quality will have an indication on them of the difference in degrees between true north and magnetic north. This is called the *magnetic declination* and is expressed as degrees east or west of true north. An area where your compass needle points east of true north is *easterly variation*, and if it points west it is *westerly variation*. Where true and magnetic north appear to be the same, it is *zero*.

To apply variation when working from a map to a compass, do the following.
1. Determine the variation from the map being used.
2. If it is easterly variation, deduct it from the bearing you require on your compass.
3. If it is westerly variation, add it to the bearing required on your compass.

Using your compass

Setting a bearing Turn the dial until the bearing (the degree number or the compass point) you desire is shown at the index pointer.

Facing a bearing Let us assume the bearing is set for 60°. Hold the compass in your hand, level enough to permit the magnetic needle to swing freely, and have the direction arrow point straight ahead. Orient the compass (and yourself) as follows: while holding the compass as in the previous paragraph, turn yourself around together with the compass until the north end of your compass needle points to the letter 'N' on the dial.

Now look up along the direction-of-travel arrow—you are now facing a *bearing of 60 degrees*.

To walk a bearing Look straight ahead (the further the better) and choose a landmark or a spot that is in the direction you are facing, as pointed out by the direction-of-travel arrow on the compass. Walk to that landmark or spot

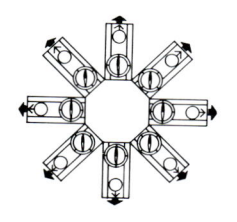

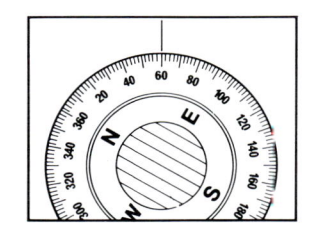

Facing a bearing

without looking at the compass. When you get there, again use the compass to locate the next landmark along the bearing of 60°, and repeat this until you reach your destination.

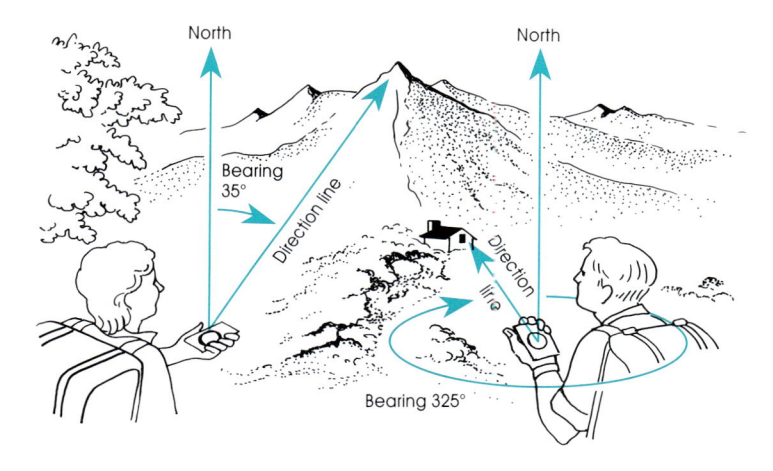

Using map and compass together

Now that you have your map and know how to read the symbols on it and have your compass and know how it works, it is time to take them along on a hike and make use of them.

Orienting a map

Once you are at the starting point and ready to go, it is necessary to *orient* your map. If you are at a road crossing, for example, do you go straight ahead or to the left or to the right or backward? You will know as soon as you have *oriented* your map. To orient a map means to line up all the directions on it with the same directions in the landscape.

   Study your surroundings for some prominent landmark that will be shown on your map—a hill or a building or a bridge. Inspect your map and find the map symbol for the landmark on it. Then turn the map until the line from the spot where you are standing and the map symbol lies in the same direction as the line from your actual position to the actual landmark. You have now oriented your map *by inspection*.

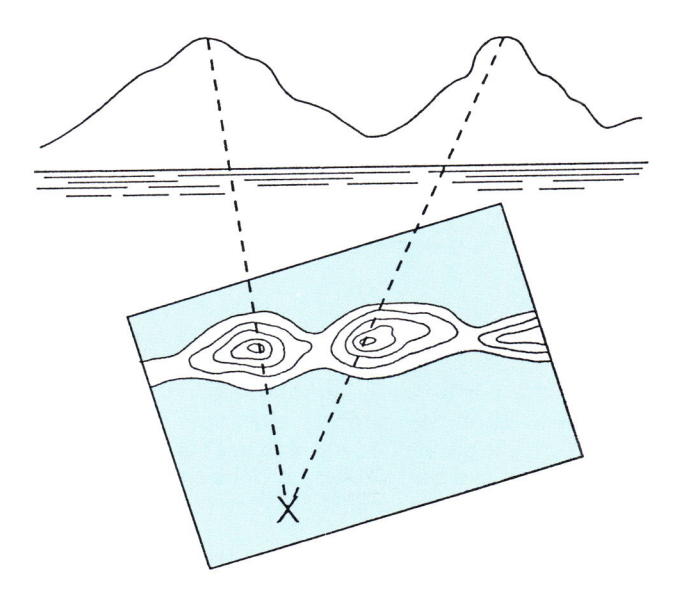

Map your position from some features

If you cannot find any features on your map to correspond with those on the ground, rest your compass on the map and turn the map under it until the magnetic-north arrow on the map points the same way as the north end of the compass needle.

Nature's compasses

Scouts should know how to find north by using the sun or stars as well as by using a compass. This is possible when you know the time of day or night. It is also possible for you to tell time by the position of the sun and the stars.

The sun moves 15° each hour, that is, 1° each 4 minutes. In the diagrams, the sun is 34° from the north–south line. It is morning, because the

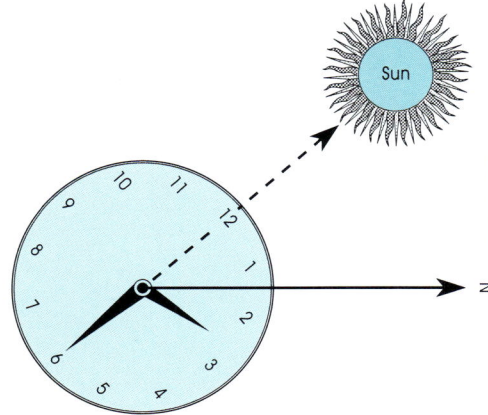

To use your watch to find north, point the 12 to the sun. Draw an imaginary line halfway between the 12 and the hour hand. That will be approximately north. If you are suffering daylight saving, think of the hour hand being an hour earlier

Finding north

Bushcraft

67

Fieldbook for Australian Scouting

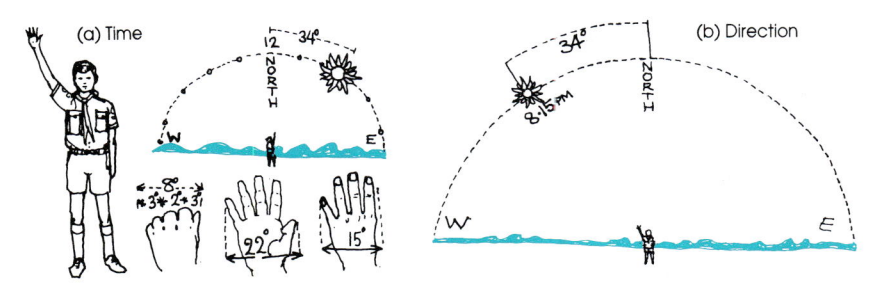

(a) Time   (b) Direction

Time and direction from the sun

sun is on the eastern side of the north–south line; 34 × 4 = 136 minutes before noon. It is 16 minutes to 10 in the morning, sun time. Standard or zone time (the time to which we set our clocks and watches) is fixed over a wide area. Noon by the sun may in fact be 11.20 or 12.35 by the clock. Find out what this difference is in your own area, and allow for it.

Direction from the sun

Example It is 2.16 p.m. sun time, calculated from your watch, therefore the sun is to the west of the north–south line; 2.16 p.m. means the sun has travelled 136 minutes of time past the north–south line. Because the sun travels 1° along its curved path in the sky every 4 minutes of time, it is 34° along its path past noon. Measure this back along the sun's path and you will have true north.

Direction by the stars

The stars are grouped into constellations named by the 'wise men' of thousands of years ago. Modern astronomers identify separate stars by adding a Greek letter to the name of the constellation. The brightest star is called 'Alpha' (A), the next brightest 'Beta' (B), followed by 'Gamma', 'Delta', and so on.

The pointers of the Southern Cross belong to the constellation of the Centaur, and are known as Alpha Centauri and Beta Centauri. Beyond the end of the long arm of the Cross is a group of four small stars called Musca (the fly), and near it are the three brighter stars of the Southern Triangle. Alpha and Beta Centauri are the Centaur's feet.

There is a fairly bright star on the other side of the Celestial South Pole to the Southern Cross, and approximately the same distance from the Pole as the Cross. This star is called Achernar.

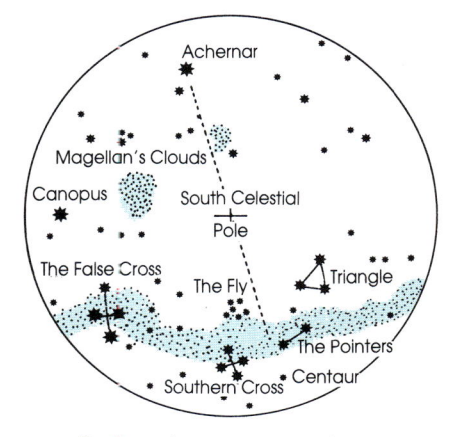

Southern stars: summer evening

Bushcraft

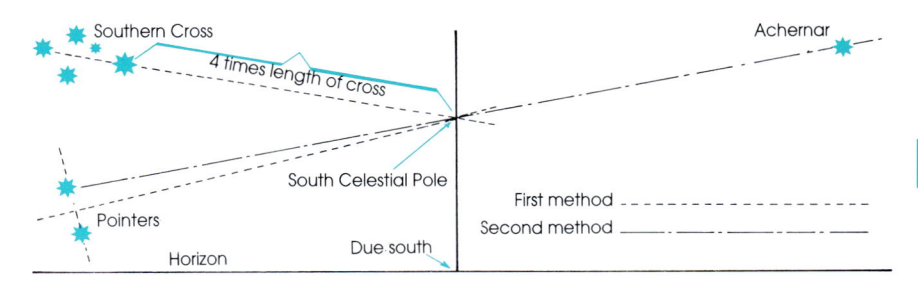

First method Imagine a line drawn through the long arm of the Cross, and continued for a distance equal to four times the length of the Cross. Where this line ends is the South Celestial Pole.

Second method Imagine a line drawn between Achernar and the pointer nearest the Cross. Halfway along this line is the Celestial South Pole.

All methods All methods require practice, particularly in recognising the Southern Cross and its associated stars.

Time from the stars

In the southern sky, the stars appear to revolve clockwise round the Celestial South Pole. When you have practised finding south by the Southern Cross, you can imagine the Celestial South Pole as the centre of a 24-hour clockface, and use the Southern Cross itself as the ends of the imaginary hour hand to tell the approximate time. The Cross is at its highest point at midnight on 1 April, and for every month later it is at the highest point 2 hours earlier; that is, on 1 May it is at its highest point at 10.00 p.m.

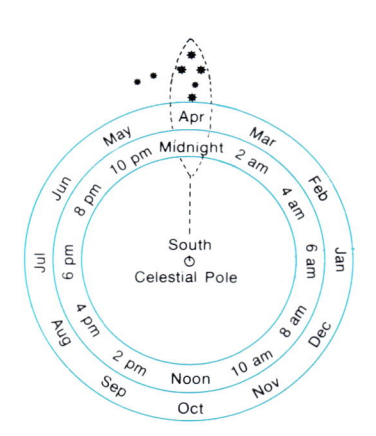

Time from the Southern Cross

Copy this diagram on a piece of cardboard; face south holding the cardboard with the date at the highest point and its centre covering the Celestial South Pole. You should be able to tell the time to the nearest half hour.

Making a map

The making of a sketch map can be a very interesting project, even by using very little gear. A sketch map is not intended to be extremely accurate, so do not be too ambitious in your early attempts, and do not expect to produce something as good as a military map.

A sketch map is made by determining the position of key landmarks as accurately as you can, then filling in the rest of the detail by approximation. For your early attempts, select an area that has some definite landmarks: fences, roads, buildings, water courses, and so on, but one that is not too hilly.

69

Sketch maps are usually prepared in the field, but you should develop the habit of recording distances and bearings in a notebook in order to check your work at home.

There are many methods: *base point, base line, double base line, plane table* and *traverse mapping*.

When starting to put the details on paper, make sure the paper you are using will be big enough, and select a scale that will fit inside the boundaries of the paper. Preferably draw the map so that north (either true or magnetic) will be up one side of the page. Leave your construction lines in light pencil, and go over the permanent detail in firmer pencil or ink.

Remember that no map is complete unless it carries the following essentials:

1. the name or title showing what it represents
2. details of the scale used
3. a clear indication of north, shown as true or magnetic
4. a legend, showing an explanation of any signs and symbols used on the map
5. date drawn (because some details may change over the years)
6. who drew the map.

Base point

This mapping system can be used for small areas and where the objects make it easy to measure the distance. The measurement to the bases can be in metres, paces, and so on.

1. Select a point (A) central to your objects to be marked on the map.
2. Draw up a chart (*see* illustration).
3. Take bearing on objects and mark on chart.
4. Measure distance to objects and mark on chart.
5. Mark point on your map paper and select scale to fit map.
6. Identify the North Point on your map.
7. Mark out bearings from the point and measure off (using scale) distance to locate object on your map.
8. Finish map (date, legend, and so on).

This is a good mapping exercise to start on if you are unfamiliar with mapping.

Base line

This mapping system is used when the objects are inaccessible and a large area is to be mapped. There is no measuring to the object because the position of the object on the map is located by cross-bearings.

1. Select a line (X–Y), which you measure. This line should be central to the area to be mapped or on one side.
2. Draw a chart (*see* diagram).
3. From Point X, take bearings to objects and mark on chart.
4. From Point Y, take bearings to objects and mark on chart.

Bushcraft

Big tree

N

Windmill

A

Big rock

Base point

Base–point chart

Object	Direction	Distance
Tree		
Windmill		
Rock		

Big tree

N

Windmill

Take cross–bearings to each landmark from both ends of measured base line. The big rock would be hard to sight on map–double base line would have to be used.

Big rock

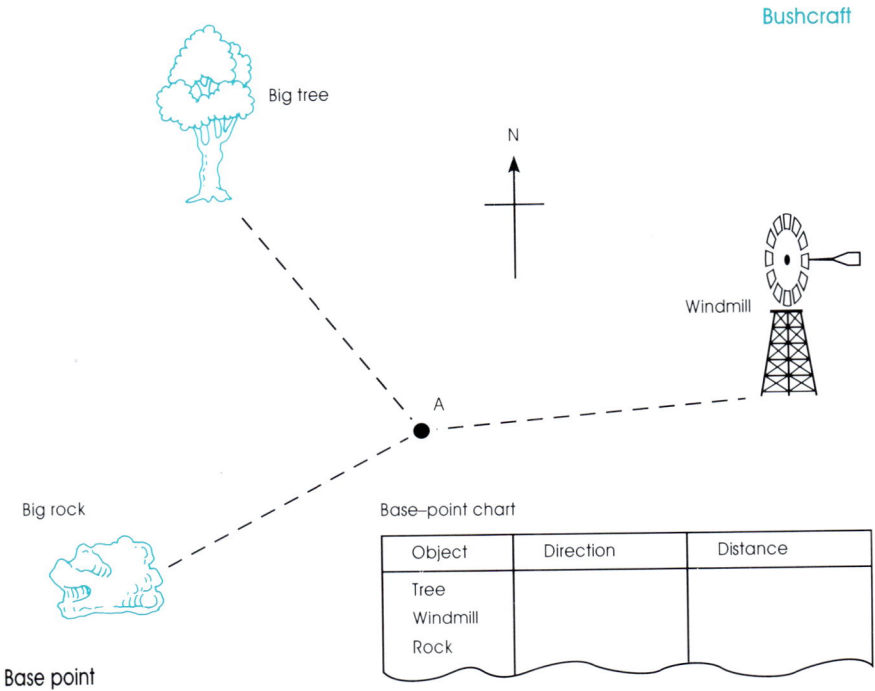

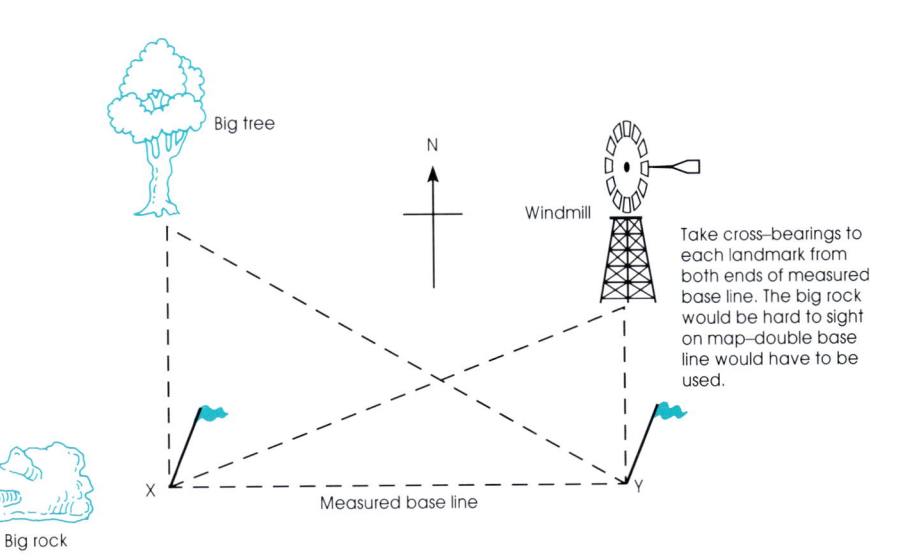

X — Measured base line — Y

Base–line chart

Object	Direction (X)	Direction (Y)
Tree		
Windmill		
Rock		

Base line

5. Mark the X–Y line on your map paper to the scale you require. Remember the location of your X–Y line in the field and place it on the map accordingly.
6. Identify the North Point on your map.
7. From Point X, draw in the bearing lines from the chart and write the name of the object on to the line.
8. From Point Y, draw in the bearing lines from the chart and write the name of the object on to the line.
9. Now mark in the objects by locating the intersection of the object bearing lines.
10. Finish the map with details.

This map-making system has one fault: if an object is almost in line with your base line, it will be hard to arrive at a cross-bearing with any accuracy.

Double base line

This system gives a method of producing a map that is more accurate than the previous systems. There are two methods that can be adopted, as follows.

System A

1. Set a line (X–Y), which you measure. This line should be central to area to be mapped.
2. From Point Y, set up a line of same length as X–Y and at right angles to X–Y line.
3. Draw up chart (*see* diagram).
4. From Point X, take bearings to objects and mark them on chart.
5. From Point Y, take bearings to objects and mark them on chart.
6. From Point Z, take bearings to objects and mark them on chart.
7. Identify North Point on your map.
8. Mark your X–Y and Y–Z lines on your map paper to scale you require and that will fit. This should be in centre of your mapping sheet similar to location in field.
9. From Point X, draw in bearing lines from chart and write name of object on to line.
10. From Points Y and Z, draw in bearing lines.
11. Now locate objects on your map where bearing lines intersect. You may find three bearing lines do not cross in one spot but form a small triangular area. Take centre of triangle as your intersection. If triangular area is large, recheck your bearings.
12. Finish map with details.

System B

This system does give you a more accurate method of identifying the location of objects on your map.

1. Set two lines of equal length and crossing in centre and at right angles; lines formed are W–X and Y–Z.
2. Draw up chart (*see* diagram).
3. You can now take bearings of objects from all four points (W, X, Y and Z) and mark them on your chart.

Bushcraft

Double base line system A

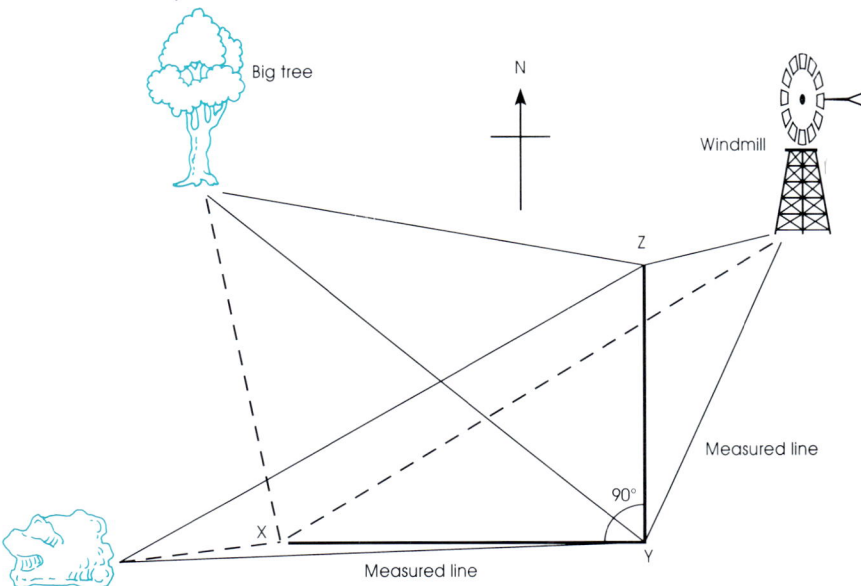

Big tree

N

Windmill

Z

Measured line

90°

X

Y

Measured line

Big rock

Double–base–line chart

Object	Direction (X)	Direction (Y)	Direction (Z)
Tree			
Windmill			
Rock			

Double base line system B

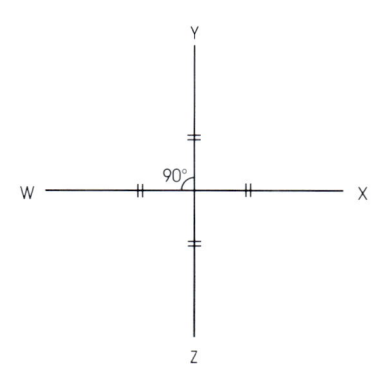

Y

W — 90° — X

Z

Double–base–line chart

Object	Direction (W)	Direction (X)	Direction (Y)	Direction (Z)
Tree				
Windmill				
Rock				

Fieldbook for Australian Scouting

4. Mark your W–X and Y–Z lines on centre of your mapping paper to scale to fit.
5. Identify North Point on your map.
6. Draw in your bearing lines and identify them as before.
7. Mark in your objects at intersection of bearings.
8. Finish map.

Some people use this method simply by using the two baselines as two single base lines and do not have four bearings for each object. This defeats the purpose of this system and reduces its accuracy.

Plane table

1. Take a flat piece of cardboard or light 3-ply about 80 cm × 80 cm; put it on a sheet of paper. Place two pins or nails firmly as shown. Use in conjunction with a small table, for example, a card table.

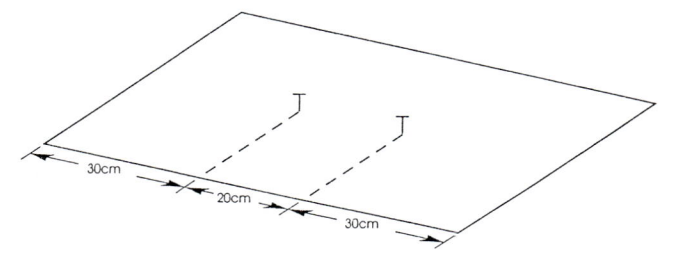

Or
Use a tripod such as a projector stand, and drawing board, with paper firmly fixed with drawing pins.

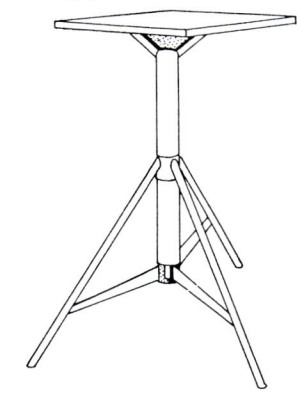

You can also construct a sighting rule as follows.
Two school rulers fixed parallel with enough space between to draw a

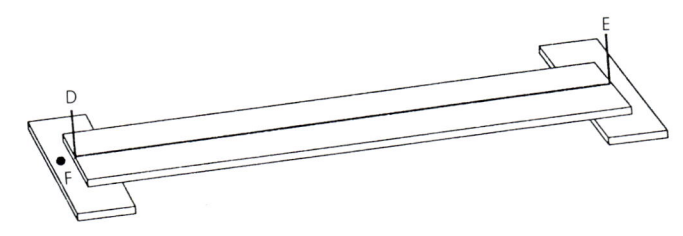

line on two cross-pieces of wood or cardboard 2 cm × 8 cm, nails D and E upright on centre line, hole F at one end also on centre line.

The plane table must be level to use, and, if you do not have a spirit level, you can make simple level by using a junket tube or medicine bottle almost filled with water strapped on its side to a piece of wood or stiff cardboard.

2. In the area you have chosen to map (let us say a football oval), choose two points a suitable distance apart. These will correspond with your points A and B on your board, so estimate the distances relative to your planned map; 40 metres would be a good distance in this case.

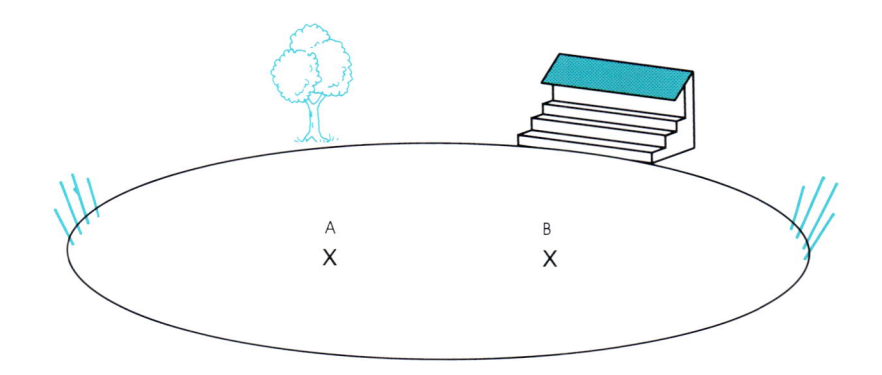

3. Take your board to point A and place it flat. It is easier if you use a card table. Orient the board so A and B pins are in the same line as A and B in the oval. Set a compass in one corner and mark an 'N' arrow.

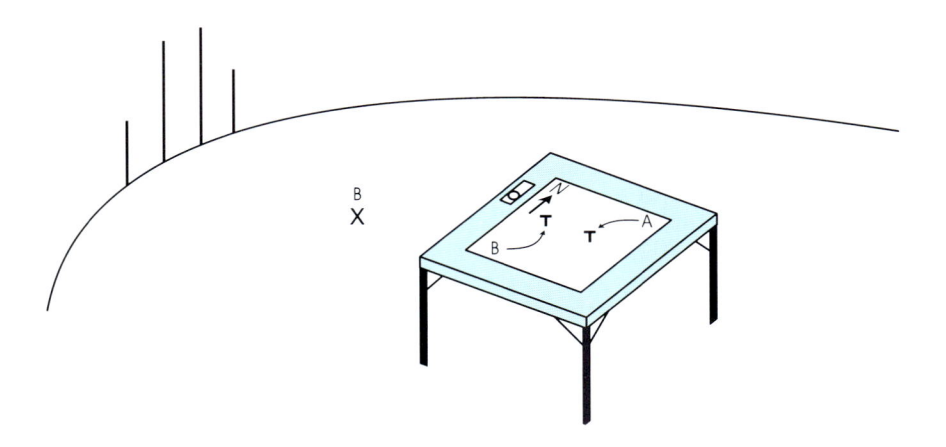

4. Line up a landmark from the pin A and pin a piece of cotton like on the following page. Pencil in the name of the landmark.

Fieldbook for Australian Scouting

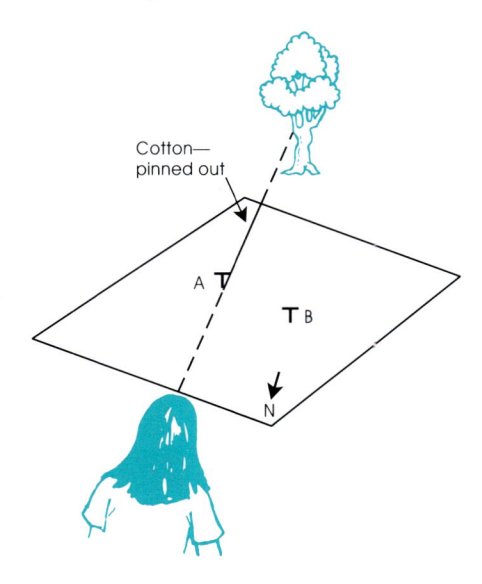

If using a sighting rule, pin through hole F to point A on board. Sight landmark with nails D–E and draw a line in pencil along slot. Name line with name of landmark.
5. Do the same for all the main landmarks. Your map will then look something like this.

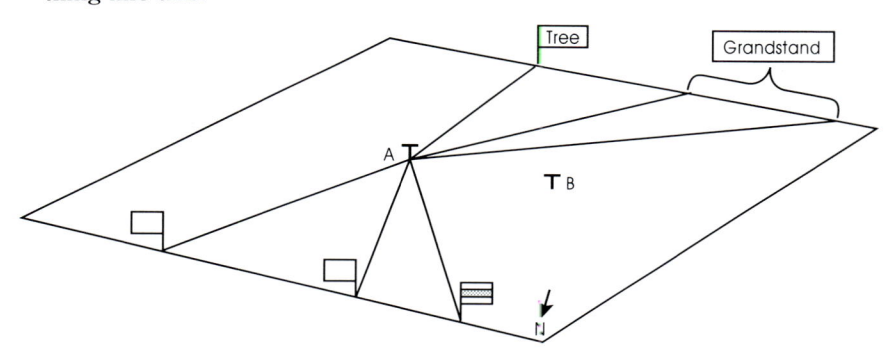

6. Take your table and set up at point B in the oval. Set your map according to your N arrow. If you line up each landmark, you can pinpoint them like in the picture at the top of page 77.
7. When you have done all the landmarks, you will have your map. Mark the spots on the map.
8. Scale: Scale is a ratio between two numbers. You can work out your scale for your map like this:
   (a) Distance on your map: Actual distance.
   For example, (in our example)
   20 cm : 40 metres
   This means 20 cm on our map is the same as 40 metres in actual distance.
   (b) Make the units of measurement the same, that is,
   20 cm : 4000 cm

Bushcraft

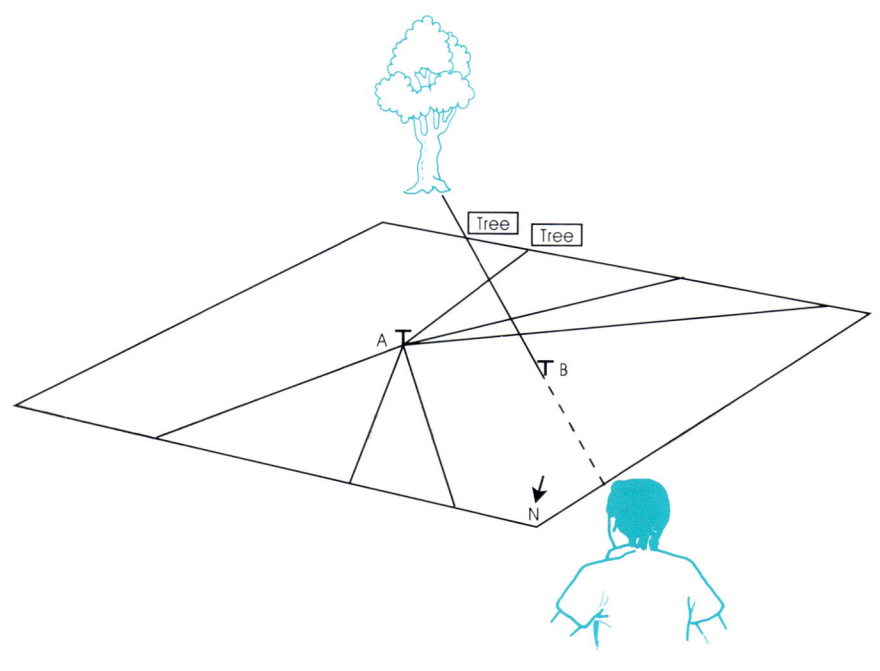

(c) Make the first figure a '1'. We do this by dividing it by itself (for example, 20 ÷ 20 = 1). Now what we do to one figure we do to the other (in our example, 4000 ÷ 20 = 200). This gives us our scale. That is, in our example, 1:200. We say this is a scale of '1 to 200'. For our example, 1 cm on the map is equivalent to 200 cm (or 2 metres) in actual fact.
9. Mark the map properly like this:

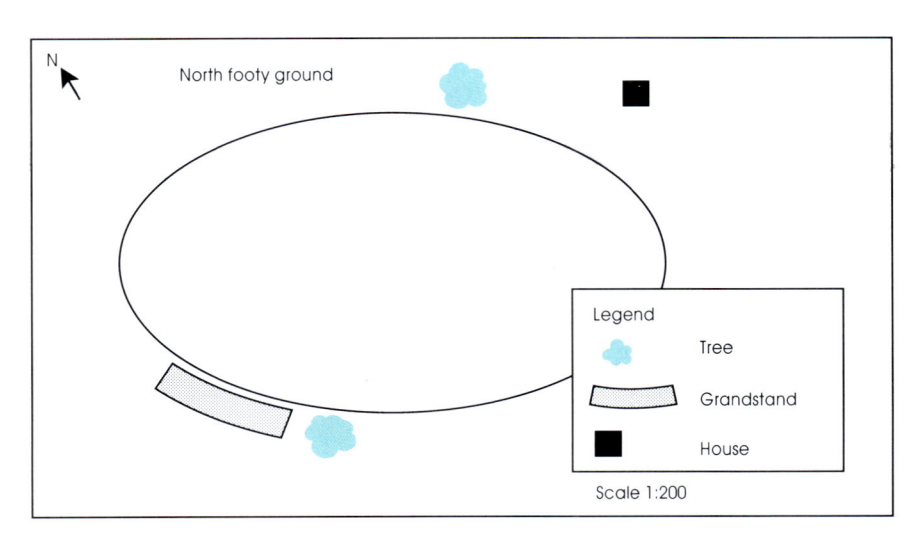

Note: There is a title, a direction arrow, a scale and a legend.
10. Practise in a park or a big paddock.

Traverse

This type of map is made as you go along. Each time you move in a certain direction, you make a note in your log book. Measure (using your pace) the distance to your next turn. Make notes of features as you go along. Your log will look like this:

(a)

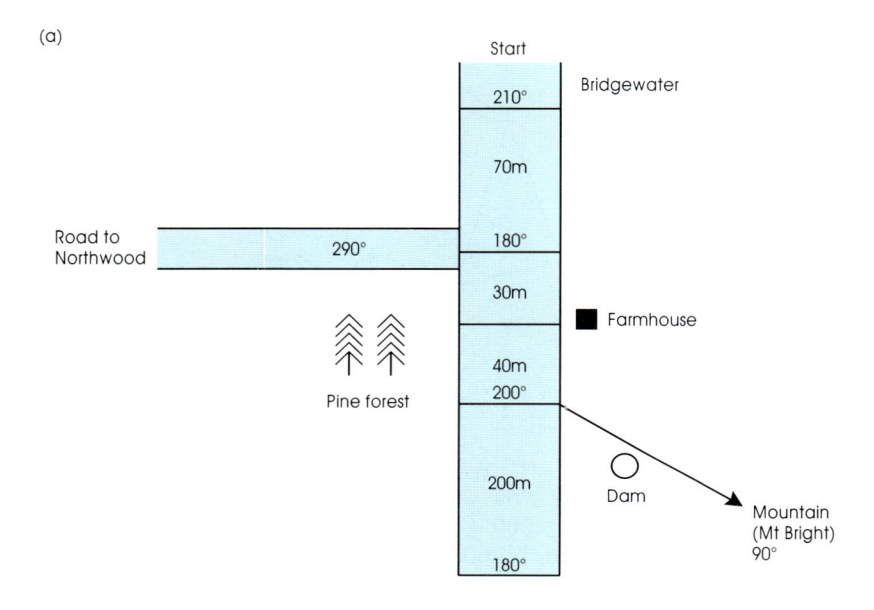

[Traverse log diagram showing:
- Start at Bridgewater, 210°, 70m
- 180°, 30m
- Road to Northwood at 290°
- Farmhouse
- Pine forest
- 40m, 200°
- 200m
- Dam
- Mountain (Mt Bright) 90°
- 180°]

Your map will look like this. (*Note*: Title; North; Legend):

(b)

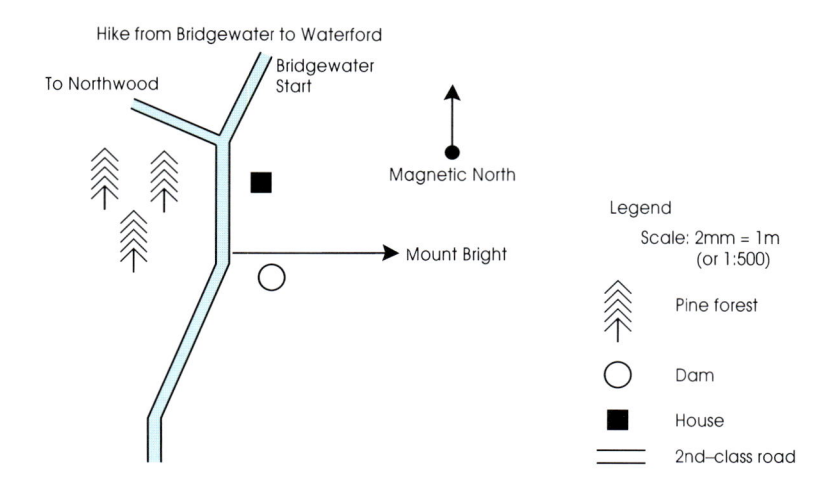

[Map showing Hike from Bridgewater to Waterford, with Bridgewater Start, To Northwood, Magnetic North, Mount Bright, and Legend:
Scale: 2mm = 1m (or 1:500)
Pine forest
Dam
House
2nd–class road]

Bushcraft skills

Scouts should always try to improve their outdoor skills. Besides the experiences of camping, there are many books and other aids available at recognised Scout Outdoor Centres.

Bushcraft skills are best learnt when you are out camping and hiking. *Remember to look and listen* when you are in the bush.

Weather

'Keeping your weather eye open' is sound advice while you are in camp. To be caught by a sudden and unexpected change in the weather can be uncomfortable at least, and perhaps even extremely dangerous.

Through observing the weather pattern of the area you live in, you will soon learn to recognise the signs that indicate a change in the weather and how big a change it is likely to be.

The clouds and wind are the two aids that will warn you of weather deterioration. Barometer readings are also reliable, so study the barometer before you leave for camp and you will have an idea of whether the weather is likely to improve, deteriorate or remain steady for the next day or two.

Learn how to read the weather maps published in the local papers. Remember that in the southern hemisphere, winds blow inwards, clockwise around a low, and outwards, anti-clockwise around a high. The lines around them are called *isobars* and mark places where the barometer has the same reading. Close isobars, then, mean rapid pressure changes and strong winds. Over southern Australia, these systems usually drift from west to east; in the north they often, but not always, move from east to west.

To forecast weather, first work out the wind direction that the map shows as likely. Air moving from sea to land will be moist; air moving from the land will be dry, and, in summer at least, warmer than air from the sea. The closeness of the isobars will given an indication of the likely wind strength. Follow around the isobars in the direction from which the wind is likely to blow, and see where that air was yesterday; this will give some idea of whether it will be hot or cold, dry or moist. The closeness of the isobars will tell you something about the probable wind strength.

Rain is more difficult to forecast, but if the weather map suggests onshore winds, and you see thick low clouds building up in the windward direction, be prepared! Clouds can give you much information—study them and note the weather that goes with each type. Practise your own forecasting whenever you go to camp. You will often be wrong, but you will learn a lot.

Keep your eyes on the sky for the best signs of weather change while you are in camp or out on any Scouting activity. (*See* 'Meteorology' section in Chapter 1: Air activities, page 11.)

Estimation

How high is that cliff? How wide is that creek? How far off the ground is that branch? How far apart are those trees? How far away is that hill? How long will it take us to reach it? These are a few of the questions you might have

Personal measurement chart

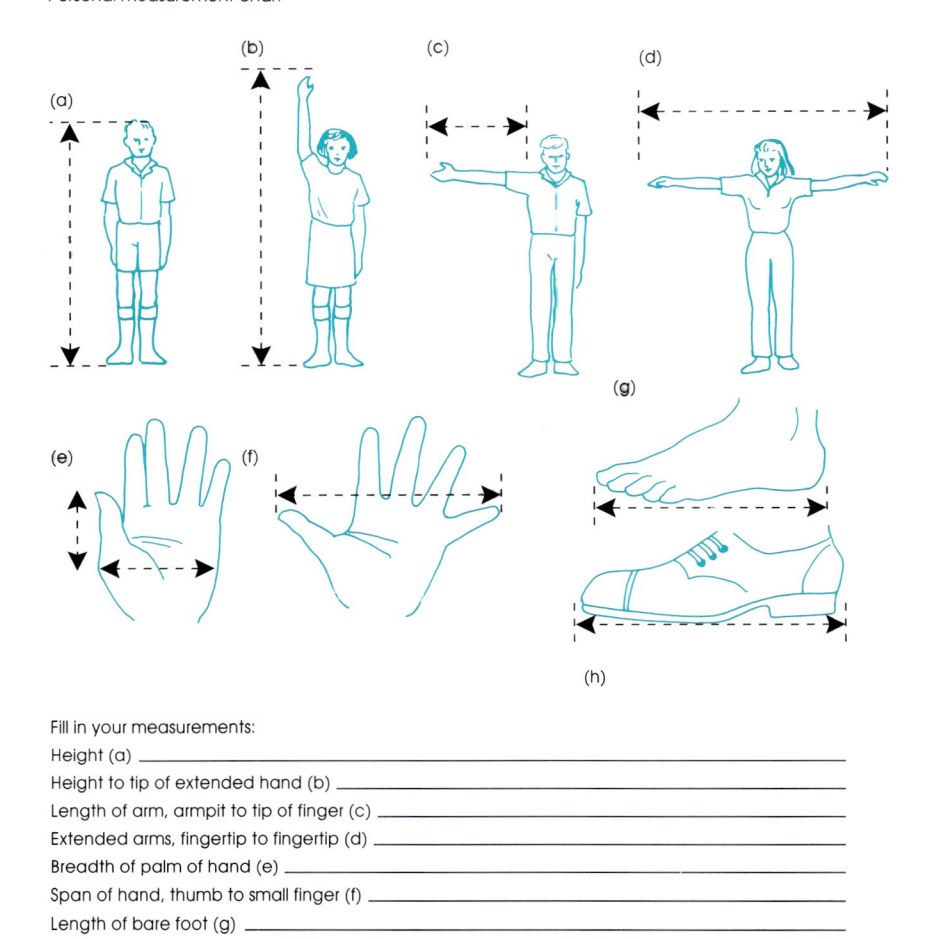

Fill in your measurements:
Height (a) _____
Height to tip of extended hand (b) _____
Length of arm, armpit to tip of finger (c) _____
Extended arms, fingertip to fingertip (d) _____
Breadth of palm of hand (e) _____
Span of hand, thumb to small finger (f) _____
Length of bare foot (g) _____
Length of boot (h) _____
Elbow tip to forefinger (cubit) _____
Length of pace on level ground _____

to answer while on your activities. The way to find the answers is not to guess, but to use known measurements to compare and estimate distances and heights.

Learn your own personal measurements—height; hand span; length of arm, foot, finger; reach. Know the length of your usual walking pace. Fix in your mind the length of your playing fields—a cricket pitch, tennis court, football field, Olympic-size swimming pool.

Know exactly the length of a kilometre from your front gate and how long it takes you to walk it. How far from home is your school, or your Scout Headquarters (HQ), and how long does it take you to walk that distance?

Learn the measurements of some everyday objects—the height of your house to the guttering and to the top of the roof; the height of the streetlight poles in your street; the length of the family car; the diameter and circumference of a 20-cent coin and the wheel of your bicycle.

Being familiar with these things will help you to estimate heights and distances with a reasonable amount of accuracy.

Finer points in estimating

After you have practised estimating and measuring distances, a number of interesting things will become apparent to you. An object will appear to be at varying distances according to whether the sun is shining behind it or behind the observer or whether the weather is overcast. Backgrounds affect estimation, and so does the slope or nature of the intervening ground.

Distances are overestimated when you are lying or kneeling; when background and objects are of similar colour; over broken country; when you are looking over a valley or undulating ground; in avenues, long streets or ravines; when the object is in the shade, in mist or failing light; when heat is rising from the ground, or when the object is only partly seen.

Distances are underestimated when the sun is shining behind the observer; in clear atmosphere, or on a bright sunny day; after a heavy shower; when the background and the object are of different colours; when the ground is level; when looking over water or a deep chasm; when looking upwards or downwards, or when the object is large compared with its surroundings.

Measuring distance across a river

There are two easy ways of doing this, but both require practice for results to be accurate.

The 'Napoleon' method   Stand on one shore. Place a flat hand against your eyebrows, palm down. Slant the hand until its outer edge seems to touch the opposite shore. Turn 90°, transferring the distance across the river to your side of the river. The distance to the point on your side of the river that the edge of your hand now seems to touch is the width of the river.

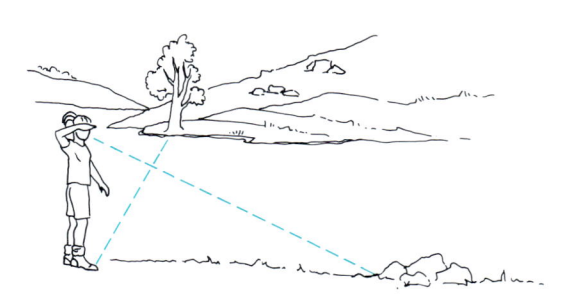

A more accurate method   This requires a lot of open space on your side of the river. Select a landmark, such as a tree, on the water's edge on the opposite bank of the river at a spot where the river's course is fairly straight; we call this point 'X'. Now place a stone or a peg at a point 'Y' exactly opposite it. Pace out 20 paces at right angles to the line X–Y and put a peg or a stone at this point 'A'. Pace out a further 20 paces in the same line. Put a peg or a stone at this point 'B'. Turn and walk at right angles to the line

Y–B and stop when the points X and A are in line; this is point 'C'. The width of the river is equal to the distance B–C.

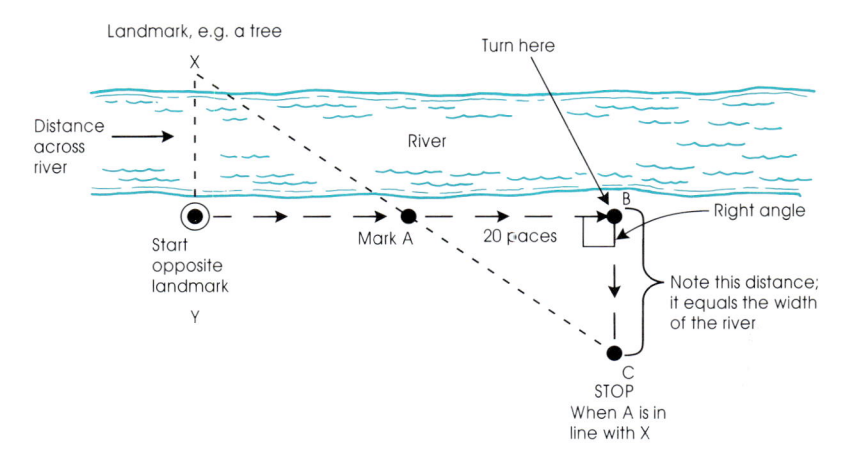

Estimating heights

There are a number of methods of estimating heights, and it is good practice to measure each height by at least two methods. Note that the slope of the ground may affect your results, so it is better to check your answer from two positions and take the average.

Following are two methods to try.

Lumberman's method Stand well away from the object and hold a twig at arm's length from your body. Arrange the twig so its tip is in line with the top of the tree being measured, and move your thumb up or down until it is in line with the base. Now swing the twig through a right angle, keeping your arm steady, so your thumb remains level with the base of the object. Observe the point on the ground at right angles to the tree where the tip of the twig now appears to rest. The approximate height of the object can be measured by pacing the distance from the base of the object to this point.

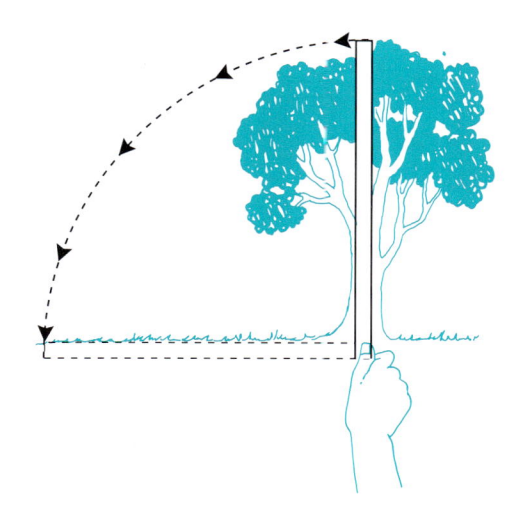

Bushcraft

Artist's method   At the base of the object, place an article (such as a staff or a person) of known height. Stand well away from the object, then, holding a pencil or twig at arm's length, arrange for the tip of the pencil to be in line with the top of the staff or person and the thumb to mark the ground level. Next, estimate how many times this distance will go into the height of the object, and multiply by the height of the article.

Using a known height

Hygiene

It is not unusual, when you are exploring, to build latrines such as you would at a fixed campsite; nevertheless, the same principles apply. Whenever you have a need to relieve yourself, you must first dig a small hole, either with a sharp stone or stick, and fill it in again after use. Some hikers carry a small trowel for this purpose. Needless to say, this sort of hole should be in an out-of-the-way place.

Also, you do not have to dig a pit to dispose of food scraps; these should be placed around the fire so they will be burned away.

Washing yourself and your dishes while you are out exploring, and where water is scarce, is also a trick you should learn. You can either use one of your deeper plates as a bowl or make a bowl in the sand, as in the sketch.

You must never use soap in a waterhole because it will pollute the water, making it undrinkable for hikers, not to mention the animals that rely on it to live. Use your soap and rinse off well away from the waterhole.

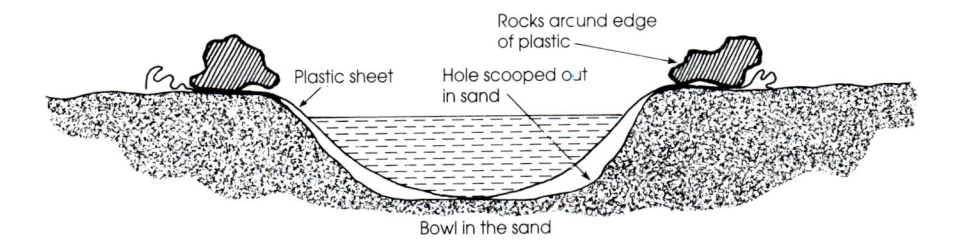

Bowl in the sand

Tracking and trails

Some hints for trailing

When looking at tracks, remember to always look into the eye of the sun. With the light in front of you, the shadows will accentuate the outline of any prints.

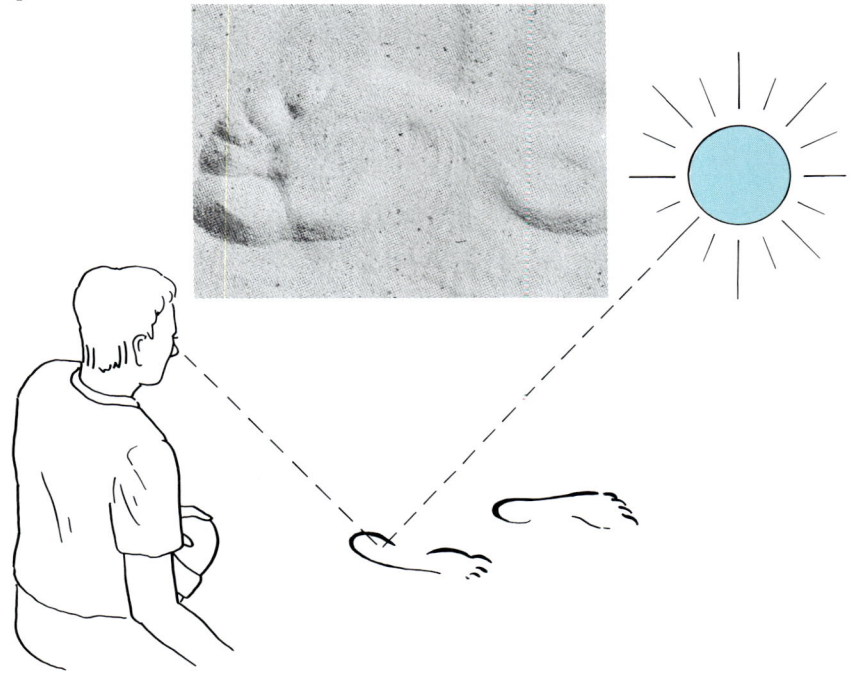

Bushcraft

A selection of common tracks

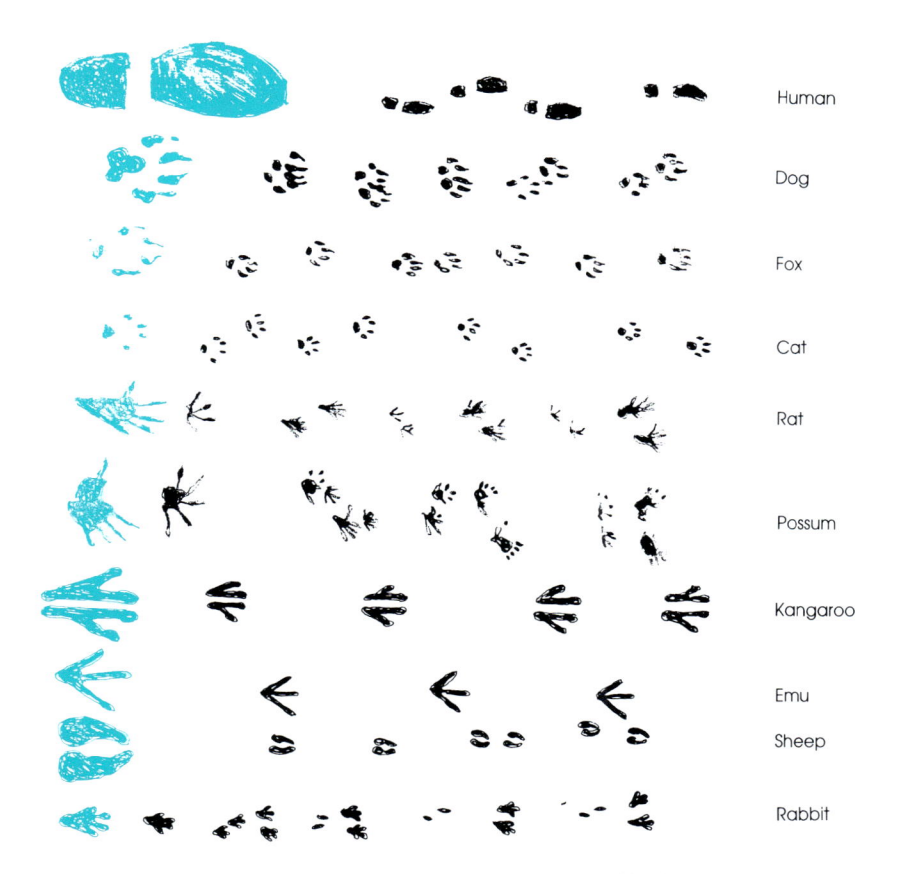

Human
Dog
Fox
Cat
Rat
Possum
Kangaroo
Emu
Sheep
Rabbit

Note Tracks are not to same scale

In the case of prints made by a bare foot, a quick method of identification is to draw a line from the tip of the big toe to the tip of the little toe, and then notice to where the other toes come with reference to this line. The toes, in fact, give you many characteristics that enable you to identify one footprint.

If you are a person who has reasonable eyesight, and a wide-awake mind, you can train yourself to see the smallest track of the smallest animal — and to work out what the animal is doing.

Have a look around your campsite for animal tracks. There is probably a patch of soft dirt or sand not far from your camp, perhaps near the creek, and no doubt animals have walked across it at some time. Study it carefully, and try to work out the meaning of the tracks you see.

How many animals and birds have left their tracks? Can you recognise any of them? A close look will tell you how old the tracks are. The ones that are clear and sharp will be fresh. If the edges are blunted and rounded by rain, it must have rained since the tracks were made. Ask yourself, 'When did it last rain?' The wind may have blown grass seeds or leaves into it: 'When did the wind blow?'

Fieldbook for Australian Scouting

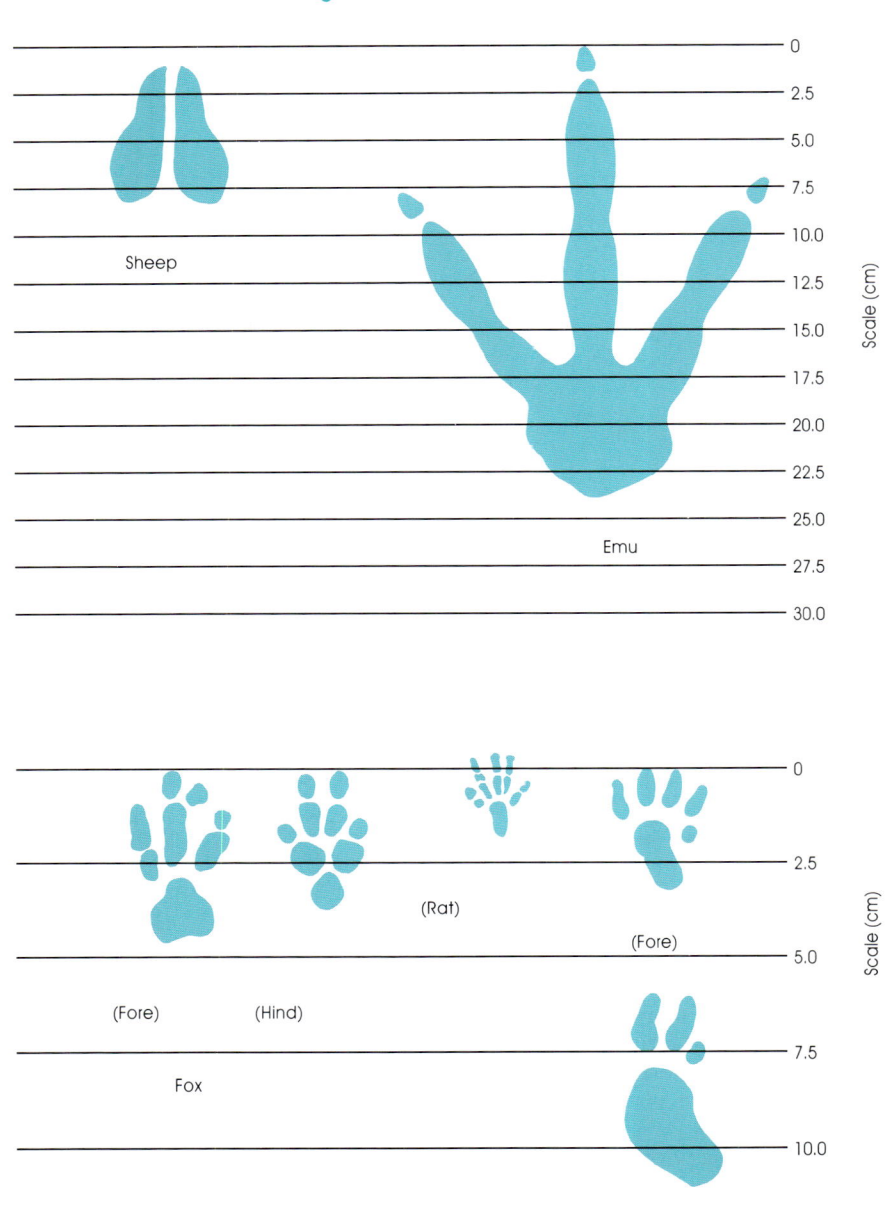

Sheep

Emu

Scale (cm): 0, 2.5, 5.0, 7.5, 10.0, 12.5, 15.0, 17.5, 20.0, 22.5, 25.0, 27.5, 30.0

(Rat)

(Fore)

(Fore) (Hind)

Fox

(Hind)

Possum

Scale (cm): 0, 2.5, 5.0, 7.5, 10.0, 12.5

Look for other signs besides tracks—animal droppings and bird feathers on the ground can reveal the type of creatures that are in the area. This can help you to complete a picture or reach a conclusion from what you have observed.

With only a little practice, you can work out the meaning of human tracks. Was he/she walking or running? carrying a heavy load or travelling light? hurrying, staggering or limping?

Bushcraft

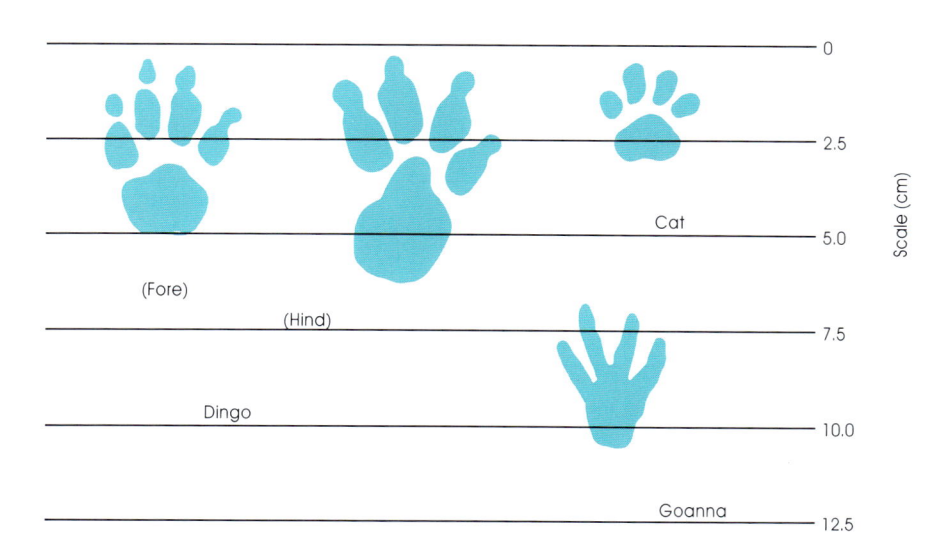

Kangaroo or wallaby

(Fore) (Hind)
Dingo

Cat

Goanna

Find a patch of sand or soft earth, and make your own tracks doing all of these things, and you will then be able to work out what other people are doing by observing the tracks they leave.

(a) Ordinary walking

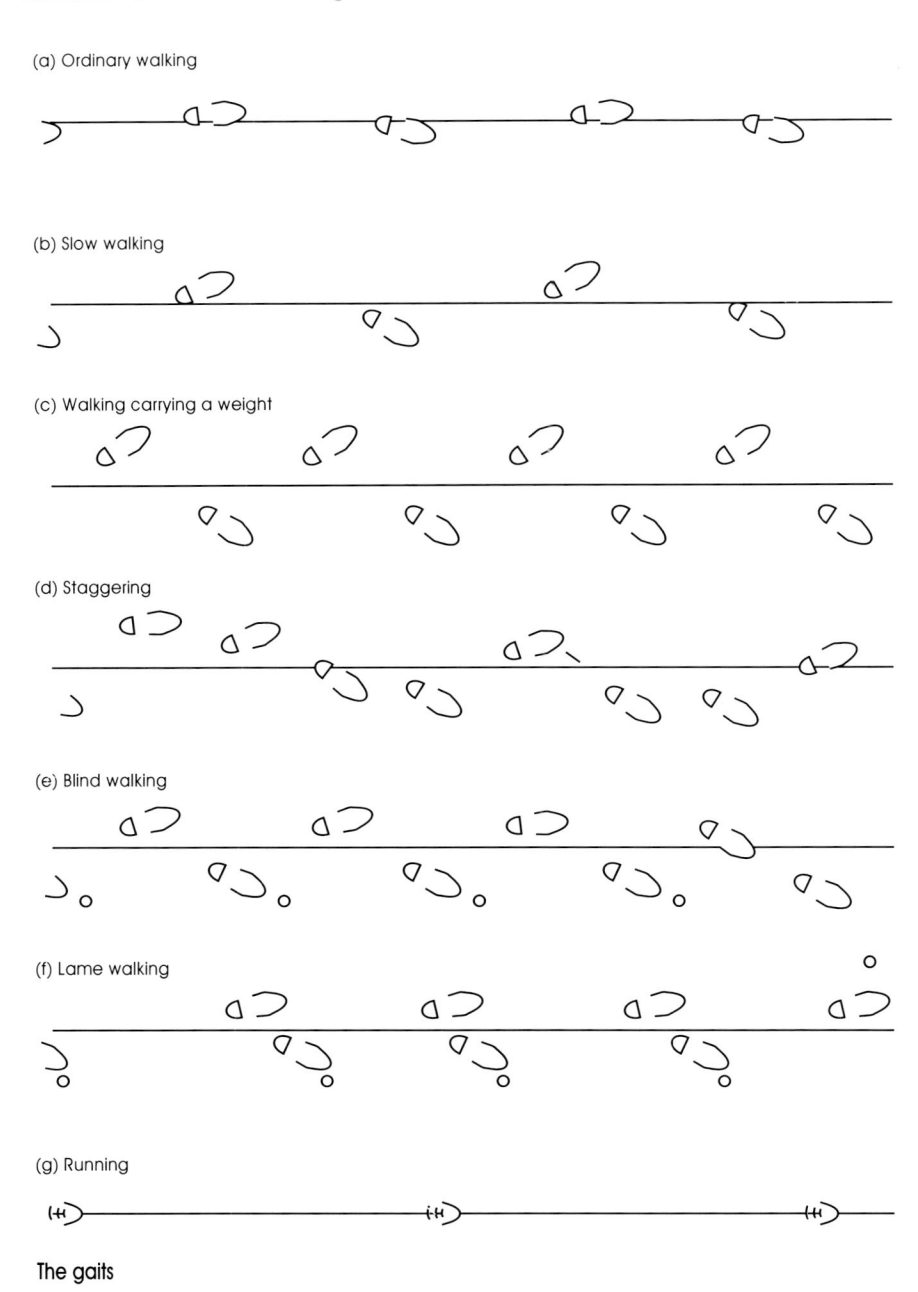

(b) Slow walking

(c) Walking carrying a weight

(d) Staggering

(e) Blind walking

(f) Lame walking

(g) Running

The gaits

Trail signs

Scout trail signs are scratched in the ground with the point of a stick, or are shaped from twigs or pebbles. A small arrow means *This is the trail*. An 'X' is a warning: *This is not the trail—do not go this way*. A square with a number in it and with an arrow means *I have hidden a message in this direction, as*

Bushcraft

many steps away as the number says. A circle with a dot in the middle reveals *This is the end of the trail* or *I have gone home*.

When you follow a trail made up of trail signs, use your eyes and take it easy. Be sure each sign is actually a sign and not one you are only imagining. If you think you have missed a sign, go back to the spot where you brushed out or undid the last one, and start off again.

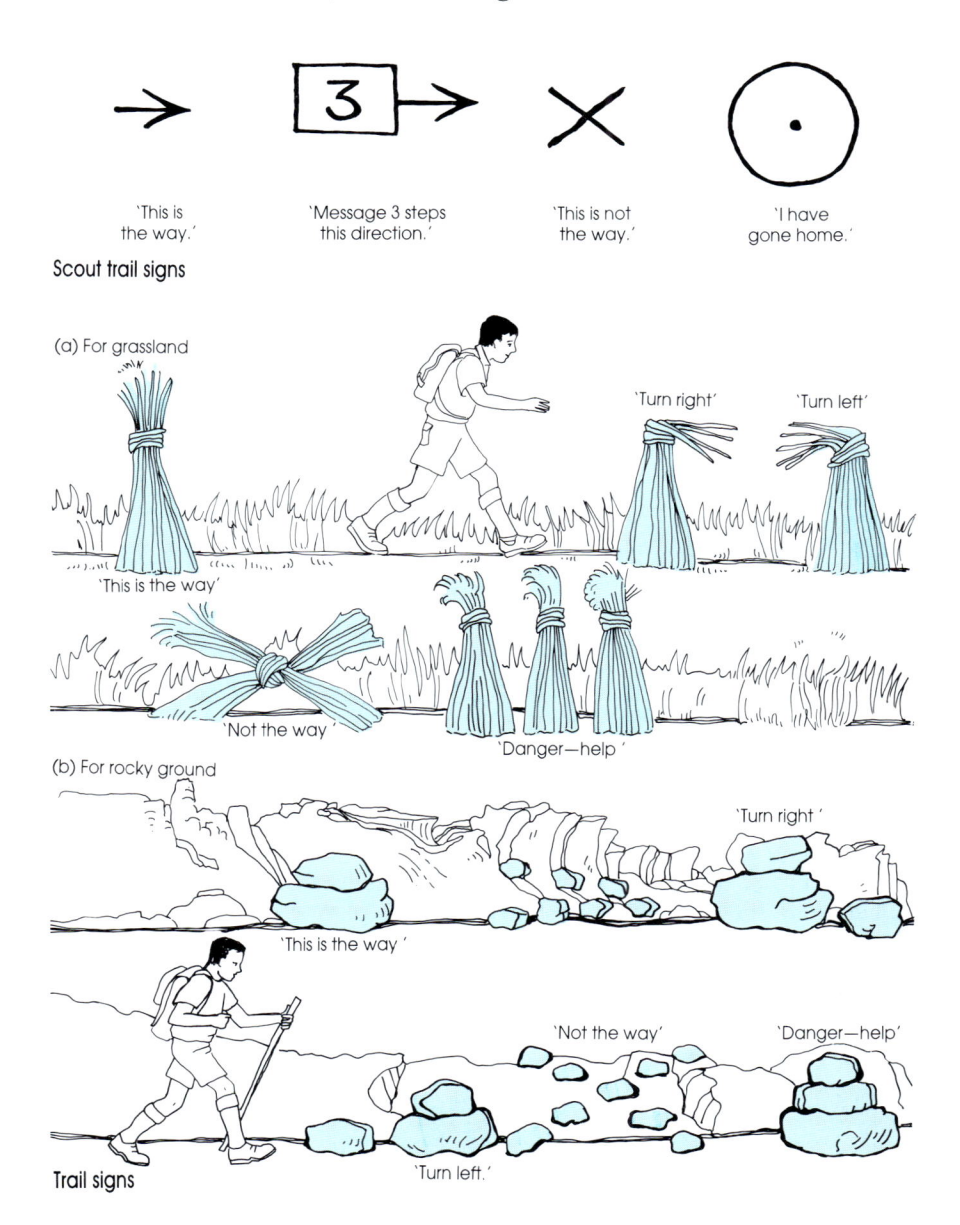

'This is the way.'

'Message 3 steps this direction.'

'This is not the way.'

'I have gone home.'

Scout trail signs

(a) For grassland

'This is the way'

'Turn right'

'Turn left'

'Not the way'

'Danger—help'

(b) For rocky ground

'This is the way'

'Turn right'

'Not the way'

'Danger—help'

'Turn left.'

Trail signs

If you do not wipe out the signs as you go along, you may cause a lot of confusion for other Patrols or even for yourself the next time you hike through the same place.

Fieldbook for Australian Scouting

When you have used the Scout trail signs for a while, you will probably want to learn to use other trail signs. American Indians made their signs by placing small stones in particular ways, or by knotting grass into small tufts, or by pushing sticks into the ground. Study the illustration on these pages and pick the trail signs you believe are best suited to you and your Patrol.

Instead of using trail signs, you can also make a trail with a *whifflepoof*. This 'animal' is a log, hammered full of nails (leave the nail heads protruding about 1 centimetre) and provided with a screw eye to which a rope is attached. When dragged along, it jumps about and makes an erratic trail.

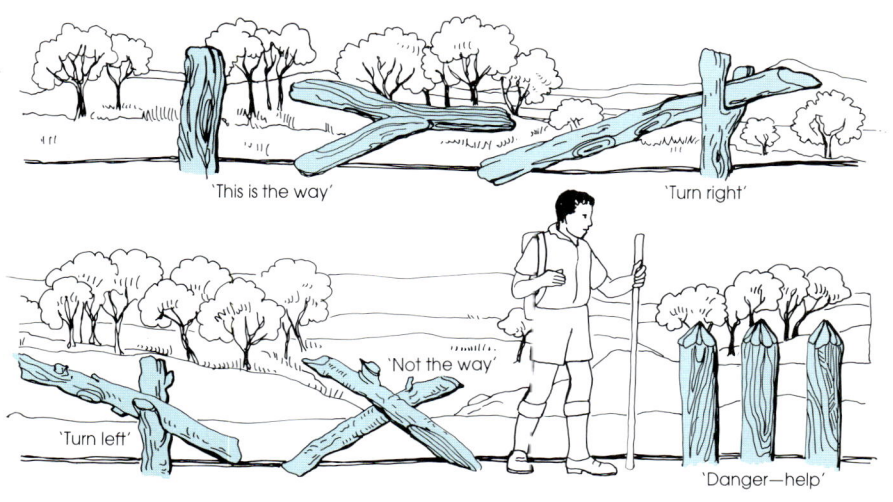

Trail signs for bushland

Trailing fun

A whole Patrol can have a lot of fun playing games that make use of trailing. Following are a couple of them:

1. 'Hare and hounds'
   In this game, one Scout is the 'hare' and is sent ahead to lay a trail using trail signs or with a *whifflepoof*. Give the hare five minutes to get going, then set out in pursuit. Use your tracking skills to trail the Scout down before he/she reaches the objective 1 kilometre away.

Never look over a rock. Look from the side

Looking from behind the tree, keep close to the ground

2. 'Wounded spy'
   In this game, the Scout playing the 'spy' drops a few drops of 'blood' (corn or chickenfeed dyed red) every couple of steps. The 'spy' has a 1-minute head start and must cross the 'border' (a creek or road) 1 kilometre away before the 'cops' (the rest of you) can make an arrest.

Plaster casts

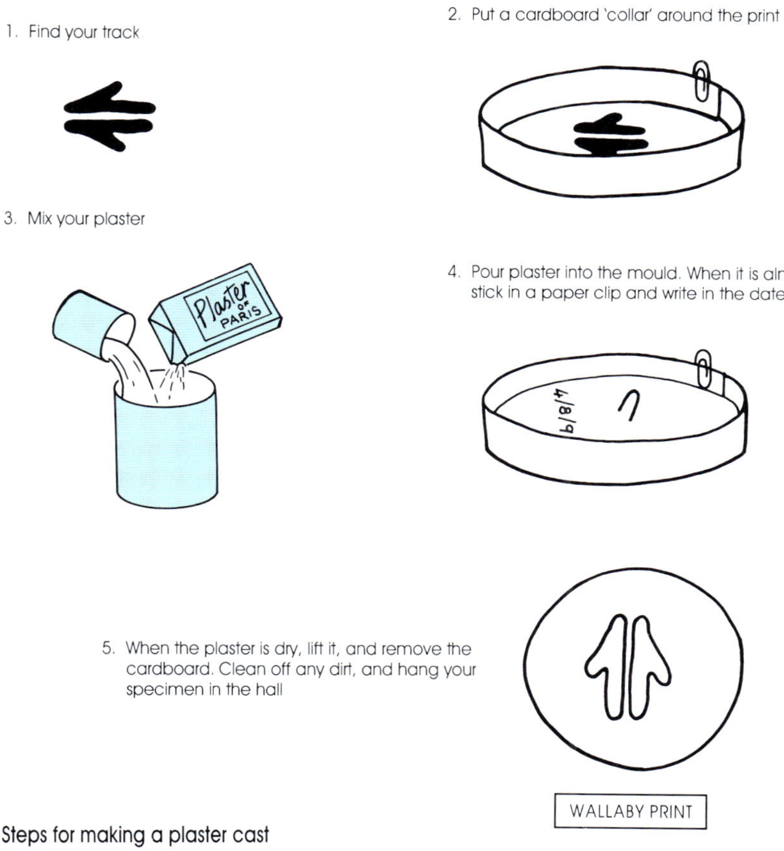

1. Find your track

2. Put a cardboard 'collar' around the print

3. Mix your plaster

4. Pour plaster into the mould. When it is almost dry, stick in a paper clip and write in the date

5. When the plaster is dry, lift it, and remove the cardboard. Clean off any dirt, and hang your specimen in the hall

WALLABY PRINT

Steps for making a plaster cast

Lightweight food

There are special points to consider in planning what food you will eat and cook while on a hike. You will need a good breakfast to get you going in the morning and a hearty meal in the evening. Cooking is usually confined to these two meals which are usually prepared at your overnight camping spot. Lunch should be a light meal or, alternatively, you may like to carry *scroggin* which you can nibble along the way. Scroggin can be made by mixing together or mincing a concoction of sultanas, raisins, mixed peel, peanuts, chocolate and dried oats.

In planning your menu, special consideration will have to be given to the following points.

Weight

At home, your daily intake of food might normally weigh over 2 kilograms. Using dehydrated and dried foods available today, your hike rations should weigh no more than 1 kilogram per person per day. Fresh fruits, for example, have as much as 95% water content, and because you can usually expect to pick up water along your way, the use of dried fruits (apricots, apples, sultanas, and so on) and dehydrated vegetables (peas, beans, mashed potato) can save a great deal in back-breaking weight. Consider, for example, the difference between carrying a 500-gram can of soup and a small packet of soup cubes.

Bulk

Space is also critical in your rucksack, and, in general, the abovementioned dehydrated foods also cut down on space.

In planning your breakfast, consider the space taken up by instant oatmeal compared with that of cereals. Bread is also much too bulky when compared with packets of crispbread. Damper made from flour offers an even greater saving in terms of weight and space.

Keeping value

If your hike is to take longer than one day, fresh meats have to be avoided. Substitute bacon, meatwurst or prepared dried varieties. In hot weather, margarine keeps better than butter, as does powdered or condensed milk compared with fresh milk.

Ease of preparation

Expedition food must be easily and quickly prepared. At the end of the day, hikers are tired and need food quickly, and it may have to be prepared under difficult conditions such as rain and wind. This is a reason in favour of having soup, made from cubes or packets, for your first item on the evening-meal menu. Once your billy is boiled you have soup-all-round to keep you going while you prepare the rest of your meal. A surprising number of items are available from your local supermarket in freeze-dried form. Delectable meals can be prepared in 15 to 20 minutes from packet foods such as beef curry and rice, chicken supreme, and even smoked lobster with rice. Ease of washing up is also worth considering; for example, if you fry foods rather than boil them, you have the task of washing greasy frying pans.

Backwoods cooking

What sort of meal can you cook without your billies and frying pans? It is surprising what a little imagination and practice can achieve, especially with the help of aluminium foil which is light and easy to carry.

By using foil, you have no utensils to clean afterwards and a wide variety of menus from which to pick. You simply wrap the food in a double thickness of foil, shiny side inwards, folding the edges carefully so the steam cannot escape. When the food is cooked, unwrap it and the foil becomes your plate.

Bushcraft

Meat and vegetables can be wrapped in the same parcel. Apples and bananas make an enjoyable dessert. Carefully remove the apple core, and fill the hole with chocolate or sultanas.

You can use foil to make small pans if you wish to fry something. If flames come in contact with the foil it will oxidise and become useless, therefore a bed of hot coals is essential for successful cooking. With practice, you will soon learn how long you have to leave the food in the coals.

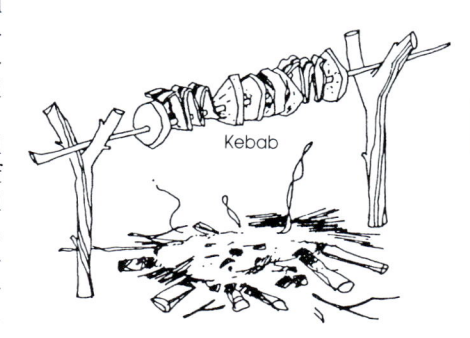

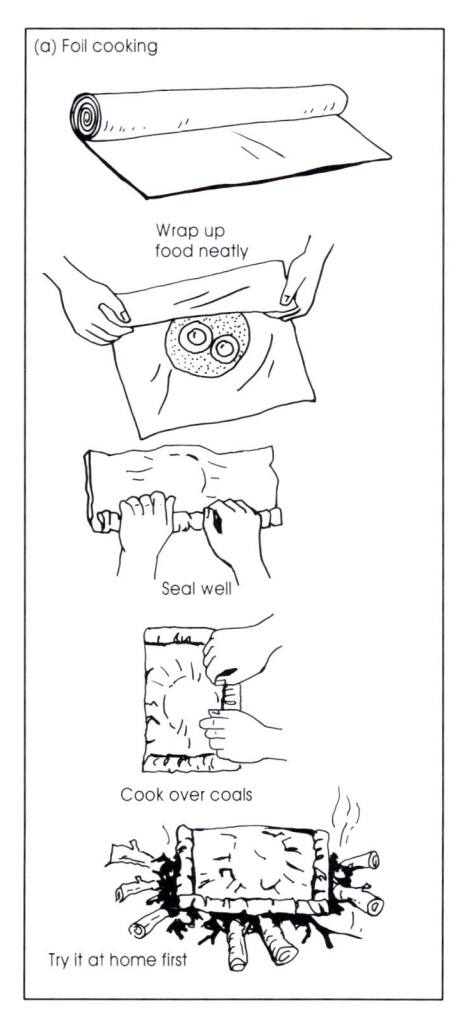

Kebab

(a) Foil cooking

Wrap up food neatly

Seal well

Cook over coals

Try it at home first

(b)

Seal your food in plastic bags. Boil the lot in one billy. Try peas, potato, carrot and egg. Try it at home—it really works

(c) Make up instant pudding in a plastic bag. Prepare at home

Powdered milk

Pudding

Plastic bag

Add water at camp. Shake up well in bag. Let it set and eat from bag

93

Baked potatoes

Wash the potatoes. Take a double sheet of foil of a size big enough to more than cover the potato. Bring the two sides of foil above the potato and fold them together three times, making sure there is an air space around and above the potato. Twist the open ends of the cylinder you have formed, like a Christmas bonbon. The important thing is to leave an airspace all around so you have made, in fact, a primitive sort of pressure-cooker. Cook for about half an hour. To test whether the potatoes are ready for eating, gently squeeze them without removing the aluminium foil. Serve with butter.

Spud egg

Cut the top from the potato and remove the centre with the corer. Break an egg into the hole, replace the top, secure with a couple of twigs, wrap in foil as before, and cook.

(a) Egg in potato

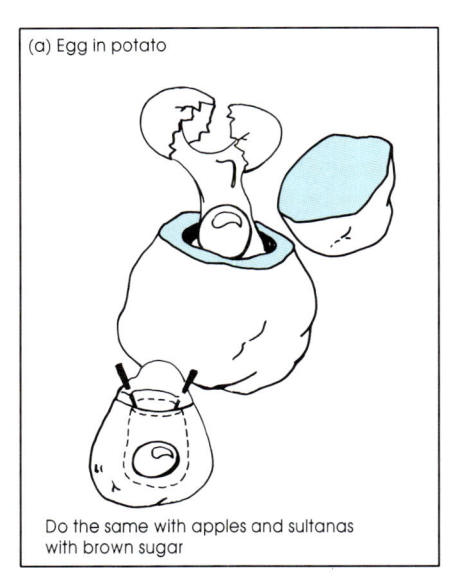

Do the same with apples and sultanas with brown sugar

(b) Kebabs

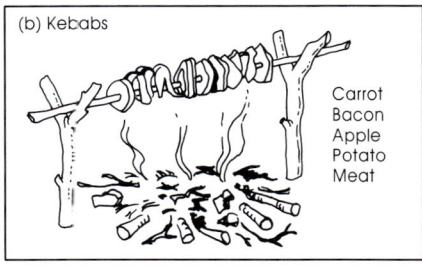

Carrot
Bacon
Apple
Potato
Meat

(c)

Halve an orange, eat the fruit. Use the skins to poach eggs

Kebab

A kebab consists of small pieces of carrot, bacon, apple, potato, meat, and so on, spiked on to a thin green stick with the bark removed. Roast slowly.

Cooking apples

Wash and remove cores. Fill the centre with brown sugar and sultanas and cook as for potatoes. They take 10 to 15 minutes.

Banana bliss

Another good dessert. Slit a banana lengthways and place chocolate pieces in it. Wrap in foil and cook for 10 minutes.

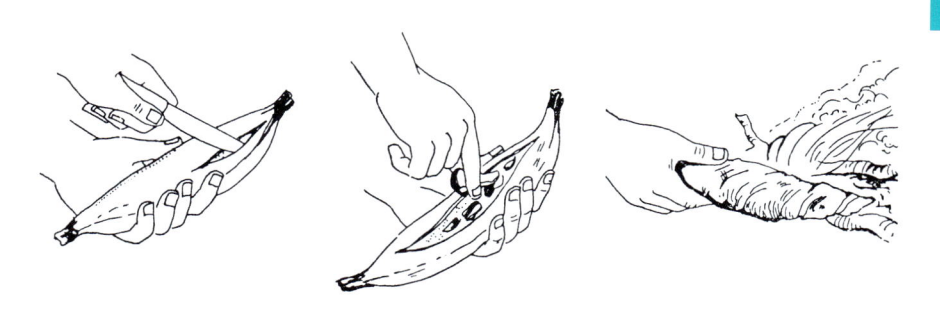

Onion egg

This is the same as spud egg but using an onion instead!

Orange pot

Halve an orange, eat the contents, and use the skin halves for poaching eggs.

In the embers

Potatoes, apples, bananas, sausages in a banana skin, and eggs with the shells covered in mud, can all be cooked in the embers.

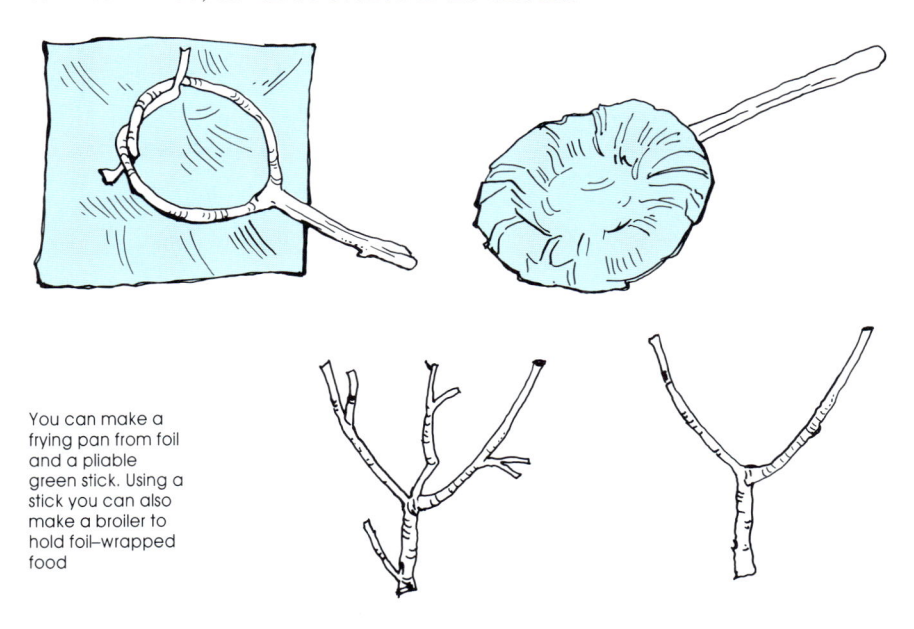

You can make a frying pan from foil and a pliable green stick. Using a stick you can also make a broiler to hold foil-wrapped food

Many foods can be cooked on a skewer

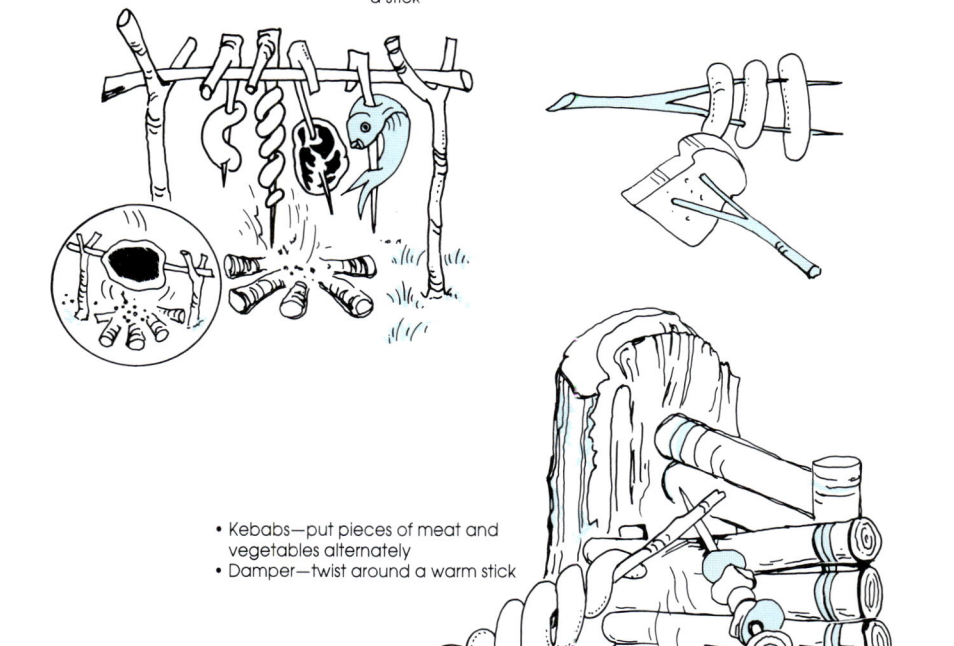

Apples, sausages, toast, marshmallows and even eggs can be skewered on a stick

- Kebabs—put pieces of meat and vegetables alternately
- Damper—twist around a warm stick

Cooking on a stick

Drinking water on hikes

Water is often not readily available. For this reason, on hikes you should carry in a plastic container in your rucksack about 1 litre per person for use between campsites. Always conserve your water by not drinking before it is truly necessary, and then keep in mind how far you have to go before your stocks can be replenished.

Hike tents

When selecting a hike tent for your expeditions, you must choose one that is light but that will provide you with the protection you need from rain, wind and snow. Hiking in harsh weather conditions requires your tentage to be of strong construction and made of quality material.

Shapes

'A' shape Traditional design; good rain-shedding ability; sloping walls reduce interior volume. Ridge has to be curved to allow this style of tent to withstand strong winds.

Wall tents A development of the 'A' shape. The walls give more usable floor area. Wall tents can be pitched tauter on uneven ground.

Tunnels and domes Very efficient at shedding rain and wind. Near-vertical walls give almost 50% more usable volume than 'A'-style tents of similar floor area. Flexible poles tension outwards to keep tent taut and prevent flapping. Because the shape is more efficient at withstanding bad weather, lighter material can be used. These tents require less pegs than traditional tents, further lightening the load. Under most conditions, guy ropes are not necessary.

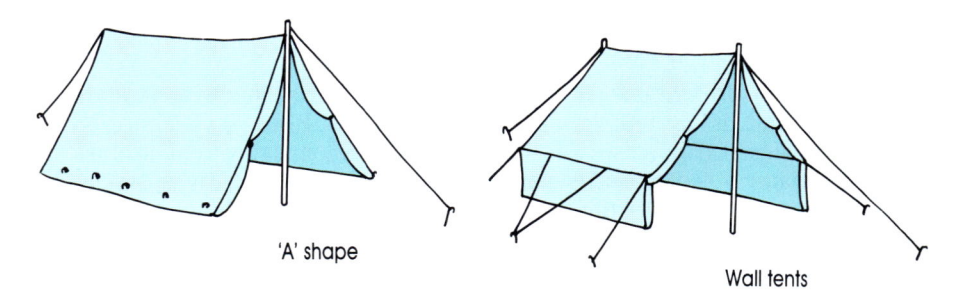

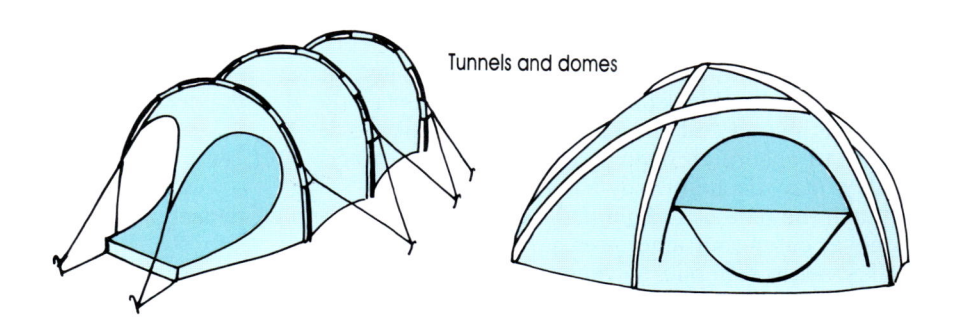

'A' shape

Wall tents

Tunnels and domes

Ultra-lightweight and bivvy sacks A compromise. To reduce weight, you must either sacrifice interior volume or durability. Fortunately, new fabrics and design are fast overcoming these limitations. However, most of these tents do not have storage space inside and must be considered only as a personal shelter.

Ultra-lightweight and bivvy sacks

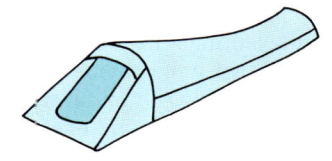

Tent poles

'A' shape and wall tents usually use mild steel poles. Dome and tunnel tents usually use thin pre-curved fibreglass or aluminium poles. Although aluminium is more expensive, it is much lighter and stronger than fibreglass and should be chosen for tents being used in extreme conditions. However, both types of poles will stand up to years of use if a little care is taken with them.

1. Always make sure all pole sections are properly mated together before inserting them in the tent sleeves.
2. Do not stand on the poles or place heavy weights on them.
3. Do not bend the poles when they are not inserted in the sleeves.
4. Do not roll the poles inside the tent—put them in their own bag in the tent bag.

Care and use of pipe tents

Before use Before use, seal all fly-sheet and floor seams with an effective seam sealant. If the tent is made of nylon, use K-Kote or Campfire Nylon Seam Sealer. Do not use wax or silicon sprays on nylon tent seams. On canvas (japara) tents, seal seams with beeswax, then lightly sprinkle the pitched tent with water until uniformly wet. This allows the cotton fibre to settle into place. Allow to dry before packing or use.

During use Remember the following points when using your tent.

1. Avoid hollows that may collect water.
2. Make sure the ground is clear of all sharp objects (stones, twigs, and so on).
3. If the tent is to be used on the one campsite for more than one night, it is a good idea to use a piece of industrial plastic cut slightly smaller than the floor of the tent. This protects the floor against sharp grit, thistles, and so on, and will aid in reducing condensation under the sleeping mats.
4. Pitch the tent end on to the wind if possible.
5. Try to ensure an even space between inner and outer tents, otherwise they may touch in windy and rainy conditions.
6. Pitch the tent as straight and as taut as possible, and condensation should never enter your inner area.
7. Try not to spill oils, solvents, acids (fruit and drinks), fuel or insecticides on the fabric because it damages the waterproofing.
8. Cook outside or in vestibules, if possible.

Emergency shelter

No matter what precautions are taken, unforeseen circumstances may make it necessary to construct an emergency shelter in a hurry. Individuals and parties lose their way—on what was meant to be a one-day trip into uninhabited country, a member of a party becomes disabled by an accident; people set off to climb a mountain and are overtaken by bad weather; the way back is blocked by a sudden flood in a river. The newspaper columns and television headlines frequently provide examples of what can happen.

If there is no cave, rock-overhang or other shelter from the elements, a lean-to must be built where it is sheltered as much as possible from stormy weather and facing away from the wind and driving rain. Inside the lean-to, put down a layer of small branches or leaves to act as insulation from the chill and damp of the ground. If possible, light a log fire in front of the lean-to; heat will radiate from the fire into the shelter.

A sheet of plastic in your kit is a valuable, lightweight resource. It does not take up much room and is ideal for constructing an emergency bivouac, and it can also be put to many other uses.

How to make tents

Trappers and drovers often made use of very simple tarpaulin tents and shelters, constructed like the half-pyramid from a tarpaulin or strip of canvas. The canvas was used as a covering for a pack-horse's load on the trail during the daytime. At night, the canvas was folded to make a shelter, and the corners that did not form part of the roof were folded under on the floor. A fire was lit in front, to burn all night and keep the sleepers warm.

Lightweight tents of these styles have been made and successfully used by Scouts who are not afraid of a little fresh air. They are very cheap and easy to make. The first is simply a 3-metre square of waterproofed tent material with a reinforced edge. Eyelets can be used to take pegs, or peg loops and rings can be sewn on. The top end of the ridge is tied to a convenient tree bough or, better still, to a pole lodged between two trees, or on one pole and a crotch. This is a one-person shelter.

The second type, an open pyramid, requires a 3 m × 5 m sheet and can sleep two people.

Because they have no doors, these shelters should always be pitched with backs to the wind.

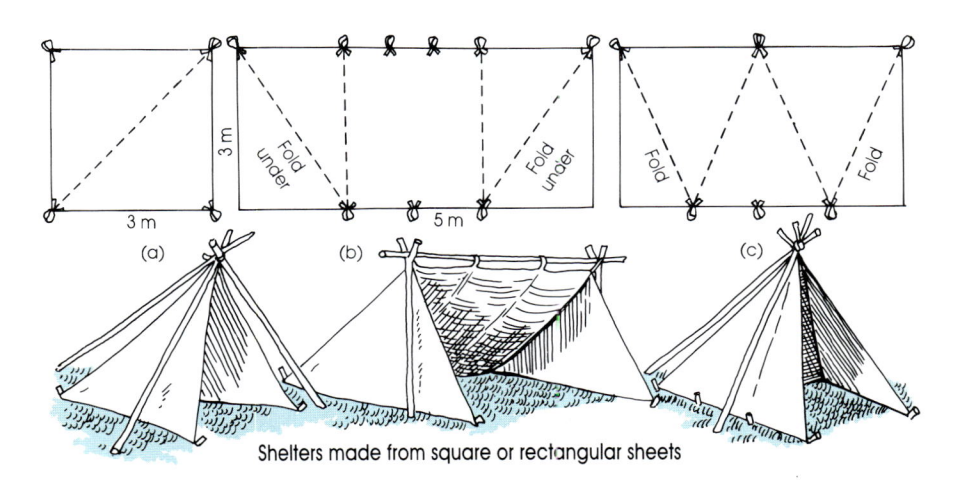

Shelters made from square or rectangular sheets

Bushcraft

The half-pyramid tent

This simple tent, illustrated as follows, can be easily made either from a canvas sheet or from lightweight material. The canvas must measure 4 m × 3 m after any necessary joining of material.

To make the tent, lay the canvas sheet flat, and mark out the dimensions shown in chalk. Strong tape loops for the pegs are required as shown. The doorway is closed with three pairs of tapes; if you also wish to tie the doors back, three other tapes are required on the inside, along the sides that have the 90° angle. Two small triangles of material at the apex, with an eyelet hole in each, are laced together with blind cord before the tent is erected if a centre pole is used. Only one pole and one guy line support the tent, but, if you wish, the tent can have a strong loop at the apex for suspending it from a tripod of saplings, or shears. Also, the tent can be suspended from a horizontal branch or a rope slung between two trees.

This gives you a tent height of 2 metres. If the material is light—balloon cloth or nylon—the corners and apex will have to be strengthened with triangular patches.

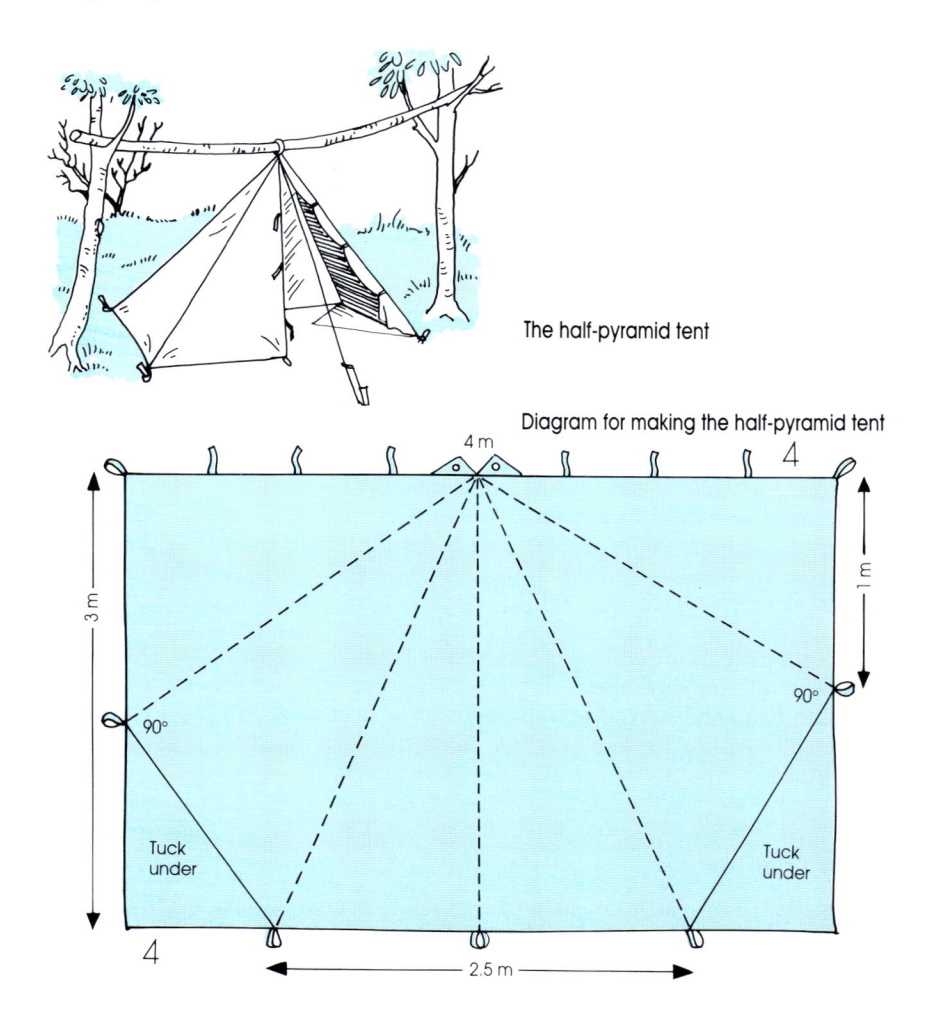

The half-pyramid tent

Diagram for making the half-pyramid tent

101

Fire making

Primitive peoples make fire by rubbing two pieces of wood together. Wood used for this purpose should be thoroughly dry; it must not be gummy or resinous, nor must it break up into fibres, but the friction should form a fine dust that does not feel gritty when rubbed between the fingers. The wood must not be too soft, otherwise the friction will not be enough to cause a spark. The wood should be hard, but not too hard, otherwise it will become polished and slip too easily. Many trees and bushes supply suitable wood from their branches or roots. The two pieces of wood may be of the same or different varieties.

There are five different methods of applying friction for firemaking:
1. the fire-drill
2. the fire-plough
3. the fire-saw
4. the bow-drill
5. the pump-drill

The fire-drill

This was largely used by Aborigines. The apparatus is very simple, consisting of: (a) a spindle, which is about 6 mm in diameter and 30 cm to 70 cm long, roughly rounded at one end (b) a hearth, which is a stick about 60 cm long and 12 mm in diameter flattened on the upper surface. A shallow basin about 6 mm in diameter is scooped out of the top of the hearth, and a V-shaped notch is cut into this from one side to allow the sparks formed to fall on to the tinder. Tinder is made out of fine dry grass, bits of the prickly tops from grass-trees, pith dust, or other suitable material. The tinder is placed in some dry grass, the hearth is placed on this, and a pinch of fine sand is placed in the shallow basin to help wear it into shape. The Aborigine then squats on the ground, holds the hearth steady with his feet, places the rounded end of the spindle in the shallow basin, and commences to twirl it rapidly backward and forward between his flat open palms, commencing on the top and pressing firmly downward all the time. At first, smoke appears, followed by a spark which falls on to the tinder. The sparks, by careful nursing, are blown into a flame, otherwise the dry grass is caught up in the hand and moved rapidly around and around at arm's length until it bursts into flame. In this way an Aborigine can make fire in less than 2 minutes.

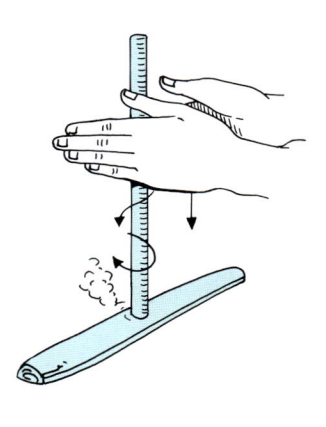

The fire-plough

In this case the hearth consists of a stick of dry wood about 120 cm long, flattened on the top in which a groove is cut lengthways. The operator sits on one end and the assistant on the other, to keep the hearth steady. The fire maker has a flattened stick dressed to a bevel so as to fit in the groove; he/she holds this stick by placing one hand on top of the other which enables enough pressure to be exerted by the fire maker who then works the rubbing stick or plough backwards and forwards, first slowly, then faster, until a spark appears. Island natives chant a song about them and the wood making fire, and they always manage it so the chant ends just as the spark appears.

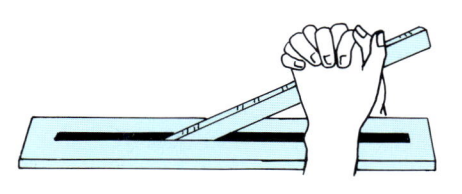

Sawing

A suitable stick is split for a part of its length and the cleft kept open by a chip of wood or stone. A notch is then cut across the split portion and some tinder placed in the split beneath it. The saw is a piece of wood 175 or 200 mm long given an edge to fit in the notch. The cleft wood is held firmly in position while the saw is moved smartly backwards and forwards horizontally in the notch. The fine powder produced soon commences to smoulder, and by careful blowing, a flame is produced.

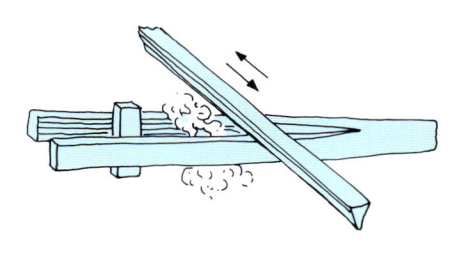

The bow-drill

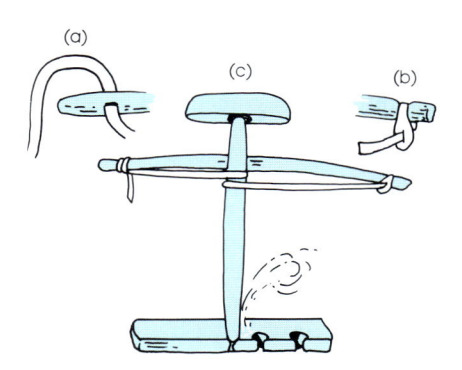

This apparatus was used by American Indians and is easier to manipulate than the Australian twirling stick. The hearth is similar to that used by Aborigines; the spindles are also alike, except that for the bow-drill it is only 30.5 cm long and can be worn down to 100 mm before being discarded. It is rounded at both ends, because the lower end turns in the hearth while the upper end turns in a hand rest of hardwood or soapstone. The bow is 45 cm to 60 cm long and curved so as to have a belly of about 25 mm in the middle. At either end of the bow a hole is made for a strip of greenhide or belt lacing about 6 mm wide to pass through. Greenhide or belt lacing is better than a cord because it is strong, pliable and capable of standing a fair amount of friction. One end of the lacing has a small slit cut in it; this end is passed through the hole at the top of the bow, and the rest of the lacing drawn through the slit. The loose end is now passed through the hole at the grip end of the bow. The spindle is placed against the lacing and twisted over so as to get a complete turn of the lacing around it; the loose end is now drawn fairly tight and fixed with two half hitches. The lower end of the spindle is placed in the shallow basin of the hearth; the hand rest or nut is placed on the upper end of the spindle which is then caused to revolve by drawing the bow backwards and forwards; at first relatively slowly with light pressure, and then faster with greater pressure. Care must be taken not to let the wood of the bow touch the spindle, which would act as a brake. Fire can be produced with this apparatus in half a minute. The proper amount of tension for the lacing, according to the pressure exerted, will be found by experience. Fine adjustment of the lacing can be made by pinching it between the thumb and forefinger of the hand holding the bow.

The pump-drill

In this case the spindle, which is about 60 cm long, passes through a 15 cm disc of wood which is jambed on to it about a quarter of its length from the lower end; this disc serves the purpose of a fly wheel. A stick about 45 cm long has a loose cord attached to its ends, the centre of the cord being fastened to the top of the spindle. The loose portion of the cord is given a few twists around the spindle; the spindle is then placed in a small depression cut in the hearth, and the stick to which the cord is attached is held horizontally and worked up and down vertically against the spindle, causing the cord to twist and untwist, which rotates the spindle rapidly. The spindle is held in position and pressure imparted to it by a hand rest on the top, as in the case of the bow-drill.

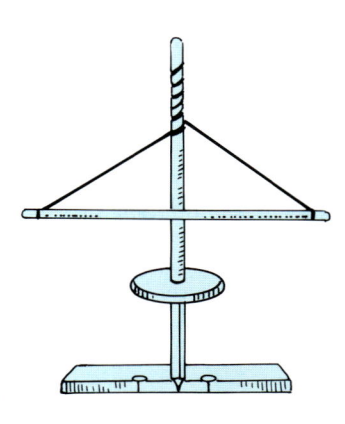

Most primitive peoples had a person selected as the fire maker, and in almost all cases this was a man. It was deemed to be a sacred ritual.

Other methods

Before the introduction of matches, fire was made in the more developed countries by striking iron pyrites with quartz, or steel with flint. It may not be easy to procure a flint-and-steel outfit at a shop nowadays, but this is not necessary, because the back of your knife and any stone hard enough to cause enough friction to heat a particle of the steel to burning point will serve the purpose. The tinder in these cases is usually a piece of charred cotton rag, which must, naturally, be kept dry.

Another method that can be used when the sun is shining is to use a magnifying glass, such as a pocket lens, or camera lens. If this type of article is not at hand, a burning glass can be made out of a bottle of clear glass, if available, filled with water. To make fire, you must hold the magnifying glass steadily, and at a distance from the tinder so the heat is concentrated on the smallest spot possible.

There are also methods of lighting fires by chemical means, and one of the most commonly used is to place some finely grounded Condy's crystals on to the tinder and add a drop or two of glycerine. After a short time this will ignite. If carrying these items, ensure they are separate, otherwise you may have a fire earlier than required.

3

CAMPCRAFT

What is camping?

Camping is fun. Camping means getting out into the open spaces, setting up a temporary home in out-of-the-way and perhaps inaccessible places, where you can study the habits of animals and birds, learn what trees are useful and what plants are edible, play wide games, climb mountains, swim in streams, and understand the noises of the night.

It means cooking over open fires, building rafts, having fun on flying foxes, and pioneering bridges over creeks. It means hiking and stalking games or sitting around a campfire singing or quietly yarning with your Patrol friends.

Camping means living in the bush, sleeping under canvas—or under the stars. It means moving around the countryside in a number of ways—hiking, canoeing, bike riding, horse riding. There are Patrol camps, backwoods camps, survival camps, parent and Scout camps, back-to-nature camps, or simple standing camps at which you enjoy a variety of activities.

Camp is where real Scouting is to be found. You will learn how to be self-reliant and resourceful. You will learn how to get along with others, how to share and to do your share.

Any type of camping is an exciting and challenging adventure. Scout camping, a particular style of camping developed by B.P. from his own experiences, is the most exciting kind, and Scouts like you all over the world enjoy the fun and adventure it offers. Scout camping means using the natural resources of a campsite to make a comfortable camp, looking after yourself regardless of weather conditions, and co-operating with your Patrol to make the camp a success.

Because it offers you fun, excitement and challenging adventure, it is worthwhile to spend some time learning the camping skills—skills that can come only from camping experience. You can learn a lot by reading about camping, and you can gain some experience from training in your headquarters or on the lawn in your backyard, but the real experience comes from getting out into the bush and camping as Scouts with your friends, camping as a Patrol.

No one will expect you to be a good camper immediately. Your Patrol Leader (PL), other experienced campers in your Patrol, or your Scout Leader, will all help you to learn. Every camp you attend will increase your camping skills a bit more. Then, as you gain experience, you will be able to help other new friends at the game.

Baden-Powell started it. He knew what an adventure it is and how Scouts like you enjoy it. By learning to be a good camper and helping others to become good campers, you are continuing where he left off.

Scouting without camping would not be half the fun.

Where should you begin?

Begin with a Patrol discussion. Intelligent planning is necessary to make any camp a success. Do it together as a Patrol and you will find that even the planning is a lot of fun (see *Camp Planning*, S.A.A. resource book).

Decide *when* the camp will be held; *what* you would like to do; *where* you will be able to do these things; *who* will be responsible for organising what; *how* you will be able to get there and back. Together, you must work out a program, a menu, a provision list, and a list of the special gear you will need for your activities.

When the general planning is completed, you as a Patrol member should take over the detailed planning of part of the camp—checking the camping gear, obtaining permission from the relevant authorities, buying the provisions, organising transport, advising parents of your plans, collecting camp fees, getting together the special gear you may need.

If you have not had much camping experience, your PL will give you one of the easier jobs, or get you to help someone with one of the more difficult tasks. Your Patrol Leader or Scout Section Leader will help you if you have difficulties.

When should you go camping?

Whenever you can. Naturally, there are some times when the weather is likely to be more suitable for camping—in northern Australia, winter is best. In southern Australia, spring and autumn are more suitable.

Nevertheless, do not let the weather influence your camping too much, because camping is possible in any season. With special training you can camp quite comfortably in the snow. Wet camps are likely at any time. With some practice you can learn to camp in the rain with very little discomfort.

Whenever three or four or more of you feel like spending some time in the bush, it is as good a time as any to go camping.

Campcraft

Where should you go camping?

Along a creek, near a waterhole, is ideal. With a bit of exploring you can probably find a suitable spot not too far out of town, with a creek, a patch of scrub, and a clearing for your tent. A polite request to the farmer for permission to camp will seldom be refused.

Try finding your own special camping spots. Do not restrict yourself to the popular places that everyone else uses. Each time you camp, try heading for new territory. The more secluded it is, the better the site will be for your activities.

Public camping areas and caravan parks are not for Scout camping. Special permission is required for camping in all areas including national parks and wildlife reserves. You must always obtain permission to camp from your Scout Leader.

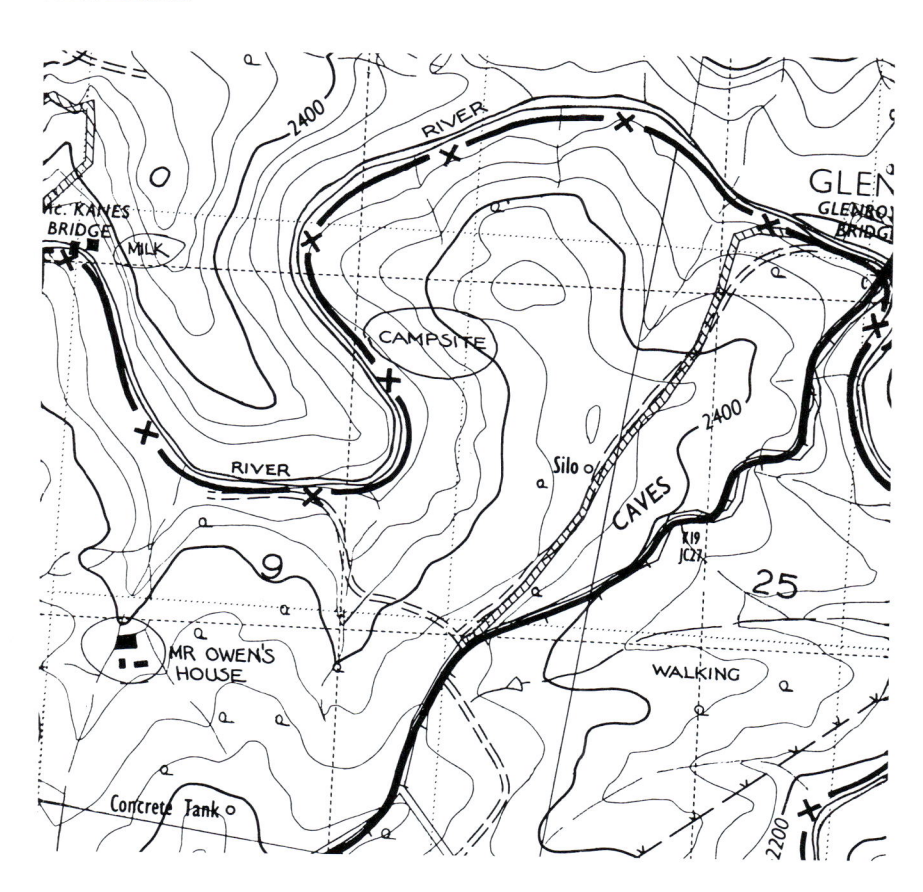

With whom can you camp?

Your Patrol is just right. Do not wait until all the Patrol members are available; four is about the smallest number that should go camping. If you have a friend in another Patrol who is interested in your camp, invite him/her if the

107

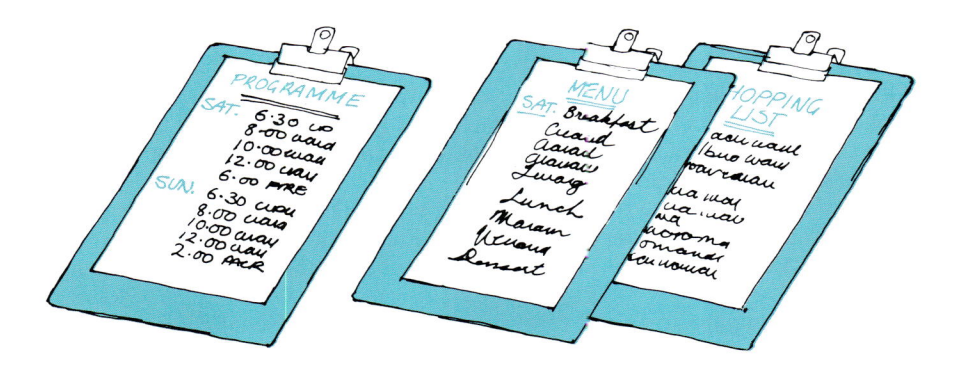

others are agreeable, or invite a friend who is not a Scout. After seeing the fun you have, your friend might join your Patrol.

You should always camp as a Patrol, but do not always camp alone; arrange joint camps with other Patrols occasionally. You can learn things from each other.

What gear will you require?

This depends on the type of camp the Patrol is planning. You will need much more gear for an eight-day summer camp than you will for an overnight camp. A hiking camp requires gear different from that for a standing camp.

Never load yourself down with so much gear that you must camp at a site reachable only by car; the best camping spots are only usually accessible on foot. Discuss this subject during your planning session. Take only the things that are essential. Make as much use as possible of the campsite's natural resources.

Patrol camping gear

There may not be much choice in the camping gear available to your Patrol, but this does not mean you have to put up with old worn-out gear that should have been discarded years ago. Always strive for improvement, and use the most modern gear the Troop can afford.

No gear list is ever finalised: some things you will want to add and some things you will discard, depending on the type of camp the Patrol is planning. So go through the list carefully during your planning session.

No matter what type of camp you are planning, your basic requirements are as follows:

- shelter for protection from weather
- bedding for rest
- clothing to protect yourself
- food and water to sustain yourself
- cooking gear, to make food edible
- tools for work, play, maintenance and emergencies.

Equipment for a standing camp

A standing camp requires the most gear. The following checklist suggests basic requirements for a Patrol on a standing camp.

General

The Australian flag, your Patrol flag, plus games gear.

For shelter

A Patrol tent with fly or waterproof roof or enough two-person tents for the people attending. Enough poles, ropes and pegs for all tents. A second fly, for dining or cooking shelter. A store tent.

For your kitchen

Fire irons or fire grill, water heater, camp oven, food-preparation table, food-box, two buckets for fetching water, one fire bucket, two dishes for washing up, one dish for hand washing, dish mops, scouring pads, steel wool.

Tools

Hand axe, bowsaw, spade, trench digger, post-hole borer, file and sharpening stone, nails and wire, tent-peg mallet, cord and rope, tent repair kit, torch.

Cooking equipment

Four cooking pots or saucepans or billies of various sizes, one large pot for heating water, one frying pan, two cooking spoons, two can openers, two mixing bowls, aluminium foil, two cooking forks, one large and one small knife, two vegetable peelers, one egg slicer and one ladle, salt and pepper shakers, food tongs, plastic bags.

Health and safety

First-aid kit, latrine gear, toilet and handwashing gear, two lanterns (including spare parts and fuel), fly-proof food storage, soap and detergent.
    There will be many times when you will go camping with only a portion of the things on this list. On occasions you may wish to add to it. For an overnight camp, select only the things you consider necessary.
    If the gear is being transported right to the site, pack it in boxes. Making a Patrol box is a good project. If you are walking to the site, you will share the gear with your Patrol friends—a bit extra for the bigger Scouts, a bit less for the smaller Patrol members.

Equipment for bike camping

Bike hiking is popular and usually involves camping. A biking camp requires much less equipment than a standing camp, and special packing arrangements will have to be made. Riding a bike with a heavy pack on your back is very tiring and can be extremely dangerous. Pack as much as you can into pannier bags beside the back wheels, and on the luggage rack. This keeps the centre of gravity low. Do not forget your bike-repair outfit.

Equipment for water camping

Your Patrol may be planning a boating or canoeing journey and have to camp for several nights.

Everything will have to be stored in watertight containers. Place individual items in plastic bags, with the top tightly secured with a strong rubber band. Place these bags inside a larger bag, made from rubberised cloth or waterproofed canvas. Securely tie the top of this bag. Unless protected by an outer skin of some other material, plastic bags are not reliable: they tear and split very easily and are then useless. Always place them inside another container.

Cans with press-on lids, such as paint cans, are handy for storing small items. Make sure some air is trapped inside your containers so they will float if you capsize. Do not forget the canoe-repair kit and any safety gear your craft may require; personal flotation devices would be at the top of the list.

Equipment for hiking camps

Because a hiking camp requires much less equipment, you will have to plan from a modified list. While each Scout must carry personal gear, several items can be shared among the Patrol. Your hike will be made more enjoyable and comfortable by reducing the weight of your pack. Aim for a pack weighing less than 10 kilograms.

Rucksacks

A comfortable pack is essential. Various types are available with or without frames. External-frame types are best suited for heavy loads in open country. Internal frames are recommended for climbing, skiing and travelling over hilly routes because of their superior comfort and stability. Frameless packs are suited for lightweight day hikes and rock climbing. Do not buy a pack that

Campcraft

Rucksack   Army pack
                              Frame rucksack

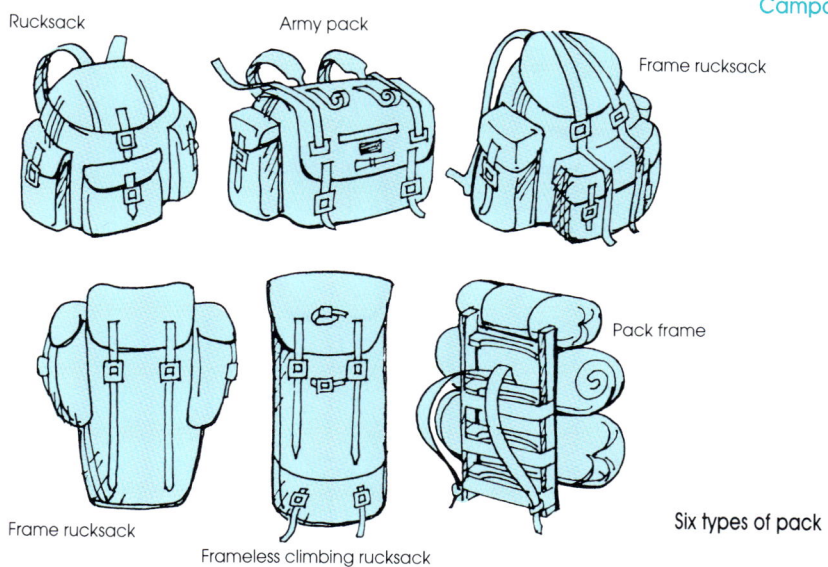

Frame rucksack
        Frameless climbing rucksack
                              Pack frame

Six types of pack

is too big—the less weight you have to carry, the better. Packs are usually made of canvas, nylon and cordura (a nylon woven material that looks like canvas but is lighter).

Packing your rucksack

A well-packed rucksack looks neat, is evenly balanced and has nothing hanging outside. In good packing, the rule is 'last wanted, first in', remembering, when possible, to place lighter bulky articles at the bottom, the heavier ones at the top, and the soft ones folded neatly at the back.

Fieldbook for Australian Scouting

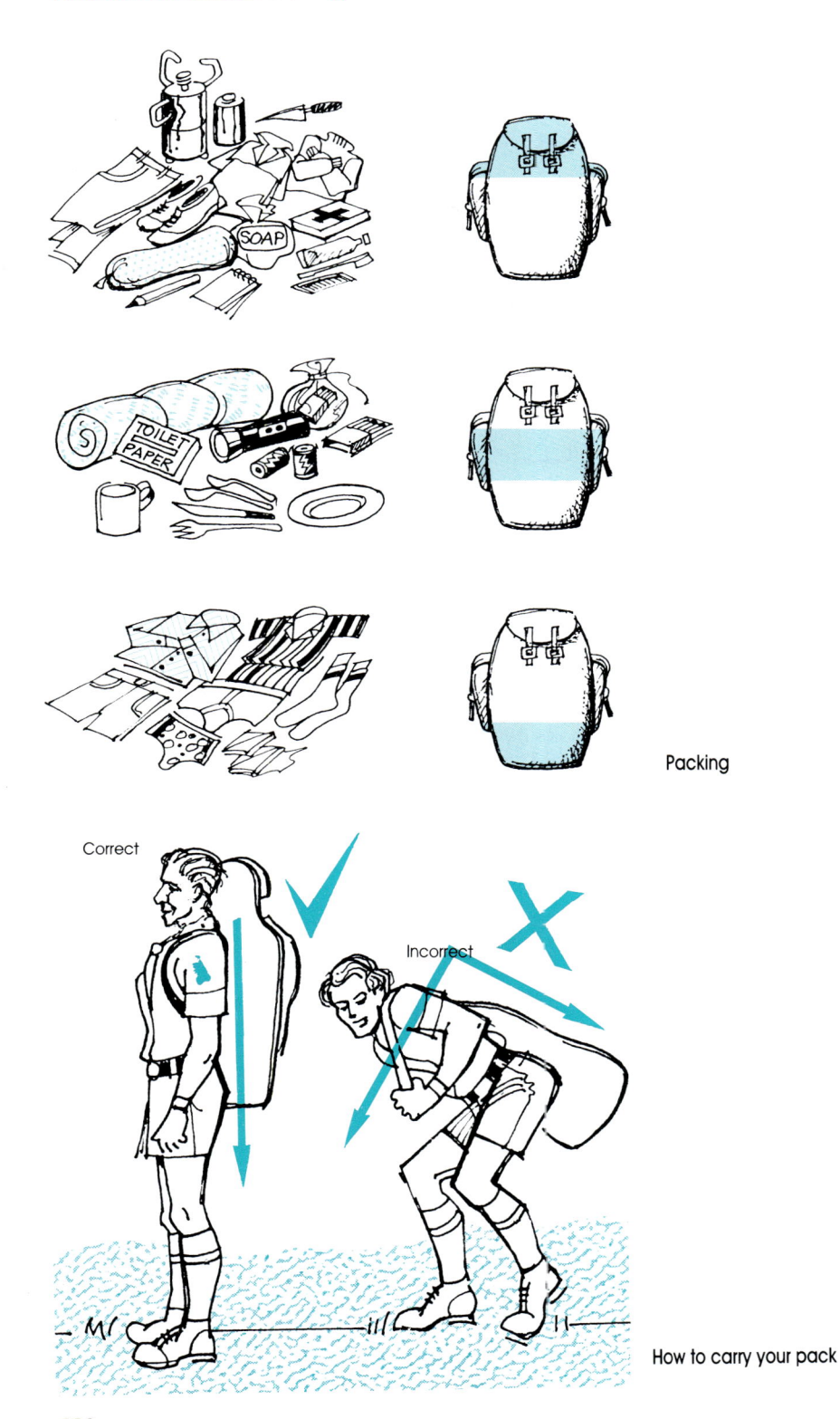

Packing

Correct

Incorrect

How to carry your pack

112

Medium items

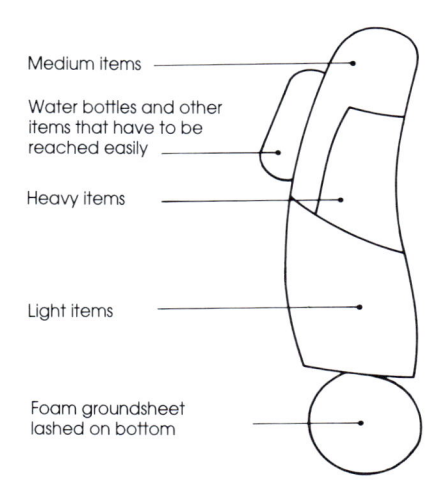

Water bottles and other
items that have to be
reached easily

Heavy items

Light items

Foam groundsheet
lashed on bottom

How to organise the pack

Place your first-aid kit in a position where it can be easily pulled out. A top-heavy pack is easier to carry. Polythene bags make packing much easier, and the kit can be easily grouped into bags. Spare bags can be taken for soiled clothes, damp articles, and the frying pan.

Groundsheets

A groundsheet is essential to stop moisture from penetrating your sleeping bag, and some groundsheets have a second use as a raincoat. Many types are available from outdoor-equipment centres. Space blankets, heavy-duty plastic sheeting, proofed nylon sheets or rain capes and urethane/polyethylene foam sheetings are all very effective and lightweight for camping.

Sleeping bags

A sleeping bag is a must for hikers. Hikers should choose a sleeping bag that is light but that retains body heat, thereby keeping the user warm. Bags may be made of either 'duck down' or synthetic materials. One made of super-down (fine duck feathers) is superior to one made of featherdown (coarse feathers).

Synthetic materials used include Dacron, Dacron Fibrefill II, Dacron Holo-fill II, Polarguard (polyester), tetron, terylene, acrylic and orlon. Other fillings can include kapok, cotton and wool, but these are more suited to warmer or tropical areas. Down sleeping bags are best in dry, cold conditions and are lighter and more compact than synthetics. In damp conditions, synthetic bags are better because of their ability to repel water and their quicker drying times.

Remember to choose a bag with a hood, because up to 40% of your body heat can be lost through your neck and head. More details on sleeping bags can be found in the 'Sleeping gear' section on page 147 later in this chapter.

Cooking gear

Aluminium or alloy is the best material because of its light weight. A 'Gilwell' cooker or similar mess kit contains two plates, one of which has a handle and can be used as a frying pan as well as a small billy can. A large 1-to-1.5 litre billy may be shared by the Patrol.

An enamel mug, 0.5-litre size, acts as an additional cooking pot as well as a drinking cup. Aluminium mugs are useless except for cold drinks; tin rusts, and plastic cannot be put on or near the fire.

Containers for food and equipment

Pack perishable foods and fragile items in plastic or aluminium screw-type containers. Avoid carrying bottles, tins and packets that are either heavy or likely to spill food. Drawstring cloth bags are useful for rice and similar dry foodstuffs.

Personal gear

Use the gear list on pages 152–3 as a checklist, but make sure you include your hiking boots and spare laces. A water-bottle will also be necessary in most places. Take a notebook and pencil; a log of your hike will be valuable later, both for reviving your own memories of it and for helping other Scouts in their planning. A camera will help you make the log more interesting.

Shared gear

The following items can be divided among the members of the Patrol:

- first-aid kit
- tents
- toilet paper
- maps and compass
- shoe-cleaning gear
- billy
- rucksack-repair kit.

Tents

The main function of a tent is to provide shelter from the rain and wind, and peace from mosquitoes and other airborne pests. Modern technology has given us tents that will protect us from the elements and the attendant flying and crawling insects, whether the campsite is on the edge of a swamp, up the side of a snow-covered mountain, or in a tropical rainforest in the wet season.

Campcraft

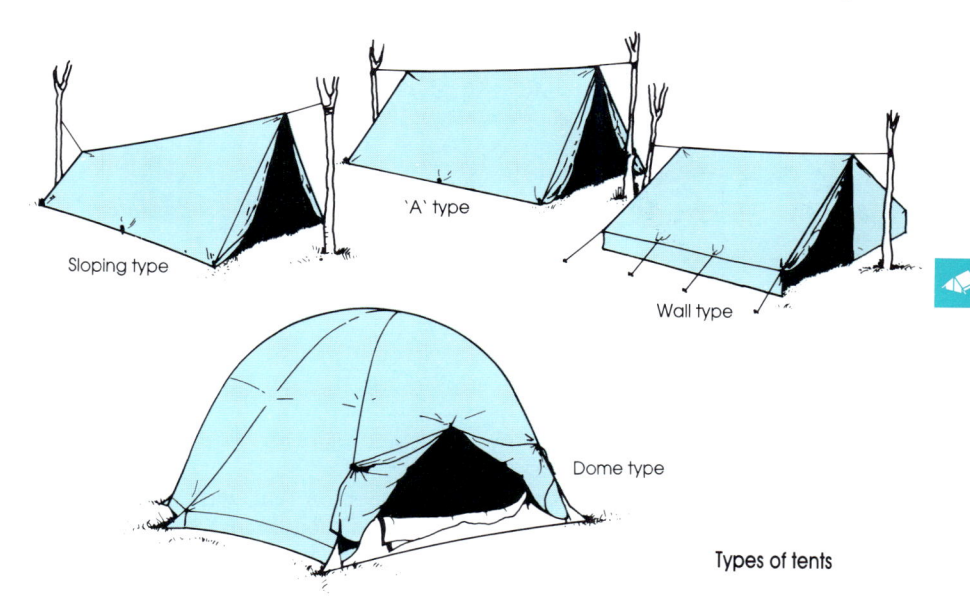

Sloping type 'A' type Wall type

Dome type

Types of tents

As a Patrol, you may not have much choice in the tents you will be using—you will have to use whatever the Troop owns. However, the tent is the most important piece of equipment in your store, so make sure you look after it at all times.

Selecting a tent

There are many styles of tents. Ridge tents, marquee type, bell shaped, hike tents, continental style, and others, but the same care is necessary for all of them. Selecting a tent is usually a compromise between size, weight, bulk, stability, quality and cost.

To help you choose a tent to fulfil your needs, some thought should be given to some relevant factors listed as follows.
- Where will the tent be used?
- At what time of year will the tent be used?
- What will the weather be like?
- How many people will use the tent at any one time?
- Are your camping needs likely to change in the near future?
- How will you transport your tent—on your back? by car? and so on.
- What is your budget?

Your tent should be light yet strongly made and waterproof. It should be roomy enough to provide enough space for sleeping, dressing and storing the personal gear of the number of people using it. It should be high enough for the average Scout to stand up in. A built-in groundsheet can be an advantage, and in some areas insect screens may be necessary. If possible, select the tent that best suits the camp being planned. Ridge tents and marquee-type tents, large enough for a whole Patrol, are suitable for long camps, but they restrict your camping to sites accessible by transport. They are too heavy and bulky to carry over long distances.

(a) Brailed ridge tent

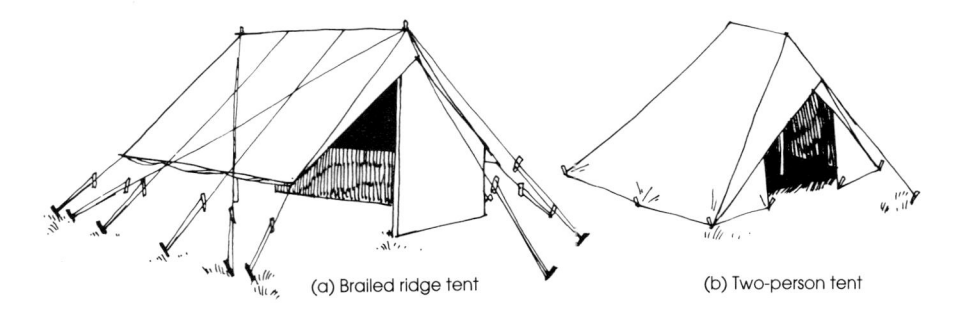

(b) Two-person tent

Brailed ridge tent and two-person tent

Pup tents are not satisfactory, but a two-person tent with about 2.0 × 2.5 metres of floor space and 1.75 metres of head room is just about ideal for any kind of camp. 'A'-type tents are usually cheap but can be small inside. Wall-type tents are roomier and adapt better to uneven sites. Dome styles have a good living space, tolerate high winds, and shed rain easily because of their shape.

For an overnight hiking camp, why not try for a bush shelter or a light fly or piece of heavy plastic to make a simple lean-to? When using a piece of plastic or similar material, fold a handful of grass or a small stone in the corner of the material before attaching your guy rope to it.

Considering these points should help you to define your needs. However, the environment in which you do the greater part of your camping should be the main consideration for the type of shelter you choose. The limitations of your shelter will not be as evident in fine weather conditions, when it is almost superfluous, but will be most evident in poor conditions, when you are most dependent on it.

Condensation

This is sometimes a problem with some tents. During the night, the human body gives off about 600 millilitres of water vapour (from perspiration and breath). Add to this the evaporation of water from wet clothing, and so on, and a very humid environment is produced.

A waterproofed and closed tent traps this moisture vapour, which on a cold or wet night will condense into dew drops on the inside of the roof of your tent. These drops will then drip down, wetting you and your sleeping bag.

The most efficient way to eliminate condensation is to have a well-ventilated double-skin tent consisting of a heavily waterproofed fly completely covering an unproofed nylon or cotton tent with a space of about 10 to 15 centimetres left between the fly and tent. The fly can be held off the tent by two cords crossing from the top of the tent down to the pegs holding the corner guys. A fly also allows the tent's occupants to touch the roof without causing leaks.

Materials

Tents are made from several types of materials, as follows.

Nylon   Nylon, in its many forms (nylon, taffeta, taslan, and so on) is used extensively in the manufacturing of tent flys, walls and floors. It is highly abrasion resistant, rot and mildew proof and quick drying. Constructed in a variety of thicknesses (deniers), it is also highly breathable unless coated with one of the waterproofing compounds, that is, silicon or polyurethane (K-Kote) to make it impervious to water.

Because of its light weight, it is fast becoming the material to select when bulk and weight are the main considerations.

- Fire danger: **Nylon tents are very susceptible to flames and sparks from a campfire which can easily burn holes or set the tent alight. Remember not to cook in tents, especially hike tents.**

Cotton   Cotton has been the traditional material used in the manufacture of tents. Japara and canvas tents remain popular today in the large family tents, but in the lightweight- and car-camping market, it has been superseded by later developed fabrics with superior weight and waterproofing characteristics. Cotton is not waterproof unless treated with waterproofing compounds (Birkmyers, Dry Coat, and so on) and even when treated this way, is never 100% waterproof if it is to maintain breathability. Lightweight unproofed cotton is used as inner tent material in the cheaper double-skin tents designed for applications when weight is not the main consideration.

Gore-tex   Gore-tex fabric is usually used only in the smaller bivvy-sack-type tents. Gore-tex fabric is composed of a micro-porous membrane, protected by fabric on one side or both sides. This membrane is popularly known under the DuPont trade name of Teflon. Gore-tex fabrics are waterproof and 'breathe-able'. They are also highly windproof and remarkably lightweight. Gore-tex requires heat (for example, body heat) to transpire water vapour through the membranes' pores, and in a tent (unlike clothing), there may not be enough warmth, while you are insulated in your sleeping bag, to transpire moisture. Condensation may form on the inner walls of the tent. Because of this, Gore-tex is usually used only in the smaller bivvy-sack-type tents where body heat can easily warm up the smaller volume.

Transporting

Keep your tent in a strong bag for transporting it. The poles and pegs should be in a separate bag because they might rub a hole in the tent. Do not put other heavy gear on top of the tent.

In camp

Do your part in making sure that the tent is properly pitched. If a strong wind gets up, fit extra guys to brace it. A collapsing tent is likely to tear. Waking up with a wet tent draped around you and a ridge pole pinning you to the ground is not very amusing.

When it rains, slacken the guy ropes. Sisal shrinks when wet and will pull the canvas out of shape, or the pegs out of the ground. This does not happen with synthetic ropes.

Do not walk over canvas while it is on the ground—you might force a stick through it.

Storing

If you have to pack up in the rain, roll the tent up loosely to transport it. As soon as possible when you get back, hang the tent up to dry out thoroughly.

Before storing, pitch your tent, and clean it, if necessary, by sponging with mild soap and water. To avoid mould or mildew, make sure the tent is thoroughly dry before storing it.

Fold or roll the tent loosely and store it on a shelf in a cool dry place. Do not store in direct contact with concrete, because the lime used in the manufacture of concrete will weaken the fabric and waterproofing agents used in the tent.

Protect canvas from nesting mice and rats: they will chew holes in it.

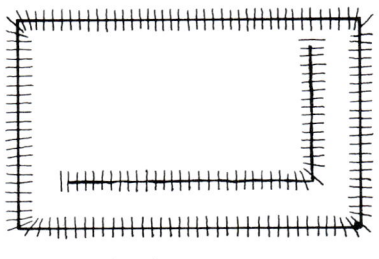

Mending a tear in canvas

Maintaining

Mend all tears as soon as they happen, no matter how small. Sew the tear together, then sew a patch over the torn area to strengthen it. Keep the guy ropes in good condition, free of knots.

Pegs

A brightly coloured paint stripe on pegs will often help in recovering them when you are striking camp (packing up).

Pitching a tent

Whatever kind of tent your Patrol uses, make sure you do your share of erecting it properly and quickly. If you practise this before you go to camp, you will save time when you get there. Sometimes you will have to put your tent up in the dark, therefore you will want to know exactly how to go about it. Pitching a tent is a team effort, whether it be a two-person tent or a Patrol marquee.

When pitching a tent, close the tent door. If the tent does not have a ridge pole, peg down all four corners, pulling front, back and sides taut. Drive pegs in the front and back of the tent. Tie the guy ropes down loosely and then raise the tent poles into position.

During the day, brail (truss) up your tent, or open it up to let the sun and breeze in, to dry out the ground and freshen everything inside.

Campcraft

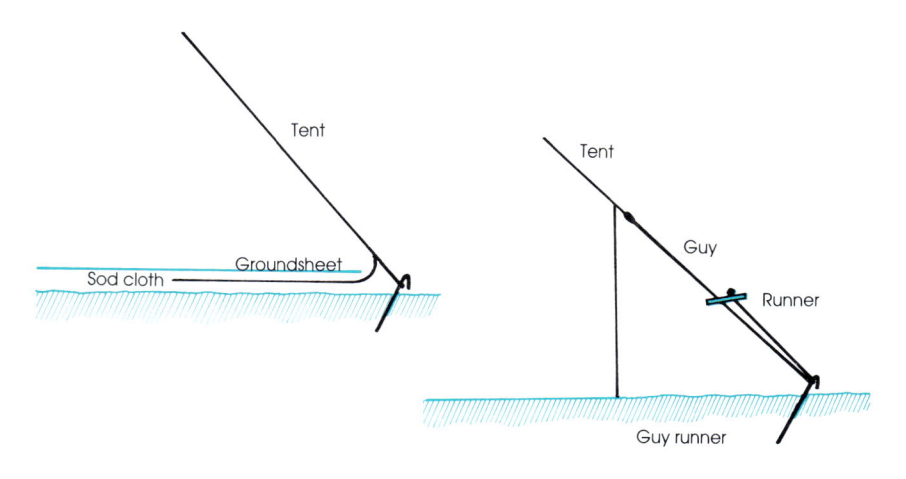

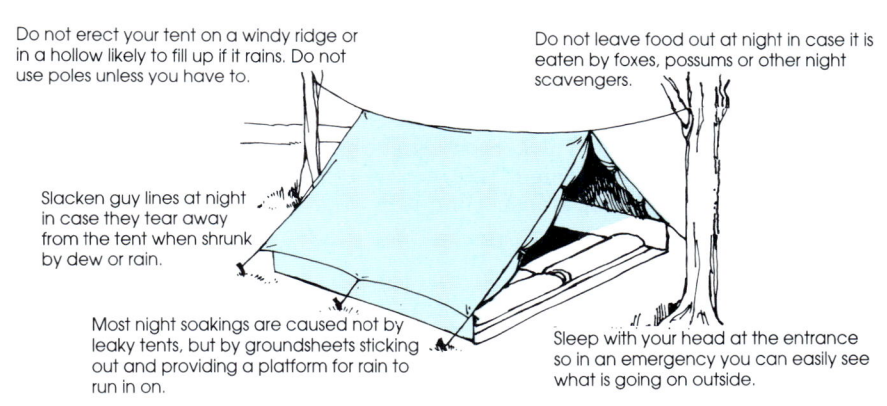

Tent

Sod cloth — Groundsheet

Tent

Guy

Runner

Guy runner

Do not erect your tent on a windy ridge or in a hollow likely to fill up if it rains. Do not use poles unless you have to.

Do not leave food out at night in case it is eaten by foxes, possums or other night scavengers.

Slacken guy lines at night in case they tear away from the tent when shrunk by dew or rain.

Most night soakings are caused not by leaky tents, but by groundsheets sticking out and providing a platform for rain to run in on.

Sleep with your head at the entrance so in an emergency you can easily see what is going on outside.

Cooking gear

A list of suggested cooking gear that may be needed by your Patrol has been given on page 109 earlier in this chapter.

The pots and pans you use around the fire are best made from heavy-gauge aluminium. If you cannot afford these, make your own from large cans and fencing wire. This makes a good Patrol project. Rub detergent or soap on the outside of your pots before placing them over the fire—this will save a lot of scouring later. Also keep your cooking pots clean on the inside. Stand them upside down on a couple of small logs, or in the Patrol box.

Plastic

Plastic is more durable than glass for Scout camps and is lightweight. Use plastic dishes and containers, because they are very good for food preparation and food storage, but keep them away from the fire or hot billies, and so on. Clearly mark them with what they contain.

Fieldbook for Australian Scouting

(a) Plastic containers

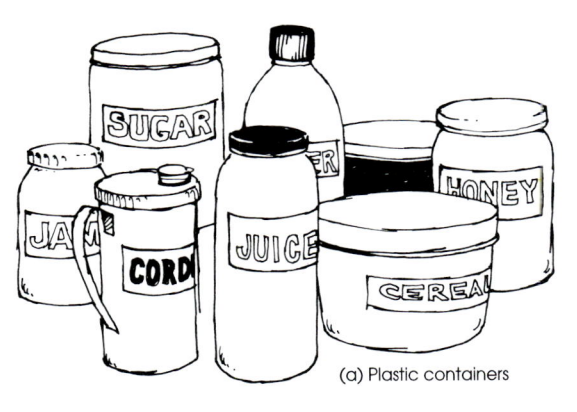

(b) Cooking tools

Plastic containers and cooking tools

Cooking tools

Utensils such as spoons, forks, knives and ladles are best kept together in a kit made from canvas or vinyl; each article has a compartment or pocket. Hang the kit from a convenient tree while in camp, and roll it up to keep everything together while transporting it. If your Patrol does not own one, you might like to make one.

Patrol box

Most Patrols have a box in which they keep the cooking gear in between camps. If transport is available to the camp, take the box for transporting and storing the gear. Remember, though, that two small Patrol boxes are much easier to transport than one large heavy one!

A box with a shelf and hinged lid is ideal. Lay the box on its side, and raise the lid to make a table. This way you have a table and a storage cupboard for your standing camps. A camp foodsafe, or a small box, can be suspended in a rope framework from a tree in order to provide food storage away from ants. (See page 94 of the publication *The Patrol System*.)

Patrol box on side. Lid raised to make cupboard with pots, pans and food containers stored inside

Camp ovens

Roast leg of lamb with baked potatoes, pumpkin and carrots, with mint sauce, in camp? Why not? Apple pie and custard too! Meals served on warm plates. Food kept hot between cooking and serving it. How? Simply with a camp oven, an asset on any long camp.

Drum oven

A 25 litre drum, with removable lid, laid on its side across a trench fire (check local fire regulations on trench fires), is all that you need. Make a flat shelf by cutting a piece of steel plate or fence panel to the required size. Covering the drum with mud and straw or grass will improve its insulation, and you will be able to eat in style.

Reflector oven

A reflector oven is also easy to make by cutting a kerosene tin in half, fitting a wire shelf to hold the food, and placing it close to the fire.

Dixie oven

A bush oven is simply a heavy 'dixie' or billy with a tight-fitting lid placed in a hole in the ground and plenty of hot coals shovelled all around and over it. Stews, casseroles, pot roasts, camp bread, cakes, and so on, can all be cooked in this oven, and you can be off on some activity while the cooking is being done. Do not forget to place the food in the dixie first, and you will do a better job if you cover the hot coals with a layer of dirt.

Hay box

Any food—such as stew, soup and porridge—that is cooked by a simmering process can be cooked in a hay-box oven. A billy packed in the centre of a large box, an esky, a garbage bag or similar large container, tightly packed with straw, dry grass, shredded paper or similar material around the billy, will store the heat and cook the food. Get the food boiling very hard, jam the lid on, pack more straw on top of the billy, and come back from your wide game or swimming excursion to find the tea cooked to perfection.

To make a hay box, follow steps 1 to 6

1. Line box with old blanket or several layers of newspaper.
2. Pack thick layer of hay (or balls of newspaper) in bottom of box.
3. Place pot in centre, resting on bottom layer of packing.
4. Pack hay (or balls of newspaper) tightly around pot, to brim level.
5. Put cushion filled with hay (or kapok) over the top of the pot.
6. Place lid on box, firmly closed, or held down with a weight.

Fieldbook for Australian Scouting

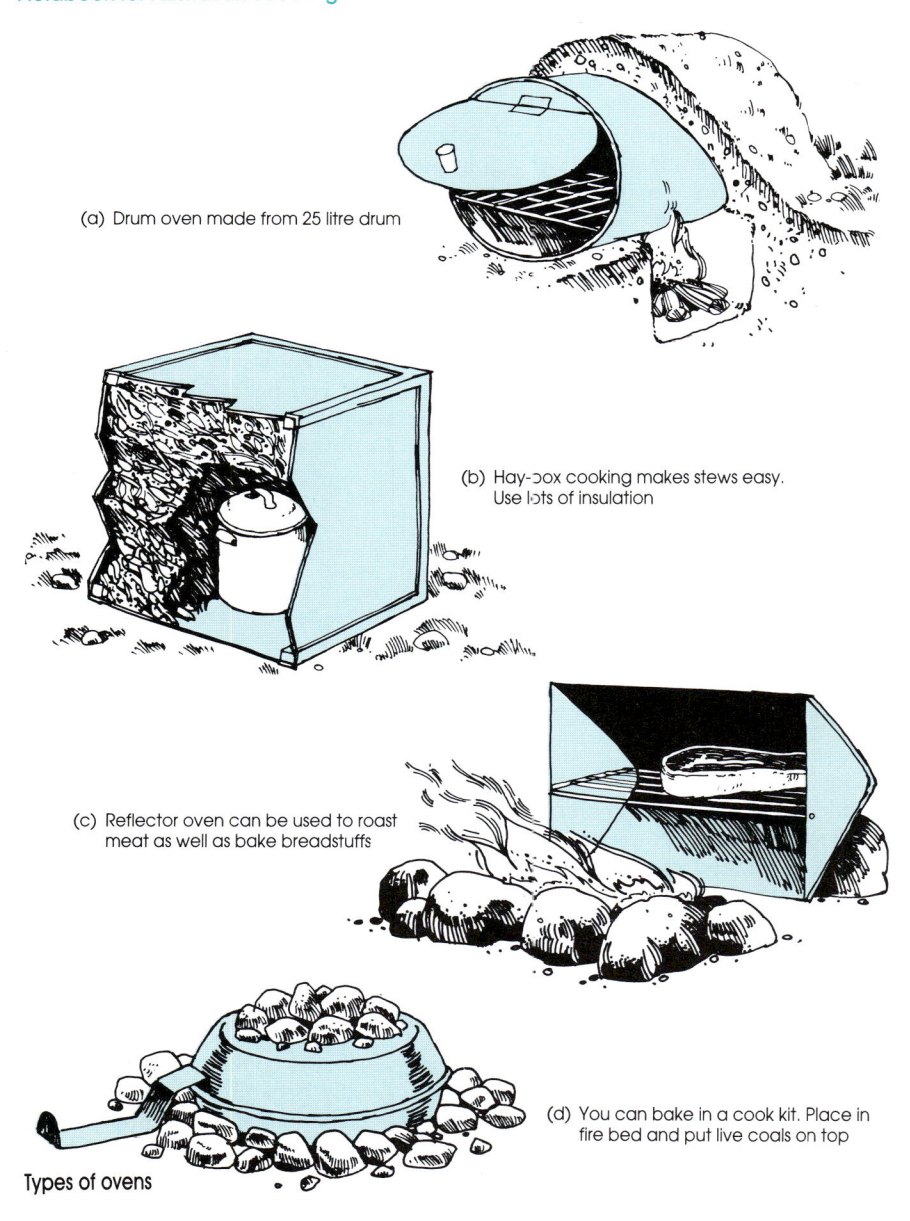

(a) Drum oven made from 25 litre drum

(b) Hay-box cooking makes stews easy. Use lots of insulation

(c) Reflector oven can be used to roast meat as well as bake breadstuffs

(d) You can bake in a cook kit. Place in fire bed and put live coals on top

Types of ovens

The hay-box oven had its origins a century and more ago, in Norway, when a stew pot, having been brought to the boil, would be wrapped in thick felt. This minimised the escape of heat, and the food continued to cook, without fire being applied.

Later, in the 1880s, a device was constructed in Norway which was called the 'Norwegian oven'. This was a wooden box thickly lined with felt, with a tight-fitting lid that was also felt lined. A stew or other dish would be brought to the boil on a fire, in the ordinary way—then the pot, lidded, would be deposited in the box, and the lid tightly closed. A few hours later the food would be thoroughly cooked and be ready for eating, piping hot.

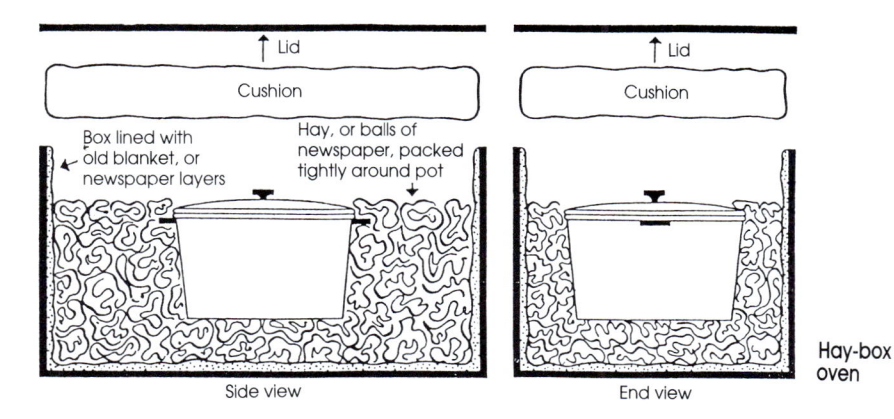

B.P. recommended it

In 1908, in his famous book *'Scouting for Boys'*, Baden-Powell strongly recommended the above type of fireless cooker—which had by then become known as the 'hay box', because hay instead of felt was used for insulation. Well into the 1920s, the hay box was in wide use in Scout camps—usually a wooden box lined thickly with newspaper, with hay packed tightly around the pot.

In 1918, in his manual for Girl Guides, B.P. wrote, 'A jolly useful thing for saving coal, saving time and saving money is a hay box.'

Dutch oven

Scouts and other campers of all types have found the Dutch oven a most useful utensil. It is probably the most versatile cooking tool of all, because it can be used for frying, browning, steaming, stewing and baking. Almost anything that can be cooked in, or on, the kitchen stove at home, can be cooked at camp in a Dutch oven.

The Dutch oven

The Dutch oven is made either of thick cast iron or aluminium alloy with a recessed or flanged cover that enables you to place hot coals on top, while the oven rests on three legs or rocks above the heat of a bed of coals, to prevent the food burning or sticking to the bottom of the oven.

The best ovens have a vertical lip (flange) around the edge of the lid, which is most important in retaining coals on the top of the oven. The rounded, domed lid works well in the kitchen at home, but is not very efficient in camp.

Buying a Dutch oven Dutch ovens are available in several sizes, their diameters ranging from around 25 to 40 centimetres, with sides varying from about 10 to 16 centimetres in depth. For cooking for a Patrol of eight persons, a 30 cm oven is fine. A 25 cm oven works well for pies and cakes.

Seasoning and cleaning a Dutch oven It is most important to 'season' your Dutch oven before you use it. This simple process also helps prevent the cast iron from rusting—as does the proper cleaning method.

Fieldbook for Australian Scouting

Old-style Dutch oven

New-style Dutch oven

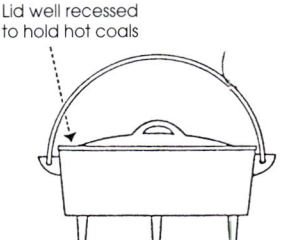

Lid well recessed to hold hot coals

Dutch oven buried in 'conservation-conscious' pit fire, made from end of oil drum

Grass and soil protected!

Makeshift Dutch oven

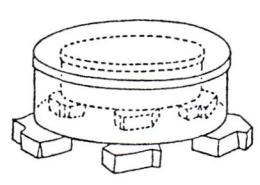

Makeshift Dutch oven

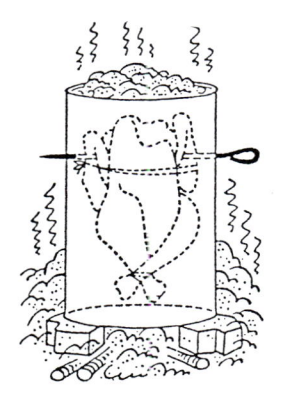

A small biscuit tin, placed inside a larger biscuit tin, on low rocks to provide air all around, makes a splendid makeshift Dutch oven. The big tin should also stand on low rocks. Hot embers are banked under, around and on top of the big tin. (Any suitable small can, within a larger one, provides a makeshift Dutch oven!)

A tin can or small drum may be used for roasting chicken or other meat. Suspend chicken in drum on a wire skewer. Raise can above fire on low rocks. Bank embers under and around can and on top.

- First, place the new oven in your campfire. When it has been well warmed, remove it, and rub every part if it—inside and outside, and including the lid—with cooking fat or cooking oil. Do this very thoroughly, using a piece of cloth, before you use it for cooking. (Alternatively, you can season it in your home oven, before leaving for camp.)
- Because it is made of cast iron, your Dutch oven should *never* be cleaned with soap and water, or detergent, or scouring powder, and so on, otherwise it will rust. Clean it by placing it in the fire so the remnants of food can burn away. Then wipe it well with newspaper or any other suitable paper that has first been soaked in cooking oil or cooking fat. (If your Dutch oven is made of aluminium alloy, and therefore rustproof, you can clean it with soap and water).

Cooking on charcoal fires

In many public parks, open wood fires are prohibited, and in many camping areas, firewood is so scarce you have to pack in your own fuel. You can solve these problems by using charcoal, or, better still, charcoal briquettes. You can buy them in convenient packages.

Charcoal stoves

Unlike a wood fire, a charcoal fire requires some type of stove. What type? There are dozens on the market. But why buy one when you can make your own?

For cooking a meal in a single pot or a small pan, you can turn a tin can into a charcoal stove. Cut off the top completely. Make holes for draught along the bottom with a juice-can opener. Make similar holes along the top edge, from the inside out. Cut off with tin shears the sharp tips of the tongues that result. To save charcoal, make a perforated grate from a can top. Rest it on a couple of wires pushed through the stove one-third or halfway down.

For broiling, barbecuing and frying, you can make a larger, trough-shaped stove by cutting open a large cooking-oil can.

Charcoal tips A charcoal fire is different from a wood fire. Using wood, you have a hot fire to start with, a slower fire later; using charcoal, you have a slow fire in the beginning, a hot fire later.

- Guess how much charcoal you will need for the whole cooking job; ignite that much from the start.
- For a sure, safe start, use twigs and wood shavings; never use flammable fluids to start a charcoal fire.

You can make a small charcoal stove from a tin can (a), and a larger one from a cooking-oil drum (b)

Hot water

Even on the shortest camp, you will need hot water. Keeping a billy or large can on the fire at all times will give you plenty of hot water, provided you remember to fill it up as soon as you take water out of it and remember to keep the fire under it.

Cold water goes in here

Hot water comes out here

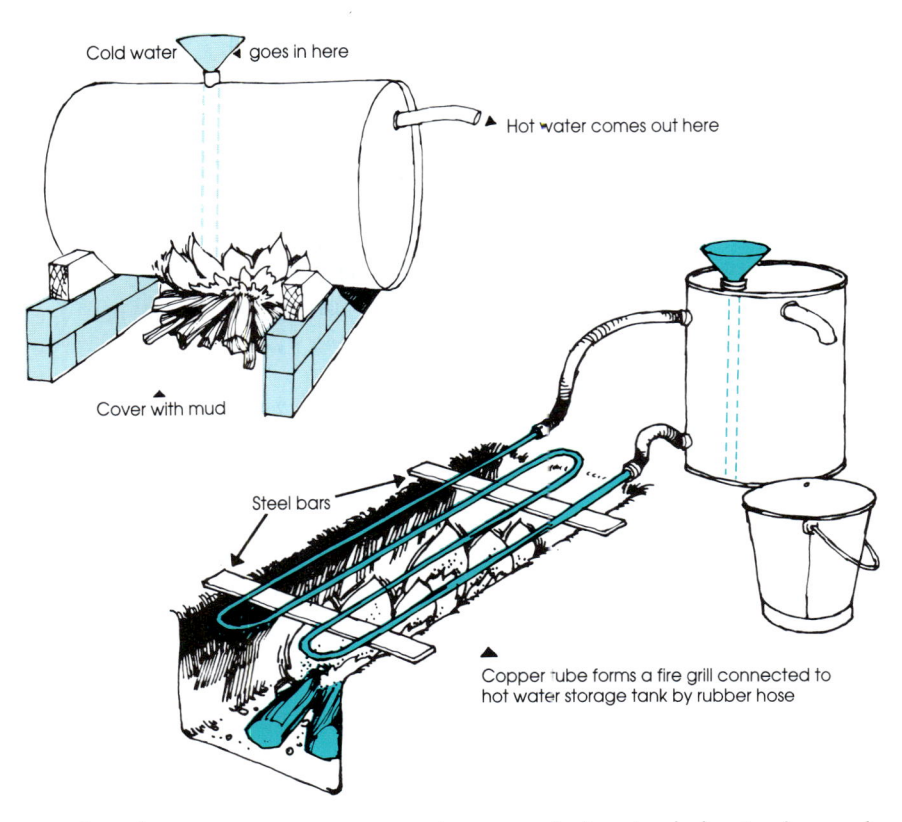

Cover with mud

Steel bars

Copper tube forms a fire grill connected to hot water storage tank by rubber hose

On a longer camp, an easy way to ensure hot water is in steady supply is to make up a drum with a filling pipe that goes almost to the bottom and a spout near the top for the water to come out of. By pouring cold water in through the filling pipe, hot water will run out of the spout and the drum remains full. The drum is laid across the trench fire, and may be covered with mud and straw or grass to insulate it. The whole time you have a fire, you will have hot water.

Camp gadgets

Scouts have always made their camp comfortable by using a few simple gadgets. Some of these you can make at home and bring along with you, others you can make quickly in camp. Some strong string or cord, a few light dead branches, and a bit of imagination, are all that is required.

Do not spend a lot of time building elaborate gadgets. Make the best use of the natural resources around the campsite. Logs, tree stumps, larger stones, a small embankment, and overhanging branches, can all be used to make your camp more comfortable.

Living timber should never be cut to make gadgets. Use what is lying around the site, or take some gadget wood to camp with you. Bamboo is

Campcraft

straight, and is strong enough for most gadgets and light enough for you to carry a decent-sized bundle with you. Old broom handles or staffs are a very good alternative.

Gadgets can be useful as follows.

- In your tent: a shoe rack and a pack rack to keep your personal gear off the ground; a clothes hanger, if there is room in your tent to hang it; a boot scraper outside the tent door.
- Around the kitchen: a rack for your pots and pans to keep them out of the dirt; a tripod for water basins and one from which to hang a food safe; a revolving clothesline for the tea towels.
- In the dining shelter: on a long camp, pioneer a table and seats if there is suitable timber available, but do not cut down a young forest to build it! On shorter camps, sit on logs, stones or the ground. A small table or a rack for standing food containers on is useful; sugar, salt, sauces and other foods in plastic or metal containers can be kept on it.

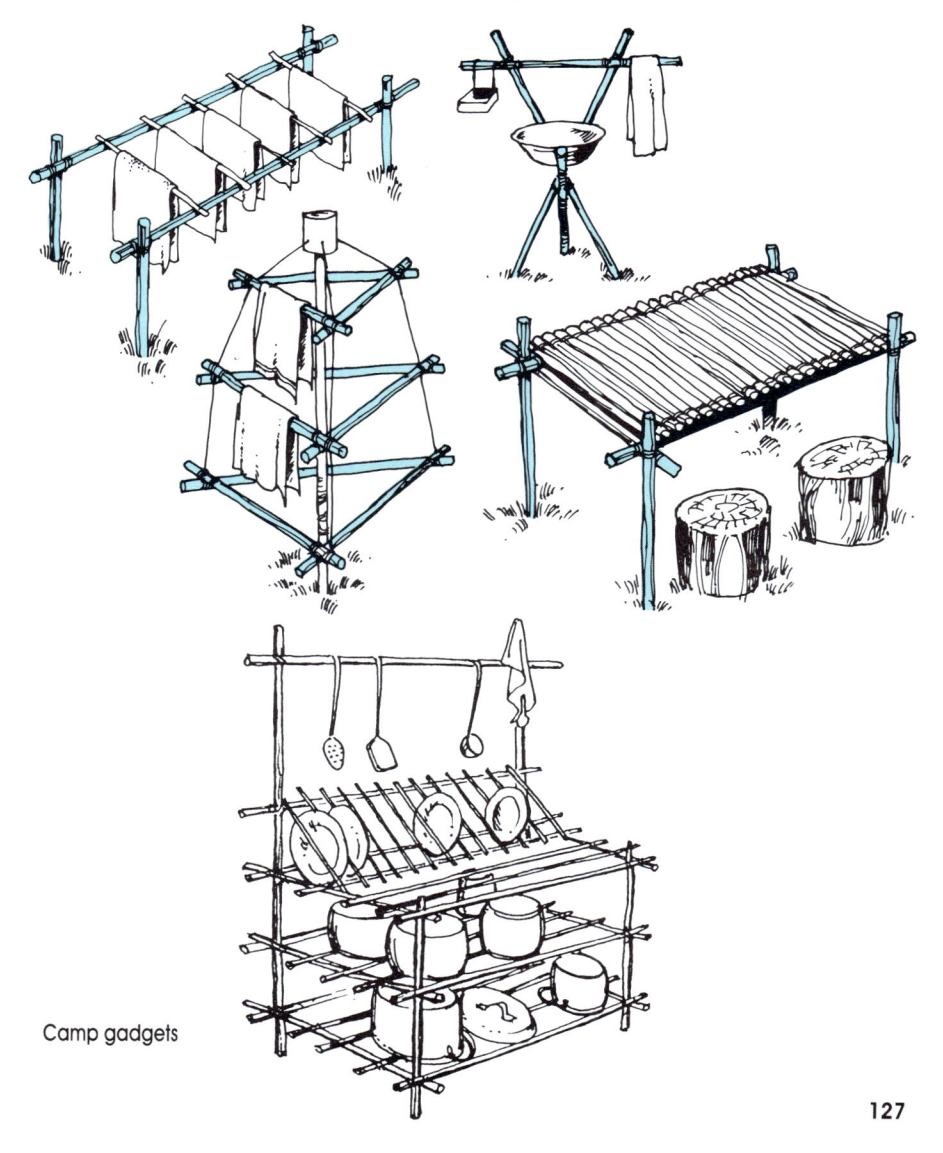

Camp gadgets

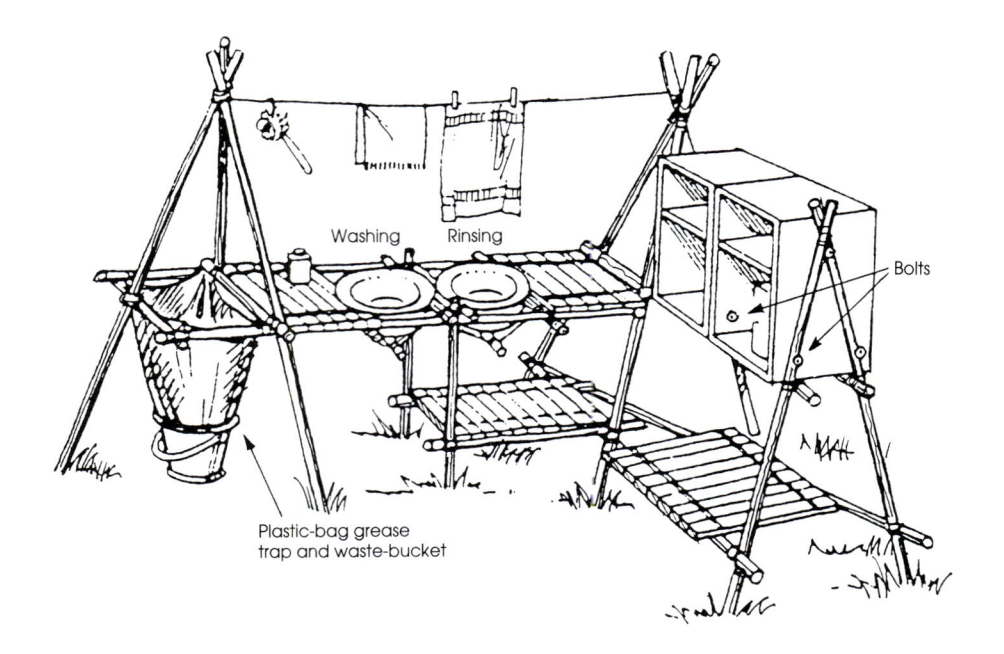

Camp loom

This is a very useful item for camp if you wish to make table tops, walls, placemats, bedding, and so on. Your need will determine the width and length of the loom.

The loom consists of a row of vertical posts spaced evenly apart. This is the width you require.

A distance away (the length you require), two vertical posts are placed in the ground, and a spar is lashed between them to form the holding spar.

A length of sisal, or similar material, is tied to the top of the vertical post, taken to the holding spar and fixed with an overhand knot, then taken back and attached to the weaving spar. This length of sisal is called a runner. Each vertical post is to have its own runner of sisal.

To operate, lift the weaving spar up and place the material for weaving between the runners. Then take the weaving spar down below the other lines, and place more material between the runners. Each time the weaving spar is brought down, you alternate each side of the vertical posts.

If you wish to make a wall, you will have to strengthen the weave by occasionally adding a strong stick to the material. You will also have to add a small spar, sharpened on one end. This can be hit into the ground to form a post when you are erecting the wall.

When the loom is full or you have reached the required length, tie off the ends together, then cut the overhand knot on the holding spar and finish off the reef knot.

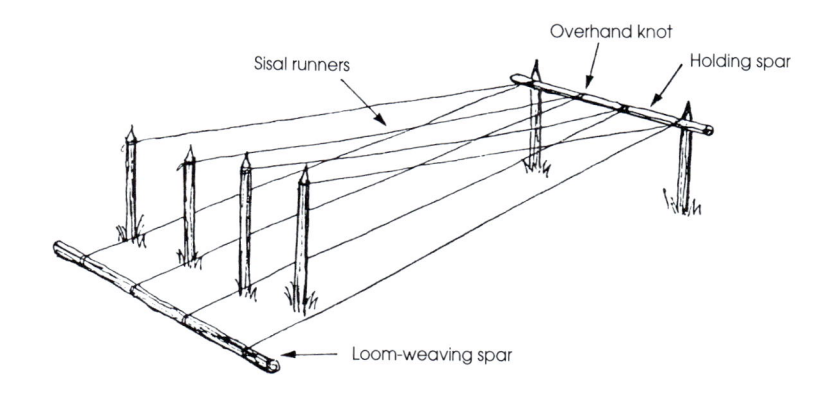

Campcraft

Overhand knot
Sisal runners
Holding spar
Loom-weaving spar

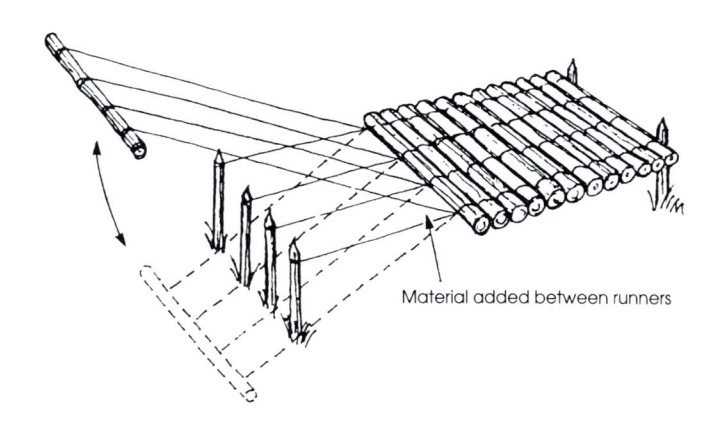

Material added between runners

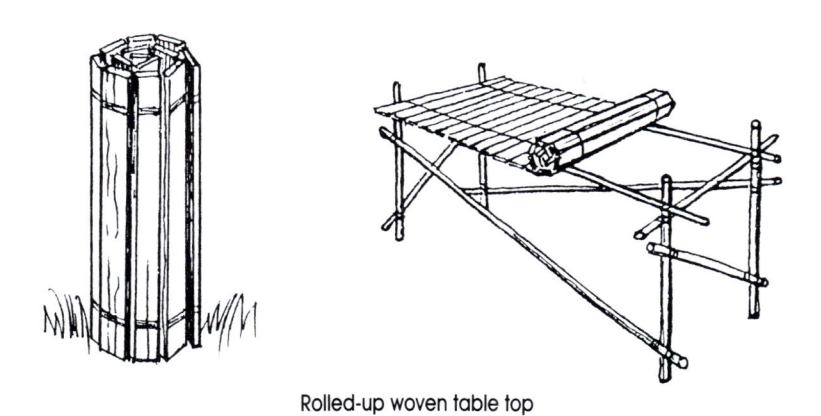

Rolled-up woven table top

Fieldbook for Australian Scouting

Fires and fuel

Because part of the fun of camping is cooking over open fires, knowing all about fires is important. How to build a fireplace, how to light a fire, how to control it, how to put it out, which woods burn best, and what the regulations state, are things you will want to know about.

Knowing exactly what the regulations state is probably the most important thing. Find out exactly what the law states you can do, cannot do and must do. Because this varies widely from place to place, it is up to you to find out these details for the place where the camp will be held. The rules will also vary from season to season.

Star fire

Hunters' fire

Trench fire

Crane fire

Bridge fire

Gypsy fire

Reflector fire

Nomad fire

Altar fire

Types of fires

Commonsense routine

Commonsense is necessary when using fire. Adhere to the following commonsense routines.

Before lighting

- Check for total-fire-ban announcements.
- Be aware of any local-council fire restrictions.
- Choose a fireplace away from dried bush and grass.
- Clear a circle 7 metres in diameter around the fire.
- Have a bucket of water handy in case of accident.
- Dig a trench for the fire.

After lighting

- Keep the fire as small as possible.
- If a strong wind or 'whirlie' wind springs up, put the fire out.
- Never leave a fire unattended.
- Burn cans, paper and all food scraps at the end of each meal.

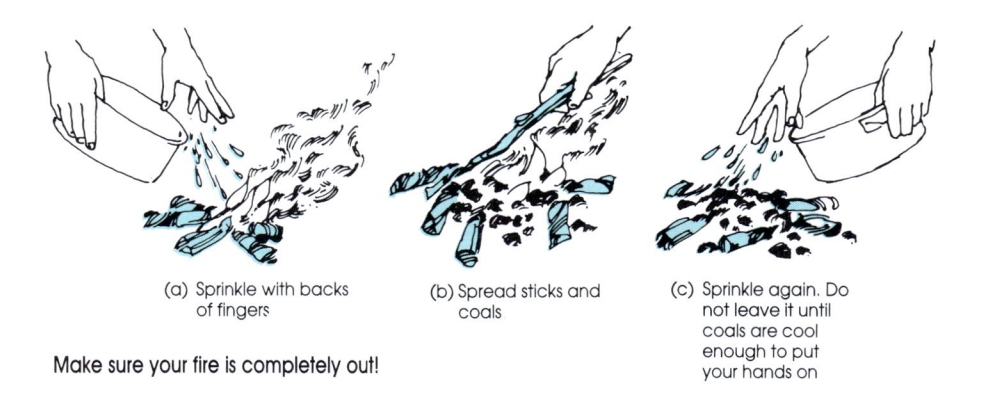

(a) Sprinkle with backs of fingers

(b) Spread sticks and coals

(c) Sprinkle again. Do not leave it until coals are cool enough to put your hands on

Make sure your fire is completely out!

After use

- Dig a hole and push the remains of the fire into it.
- Extinguish all lit pieces of wood, embers, and so on, with water.
- Bash cans flat and carry them home.
- Fill in the hole, stamp down firm, and smooth off the surface.
- Fill in the fire trench, and replace the topsoil sod so the trench is not easily visible.

There are many methods for lighting a fire without matches, but they do require practise for you to become a skilled fire lighter. (*See* 'Fire making' section in Chapter 2: Bushcraft, page 102). Take spare waterproof matches and keep them dry. You can coat them with candle wax or nail polish and seal them in plastic bags; do not forget to also put the striker in the bag. If the matches become wet, dry them in your hair for, say, 20 minutes, or put them next to your skin where your body heat will eventually dry them.

In wet weather, the dead wood on trees is usually dry compared with that lying on the ground. Large logs always have dry centres, and, if they can be split, the splinters make good kindling. It is easiest to light wet kindling with a candle or solid-fuel tablet.

How to build and light a fire

Light the smallest fire you can to suit your needs. A fire 20 centimetres across is big enough to boil a billy. A fire 50 centimetres long with a 10 cm log each side is big enough to do the evening's cooking. Most of the sticks should be laid parallel, not criss-crossed; one cross-stick should be enough to get air through the wood—otherwise you will have a wild blaze that throws the heat on you and not where you want it, that is, under the billy or food.

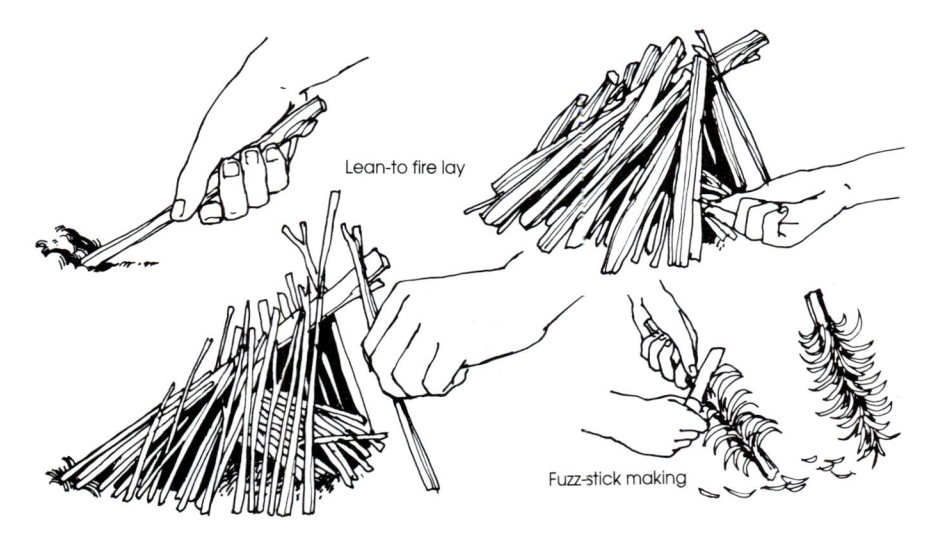

Building and lighting a fire

Fireplaces

Trench fireplaces are the safest. Dig a trench 30 centimetres deep, the width of your spade, and up to 1 metre long. Take care in removing the sod of turf. Store it carefully for replacing when you fill in the fireplace. Pile the dirt up in a heap, away from the fire, to refill the trench when you are breaking camp.

If you have to cook only one or two meals, and your commonsense tells you there is little risk of bushfire, a fireplace above ground may be used. A simple fireplace made from stones can be made quickly. Take care when you select stones for your fireplace, because some stones explode when heated.

Campcraft

A trench fireplace is safest

Clear a 7-metre circle of anything likely to burn (check local fire regulations for clearance area), make your fireplace in the centre, gather your firewood and place it in a pile outside the circle, and you are all set to light your fire.

Firewood

Because the most elaborate or correctly made fireplace is useless without a fire, making a fire is an art worth learning properly.

The first thing to learn about is firewood. Learn which woods in your area burn best, which ones are poor burners, which ones burn quickly for getting a fire going, and those that burn slowly and make a good bed of coals for long cooking.

Woods from most of our native trees burn well. Poplars and willows, often found along creeks, are poor burners, tending to only smoulder and smoke. Pines, pine cones and wattles are usually good for starting, while eucalyptus provide better cooking wood.

Fire lighting

To get a fire going, you will need tinder and kindling, then heavier wood to keep it going. For tinder, find very dry grass, dead leaves, crushed bark and tiny twigs. Kindling is thin sticks, about as thick as a pencil. Small dead branches that remain on the tree are ideal, or split heavier timber if that is all you have.

Lay the tinder in a loose pile on the ground, then lay the kindling gently on top, thinnest pieces nearest the tinder. Keep it in a loose pile so air can circulate through it. With your back to the wind, strike a match. When it is burning well, touch it to the tinder, close to the ground; the tinder will flare up. Let the kindling get burning well, and then gradually feed larger sticks until you have the size of fire you require.

Flames will boil water quickly; coals or embers are best for all cooking, and a must for foil cooking. Practise your fire lighting under all conditions. You need a fire most when the weather is wet and cold, and that is when it is hardest to get one going.

Look on the trees for the driest wood on a dead branch.

If the wood is saturated, peel off the wet bark and trim off the outside wood. You will find the inside wood dry. Make a couple of fuzz sticks, split some other branches to expose the dry centre, and you should get a fire going with very little trouble.

Practice is the key to achieving success. Naturally, if you carry a couple of 'Meta' tablets, or fire starters, in your pocket, you will not have much trouble in starting a fire under any conditions.

Stoves and lanterns

Scouts have always prided themselves on being able to cook successfully over open fires. However, there may be occasions when you will wish to concentrate on a special activity and spend less time preparing meals.

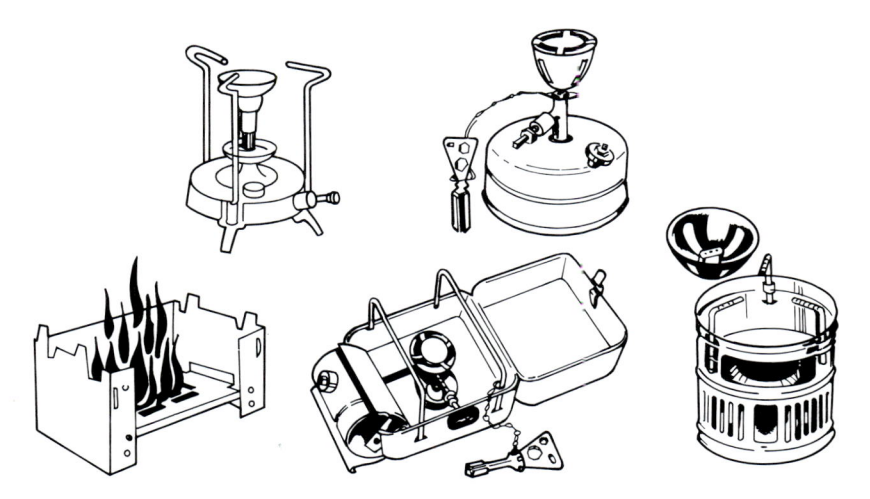

Stoves and lanterns

Using kerosene pressure stoves and liquefied-petroleum-gas (LPG) stoves will enable you to do this. Learn how both systems work so that if you have the opportunity to use them, you will know exactly what to do. With both systems, a certain amount of assembly is necessary. Know how the various types are assembled. Preheating is necessary for the pressure stoves, usually with methylated spirits, which can be dangerous. Always do this out in the open. Learn the correct way to preheat.

Each system can also be used for lighting. Each type depends on a very fragile mantle that is easily broken. Make sure replacements are available and you know how to fit them. Avoid inhaling the fumes of these mantles when they are being 'burnt in'.

Do not attempt to use either system until you have been properly instructed in its use. The systems are not hard to operate once you have been shown the correct way. Never fool around — if misused, the systems can be dangerous.

Fuels

Stoves and lanterns can be powered by many fuels. The most popular fuels are listed as follows.

Propane (LPG)

Availability: good (most service stations). Appliances may be removed and replaced as required; cylinders are large and heavy but are available in different sizes to suit individual needs. Quick lighting and clean burning. Cylinders must be tested or replaced after 10 years.

Butane

Availability: good to fair (camping stores, supermarkets, hardware stores). Lightweight disposable cartridges are much cheaper than propane cylinders and are available in an assortment of sizes. 'PRIMUS' cartridges allow removal and replacement of different appliances. 'GAZ' appliances must remain on the cartridge until fuel is exhausted. Quick lighting and clean burning, Butane loses efficiency when cold or at high altitude.

Alcohol (methylated spirits)

Availability: good (supermarkets, service stations, hardware stores). A hot, low-volatility fuel; evaporates quickly when spilt; not very thermally efficient (requires more fuel to heat a given object than kerosene or Shellite). It performs very well when used in stoves and cooksets that are designed to effectively trap and channel all the available heat to the pot.

Kerosene

Availability: good (supermarkets, service stations, hardware stores). In many third-world countries it is the only fuel available. Not as thermally efficient as Shellite; has an unpleasant odour, and does not evaporate quickly when spilt. Appliances require preheating to light, even at room temperature.

Shellite (white spirits)

Availability: fair (supermarkets, service stations, camping and hardware stores). A high-energy low-cost fuel that evaporates quickly when spilt. The best fuel for cold weather. Some stoves need preheating to light.

Multi-fuel stoves

Note that all multi-fuel stoves will not give as much heat output as a single-fuel version of the same stove. If you do not intend to use the stove outside Australia, choose a single-fuel stove.

Solid-fuel stoves

Solid-fuel stoves are ideal for emergencies, and the solid-fuel tablets make ideal fire starters when wood is damp.

Camp tools

The main tools you might require in camp are an axe, a saw, digger, post-hole borer, and perhaps a rake. Your Scout knife might also be useful. Naturally, a tent-peg mallet would be essential. On an overnight camp, or if you have to hike to the site, you will probably settle for a hand axe and a small shovel.

Rake

This tool is handy for clearing the fire circle and the tent floor and for keeping the campsite tidy.

Post-hole borer

On a standing camp, you will find plenty of use for this tool if the soil is easy to dig. Use it for digging a hole for the urinal and for holes for posts to fence off your kitchen fireplace. After you have lifted out the turf sod with a spade, bore a series of holes side by side along the trench, then finish it off by squaring it up with a spade. If you decide to make an underground cool store for perishable foods, the borer will do most of the work.

Digger

The most useful digging implement to take on a standing camp is a garden spade. If you know the ground is stony, a pick or mattock will also be handy. Small collapsible shovels are good if you are on the move.

Campcraft

Camp tools

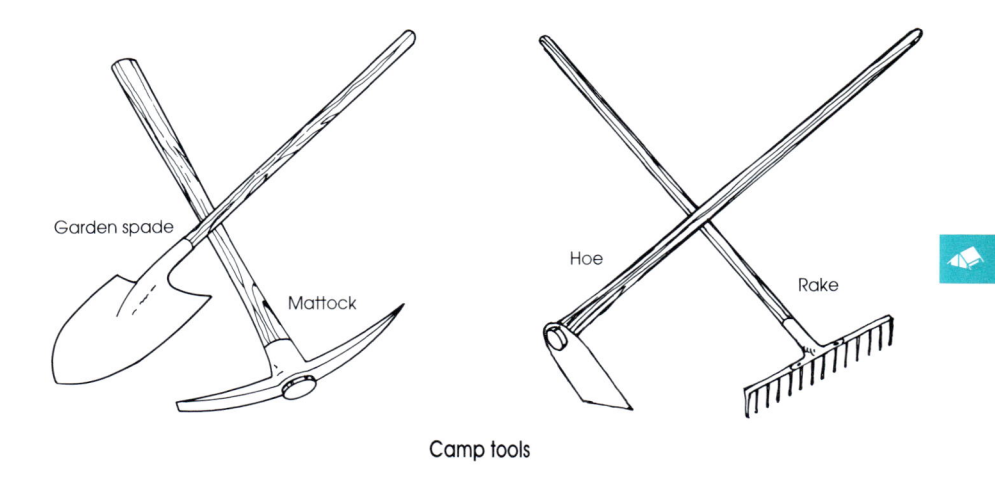

Saws

Saws are very useful things in camp, and you should have one at least in your Patrol box. The best sort for your Patrol is probably a bush saw or Swedish-bow saw.

A bush saw will produce firewood more quickly with less effort and less waste than an axe. If there is a lot of wood to cut, a Scout on each end will whiz through it with ease.

With a bush saw, you will find it easier to cut firewood than with an axe. Naturally, you will still need an axe to split it, but a bush saw will cut it to length faster and with less chips.

Following is what a bush saw looks like.

As with every other tool, you have to keep it sharp and look after it. It is fairly difficult to sharpen a bush saw, but new blades are very cheap and easily fitted. Make sure you wipe it dry after using it, and oil it before you put it away.

When using the bush saw, start very slowly, otherwise it may jump out of its groove and may easily cut you. Once the edge of the saw has a firm grip on the wood, you can go as fast as you like.

Because of the very coarse teeth, it can be a dangerous tool unless properly used. Keep your hands well away from the blade. Always make sure you are cutting away from your body, particularly your legs.

Remember also that it is quite an awkward shape, and do not leave it lying around on the ground or someone—even you—is likely to fall over it.

When the saw is not being used, protect the blade (and yourself) by sliding a length of split hose over the teeth.

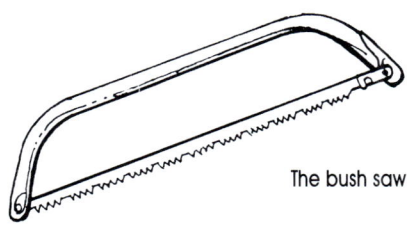

The bush saw

Hand axes

For most of your requirements in camp, a hand axe or tomahawk is all you will require. A full-size or felling axe is necessary only if you are in heavily timbered country and have to clear an area, which is most unlikely for Scouts. Concentrate on becoming expert with a hand axe, and leave the felling of trees to the timber cutters.

A hand axe or a half-axe is a vital part of a backwoods person's equipment, and it is important you should know how to use them safely and effectively.

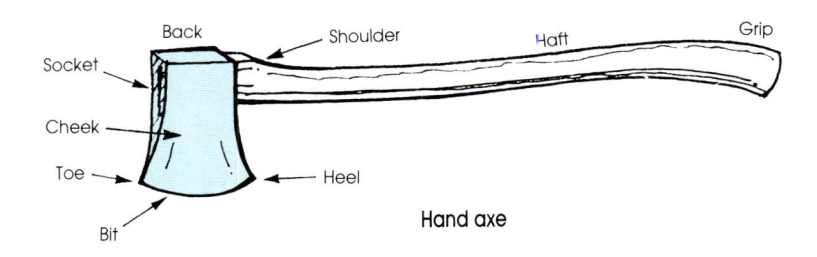

Hand axe

First of all, care must be exercised in the choice of an axe to see that the head is of good steel, and the haft is sound. What is known as the Canadian dog-legged haft is most suitable, the wood used being ash or hickory. The head should be firm on the haft, the wedge solid and of one piece, and the axe true; that is, the edge of the blade should be in the same straight line as the centre of the haft.

Hafts sometimes break, but spare hafts can always be obtained and inserted in the old head.

The edge of the axe is sharpened by grinding it on a grindstone. Thereafter, unless the axe has been abused, it should not require more than an occasional touching-up with a piece of carborundum stone, which is worked over the cutting edge with a circular motion. If the edge has been nicked, a flat file will have to be used, working from front to back, in order to take out the nick.

Sharpening an axe

This diagram shows how to use a grindstone to sharpen an axe.

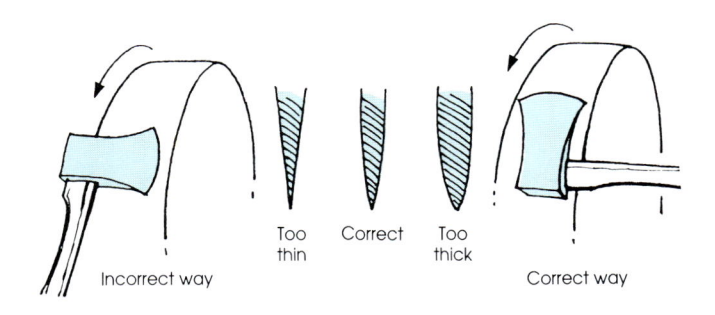

This diagram shows how to use a file for sharpening.

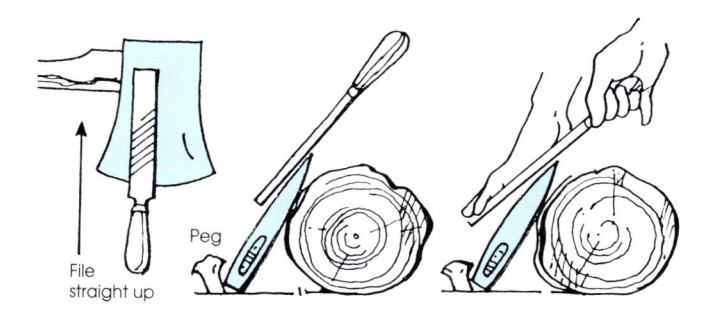

File
straight up
Peg

This diagram shows how to use an axe stone for the final keen edge.

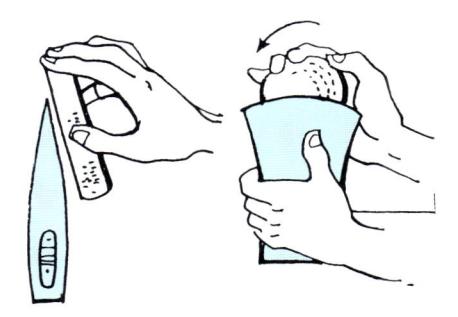

Care of an axe

- Keep the edge or 'bit' sharp—sharp enough to bite!
- Keep the handle tight—if it gets loose, drive the wedge in further. Some axes have a bonded head which is very much less likely to come loose.
- Do not let your axe touch the ground—driving it into the ground may nick it; leaving it on the ground will rust it.
- Always have a chopping block under the wood you are chopping or splitting.
- When you have finished using your axe for a while, mask it in the chopping block. When you have finished with it for the time being, put it in its sheath.
- Rub the head of your axe with oil to stop it rusting, and rub a little *raw* linseed oil on the handle from time to time.
- Never touch a living tree with an axe unless you have permission to do so and you have a definite use for its wood.
- When an axe is being stored away, the haft should be oiled, and the head greased and wrapped in sacking. It will then be ready for use at any moment after the oil and grease have been wiped off.

Safety rules

Remember always that an axe improperly used is a very dangerous tool.

- See that the axe head is tight.
- See that the edge of the axe is sharp.
- Sheath the axe when not in use.
- Keep onlookers at a safe distance—at least two axe lengths clear.
- Clear overhanging branches of nearby trees or bushes.
- Secure a firm footing—always wear boots or shoes.
- Remove your scarf and loose clothing.
- Stop and rest when tired.

Using a hand axe

Chopping firewood Adhere to the following advice.

- Always use a chopping block.
- Never cut unsupported wood.
- Split cut logs as follows.
- For thick pieces, cut a 'V' notch. The top of the V should be as wide as the branch is thick.

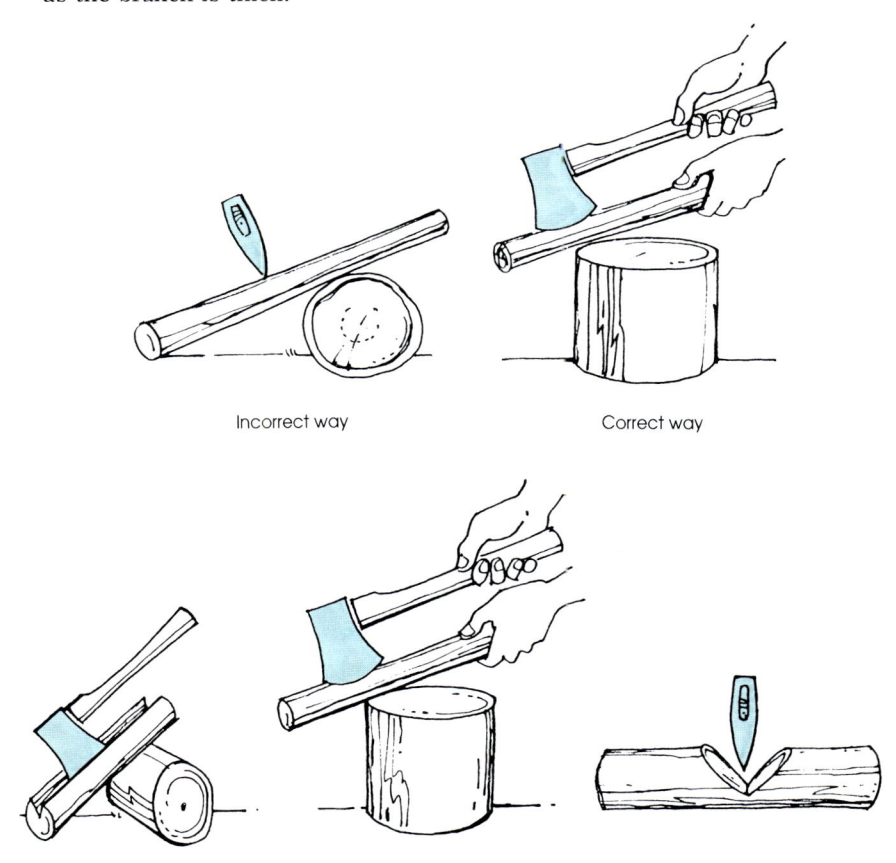

Incorrect way

Correct way

Campcraft

A good tip when a number of pickets or stakes have to be sharpened is to burn the end in a good fire so they are charred evenly all around. The removal of the charcoal portion leaves a fine pointed stake, with a hardened surface.

Hand axes are very often misused, and the following 'do nots' should be remembered.

- In the first place, do not use an axe as a mallet for knocking in tent pegs and the like; in particular, using the face of the axe as a mallet is dangerous and bad for the axe.
- Do not indulge in the practice of axe-throwing or knife-throwing, especially at living trees; the danger of someone getting hurt is great, and it is also bad for both the axe and the target.

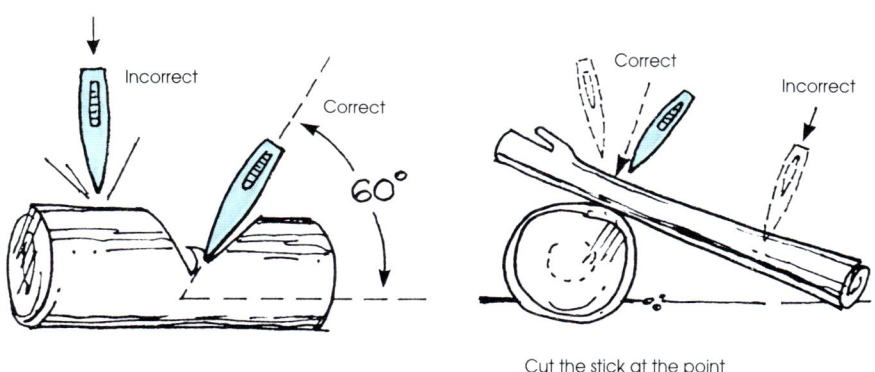

Cut the stick at the point supported by the log

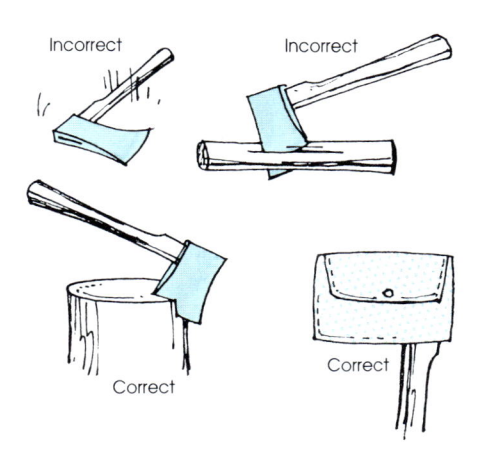

Correct use and care of an axe

Knives

The Scout knife is the most popular knife among outdoor people. It has a strong cutting blade, and some types have various tools as well—a can opener, screw driver, leather punch or awl, and so on. Your knife is a valuable tool, so take good care of it.

If knives are to be of any use at all, they must be kept sharp. Knives are needed by the pioneer to cut cords and lashings and wedges, and for various other purposes. The Scout clasp knife, with a marline spike, is of much more use to the pioneer than the sheath knife, which is the tool of the hunter.

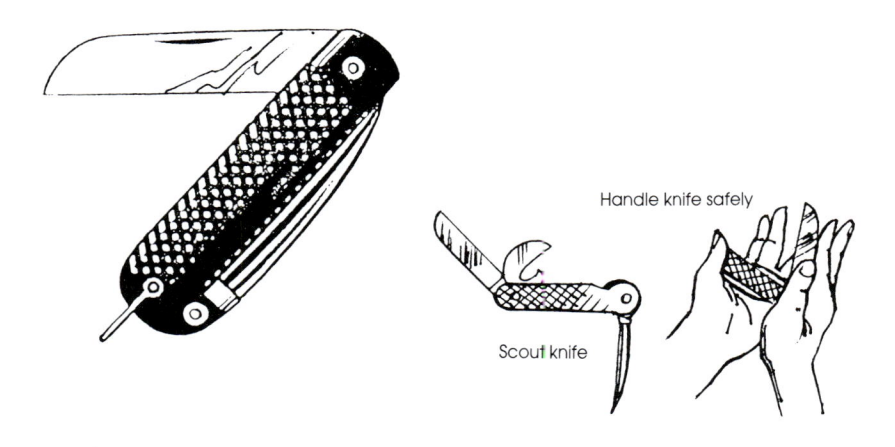

Scout knife

Handle knife safely

Keep it clean, dry and sharp. Do not use it on things that will dull or break it. Keep it off the ground—moisture and dirt will ruin it.

Keep it out of the fire—the heat draws the temper of the steel and makes the edge soft and useless. Wipe the blade clean after using it, then close the knife. Oil the joints and springs occasionally. Keep knives folded when not in use.

Do not throw or fool with knives; this is hard on knives—and people!

There should be, in each Troop, some type of a stone, carborundum or other, that can be used by the Troop members to sharpen any knives they may possess.

Safety rules apply just as much when using a knife as when using an axe. In particular, never cut towards your body when whittling, and always keep the knife in front of your knees when you are seated.

Sharpening your knife

The keener the edge, the safer your knife.

A dull knife is always dangerous, because it does not cut into the wood properly and therefore cannot be controlled. Also a dull knife gives you a lot of extra work even if you do manage to whittle with it. Sharpen your knife on a dry sharpening stone.

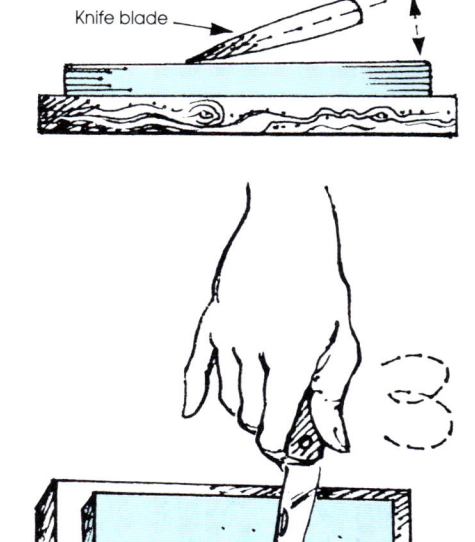

When sharpening your knife, hold the blade of knife at an angle of 20° to 25° to the sharpening stone, and draw against the edge from heel to point. Do not lay the blade flat on stone, because this gives an edge too fine for general use.

After a few strokes on one side, turn the blade over and give it the same number of strokes. Continue back and forth until the edge is sharp.

Camp cleanliness

Waste disposal

Food and rubbish

Scouts the world over are renowned for their clean and tidy campsites and for leaving the site in better condition than it was when they arrived. If someone before you has left a mess, clean it up and then make sure you do not leave a mess for someone else. 'Keep the scene clean' should be your camping motto.

Do not throw rubbish down and it will not have to be picked up. Wrappings and food scraps thrown around the site will soon make a mess. Be considerate of others—they have to live there too.

Spend a bit of time thinking about rubbish disposal. If you bury it, will it rot away? Is it safe to bury raw-vegetable peelings—they will make compost. Orange and lemon peel, however, do not break down quickly, and it is best to take them home and dispose of them with your domestic rubbish. Other garbage, unless buried deeply, is likely to be dug up by fossicking animals.

If you burn it, will you pollute the atmosphere? Because some plastics pollute the atmosphere heavily, do not burn them. Other garbage, if dried first, burns with almost no pollution, and burning is the best way to dispose of it. Take aluminium foil home.

If it will not burn or rot away, what can you do with it? Take it back home with you! If you can carry a glass or plastic container full of food into camp, you can easily carry an empty one home for disposal with household rubbish. Cans may be burned and bashed flat, but take them home with you also.

Water

Unless you treat it properly, waste water can make just as much mess around your camp as the solid rubbish will.

The washing-up water is the dirtiest water you will have to dispose of. Unless given special treatment, the grease and food scraps in it become a problem. They not only become smelly; they attract flies. Work out your own hygienic disposal method. One way, however, is to strain the dishwater through a strainer of grass to trap the grease and food scraps before broadcasting the water well away from your campsite. The grass used as a strainer can then be burnt to dispose of the grease and food scraps.

Your local environmental health officer may also offer some suggestions.

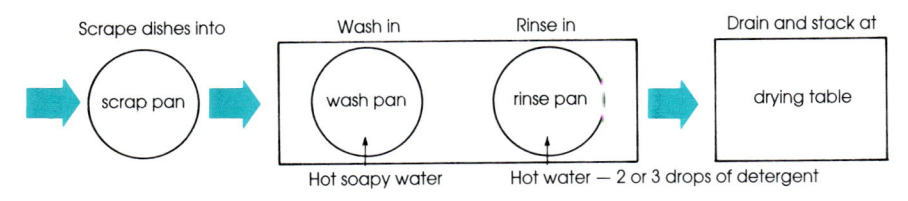

Scrape dishes into → scrap pan → Wash in wash pan (Hot soapy water) Rinse in rinse pan (Hot water — 2 or 3 drops of detergent) → Drain and stack at drying table

Dishwashing production line

Grease pit

Before considering building a grease pit, you will have to check with the local health-department regulations.

Here are two alternative methods for building a grease pit.

First method Dig a hole, about 60 centimetres deep, with your post-hole borer. Suspend a can, about the same diameter, in the top of the hole. The can must have the top removed, holes punched in the bottom, and be 75% full of small stones. Place a straining mat made from interwoven reeds, bracken

Campcraft

fern, long grass, or leafy twigs, over the top of the hole. Pour the dirty water through the strainer, which will catch the food scraps. As the water runs through the can, the grease will congeal on the pebbles, and relatively clean water will run into the bottom of the hole to soak away. Change the strainer after each meal, and burn the dirty one.

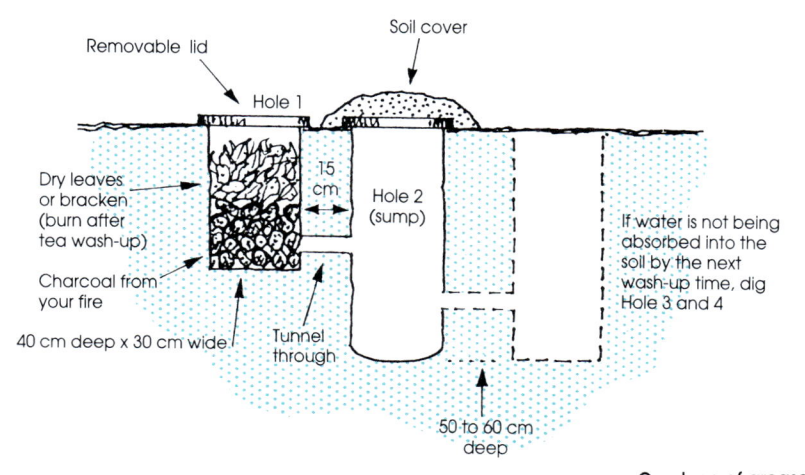

One type of grease pit

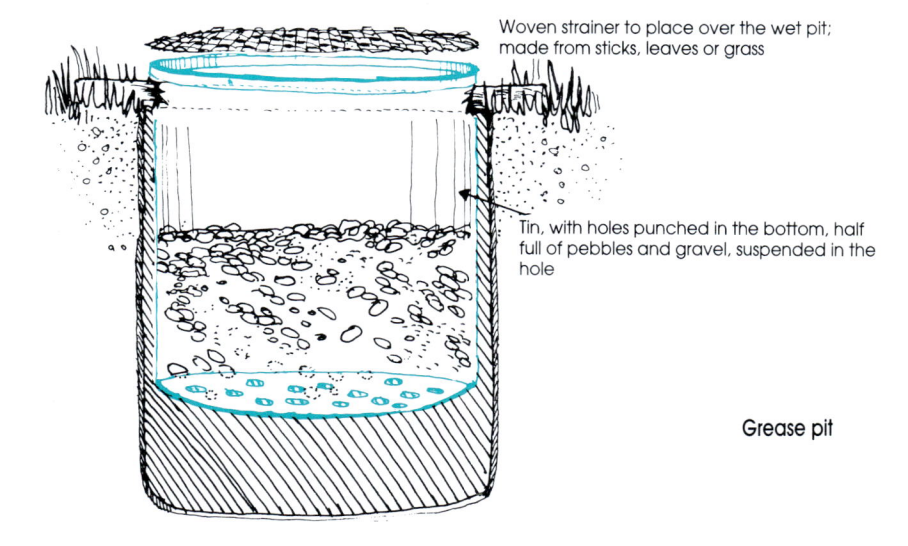

- Removable lid
- Soil cover
- Hole 1
- Dry leaves or bracken (burn after tea wash-up)
- Charcoal from your fire
- 40 cm deep x 30 cm wide
- 15 cm
- Hole 2 (sump)
- Tunnel through
- 50 to 60 cm deep
- If water is not being absorbed into the soil by the next wash-up time, dig Hole 3 and 4

Grease pit

- Woven strainer to place over the wet pit; made from sticks, leaves or grass
- Tin, with holes punched in the bottom, half full of pebbles and gravel, suspended in the hole

145

Second method Another method, useful if you are camping on clay soil where water will not soak away, is to dig a second trench under your fire trench. Cover the second trench with a steel plate on which you light the fire. Channel the water into the bottom trench, and the fire will evaporate the dirty water. Make sure waste water does not run into your usable water supply.

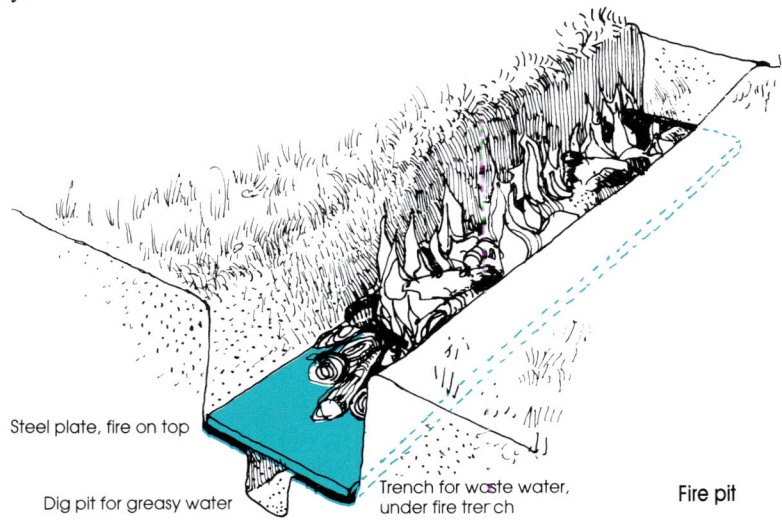

Steel plate, fire on top
Dig pit for greasy water
Trench for waste water, under fire trench
Fire pit

Latrines

Build your latrine in a secluded spot with a natural shielding or a light canvas surround, at least 20 metres from your water supply. A narrow trench, about 30 centimetres wide and at least 40 centimetres deep, which you squat over with one foot on each side, is the most satisfactory camp toilet. Pile the dirt from the trench at one end and provide a small spade to cover excreta each time the latrine is used. Keep the toilet paper in a plastic bag, close by the trench, and a basin of water, and soap, in the toilet area for handwashing. It is more hygienic to shake-dry your hands than to provide a towel for all to use. Provide a lantern at night.

A hole in the ground, filled with stones, in the same area but shielded from the trench, is the most suitable urinal.

Personal cleanliness

Having fun in camp usually means getting grubby. Do not forget to wash the dirt off. A bucket of hot water, a washing cloth, and a cake of soap, will do a good cleaning up job. A bush shower will give you the comforts of home. Swimming will get only some of the dirt off, and using soap while swimming will pollute the stream.

Wash your hands after every visit to the latrine and before you commence cooking and eating. Keep your eating utensils and cooking gear clean.

Campcraft

Make a straddle latrine. Pile up dirt at one end and throw in dirt after each use

Earth
Trowel
Toilet paper
Trench
Urinal filled with pebbles

Latrines

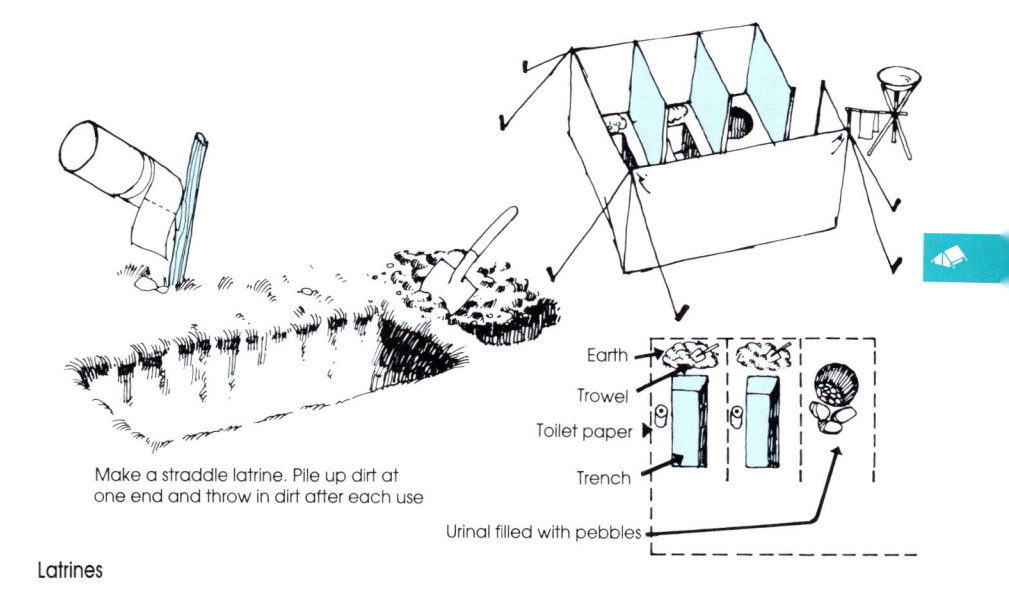

Dish washing should be shared by everyone in the Patrol and is an important part of camp hygiene. Make sure you do your part of it properly.

Sleeping gear

The fun, excitement and activities of life in camp require a lot of energy. It is essential that you get a good night's sleep, but you will not sleep well unless you are comfortable. Make sure your head is higher than your feet, there are no sticks or stones under you, and you have a waterproof sheet between your bedding and the ground.

The time of year and the part of Australia where you are camping will decide the amount of bedding you will require to keep warm. A sleeping bag is most suitable, but if you have only blankets, fold them so they make a bag. Experienced bush people know you need as much bedding under you as on top in order to keep truly warm. Always use a groundsheet under your bed. Change into pyjamas or a tracksuit. Never sleep in the clothes you have been wearing all day. Air your bedding every morning, and keep it dry at all costs.

Sleeping bags

When choosing a sleeping bag, buy the best one you can afford. Look carefully at its construction. The 'sewn through' (or quilted) types lose body heat at their seams. Bags using the 'box wall' construction have fewer heat-loss points, but effectiveness is related to the thickness of the filling. Use of the 'double quilted' technique provides a very warm bag, but these bags are bulky and heavier.

Shape

Rectangular Most common style. Gives room at the expense of weight and packed size.

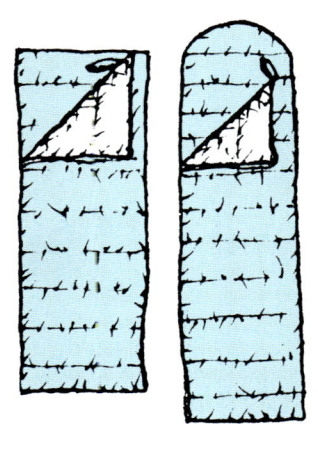

Tapered rectangular Probably the best compromise in weight for room. Requires less body heat to warm than the rectangular shape.

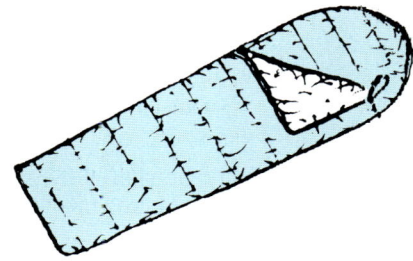

Modified tulip A good compromise in weight for room, and gives more space around the shoulders; but thinner at the knees and foot than the tapered rectangular shape.

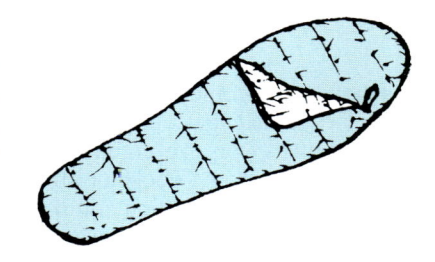

Mummy/tulip with box foot The shape when weight is the main consideration. Warms quicker than other shapes at the expense of movement inside the bag. Box foot keeps feet warmer than bags with full zippers.

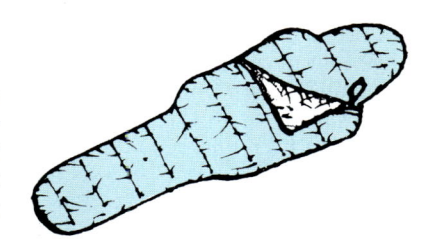

Construction

All insulation material must be held in place to allow for uniform warmth over the bag. Following are some of the methods.

Sewn through or quilting Lowest cost of manufacture. The filling is sewn between the inner and outer shells of the bag. Not recommended for temperatures below 5°C because cold spots will form where inner and outer shells are sewn together. Used mainly in synthetic bags. Rarely used today in down bags.

Double quilting or slab construction Mainly used in synthetic bags. Top layer is sewn to outer shell and bottom layer to inner shell. Quilting overlaps to prevent cold spots.

Box wall or box section Baffles are sewn between inner and outer shells to separate the down. Eliminates cold spots. Used in most down bags.

Slant wall More expensive to manufacture than box walls but slightly more effective. Mainly used in down bags meant for snow use or very low temperatures.

Vertical baffles The baffles in the top half of the bag are at right angles to the lower baffles. This prevents down shifting from the chest and waist in the body-hugging 'mummy'-style bags.

Chevron baffle construction The baffles on the upper shell of the bag are arranged in a 'V' formation, instead of going straight across. This keeps the down where it is required by allowing very little unintentional down shift while sleeping, enabling restless sleepers to stay warm throughout the night.

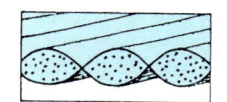

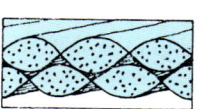

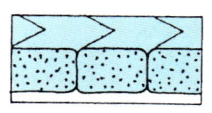

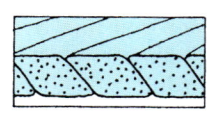

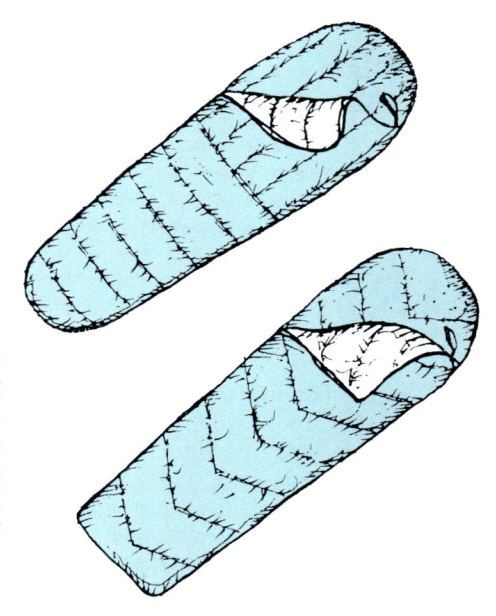

Draught tubes Used on sleeping bags for use in low temperatures. This tube is sewn to the top of the bag, and hangs over the zipper to prevent heat loss.

Zip glide A length of nylon tape sewn next to the zipper to prevent snagging on the draught tube.

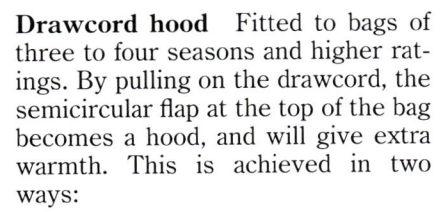

Drawcord hood Fitted to bags of three to four seasons and higher ratings. By pulling on the drawcord, the semicircular flap at the top of the bag becomes a hood, and will give extra warmth. This is achieved in two ways:

1. A very high percentage of the body's heat is dissipated by the head and neck. The fact that the head is now insulated means it will allow the body to retain more of its heat.
2. Each time you turn over you create a 'bellows' effect within the bag, sucking in cold air and pumping out the warm. Drawing the hood around the head eliminates this effect.

Remember: If your feet are cold, do up the hood.

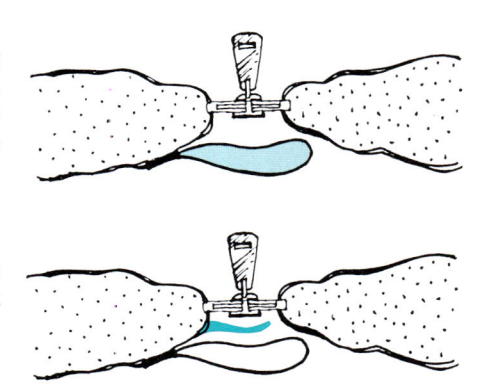

Some general information about sleeping bags

1. A sleeping bag does not produce warmth; it traps air and slows down the rate of loss of heat from your body.
2. Excluding natural and human factors, it is usually accepted that the insulating value of a sleeping bag (its warmth) depends on the loft or thickness of the filling; that is, among bags of the same type of filling, the thicker the bag, the warmer it will be.
3. All sleeping-bag fillings compress, lowering the thickness of insulation under the body. Use of a closed-cell foam mat or a Therm-a-Rest Mat will minimise heat loss to the ground. (An air mattress is unsuitable at lower temperatures.)
4. Cut down on radiated heat loss by sleeping in a tent or under some shelter.
5. Moving air conducts heat away, so avoid draughts.

6. Sleeping bags have to 'breathe' and are not waterproof unless covered with Gore-tex, Milair or Reflex breathe-able waterproof fabric, and even then the bag would let in rain around the zip and the hole for your face.

   If you do require a waterproof bag, a Gore-tex bivvy sack is recommended. This sack is a one-person shelter made from Gore-tex with nylon-waterproofed floor. Seam-sealed at the factory to prevent leakage, this sack will protect your expensive sleeping bag and increase its warmth. It is light enough to be taken anywhere for personal shelter.
7. While synthetic-filled sleeping bags dry quicker and are warmer, when wet, than down, a wet sleeping bag is still a wet sleeping bag and is uncomfortable. Take care to keep your sleeping bag dry no matter what its type of insulation.

Care and cleaning

A sleeping bag will last for years with a little care, so to get the best out of your bag, the following advice is given.
1. Allow the bag to air for at least 15 minutes before use.
2. Always use a groundsheet or tent floor.
3. After use, open the zipper completely and leave the bag in the sun for a while before packing away.
4. On arriving home, allow the bag to air for at least 24 hours (some of this time should be in the sun) before storing.
5. Store your bag in a loosely packed way. Do not store it in the stuff sack for long periods.
6. Do not store against a concrete wall or floor.
7. Do not roll up your bag; just cram it into the stuff sack.
8. Use an inner sheet to help keep the bag clean (it is easier to wash than a sleeping bag).
9. Clean your bag after about two or three years or when necessary.

   For more information and selection of sleeping bags, contact your Scout Outdoor Centre.

Personal gear

Give some thought to the personal equipment you take to camp. Ask yourself, 'What do I really need?' and remember that you have to carry it.
   You will need something to:
- eat with
- sleep in
- keep you dry
- keep you warm
- have fun in
- keep clean with.

   A rucksack is the most suitable thing in which to carry your gear to camp. You will want one that is large enough to hold your necessary gear, but not so large you have difficulty carrying it when it is full.

Fieldbook for Australian Scouting

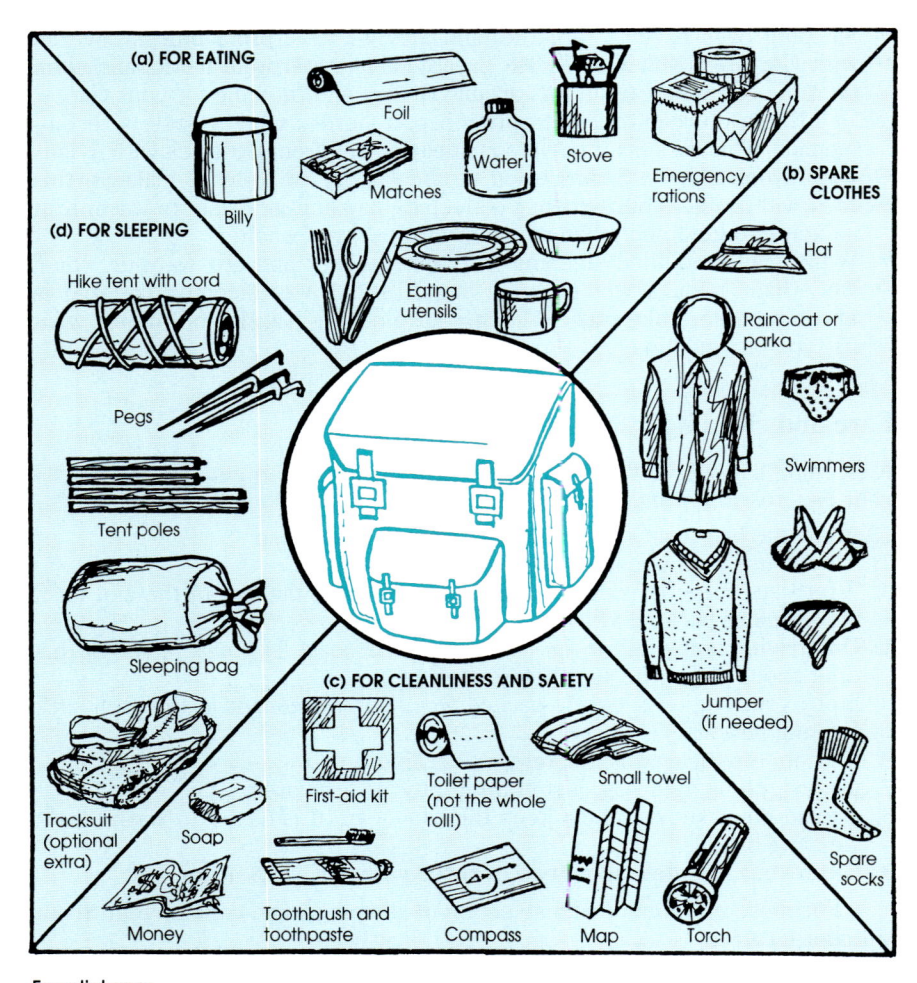

Essential gear

Before going to camp, get your gear together and practise packing it. The things you might need urgently go on the top or in an easy-to-get-at pocket. Pack something soft against your back, and distribute the load evenly through the rucksack so it is comfortable on your back and shoulders.

Gear list

The essential gear you will have to pack should be on a list that you check off as you pack:
- sleeping bag or blankets
- waterproof groundsheet
- pyjamas/tracksuit/sleeping gear
- cutlery, cup, one cereal bowl, one dinner plate

- soap, towel, wash cloth
- comb, toothbrush and toothpaste
- spare shirt, pants, underwear
- raincoat or windjacket
- jumper, two extra pairs of socks
- light shoes for around camp
- sunhat, sunscreen
- torch
- handkerchiefs
- teatowel
- insect repellent
- swimmers
- nature books
- this fieldbook
- notebook and pencil
- watch
- personal first-aid kit.

If you have room, you may think it worthwhile to pack some of the following items:

- camera and film
- campfire blanket
- songbook.

Wear your uniform to and from camp. Let everyone know you are proud of being a Scout. Your uniform is a serviceable set of clothing designed for outdoor activities.

In your pocket, carry a pocket knife, matches in a waterproof case, a handkerchief, compass, money (including the correct amount for a phone call), two or three adhesive bandages, a fire starter, and a piece of string.

Food storage

If the meat goes bad or gets flyblown, or the paper bags get wet allowing salt and flour and sugar to get mixed into a gooey mess, or the eggs all break, or the possums get in and mess over everything, you might go hungry!

At home, you do not have to worry too much about how or where food is stored. In camp, it is your responsibility, so give it some attention.

All fresh meats are perishable and must be used very early in the camp. Processed dairy foods require special care or they will soon turn bad. Canned foods last indefinitely until the can is opened. If you have to carry them, remember they weigh a lot. Dried foods, now available in a wide variety, last well, are extremely light, and take up very little space. The addition of water, or the cooking process, restores them to the equivalent of fresh food.

The every day foodstuffs, such as salt, flour, sugar, cocoa and sauces, are best kept in plastic containers, clearly marked with their contents. Bread, vegetables, fruit, and so on, can be packed in plastic bags and kept in a meat safe, hanging in the shade. Wrapped bread costs more but keeps well. Butter, cheese, eggs, bacon, milk, and so on, which have to be kept cool, will have to

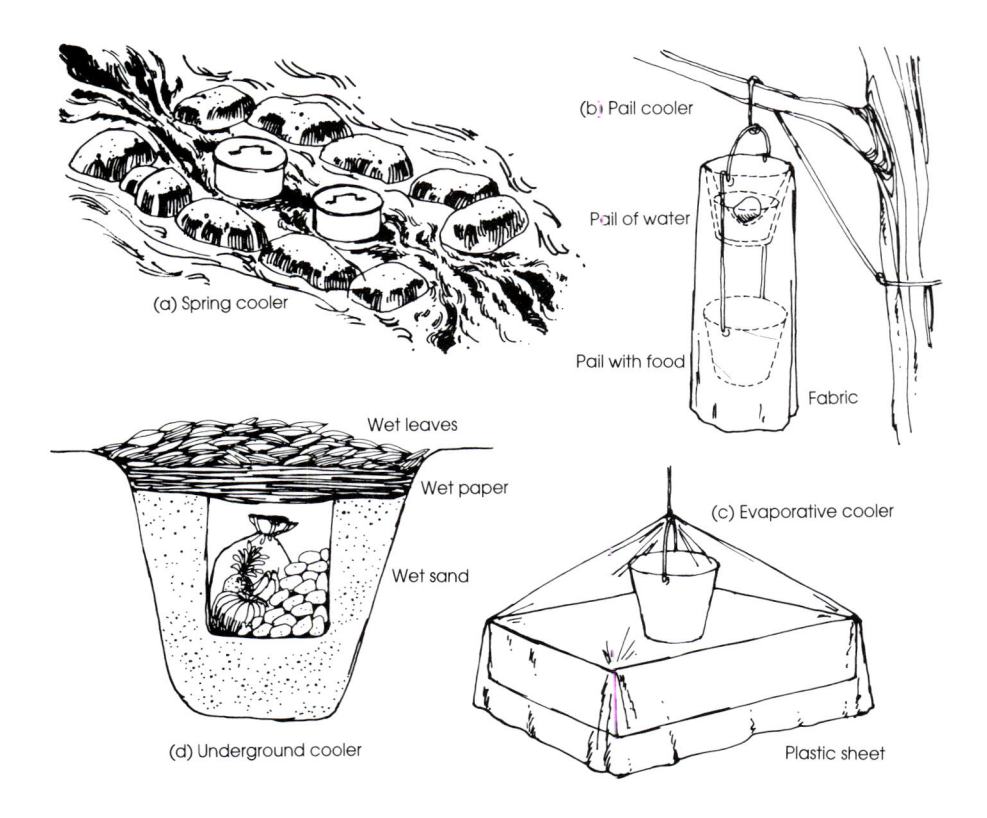

(a) Spring cooler
(b) Pail cooler
Pail of water
Pail with food
Fabric
Wet leaves
Wet paper
(c) Evaporative cooler
Wet sand
(d) Underground cooler
Plastic sheet

Types of coolers

be kept in an icebox, or in a camp refrigerator, or in a watertight container submerged in a nearby stream. In a long camp, a hole in the ground lined with rocks, and a substantial cover, will keep food cool.

Bush animals can make a mess of your supplies. Keep lids on your food containers, and your foodbox closed. Flies and ants also like your food. Store it in a fly-proof safe, hanging from a tree or tripod.

Cooking

B.P. told his story of the first time he went camping with his brothers and cooked his first camp meal: 'Well, you know what it is when you begin as a Scout to cook your food; it is not quite a success at first. Mine was not either. The dinner was not good. I know it, because I ate the whole of it myself—not because I liked it, but because I had to. My brothers could not eat it, so they made me do so, just as a reminder that I must learn to cook better.'

He did learn to cook better, and so can you.

How to begin before you start

Plan your menus in connection with your program. If you are not sure of quantities, ask someone. One of the adults at home will have a good idea of how much you will need of this and that. Your Scout Leader or the shopkeeper will help you if you have difficulty.

Always have hot water available so you can clean up as you go along. There is no need to have a mountain of dirty utensils. Detergents make washing up quick and easy. When you have finished with a billy, fill it with water immediately. Wooden spoons are best for beating and stirring.

Keep your camp kitchen tidy. It is better to have it large rather than small, and keep everything in its proper place. Only the kitchen staff should be in the kitchen. Keep your meals well balanced, with proteins (meat, fish, cheese, eggs, milk), carbohydrates (flour, rice, potatoes, sugar) and plenty of fruit and vegetables for vitamins.

Food is used by the body in the following three ways:

1. Bodybuilding: The proteins and minerals for this function are provided by meat, fish, cheese, eggs and milk.
2. Health and energy: The carbohydrates for this function are provided by fats, dairy products, sugar, potatoes and bread.
3. Protection: The vitamins for this function are provided by fresh fruit and vegetables.

Good menus will include food types that cater for all bodily needs. Remember that energy requirements will be particularly high. Remember also that some foods will be *off-limits* to some Scouts due to health or religious criteria.

When catering, some points to be kept in mind are:

- cost
- availability of foods
- cooking abilities
- Scouts' eating habits
- safe storage life or resupply access
- available time for preparation
- the program (menus should be planned after the program is set).

Menu

Table 3.1 Sample weekend menu

	Meal	*Ingredients per person*
Dinner:	■ Mixed grill	200 g steak; 45 g sausages; 1 egg; 140 g tomatoes; 60 g potatoes (or chips)
	■ Lemon sago	45 g sago; half a lemon; 20 g sugar
	■ Tea or coffee	5 g tea (or 1 teabag) or 5 g coffee; 560 ml milk to cover all meals; 45 g sugar
Evening snack:	■ Chicken biscuits or fruitcake	80 g biscuits or 60 g cake (*see* milk above)
	■ Tea, coffee or cocoa	(continued)

	Meal	*Ingredients per person*
Breakfast:	■ Cereals with sultanas and milk	60 g cereal; 20 g sultanas; 30 g sugar (see milk above)
	■ Scrambled onion-eggs on toast	2 eggs; quarter of an onion; 50 g toast
	■ Bread, butter, jam	120 g butter, 60 g jam per day
	■ Tea or coffee	
Lunch:	■ Sliced corned beef and salad	140–170 g canned beef; 45 g cheese; 140 g tomatoes; 85 g canned potatoes; 120 g canned pineapple
	■ Bread, butter, jam	See above
Additional Information:	■ Allow 15 g salt per day; pepper if required. ■ A 680 g loaf of bread provides 28–30 slices and each slice weighs 22–24 grams. Allowing for one-third of a loaf of bread per person per day, you need, on average, 8–9 slices or 176–212 grams. ■ Vegetarians will need to be catered for. ■ While all weights are given as average, you will have to make compensation for big bread and sugar eaters, those who are diet conscious, and so on. ■ Multiply the quantities given above by the number participating, allow compensations, and you are ready to cost and purchase your food requirements.	

Have a cooking plan

The secret of preparing a meal successfully and on time is to do things in the correct order. It is no use having the vegetables burning while the meat is cooking. Get your fire going in plenty of time. A simple meal will probably take you an hour to prepare and cook.

Cooking timetable

Clock diagram (60-minute cooking timetable):

- 60/0 — Start fire
- 5 — Put on wash-up water
- 10 — Prepare vegetables
- 15 — Put on water for potatoes, peas and beans
- 20 — Add more fuel to fire
- 30 — Put on water for tea; Boil potatoes
- 35 — Boil peas and beans
- 40 — Set table. Heat milk for custard
- 45 — Grill chops and steak
- 50 — Make custard; Fry sausages
- 55 — Make tea and mash potatoes
- 60 — Serve hot, say Grace or prayer

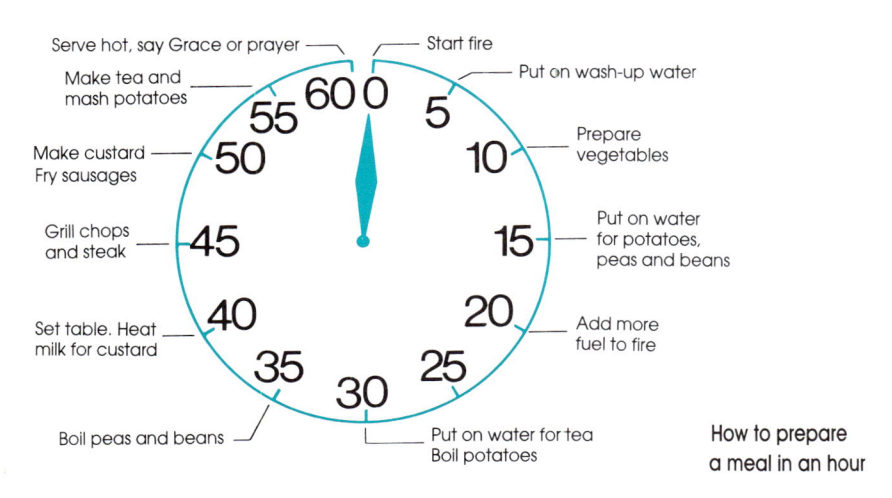

How to prepare a meal in an hour

Campcraft

As a guide, following is a cooking plan on a clockface. *Note:* This menu was all cooked in 1 hour. Some menus will take longer, so you must make the appropriate changes to your plan. Remember, though punctuality of meals is desirable, it is better to have well-cooked meal late (or early) than to have a badly cooked meal on time.

Table 3.2 Timetable

Item	Method	Cooking time
Soups		
Vegetable	Simmered	2 hours
Canned and packet	Simmered	As directions
Fish:	Boiled	10–15 mins per 450 g
	Fried	5–10 mins per 450 g
Poultry:	Boiled	20 mins per 450 g
	Roasted	20 mins per 450 g
Eggs:	Fried	2–3 mins
	Boiled	3–3.5 mins
Meats:		
Beef	Roasted	25 mins per 450 g
	Boiled	20–30 mins per 450 g
Mutton, lamb, veal	Roasted	20 mins per 450 g + 20 mins
	Boiled	20 mins per 450 g + 20 mins
Pork	Roasted	25 mins per 450 g + 20 mins
Sausages	Fried	15–20 mins
Saveloys	Boiled	20 mins
Stews	Simmered	2–2.5 hours
Vegetables:		
French beans	Boiled	20–25 mins
Broad beans	Boiled	20–30 mins
Brussels sprouts, cabbage	Boiled	20–25 mins
Carrots and parsnips	Boiled	20–30 mins
Cauliflower	Boiled	20–30 mins
Marrow and pumpkin	Boiled	20–30 mins
Mushrooms	Simmered	20–30 mins
Onions	Boiled	30–40 mins
Peas	Boiled	20–25 mins
Potatoes	Boiled	30 mins
	Roasted	45–50 mins
Silverbeet, spinach	Boiled	15–20 mins

Food allowances: rationing and packaging

The amount of food allowed for each person in the Patrol is important. If you allow too much, it will be wasted and the camp will cost more. If you allow too little, you and your Patrol might go hungry.

The following tables are a guide to rationing and packaging requirements, but do not be afraid to alter these quantities to suit the needs of your Patrol. For each Scout, allow the following quantities per meal.

Table 3.3 Ration guide

Item	Quantity per head	Per meal/day
Bacon	60 g	per meal
Biscuits	60 g	per meal
Bread (ordinary)	360 g	per day
(milk/wrapped)	180 g	per day
Butter or margarine	60 g	per day
Baked beans	120 g	per meal
Cake	90 g	per day
Cereals	40 g	per meal
Cheese	30 g	per meal
Cocoa	4 g	per meal
Coffee	4 g	per meal
Custard powder	7 g	per meal
Eggs	(1 only) 50 g	per day
Fish (fresh or frozen)	180 g	per meal
Fish (smoked)	120 g	per meal
Fish (canned)	180 g	per meal
Flour (self-raising)	60 g	per meal
Fruit (fresh for eating)	(1 apple, orange or pear, and so on)	per day
Fruit (dried)	60 g	per meal
Fruit (fresh for stewing)	120 g	per meal
Fruit (canned)	180 g	per meal
Honey	30 g	per meal
Jam	30 g	per meal
Lettuce	60 g	per meal
Macaroni	40 g	per meal
Milk (fresh)	500 ml	per day
Milk (powdered)	35 g	per day
Milk (condensed)	120 g	per day
Meat (fresh for stewing)	120 g	per meal
Meat (fresh for grilling)	180 g	per meal
Meat (minced)	180 g	per meal
Meat (cooked)	90 g	per meal
Meat (canned)	120 g	per meal
Oatmeal	30 g	per meal
Peas (dried)	30 g	per meal
Peas (in shell)	150 g	per meal
Peas (frozen/canned)	90 g	per meal
Prunes	60 g	per meal
Potatoes (fresh)	180 g	per meal
Potatoes (dried)	30 g	per meal
Rice	30 g	per meal
Sausages	150 g (2 large)	per meal
Sausage (luncheon)	90 g	per meal
Spaghetti (raw)	45 g	per meal
Spaghetti (canned)	120 g	per meal
Sugar	90 g	per day
Syrup	15 g	per meal
Tea	15 g	per day
Vinegar	10 g	per meal
Vegetables (salad, excluding lettuce)	180 g	per meal
Vegetables (boiling, excluding potato)	120 g	per meal

Table 3.4 Packaging

Item	Quantity
Bread	1 kg or 500 g
Dairy products	
Butter or margarine	500 g or 250 g
Cheese, cheddar	500 g
Milk, powdered	1400 g or 350 g
Cereals	
Rice bubbles	350 g or 250 g
Cornflakes	750 g, 500 g
Weet Bix	700 g and 350 g
Muesli	350 g
Dry foods	
Custard powder	375 g
Oatmeal	750 g
Rice	1 kg
Beverages	
Tea	500 g or 250 g
Coffee (instant)	500 g or 250 g
Cocoa	500 g
Dripping	500 g
Vegetable oil	750 ml
Condiments	
Honey (canned)	500 g or bulk
Jam	750 g or 250 g
Tomato sauce	500 g or 250 g
Vinegar	500 g or 350 g
Fruit (canned)	500 g or 750 g
Vegetables (canned)	750 g or 500 g
Meat	
Fresh sausages	13 per 1 kg (large)
	22 per 1 kg (small)
Meatloaf type	350 g
Camp pie	500 g, 250 g, 100 g
Fancy grades	500 g, 250 g, 100 g
Fish	
Fish (canned)	500 g, 350 g, 250 g, 100 g
Sardines	80 g or 30 g
Other canned foods	
Baked beans	750 g, 500 g, 250 g, 100 g
Spaghetti	750 g, 500 g, 250 g, 100 g
Basic foods	
Flour	1 kg, 2 kg
Sugar	1 kg, 2 kg

Note: It is often easier to work in 'slices' or 'pieces' instead of 'grams'. The lists in the tables can then be adjusted according to the size of the slice available; for example, for cold meat, you might buy one large slice or two small slices per person.

It also helps to know that there are approximately:
- 24 slices in a loaf of bread
- 500 grams of butter to 4 loaves of bread
- 5 serves of custard per litre.

Build up your own list. Much helpful information is contained on the product labels.

A checklist such as the following could be used to make sure you take whatever you need:

- salt
- pepper
- vinegar
- sauce
- detergent
- pot scourers
- matches
- tea
- coffee
- Milo
- alfoil
- Gladwrap
- cordial
- sauce
- disposable wipes

Meals

Breakfast

Breakfast will give you the right start for the day. It is worth going to the trouble of preparing a good meal, but use easy-to-cook meals. Fruit juice contains plenty of vitamins and is a pleasant start to the day—open a can, or use the concentrated form which requires the addition of water. Cereal puts some bulk under your belt—there is a wide variety of prepared cereals to choose from, or use the easy-to-cook instant porridges.

Follow this first course with one of the following:

- sausages (boiling them for a little while before placing them in the pan will lessen the possibility of the sausages bursting), or chops with an egg (boiled, poached, scrambled or fried with bacon)
- fried tomatoes, fried leftover vegetables
- rissoles, spaghetti or baked beans on toast
- perhaps a combination of these.

Get out of the rut and try something different, as in the following.

Egyptian egg   Cut a hole in a fairly thick slice of bread. Place in frying pan with a little cooking oil; break an egg into the hole, cook until the egg white sets. Turn it over and cook the other side.

Scotch eggs   Hard boil an egg for each person the night before. Shell the cold eggs and enclose them in a mixture of sausage mince, breadcrumbs and raw egg. Fry them in deep fat; serve hot with tomato sauce. For a Patrol of five or six, you will need 350 grams of sausage mince, half a cup of breadcrumbs and one egg all mixed together. The mixture should form a half-centimetre covering around the egg.

French toast   Beat an egg into a cup of milk. Dip—do not soak—a slice of bread in the mixture, and fry it in a hot greased pan, first one side, then the other. Watch a loaf of bread disappear.

You can finish your breakfast with a hot cup of tea or coffee, and toast and jam. Flapjacks will help to fill up those few empty corners.

Lunch

You will not want to spend a lot of time on lunch. It will interfere too much with your fun activities. You will probably settle for a cold meal, although a mug of hot soup and a hot drink will be welcome if the weather is cool.

Cooked cold meats, or canned meats or fish, with salad vegetables, cheese and fruit, will keep you going until dinner. Small jacketed potatoes, boiled at breakfast time, provide variety at lunchtime. Bread and a variety of spreads will help make the meal interesting. Soak the salad vegetables for an hour or so beforehand so they are fresh and crisp. Keep the meat in a cool place, and do not serve it until everything else is prepared.

Dinner

This will be the main meal of the camp day. It is your golden opportunity to prove your cooking skills. No self-respecting camp cook would consider less than three courses, and an expert cook will make use of different heating methods.

Cooking methods

You can cook by the following methods.

Direct heat Boiling and frying in pots and pans, grilling and toasting; backwoods-style cooking; foil cooking.

Reflected heat Baking and roasting, using an oven; a reflector oven.

Stored heat Hay-box cooking; bush oven; burying food under hot coals; cooking on stones heated in the fire.

Besides the various cooking methods, you have a wide variety of foods and dishes to select from.

You will probably begin your meal with soup. The packet varieties are good, but be adventurous — try to make it yourself with your own ingredients.

Follow this with meat and vegetables. Stew is meat and vegetables cooked together. Some other ideas include fried or grilled chops or sausages; boiled potatoes, carrots, peas, beans; kabobs; roast lamb or chicken and baked vegetables; meat or fish rissoles, with peas and carrots, and potato chips.

Stew takes time to prepare and should be cooked slowly. Prepare the meat and vegetables at lunchtime; place them in a billy, just covered with water; add a teaspoon of salt; bring to the boil, and leave over a dying fire to simmer. Stir occasionally to prevent it sticking, keep a little bit of fire under it during the afternoon, and it will be well cooked by dinnertime. Another way is to cook it in a hay-box.

Partly processed vegetables are readily available and cut down on your cooking time, but are more expensive than fresh vegetables. Freeze-dried peas and beans are worth purchasing, but fresh potatoes, onions and carrots are best for camp cooking.

No dinner is complete without a dessert, and again your choice is very wide. Try some of the wide variety of canned desserts and instant puddings that require only heating, or try to cook any of the following: stewed fruit and custard; steamed pudding and custard; apple fritters or banana fritters; pancakes; boiled rice, with prunes or other dried fruits.

Custard improves any dessert and is easy to make. For a Patrol of six, you will need 750 millilitres of milk, 2 level tablespoons of custard powder and 2 tablespoons of sugar. Mix the custard powder to a thin paste with a little milk, making sure there are no lumps. Put the rest of the milk on to heat. Just before it boils, take it from the fire and stir in the sugar and the paste. Return it to the fire, stir continuously until it boils, then take it from the fire. Keep it warm until needed, by standing it beside the fire.

Cooking with a Dutch oven

Most of the skill in using a Dutch oven successfully lies in accurately judging the heat output of the cooking fire. Heat control is important and comes with experience. You need to know roughly the amount of coals to use to produce the required degree of heat. The most common error is the use of too many coals, which results in burned food. It is much better to have fewer coals than necessary than too many.

Preheating the oven For many recipes, it is necessary to heat up the oven before starting to cook. This is done by placing the oven on a bed of coals with additional coals piled on the lid. Note this is the only occasion the oven is placed directly on the coals—when cooking, there should always be a space between the bottom of the oven and the coals. If your oven does not have legs, stand it on a grid or a few small rocks to raise it above the bed of coals. This will help to prevent the food burning in the oven.

Using your Dutch oven

For boiling Use heat underneath only—a moderate heat that will give you a slow, steady boil.

For stewing Use heat underneath only — although you can bank embers around it too, and place some on the lid, if you wish.

For frying Use heat underneath only; the same applies for deep-frying. The lid, reversed, can also be used as a frying pan.

For roasting First warm your Dutch oven on the fire, and then put in a little cooking fat, and, when this begins to smoke, add the meat and sear it on all sides by turning it a few times. Then pour a little *hot* water over the meat—about half a mugful will do—and add seasoning; put the lid on. Now surround the Dutch oven with hot coals, beneath and around it, and rake some on top of the lid. Keep the fire moderately hot. You can add vegetables for roasting—such as potatoes and carrots—when the meat is about half done.

For baking Line the inside of your Dutch oven with heavy-duty household aluminium foil; remember to have the foil shiny-side up. Then place the item|s to be baked on the foil, directly, or in foil pan|s or wrap|s, depending on the requirements of the dish you are baking. You can often bake more than one type of food at once. For baking, have coals under, around and on the lid, for all-round heat.

Cooking times

As a rough general rule, for baking and other kinds of cooking, the cooking times will be much the same as for an ordinary stove at home. Experience will teach you best.

Use various fires Depending on your cooking requirements, you can use your Dutch oven with different types of fire. It can, for example, be suspended over an open fire, or be stood on its legs over a fire, or be used on a trench fire, or in a pit fire. For fuel, use wood or charcoal.

Recipes to try

Anzac biscuits (to be cooked at home before the hike). *Ingredients:* 1 cupful each of plain flour, rolled oats, sugar and coconut, half a cupful of butter, 1 tablespoon of treacle or golden syrup or honey, 2 tablespoonfuls of boiling water, and a teaspoonful of bicarbonate of soda. Mix together dry ingredients with exception of soda. Heat the butter, water and treacle together. Take off the heat and stir the soda into the liquid. Mix this with the dry ingredients. Roll out. Cut into rounds about 80 millimetres in diameter and slightly less than 100 millimetres thick. Bake in a moderate oven for 30–40 minutes until a pale brown. These quantities will make just over half a kilogram of biscuits.

Steamed puddings These can be easily made in camp. Add a dessertspoonful of sugar to a mugful of self-raising flour and then a pinch of salt. Mix in a heaped dessertspoon of butter or dripping. If desired (and available), a few raisins, sultanas, chopped-up dates or currants may be used. This should be mixed into a dry dough as for a damper, and placed in a well-floured ration bag, big enough to allow for swelling. The bag should be tied up and dropped into a billy of boiling water. The billy must then be kept boiling until the pudding is served. Allow half an hour for a mugful of flour, and longer for a bigger pudding. Over-boiling (within reason) will do no harm.

Salmon and rice with cheese sauce Put 1 cupful of rice into plenty of boiling salted fresh water. The rice is cooked when a grain can be squeezed out flat between the fingers. This takes about 10 minutes from the time the billy has come to the boil again. As soon as the rice is cooked, drain the water as thoroughly as possible. Remove the salmon from the can, mash it up, juice and all, and mix in a little thinly sliced raw onion and heat it in a lightly greased pan. Make cheese sauce similarly to Welsh rarebit, but with only 1 tablespoonful of cheese and more milk. Serve the rice on the plate, place the salmon on top of the rice, and then pour sauce over the top.

Welsh rarebit (modified) Slice a cupful of cheese thinly and lay it in the bottom of a cooker similar to a 'Gilwell' cooker. Add cold milk until the cheese is covered and about half a centimetre under the level of the milk. Heat until the cheese is thoroughly melted. Salt to taste, and thicken with flour. Serve on buttered rye biscuits with a slice of fried bacon.

Dried apricots For a Patrol, soak 1 cupful overnight and add half a cupful of sugar, or more if desired very sweet. Bring to boil and allow to simmer for 25 minutes. Drain and serve with custard or cereals.

Novel cooking ideas

1. Caramel made from an unopened can of sweetened condensed milk boiled in a billy of water for an hour or two
2. Pancakes made from packet mixture
3. Popcorn: Purchase a packet from your local supermarket and fry in a *covered* lightly greased pan
4. Donuts: Buy a 'tube' of donut mix and deep-fry in a billy
5. Eat a flame thrower: Take a rye biscuit, spread with butter and vegemite, add a thin slice of raw onion and a slice of metworst. Cap with another biscuit. Eat and breathe out
6. Apple fritters: Slice apples (or whatever you are using) into thin slices. Make up a thin batter of flour, salt and milk. Dip the apple into batter and fry in hot fat

Dutch oven camp recipes

Just about anything that can be cooked in an oven at home can be cooked in a Dutch oven, so your choice of what to cook is virtually endless. However, following is a basic dough recipe that is a useful standby, because with a few variations it can be used for many purposes.

Basic dough *Ingredients:* 2 cups of flour; 1 rounded teaspoon of baking powder (at lower altitudes use more); half a teaspoon of salt; 2 rounded tablespoons of shortening; 2 rounded tablespoons of sugar.

This mixture will make about 25 to 30 biscuits, or fill a 30 cm Dutch oven.

Biscuits To make biscuits, melt the shortening. Mix the flour, baking powder, salt and sugar together by stirring. Add a little water at a time until you get the right consistency (thicker than pancake batter, but not quite as thick as rolled dough). Pour the melted shortening into the mixture with the water, stirring it quickly so the shortening does not harden.

Your oven is hot enough when the grease begins to spread apart and smokes slightly. The lid should be hot to the extent that water sizzles on it if dropped on to it. Drop the biscuit dough a spoonful at a time into the oven. Replace the lid and place coals on top after placing the oven above some hot coals.

If the temperature is right, the biscuits should be ready in about 15 minutes. Do the 5-minute inspection. If they have risen and are starting to brown, they are coming along nicely. If already brown, the oven is too hot; lessen the heat. This basic recipe can also be used for the following.

Cobbler dough Add an egg and a pinch of nutmeg for each cup of flour and double the sugar. For *pancakes* follow this, but add more water or milk to make a thinner batter.

Cobblers Cobblers are easy-to-make desserts and are very popular. They basically consist of a layer of fruit with a cake covering. They taste really good.

Trail cobbler *Ingredients:* 2 cups of biscuit mix (see above); 2 cups of milk or water; 1 cup of shortening; 2 cups of sugar; 1 large can of fruit (drained of juice), for example, peaches, apples, pears.

Mix the biscuit mix, sugar, milk and shortening. Then add the canned fruit and stir. Bake in a covered Dutch oven for about an hour. Serves 8 people.

Philmont Ranger cobbler *Ingredients:* 2 × 820g (2 lb) cans of fruit such as peaches, cherries, fruit cocktail. Enough biscuit mix (see above) to just cover fruit, 1 teaspoon of cinnamon; quarter of a cup of sugar; butter.

Preheat the oven. Place oven over coals and pour the canned fruit with the syrup into the oven. Replace the lid and bring the fruit to a boil (no coals are required on the lid at this point). Make a crater in the biscuit mix and add water, stirring with a stick to make dumpling-sized balls of the mix, about 3 centimetres in diameter. Drop these into the boiling fruit to cover the top of the fruit. Let the coals under the oven die out, but add plenty of coals on the lid of the oven. Replace the coals often to make sure you get a good heat, because you cannot burn this cobbler by having too much heat on the lid. Add some butter to the top of the dough; sprinkle with cinnamon and sugar mixed together, and replace the top of the oven.

Oven-fried chicken Use about half a chicken per person and cut it into two pieces. Dip the pieces in cold water, wipe them dry, and then shake them in seasoned flour in a plastic bag. Place two tablespoons of fat or cooking oil in the hot oven, and brown the floured chicken pieces all over. Then turn the pieces skin-side down, cover the oven with the lid, and add coals. Bake, basting the pieces of chicken with the juices occasionally, for 15 minutes. Turn the pieces over and cook until tender, about 25 minutes.

Pot roast Rub a 1.8 kg piece of meat in flour, and brown all sides in hot fat in the oven. Add about 13 millimetres of water and replace the lid. Add more hot coals to the lid. Simmer for from 2 to 3 hours, adding water as needed, until the meat is tender. Add a peeled potato, onion and carrot for each person for the last 45 minutes of cooking.

Deep fruit pie Start by mixing the piecrust dough, using either bought readymade dough, or by mixing your own as follows (this is enough for a 25 cm double-crust pie).

2 and a quarter cups of self-raising flour; 6 tablespoons of margarine; 1 teaspoon of salt; about a quarter of a cup of cold water.

Thoroughly mix the salt into the flour and then add the margarine cut into pieces the size of peas. The edge of a fork works well for doing this. Sprinkle water on the mixture, stirring with a fork, until you think the dough can be formed into a ball. Handle it very lightly.

Divide the dough into two parts. Roll one part 3 millimetres thick and 203 millimetres wider than the oven. Fold it once and place it in a cold oven. Unfold it and mould it into shape to cover the bottom and sides of the oven. Do not stretch it, otherwise it will shrink on baking. Bake the pie shell in the oven for about 10 minutes, and then inspect it—starting with a cold oven, the dough should be firm but not cooked.

Rub the bottom lightly with margarine. Now add the fruit-pie filling, up to the rim of the pastry shell (about two cans of fruit, unless you have fresh fruit, in which case you must add sugar). Do not break the crust, otherwise the filling will leak through and burn on the bottom of the oven.

To make a lattice-work crust, roll out the other part of the dough 3 millimetres thick and 26 millimetres wider than the oven. Cut the dough into narrow strips and cover the top of the pie in a criss-cross pattern. Moisten the ends with water and press them to the crust lightly. Leave some slack for shrinkage. Replace the hot lid and bake the pie until the lattice is browned. The filling should be hot by then, because the contents of cans are already cooked and do not require further cooking. Remove from oven and eat.

If you want to bake a pie completely covered with pie crust, both the shell (bottom and sides) and the top crust, with the filling, are baked at the same time, starting with a cold oven. Do not forget to make slits in the top crust to let the steam out. With raw fruit, bake the entire pie all at once so the filling is cooked. A closed crust is best for firm fresh fruit (for example, apple).

Pineapple upside-down cake   Serves 8 persons. *Ingredients:* quarter of a cup of butter; 1 can of pineapple (rings or crushed); 1 egg; half a cup of brown sugar; 1 cup of vanilla cake-mix.

Place the butter and brown sugar in the oven and stir the mixture until thoroughly mixed. Add the pineapple to the butter and sugar mixture in the bottom of the oven. In a separate bowl, stir the egg into the cake-mix, and pour this batter over the pineapple in the oven. Cover the oven with the lid and bake for about 30 to 40 minutes. To test whether it is cooked, prod with fork or stick.

When the cake is cooked, remove the coals from the oven, remove the lid, and let the oven cool for about 10 minutes.

Using a large board or other suitable support, hold the board on top of the oven and turn the oven upside-down quickly, to allow the cake to fall on to the board. The pineapple will now be on top. A more clever way to do this operation is to have a board (or cardboard) a round shape so that it fits into the oven on the cake. When the oven is inverted, the board can be held directly under the cake with safer results.

Baked potato   Scrub well one big potato per person. Prick skin with a fork and grease lightly, wrap tightly in foil, place on a metal plate or pan, and set on pebbles in hot Dutch oven. Cover, add coals to lid, bake for an hour or so. Test with splinter—mealy crumbs sticking to wood show potato is done. Slash an X in foil and potato, and pinch to push it open. Add butter and salt.

Camp scones   *Ingredients:* 500 g of flour; 1 teaspoon of baking powder; pinch salt; 2 tablespoons of butter; milk.

Method: Sift flour, salt and baking powder together. Rub in the butter, and mix to a dough with milk. Make a ball of the dough and roll it out to form a circle about 1 centimetre thick. Cut circle into 16 wedges. Place on lightly greased baking sheet, on pebbles in bottom of foil-lined Dutch oven, and cover. Use all-round heat with hot coals underneath, all around, and on lid. Bake for 15 to 20 minutes, turning wedges once or twice.

Bread-and-jam pudding   *Ingredients:* 1 litre of milk, or a little more; 16 slices of bread; enough jam to spread 8 slices; a little margarine; 1 or 2 eggs.

Method: Spread 8 slices of bread with jam, and place the other 8 slices on top, sandwich style. Grease pie-dish with margarine. Cut the bread slices into squares (removing the crusts if you wish), and lay them in the dish. Beat up the eggs, and pour over the whole. Place in foil-lined Dutch oven—shiny side up—on pebbles in bottom of oven, and cover with lid. Use all-round heat—underneath, around sides, and on top. Bake for about 1 hour; top should be slightly browned.

Stuffed fish   First, catch yourself a fish. Ours was a small 6.6 kg grouper. Scale and clean in the customary way, and rub inside with a little salt. Make a stuffing of 2 or 3 tomatoes, 1 finely chopped onion, and 1 cup of prepared seasoned stuffing.

Mix all together and pack into fish cavity, and tie with string to keep mixture in while cooking. Heat 2 or 3 tablespoons of dripping or margarine in Dutch oven, and brown fish on both sides. Cover with lid and cook for 20 to 30 minutes or until cooked. For added flavour, lay sliced lemon on top while cooking second side.

Chicken sweetcorn bake *Ingredients:* For 4 people: 2 × 420 g cans of sweetcorn; 450 g cooked chicken, chopped; 3 cups of cooked and mashed potatoes; a quarter of a teaspoon of Worcestershire sauce; salt and pepper to taste; butter, or margarine.

Method: Drain sweetcorn and place in baking dish with chopped chicken. Add salt and pepper, and teaspoon of butter or margarine, and sprinkle Worcestershire sauce over all. Cover all over with 2 cm-thick layer of mashed potato. Place dish on pebbles in bottom of a hot foil-lined Dutch oven. Bake with all-round heat for about 25 minutes, until potato layer has browned a little.

Baked apple Wash and core one large apple per person. Fill hole with sugar, raisins, and dab of butter, plus cinnamon if desired. Put apples on greased metal plate or pan and add some water. Put plate in hot Dutch oven, on three or four pebbles, to prevent burning. Cover and bake for about 20 minutes.

Bread pudding *Ingredients:* half a loaf of bread, dry or stale; 2 tablespoons of sugar; 2 tablespoons of margarine; 1 cup of currants (or raisins, sultanas, or mixture); a quarter of a teaspoon of spice.

Method: Break up bread and soak in water. Wash currants and dry well. Press surplus water out of bread. Melt margarine, and rub into bread. Add sugar, spice and currants, and mix well together. Put in well-greased pie-dish; level it down. Place on pebbles on bottom of foil-lined Dutch oven and cover with lid—use all-round heat with hot coals underneath, around and on top. Bake for about 1 hour; top should be lightly browned.

Lid of Dutch oven This makes an excellent griddle (upside-down) for making pancakes, broiling steak or frying bacon, and so on.

One last word There are two ways you can break Dutch ovens. One is to put it on the fire with part of the oven on the fire and part of it out where the air is cold. The unequal expansion can crack the cold side. The other is to pour cold water in it when it is hot—as in making gravy. You should either use hot water, or move the oven off the fire to let it cool off before pouring in cold water.

Water

One thing you must always have in your camp is a good supply of safe drinking water. Running water, or still water that does not smell bad, will be all right for swimming or washing, but do not take any chances with it for drinking or cooking. Animals, either domestic or wild, are sure to be sharing the water supply with you. As you know, they are not fussy about using their drinking water as a toilet. Even clear running water may contain

Fieldbook for Australian Scouting

Straining muddy water

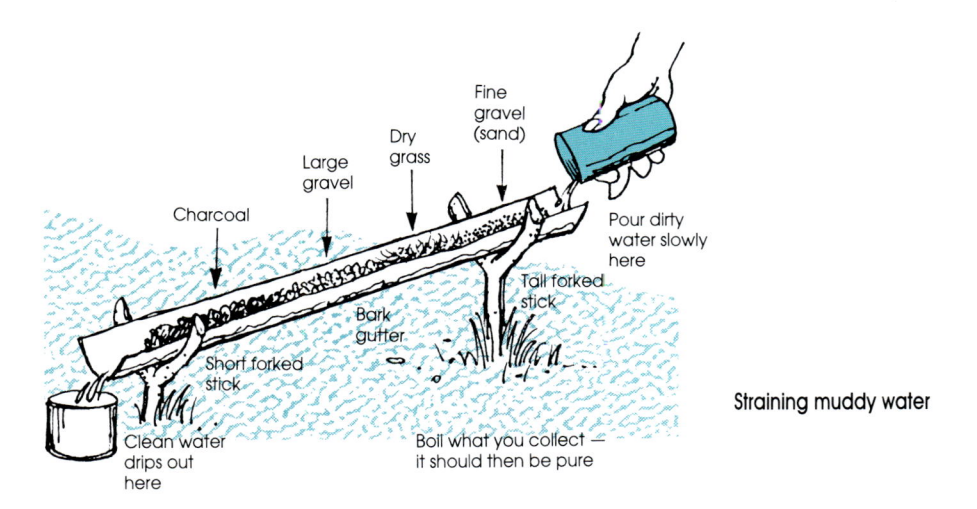

dangerous germs. Therefore, treat all surface water with suspicion, and make it safe for drinking by killing any germs it might contain.

When purity of water is not known, boil it for five minutes. Because this drives the air out and gives the water a flat taste, aerate it by pouring rapidly from one clean container to another several times.

Small capsules, 'Stericaps', are available from Scout shops and are used for treating impure water when it cannot be boiled. Brackish or poor-tasting water can be made more palatable by adding fruit saline crystals.

Muddy water can often be cleared by boiling it hard for 10 minutes and then letting it stand until it is cold. The mud will settle in the bottom of the container. Pour the clear water off the top. Excessive mud and debris can be removed by pouring the water through clean sand, but you will not get completely clean water by this method.

A safe but slow method of cleaning and purifying water is to use a plastic sheet to make an evaporator.

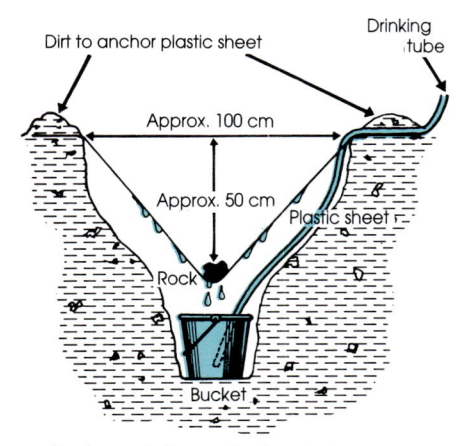

Collecting water by evaporation

Fresh vegetation under the plastic will help

Insects

No matter where you make your camp, there are bound to be insects. Some will be dangerous, others will be a nuisance.

The nuisance varieties, such as mosquitoes, midges, sandflies and ants, can usually be kept at bay by using repellents, sleeping under nets, or making sure you do not pitch your tent over an ants' nest.

Some of the dangerous types are dealt with in the 'Bites' and 'Stings' sections in Chapter 6: Emergencies, pages 298–302, and you should learn how to treat these bites and stings.

Your campsite

The word camp immediately brings to mind the fun and excitement of living in the bush. The word campsite will make you think of a secluded spot in the bush, on a grassy bank near a clear running stream — your perfect camping spot.

The perfect campsite — is there a place of this type? Well, following are the good and bad points to look for.

Good points

- It will be a secluded spot, but reasonably open.
- It will be elevated and gently sloping, so rainwater will run off, yet level enough for comfortable sleeping.
- The ground is grass covered, and sandy or gravelly to absorb the rain.
- There will be shelter from the prevailing winds, and trees or scrub to the south and west so your tent will catch the morning sun and be sheltered from the hottest sun and worst winds.
- There will be water close by, not only for drinking, but for safe swimming.
- Wood for fuel, and perhaps for gadget making, will be plentiful.
- The surrounding countryside will be beautiful, far enough from people for privacy, yet close enough to town to be reached without spending too much time and money on travelling.

Bad points

- Avoid clay and black soil because it will turn to mud in rainy weather. Also avoid loose sand — it has a way of getting into everything, including your food and clothes.
- Do not camp directly under trees — they may protect your tent in a heavy rainstorm, but when the rain stops they will go on dripping for hours afterwards. Falling branches are also a danger to be reckoned with.
- Do not pitch your tent in a gully or dry creek bed — flash floods do occur.
- Avoid falling stones from overhanging cliffs.
- Do not go into forest or scrubland if the country is tinder dry in the middle of summer — you may be trapped by a bushfire.

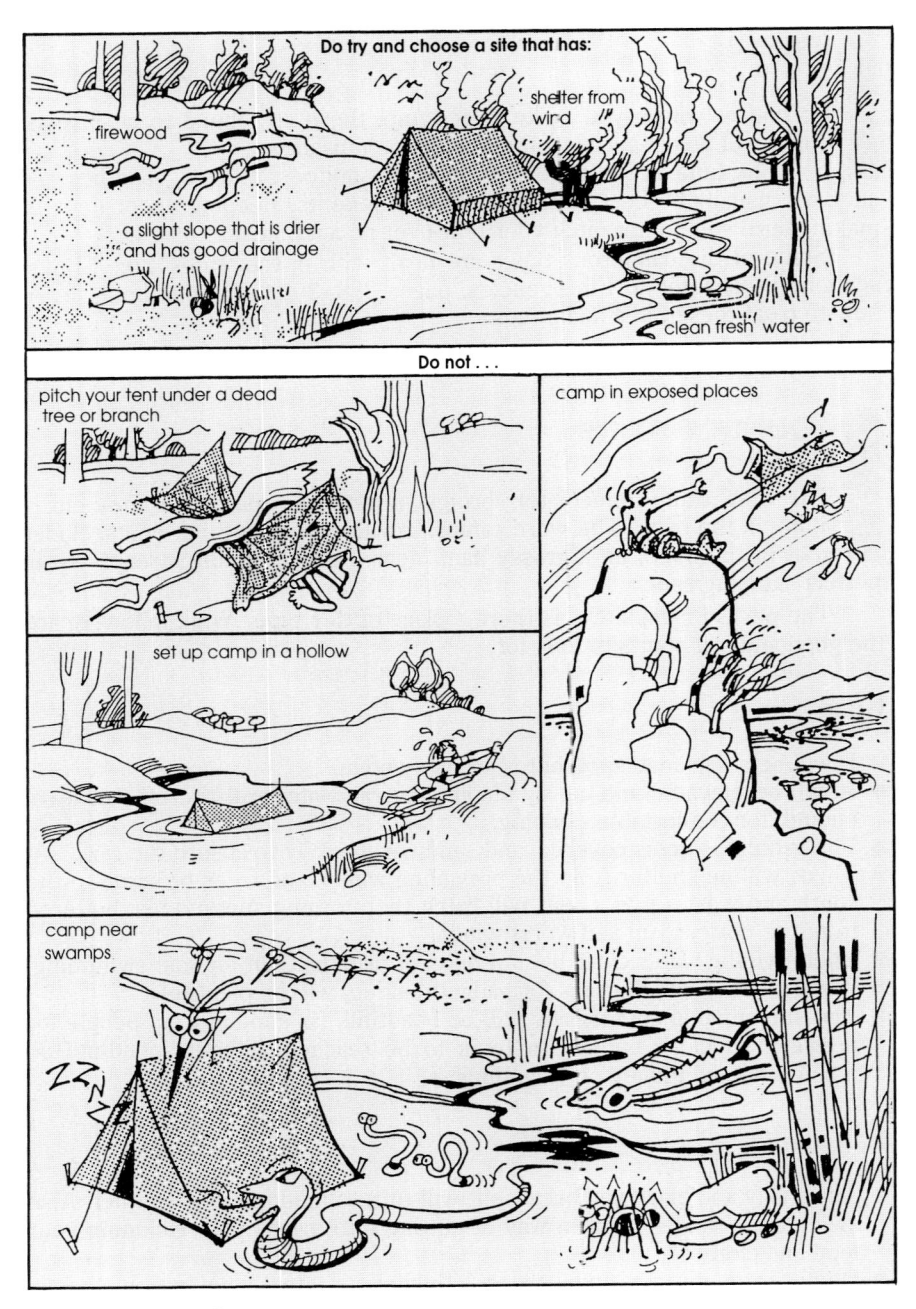

Choosing your campsite

If you can find a spot that has all these good points and avoids all the bad points, you certainly have found the perfect camping spot. Very often you will have to settle for a site that has only a few of the good points, but always keep looking—near-perfect spots do exist!

Campcraft

When you arrive at the campsite, the Patrol will discuss the camp layout. Where is the best place for the tent? Select somewhere level and free of stones and sticks or small bushes. Place your fire where the prevailing wind will blow smoke away from the tent and dining area. The latrine must be situated at least 50 metres away from the camp and water supply. If the whole Patrol discusses it, you should get the best use of the site.

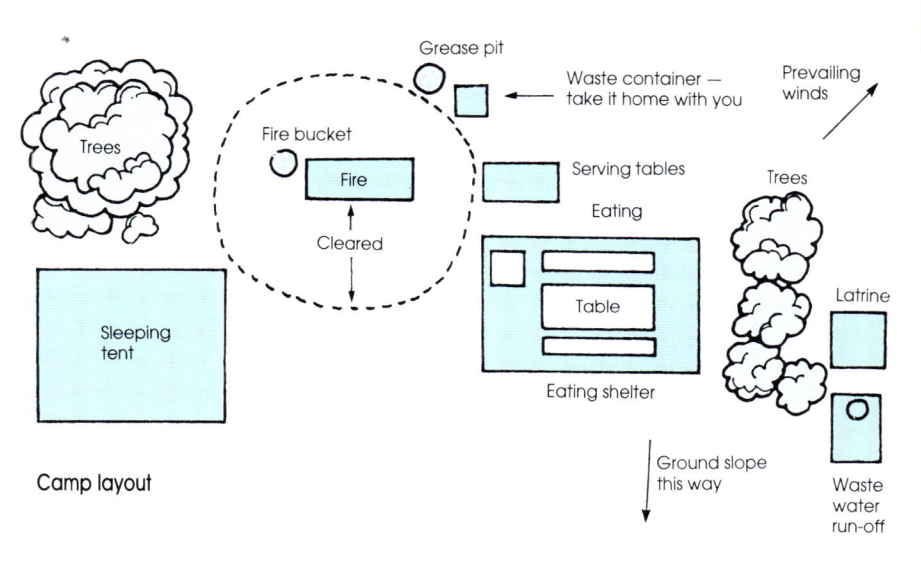

Camp layout

Look and listen

Camp is a golden opportunity for you to develop and improve your senses. Look at something, notice the small detail, and remember what you saw. Remain quiet, and listen to the noises of the bush, then interpret the sounds you hear. Smell the scents that come on the breeze, and recognise their sources.

These are things Scouts should train themselves to do. Scouts should be very proud of their ability to see things other people miss, tell what is going on around them by listening, recognise various smells, and recognise articles by feeling them.

Practice is necessary if you intend to develop these senses as B.P. developed them. Being in camp gives you the opportunity.

Observation in camp

Questions will immediately come to an observant Scout in camp, not only 'What sort of tree is that?' but 'Why does it grow beside the creek and not up on the ridge?' Not only 'What bird is that?' but 'Why does it live here?' Also, 'Why don't we see such and such an animal here?'

An inquiring mind is a necessity if you intend to be good at observation. Ask yourself the question, then try to find the answer. True bush people know so much about nature because they have taken the trouble to find the answers to things they have seen and not understood.

By being observant and trying to understand what you see, you will enjoy more of the world around you, particularly the world around your camp.

Camp adventures

Setting up your camp, keeping it clean and tidy, cooking your meals, packing up at the end—these are things that have to be done in any camp. It is the other activities, however, that make a camp exciting. What are some of the things you can do?

You can organise wide games, stalking games, ball games; practise orienteering and map making; take part in a conservation project or a good-turn project.

If there is water near the camp, you can have swimming activities, raft making, canoeing, or go fishing. There are so many things you can do it is best to make a program of the things you would like to do when you go to camp. You will probably not stick to it completely, but that does not matter.

Leave some time free when you are on any planned activity—lazing around in the middle of the day, or relaxing in the cool of the evening after dinner, can be every bit as enjoyable as any other activity.

Wide games

Wide games provide a source of fun and adventure and help develop skills of concealment, observation, deduction, tracking and so on.

There are three basic types of wide games:

1. a treasure hunt or competition to locate a specific treasure
2. a spoils-of-war game involving the capture of each other's belongings
3. a conquest or occupation of territory that must then be defended.

Night games usually require more self-control than daylight games, which require more skill.

It is essential to develop rules about how and when the game will start, how and when the game will finish, methods of capture, and so on.

Precautions must also be taken to avoid injury. Check the area for dangerous obstacles such as holes, steep banks and barbed wire. Make sure your Patrol understands the importance of the Country Code.

Try the following wide games.

Secret camps The Patrols go out for a one-night camp within a 1 km radius from an agreed spot. Time limits are fixed, but details can be fixed to suit the country. The aims are:

1. to discover the opponents' sites
2. to put opponents out of the game by taking their 'lives' (pieces of coloured wool tied around the wrist)
3. to capture any agreed articles of equipment without being caught.

In country that has plenty of cover for stalking, this game can be played in daylight using a wider area—say, a 2 km radius.

Spies Two sides start from points about half a kilometre apart. Each Scout is given half of a message written on a slip of paper. The object is for the members of one side to meet members of the other and find somebody who has the missing half of their particular message. Before comparing notes, however, a sign is given by each Scout to prove that he/she is willing to risk the exchange. It is a risk, because on each side there is a spy. Instead of having half a message, the spy has the word spy written on the piece of paper. Therefore if, after agreeing to compare notes, Scouts get caught by a spy on the opposite side, they must give up their slip of paper to the spy, and return to a pre-arranged base without revealing the spy's identity. The first pair to reach the base with the message completed are the winners. Other wide games appear in 'Campfire yarn 14' of Baden-Powell's *Scouting for Boys*. For more ideas, read the publication *Wide Games*.

Pioneering

Pioneering is an activity that will test many of your Scouting skills. If you build a swing or tower or bridge, you will be using your knotting and construction skills and having fun at the same time. An aerial runway or flying fox will give you hours of enjoyment, and will certainly add to your camp adventures. *See* Chapter 5: Construction, page 203.

Campfires

Some of your happiest times in camp will be spent around the campfire watching the flames, singing and play-acting, or planning what the Patrol will do tomorrow. Baden-Powell, at the first Scout camp on Brownsea Island, gathered the boys each evening for exactly this purpose—to meet around a fire, to sing and to give them his campfire yarns.

How does a Patrol or a Troop take up singing? It is helpful to have 'learning sessions' at meetings. Books can be used for these, or large charts with lyrics (song words). The aim will be to become familiar with a variety of songs. it is not good to be over-reliant on books, however, because when you are singing outdoors, books become a nuisance.

When you are camping with other Patrols, a truly spectacular campfire can be organised, including impressive opening and closing ceremonies, Patrol stunts and community singing (see *Campfire Leader's Handbook*, S.A.A. resource book).

Having a campfire

If you are asked to prepare a campfire program, following are several points to guide you.

- Have one or two boys or girls responsible for the fire—to build and sustain it.
- Have somebody to open your campfire officially with a few simple opening words.
- Have a selection of songs that provides variety. Start with rousing, boisterous, well-known songs. Move to songs that have humour and actions. Then try some songs that have leader and chorus sections, or that have solo sections, which are not so boisterous.
- Move to quieter songs and spirituals as the program draws to a close. Try to 'feel' what these quieter songs mean in order to best enjoy them.

In other words, follow the mood of the fire itself.

In the program, include several short sketches or items by individuals or Patrols. Towards the end of the singing, you could ask a Scout Leader to tell a yarn, but ask in plenty of time so he/she can prepare.

You will find a wide selection of songs in Scout songbooks. Try to become familiar with a range of these. There are many fine songs, especially folk songs, which you may discover elsewhere. Learn these too.

Become a singing Patrol and you will find deep enjoyment together. Not only that, you will be able to make a big contribution to the campfires of your Troop or your District or at the great assembly at a Jamboree.

For more ideas, read the *Australian Scout Songbook* published by The Scout Association of Australia.

Breaking camp

The worst part of any camp is packing up: you have had a terrific time, you have learnt some new skills, you are now a bit more confident you can look after yourself in the bush; but all good things must come to an end.

Being an expert camper, you will take as much pride in cleaning up your campsite as you did in setting it up. You will make sure all trenches are properly filled in and the turf sods re-laid so the grass will grow again. All the litter will be packed up and burned, buried, or put in a bag to take home.

The dried grass, leaves and twigs you raked from around your fire circle will be raked back, in order to restore the area. The fire will be dead out, and in many respects the campsite will be better than how you found it. You will thank the owner of the property and everyone who has made the camp possible.

Having set up a good camp, had a terrific time, and cleaned up properly, you will be able to enjoy that sense of achievement and pride that comes to all expert Scout campers.

Scouts leave nothing but their thanks

4

CITIZENSHIP

Aim of the Association

The aim of The Scout Association of Australia is to develop good citizenship. Why? You will be an adult in a few years. What type of adult do you want to be? Look around and find the qualities you would like to see in yourself.

First, you will want to be as fit and active as the body you have been given will allow you to be: the person who cannot jump up and run a message for their mother because they are too tired is not worth their salt. Second, you will want to complete the message to the best of your ability: if the shop does not have the article you want, you will choose the closest alternative or try the shop down the road. In this simple task, therefore, are some of the ingredients of a good citizen:

- obedience: you went off immediately
- self-reliance: you knew where to go and how to get there
- thoughtfulness: you were asked only once
- dependability: you certainly carried out the job
- co-operation: you would help anyone to the best of your ability.

What other qualities do you see around you? Your parents' devotion to the family, your religious leader's understanding, your Scout Section Leader's perseverance, your teacher's enthusiasm. Athletes, war servicemen and servicewomen, scientists, writers, tradespeople, all have worthwhile qualities. Make your own list.

If Scouting helps you achieve some of these qualities, you will have become a better citizen—and in doing so you will have a lot of fun. Why is it so necessary to become a good citizen? You are part of Australia, and as you grow up, you will want to take your share of what life can offer you. What you take and give will depend on the qualities you put to work for yourself. Let us look at how you fit into the picture.

Scouting

You are a member of your Patrol and the Brownville Troop. The Troop is a good one, but can you improve it? There are thousands of Troops, and each Troop is combined with a Joey Scout Mob, a Cub Scout Pack, a Venturer Unit and a Rover Crew using the Group headquarters as home base. The Group is part of a District or Area shown by the badge you wear. Many Areas combine to make a Branch, and the Branch Headquarters are in your capital city. When we put all the Branches and states together, the result is the national organisation: The Scout Association of Australia, some 150 000 members-strong!

Australian heritage

United Nations

In 1945, 51 nations, including Australia, signed the *United Nations Charter*; at the time of writing, there were 140 members. The aims of the United Nations (UN) are:

1. world peace and understanding
2. to help nations work together
3. to free the world of poverty, misery, hunger and ignorance.

United Nations logo

The UN Security Council consists of five permanent and 10 temporary members. The Council's main purpose is to keep peace between the nations. Do you know who are the present members of the Security Council?

The General Assembly of the UN meets in a building in New York. The meeting places are decorated with crafts and materials from member nations.

An office building behind the main building houses some of the agencies of the United Nations.

Commonwealth of Nations

Thirty nations that were once colonies of Great Britain joined together with Britain as equal partners in the Commonwealth of Nations. Some of these countries are republics, others recognise the Queen as their head of State. The organisation has no Constitution, but meets to consider matters of defence, trade, migration, investment and culture. The Secretariat in London arranges meetings for the prime ministers and groups such as conferences and university commissions. Diplomats who liaise between these countries are called not ambassadors but High Commissioners.

Parliament

Federal Parliament

The states of Australia were granted a Constitution to form a government for all Australia in 1901. The first parliament met in Melbourne, and in 1927 it moved to Canberra. When you reach 18 years of age you will be required to vote for candidates for the House of Representatives and the Senate. When a

Australian Coat of Arms

proposed law or Bill is passed by both Houses, it is signed by the Governor-General (the Queen's representative) and becomes law. The Governor-General invites the leader of a political party to form the government, and if he/she has the backing of a majority of the members, he/she becomes the prime minister. The prime minister and ministers are the heads of departments called ministries. Can you name some of these ministries?

Judicial system

Each state and the Commonwealth have separate laws, so the judicial system is very complex. Common law is the law that applies by tradition; that is, it has been decided before in a court of law. Statute law is the law laid down by Acts of Parliament and interpreted by the courts. All English law that was in force when your state was proclaimed still applies to you, unless it has been repealed.

The strength of the British legal system we use is based on the idea that judges are completely free from influence of the government. The courts are Australia's conscience.

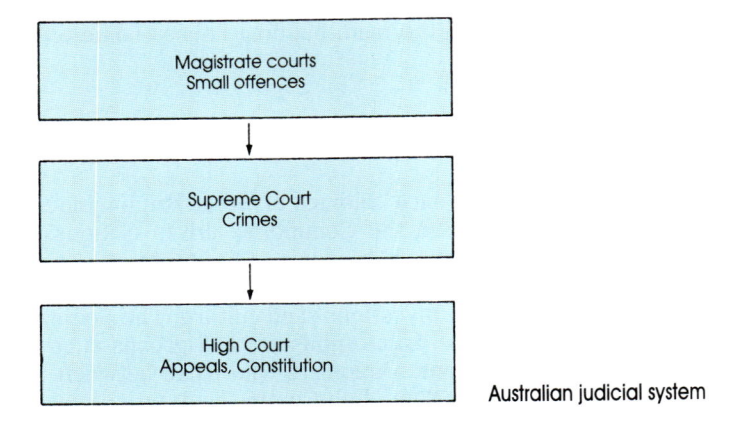

```
┌─────────────────────────┐
│   Magistrate courts     │
│    Small offences       │
└───────────┬─────────────┘
            ↓
┌─────────────────────────┐
│    Supreme Court        │
│       Crimes            │
└───────────┬─────────────┘
            ↓
┌─────────────────────────┐
│      High Court         │
│  Appeals, Constitution  │
└─────────────────────────┘
```

Australian judicial system

State Parliament

When you reach 18 years of age, you will also be required to vote for your chosen representative in the State Parliament. State governments were first formed last century when the states were colonies of England. When Australia became a federation in 1901, the state governments continued, but became involved in matters affecting individual states, for example, education, health, railways and police. Most states have two houses, a lower house and an upper house, as in Federal Parliament. The exception is Queensland, which only has a lower house. It would be educational and a challenge to organise a Patrol visit to your parliament while it is sitting.

Local government

Your local-government area is called a city, shire or municipality. Each area is ruled by a council. Members of a council are elected by the ratepayers. Council is responsible for roads, lighting, parks, sanitation and health. Are there any other responsibilities? There are at least three permanent officials—clerk, engineer and health officer. Does your council have a lord mayor or mayor? One of the activities you may care to undertake for this chapter on citizenship is a visit to your local council.

You as a citizen

Eventually your days as a Scout, Venturer or Rover will be over... they will have been years of fun, and if you were able to keep a log or a few photographs, you will be able to recall some of your adventures. You may want to continue with Scouting as an adult Leader; a Leader of a Joey Scout Mob, a Cub Scout Pack or a Troop; or on a committee that helps Scouting, or even become a Professional Scouter. Whichever you choose, we hope to see more of you when you leave. What you have learnt as a Scout will stay with you always. When you reach voting age you will know the full meaning of democracy and will be able to carry out your duties to your country: obeying its laws, and taking your place in the community.

Be a thinking citizen, not a thoughtless one. Keep yourself informed on the happenings of the day, in your own community, your country, and throughout the world. Learn how your country, your state, your city, town or shire is governed, and how you fit into that government. Discover where that government is strong and where it is weak. Do your part as a citizen in the task of upholding its strength and overcoming its weaknesses.

Be prepared to do your part in the smaller tasks—in the many everyday things such as obeying traffic regulations, observing laws of games, and serving on a jury when called. Find out about our political parties and what they stand for—all of them. Study all sides of their policies; then vote as your conscience tells you.

This is the way to make democracy work. We must work for it in order to deserve and enjoy our heritage, as expressed in Kipling's verse:

'If you can fill the unforgiving minute
With sixty seconds' worth of distance run,
Yours is the earth and everything that's in it.
And—what is more—you'll be a man, my son.'

Kipling's verse is now very dated and social attitudes have changed. However, the basic value—that all people, of both sexes, should participate fully in their communities—has not.

Your future

Soon you will have to make one of the most important decisions in your life: What will you do to make a living?

First, find work you can enjoy: if all you can get from your work is money, you have not found the right job. Second, spend lots of time finding out more about the occupation you would like to do. Ask people about the job they do. *Remember:* it is an important decision. Let us look at some of the people who are happy in their jobs, people who serve other people . . .

In schools

Your teachers have a great responsibility and have a big influence on your life. What is their responsibility?

There are various teachers who teach almost any subject you can name and at all levels: kindergarten, primary school, secondary school, college, university and adult education. The first requirement for teachers is that they are experts in their subject. For primary schools, secondary schools and universities, the teacher has a university degree or a Diploma of Education. Teachers respond to your interest in the subject; you will want to learn, so helping the teacher also helps you.

In the community

Helpful people are to be found everywhere. Have you ever asked the librarian for a book and not been able to find it? Shopkeepers will try to get you something they do not have, provided you have the patience to wait. Police not only enforce the law but listen to your complaints and attend accidents. Everyone has a job to do, and they all fit neatly into our pattern of life.

In the government

You probably travel on a road, bus or train every day. Behind the road is someone who planned it, someone who put aside the money for the materials, and many people who operated the bulldozers and graders to make it. There are also teams of people working together to provide you electricity, water, gas and sewerage. We could go on: the post office, defence forces, taxation office. A lot of these people we never see, yet they serve us.

In communication

We are familiar with the telephone and how quickly we can phone a friend. There are also the unseen people who lay cables across the land and under the sea, people who send up rockets to launch communication satellites. There are newspapers, radio and television. This is only a small portion of the thousands of jobs available—make sure you are careful to choose the right one.

Religion in your life

Many questions arise out of normal and natural experiences of life. The answers are always 'of faith'. Nobody knows what the correct answers are. They can be given only on the basis of a person's belief—answers of faith. To say, 'I believe there is no meaning in life' is a belief, as surely as saying, 'I believe in a God who made me and loves me.' You can never find proof of either statement. What we believe determines what we do in our lives.

Blondin was a famous acrobat who used to carry people across America's Niagara Falls in a wheelbarrow on a strong cable. This, naturally, was a brave thing to do, both for Blondin and the people who got into the wheelbarrow! One day he asked a person standing by whether he believed he could carry him across the Falls. The man replied, 'Yes, I have seen you carry others across; I certainly believe you could also carry me.' 'Right,' said Blondin, 'hop in . . .' The man ran away: he was prepared to believe intellectually that something was possible, and not convinced enough to commit himself in the hands of another person.

There is a tremendous difference between believing something about a thing and believing in that something. Faith is believing in your God like that, trusting Him in everything, and committing yourself into His hands. If things go wrong for us, it is no use asking, 'Why does God allow this to happen to me?' That is the shallow way—you are not going deep enough into it. People who believe in God for what they can get out of Him (protection or material blessings) remain beginners. We cannot argue that there are advantages in loving God and serving your neighbour. In many cases the wicked flourish and the good suffer. Yet people still do good, even when there is nothing in it for them. Believing in God also means following the commandments and discipline.

'Love the Lord your God . . . and your neighbour as yourself.' There is an old Hebrew proverb that states, 'The heart is half prophet.' This means you know already what is required of you. Be faithful, then, to your God, your faith; attend Scout's Own and the services of your faith when they are held. Scouting embraces all faiths, Christian and non-Christian. Every religious faith has its own particular discipline. Know what it is and practise it well, because beneath the outward signs of religion can be a great depth of meaning.

The Australian flag

At Eureka Stockade in 1854, 500 men were sworn by Peter Lalor under the Southern Cross flag. The rebellion against goldmining taxes was defeated, the bullet-ridden flag torn down and dragged behind a horse. In 1901, 3200 entries were sent in to a competition to design a flag. Five identical designs were chosen, and in 1903, permission was given to fly this flag.

When Her Majesty Queen Elizabeth II visited Australia in 1954, she signed the *Flag Act*, which established the official Australian flag.

The Australian national flag is a dark-blue flag on which the Union Jack occupies the upper hoist, a seven-pointed white star (the Federation star) in the lower hoist points directly to the centre of the union, and, on the fly, five

Fieldbook for Australian Scouting

The Southern Cross

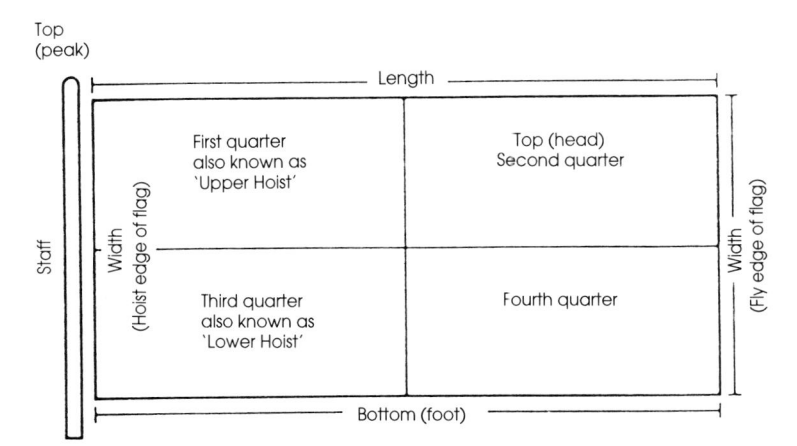

The Southern Cross has long been a navigation aid to mariners and travellers. This constellation had a place in Aboriginal legends before the coming of Europeans to Australia. The stars are called after the first five Greek letters of the alphabet:
- a = alpha
- b = beta
- c = gamma
- d = delta
- e = epsilon.

a, b, c, and d have seven points and e has five points.

182

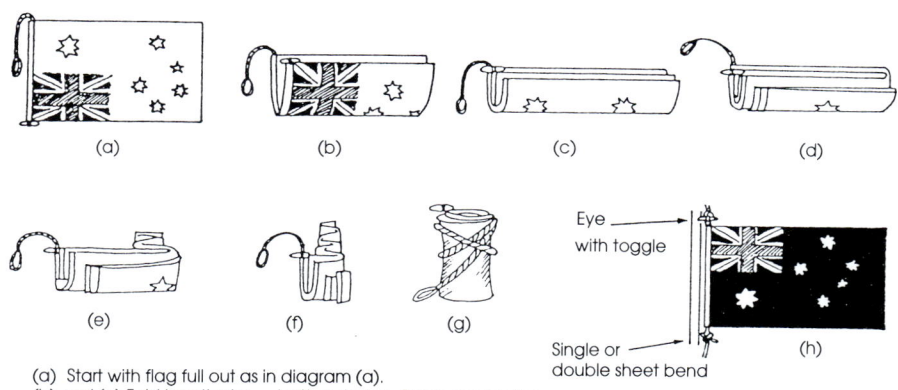

(a) Start with flag full out as in diagram (a).
(b) and (c) Fold lengthwise — bottom to top. This is done twice.
(d) Fold in half across the length.
(e) and (f) Fold in a concertina fold backwards and forwards.
(g) Hold the flag firmly, and wind the rope around and then under itself.
(h) The toggle is placed in the eye of the halyard, and the halyard is attached to the bottom of the flag rope with a sheet bend or double sheet bend.
Care should be taken whenever preparing the flag to ensure it does not touch the ground.

Rolling the Australian flag for 'breaking'

white stars represent the constellation of the Southern Cross, the four larger stars being seven pointed and equal in size, the small star five pointed. In each star, one of the points is at the very top. The seven-pointed Federation star represents the six Australian states and the Commonwealth territories. The flag should be flown only between 8 a.m. and sunset. At flag-down, it should be lowered steadily. The flag should never be allowed to drag on the ground, but should be caught up by the hand as it approaches the ground. The *Ceremonies Book*, published by The Scout Association of Australia gives the details of flag protocol.

Australian national anthem

'Advance Australia Fair'

Australians all let us rejoice,
For we are young and free;
We've golden soil and wealth for toil;
Our home is girt by sea;
Our land abounds in nature's gifts
Of beauty rich and rare;
In history's page, let every stage
Advance Australia Fair.
In joyful strains then let us sing,
Advance Australia Fair.

Beneath our radiant Southern Cross
We'll toil with hearts and hands;
To make this Commonwealth of ours
Renowned of all the lands;
For those who've come across the seas
We've boundless plains to share;
With courage let us all combine
To Advance Australia Fair.
In joyful strains then let us sing,
Advance Australia Fair.

Aborigines

There are some 238 000 Aborigines scattered throughout Australia. Today tribal life exists only in remote parts of the continent.

The Aborigines were nomadic hunters and their skills at hunting and tracking were truly wonderful. From a very young age an Aboriginal boy learnt the tracks of people and then of every animal. He would eventually be able to follow the tracks even on stony ground. When old enough he would be allowed to help his father hunt for food—until he was able to stalk close enough to a kangaroo to spear it.

Besides tracking, the Aborigines had to know the habits of the wild creatures: where they could be found and where they laid their eggs. The women knew what plants were edible and how to prepare them for eating. Not many of us could survive at all if we became lost in the bush.

Some early explorers, such as King of the Burke and Wills expedition, were lost and starving, but kind Aborigines took them into their tribe until help was found. Other Aborigines objected to the early settlers' claims on domestic animals and land. Much fighting took place and many people were killed on both sides.

Aborigines believe that mountains and rivers, trees and animals, were made by their ancestors long ago in what was known as the Dreamtime. These spirit ancestors had the form of huge animals of the types that live on the earth today, and could also behave like people, although they were much more powerful. The customs and ceremonies carried out by Aborigines had their beginnings in the Dreamtime. When the ancestors died they became stars in the sky, or rocks and other features of the landscape, but their spirits continued to influence life on earth.

All ancestors gave their individual animal name or 'totem' to all their descendants, and people of the same totem were not permitted to marry. They could not eat the animal that gave their totem its name.

If the Dreamtime ancestor had become a rock, the area near that rock was sacred, particularly to people of that ancestor's totem, but it would be respected by all other tribes as well.

Ceremonial corroborees were used to re-enact the life of a Dreamtime ancestor, and in this way Aborigines felt themselves to be part of their history. You can see why they would object if a mining company or station owner wished to drive them away from their territory and its sacred places.

To many Aborigines, the sacred places of the Dreamtime are very important. Contact your local Aboriginal Affairs office to find out your local heritage.

Good turns and service to others

By doing a good turn every day, we as Scouts are carrying out service to other people. The good turn is something that happens, and you will do it without thinking, but service to others is a bit more. Service to others has to be planned carefully—and as you go through Pioneer, Explorer and Adventurer, you will want to improve on what you have already done.

Citizenship

In doing a service to someone else you will truly be living the Scout Promise. What is more wonderful, you will find that by doing a service project you will get a great deal of satisfaction in the process of giving. And sometimes you will get thanks that you will truly appreciate.

There are 101 ways to give service to others. Look around; a lot of people are doing it all the time. The people who wrote this book; your Leaders who are the mainstay of the Troop—these are people giving service to others.

How you can tackle it

First, Patrol or individual or pairs? This will depend on circumstances. If the Patrol is easily got together and you can all join in cleaning the windows of the pensioners' home, do it as a Patrol. If some of the Patrol are doing part of an Award and some have just joined, however, you will have to go by yourself or in pairs. Anyway, the older Scouts can always give you ideas.

Do you get paid? Whatever you do, payment must not be expected. You may get expenses for the train fare on the excursion with Joey Scouts or Cub Scouts or the cost of the lawn seed for planting the local community-hall lawn; but your own labour is freely given. If you get a cool drink or cup of tea and a biscuit, however, that is fine.

How much service? A lot will depend on the type of job you tackle.

If you are completing part of your Target, check time requirements in the segment you are working on.

How to start Your P. L. may organise the job. If you intend to tackle it yourself, see the people in charge first to organise what you do and when to do it. Then collect the tools before the day.

What type of service?

You will have a lot of fun trying out some of the following activities.

Your own Scout Group

- painting the headquarters
- fixing things — the sign
              — the flagpole
- cleaning the sinks and toilets
- beautifying the surroundings with trees or shrubs
- making a street sign to help people find the headquarters
- making tea or supper for the annual general meeting (AGM)
- getting things ready for the big do: picnic, sausage sizzle, fundraising effort
- printing and distributing pamphlets.

The Joey Scouts

- helping at a Mob meeting going on a day activity or a sleepover.

The Cub Scouts

- making boxes or display boards
- helping the Cub Scout Leader with a special program, tests, badge work
- going to camp with the Cub Scouts and being general dog's body, cook's help, washer-upper and games organiser
- making campfires and cooking outdoors.

Area and District

- helping with the Gang Show
- patrolling check points for rallies
- preparing areas for District rallies
- getting markers and gear ready for large camps — the organisers will give you lots to do.

Now let us get away from our own organisation.

Old people and very young people

Everywhere in your neighbourhood you will find older people. As they get older their gardens and houses are not looked after as well as they sometimes could be. You may know of an invalid pensioner or elderly widow. The Patrol or you can always offer to:

- weed the garden
- cut back the shrubbery
- cut and trim the lawns
- paint the front fence
- fix the leaky taps
- take the dog for a romp
- do some shopping.

For very young people, you will have to confine yourself to the parents who know you — and you should be very careful and alert. Take the little children to the park for a play. Organise games to keep them amused, or read stories.

Community service

The place to find out about what you can do is the local council. In fact, they will have some big jobs the whole troop can join in on doing:
- cleaning up—the main street, the oval, forgotten corners of public property
- painting benches, cleaning signs
- helping the council gardener

The council will also give you a list of who to ask from the following list of charitable organisations.

Charitable organisations

- Animal-welfare leagues
- Hostels and homes
- Aged and invalid pensioners
- Rehabilitation centres
- Hospitals
- Religious societies caring for the aged
- Senior Citizens' Clubs
- Churches
- Red Cross and Junior Red Cross
- ...
- Orphanages
- ...centres
- Youth Movement (Junior ...)

- A disadvantaged organisation
- School library
- Holiday camps
- Prisoners' Aid Association
- Salvation Army Social Services
- St John Ambulance Brigade
- Invalid clubs
- Country Women's Association
- Meals on Wheels
- Good Neighbour Council
- War Widows' Guild
- Apex Clubs
- Junior Chamber of Commerce
- Lions International
- Rotary Clubs

These organisations will have jobs to do, as well as special occasions when Scouts can form a guard of honour or simply be seen by the public

... mention it, but there are a lot of worthwhile service jobs at ... inside and outside school and during and after school.

Fieldbook for Australian Scouting

Real service

Sometimes when you are out among people, perhaps helping someor
may happen to be on the spot to give first aid to someone in trouble.
'be prepared?' It would be a free service and something you will nev

Following is a true story of real service: Phillip was a 13-year
Leader in Tasmania. That year he went to a swimming carnival
a drowning girl in the public swimming pool. Later that year he
helping a child who was exhausted and distressed while swim

In the following year, Phillip was helping his father wit
on their farm. When his father was hitching up the trailer
slipped and broke both legs. Phillip, without help, assisted
on the trailer and into a comfortable position. Then he d
trailer home and called an ambulance. Phillip showed re
ing with a tense situation and was highly commended for
awarded the Certificate for Meritorious Conduct.

Preparing a talk

In Citizenship you may tell the troop an A
report to your Patrol or Troop about a given

It is easy to give a talk, but it takes pr
will make the attendees sit up and listen. Try

1. Know 10 times more about your subject
   prepared, you will know all about it and
2. Never write out your talk and then re
   Anyway, you know all about the subje
   to, make brief notes on a small piece
   esting things or the facts.

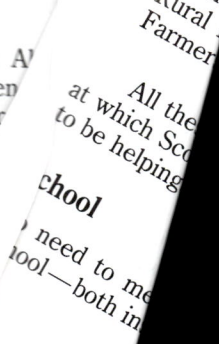

3. Find illustrations and examples for your talk. You can use a host of aids — blackboard, whiteboard, charts, illustrations, slides, tape, models and exhibits. (Bring these out only at the right time in your talk, however, otherwise your audience's attention will be diverted — it would ruin your talk if the pet mice escaped into the Troop Headquarters just as you were starting.) Then prepare examples for your talk.
4. Now you are set — go hard into the talk. In other words, 1, 2, 3 go!

When actually speaking, if you are enthusiastic about the bicycle camp to the ranges, no one will notice if you are buck-toothed or cross-eyed. You had a great time pushing (*puff*) the bicycle (*push hard*) up the hills. And imagine the time when Rachel got a puncture (*sssst*) and had to mend it twice because she pinched the tube (Rachel is in the audience and the laugh's on her). And then David tried to make pikelets like this (*actions*) but he forgot he should have used *self-raising* flour and we used them for a game (produce one and drop it on the floor — *clunk!*).

And you've given a successful talk!

Take part in meetings

Your Patrol will often have meetings. Make sure you know what the meeting is about and bring along some ideas. It may be to decide about the next Patrol activity, camp or hike. Bring a map and suggest a campsite or an activity.

The meeting should not be formal. You will certainly not want to read and confirm the minutes of the last meeting or have a session on 'any other business arising from the minutes'. But make sure that you or the Patrol scribe brings the Patrol log book or at least some paper and pencil. Take a note of what everyone decides to do. Your P. L. will nominate somebody to do the things you must decide on before the activity, camp or hike. It is not much of a meeting if nothing is decided.

Patrol Programs

Each evening there are two programs — the Patrol and the Troop. The Troop Council plans the Troop Program when it meets with the Scout Leader. Make sure your Patrol Leader talks over with you and the Patrol what ideas would suit the Patrol before the Troop Council meets and before deciding the Patrol Program.

Self-discipline

Lack of discipline will result in your leaders telling you off and in the Troop Council banning you from the next Scout night or special event. Self-discipline is when you toe the line to your own requirements. If you do not achieve the aim or goal, you can punish yourself — the fact that you have not achieved the goal automatically punishes you. How can you achieve some self-discipline?

Target Write down your aims, for example:
- Understand the Scout Law at Adventurer level.
- Become better at sport.
- Get up earlier.

Timing Put down the time scheduled and how to get to these targets.

Scout Law Read one Law every night and find an example of each in your own life.

Sport As well as practise, get Steve to help for one hour each week, four weeks, kicking at goal.

Getting up Try different methods. Next week, repeat at bedtime: 'Get up quickly because I am going to . . .'
Then, between you and your conscience, you will get there.

There are some general things for which you need self-discipline. Sometimes you may feel like lashing out in a temper, or you may be too lazy to do anything. Or you may be irritated and turn sour. This happens to all of us.

To stop this, you have to 'think before you act' or stop and look at yourself doing things that then look silly.

Sometimes you will disagree with a friend. Listen to her proposal first and then present your own view in an agreeable way, as an alternative, not as direct opposition. She will then listen. But if you tell her she is wrong, she will not listen, and you will have lost outright.

Learn to take knocks that come in good spirit. Forget yourself—get into the habit of thinking of other people. Keep busy doing interesting things, and the worries will disappear.

With a little self-discipline, your life will be so full of things to do there will not be time to fit them all in.

Fitness

What is fitness?

Long ago, human beings' survival depended on their physical fitness, their strength and stamina to hunt and trap and explore, their ability to fight, and if necessary, escape. Because primitive people spent most of their time in physical activity, they automatically had a high level of fitness.

In today's society, although we can exist by having a lower standard of physical fitness, we have to keep fit to survive. We have new problems: lack of exercise, poor eating habits, nervous strain, smoking and substance abuse.

Too many people spend their lives sitting down, and the number of people depending on physical work for a living is becoming smaller every day. While machines do the work, modern people pay the penalty for soft living in several ways: they develop flabby muscles, are overweight, and have tension and heart disorders. To survive, we have to make up for our lack of physical work by using our leisure time in a more active way, participating in exercises, games and sport.

Fitness is hard to define. To some people it simply means freedom from disease; others expect a fit person to be something like a superperson, capable of running a marathon and lifting your own body weight above your head.

As a compromise, it can be stated that a fit person is usually healthy. Our physical strength and stamina allows us to live and function close to our peak for a particular age. We can work or study efficiently, participate in games and sport, enjoy our leisure, and nevertheless have enough reserves for an emergency.

Your fitness depends entirely on you: it is a personal matter. You yourself need to learn a variety of physical skills and activities and to participate in them regularly.

Your health

Health is closely related to physical fitness, but keep in mind that the presence of certain diseases does not necessarily preclude fitness. Many famous sportspeople have been diabetics, suffered from asthma, or been survivors of polio. Their sporting achievements show that not all diseases are barriers to physical fitness.

Nevertheless, health is a key part in fitness. It depends on the working order of your body and is not measured by the number of bulging muscles you have. To keep the body functioning well is mostly a matter of good living habits and commonsense.

Good habits include eating proper food, keeping clean, having regular exercise and having adequate sleep. Regular checkups by your doctor and twice-yearly visits to the dentist are important.

Scouts might not always have their own choice of food, but they can avoid satisfying their hunger with large quantities of sweets, biscuits, potato chips and softdrinks; these supply useless calories and cause tooth decay. Keep in mind that what you eat must both provide fuel for energy and growth and keep your body in good repair.

Four main groups of food containing proteins, fats, carbohydrates, vitamins and minerals, are necessary for good health. A satisfactory Australian diet contains a variety of foods from the following categories:

- milk in any form, at least 500 millilitres per day for Scouts. Cheese, powdered milk or unsweetened evaporated milk. Milk and cheese provide *protein* and *vitamins* and are the best source of *calcium*
- meat, fish, poultry and eggs; dried beans and peas, lentils and peanuts. These foods provide *protein* and also contain *vitamins* and *minerals*
- bread, flour and other cereals. Wholemeal varieties are better food value. These foods supply *carbohydrates*, several *B vitamins* and *minerals*
- vegetables and fruit. Leafy green, orange, or yellow vegetables for *vitamin A*, fruit or vegetables rich in *vitamin C*, and two other servings of vegetables or fruit, including potato. This group provides *vitamins* and *minerals*
- butter or table margarine. These are sources of *vitamin A* and *calories*.

Without adequate sleep you will never be truly fit, and your growth and health may suffer. While you are growing, the body uses a lot of energy and getting enough sleep is an absolute necessity; you will need nine to ten hours every night.

Your body

Have you ever stopped to look at older people and tried to guess their age? Some age quickly whereas others continue to look active and robust despite their years.

The body ages or wears out by lack of care, lack of use, or abuse. We may not appreciate many of the advantages of a well and fit body until an accident, a disease or lack of care has made a part of our body incapacitated or useless. Watch an overweight middle-aged person running for a bus, or look at someone with false teeth trying to bite a fresh crisp apple.

The skin, besides being a protective covering for the body organs, preserves heat and can close its pores (goose pimples) when necessary. The skin has to be kept clean, and any cuts or abrasions treated carefully to prevent infection occurring. Nail wounds can harbour tetanus germs because these grow without oxygen. Seek help if your skin becomes 'pimply' as you get older.

Hair and nails can harbour germs, and regular washing is therefore necessary. Bowel upsets are usually due to dirty hands contaminating food. Some people can be 'carriers' and transmit diseases to others although they do not suffer from it themselves; this happens with typhoid fever.

Being able to see and hear are great assets. The eye is placed in a protective socket in the skull and escapes injury very easily. Care must be taken when welding and when handling lime or caustic or any other material that may splash into the eye. Wash the eye out with plenty of water in case of an accident and seek help immediately, remembering what has gone into it. Excessive noise for a long period can cause deafness, but the most common cause is an ear full of wax. Clean the ears regularly, especially in dusty conditions. Do not let the ears remain full of water after swimming or showering.

Special care has to be taken in understanding changes in the body when you mature. When a boy becomes a young man, the voice deepens and hair grows on various parts of the body. The testicles in the scrotum, and the penis, enlarge. When a girl becomes a young woman, her breasts develop and menstruation starts. Some young people sweat copiously, and pimples develop on the chin, neck, chest and back. These are all changes due to the release of hormones from the pituitary gland situated in the base of the brain. Ask your parents about these changes if they worry you.

Continued abuse of the body leads to a partial or complete unfitness. While we are young, our body has a large reserve and can overcome assaults; as we become older, continued assaults result in poor health and lack of enjoyment of living.

A young person who has a heart complaint, or rheumatic fever, needs complete rest otherwise she could become a 'cardiac cripple'. A broken leg has to be set and placed in plaster until it heals, in order to prevent deformity. With reference to substance abuse, (see next section) smoking causes 'pollution' of the lungs and can lead to bronchitis and more serious chest diseases later. Continued alcoholic intake leads to trouble in the liver besides being a causative factor in many accidents and broken homes. Hard drugs (narcotics), amphetamines (stimulants) LSD (hallucinogenic drugs), and so on, are taken to give you a lift or help you to forget. Repeated use leads to addiction, and changes occur not only in the person's physical makeup but in his thinking or mental makeup.

Scouts have to use and not abuse their body so they may work in as fit a condition as possible.

Substance abuse

There is a puzzling fact about people who swallow, inhale or inject drugs into their bloodstreams in order to change the way they feel. Men and women, young and old, intelligent and dull: these people know that 'doing drugs' can hurt them, if not in the short term, certainly over long-term use, yet they persist.

The most common drugs are alcohol and nicotine, even though many people do not think they are. Drinking beer, wine or liquor, and smoking cigarettes, cigars, or a pipe, are not usually considered to be drug taking even though they are chemicals that affect the central nervous system and influence the way people feel and react. Even though alcohol and tobacco are legally used by many people, this does not mean they cannot hurt you. Alcohol-related accidents kill thousands of people a year, and many smokers die from lung cancer and associated ailments.

These days, much has been said about the harmful effects of these drugs, yet people continue to use them, and more young people are developing the nicotine and over-drinking habits. The most likely reasons are 'social' ones: boys and girls like to be with the 'in' group, to feel more like one of the gang, to feel and look at ease and to be less self-conscious. Because so many adults drink and smoke, young people tend to think behaving in the same way will make them adults too. Most people want others to think they are mature men and women who know the right things to say and do.

Experimenting with these drugs, may at first be unpleasant, but young people continue to 'get used to it' and go on to develop addictions. Magazines and newspapers print a small line of type in their large cigarette advertisements that reads: 'WARNING: Health agencies advise that danger to health increases with the amount smoked.' It is not only smokers who run this risk; non-smokers who are exposed to secondhand smoke in their work, school, and social environments are also susceptible. No warning of this type is required by law on the beer, wine and liquor advertisements, although most states require a temperance or moderation message be run at the same time. It may sound cynical, but warnings would probably make no difference to liquor sales. Not many people take the time to even read the warning labels on their medicines. These are drugs too—whether you buy 'cold' tablets or capsules by prescription or over the counter, they are potentially dangerous if taken in too heavy a dosage or if taken too soon before drinking alcohol.

The main danger from some drugs found in your medicine cabinet is that they slow down your reaction time: they can make you drowsy. Another danger is in consuming too much alcohol at one time, or in drinking alcohol and taking drugs together. All types of accidents are more likely to happen to people when they are drinking. Then there are alcoholics—people who have become addicted to the drug alcohol. They give up school, job, family, money and health in order to get enough alcohol to satisfy their need. Even if you are not a heavy drinker or alcoholic, long-term damage to your liver can result. Because alcohol cannot be broken down by the stomach's digestive juices, it passes into the bloodstream and must be filtered out by the liver. Eventually the liver cannot cope with the amount of alcohol it must remove and breaks down; this is known as cirrhosis.

Alcohol and tobacco are not the only drugs available. Substances such as butane gas, glue, marijuana, LSD and heroin and 'ecstasy' are mood- or mind-altering drugs. More young people are smoking, eating and even injecting these drugs for the effect, however temporary, they produce. The community and Scouting is concerned about the threat to young people. It does not make sense to use anything that may cause serious or permanent damage to your body. Unfortunately, young people go right ahead and do it; some have lived to regret their mistakes, others have not.

The sensible person realises it is not worth trading a few minutes or a few hours to do something illegal and dangerous. If friends challenge your right to make a wise decision not to smoke, drink little or nothing and refuse illegal and dangerous drugs; they are not very good friends to have. You are first responsible to yourself for your well-being; you must maintain the strength of your conviction to refuse alcohol and drugs.

Scouts against smoking

Following is an article adapted from a speech made in 1991 by Mr Jacques Moreillon, Secretary-General of the World Scout Movement.

Baden-Powell, founder of the Scout Movement almost a century ago, once said, 'No boy ever began smoking because he liked it, but generally because either he feared being chaffed by the other boys as afraid to smoke, or because he thought that by smoking he would look like a great man—when all the time he only looks like a little ass'.

He believed that simply ordering a young person not to do something would be seen by that young person as an exciting challenge. Instead, he offered exciting challenges of a healthier kind—Scouting.

Of course, many of the programs and activities Scouting offers today have been developed considerably and adapted since the early part of this century, but Scouting's purpose has not changed: to help young people, starting with the youngest Scout, to develop their full potential in every aspect of their lives—to strive towards physical, mental and social well-being, in other words, health.

In more concrete terms, health education itself plays an important role in Scouting throughout the world, and in many countries Scouts are involved in all kinds of projects to promote health in their communities. In a number of countries, this includes creating a greater awareness of the dangers of tobacco.

In Egypt, for example, Scouts organise sports competitions, such as football matches, between teams of smokers and non-smokers. The spectators of these football matches are not only Scout groups but very often the entire village, from the very young to the very old, laughing and cheering. An amusing activity, with a clear message. Especially so as it is always the non-smoking teams that win.

For Scouts in Nepal, drug-abuse prevention is part of their Scout program, and they can even earn a badge for their efforts.

Of course, it is one thing to know, and agree, that smoking is bad for your health, and quite another, particularly for young people, to have the courage of their convictions and actually say 'no' when offered a cigarette. 'No' can be one of the most difficult words any of us, even as adults, ever have to pronounce.

I sincerely hope more and more young people will be encouraged to say no to tobacco, and helping young people to say no is one of the aims of the Scouts' anti-drugs campaign.

In fact, everything depends on the art of saying no. To be able to say no calls for a strong character, a fact that the Scouts of America realised when they decided to call their education campaign 'Just Say No'.

Scouting is about education—and for the many adult leaders who are in direct contact with these young people, helping them to grow up, which means truly understanding the young person. Education about the dangers of tobacco must start early in a young person's life. The Scouts' responsibility as an educational movement is evident.

It is for this reason I have accepted on this third World No-Tobacco Day, the Tobacco or Health medal on behalf of the 16 million Scouts worldwide. This medal for us represents not only a reward for the global dedication of the Scouts to health education and community development but an incentive for our continued action enabling young people to grow up without tobacco.

The body — how it works

The human body is a complicated machine. To get fit and keep fit you must understand what goes on inside the body, how the muscles work, why the heart pumps blood to the muscles, what happens to the air in the lungs, and so on.

Let us begin with the *skeleton*, the structure of bones that forms the framework for the human body. The skeleton is composed of hundreds of bones, each of which has a specific task for movement and/or protection of vital organs.

The bones meet in areas called joints. At the joint, muscles are attached to the bones by tendons, making movements possible. When a muscle con-

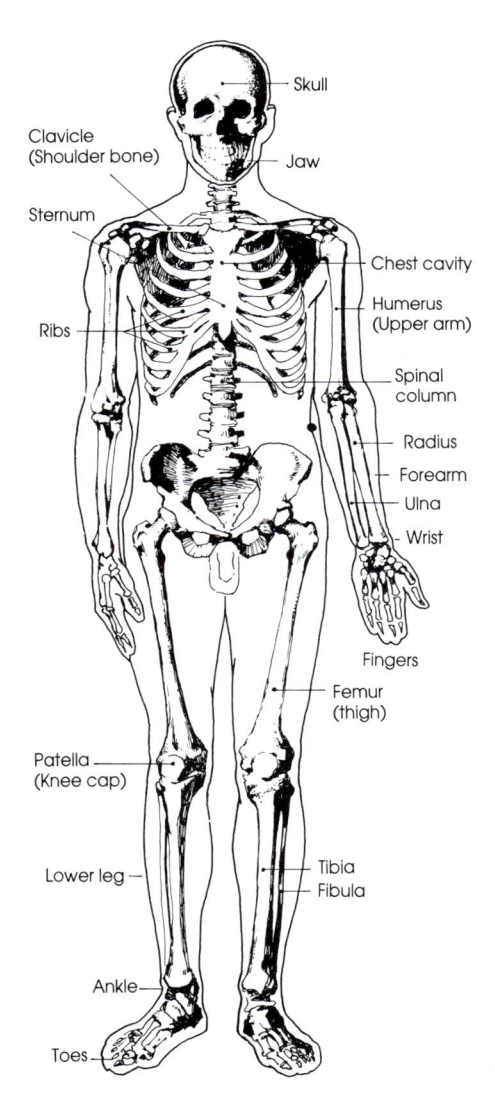

The human skeleton

Citizenship

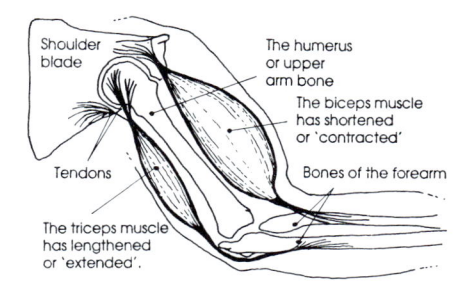

Flexion of the arm

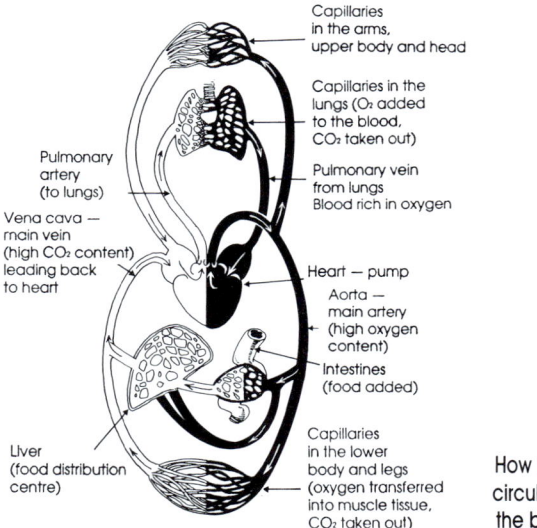

How the blood circulates around the body

tracts or shortens, the bones to which it is attached move together. When a muscle relaxes, it increases in length and allows the bones to extend.

For every muscle that bends a joint there is a muscle that lengthens to let it bend. The muscles work together in pairs: one must relax while the other is doing the work. The muscles are made of small fibres that are pulled together and stretch like elastic. When a muscle becomes stronger, each of these fibres becomes thicker and can contract faster and with more force.

The *brain* and *nervous system* control the working of the muscles. The brain is like a control tower: it receives messages, sorts them out, and signals the decisions to the appropriate muscles. The signals are received and delivered through the spinal cord, the main cable through which the messages flow.

When the muscles receive signals to work, they require an adequate supply of chemicals in order to get into action. The two important chemicals are glucose and oxygen. They are brought to the muscles through the blood vessels.

Blood vessels are part of what is called the circulatory system. The centre of this system is the *heart*, acting like a pump. The heart circulates the blood, pumping it into the lungs to receive oxygen and to pick up glucose, poured into the bloodstream from the liver.

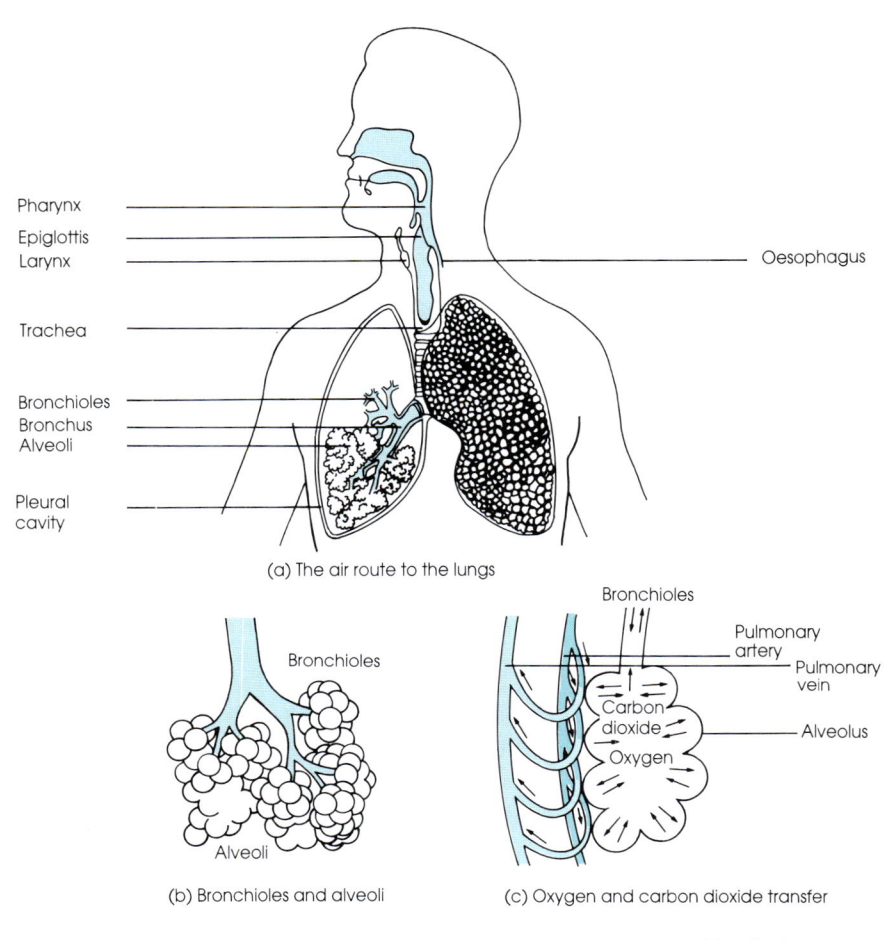

How the lungs work

(a) The air route to the lungs

Labels: Pharynx, Epiglottis, Larynx, Trachea, Bronchioles, Bronchus, Alveoli, Pleural cavity, Oesophagus

(b) Bronchioles and alveoli

Labels: Bronchioles, Alveoli

(c) Oxygen and carbon dioxide transfer

Labels: Bronchioles, Pulmonary artery, Pulmonary vein, Carbon dioxide, Oxygen, Alveolus

---

Oxygen is one of the two main ingredients for the muscles for energy. The source of our oxygen supply is the air we breathe. When we breathe in, muscles expand the ribs, leaving a partial vacuum to drag air into the *lungs*. While the air is in the lungs, part of the oxygen is extracted and carried by the blood to the working muscles.

Glucose, the other ingredient for muscular energy, is sugar derived from various sources but mainly from the food we eat. The food is broken up by the *digestive system* into simple chemicals. The chemicals, including glucose, are absorbed from the intestines into the bloodstream and taken to the liver for storage.

When energy is required for muscular work, glucose is released from the liver and carried by the blood through the arteries to the muscles. There it is broken down in chemical processes with the aid of oxygen. It is like splitting an atom: the chemical processes within the muscle split the glucose and release the energy to be used as fuel.

The value of exercise

Our whole body needs regular exercise. Take the muscles, for example. They have to be used to be kept in shape; lack of use soon leaves them weak. A bus or car trip to school and short physical-education lessons are not enough to work the muscles.

The heart is the most important muscle in our body. Lack of enough exercise is one of the heart's worst enemies. You will soon find it out when a run leaves you winded or when you find it hard to continue while on a hike, climbing a hill.

There are many other signs constantly telling you that the modern person needs exercise to keep fit for life. You cannot function properly for long on the meagre amount you obtain by working or studying. The deficiency must be made up by regular participation in sports, games and physical activities.

By having regular exercise, the body adjusts itself to new tasks and becomes more efficient. It can do more work in a shorter time; that is, it works with greater economy and recovers faster from the work done.

Many changes take place: the heart becomes stronger and pumps more oxygen to the muscles; the muscles become stronger, the joints more mobile, ligaments and tendons tougher. Several other changes take place, all contributing towards well-being, fitness for daily living, and improved sporting ability.

If you want to be truly fit, you will have to improve all the components of physical fitness listed as follows. This probably means exercising much more than you are used to, but do not worry: once you have started, you will enjoy every part of the challenge.

Components of fitness

Every exercise program should aim to improve all aspects of physical fitness. The components that make up the hard core of fitness can be classified as follows:

- endurance or stamina
- strength
- muscular endurance
- muscular power
- mobility.

Endurance is the ability to keep on performing movements such as running, swimming, cycling and walking, for a long time. Endurance, often also called stamina, depends on how well your heart and lungs can deliver oxygen to the working muscles.

When you run, your heart speeds up, blood flows quickly, and lungs work hard. If you are fit and have good stamina, you can keep on for a long time. However, if your endurance is low, you will be gasping for breath soon after you start the exercise.

Strength is the muscles' capacity to exert force when they contract. Strength is determined, among other factors, by the size of the muscles. If you are very strong, the thousands of movements that occur every day become a lot easier and more efficient.

Fieldbook for Australian Scouting

(a) Running develops stamina

(b) Weight training develops strength

Running and weight training

The work a muscle does in one single contraction, such as lifting something heavy, is called pure strength. If the effort is repeated many times, such as when you are chopping wood, the movement depends on *muscular endurance*.

The strength that makes it possible to move your body very fast and suddenly explode into action is called *power*: the ability to use maximum strength in the shortest time possible. The standing long-jump is a good example of power.

As you have noticed, all three variations of strength—pure strength, muscular endurance, and muscular power—are important in work and play. If you are stronger, you can lift heavier weights, throw, kick, jump, run, climb and propel your body weight more efficiently.

Another important factor of fitness is *mobility*. It depends on flexibility, suppleness, balance, and the agility to change direction quickly. Suppleness and flexibility decide the extent of movement in the joints. An agile and

(a) Push-ups develop muscular endurance

(b) Jumping develops power

Push-ups and jumping

Exercises develop mobility

supple person can perform a wide range of movements without strain on muscles and ligaments.

Training

Before you begin your keep-fit campaign, remember the following golden rules.
1. *Train—don't strain.* If you find your training leaves you exhausted the next morning, check your program. Do not be lazy but do not try to become fit in a day or two.
2. *Be dedicated.* You will have to keep at it. Peak physical fitness may take a long time to reach, but once you stop training, your fitness level will drop very rapidly.
3. *Start gradually.* Be patient. Work hard and regularly but do not start by working until you drop exhausted. At the outset, take it easy and allow your body to adapt to the new demands.
4. *Be progressive.* After you have reached basic fitness, set yourself progressively harder tasks. You can improve your fitness only by steadily increasing the amount of training.
5. *Be regular.* Haphazard training has no value and it is always better to work a little every day rather than have long sessions once or twice a week.

Living in a community

REMEMBER: Part of being a good citizen means knowing how to live within a community. No matter how large or small, Australian communities depend on people to help them run and function well. The same can be observed in your Troop, where your members must work together to reach specific goals.

One of the most important things about a community is helping other people and sharing knowledge. Young people are particularly valuable to a community for their contributions as volunteers. A person living within a community also has the responsibility of obeying the laws of Australia and its governments. Laws stand for what a community thinks is right and safe for the people living there. In return for certain advantages from the community, an individual must accept what the majority has decided through the democratic process. Young people can sometimes be subjected to pressure from their friends to do things that entail breaking the law. An individual should use commonsense and be courageous and honest enough to say no to illegal actions.

Although people should obey laws, they have an equal responsibility to try and get bad laws changed. A community can be a democracy only if everyone voices an opinion about the governments and the laws they have made. A true citizen is concerned about others. If a person is not served well by a law because it is not fair, adults should work together to change it. Australians have also been given guarantees against many forms of discriminations. An employer can no longer refuse to hire a person because that applicant is male or female, an ethnic Australian, and so on. Australians also have an unwritten right to economic security and social welfare. This means Australians who are unemployed, disabled or poor are able to get help from the government to see them through hard times. Taxes are collected from citizens, and this revenue pays for unemployment, pensions and welfare.

The Scouting movement is a community, and it provides services to its members. Being a good citizen in it means doing a fair share of the work, being careful of other people's property, and co-operating with Leaders and other members.

The best way to learn citizenship is by doing!

5

CONSTRUCTION

Construction through the ages

Construction is one branch of human activity that has been pursued from prehistoric times when human beings began to adapt their environment to suit their needs. Perhaps by accident or even by experiment, stone-age humans found that sticks and stones could become useful tools, enabling them to perform tasks that could never be attempted using bare hands alone. It is amazing to realise that modern engineering principles involving stress and strain can be recognised in the manufacture of some stone-age tools and weapons. The earliest materials available to humans for construction were earth, stone and timber. By 4500 BC, the practice of moulding mud into bricks had developed to such an extent that large buildings could be erected.

The ancient Egyptians were able to work in stone with both stone and copper tools, and later the Greeks had the benefit of iron as a material for tools. The greatest contribution of the Romans to the art of construction was their development of cement, which enabled them to erect structures many of which have outlived the centuries and continue to stand today.

The discovery and working of iron was a major step in the history of humankind. The Egyptians had used iron for small implements and weapons, whereas the Greeks were able to make iron tools and understood how to make steel.

Mid-seventeenth-century engineers and architects recognised the importance of testing materials in order to determine their strength.

Iron was much used as a construction material during the nineteenth century, and great bridges were erected throughout England. The age of steel was heralded by the introduction of the Bessemer furnace in 1855, and by the turn of the century, the great Forth Bridge made of some 50 000 tons of steel had been completed.

Concrete made from cement was first used as a construction material in the final years of the nineteenth century and provided a method of casting structures to any shape desired. It remains one of the most important construction materials.

Since 1900, engineers have been able to develop a number of versatile materials including alloy steels, high-strength concretes, and plastics, which have revolutionised all forms of construction and construction methods. Naturally, we have not discarded the old methods of building such as brickwork and timber construction, but it is true that the spectacular bridges and buildings of recent times have been achieved only as a result of the modern developments of materials and methods.

The following table shows how construction has proceeded throughout the years.

Table 5.1 History of construction

Date	Materials	Methods of construction
5000	Brickwork	
	Masonry	Mass slave labour
	Timber	Elementary surveying
	Copper	Animal power
0 BC	Bitumen	Water power
	AD Pozzolith cement	Cranes
	Iron	Coffer dams
	Steel	Ropes, pulleys
1000		
		Craft guilds
1500		
	Charcoal iron	Treadmill
1650		
1700		
	Coal smelting of iron	Diving-bell
	Tensile tests of materials	Clay puddling
1750		

Construction

Table 5.1 (*continued*)

	Malleable iron Soil testing Hydraulic cement	
1800		
	First iron rolled sections Portland cement	Tunnelling under compressed-air Steam-powered machines
1850		
	Bessemer steel Reinforced concrete	Hydraulic power tools Steam excavators
1900		
	Welding Aluminium	Internal-combustion machines Tracked vehicles
1920		
1970	Prestressed concrete High-strength steels Epoxy resins Plastics	Precasting Premixed concrete in trucks
	Fibre-reinforced concretes	Prefabrication
2000		

ANCIENT

Babylonian brickmaking

Building the Great Pyramid in Egypt

MODERN

Sydney Harbour Bridge

Sydney Opera House

Ancient and modern building

Most construction projects are undertaken in order to raise the standards of living for communities of people. It is important, therefore, that construction in all its phases, should be aimed at an improvement of people's environment. As our levels of material well-being are rising, it is to be hoped this progress is matched by humankind's moral and spiritual standards.

How strong are materials?

If you observe carefully any building or structure, you will notice it is composed of a number of components or elements. In a house, for example, the weight of the roof cladding and ceiling is carried on a truss made perhaps from timber. This truss, in turn, may be supported on the outside walls, which could be of brick. The floors that carry the loads of furniture and people are carried on beams, which may be supported on the walls or on separate piers.

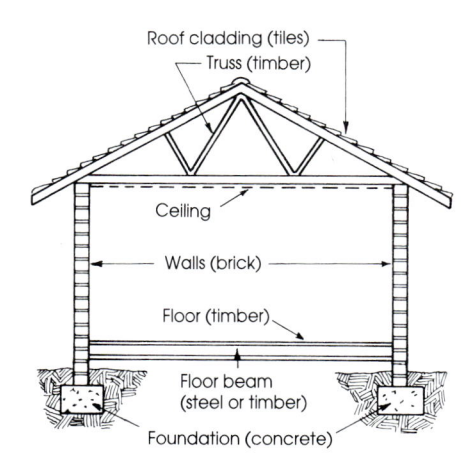

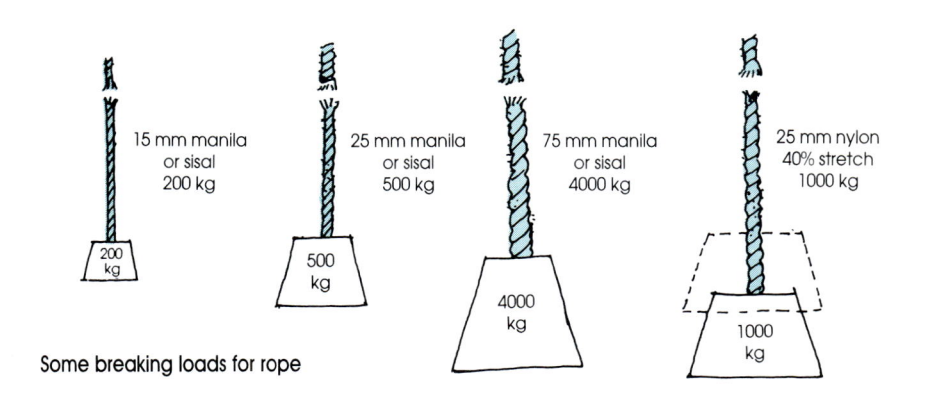

- Roof cladding (tiles)
- Truss (timber)
- Ceiling
- Walls (brick)
- Floor (timber)
- Floor beam (steel or timber)
- Foundation (concrete)

15 mm manila or sisal
200 kg

25 mm manila or sisal
500 kg

75 mm manila or sisal
4000 kg

25 mm nylon 40% stretch
1000 kg

Some breaking loads for rope

Construction

The whole building is built on a foundation, which transmits the loads to the ground. The various elements may therefore be of diffferent materials, and they each act in a different way. It is important to understand how parts of the building carry the loads that arise. It is also necessary to find which materials will be strong enough for these loads.

Whatever the structure, be it a cycle shed or a mighty bridge, safety is paramount so neither life nor property is endangered. On the other hand, a wise choice of materials is essential if the structure is to be built economically.

In this section we will look at ways of getting the best out of various materials. We will also see how the various types of structural elements work, and how we can join them to produce safe structures.

Tension members

We often see examples of simple tension members. When a rope is used to lift a weight, the rope exerts a *pull* on the weight and is said to be in *tension*. Engineers measure forces such as the tension in a rope in units called Newtons (N). A mass of 1 kilogram is attracted to the earth by a gravity force of almost 10 Newtons, so that when you pick up a mass of 1 kilogram, you are exerting a pull of about 10 Newtons.

Scouts use ropes for a variety of purposes, and it is often important to know how much load a rope of a given size can carry. Naturally, this depends on the material in the rope and the way in which it is made. The size of a rope is usually given as its *circumference* rather than its thickness. For sisal or manila ropes, which are often used in Scouting, the load required to break a rope can be found approximately by taking the *square* of the circumference in millimetres and multiplying the result by 7 to give the breaking load in

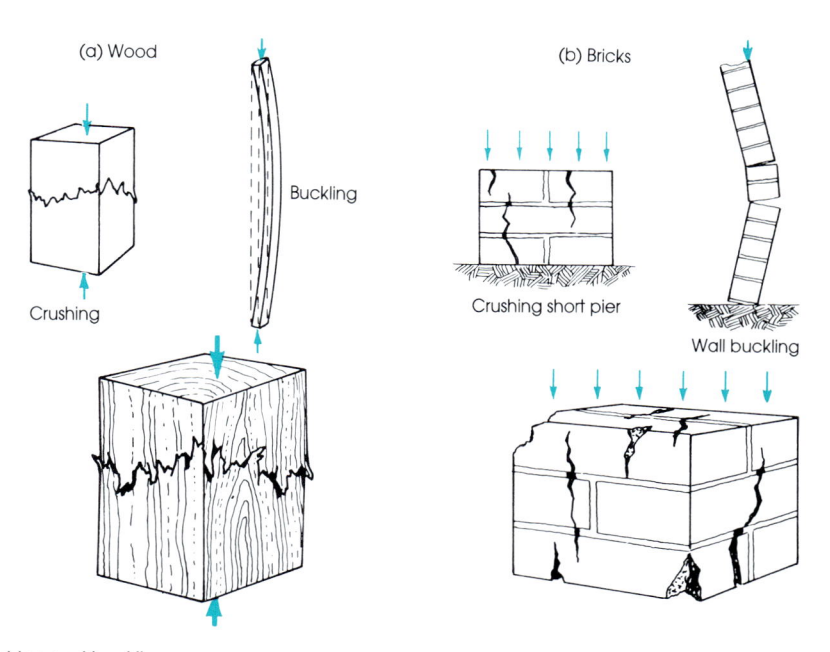

(a) Wood

Crushing

Buckling

(b) Bricks

Crushing short pier

Wall buckling

Crushing and buckling

Newtons. Therefore, a rope having a circumference of 50 millimetres will take a load of about 50 × 50 × 7 = 17 500 Newtons to break it. The modern synthetic ropes now available are somewhat stronger than manila and sisal.

Let us look at the safety aspect. Once we have worked out the breaking load of the rope, the actual load we can put on it must not exceed one-sixth of the breaking load. Ropes become strained with use, and the safe working capacity reduces with age, so we use an adequate factor of safety. In practical terms, a monkey bridge using an 80 mm rope as the foot rail will take a load of about 7500 Newtons if used properly.

This also brings us to the problem of joining and knotting. *Any knot weakens a rope!* The loss of strength of a well-made splice may be 20%. A hitch causes a loss of about 25% and a reef knot 50%, so watch the safety margin!

Other materials that are not flexible like rope may be used as tension members. Their strength is usually given in terms of the breaking *stress*, which is the force required to break each square millimetre of the material. For timber, the breaking stress varies from about 35 Newtons per square millimetre for softwood, such as oregon, to about 70 Newtons per square millimetre for hardwood, such as Australian oak.

The figure for steel varies from about 400 Newtons per square millimetre for mild steel to about 1700 Newtons per square millimetre for high-strength steel. The huge cables that support suspension bridges are made from the latter material. In the Golden Gate Bridge spanning 1280 metres over San Francisco Bay, the cables are 920 millimetres across and carry a tension of about 300 million Newtons at a stress of 600 Newtons per square millimetre.

Compression members

Compression members, or columns, act in the opposite sense to tension members; that is, they are *compressed* under load. The strength of these members is related to their *slenderness*. Therefore, a short stocky piece of softwood may take a breaking or crushing stress of 35 Newtons per square millimetre before it fails, but a long slender piece will *buckle* sideways at only a small load. This is the reason why we have to *brace* the uprights in our towers to avoid buckling.

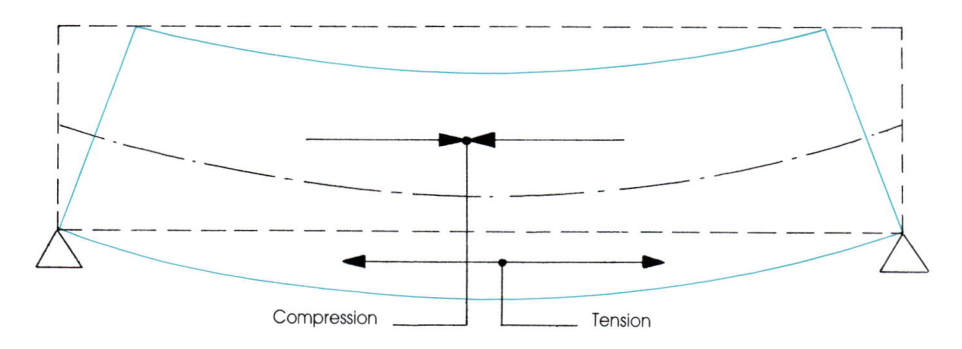

Compression and tension

Similarly, a small brick pier may have a strength of about 15 Newtons per square millimetre before it crushes, but the strength of a slender wall may be only a very small proportion of this value, depending on its height and thickness, because it suddenly buckles outwards on failing.

Beams

Beams carry loads by bending. When we bend a beam, the top fibres tend to shorten (or compress), and the bottom fibres stretch (or extend) along the length of the beam.

We therefore have a combined compression–tension action, and the beam breaks when either the compression strength or the tension strength of the material is exceeded. The bending of a beam is influenced by the way we place the load on the beam. For example, if the load can be placed uniformly along the length, the stresses in the beam and the sag are smaller than if the same load is concentrated in the middle.

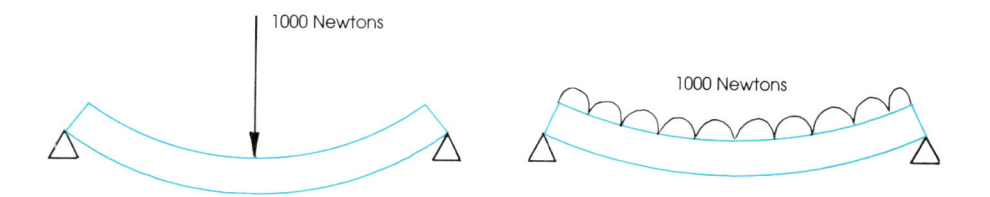

Concrete and bricks

Concrete is extremely useful in all forms of building. It is a mixture of cement, sand, gravel and water, and the proportions used vary according to whether a mighty dam, a concrete driveway or a foundation is to be poured. A standard mix for most household projects would be a 1:2:3 mix, which means 1 part cement, 2 parts sand, and 3 parts clean gravel, all measured by volume. An exact amount of water cannot be specified because the other materials, especially the sand, contain some water themselves. The dry ingredients are first mixed thoroughly together in the correct proportions with a shovel. The mixture is then made into a pile and a crater formed in the centre. A little water is added in the crater and mixed in thoroughly with dry ingredients.

Too much water dilutes the cement paste holding the gravel together and weakens the concrete, so avoid runny mixes. A good mixture will not be too stiff, but will 'plop' off your shovel. Whenever you are using concrete, whether it is for paving stones or for a wall foundation, it must be 'cured' properly once it has started to harden. Curing is essential in order to prevent the concrete from drying out too quickly. You do this by covering the concrete with wet bags, or even wet sand, and keeping it wet for at least a week. Lack of curing may cause the concrete to crack.

Remember, too, that good concrete work requires good forms or moulds that do not bulge when the wet concrete is placed and compacted. If you intend to use the forms many times, say, for bricks or paving slabs, you will have to oil the surfaces so the concrete will not stick to them.

Bricklaying made easy

A Scout can easily build a small brick fence or wall if he follows a few simple rules. Start by laying a level concrete footing slightly larger than the width of the wall, and about 150 millimetres deep. If the wall is more than about 4 metres long, reinforce the footing with a couple of 10 mm-diameter steel rods. Calculate the number of bricks required by laying the first course dry as shown in the illustration. Try to avoid cutting bricks, but if necessary, a cut brick can be placed in the centre of the wall.

Stretch a string along the top of one end brick to the other. Mortar for the wall is mixed from 1 part cement, 2 parts lime, and 9 parts clean sand, with enough water for a plastic, workable mix. Lay a bed of mortar, and bed the bricks in each course by tapping them into the mortar with a trowel, working from each end. The joint thickness should be 10 millimetres, and this can be achieved by building the ends of the wall first with the correct joint sizes, and stretching a string between the ends to keep the joints even along the length. Use a level to ensure the edges of the wall are perpendicular. Keep the bricks free from surplus mortar, and iron out the joints when the mortar is partly set. Brick piers should be added at each end for strength and appearance. A long wall can also be strengthened by building in additional piers which should be about 2 metres apart.

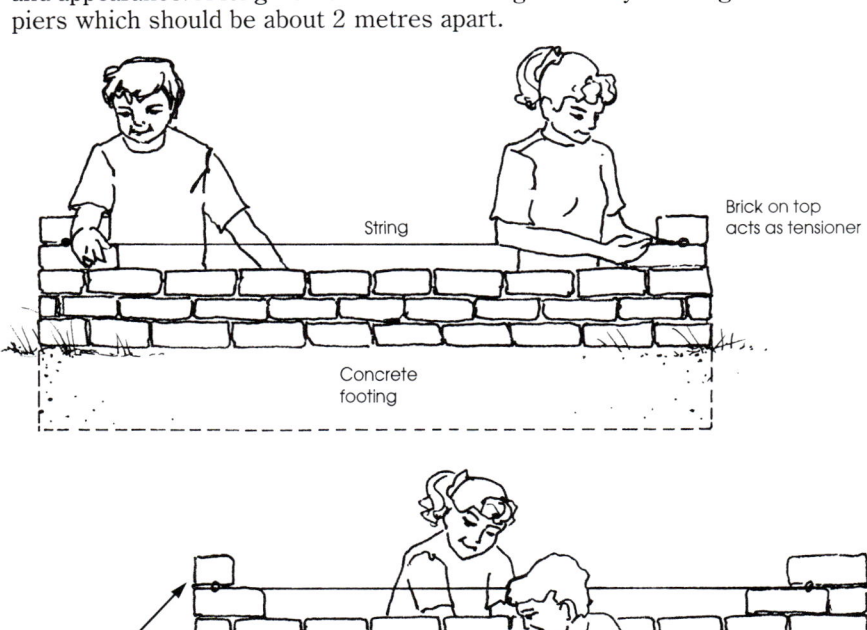

Bricklaying

Joining materials

You may have heard of the old saying, 'a chain is only as strong as its weakest link.' In a structure, all the elements have to be joined together, and the completed structure will be strong only if the joints themselves are strong.

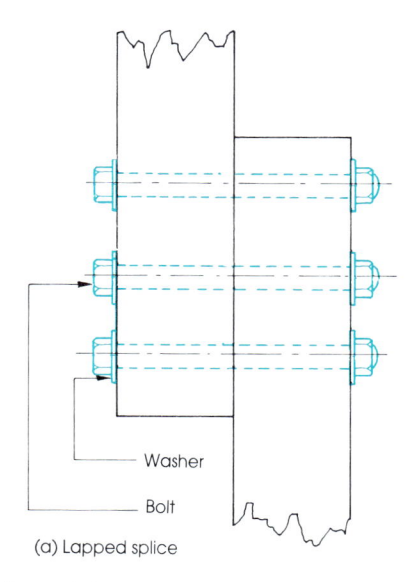

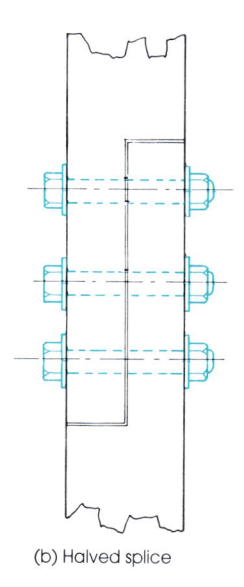

(a) Lapped splice

(b) Halved splice

Joining materials

Permanent and temporary joints

Two main types are used in construction: permanent joints and temporary joints. Each type must be designed for the particular material involved. For example, in steel structures, permanent joints may be made by welding. In this process, the steel members are fused together under intense heat, which is usually applied by either an electric arc or special gas torches. For many years, carpenters have been making permanent joints in timber construction by glueing. Large buildings, and even aeroplanes, have been made by this method, but special glues and techniques are necessary in these cases to ensure safety is adequate.

The Scout will often be required to make temporary joints in structures. In timber, bolts may be used to obtain strong joints. For most pioneering-style projects, the bolts should not be smaller than 10 millimetres in diameter, and washers must be fitted on each end. The two lengths of timber to be connected must be held together temporarily for drilling. Stronger joints are usually obtained by preventing the members from bending the bolts, so a halved splice between two timbers is often more satisfactory than a lapped splice.

: Fieldbook for Australian Scouting

Rope

What is rope?

Ropes have been found in Egyptian tombs dating from 3000 BC, so we know that people have used rope for at least 5000 years. The Egyptian ropes were made from the fibres of flax (*fibres* are the threadlike cells that form tissues or textile substances; *flax* is a plant with blue flowers that is grown for its seeds—linseed—and for the fibres obtained from its stem from which linen is made), from bullrushes and from camel hair. Ropes have also been made from animal skin and jungle creepers. Today, rope is made from materials as different as steel wire and nylon.

The ropes you will be using will probably be made from either vegetable fibres or long-chain synthetic polymeric amines of which the structural units or molecules can be oriented in one direction (that is, nylon!).

The natural-fibre ropes will be either 'hard' or 'soft'.

Hard   For example, manila, sisal and coir

- *Manila* is the name of a city in the Philippine Islands and of the material obtained from the leaves of *Musa Textillis*, a tree native to these islands.
- *Sisal* is a strong, durable white fibre of a plant that looks something like a spiky cactus, which grows in tropical regions.
- *Coir* is the prepared fibre of coconut husks.

Soft   For example, flax, hemp and cotton

- *Flax* has been mentioned previously. It is grown extensively in Ireland and to a lesser extent in England, Scotland and Wales.
- *Hemp* is an annual herbaceous plant native to west and central Asia.
- *Cotton* is the white, downy, fibrous substance that covers the seeds of the cotton plant.

How is rope made?

Yarns   A rope manufacturer starts with the fibre, which he spins into yarns. The twist is in a clockwise (right-handed) direction. Examples of yarns are cotton in your repair kit and thread.

Strands   When several yarns are twisted together in an anticlockwise (left-handed) direction, a 'strand' is made.

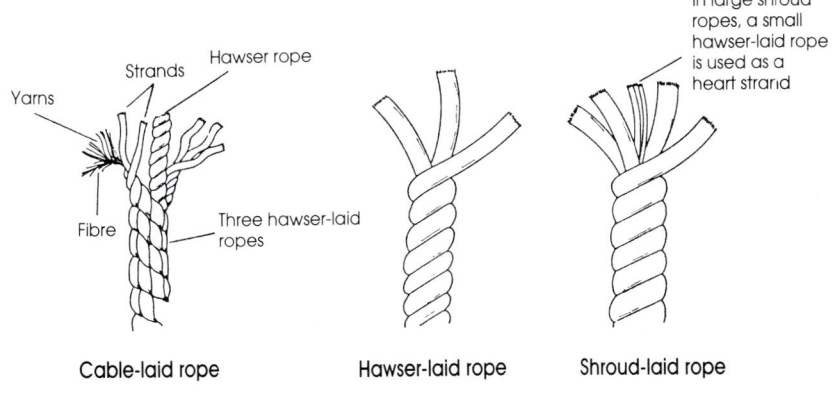

Cable-laid rope — Yarns, Fibre, Strands, Hawser rope, Three hawser-laid ropes

Hawser-laid rope

Shroud-laid rope — In large shroud ropes, a small hawser-laid rope is used as a heart strand

Hawser-, shroud- and cable-laid ropes Twist three strands together in a clockwise direction and you have a hawser-laid rope; four strands twisted together are called shroud-laid, and three hawser-laid ropes twisted together are called a cable rope! Of course, these are only the main types of rope ... there are numerous other varieties.

Synthetic rope As has been mentioned, nylon, like other synthetics, neither grows on nor is derived from, trees or plants; it is manufactured. Synthetic rope has the following advantages.

- It is twice as strong as ordinary hemp rope.
- It is 'elastic' (this is important for climbers in particular, because it helps to lessen the shock following a sudden fall).
- It is lighter than hemp.
- It is easier to handle.
- It does not rot (although some ropes do deteriorate at very high temperatures, which can be caused by excessive friction).

Rope making

Why not make your own? Following are a few things you have to keep in mind when making rope.

1. The finished rope will be only two-thirds as long as the strands you use.
2. As you wind the handle, keeping the blade parallel to the floor, take care to use the wrench in order to prevent the strands from tangling.
3. When the strands start to take shape, the weight box will begin to move on its own. Let it; if you try to stop it you will lock the swivel, which has to spin.
4. As raw material for your rope, you can use binder twine or ordinary counter string available at any wholesalers. Avoid synthetic fibre, because it sets up static electricity and makes the process very difficult.

Rope-making machine

To make your rope

1. Place the weight box (b) at one end of a smooth uncarpeted floor or on the ground. Place books or a 4 kg bag in the box.
2. At some distance away, set up the machine (a), lining up the hooks (f) with the swivel (e) on the weight box.
3. Work the handles of the hooks through the three holes in the winding handle (c).
4. Make a small loop in the end of a ball of counter string, or one-ply sisal binder twine and thread it on to the swivel.
5. Stretch three double strands to each of the hooks, keeping the tension even. You may have to have someone hold the machine still.
6. When all three hooks have six pieces of string on them, start to wind the handle, keeping the blade parallel to the floor and always turning in the same direction.
7. When the strands begin to wind together, use the wrench to pack the turns evenly. You may have to slow your winding.

Fieldbook for Australian Scouting

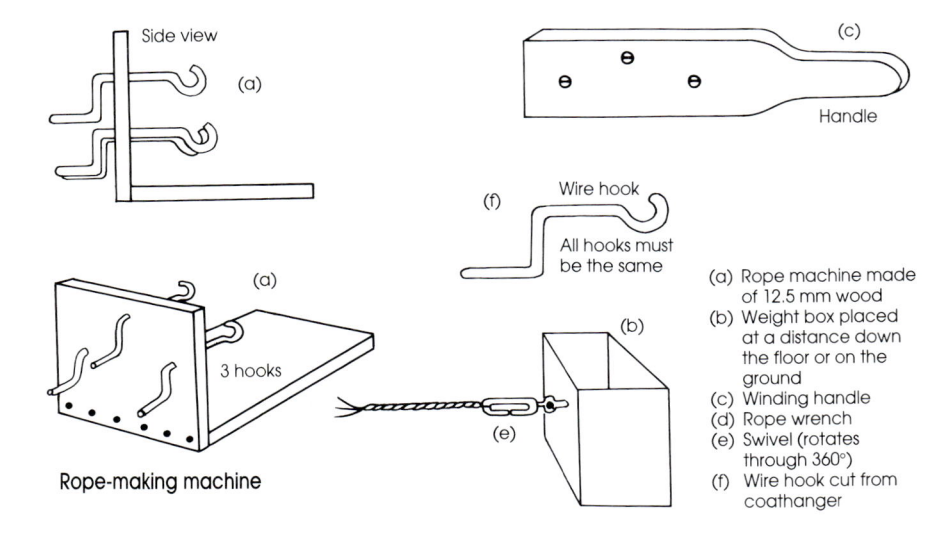

Rope-making machine

(a) Rope machine made of 12.5 mm wood
(b) Weight box placed at a distance down the floor or on the ground
(c) Winding handle
(d) Rope wrench
(e) Swivel (rotates through 360°)
(f) Wire hook cut from coathanger

8. When the rope is almost complete, take out the wrench and turn the handle very slowy to ensure the strands do not form knots.
9. Using a length of the string, whip the ends of the rope very tightly before cutting the rope from the machine with a sharp knife. Snap the rope to even out the turns. If you wish, dip the rope ends in varnish to seal the whipping.

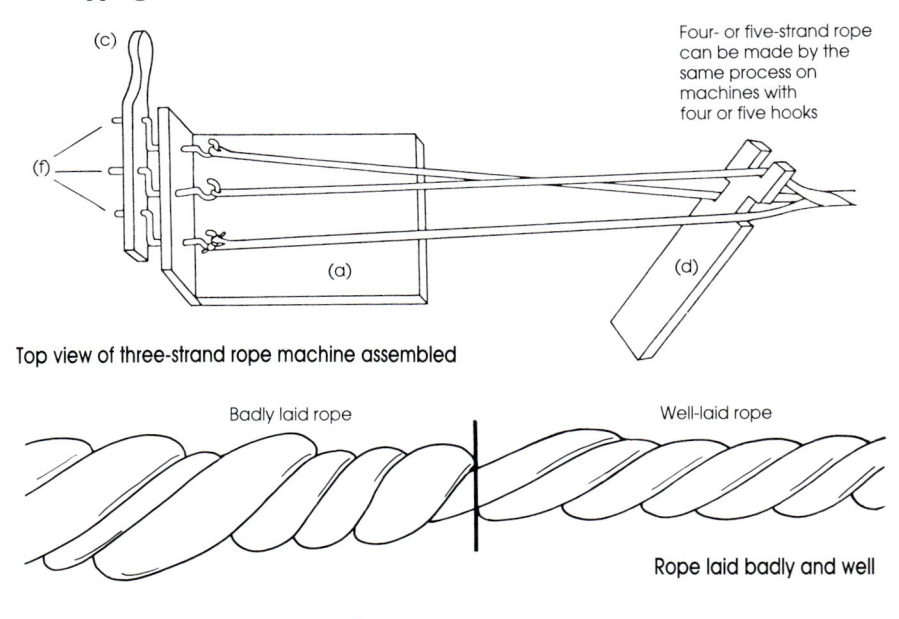

Four- or five-strand rope can be made by the same process on machines with four or five hooks

Top view of three-strand rope machine assembled

Rope laid badly and well

How is rope measured?

Rope can be measured by either its circumference or its diameter. You want to be quite sure which method you are using, otherwise you might not get what you bargained for!

Care of rope

A Scout is thrifty, so you should learn how to look after rope. There is nothing wrong with rope being worn out through use, but unfortunately most rope is lost, destroyed or damaged so much it has to be discarded long before it has reached the end of its expected life span. Following are some rules for caring for ropes.

- *Do not walk on rope*. This grinds dirt and grit into the rope, cutting the fibres.
- *Do not drag rope along the ground*. This is often more severe than walking on it, damaging the fibres with dirt and grit more rapidly.
- *Do not coil or store wet rope*. Rope requires complete drying before putting away. Natural-fibre ropes will rot if left wet.
- *Do not leave knots in rope*. All knots in rope weaken it, some more than others. Leaving knots in rope creates kinks, which permanently weakens the rope.
- *Do not allow rope to chafe over rock*. It should be obvious that allowing a rope to chafe on a rock will wear the rope, but some fools do it. Place sacking, canvas or similar protection between the rope and the rock.

Coiling rope

- *Coil* ropes clockwise with the lay of the rope. Coils should be at least 0.5 metre in diameter and wider for larger ropes. Secure with a strop for hanging.
- *Hang* the coils; do not leave them on the ground. Hanging will enable air to circulate round the rope.
- *Hank* coil rope over left-hand small coils, depending on size of rope. When near the end of coiling, take a turn around the hank, then a half hitch, pulling it tight. The hank should be compact, not floppy.

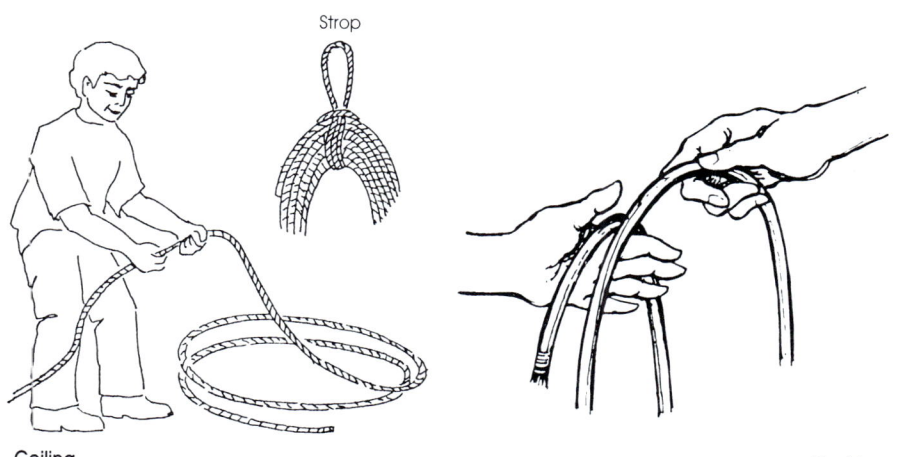

Strop

Coiling

Hanking

Knotting

A knowledge of knots is useful if not essential for a range of Scouting activities such as camping, boating, rock climbing, abseiling and caving.

It is important to realise that two categories of rope are available: natural and synthetic. Natural-fibre ropes include the traditional sisal and manila used for camping and construction. The newer synthetic-fibre ropes are used for rock-craft activities such as climbing, and, these days, often also for yachting. The two categories require different knots, and it is important that the correct knots are used on the appropriate rope.

In order to be a successful knot tier, you have to know the correct *use* for the knots and the category of rope for which the knot is designed. It is more important to know the use of a knot than to remember its name.

By tying the correct knot for the specified use, you are sure it will hold for your purpose and that you can untie it when you have finished. Tying an incorrect knot means you run the risk it will slip as soon as you put any strain on it or it will jamb so badly you will be unable to untie it.

Terms

Before learning knots, it is useful to know a few terms, listed as follows:

standing part   the main part of a rope, irrespective of length other than the ends

standing end   the end of a rope that is made fast to any object

running end   the end opposite to the standing end

a bight   a loop formed in the standing part or at the running end—no definite size. Part of the rope used double when the ends are not available

to bend   to join or make fast two ropes with a definite and recognised knot

hitch   knots used to attach a rope to a spar or similar object

round turn   one complete turn taken with a rope around a spar or picket

riding turn   as in a round turn, but the turn or bight is allowed to rest over the first part of the turn and jamb on it, thereby giving greater holding power temporarily

half hitch   a single turn taken around a spar or object so the weight jambs the running end. The half hitch is the essential locking feature in many hitches and bends

whipping   securing the ends of a rope with fine twine in order to prevent it from fraying or unlaying

frapping turns   two or more turns taken over or around the returns of any lashing, and so on, to hold them together securely

returns   the rope passing from one object to another; for example, the spars in a lashing

Technically speaking, a *bend* joins two ropes, a *hitch* makes fast a rope to something else, and a *knot* is an interweaving of one rope only. There are

Construction

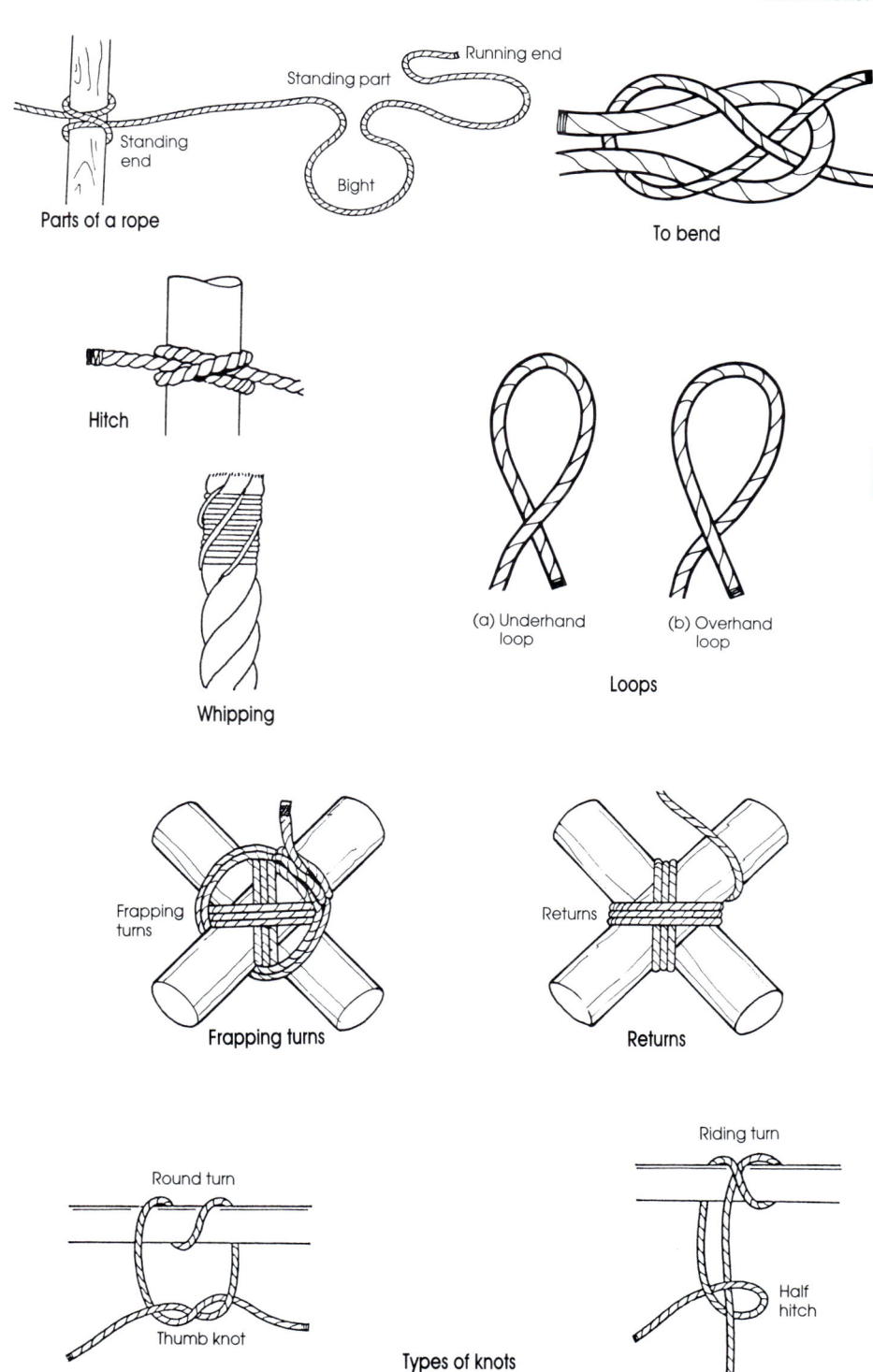

Parts of a rope
- Standing end
- Standing part
- Bight
- Running end

To bend

Hitch

Whipping

Loops
(a) Underhand loop
(b) Overhand loop

Frapping turns

Returns

Types of knots
- Round turn
- Thumb knot
- Riding turn
- Half hitch

217

exceptions, however: the *fisherman's knot* is a bend, and the *fisherman's bend* is a hitch, to name two that do not comply with the rules.

Bends

Sheet bend (single and double)

This is used to join two natural-fibre ropes of equal or unequal thickness. If one of the ropes is thicker than the other, the initial bight is made in the thicker rope. This bend can also be used to join a rope to a loop, in which case the initial bight is already made. It gets its name from the rope attached to the corner of a sail; this rope is called the *sheet*. The *double* sheet bend is the strongest knot for joining natural-fibre ropes, and is used when there is a great amount of movement on the ropes or when they are wet (*see* next subheading).

- *To tie the knot:* Form a bight on the heavier end of the rope and hold this in your left hand. Pass the end of the thinner rope up through the bight from below.

   Bring the end of the thinner rope over, around and under the bight, then slip it under its own standing part where this enters the bight, then up over the bight (note that both rope ends are on the same side.)

   Hold the bight with one hand, and tighten the sheetbend by pulling on the other rope's standing part.

Double sheet bend

- *To tie the double sheet bend:* Complete a *single* sheet bend as described (but do not tighten). Then take the running end of the thinner rope around the bight again and under its standing part, working towards the end of the bight and not riding on itself. Tighten as for the single sheet bend.

Heaving line bend

This is used for joining a light line to a heavy rope (for example, attaching a throwing line to a heavy hawser rope in order to take it across a gap) when there is a great difference in thickness.

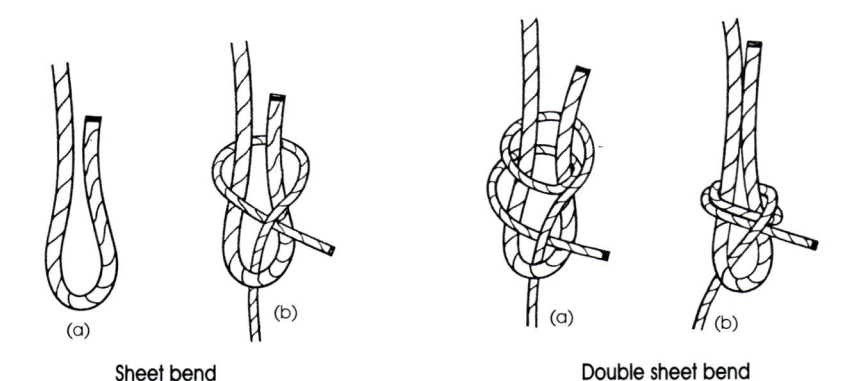

Sheet bend

Double sheet bend

To tie the knot: Form a bight in the heavy rope; take the end of the light rope through the bight over the side of the bight, then back up through the bight, then over the other side of the bight, as in a figure-of-eight pattern. Continue to do this (at least six times) until the running end of the thick rope is parallel to its standing part. Finish with a half hitch round both parts of the thick rope.

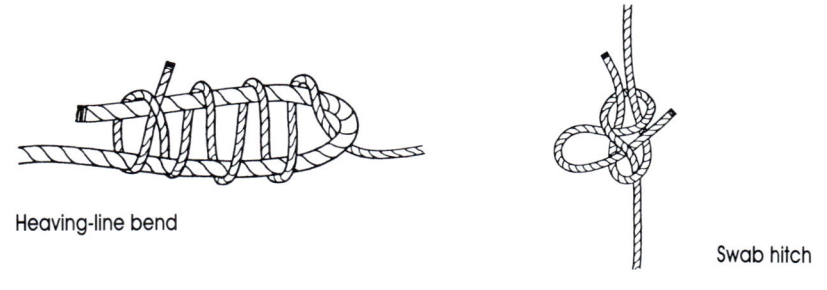

Heaving-line bend

Swab hitch

Swab hitch

This is used for joining two ropes securely together when a quick release is required.

- *To tie the knot:* Commence as for a single sheet bend, but instead of placing the running end of the thinner rope under itself, use a bight of the rope.

Hunter's bend

This is for use with slippery cord or light rope. It is easy to tie, and when made, is completely stable and will not distort under strain; it can also be readily untied. Its only fault, perhaps, is that it is somewhat bulky and takes about twice as long to tie as, say, the sheet bend. With its multiple locking points, it should prove an excellent bend for nylon ropes, in which case extra turns are always advisable due to the slippery nature of the surface.

- *To tie the knot:* Lay the two ends together with the ends opposed (a), and take a turn in the dual ropes (b). Next, pass each end through the turn in opposite directions, as shown by the arrows in diagram (b) in order to give you the position shown in (c). Carefully work up tight to produce the finished knot. Diagrams (d) and (e) show the two faces of the completed knot.

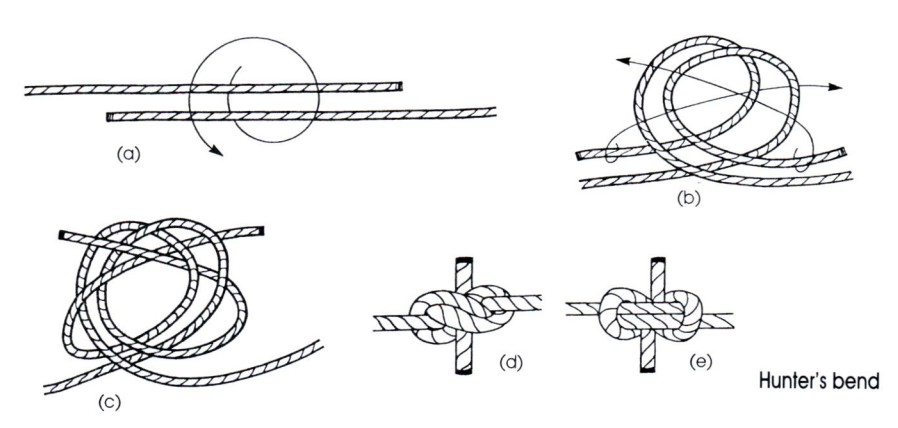

Hunter's bend

Rolling hitch completed

Rolling hitch

(a) load
(b)
(c)
(d)

(a) (b) (c) (d)

Rolling hitch on a guy

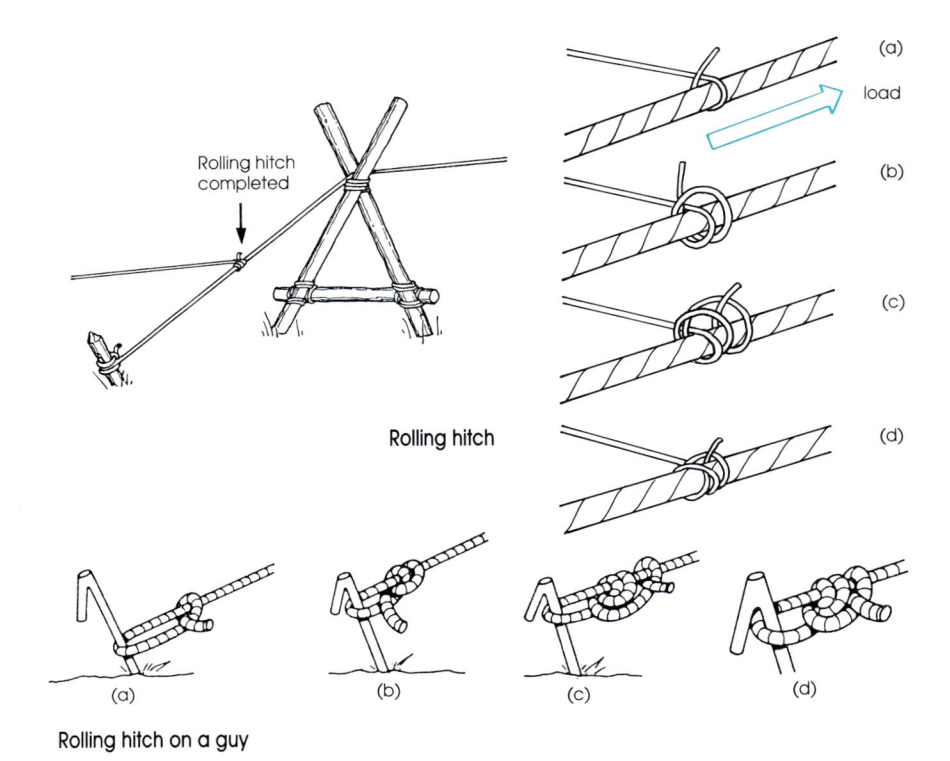

Rolling hitch

This is used in order to make fast a rope to another rope that is under tension; for example, to relieve the strain on a laden rope while adjustments are made to it.

Because of this property, the rolling hitch can be used to make fast a rope to an anchorage when the load is not great and the knot requires frequent adjustment, as in tent guys, and so on. If the guy is not at right angles to the picket, put a round turn around the picket.

- *To tie the knot:* Place a riding turn over the rope in tension (as in the diagram), and take your rope back up between your riding turn and the standing part. Finish by taking the running end over the knot tied, and complete with a half hitch on the load side.

If used on very light lines as on hike tents, use the bight of the light line to tie the final half hitch. This will convert the knot into a slip rolling hitch and is easy to untie if the light line is wet.

Bowline bend

This is for joining two heavy hawser ropes together, and is one of the strongest methods of joining heavy ropes.

- *To tie:* Form a bowline in one rope, then take the running end of the other rope through the loop formed, then tie a bowline in the second rope to form interlocking bowlines.

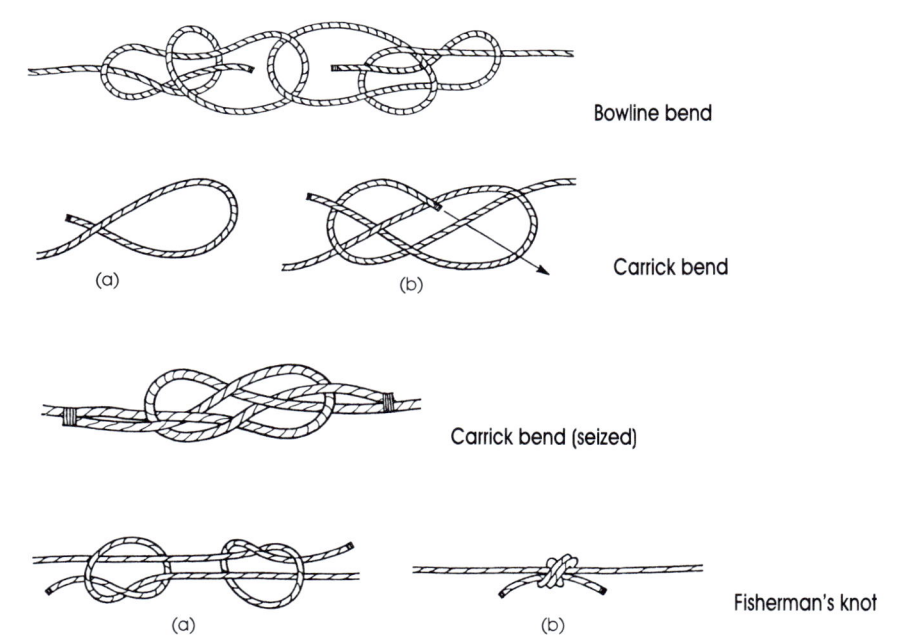

Construction

Bowline bend

Carrick bend

(a)   (b)

Carrick bend (seized)

(a)   (b)   Fisherman's knot

Carrick bend

This is for joining two heavy ropes together when there is a need for a flat flexible knot to run around an object (for example, mooring ropes running around a bollard).

- *To tie:* Lay one rope down, and form a loop with the running end and standing part on the same side. Then lay the standing part of the second rope on the same side of the loop as the first running end. Run the second running end over the standing part, then under the running end of the first rope. Take the running end over one side of the loop under its own standing part, then over the opposite side of the loop. Running ends should end on opposite sides.

The running ends are usually seized to their standing parts in order to finish the knot. If tightened by pulling on the standing parts, this knot will become one that will hold under tension but that will not jamb.

Fisherman's knot

This is used for joining synthetic ropes. The *double* fisherman's knot is the bend most commonly used to join ropes when you are rock climbing, abseiling and caving.

- *To tie:* Overlap running ends in opposite directions. Tie an overhand, with each running end incorporating the other standing part, and the running end to run parallel with the standing part.

To tighten the pull on the standing part, the overhand knots should lock into one another.

221

Blood knot

This is another bend for synthetic ropes or fishing line, and there are a number of variations.

- *To tie the basic blood knot:* Overlap the ends to be joined, then, from the centre of the overlap, twist the running ends around the standing part of the other rope. Then take the running ends through the centre of the overlap in opposite directions, and pull the standing parts in order to tighten the knot.

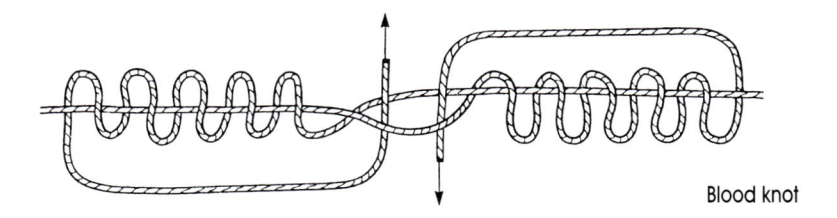

Blood knot

Knots

Overhand or thumb knot

This is a simple knot on the end of a rope in order to temporarily prevent fraying or unlaying or to stop the end of the rope from passing through a small eye or a block. It is also tied with two ends as part of other knots such as a reef knot.

- *To tie the knot:* Take the running end over the standing part and then through the loop formed.

Multi-overhand knot

This is a simple knot in order to form a light weight in the end of a rope or as a decorative knot.

- *To tie:* Start as for an overhand knot, and continue to take the running end through the loop formed; double fold, triple fold, and so on. Then ease the turns together and tighten.

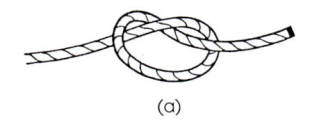

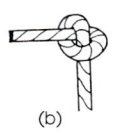

(a)   (b)   Overhand or thumb knot

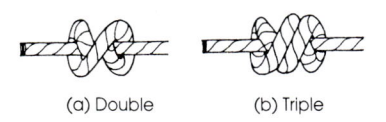

(a) Double   (b) Triple   Multi-overhand knot

Construction

Figure of eight   Figure of eight (upset)

Figure-of-eight loop knot or Flemish eye knot

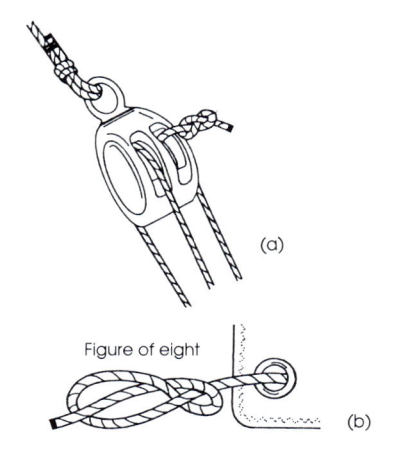

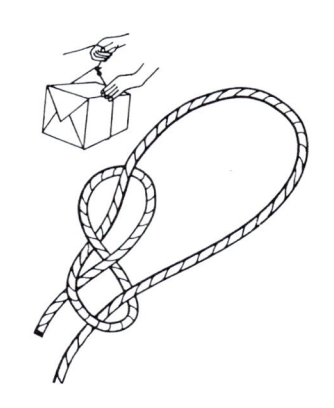

(a)

Figure of eight
(b)

Figure of eight

Packer's tie

Figure-of-eight knot

This is a knot tied in the end of a rope in order to give a larger, flat stopper knot to prevent a fall running through a pulley or block.

- *To tie:* Take the running end over the standing part, and give the loop formed a half twist before bringing the running end through the loop.

This has to be tightened by running your hand along the standing part towards the end, pushing the knot tight.

Figure-of-eight loop knot or Flemish eye knot

This is used when a small, quick eye is required in the end of the rope. It will jamb under strain.

- *To tie:* Take a long bight in the end of the rope, and tie as a figure-of-eight knot.

Packer's tie knot

This is used when you are tying up packages, and so on, when tightening will jamb the knot in order to prevent untying.

- *To tie:* Take a loop around the standing part, and continue to form the loop into the figure-of-eight knot. You should have a long running end. Pull on the other running end to tighten the figure of eight. When tight, lock with a half hitch.

Reef knot

This is used in order to join two ends of a light rope or other material, such as twine, in whipping, and in first aid for bandages and slings. It is a flat knot that can be tied so the standing part is tight. It is important that the knot must have something behind it, because a reef knot in mid-air may slip. This knot is easily untied when required.

It gets its name from the reef points of a sail—the lines used in order to tie up the bundle of sail to the boom when you are shortening sail.

- *To tie the knot:* Take one end over and under the other end, and pull both ends as tight as required. Take one end to run parallel to its standing part, and take the other end over and through the loop formed. Then pull both ends tight.

Note that the running ends must be on the same side of the knot, parallel to their own standing parts.

Slip reef knot

This is used when you require a quick-release knot, for example, for tent brailings.
- *To tie the knot:* Tie the first part as for a reef knot, but at the end, take a bight, instead of the running end, through the loop formed.

Double slip reef knot, or reef bow knot

This is used when a double slip knot is required, for example, for shoelaces.
- *To tie the knot:* Tie the first part as for a reef knot, then use a bight on each end, and complete as for the reef knot.

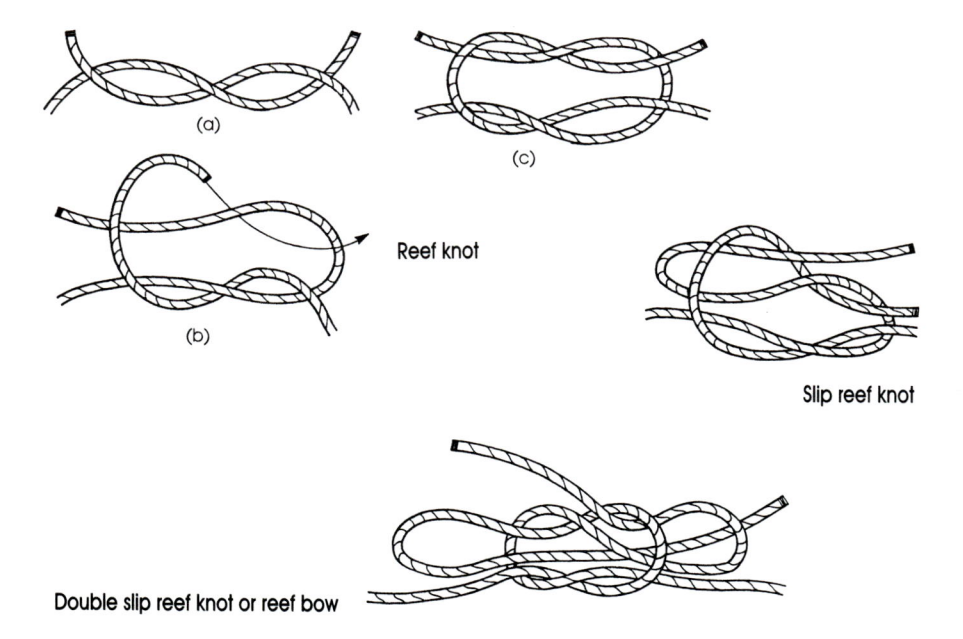

(a)

(c)

(b)

Reef knot

Slip reef knot

Double slip reef knot or reef bow

Construction

Surgeon's knot

Surgeon's knot

This is used for joining the two ends of a light line tightly around an object when the line is wet or slippery.

- *To tie:* Start as for a reef knot, and take an extra turn in the first part of the knot; this extra friction on the rope will help hold the tautness in the knot. Complete as for the reef knot.

By using the single and double bights as used in the slip reef and double slip reef, you can tie a slip surgeon and double slip surgeon knot.

Bowline knot (single)

This is the best knot for making a non-slip loop in the end of a natural-fibre rope.

The name comes from the use of a line from the bow of a boat in order to take a loop around a bollard, and so on; this line was called a *bow line*.

- *To tie the knot:* It can be made with the loop towards you as illustrated. First place the running end over the standing part, and hold with the right hand (a). Turn the right hand over. Lift the part in the left hand (labelled X in diagram (a)) and place on Y. Then, with the left hand, hold the two parts of the rope shown as XY in diagram (b).

With the right hand, take the running end on the course shown by the arrows. Do not let go with the left hand.

Diagram (c) shows how the knot is pulled tight. Gather the three ropes of the main loop in the last three fingers of the left hand while releasing the thumb and forefinger at 'XY', then pull the standing end with the right hand.

The bowline can also be made away from you (for example, around something else).

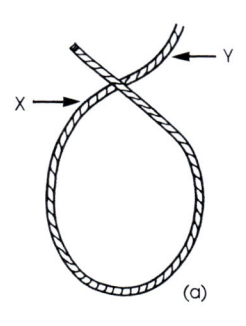

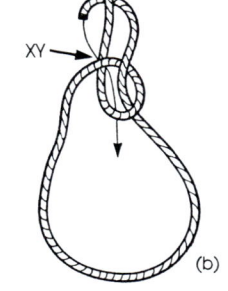

Single bowline

225

Bowline around an object

Sailor's bowline   Cowboy's bowline

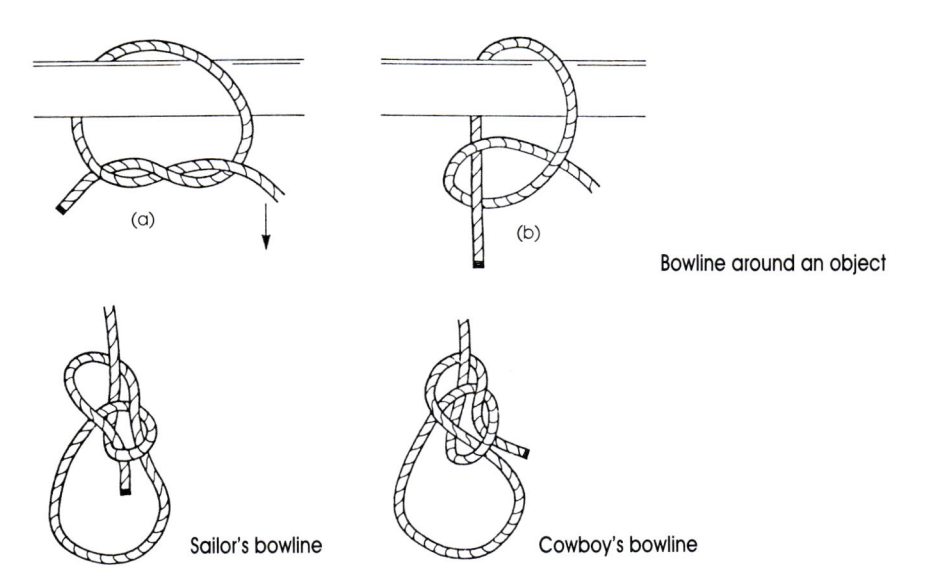

Make an overhand or thumb knot as in diagram (a). Hold one end in each hand, then pull the running end sharply towards you.

This will convert the overhand knot into that shown in diagram (b).

Now, can you complete the bowline?

The *sailor's bowline* has the running end inside the loop; the *cowboy's bowline* has the running end on the outside, and is not as secure.

Bowline on the bight

This is used when two loops are required in the rope. It is used in natural-fibre ropes.

- *To tie the knot:* Double the rope to form a long bight. Proceed to tie a bowline with the doubled rope until you reach diagram (b) as for the single bowline, then take the bight towards you and pass it down and up the back of the knot (do not let go the XY point), then tighten as before.

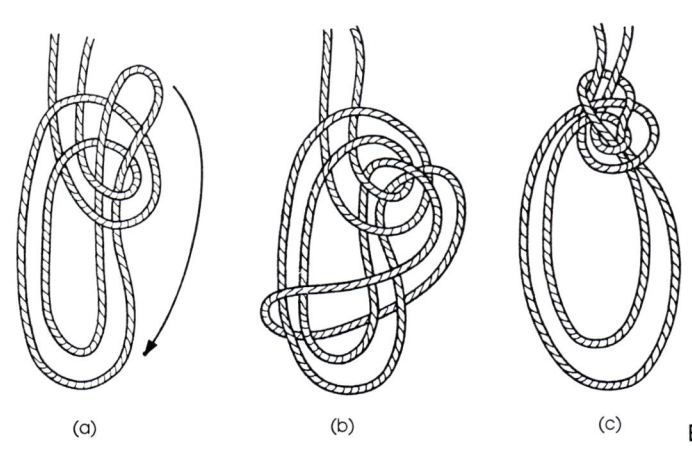

Bowline on the bight

Construction

Water bowline

Triple bowline

(a)

(b)

(c)

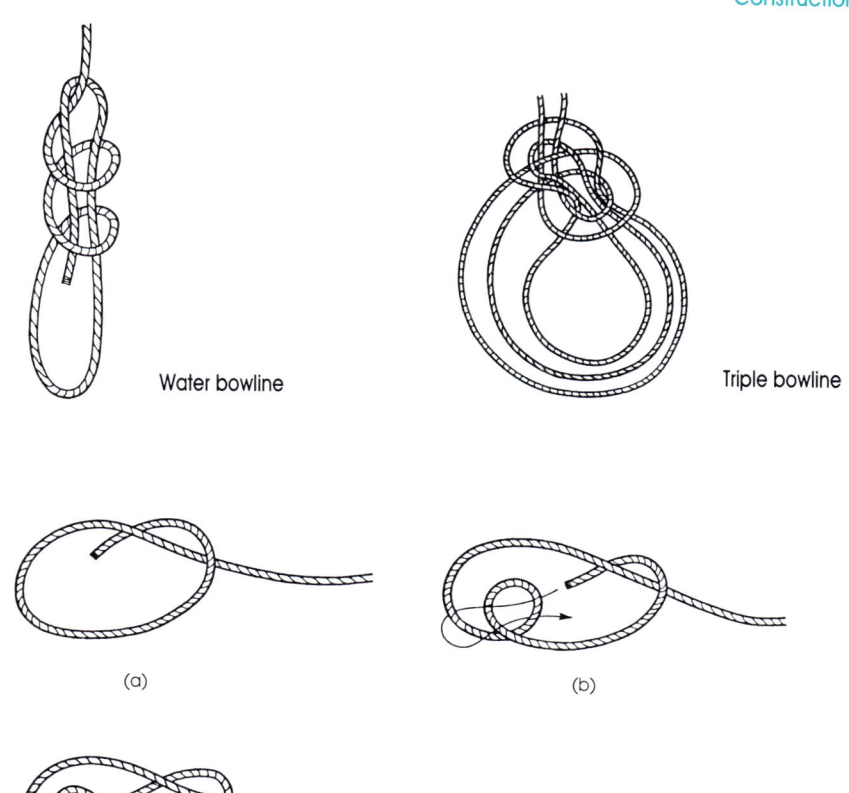

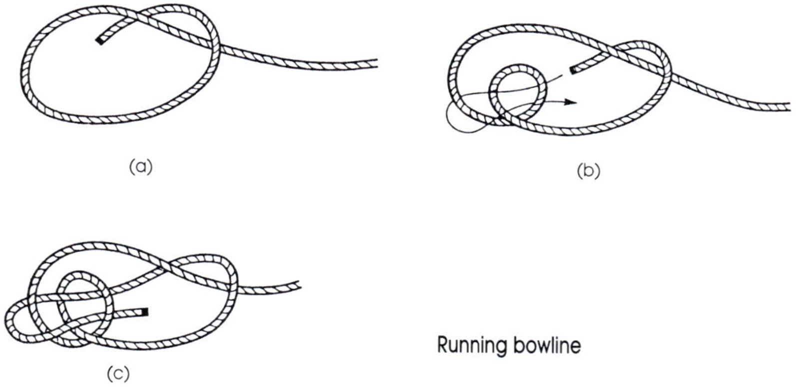

Running bowline

Water bowline

This is used when the bowline will become very wet. It is for use in natural-fibre ropes.

- *To tie:* Proceed as for the single bowline to diagram (b), then take the running end up a short distance and repeat. Now take the running end around the standing part and back through the two eyes formed. Tighten as for the bowline.

Triple bowline

This is used when three loops are required in the end of natural-fibre rope.

- *To tie:* Double the rope to form a long bight. Proceed to tie a bowline with the doubled rope; the end of the bight is to finish in the loop.

Running bowline

This is a running loop.

- *To tie the knot:* Take a loop around the standing part, then convert the loop into a bowline.

227

Heaving-line terminal

This is in order to form a soft weight in the end of a light line for throwing, as for a heaving line.

- *To tie:* Take a bight in the rope a fair way from the running end, depending on the weight required. Then fold the bights backwards and forwards, leaving the first bight longer than the others. Take a riding turn around the bights and bind the bights together, working towards the end of the first bight. When bound, tuck the running end through the bight, and pull on the standing part in order to tighten the bight on to the running end.

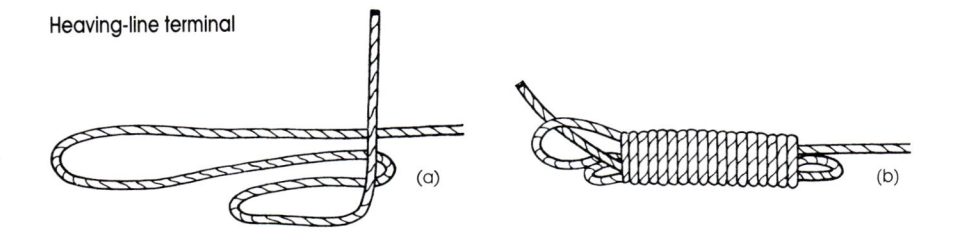

Heaving-line terminal

(a)

(b)

Sheepshank

This is used in order to tighten a rope when both ends are fixed.

- *To tie:* Form an 'S' with the slack, and make a half hitch in the standing part at one end of the 'S'; then place the bight into the half hitch. Pull the half hitch tight. Take up all the slack, and with the remaining bight, tie a half hitch on the taut standing part. Pull hard on the bight, and convert the half hitch on to the standing part.

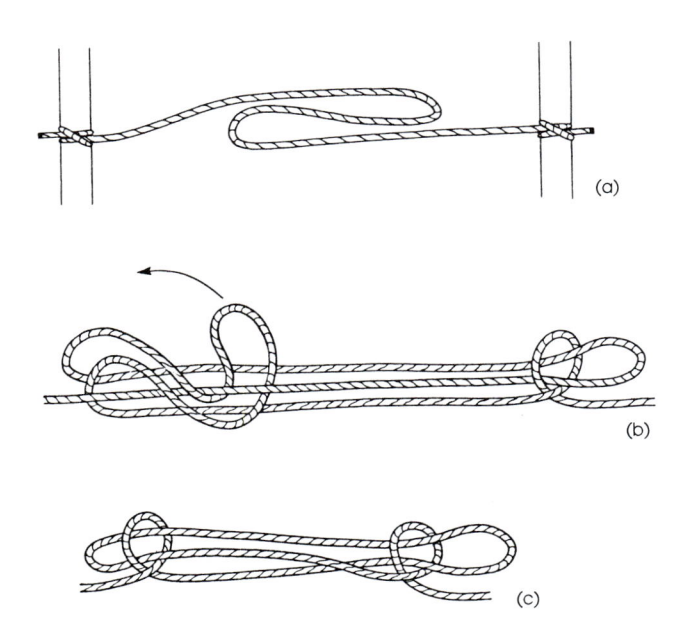

(a)

(b)

(c)

Sheepshank

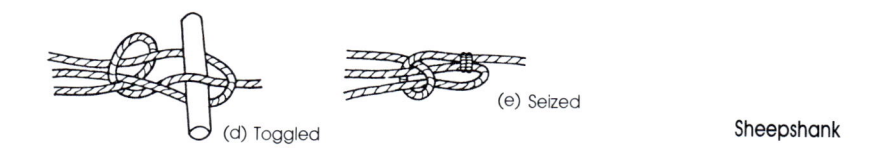

Construction

(d) Toggled (e) Seized

Sheepshank

Sheepshank knots do not strengthen ropes; each knot tied in a rope weakens it. If a rope has a weakened part or is starting to break, it should be cut and whipped and a suitable knot tied in order to suit the purpose for which the rope is being used.

Sheepshanks should be toggled or seized, because movement could cast the half hitches undone.

Hay hitch

This is used as a rope tackle when there is constant strain, for example, in the case of a trailer load.

Hauliers use it to secure their loads, and call it a *truckie's hitch*. It resembles one end of a sheepshank.

■ *To tie it:*

1. Fix one end to the load to be moved or to the bar on the far side of the load.
2. Pass the rope around the anchorage (a tree) or bar on the trailer.
3. Pick up a bight in the standing part, and make a half hitch around it in much the same way as one end of a sheepshank. This must be toggled or seized.
4. Pull the running end through the bight towards the anchorage. The power gained is three to one, there being three returns on the moving part.
5. The running end is secured around the anchorage, then two half hitches around the standing part of the rope, and back against the anchorage.

Clearly, there could be wear and strain caused by the rubbing of the rope in the bight.

Care should be taken if a tree is used as an anchorage. In order to prevent damage, sacking should be wrapped around the tree, under the rope.

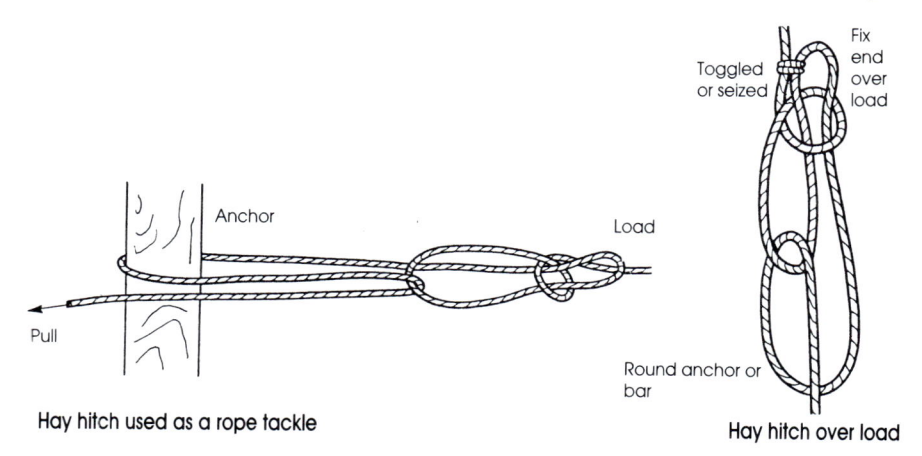

Anchor   Load

Pull

Toggled or seized

Fix end over load

Round anchor or bar

Hay hitch used as a rope tackle

Hay hitch over load

Fieldbook for Australian Scouting

Manharness hitch

Manharness hitch with thimble

Manharness hitch

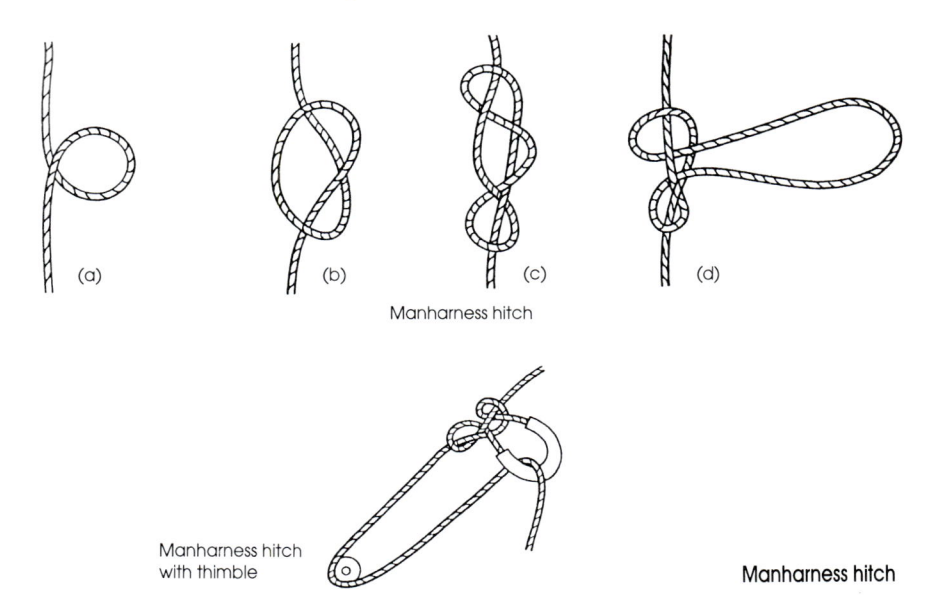

Manharness hitch

This is used to form a loop in the centre of a rope for hauling or to make a rope tackle.

- *To tie:* Make a loop, then lay it back over the standing part. Then take one side of the loop, and take it under the standing part and through the loop to form another loop; pull tight. The loop should be pulled against the half hitch in the rope. When hauling, the loop should be about 1 metre, and only used over one shoulder, in case the load gets away. If you use this knot as a rope tackle, a small thimble should be used.

Butterfly knot

This knot will give you a loop in the centre of the rope for hauling, and has more security especially if the rope is slippery.

- *To tie:*
    1. Make a bight in the rope in one hand and hold it as shown.
    2. Make one twist in the bight to form eyes X and Y.
    3. Make another twist in the same direction and produce eye Z.
    4. Fold bight up to Y.
    5. Pass X down through eye Y and up through eye Z.
    6. Pull the bight through and tighten it.

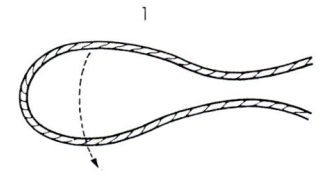

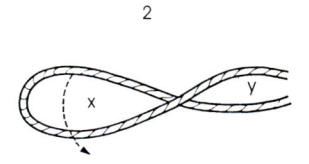

Construction

Butterfly knot

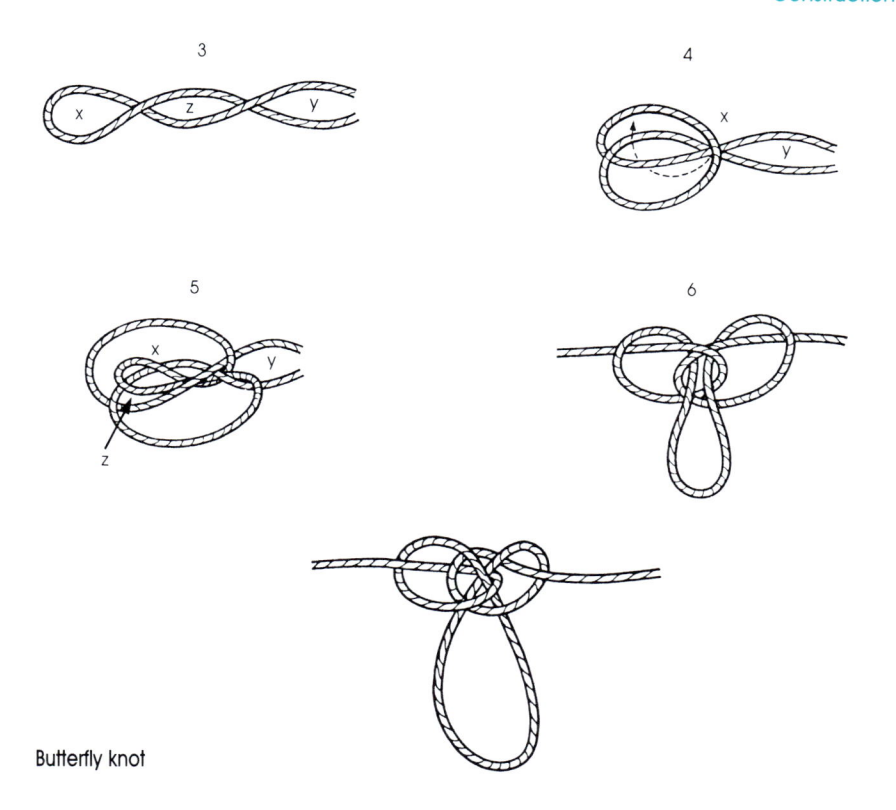

Hitches

Clove hitch

This is used in order to start almost all the 'standard' lashings. It is also used for attaching a rope to a spar when a strain on the rope not at right angles to the spar is expected. It is necessary to 'lock' the running end with one or two half hitches around the standing part in the same way as the round turn and two half hitches. It is not possible to tie a clove hitch and finish with the rope tight; this is not to say the rope cannot be tightened later by pulling on the standing part (or the standing end).

When used in a lashing, the running end is twisted with the lay of the rope enough distance to lock around the next spar.

- *To tie the knot:* There are two ways, as follows.
  1. Tying in the end of the rope when the ends of the object are not accessible, or placing the running end over the object you are attaching it to (usually a spar), then taking it around and then back up over itself as a riding turn. Continue around, and come through on the side of the standing part other than that you came before; then take the running end under the riding turn. Pull both the running end and standing part in order to tighten knot.

231

Clove hitch

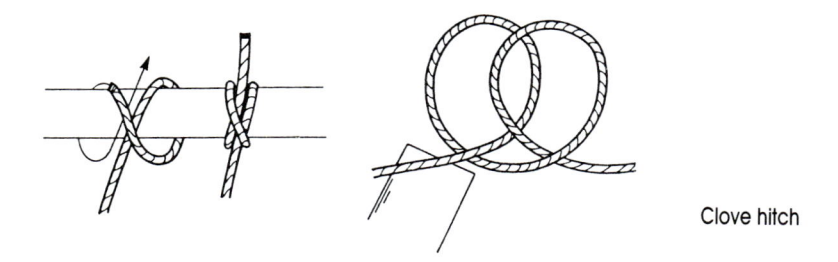

2. Tying in the middle of the rope. Make a loop with the rope on one side of the standing part, then make another loop in the opposite direction, ending up with the rope on the other side of the rope. Then bring the loops across the standing part and lay them on one another. Slip the two loops over the object. Pull tight.

Magnus hitch

This is similar to a clove hitch but has an extra turn. It is able to take a pull along in the direction of the extra turn without slipping.

- *To tie the knot:* Start as for a clove hitch, but before making the riding turn, take two or three turns towards the load side. Then make the riding turn, and complete as a clove hitch.

Constrictor knot

This is another hitch that is similar to a clove hitch. Its advantage is that the object around which it is tied is gripped very firmly. It can be used in order to hitch a rope to a spar or to tie up the top of a sack. A tightened constrictor knot can be difficult to untie.

- *To tie:* Tie a clove hitch, then take the ends across under the riding turn and through under the turn; then tighten in the same direction as before.

Two half hitches

These can be tied around the standing part of a rope after passing the rope around a spar, or can be tied directly on to a spar as when you are finishing most lashings. In either case, the first half hitch should be tied and the rope worked tight, then the second half hitch added in order to secure the knot and retain the tightness.

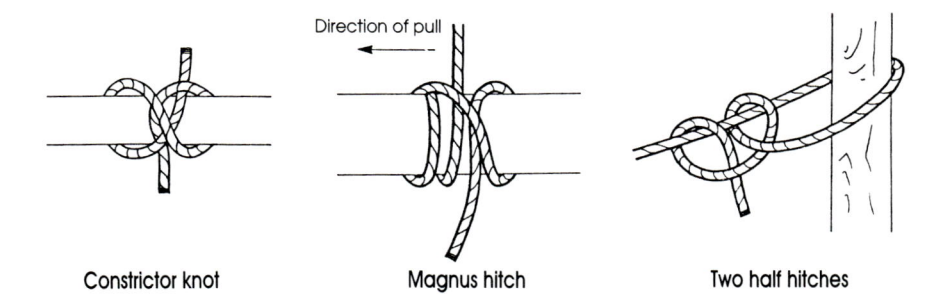

Constrictor knot   Magnus hitch   Two half hitches

Construction

Round turn and two half hitches

This is a useful hitch for joining a rope to a spar when the pull will be more or less at right angles to the spar. The round turn can be tied and the standing part worked tight, and the friction of the round turn helps in holding the tightness.

- *To tie:* First, one half hitch can be tied and tightened, followed by the second. The two half hitches should be tight against the spar, not part way along the standing part.

When tying the half hitches, the running end must always continue in the same direction. If you change direction after the first half hitch, the second half hitch will be useless.

Anchor bend or fisherman's bend

- *To tie:* This is actually a hitch similar to a round turn and two half hitches, the difference being that the first hitch is tied through the round turn as well as around the standing part.

This hitch is less likely to work loose when there is a lot of give-and-take motion such as can occur when a rope is attached to an anchor. When mooring a boat, the anchor bend is used for hitching the painter to a ring or other object on land.

Timber hitch

This is used in order to start a diagonal lashing. The two spars to be lashed are pulled together by tightening the timber hitch. A timber hitch on a log, plus a half hitch towards the end of the log, is called a *killick* hitch and is useful for dragging logs along the ground.

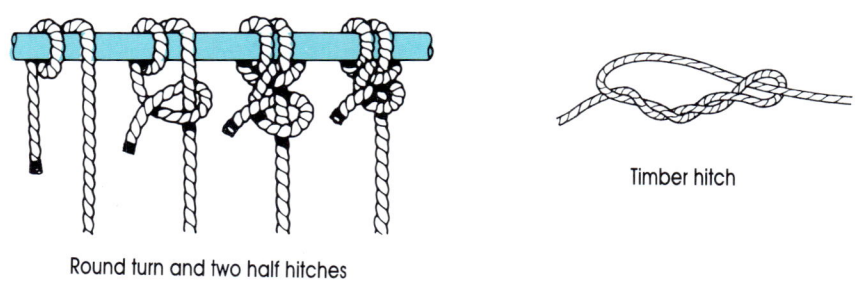

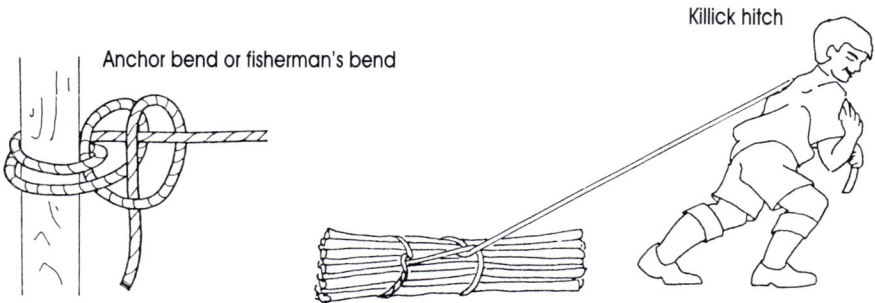

Round turn and two half hitches

Timber hitch

Anchor bend or fisherman's bend

Killick hitch

Fieldbook for Australian Scouting

- *To tie the hitch:* Take the rope around the spar or log, and so on. Then take the running end around the standing part, forming a bight with the standing part running through it. Then twist the running end back around itself six to eight times. This forms a hitch that should pull tight.

Prussick hitch

This is used for joining a loop to the standing part of a rope. It holds fast when a load is applied to the loop but can be quickly adjusted along the length of the other rope when unloaded.

- *To tie:* Take a loop up one side of the main rope, and form a bight in the rope on the other side. Then pass the bight through the loop three or four times, and pull the bight to tighten the knot.

The prussick hitch can be used for climbing a rope, and this is called prussicking.

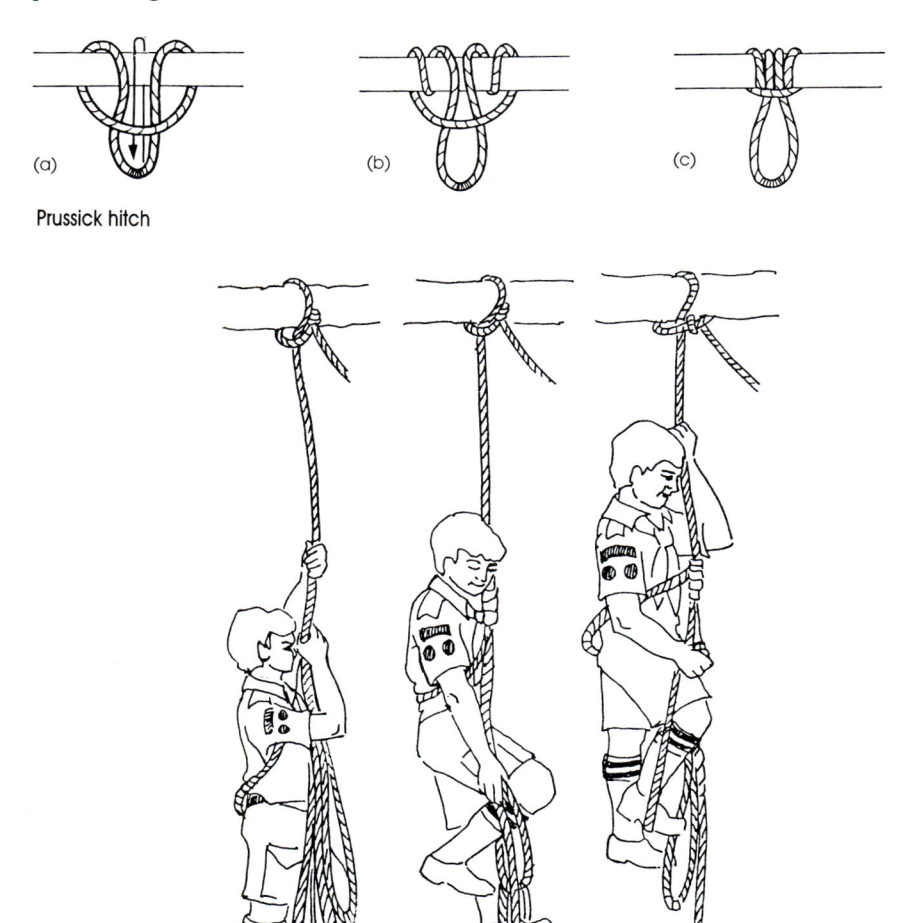

Prussick hitch

Prussicking

Prussicking

This involves climbing a rope using three loops attached to a climbing rope with a prussick knot. The loops can be made from three ropes joined into a loop with a fisherman's knot.

- *To tie:* Bend your three strops on to the rope, one above the other at intervals of about 30 centimetres. Grip the rope, and put your foot into the *bottom* loop so you can raise yourself clear of the ground. Slip the *top* loop around yourself under the armpits. Now push the *middle* loop up the rope, and put your other foot in the loop. Transfer your weight to this leg, and push the *top* loop up until it again grips under the armpits. You will find you are supported by this loop and have both hands free to reach down and raise the *bottom* loop. Continue this process, working your way up the rope.

It is preferable that the size of the rope for the loops is smaller than the climbing rope, because the closer the sizes are, the greater the danger of slipping.

Scaffold hitch

This is used in order to attach a rope to a plank to form a boatswain's chair.

- *To tie the knot:* Lay the rope over the end of the plank, and take two turns around the plank to finish with three ropes on top (two under). Working towards the end of the plank, take the inside rope over the next rope and between the other two ropes. Then take the inside rope over the two ropes and underneath the plank. The running end is then used, and the standing part is finished as a bowline. You will have to repeat the hitch on the other end of the plank in order to form a seat.

If the seat is to be used on the hook of a block, the rope should be attached with a catspaw-on-the-bight hitch.

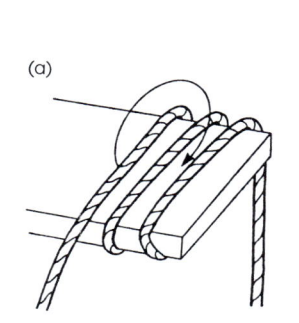

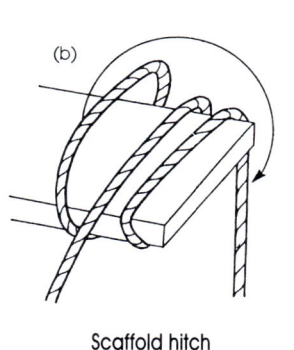

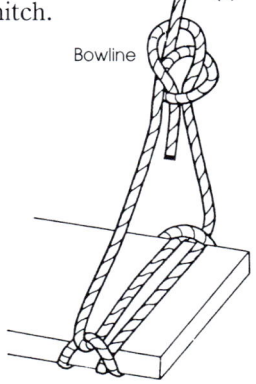

Bowline (c)

(a) (b)

Scaffold hitch

Catspaw-on-the-bight hitch

This is used in order to attach the bight of a rope to a hook when both ends are under tension.

- *To tie:* Make two loops with the ropes on the same side of the standing part. Continue to twist the loops evenly until four to six turns have been completed. Place the two loops on to the hook and place a mooring on the hook.

Fieldbook for Australian Scouting

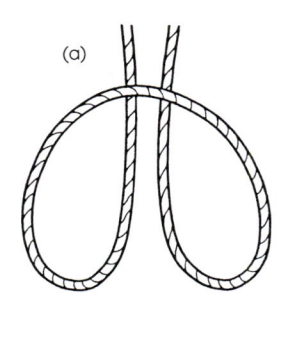

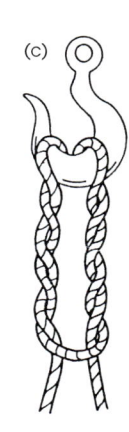

Catspaw on the bight

Draw hitch

This is used to attach a rope to an object (for example, a spar or ring) when there is a variable movement on the standing part but a quick-release knot is required.

- *To tie the knot:* Place a bight of the rope behind the object. Make a bight in the standing part, and take it across the front of the object and through the first bight. Pull down on the running end. Take a bight in the running end, place it through the second bight, and pull down on the standing part. To release the knot, pull on the running end. The rope should slip easily off the spar or ring.

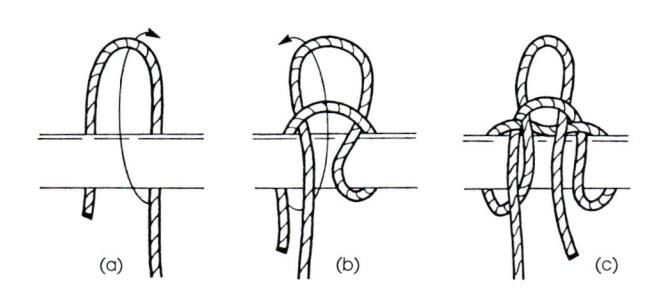

Draw hitch

Marline spike hitch (sometimes called a lever hitch)

This is used in order to form a knot in a rope and insert a spar or marline spike, and is then used in order to tighten, for example, lashing, or in order to form a ladder rung.

- To tie: Form a loop and fold it back over the standing part, holding the rope at the point of the loop. Then feed the rung or spike across the loop and under the standing part. Release, holding the rope as it tightens. The extra twist formed on one side has to be pulled against for tightening or under the ladder rung.

Construction

(a) (b)   (a)   (b)

Hold!

Twisted part of
knot under rung
to lock knot

Marline spike hitch   Marline spike hitch

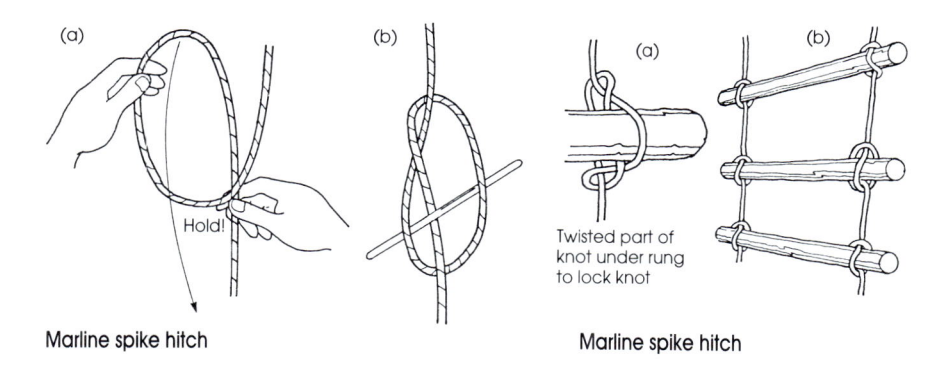

Whippings

Whippings are the most effective method of preventing the end of a rope from fraying or unlaying. A *stopper knot* such as an overhand knot is quick and can be used when you are in a hurry in the middle of a project. A *back splice* can be tied quickly and without twine, but it doubles the thickness of the rope and makes it hard to tie knots or to pass the end through blocks or eyes. A properly tied whipping should last as long as the rope.

Whipping materials

The best thread for whipping is three-ply seaming twine, and you will also need beeswax. Cut your whipping thread to length, then run it through the beeswax in order to coat the thread before whipping.

Synthetic-fibre ropes can be prevented from fraying or unlaying by fusing the ends with a flame or hot iron. With some of these ropes, plastic sticky tape provides a serviceable means of holding the end of the rope together.

West-country whipping

- *To tie:* This is formed by passing the twine around the rope about two rope diameters from the end and making a thumb knot leaving both ends of the twine equal in length. Tie another thumb knot on the side of the rope opposite to that of the first, then continue with alternating thumb knots, working towards the end of the rope. Tighten each knot in turn. When the

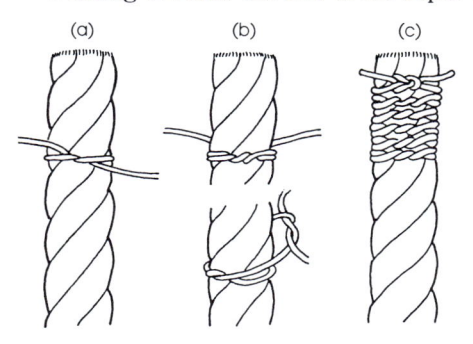

(a)   (b)   (c)

West-country whipping

237

length of the whipping is approximately equal to the diameter of the rope, tie a second thumb knot on top of the last, forming a reef knot.

Sailmaker's whipping

- *To tie:* Unlay the end of the rope for about twice the rope diameter. Pass a loop of the whipping twine over one strand, with the two ends emerging together between the other two strands. Hold the loop and the ends of the twine together with the rope, and relay the strands carefully. Wrap one end of the twine tightly around the relayed rope, working towards the end, until the length of the whipping is equal to the diameter of the rope. Hold the end of the twine tight, and bring the loop up and over the end of the same strand it is straddling. Pull the end at the bottom so the loop tightens, each side of the loop settling in the groove of the lay of the rope. Bring the end from the bottom to the top up the third groove. Join the two ends in the centre of the strands with a reef knot or a surgeon's knot.

Palm-and-needle whipping

This whipping is the most enduring because it is sewn into the rope, and if done well, will last the rope out.

You will need a sailmaker's or packer's needle, and a palm—this is an apparatus that fits on your thumb and covers your palm and enables you to push the needle through the rope. If this is not available, it will take a little longer to do the whipping and whipping twine.

- *To tie:* After threading the needle, pass the needle through a strand of the rope near the lay grooves, and continue until the twine is through all three strands; this is the base of the whipping. Then bind the rope as tight as possible with the lay of the rope until the width of whipping is reached. Then pass the needle through a strand coming out in the lay groove, take the twine down the groove, and sew the twine through a strand. Then run the twine up another lay groove. Continue until a twine is running in all lay grooves and it looks like the sailmakers'. To finish, sew the twine through the strands again, then trim the twine flush with the rope.

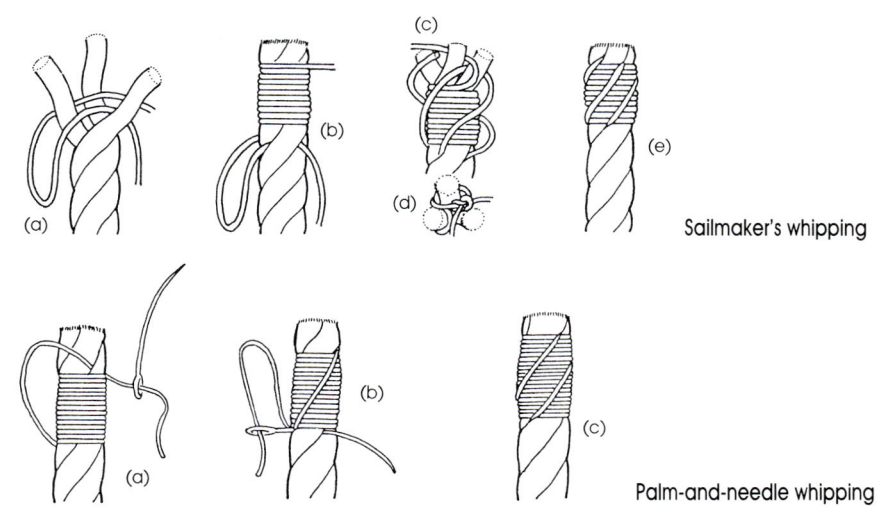

Sailmaker's whipping

Palm-and-needle whipping

Construction

Splices

Splices are used in order to mend a damaged rope or to fasten one rope to another. A good splice may have about 80% of the rope's strength, whereas a knot's efficiency varies from only 45 to 60% of the rope. The *long splice* allows the rope to run through a block, and should be made only with two ropes of the same size; however, it is time consuming to make and uses a lot of rope. The *short splice* is the strongest way to join two ropes, can be made quickly, and involves little rope waste—its disadvantage is that it cannot pass through a block. The *eye splice* is used in the end of a rope for mooring or when a permanent loop is required. The *back splice* is used for a temporary finish to the end of a rope.

Back splice

This is used in order to temporarily prevent the end of a rope from fraying or unlaying. It does not require twine, and a competent splicer can tie a back splice more quickly than can a competent whipper.

- *To tie:* It is commenced with a crown knot. To make this, unlay the rope for a distance about two and a half times the circumference of the rope, and hold it so the middle strand is away from you, as in diagram (**a**). Bring this middle strand down towards you to form a loose loop, as in diagram (**b**). Take the left-hand strand and pass it towards you over the loop and then back between the loop and the right-hand strand, as in diagram (**c**), pulling tight. Pass the right-hand strand through the loop as in diagram (**d**), pulling it tight, then pull the loop tight. Even it up by pulling on each strand in turn.

After forming the crown knot, each strand is, in turn, tucked over one strand and under the next against the lay of the rope, that is, at right angles to the grooves in the rope. The splice is complete after two tucks in each strand. At this stage the ends can be trimmed off neatly or the strands halved and tucked again in order to provide a taper.

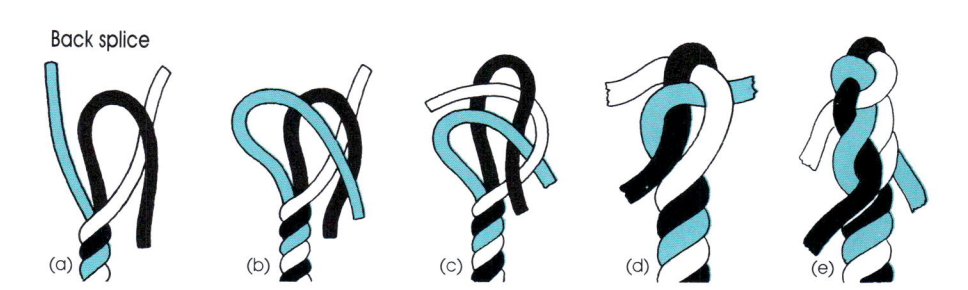

Back splice

Eye splice

This forms a permanent loop in the end of a rope.
- *To tie:*
   A. Unlay the end.
   B. Strand **2** is tucked over strand **c** under **b** and out between **a** and **b**.

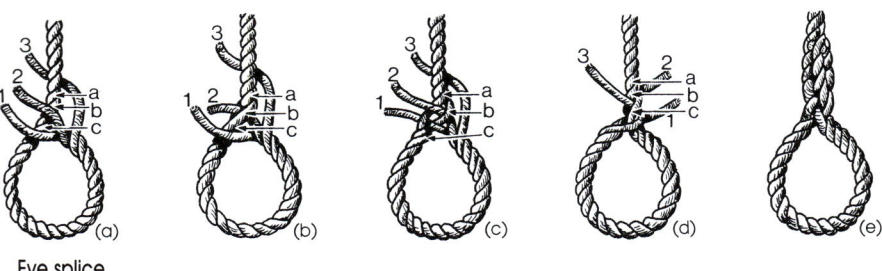

Eye splice

C. Strand **1** is tucked over **b** and under **a**.
D. Turn the splice over, and tuck strand **3** by passing *around* then under **c** and coming out between **c** and **b**.
E. Tuck each strand, in turn, two more times. Trim ends or taper as in the back splice.

Short splice

This is the strongest method of joining two ropes together. However, because the rope thickness is increased, it is not suitable for ropes that are to pass over the sheaves of blocks.

■ *To tie:*

A. Unlay the rope a few turns and alternate the strands.
B. It is sometimes an advantage to tie the strands down in order to prevent further unlaying.
C. Tuck one strand (**1**) over an opposing strand and under the next strand.
D. The tuck of strand **2** goes over the first strand (**5**), under the second and out between the second and third.
E. Repeat the operation with the other two strands (**1** and **3**) from the same rope end. Then repeat the operation on the other rope end (after removing the tie, if used).
F. Work the strands in. Cut ends.

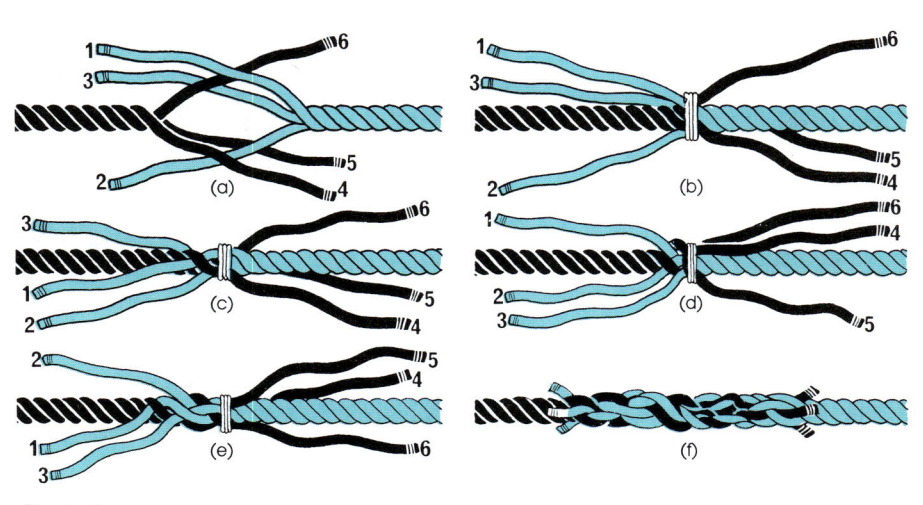

Short splice

Construction

Long splice

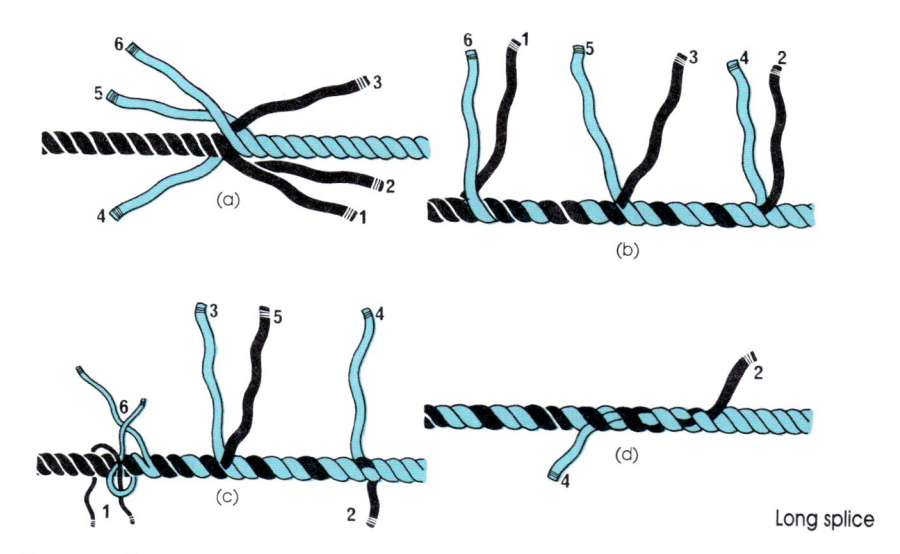

Long splice

This is used for joining two ropes together when the join may have to pass over the sheave of a block. This splice requires a lot of rope because the full length is about 100 times the rope diameter, and is not as strong as a short splice.

- *To tie:*
   A. Unlay each rope about 50 times the rope diameter and place the ropes together, alternating the strands of each end.
   B. Using opposite pairs, unlay one strand (**4**) and fill its place with its partner strand (**2**) until almost at the end of the strand being laid. Repeat the operation exactly with another pair of strands (**1** and **6**) in the opposite direction.
   C. Tie each of the three pairs of opposing strands **1** and **6**, **3** and **5**, and **2** and **4**, with an overhand knot.
   D. Make two tucks, or at least one tuck with each of the six ends. If the slight extra thickness of these tucks is unacceptable, halve the strands before tucking.
   Trim the ends.

Grommet, or rope quoit

- *To tie:* Take a strand out of a rope at least four times the circumference of the grommet required. Form a circle in the centre of the strand the size required and then relay the strand into itself. Finish as for a long splice. One piece of rope will give you three grommets.

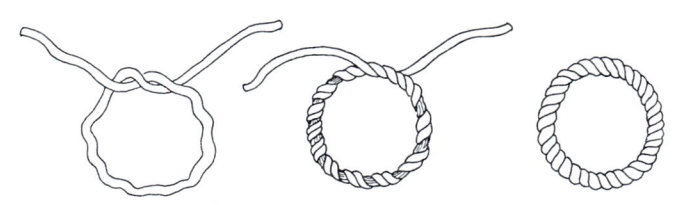

Grommet

241

Lashings

There are two distinct categories of lashings: the *'standard'* lashings, and the relatively more recently introduced *'instant'* lashings. Both have their uses. The standard lashings are more secure but take longer to tie and should be used on solid structures such as bridges and towers, particularly if you want to get your whole Patrol on top of the finished product. Instant lashings are quicker to tie but are not as strong. Lashing ropes rarely break, but lashings fail because they slip. Almost always the last thing to slip on a standard lashing is the initial clove hitch; instant lashings (with one exception) do not start with a clove hitch. Instant lashings are suitable for camp gadgets and public displays when you want to get something up and finished quickly.

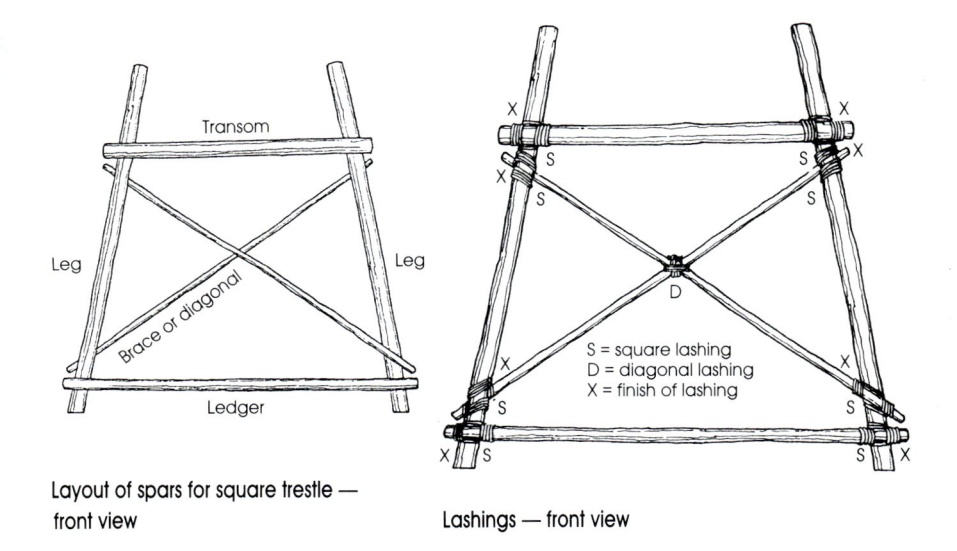

Layout of spars for square trestle — front view

S = square lashing
D = diagonal lashing
X = finish of lashing

Lashings — front view

Standard lashings

Square lashing

Whenever two spars cross and there is a need to prevent one sliding along the other, the square lashing should be used. It is not necessary that the two spars should be at right angles (or *'square'*) to one another.

- *To do:*
    1. It is started with a clove hitch around the upright spar immediately under the spot where the cross piece is to be and on the side opposite to the force.
    2. Twist the running end of the rope with the standing part, then *'wrap'* the rope around the cross-piece and upright binding them together. This turn should start around the spar where you intend to finish.
    3. Pull tight after each complete turn.

Construction

4. With wrapping turns, the rope goes outside the previous turn on the cross-piece and inside the previous turn on the upright (clove hitch).
5. After four wrapping turns, make two *'frapping'* turns between the spars. Pull each frapping turn tight. After the fourth wrapping turn, you will have to take a quarter turn in order to change direction to start the frapping turns.
6. Finish with two half hitches around the end of the cross-piece. Tie the first half hitch and work it tight against the last frapping turn, then tie the second half hitch and work it tight. The completed half hitches should look like a clove hitch, but it is not a clove hitch.

Note: The most effective lashing is produced with four wrapping turns; however, an often acceptably strong lashing can be tied with three wrapping turns. The number of frapping turns should remain two. Remember you should finish out spar or up spar.

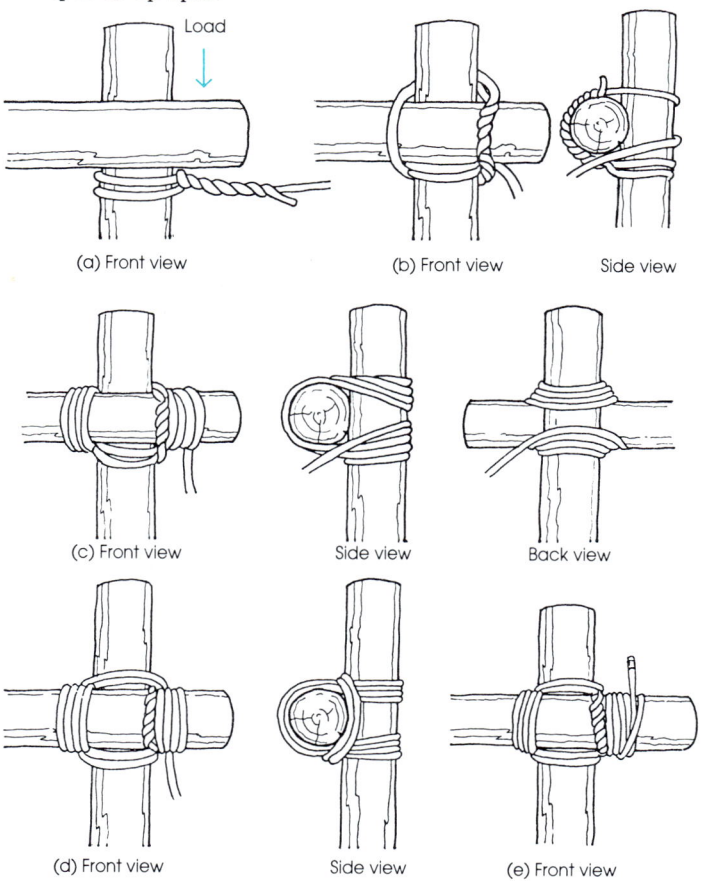

(a) Front view   (b) Front view   Side view

(c) Front view   Side view   Back view

(d) Front view   Side view   (e) Front view

Square lashing

Diagonal lashing

This is used to hold together two spars that tend to spring apart or do not touch. It is required in the centre of a square trestle where the two diagonal braces cross.

Fieldbook for Australian Scouting

Diagonal lashing

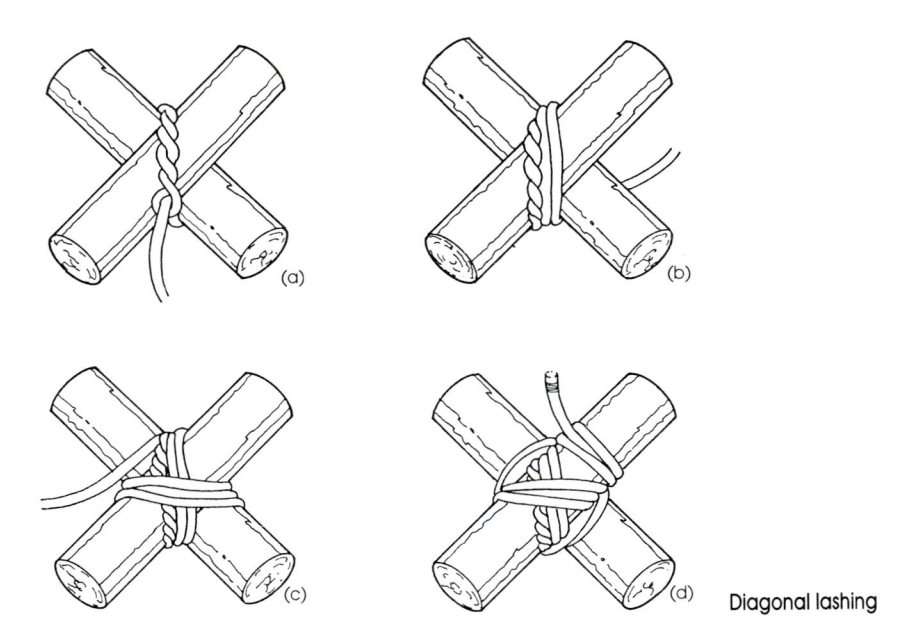

- *To do:*
  1. The lashing is started with a timber hitch around both spars, usually on the vertical crutch.
  2. The timber hitch is tightened in order to bring the spars together.
  3. Three turns are taken around the fork, counting the timber hitch as the first.
  4. Three turns are taken around the fork at right angles to the first. Take a turn around the spar in order to change direction for frapping turns.
  5. Make two frapping turns.
  6. Finish with two half hitches around the most convenient spar. Tie the first half hitch and work it tight against the last frapping turn, then tie the second half hitch and work it tight. The completed half hitches should look like a clove hitch. Remember to finish up spar.

Shear lashing

This is used for lashing two spars together in order to form shear legs when the load will be between the legs, such as for rope bridges.

- *To do:*
  1. Place the spars together with the butts (bottoms) flush and the lashing centre marked for correct splay.
  2. Chock the spars apart using pegs or similar material a little larger than the diameter of the rope being used.
  3. Tie a clove hitch around one spar, and twist the running end of the rope with the standing part enough to go around the other spar.
  4. Take six to eight turns around both spars, working towards the tips. Tighten each turn as it is made.
  5. Make two frapping turns between the spars.

Construction

Shear lashing

Round lashing

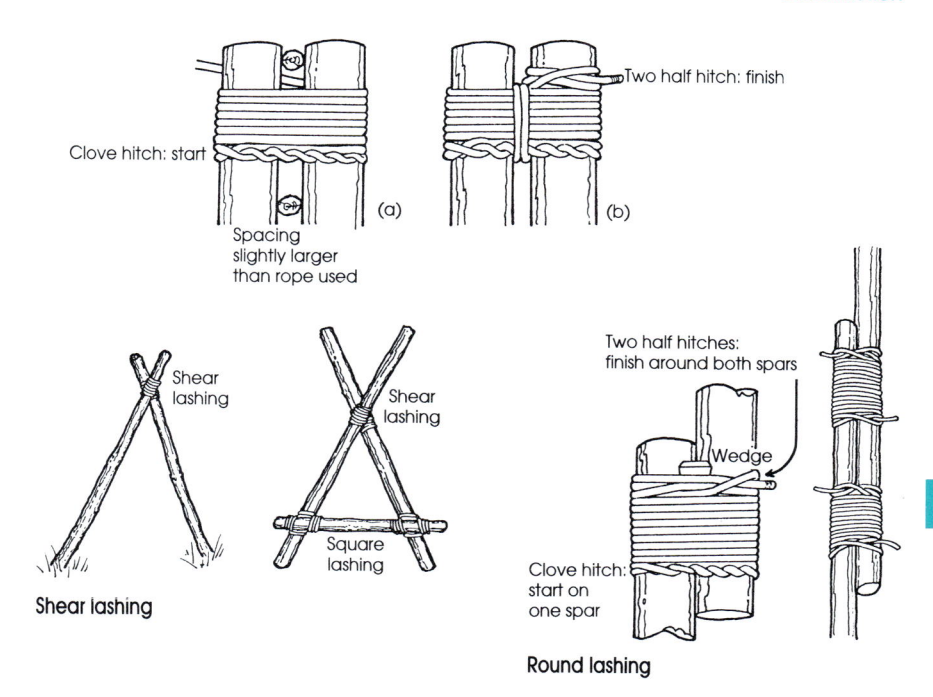

6. Finish with two half hitches around the spar you did not start on. Tie the first half hitch and work it tight against the last frapping turn, then tie the second half hitch and work it tight. The completed half hitches should look like a clove hitch.
7. Spread the legs in the direction of tightening the lashing. The splay of the legs are as per the use to be made of them. A ledger is square lashed to the legs.

Round lashing

This is used for joining two spars together in order to extend the length, as in constructing a flag pole.

■ *To do:*
1. Place the spars in the desired position with a suitable overlap. The spars should be in line, for example, butts to the base.
2. Tie a clove hitch around one spar (the bottom spar in a flag pole), twist the running end of the rope with the standing part enough to go around the other spar.
3. Take as many turns around both spars (working towards the tips of the spars) as the rope length will permit, leaving enough for the final two half hitches.
4. Finish with two half hitches around both spars, tightening each half hitch in turn.
5. Tighten the lashing by knocking small wooden pegs down between the spars and under the rope turns.

Note: For an effective join, it is necessary to tie two round lashings a little distance apart. This will prevent the spars pivoting on a single lashing.

Figure-of-eight (or gyn) lashing

This is used in order to form a tripod (or gyn).

- *To do:*
  1. Place the spars as shown in the diagram, after measuring and marking the centre of the lashing.
  2. Chock the spars apart using pegs or small spars a little smaller than the diameter of the spars being used.
  3. Tie a clove hitch around one of the outside spars, and twist the running end of the rope with the standing part enough to go around the next spar.
  4. Take six to eight figure-of-eight turns, working towards the tips of the outside spars. Finish back at the spar on which you started.
  5. Make two frapping turns between each of the spars.
  6. Finish with two half hitches around the outside spar you did not start on. Tie the first half hitch and work it tight against the last frapping turn, then tie the second half hitch and work it tight. The completed half hitches should look like a clove hitch.

Note: To erect the tripod:
  1. Lift the spars slightly at the point where they are lashed.
  2. Cross the butt of one outside spar over the other.
  3. Continue to lift; place the butts in an equilateral triangle on the ground. The distance between the butts should be about one-third the height. The central spar would be resting in a fork formed by the outside spars.

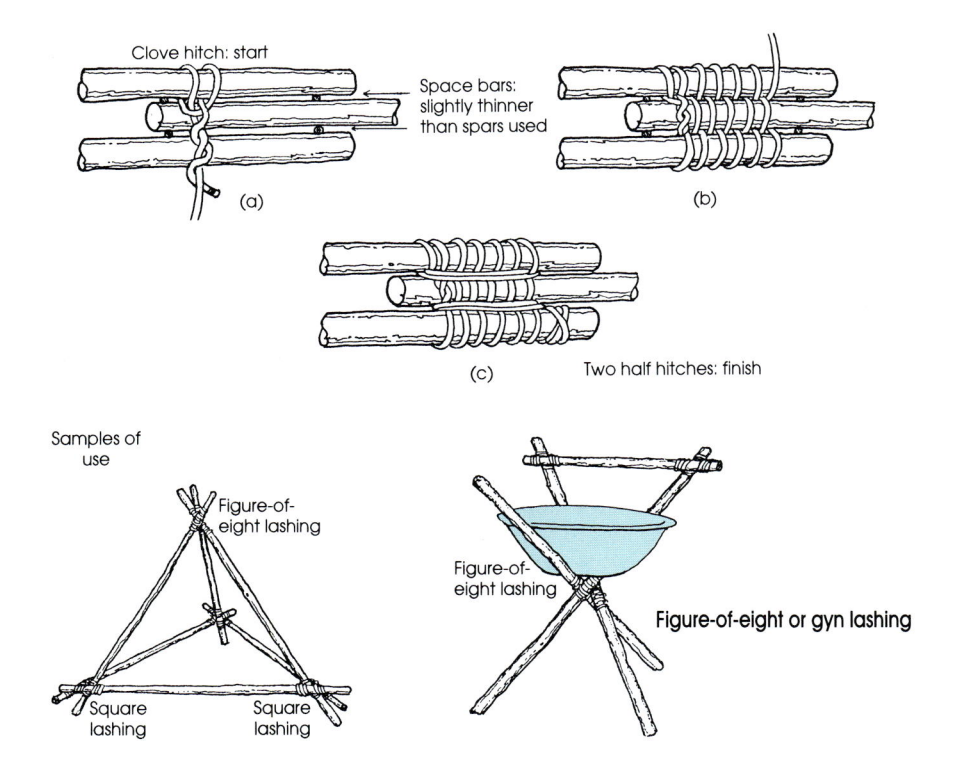

Holdfast lashing

This lashing is used in order to attach one picket to another to form an anchorage.

- *To do:* Attach the rope to the top of the first picket with a clove hitch, then twist the running end around the standing part for a distance to go around the base of the second picket.

Take six to eight turns around both pickets. Finish off with two half hitches around all turns and hard against the first picket. The lashing should run from the top of the first picket to the base of the second picket and be at 90° to the pickets.

Holdfast lashing
Clove hitch: start
90°
Two half hitches: finish

Block lashing
Clove hitch: start
Two half hitches: finish
Hook mousing

Block lashing

This lashing is used when you are attaching a block to a spar or tree (remember the sacking).

- *To do:* Attach the rope to the spar or tree with a clove hitch, then tie a half hitch to secure the knot. Then take as many turns through the block hook as is practical and around the spar or tree. Finish with two half hitches around the spar or tree above the block. The mouth of the hook should be secured with a mousing.

Instant lashings

These were developed as a fast method of lashing lightweight material together in order to form displays or some camp gadget items. It must be remembered that they should only be used in this way; the lashings will not take any major weight. The early material used with these lashings was mainly bamboo, which in itself is lightweight, and because of the shape (notches and narrow sections), the lashings held the spars together reasonably well.

There are a considerable number of instant lashings, and a description of four of them follows. Three lashings are given the prefix 'Japanese', and all are variations of the square lashing.

Japanese lashing (mark I)

1. Start with a bight in the centre of the rope around one spar, where the clove hitch would be for a square lashing.
2. Take two complete wrapping turns with the doubled rope.

Fieldbook for Australian Scouting

Japanese lashing (mark I) — square lashing

Japanese lashing (mark II) — square lashing

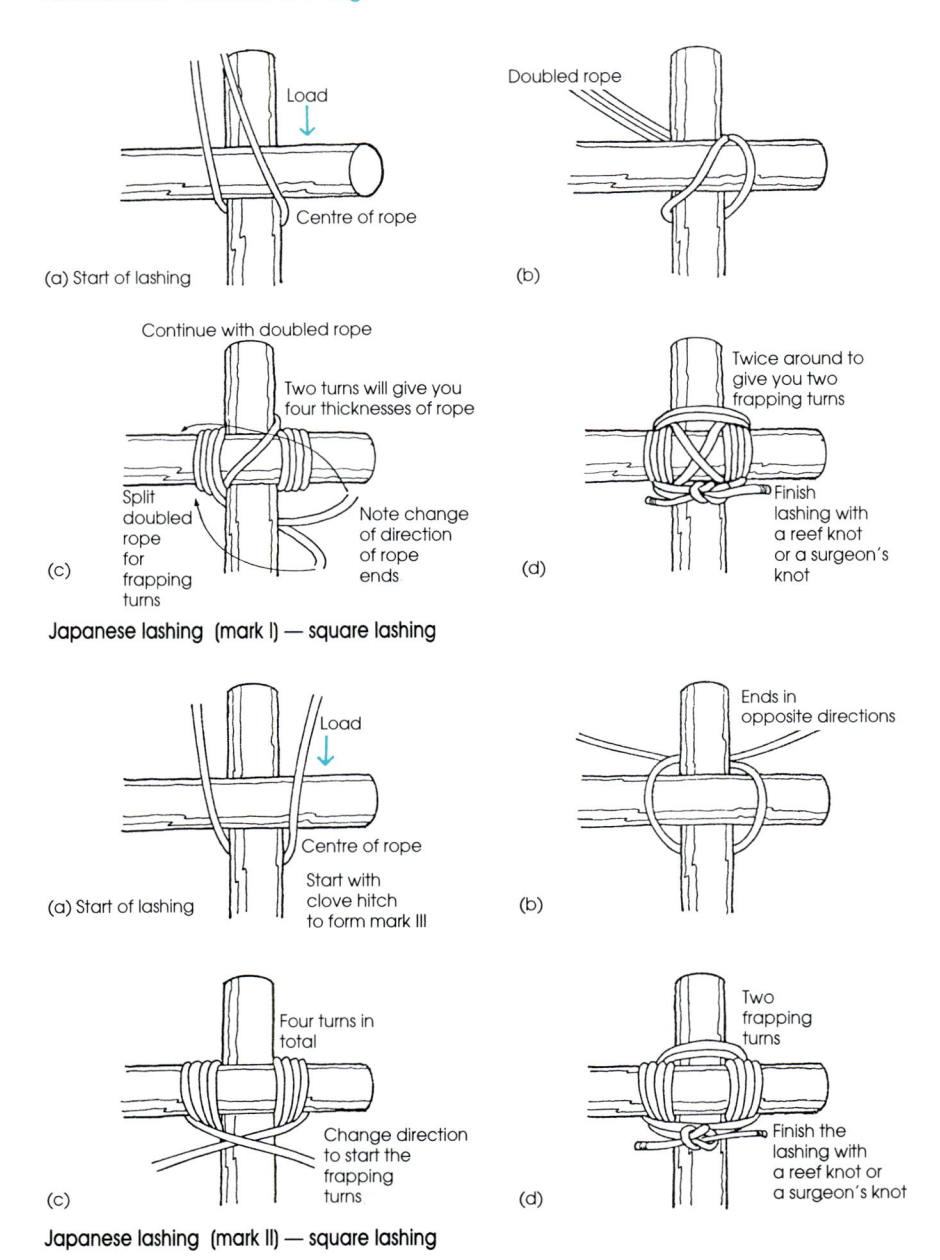

3. Take one frapping turn with each end of the rope in *opposite* directions.
4. Tie the two ends together with a reef knot or surgeon's knot.

Japanese lashing (mark II)

This lashing is tied in a way similar to that of mark I except that the wrapping turns are made with each end individually in opposite directions. This is the most popular one for Scouts to learn.

Construction

Japanese lashing (mark III)

This lashing can be tied as mark I or mark II except that the start is made with a clove hitch in the centre of the rope. It is, consequently, probably the least likely to slip of any of the Japanese lashings.

Filipino lashing

This is an instant diagonal lashing.

The lashing is started with a bight in the centre of the rope. The doubled rope is then taken through the bight around both spars (similar to a lark's head hitch) in the same way the timber hitch is used in the diagonal lashing in order to bring the spars together.

Take a turn with the doubled rope around the same fork as the start, then two turns with the doubled rope in the other fork. Divide the two ends, and take one frapping turn with each in opposite directions. Finish by joining the two ends with a reef knot or a surgeon's knot.

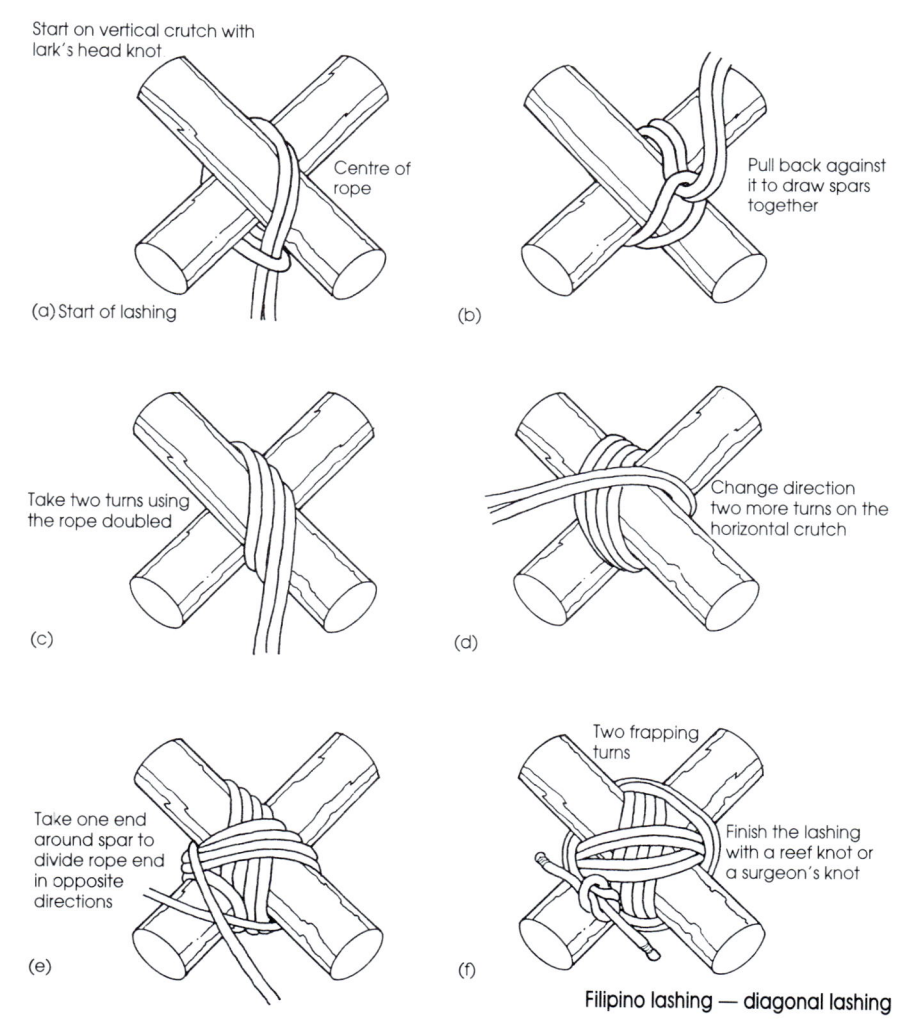

Start on vertical crutch with lark's head knot

(a) Start of lashing

Centre of rope

(b) Pull back against it to draw spars together

(c) Take two turns using the rope doubled

(d) Change direction two more turns on the horizontal crutch

(e) Take one end around spar to divide rope end in opposite directions

(f) Two frapping turns. Finish the lashing with a reef knot or a surgeon's knot

Filipino lashing — diagonal lashing

249

Anchorages

It is often necessary to form an anchorage for a pioneering structure, and trees do not always grow in the right spot and are sometimes unsuitable as an anchorage. The following are various anchorages for use in different situations.

Tree

The tree has to be well established and healthy. Sacking or other suitable material must be used in order to prevent any damage to the tree.

Holdfast 1:1

This is a basic anchorage used in heavy soils. Measure out the position of the anchorage and fix the first picket in the ground at approximately 45°. Place the second picket in the ground in line with the direction of strain and parallel to the first picket. Join the pickets together with a holdfast lashing.

Holdfast 2:1 and 3:2:1

When greater holding power is required, these anchorages can be applied. Two pickets are driven into the ground side by side, then a single picket is placed behind, or three pickets are driven into the ground together, then two, then one. The pickets are held together in line with a holdfast lashing.

Holdfast 1:2:4

This is usually used when the ground is of light texture; it helps in spreading the strain. Drive the main anchorage picket in position. Place two pickets in approximately 30° off the direction of strain. Then three or four further pickets, behind the two pickets, form a fan pattern over the holding area. The pickets can be joined with holdfast lashings or tied tightly together.

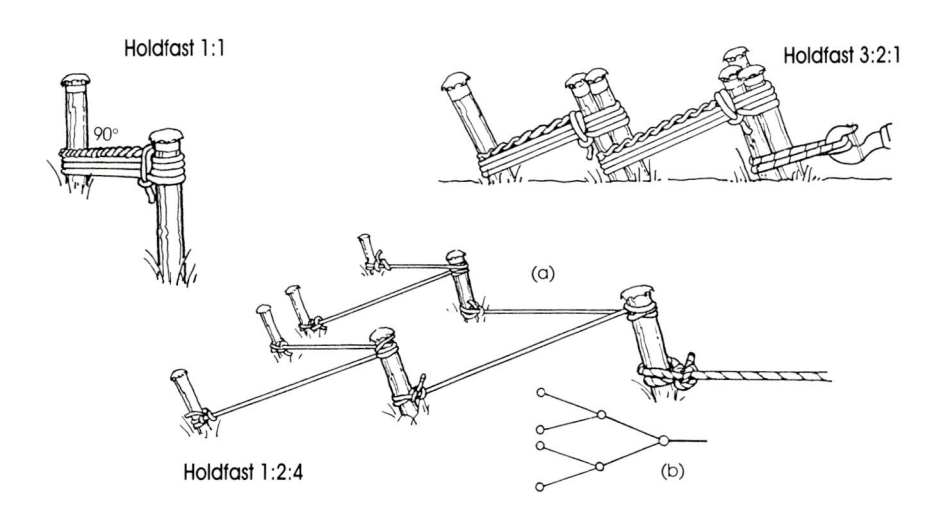

Construction

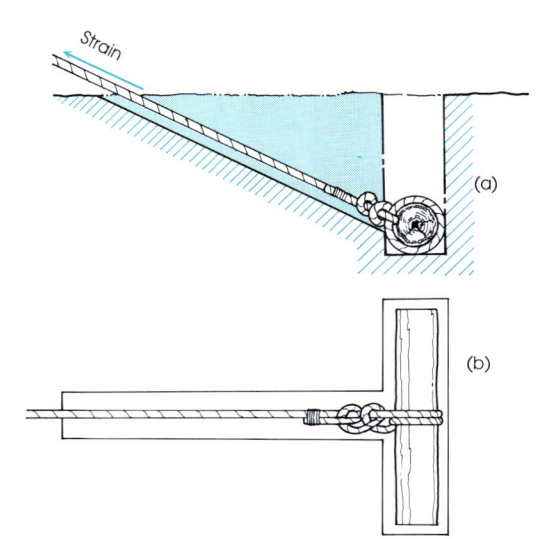

Deadman's anchorage

This is used when you require an anchorage in snow or sand, or a semi-permanent anchorage. Dig a trench at right angles to the direction of strain and a tapering trench towards the direction of strain. This should form a T shape. Place an object in the main trench (range from a spar to a log); attach a rope or wire to the centre of the object and run it out towards the construction.

For greater security, the trenches could be filled, but remember that rope should not be buried. The angle between the ground and the line under strain should never exceed 30°.

Log and picket

The anchorage for great security, if constructed correctly, is the log and picket. Four pickets are placed in line so a log can be placed behind them. The log will be at right angles to the direction of strain.

Each picket will have a second picket placed behind to form four 1:1 holdfast anchorages. A rope is then attached to the centre of the log that forms the anchor. The angle of the rope under strain should never exceed 30°.

Anchorages should be at least twice the distance from the base of the construction as the height.

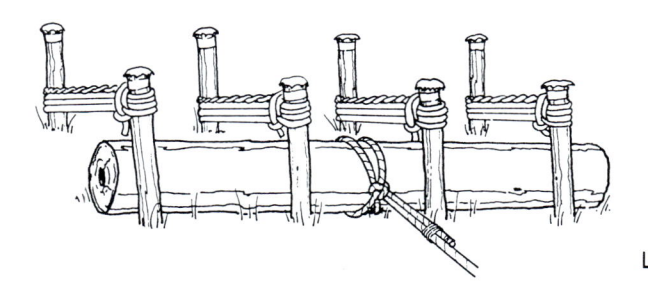

Tackle

Apart from rope tackle already covered, there are a number of ways to move, lift or tighten things. Metal or wooden blocks are mainly used. There are parts to blocks, and these are illustrated.

The rope running between the blocks is called a *'fall'*. When blocks are moved so they are at the extent of the fall, they are *'overhauled'*, when they are drawn together they are *'rounded in'* or when completed *'rounded in'* they are *'chock-a-block'*.

Blocks may be single sheaved or multi-sheaved and, depending on the combination, will depend on the mechanical advantage. The combinations also have names:

- Two single blocks form a *whip tackle*.
- A single and a double block form a *luff tackle*, also called a *handy billy*.
- Two double blocks form a *gun tackle*.
- A double and a triple block form a *light gyn tackle*.
- Two triple blocks form a *heavy gyn tackle*.
- A triple and a quadruplicate block form a *light boat tackle*.
- Two quadruplicate blocks form a *heavy boat tackle*.

When the fall is being run through the sheaves to form the tackle, this is called *'reeving'* the tackle. To reeve the tackle, place the blocks down, a distance apart, with the hooks facing outwards, and, if the blocks have becket, these should be down. The block with the mast sheaves should be the top block, and the fall passes through the sheave from right to left to run in an anticlockwise direction to start. This is easy to do with two people standing back to back between the blocks.

For the whip tackle There is no problem with reeving. To finish, tie off the fall to the becket on the top block with two half hitches and seizing.

For the luff tackle Pass the fall from the right through the bottom sheave of the top block to the sheave of the bottom block. Then change direction, and pass the fall through the top sheave of the top block from the left. Tie off on the bottom-block becket with two half hitches and seizing.

For the gun tackle Pass the fall from the right through the bottom sheave of the top block, through the top sheave of the bottom block. Change direction, then, from the left through the top sheave of the top block through the bottom sheave of the bottom block. Then pass the fall under the ropes on the left side in order to tie off on the becket of the top block with two half hitches and seizing.

For the light gyn tackle Pass the fall from the right through the centre sheave of the top block, through the top sheave of the bottom block. Then change direction and pass the fall from the left through the top sheave of the top block, through the bottom sheave of the bottom block to the bottom sheave of the top block. Pass the fall under the ropes in order to tie off on the becket of the bottom block with two half hitches and seizing.

An easy way to remember the reeving is as follows:

- luff tackle   BT → T
- gun tackle   BT → TB
- light gyn tackle CT → TBB.

Construction

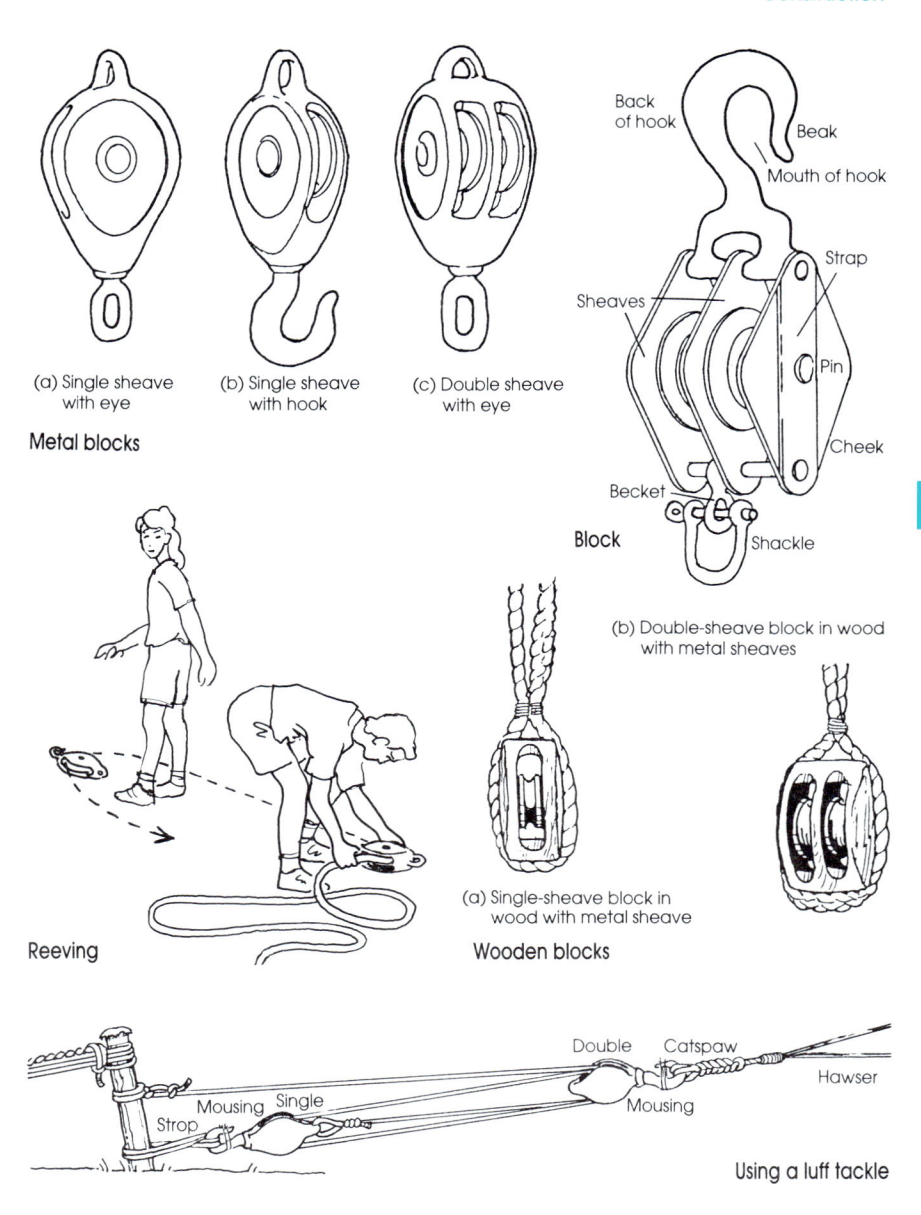

(a) Single sheave with eye
(b) Single sheave with hook
(c) Double sheave with eye

Metal blocks

Back of hook, Beak, Mouth of hook, Sheaves, Strap, Pin, Cheek, Becket, Shackle

Block

Reeving

(a) Single-sheave block in wood with metal sheave

Wooden blocks

(b) Double-sheave block in wood with metal sheaves

Mousing, Strop, Single, Double, Catspaw, Mousing, Hawser

Using a luff tackle

There is also a special reeving sequence for the heavy gyn, light boat and heavy boat tackles, but most Scout Groups would not require or have use of these.

Finishing off the tackle The end of the fall should be finished with a figure-of-eight knot (upset) in order to prevent the fall from running through the sheave when the tackle is overhauled.

The half hitches are finished with seizing.

To tie the seizing, select a length of twine and tie it to the standing part of the fall near the half hitches. Tie a clove hitch in the middle of the twine.

Seizing

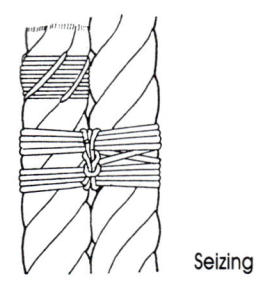

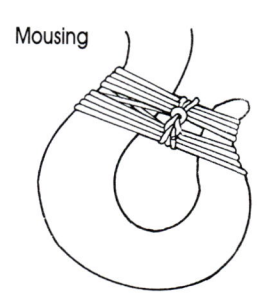

Mousing

Then bind the end of the fall on to the standing part, working each end of the twine away from the clove hitch. Take the twine around the binding in order to form two frapping turns, and finish with a reef knot.

When the tackle is in position, it is also necessary to '*mouse*' the hook. To tie a '*mousing*', take a short length of twine and tie a clove hitch on the back of the hook in the centre of the twine. Now bind across the mouth of the hook, using the beak, five or six times. Bind the turns together near the beak, and finish with a reef knot. The mousing helps to prevent the rope held in the mount of the hook from jumping out.

Trimming a tree

Give a fallen tree time to settle, because it may be resting on a limb that will break and allow the tree to roll.

Working from the butt upwards, cut off twigs and branches. Small branches can be cut off with a single blow of the axe from the underside upwards. Larger branches should be taken off by cutting a notch on the higher side and then the lower. This prevents splitting the main trunk.

Wood should be sorted into piles according to thickness. Long pieces can be cut into suitable lengths by axe or, better still, by a bush saw.

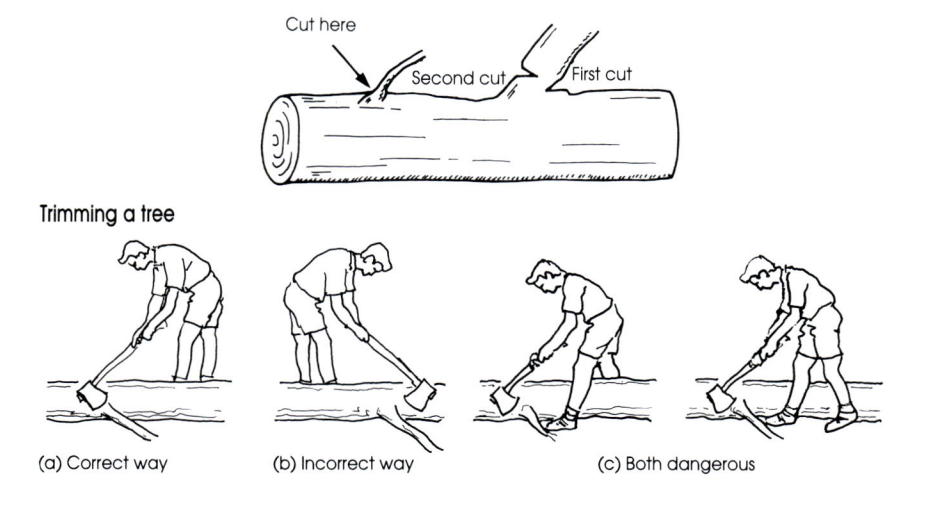

Cut here
Second cut   First cut

Trimming a tree

(a) Correct way   (b) Incorrect way   (c) Both dangerous

Logging up

Logging up a piece of timber or tree trunk is cutting it up into logs or pieces of usable size. A cross-cut saw worked by two people each pulling the saw in turn (not pushing) is often used and means less wood is wasted. Logging up can be done with an axe, scarfing the timber on both sides if necessary.

Cross-cut saws

These are large saws and are used for tree felling or logging up. You may use them for logging up, but you have to be a real expert to use them for felling a tree.

Following is what they look like.

Following is what the teeth look like:

As you can see, some of the teeth are called *cutting teeth*, and these are the teeth that actually cut the wood. The other teeth are called *rakers*, and their purpose is to clean out the saw dust and prevent the cutting teeth from becoming clogged up. As you can see, some of the larger cross-cut saws have detachable handles, and if you use one of these, make sure the handles are put properly and firmly in place.

To cut up a log with a cross-cut saw, it is a good idea to put a support under the log on one side of the cut.

Make sure the log will not roll as you start to cut it.

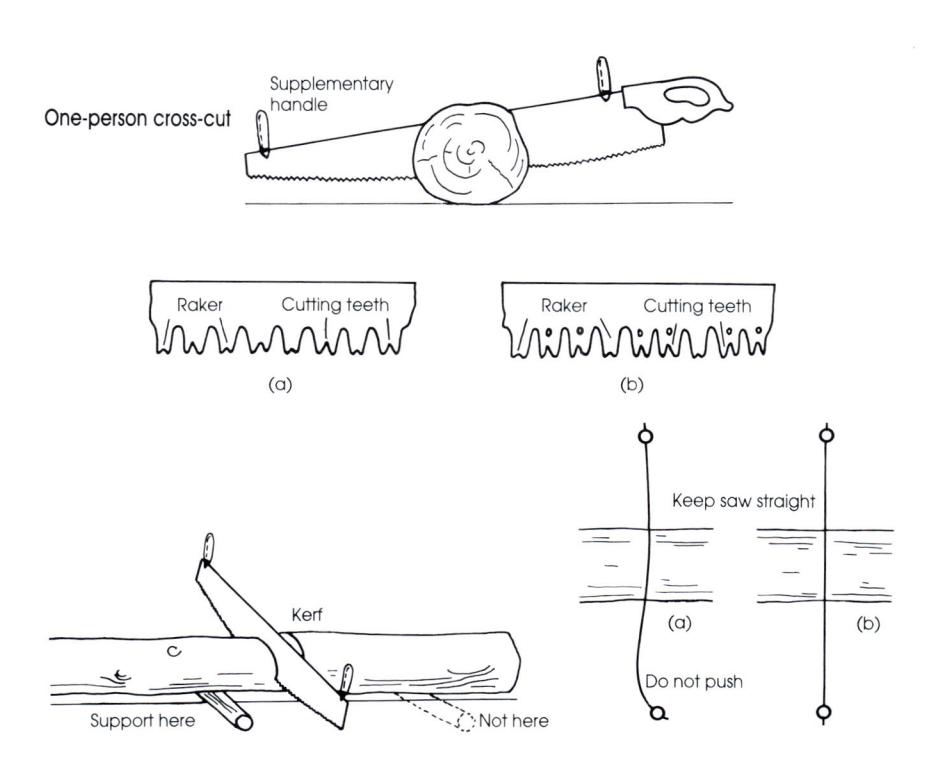

Using the saw

You will have to have another Scout to help you use the saw.
- Take the bark off the trunk where you intend to cut it with an axe.
- Put the saw on the log, and stand on opposite sides of the log with the saw in your right hands.
- Make sure you have a good solid footing.
- *Pull* the saw—never *push* it; if you push the saw it will bend, so keep it straight and pull it towards you in turn.
- Do not try to work it fast. Get a good even rhythm.
- If the log is a thick one, you may have to put a wedge in the saw cut in order to hold it open.

When you have finished, wipe the saw dry and oil it. Sometimes if you are cutting a resinous timber, such as pine, it is a good idea to wipe the saw with kerosene from time to time in order to keep the resin from clogging the saw.

Pioneering

Now you have learnt some knots and lashings, you will wish to try them out by building things. Following are some projects you can try with your Patrol.

Ideas for projects

Pioneering is an activity you can enjoy by building projects. Scouts have always had great fun by building with ropes and spars, and have displayed great ingenuity in devising structures to cope with a variety of problems. Modern materials and methods can also be applied to many Scouting projects. This section gives a few ideas on pioneering projects you can build, but remember you will get more satisfaction from inventing than from copying!

Camp projects

The step ladder requires the use of lashings—shear lashing for the legs and square lashings for the rungs. The two strings joining the feet of the ladder are essential, and a diagonal brace should be added to the legs for stability.

The foot stool is also an exercise in lashing, but the hardest part is making the seat reasonably comfortable! For the deck chair, the seat can be of either string or canvas, but get the sag correct. The gate is an exercise in the use of lashings.

Ropeways

Flying fox This is the best known and most popular of all pioneering projects. The job can be broken down into four separate parts: shear legs, anchorage, platform and fixing the rope in the tree, and bosun's chair.

Construction

Deckchair

Step ladder

Footstool

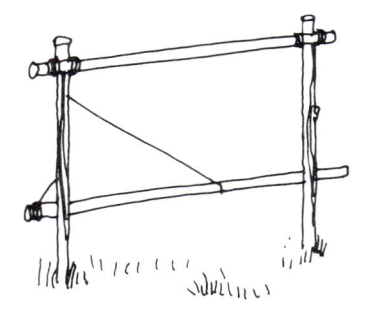

Hinged gate — the hinge is actually a rope!

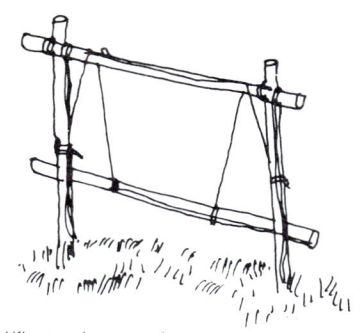

Lift-up gate — requires two sentries

Camp projects

Shelving racks

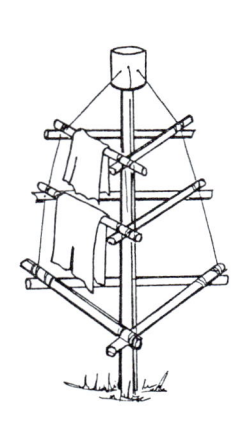

Clothesline

257

Fieldbook for Australian Scouting

Patrol name

Altar fireplace — use
100 mm mud or clay

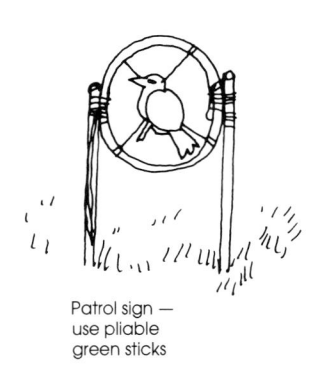

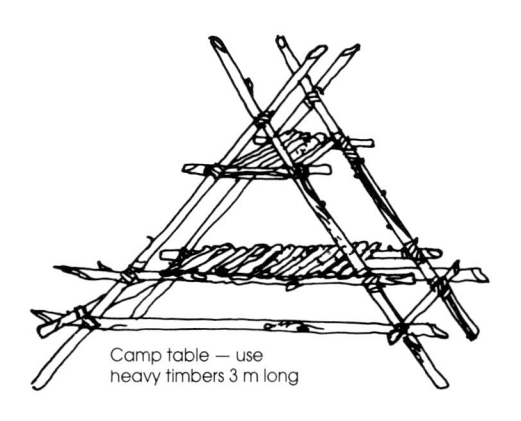

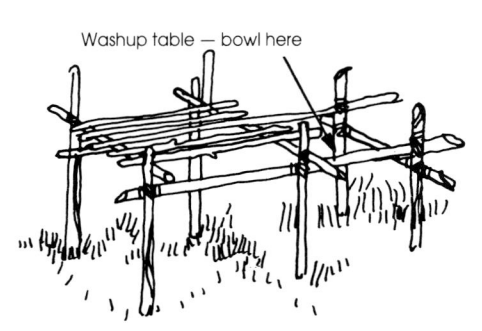

Patrol sign —
use pliable
green sticks

Patrol
flag

Patrol
flagpole

Camp table — use
heavy timbers 3 m long

Washup table — bowl here

Washup bowl stand —
with towel rail

Camp projects

258

Construction

The shear legs must be high enough for the bosun's chair to clear the ground at the lowest point. To stop the shear legs from sliding under the rope and collapsing, brace them securely with guy lines. The anchorage should be one you can tighten, because the rope stretches with use. Do not forget sacking where the main rope is fixed to the tree and at the shear legs. The main rope should not be too tight, because a small amount of slack helps in the slowing down. However, there is a fair load in the rope, so make sure it is in good condition. Keep the pulley block oiled, otherwise it will be too hard to get it back. For best results, the runaway has to be at least 20 metres long and the angle of descent not too steep.

Note: **Check with your Branch for any extra regulations for the construction of flying foxes or aerial runways.**

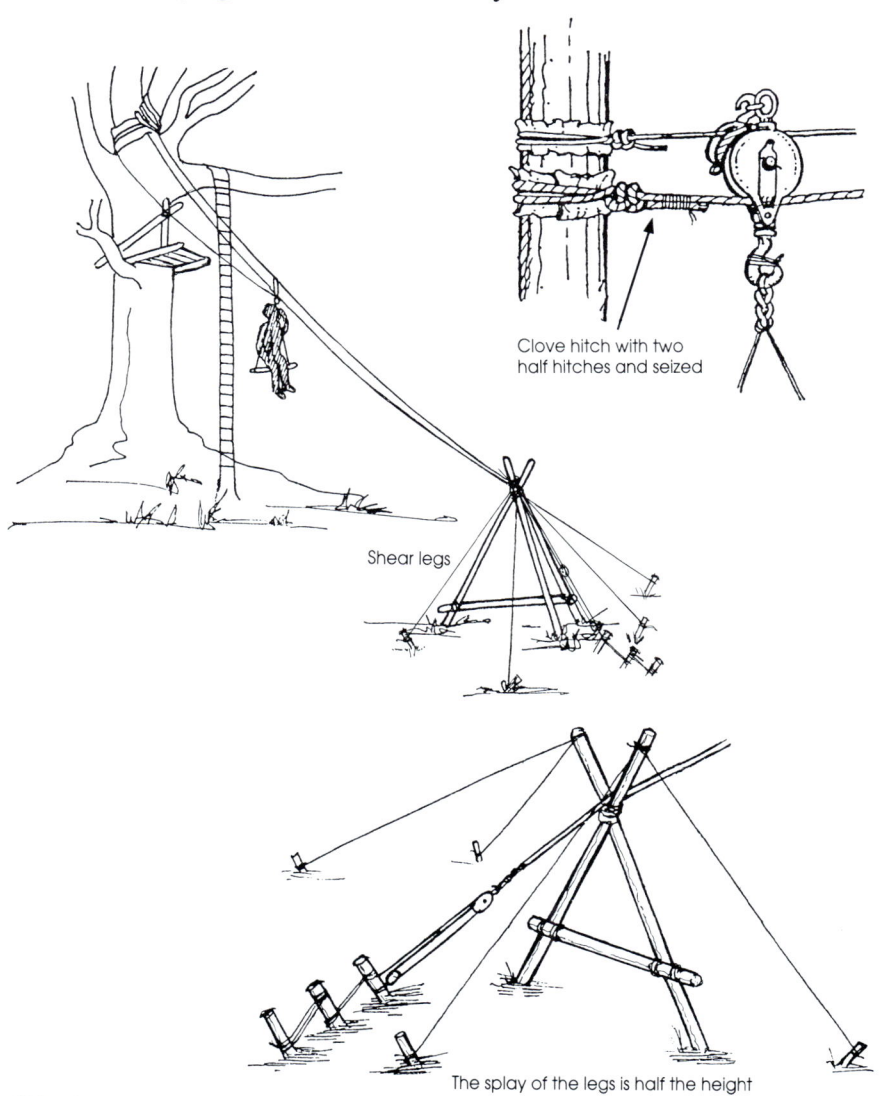

Clove hitch with two half hitches and seized

Shear legs

The splay of the legs is half the height

Flying fox

Simple rope bridge

Simple rope bridge All that is required for this bridge is two ropes and, of course, two stout trees! If the bridge is to cross a stream, you should plan a method for getting one of your Patrol members across. You may have to throw one rope into the far tree with a short stick attached so it wedges in the branches tightly, and then either swing across or go hand over hand. The most important thing is to get both ropes to the same amount of tightness. The best method of tightening would be by using a tackle. If the ropes are at all loose, the bridge will sag, and the top rope may even go out of reach! The protection around the tree is vital. To secure the ropes, make a clove hitch and two half hitches to the start, then finish by tightening with a round turn and two half hitches.

Towers

Platform The main requirements of this structure are two long and fairly stout spars to carry the platform. The whole tower can be built on the ground and pulled erect in a way so the main legs drop into holes in the ground about 30 to 50 centimetres deep. To be successful, the lashings for both the platform supports, and also the diagonal bracings, have to be well made. The rope ladder is attached before the tower is erected, but it should be pegged to the ground so it can be climbed easily. The four main guys should be tightened evenly in order to prevent the tower from twisting.

Square tower This tower has many uses, and provides a rigid platform that can be up to 6 metres above the ground. It can be made as a permanent

Construction

Platform

Splay C = A/4 + B
D should not exceed 2 metres
Crossed diagonals are stronger

(a)

(b)

Square tower

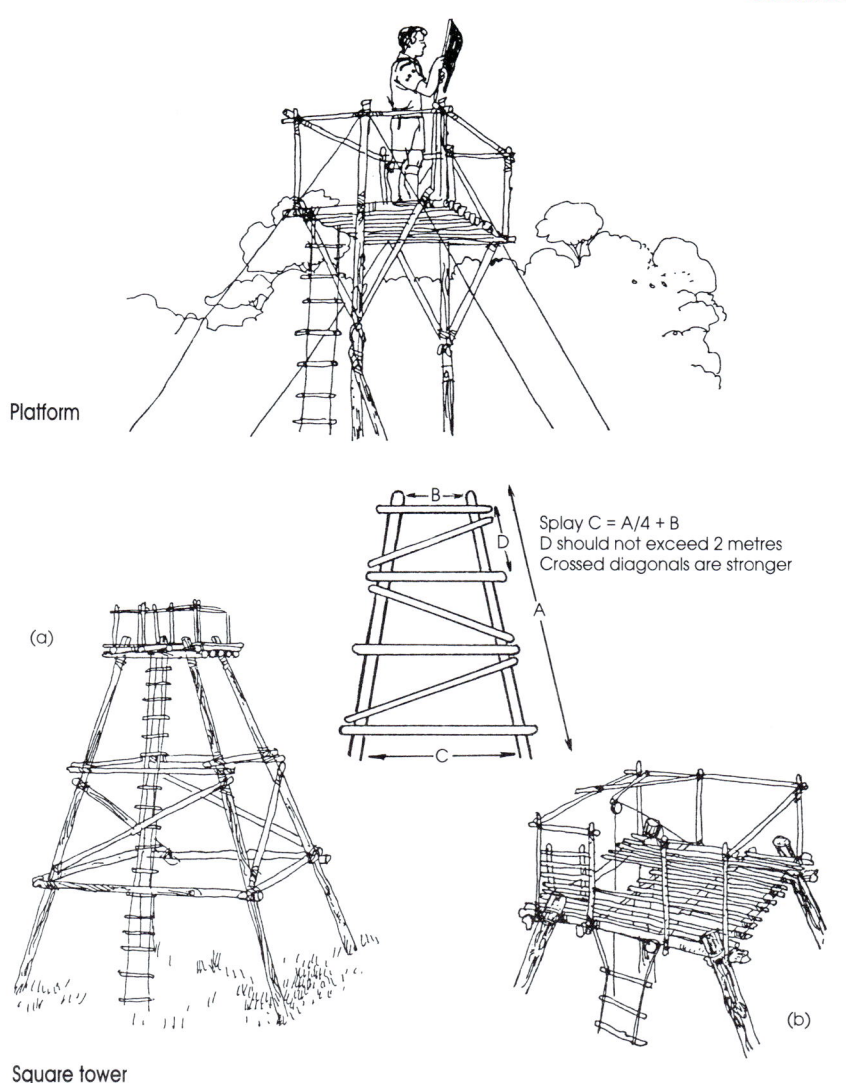

structure if the joints between the spars are bolted, or, alternatively, it can be dismantled if rope lashings are used. As in the previous tower (the platform), the actual building is best carried out on the ground and then pulled upright. You may find this part of the job is most easily carried out with the help of some auxiliary guy poles.

Pyramid tower The structure shown is composed of two similar three-sided pyramids, which are lashed together and held in place by short guy ropes. The easiest way of building it is to construct the two pyramids separately, the longest sides on the ground, and to join them with figure-of-eight lashings where the three main spars meet. The whole tower can then be pulled erect with long guy ropes. Make sure the rope ladder is in position before erection. Depending on the length of your spars, a tower up to about 6 metres high can be built.

Fieldbook for Australian Scouting

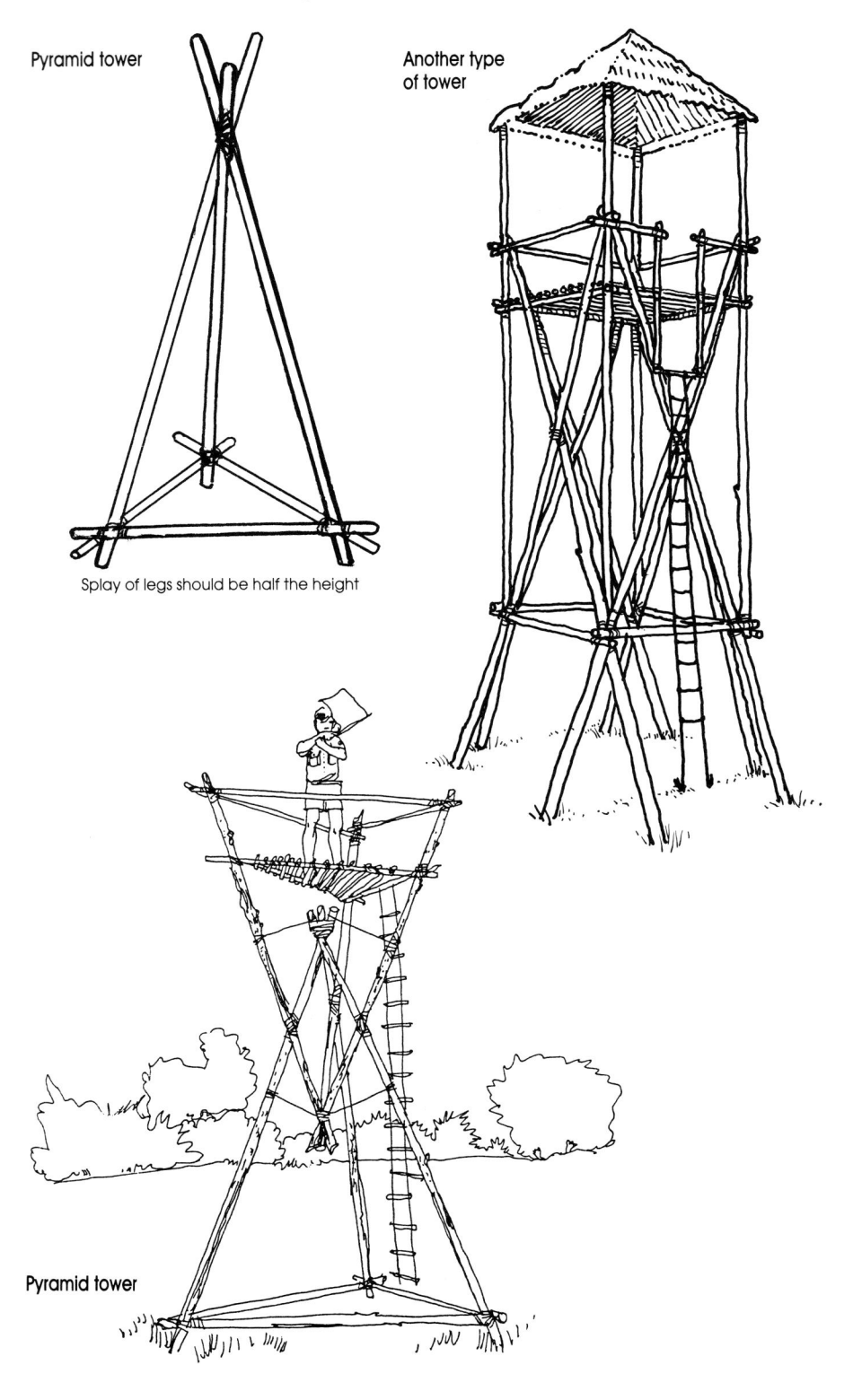

Pyramid tower

Another type of tower

Splay of legs should be half the height

Pyramid tower

262

Construction

Bridges

Rope suspension bridge This bridge uses the same principles as those in the world's great suspension bridges such as the Golden Gate in the United States, or the Forth Road Bridge in Scotland. The loads are carried entirely by tension in the main top ropes, and the footway is simply suspended from the main ropes and lightly stretched between the trestles. The loads in the main ropes are transferred to the trestles, which require some diagonal braces in order to stop them collapsing sideways, and to the end anchorages. The latter must be perfectly secure, and allow for some tensioning adjustments in the ropes. One difficulty often encountered is that of getting the strings between the top rope and the footway exactly equal on each side of the bridge. The trestles must be securely fixed in the ground so they will not slip, and must be tall enough to give sufficient clearance over the water. Remember this bridge may sag appreciably as you walk across, but if built properly, has adequate safety.

Lattice girder bridge This is a bridge that can be built with the traditional ropes and spars, or from steel waterpipe, or even from slotted-steel angle section. The latter materials would be ideal for longer lasting structures, although the project could also be constructed in timber with bolted joints. Using lashed joints, spans up to about 6 metres are easily achieved, and using bolted joints, much greater spans are feasible. If the bridge is to be built from waterpipe, standard clip fittings are available for the joints. In each panel the diagonals can be either single 25 mm × 3 mm steel flats, or they can be

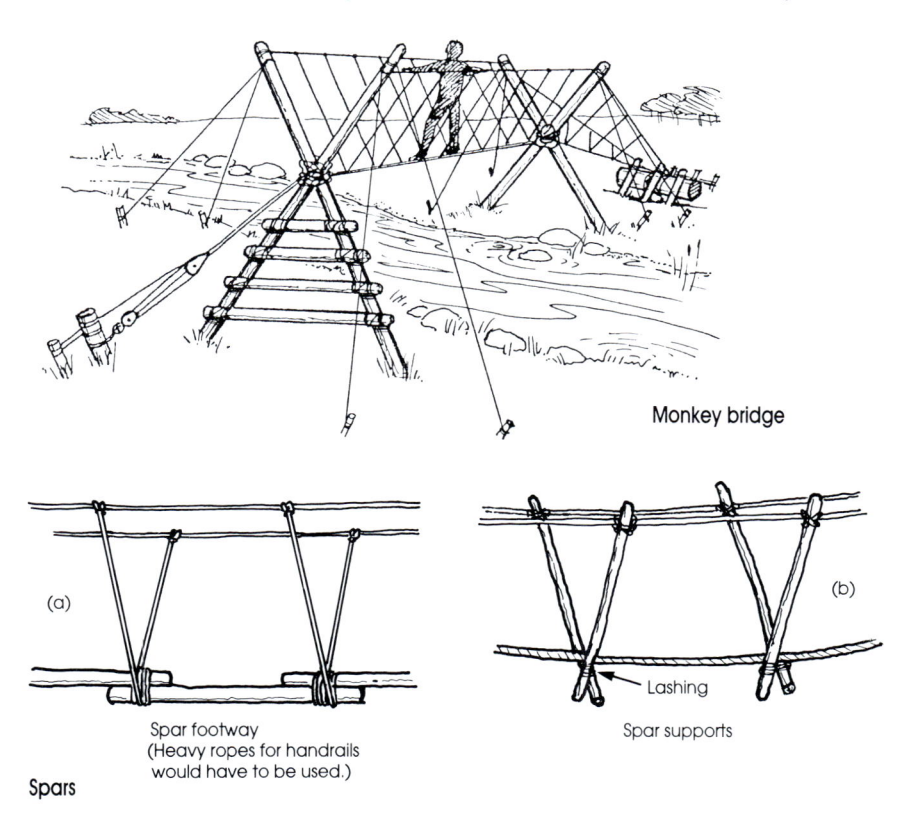

Monkey bridge

(a) Spar footway
(Heavy ropes for handrails would have to be used.)
Spars

(b) Spar supports
Lashing

263

crossed between each corner from loops of fencing wire which are tightened by twisting. Notice how the handrail can be braced by outriggers at each vertical member. This is necessary in order to prevent it buckling sideways under load. You will find it easy to build this bridge on the bank of the stream and to launch it by pulling with ropes across the stream.

Some ideas for crossing the creek

The ideas range from elaborate pioneering construction to simple single-spar operation. All the illustrations are simply ideas for you to build and have fun.
Each construction incorporates a variety of pioneering principles.

Rope suspension bridge

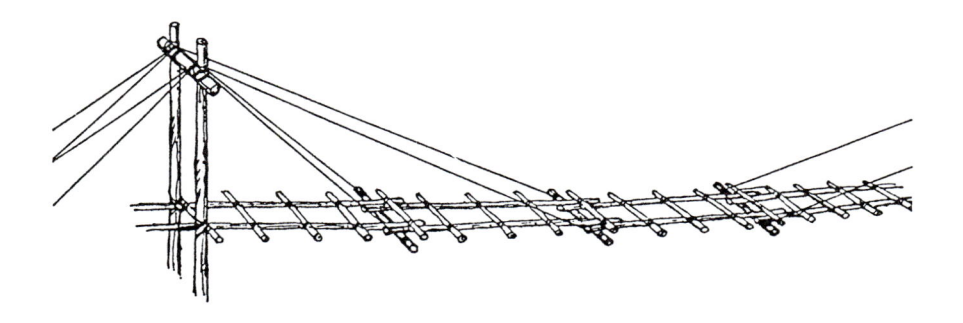

Rope suspension bridge

Construction

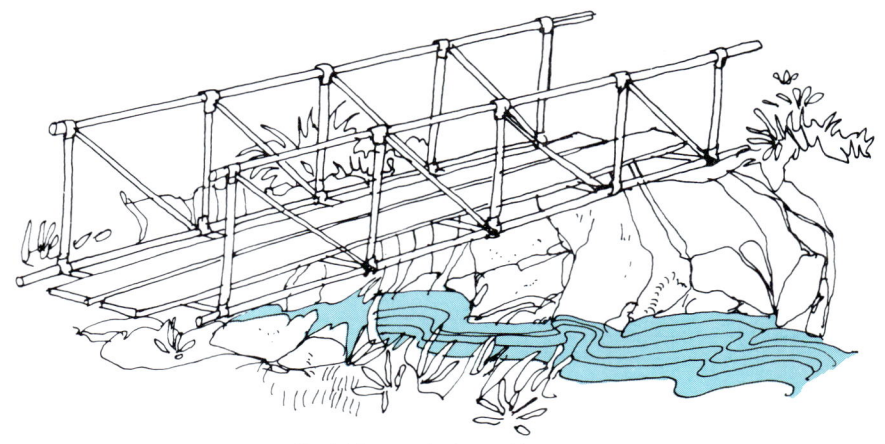

The bridge can be braced two ways:

Single diagonals,
and can also have the handrails braced

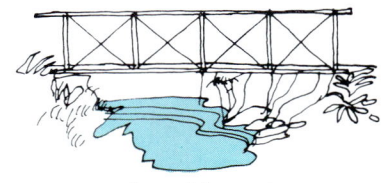

Crossed diagonals

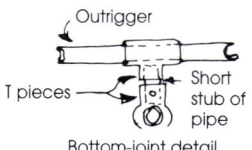

Outrigger
T pieces
Short stub of pipe
Bottom-joint detail

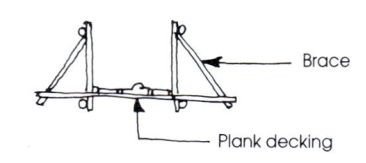

Brace
Plank decking
Lateral bracing of handrail

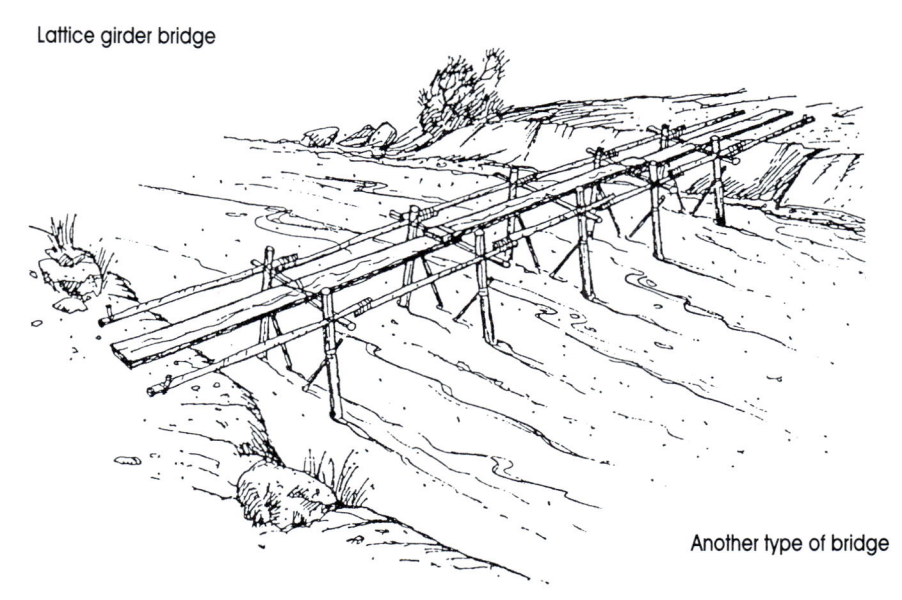

Lattice girder bridge

Another type of bridge

265

Fieldbook for Australian Scouting

B = clear roadway plus half a metre
C = B + A/3
Bay = 3 metres (Bay is the distance between trestles.)

Trestles

Hop-pole bridge

A Scout transporter

Construction

Swing bridge

Draw bridge

1 metre

A

Splay B = A/2

B

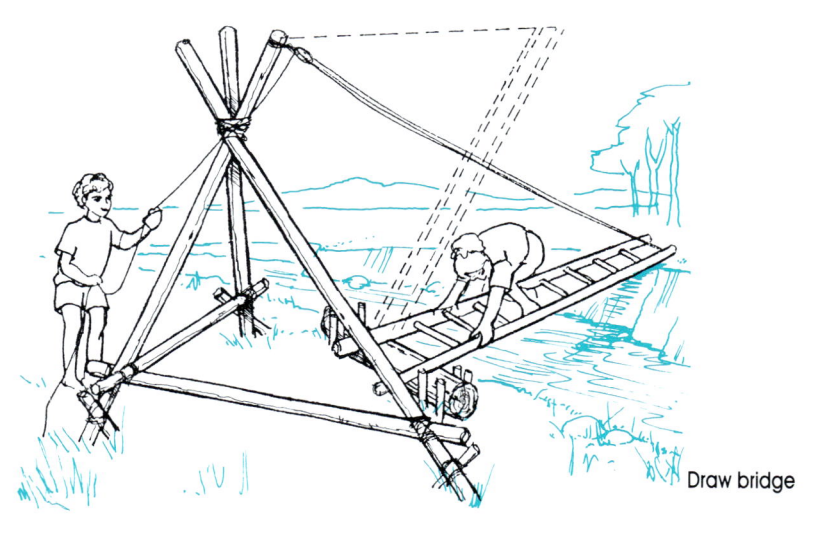

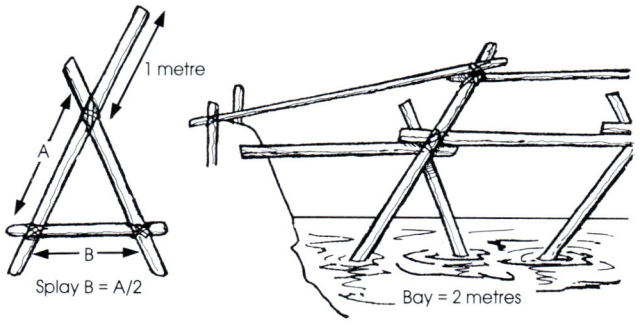

Bay = 2 metres

Light pole bridge

267

Fieldbook for Australian Scouting

Pontoon bridge with lift section

Ferry raft

268

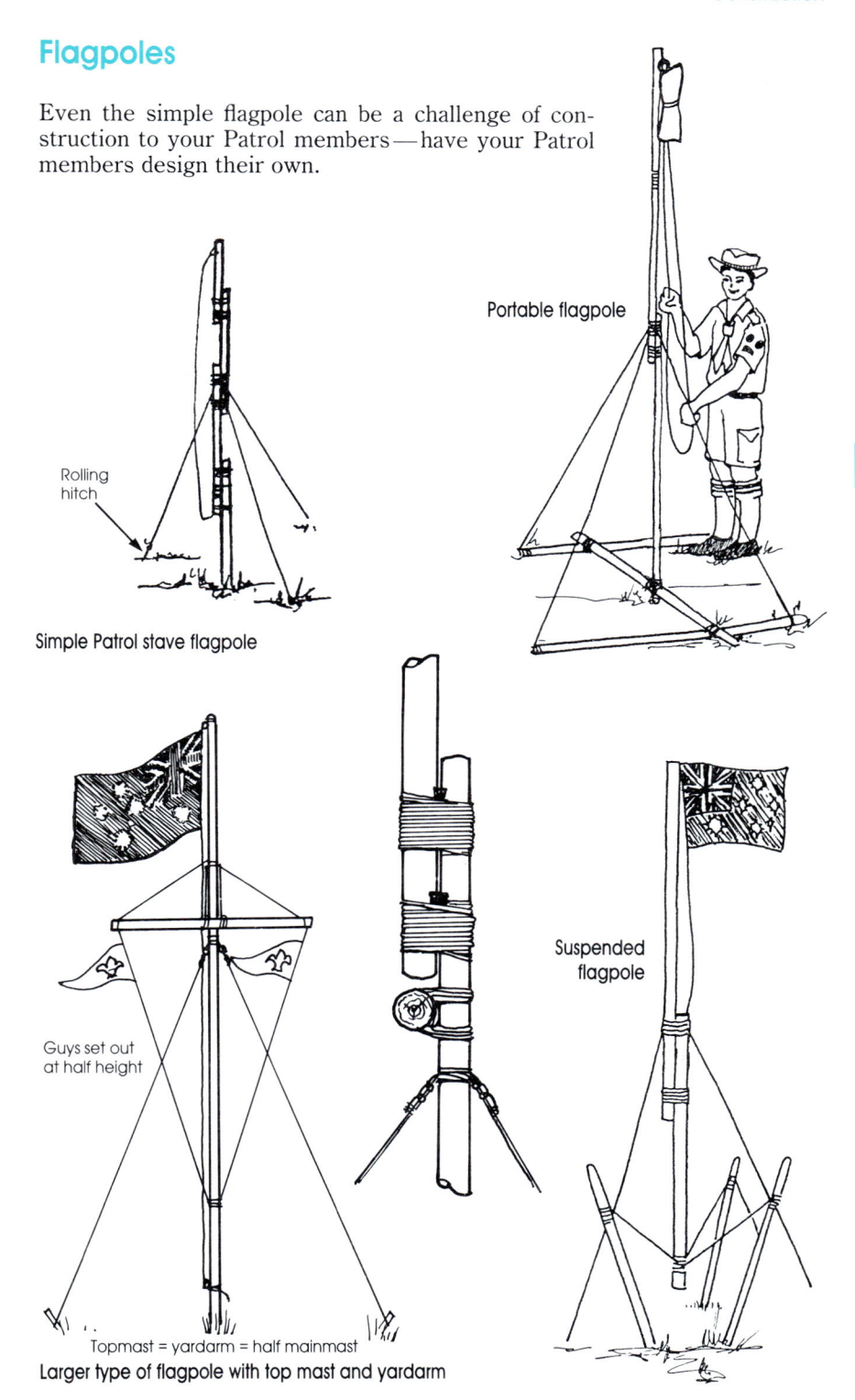

Construction

Flagpoles

Even the simple flagpole can be a challenge of construction to your Patrol members—have your Patrol members design their own.

Rolling hitch

Portable flagpole

Simple Patrol stave flagpole

Guys set out at half height

Suspended flagpole

Topmast = yardarm = half mainmast
Larger type of flagpole with top mast and yardarm

Fieldbook for Australian Scouting

Shear legs and balistas

Following are a few more ideas on things to build, from shear legs to balistas.

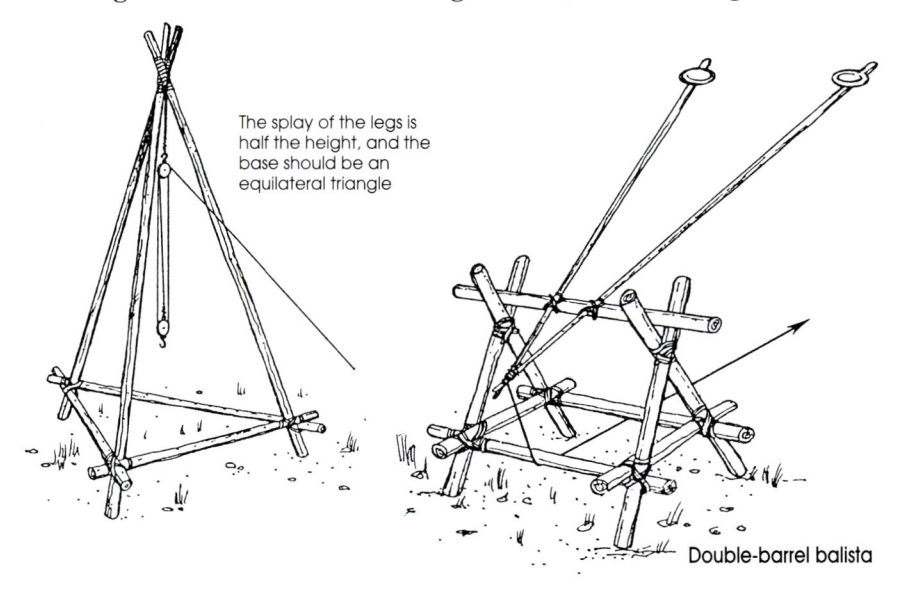

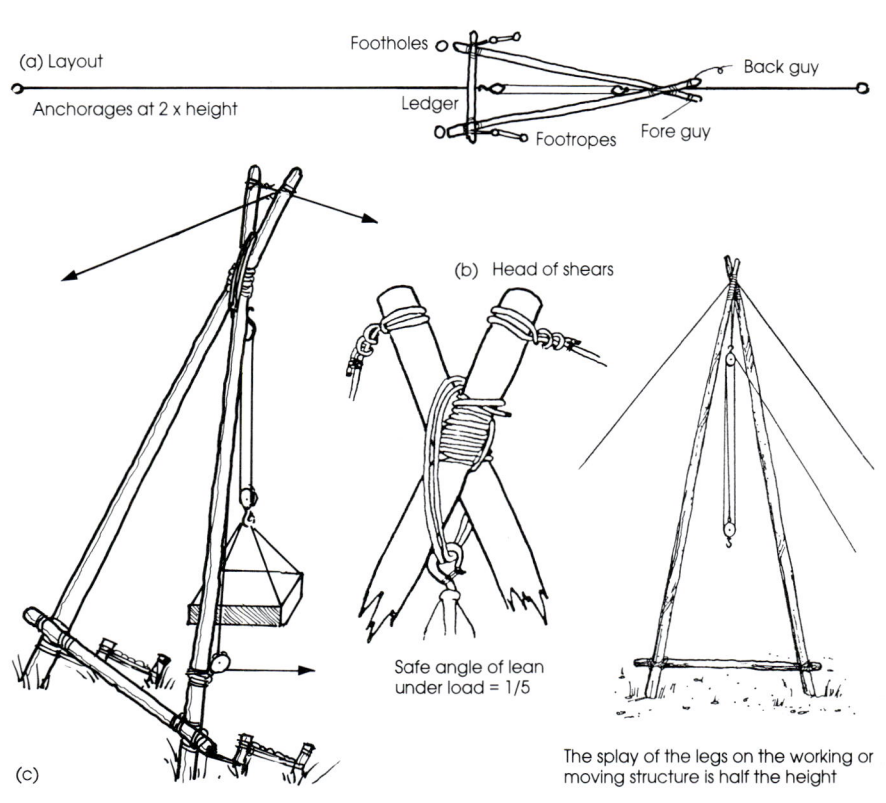

The splay of the legs is half the height, and the base should be an equilateral triangle

Double-barrel balista

(a) Layout
Anchorages at 2 x height
Footholes
Ledger
Footropes
Back guy
Fore guy

(b) Head of shears

Safe angle of lean under load = 1/5

(c)

The splay of the legs on the working or moving structure is half the height

Construction

Hyperbolic-paraboloids

For a challenge, try construction of a hyperbolic-paraboloid (HP).

You will require some spars, eye screws or staples, and lots of sisal or coloured string.

The first illustrations show a variety of simple two-spar layouts. The lines can be one way without cross-lines.

Design 1   Follow steps 1 to 3 as follows.

1. Passing the twine, as in diagram (a). Horizontal pole: 2.5 m (an eye every 10 cm, 25 intervals). Vertical pole: 4.5 m (50 cm in the ground, an eye every 16 cm, 25 intervals).
2. The vertical pole is put in place as in diagram (b).
3. The ropes are prepared, starting at one end, as in diagram (c). It must be noted that a considerable quantity of metres of sisal is recuperated.

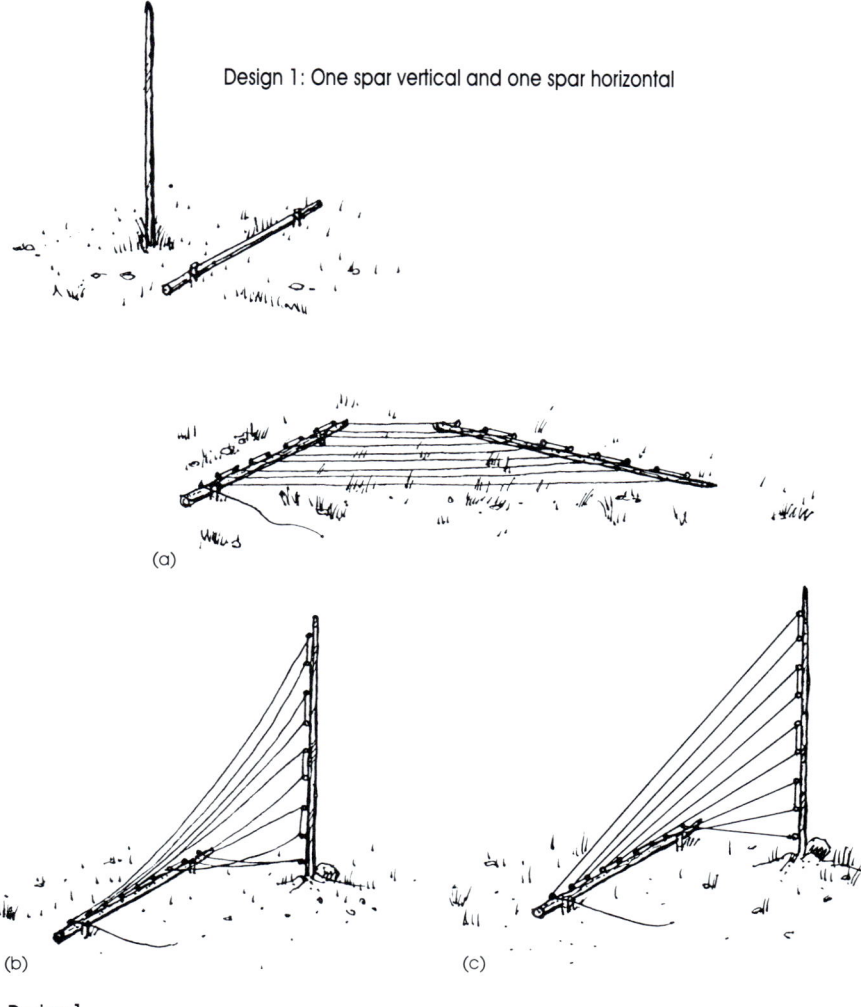

Design 1: One spar vertical and one spar horizontal

(a)

(b)   (c)

Design 1

271

Design 2 This design is another simple layout and can be altered to give various results. Follow steps 1 to 3 as follows.
1. Pass the twine through the eyes. The number of eyes will depend on the effect you wish to achieve. You can also run a second colour twine on alternate eyes, as in diagram (**a**).
2. Place one spar in place, vertically or at an angle. You now have a choice.
3. Place the second spar in place, running the twine as you finalise the angle and result required. If you run the twine in line, you will have a result as in diagram (**b**). If you reverse the second spar then run the twine, you will have a different effect, as in diagram (**c**).

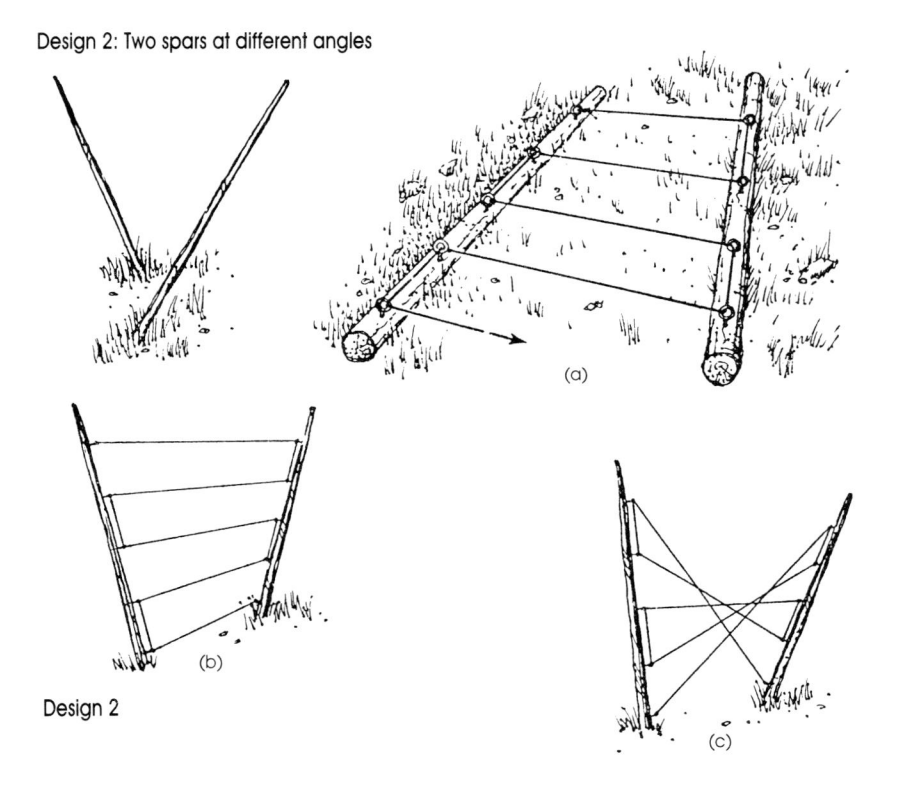

Design 2: Two spars at different angles

Design 2

Design 3 When using more than two spars, your designs can become very effective.

Construct a hyperbolic-paraboloid camp gateway. You will require four spars of various lengths. Follow steps 1 to 6 as follows.
1. Sisal or similar material is stretched from points spaced evenly along V–W to points along Y–X.
2. Similarly from points along W–X to V–Y. This can be a different colour.
3. The easiest place to start is to place spar X–Y in the ground. You may require a guy to steady it.
4. Now lift points V–X and fix with a lashing.
5. Now fix points W–Y and run the twine through.
6. Now lash points W–Y, as in diagram (**b**).

Construction

You will find that Design 3 has many applications, and they do not always have to be on the ground. *See* diagram Design 3 (b).
Some ideas for you to build on are:
(a) as a background to your flagpole: diagram Design 3(a)
(b) as a covering for a table: diagram Design 3(b). This can also be woven with vegetation for more shade, if necesary
(c) as a quiet spot for reflection: diagram Design 3(c). Note the use of some vertical lines, added to give a wall effect
(d) as a base for a dining table: diagram 3(d).

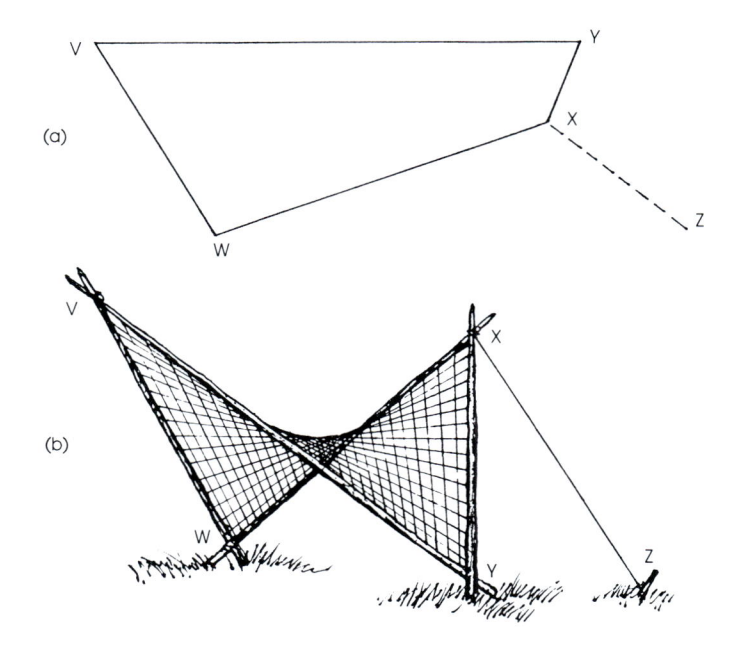

Design 3

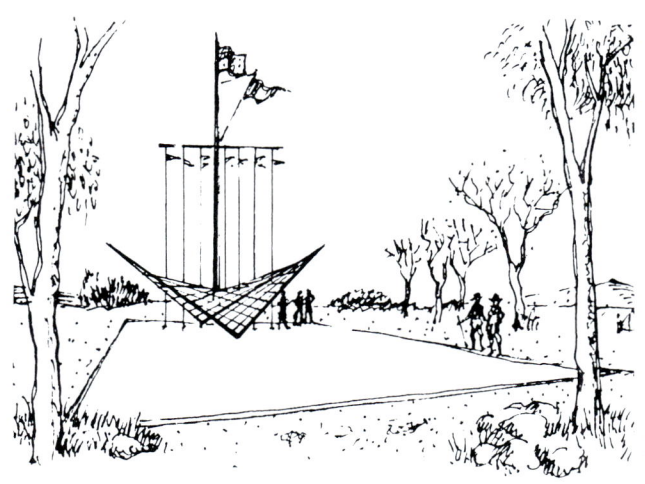

Design 3(a): as a background to your flagpole

Fieldbook for Australian Scouting

Design 3(b): as a covering for a table

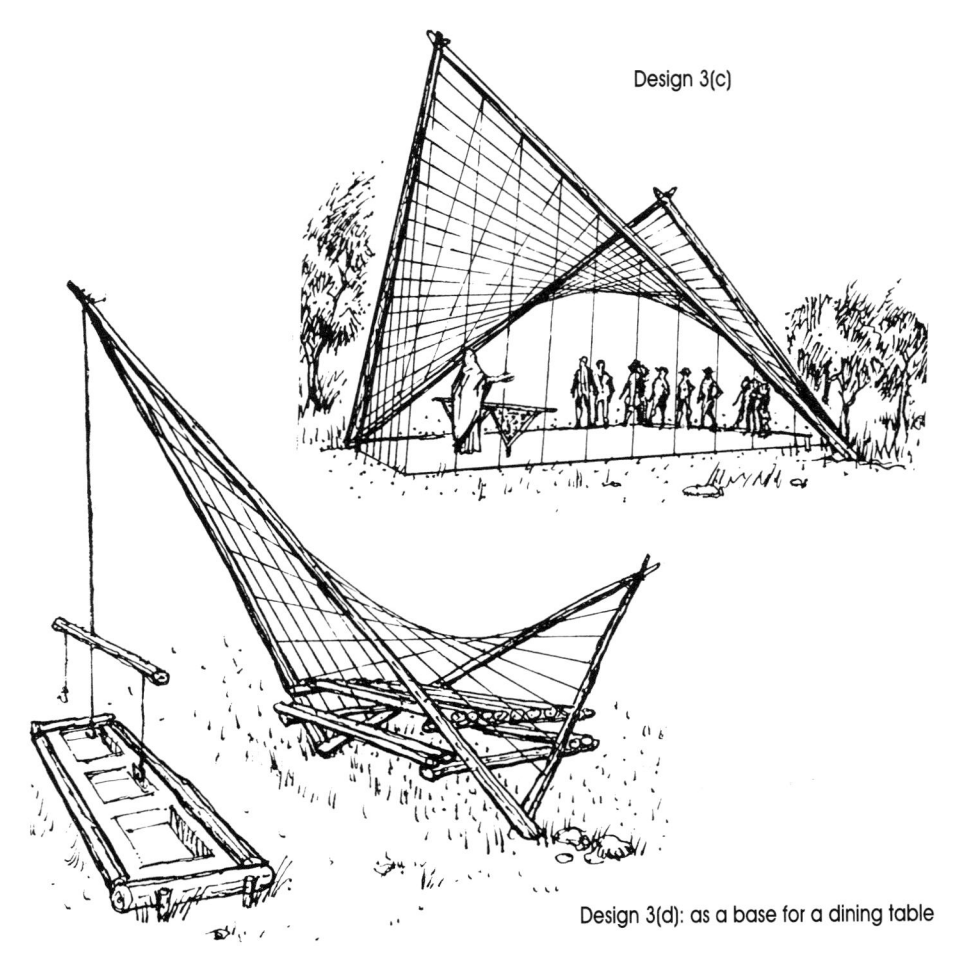

Design 3(c)

Design 3(d): as a base for a dining table

Model for Design 3

In conclusion, the HPs are only one example of all the 'regulated surfaces', that is, surfaces composed of straight lines.

If we stretch the ropes between two circles, we obtain, under certain conditions, two cones meeting at their vertex.

It we stretch ropes between a straight line and a circle (always under certain conditions), we have a cone.

Before actually putting this into practice, models should be made with assembly sets or elastic thread, which gives us a good opportunity to prepare the camp.

Rafting

Construction often includes water, not only building on dry land. We cross rivers or lakes during our activities, and one of the great fun activities in pioneering is rafting.

On the following pages are a few ideas, but you must remember two most important items in rafting:

1. flotation calculations, otherwise your fun will be shortlived
2. strong construction, because the forces on your construction will be much more variable than when it is on dry land.

Coracling

The ancient Brits used to get about on the water in coracles, and Welsh anglers continue to use them. A coracle is a cross between a raft and a canoe and is a small craft made of wickerwork covered with canvas (or animal hide).

However, you do not have to skin a cow or have a certificate in wickerwork in order to make a simple coracle! Following are two methods for making one.

Method 1 Follow steps 1 to 7 as follows.

1. Get some lengths of thick green vines or sticks about 1.5 centimetres thick, and soak them in water for about a day until they become pliable.
2. Stick the ends of the framework in the ground, bend over opposite pairs and lash overlaps, and interweave the crossings. Make sure the centre part is flat. You can do this by putting stones on the top, pulling the centre down to a tent peg: the professional coracle builder bends the wet strips in a steam jet from a kettle, or stands an old drainpipe upright in a saucepan of boiling water.
3. Weave other thinner pieces around the sides: these should be as long as possible but they do not have to go all the way around.
4. Temporarily lash the pieces near the ground so the coracle won't spring into a hundred fragments when you pull the main stakes out of the ground.
5. When you've got it out, turn it over and bend down the stakes, lashing them to their next door neighbours.
6. Stretch canvas, an old groundsheet or tarpaulin over the framework and the top edge and tie.
7. Put a woven stick mat or board in the bottom and make a paddle.

Method 2 Follow steps 1 to 3 as follows.

1. Knock two concentric circles of stakes into the ground, the outer ring having a radius of about 60 centimetres.
2. Pack in brushwood and bind with sisal string.
3. Place on canvas, old groundsheet or tarpaulin, and tie in position; put a mat in the bottom, make a paddle and you are away!

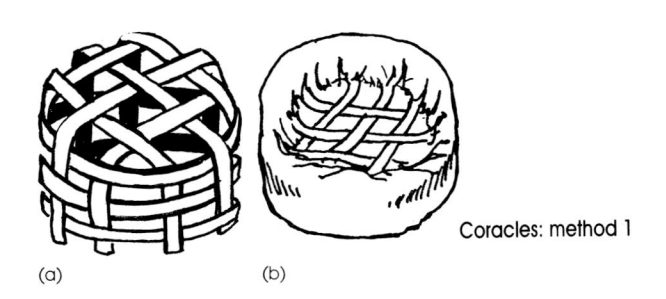

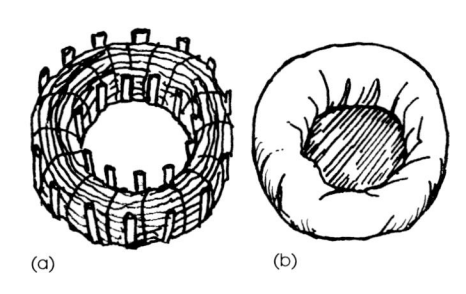

Coracles: method 1

(a) (b)

Coracles: method 2 (a) (b)

Construction

'Sausage' raft

The 'sausage' raft is also a fine raft, and can be made out of groundsheets. You will again require brush or wire netting. Make up 6 to 8 sausages, and bind the groundsheet well. Lay the sausages out with the opening on the top.

Build a light frame from Patrol staves with a light plank in the centre, then attach the sausages to the frame. Carefully place in the water, and remember that if one sausage takes on water it will start the sinking. *Always* stand or step in the centre.

Tarpaulin raft

This is like a big box, and can carry more crew. However, you have to pad the corners well in order not to damage your tarpaulin. Again, if water comes in, you have no buoyancy.

Drums and inner tubes can be used to form buoyancy, and with practice you will have a lot of fun.

Remember that there are rules for water activities, and care should be taken and the rules obeyed. Check with your Branch for local policy rules.

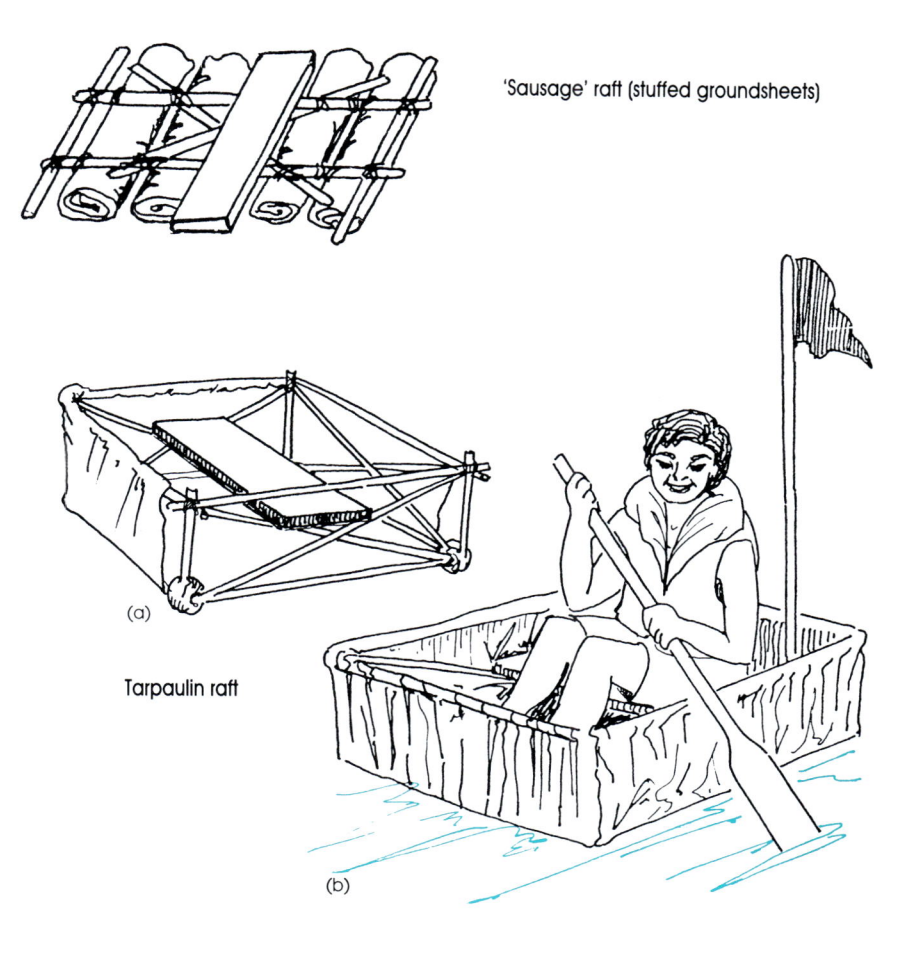

'Sausage' raft (stuffed groundsheets)

Tarpaulin raft
(a)
(b)

Fieldbook for Australian Scouting

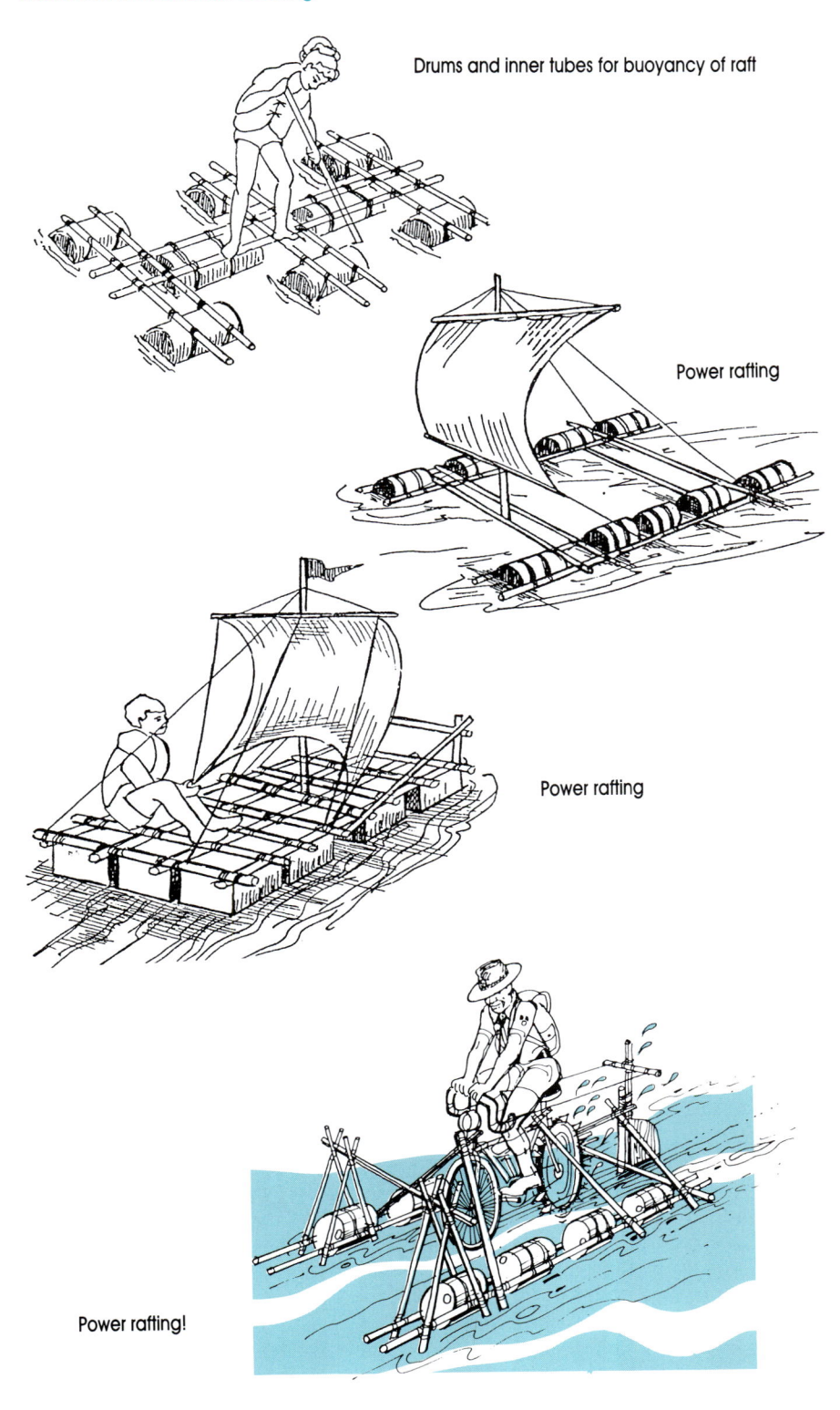

Drums and inner tubes for buoyancy of raft

Power rafting

Power rafting

Power rafting!

6
EMERGENCIES

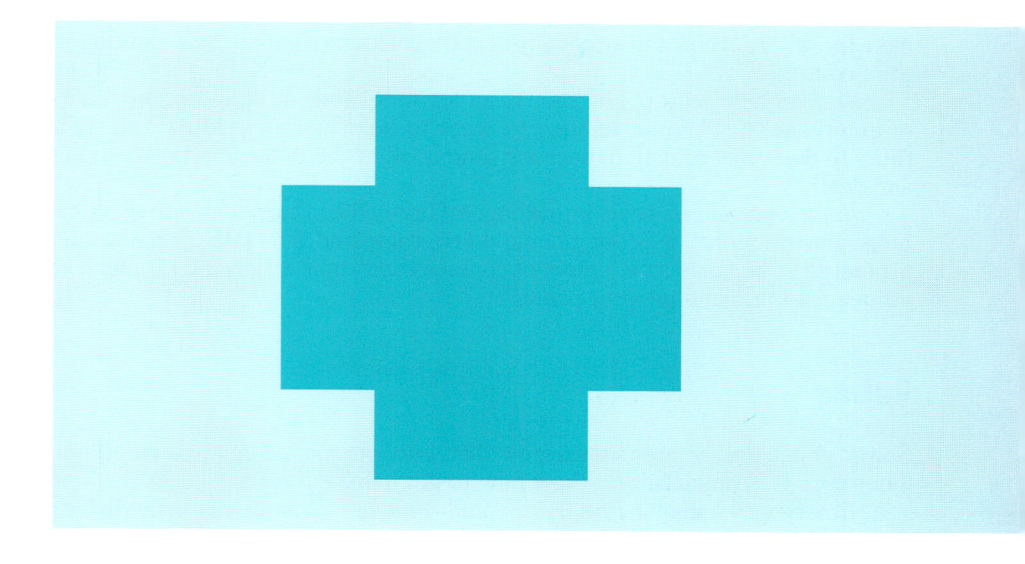

Emergency

A Patrol of Scouts was hiking along a country road. As they came around a corner, they were just in time to see a car, travelling very fast, collide with a cyclist, hurling him and his machine into the gutter. The car did not stop.

The Scouts ran up to the cyclist who was holding an arm against his chest and looking very white. The Patrol Leader quickly noticed bright-red blood coming in little spurts from the boy's leg. He took a clean handkerchief from his shirt pocket, folded it into a pad and pressed it firmly on the wound. He then borrowed another handkerchief and tied the pad firmly in place. The Scouts used their pullovers (jumpers or sweaters) to keep the cyclist warm while they decided what to do about his arm.

Just then, a car stopped near them. After examining the cyclist, the driver considered that the upper arm was broken and tied it firmly to the body. He commended the Scouts on their prompt treatment of the bleeding. He then took the cyclist in his car to the hospital in the next town, dropping one of the Scouts at the nearest telephone to report the accident to the police, while the others guarded the bicycle. One of the Scouts was observant enough to have noted the registration number of the hit-and-run car, so the police were able to trace the driver.

A doctor's report suggested that the quick treatment of bleeding by the Scouts had probably saved the boy's life.

This sort of thing could happen to any of us. Would you have known what to do? As a Scout you should be prepared for the unexpected. This means learning beforehand how to deal with emergencies, so that when time is precious you do not have to stop to think what to do. Lives have been saved by Scouts simply because they could act a few minutes before others when a serious accident occurred. Naturally, you must also be prepared to hand over to more qualified people when they arrive on the scene.

Many accidents occur because people do not observe ordinary rules of safety. What these rules actually amount to is commonsense and thoughtfulness for others. Scouts are thoughtful and considerate people by definition in the Scout Law.

We can help with public safety, by learning what to do in various kinds of emergencies. It is not enough to want to help: we must know the right thing to do in that situation, because time is often the difference between life and death.

In an emergency a basic knowledge of first aid can turn fear into practical help. Furthermore, a Scout should keep calm and act with decision and promptness, because an example of coolness and right action will do much to influence others and prevent panic.

Report

Some emergencies are so serious that one person cannot handle them. Therefore it is important to know how to get help.

Emergency calls for *Fire, Police,* and *Ambulance* can be made by dialling 000. No money is required for these telephone calls. However, it is a wise precaution to have at least 40 cents in your pocket for emergency calls that might require coins. For a manual telephone in the country, ring the local fire number, or ask the exchange for help.

When making an emergency call, remember the three Ws: *Who? Where? What?*

Who: Give your name and which service is required.
Where: State where the accident has occurred.
What: Tell what has happened, give details of number of casualties, advise whether any are unconscious, and state action taken.

Be ready to receive instructions about what to do until help arrives. If necessary, wait at an easily identified point and direct help to the scene of the accident.

Rescue

Most of us at one time or another are faced with a situation in which help and first aid are necessary—and the right action and care promptly given can minimise injuries and save lives. So there is much to be said for taking a course in rope work, rescue methods and first aid, but even without formal training there are certain things you can do in case of accidents until medical help arrives. Further reference can be made to first aid books from the Red Cross, St John Ambulance Australia or your local state ambulance authority from which amended and up-to-date treatments can be obtained.

Emergencies

Principles and practice of first aid

If you happen to discover an accident, stop, survey the situation, think, and act quickly, quietly and methodically, taking care that you do not place yourself in any danger of becoming a casualty. Remember you are not a doctor. Your role is that of a first-aider and, as such, you should be trained to give help that will:

1. remove the cause if still active, or remove the patient from the source of danger
2. preserve life by commencing resuscitation if breathing has stopped, controlling bleeding, and lessening shock
3. prevent the injury or illness from becoming worse by covering wounds, immobilising fractures, and making the patient comfortable
4. promote recovery by reassuring the patient and people around the scene and therefore help to lessen anxiety, relieving pain, handling gently, protecting from weather, and improvising if necessary.

While carrying out these four roles, ask other people to help you by giving definite instructions such as the following:

- 'Phone and notify the police.'
- 'Ask for an ambulance.'
- 'Keep the crowds back so the patient can get fresh air.'

Remember the following:
D—danger, R—response, A—airway, B—breathing, C—circulation.

Circulation of blood

The normal adult has a blood volume of about six litres that is being continuously circulated to all parts of the body by means of the heart, a muscular organ acting as a double pump, located in the chest behind the breast bone and slightly towards the left. The function of the blood is to carry oxygen from the lungs to all parts of the body and to take carbon dioxide to the lungs for discharge to the air. It also takes nourishment from the products of digestion to all parts of the body and removes waste products. In addition, it maintains the body temperature, provides the tissues with moisture, and provides a defence against infection.

Each time the heart beats, the surge can be felt in the arteries as a pulse, particularly where the artery crosses bone.

When a person receives a wound, haemorrhage (bleeding) in some form may occur. A surface wound may injure only small blood vessels, producing a steady flow of bright blood from all parts of the wound. The wound should be cleaned and dressed with a firm dressing. Clotting, which is nature's way of healing, should be encouraged, and a clot should not be moved.

A deeper wound may easily injure an artery, a vein, or both, as well as many capillaries, and a person can easily bleed to death if prompt action is not taken. Blood coming out from an artery will be bright red, in a steady stream, which may spurt in gushes with each heartbeat. Arterial bleeding is the most serious. Venous bleeding (from a vein) will be dark, deep red, almost purple, and will ooze from the wound (see Bleeding page 284).

Treatments

Unconsciousness

If you find a person who is unconscious, that is, one who cannot speak and answer your questions or does not respond if you try to rouse him/her, the general treatment is as follows.

- Place the patient in the recovery (lateral) position. This will permit secretions, blood, vomit or food to drain from the mouth and not obstruct the air passages.
- Clear any obstruction to the mouth or nose.
- Check breathing. If breathing has stopped or is failing, commence artificial respiration.
- Control bleeding.
- Quickly check for any other injuries, particularly injuries to the spine.
- Loosen clothing about the neck, chest and waist.
- Treat for shock.
- Do not give anything by mouth.
- Send for medical help.

To place patients in a recovery position: If they are lying on their back, roll them over until they are lying on their side, as shown in the diagrams.

Concussion or stunning

This is a common result of a fall or blow on the head and should be treated similarly to unconsciousness. Its symptoms are headaches after a head injury; frequently, a loss of memory for events before and after the injury; nausea and often vomiting, and blurring of vision.

It should be treated as follows.

- If the patient is unconscious, place him/her in a recovery position.
- Clear any obstruction to the mouth or nose.
- Check breathing and pulse.
- Control bleeding.
- Check for other injuries.
- Treat for shock.
- Send for medical help.

Warning

No head injury should be considered or treated lightly. Every patient who has had even a mild injury to the head is to be observed thoroughly to detect the onset of complications.

Advise the patient who has been unconscious, even for a moment, to seek medical help. A return of unconsciousness is a sign of serious danger.

Fainting

Fainting is due to a temporary disturbance of the nervous control of the blood vessels allowing too little blood in the head. The symptoms are giddiness,

Emergencies

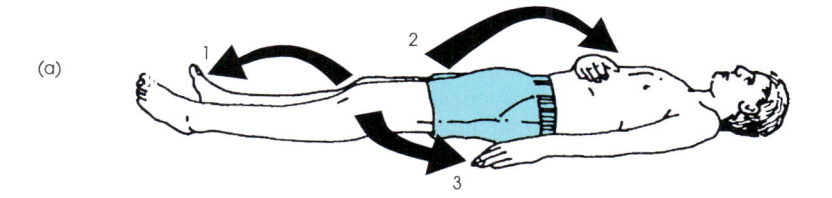

(a) Prepare to turn the patient onto their side.

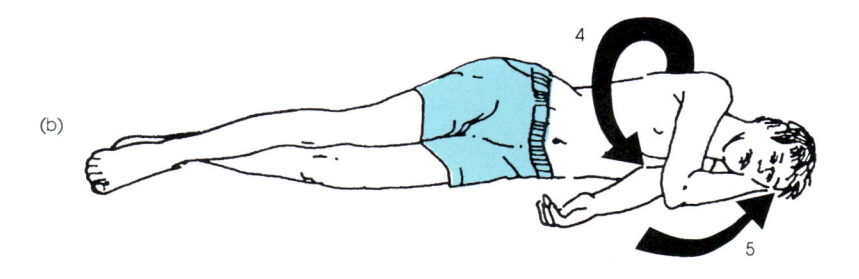

(b) Tilt the patient's head to open the airway.

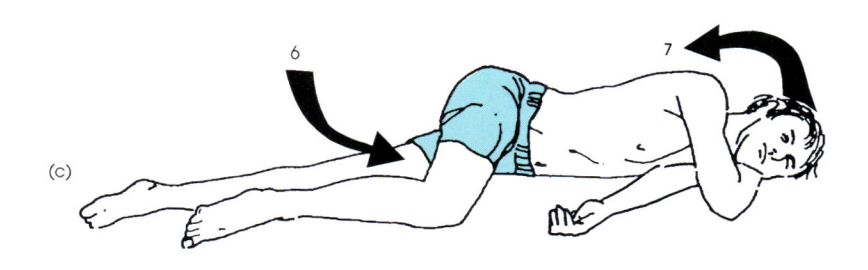

(c) Placing the casualty in the recovery position

unsteadiness and blurred vision; the patient becomes cold and clammy; yawning; weakness, and loss of consciousness.

Treatment should be as follows:
- Lie the patient down with legs raised and head lowered.
- Encourage regular breathing if conscious.
- Loosen clothing around neck, chest and waist.
- Ensure a good supply of fresh air.
- Reassure the patient.

Seizures

If a person cries out and falls and twitches and jerks their limbs about and froths at the mouth, they are in an epileptic seizure.
- Protect the patient from injury but do not restrict their movements.
- Do not try to force their mouth open.
- If the opportunity arises, remove any false teeth or plates.
- If the patient falls asleep, do not disturb them.
- Seek medical assistance.

Bleeding

Bleeding (haemorrhage) is the loss of blood from the circulation. The blood may escape through a wound or remain in the tissues. Severe bleeding leads to grave shock (see next section 'Shock').

When the blood is from an artery it spurts with the heartbeats and is bright red (oxygen rich). Blood from the veins is a continuous flow and is dark in colour (oxygen poor). The general treatment for severe bleeding is as follows.
- Act quickly—every drop of blood is important.
- Apply direct pressure to the wound.
- Rest the patient—to lower blood pressure.
- Raise the part—to decrease the bloodflow to the injured limb.
- Rest the part—to encourage a clot to form.
- Treat for shock.
- Send for medical help.

The application of direct pressure to the wound controls bleeding by compressing the blood vessels leading to the wound and by retaining blood in the wound long enough for it to clot.

Pressure is applied by placing a large dressing or pad (for example, a clean handkerchief folded up) over the wound. Bind the dressing firmly. If the dressing gets soaked, do not remove it, place another dressing over it and maintain pressure. In time, the blood should clot.

On small wounds, do not disturb any blood clot. Remove any foreign bodies, apply an adhesive plaster or a clean sterile dressing and a bandage.

Bleeding from the nose Although bleeding from the nose is usually not serious, if not stopped the patient can lose a lot of blood. Treat as follows.
- Sit the patient up with the head slightly forwards.
- Apply pressure on the flap of the nostril for at least 10 minutes.
- Loosen all tight clothing around the neck, chest and waist.
- Keep the patient cool with a free supply of fresh air.
- Instruct the patient not to blow his/her nose.
- Instruct the patient to breathe through the mouth.
- Place cold wet towels on the neck and forehead, replacing frequently.

Internal bleeding Spitting or vomiting blood means internal injury or bursting of a small blood vessel inside the patient. If the blood is light red in colour and mixed with froth, it means injury to the lungs. *In either case* keep the patient quiet and seek medical help urgently.

Bruises Ice packs or cold compresses will reduce the amount of bleeding. If the bruise is large, a firm bandage and elevation of the part may be necessary.

Shock

Shock is a dangerous condition that comes with *almost* all injuries or emotional disturbance. It is caused by insufficient blood circulation and varies in severity with the extent of the injury.

It may develop at once, or it may take time to develop, even an hour or so after the event. It is always present or likely to be present in any accident, and should always be treated even when no symptoms are present. It can be a cause of death after an accident.

Shock may vary from faintness to complete collapse. The symptoms vary and may include giddiness and faintness; thirst; coldness; nausea, and vomiting. The signs are a cold clammy pale skin; beads of sweat on the forehead; breathing quick and shallow; a slow pulse at first, becoming rapid and feeble; change in behaviour, and then unconsciousness.

First-aid treatment must be started immediately as follows.
- If unconscious, place the patient in a recovery position.
- Ensure an adequate airway through the mouth and nose, and a supply of fresh air.
- Control any bleeding.
- Elevate the legs in order to ensure maximum supply of blood to the brain.
- Do not heat the patient unnecessarily, but prevent shivering.
- Relieve pain by covering wounds, immobilising fractures, raising the injured part, resting the injured part, and handling gently.
- Reassure the patient.
- Arrange quick and gentle transport to medical help.

- Fluids may be given frequently in small quantities only if medical help is not readily available.
- Do not give fluids if the patient is unconscious; if there is an abdominal injury; if there is the possibility of an immediate operation, or the patient feels sick.
- Do not give alcohol.

Burns

Burns are the damage to body tissues caused by exposure to excess heat. They occur from dry heat from a fire; a flame; contact with hot objects; an electric current; sunburn or excess friction, and moist heat from hot water or steam (these burns are called scalds).

Burns are classified according to their depth and the area of the body surface burnt.

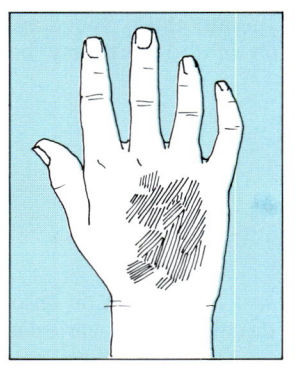

Superficial burn: The skin is reddened and the patient may feel pain.
Sunburn is usually a superficial burn

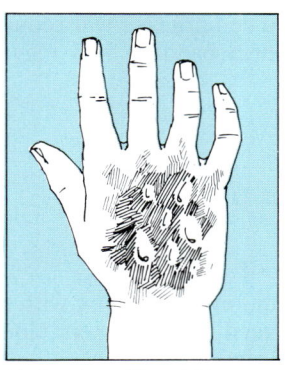

Medium burn: Where blisters have formed. Extreme care is necessary to keep the blister from breaking and wound from being infected

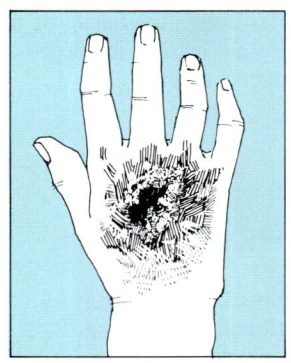

Deep burn: Some skin may be burned away and some flesh charred. This burn is very dangerous because growth cells that form the new skin are destroyed

The three types of burns

Treatment of burns

Superficial burns These occur when only the outer layers of skin are damaged and where there is reddening and minor blister formation. Treat as follows.

- Wash with cold water for 15 mins. Reapply cold water if pain continues.
- Apply a sterile dressing and bandage firmly.

Deep burns These occur when the full thickness of skin and underlying muscle are also burned. Treat as follows.

- Remove or cut away clothing over the burned area but leave clothing that is stuck.
- Wash liberally with cold water for 15 mins.

- Cover the burned area with a sterile or clean dressing and bandage lightly.
- Cover large burns with a clean sheet or towel.

In burns to the face, provide an adequate airway for breathing.

- Do not apply any lotions, ointments or oily dressings.
- Do not prick blisters.

If the patient is thirsty, or if there is a long delay, give small amounts of water unless he/she is unconscious and/or medical help is readily available.

Transport the patient to medical help without delay.

Sunburn Prolonged exposure to the sun may lead to extensive superficial burns with blister formation. The distress of sunburn without blister formation can be relieved by applying the following treatment.

- Apply cool moist compresses.
- Rest the patient in a cool place.
- Give a large quantity of fluids.

Serious sunburn with severe blistering requires medical help after this treatment.

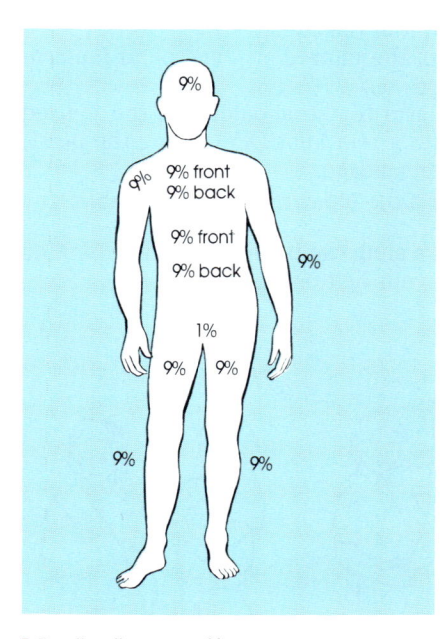

Chemical and corrosive burns
Treat as follows.

- Wash off immediately with a large volume of water for 20 mins.
- Remove contaminated clothing but avoid contaminating yourself.
- Apply a dressing.

Estimating the area of burns

Bandages

A piece of linen or calico 1 metre × 1 metre makes two triangular bandages. Your Scout scarf can be used in an emergency, but make sure it does not touch the wound, because dirt or dye from it might cause blood poisoning. To use it as a large arm sling, study the diagrams.

Fieldbook for Australian Scouting

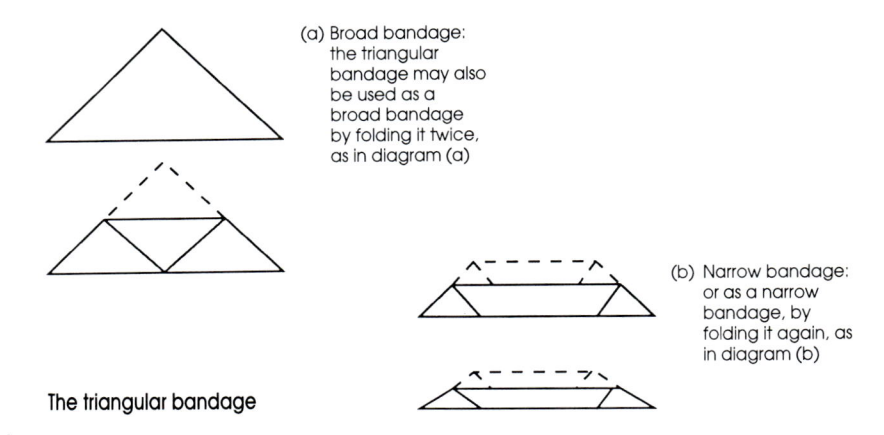

(a) Broad bandage: the triangular bandage may also be used as a broad bandage by folding it twice, as in diagram (a)

(b) Narrow bandage: or as a narrow bandage, by folding it again, as in diagram (b)

The triangular bandage

To use as a large arm sling

- Spread out a bandage. Put one end, X, over the sound shoulder.
- Let the other end, Y, hang down in front of the chest.
- Place the point, Z, behind the elbow of the injured arm and bend the arm forward over the middle of the bandage.
- Carry the second end, Y, across the arm to the shoulder on the injured side and tie it to the other end, X, with a reef knot (XY). Bring the point, Z, forward and pin it to the front of the bandage.
- Check the circulation. Ask the patient if the hand/arm is comfortable.

When there is no bandage available, a sling can be improvised by pinning up the sleeve of a coat or even by using your belt or a piece of rope.

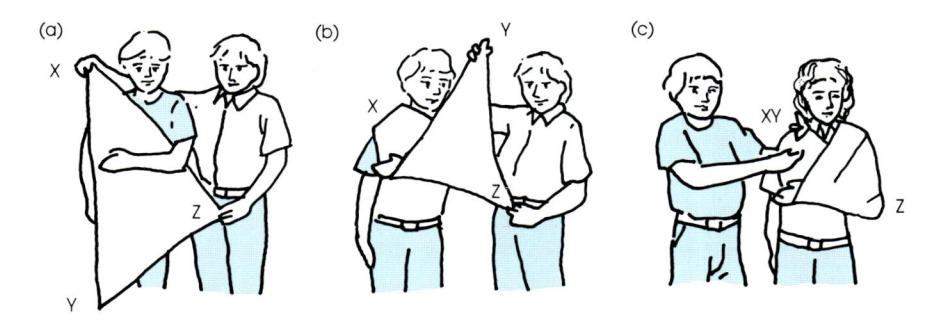

Large arm sling

To use an elevated sling

- Place the injured arm, if possible, in the position as in the diagram (**a**).
- Place point X of the bandage over the shoulder on the uninjured side.
- Support the injured arm and tuck the bandage under the arm, as in diagram (**b**).

Emergencies

- Take point Y around the back and up to point X.
- Tie XY together with a reef knot in the hollow of the neck, as in diagram (**c**).
- Bring point Z around and pin to form a pocket, or if no pin is available, twist it and then tuck it in behind the elbow.
- Check the circulation. Check the comfort of sling.

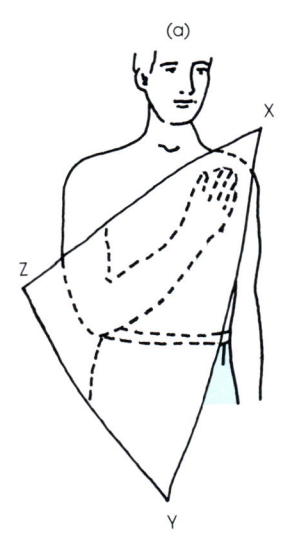

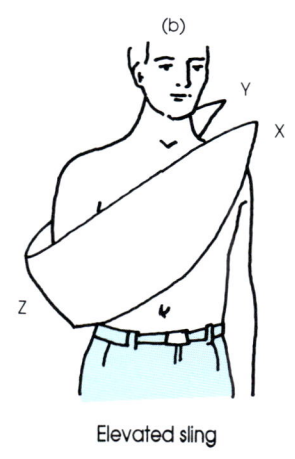

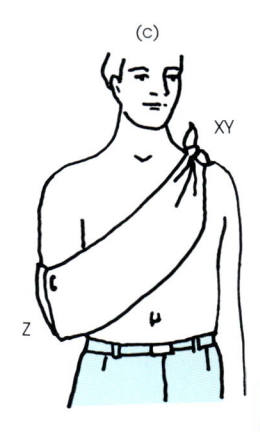

Elevated sling

Collar-and-cuff sling

This supports the wrist.

- Place the forearm across the chest with the fingers pointing towards the opposite shoulder.
- Pass a clove hitch over the hand and around the wrist, the knot of the clove hitch on the thumb side of the wrist, and a fold of the cuff on either side of the wrist.
- Tie the ends of the bandage in the hollow just above the collarbone on either side. Check the circulation. Check the comfort of sling.

Collar-and-cuff sling

For a scalp wound

- Fold a hem inwards along the base of the bandage, and place the middle of the hem over the centre of the forehead close to the eyebrows, with the point hanging over the head to the neck.
- Carry the two ends around the head just above the ears, cross just below the prominence on the back of the head, and carry the ends forward to tie in front of the forehead.
- Pull the point down, turn it over the top of the head, and pin in position.

Fieldbook for Australian Scouting

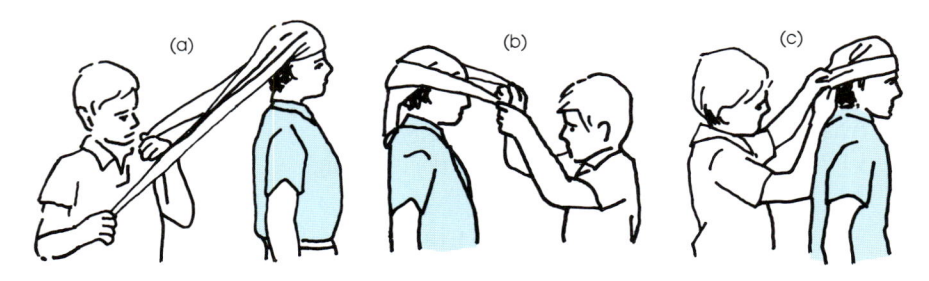

Head bandage for a scalp wound

For forehead, back or side of head, eye, ear or cheek

- Use a narrow or broad bandage and place the centre of it over a pad over the wound.
- Carry the ends around the head, cross them, and bring back to tie with a reef knot over the pad.

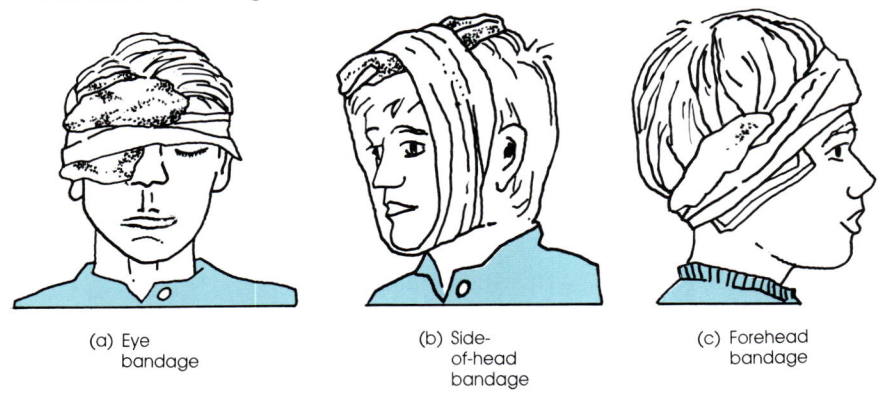

(a) Eye bandage

(b) Side-of-head bandage

(c) Forehead bandage

For a knee wound

- Bend the knee to a right angle.
- Fold a narrow hem inwards along the base of the bandage.
- Lay the point on the thigh and the middle of the base below the knee.
- Cross the ends behind the knee, then around the thigh, and tie about the knee on the front of the thigh.
- Bring the point down over the knot, and pin it in position.

For a foot wound

- Lay out bandage unfolded, and place injured foot in the centre of it with toes towards the point.
- Draw the point up over the foot, bring the ends forwards so the heel is covered, cross them, and pass the ends around the ankle.
- Cross at back, and bring them forward again to tie at the front.
- Draw the point forwards and pin over the instep.

Emergencies

(a) Fold bandage like this

(b)

(c)

(d)

(e) Bandage for knee or elbow

(a) Lay bandage flat. Put foot down with toes to the point

(b)

(c)

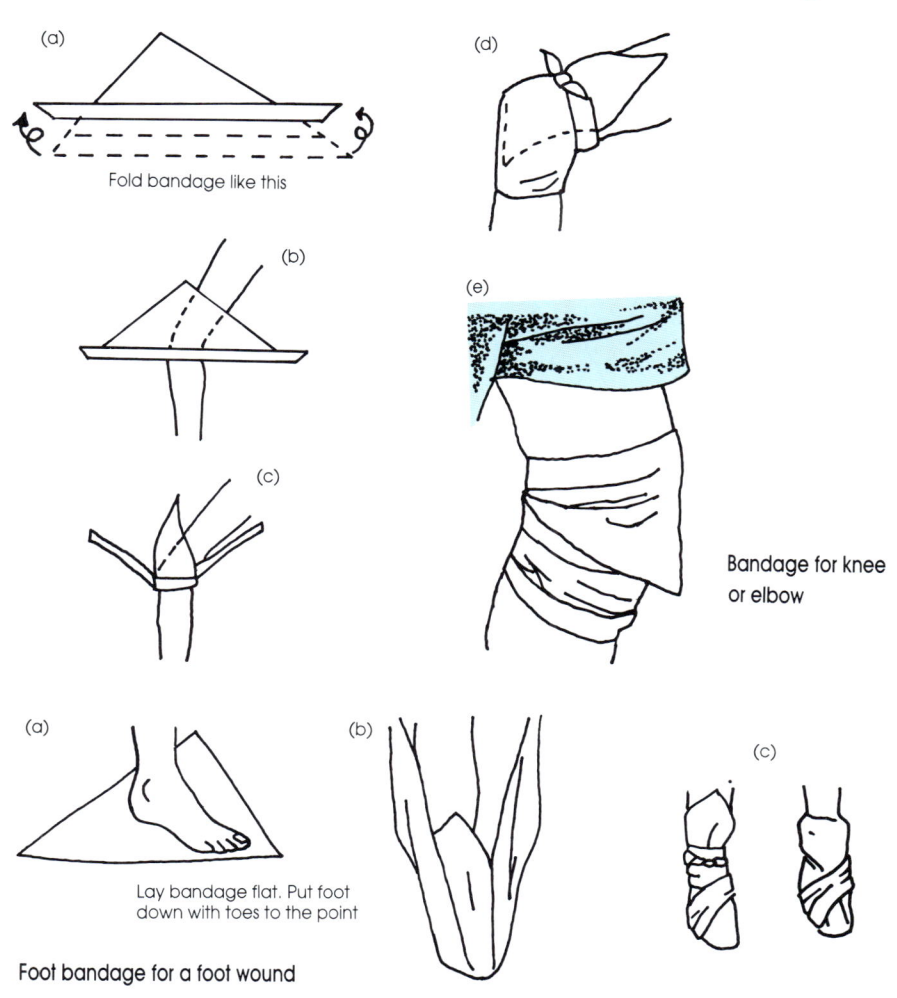

Foot bandage for a foot wound

Sprained ankle A sprained ankle is often the result of a stumble or fall. It is painful and starts to swell immediately. Do not remove the shoe — if you do, the swelling may prevent you from putting it on again. Instead, use the shoe as a support and tie the special ankle bandage (see diagram) around both leg and shoe to keep the ankle steady. If the foot is bare, lie the patient down, raise the leg and put a cold, wet towel around the ankle. If you have the slightest notion that the injury may be a fracture rather than a sprain, take no chances: treat as for a fracture.

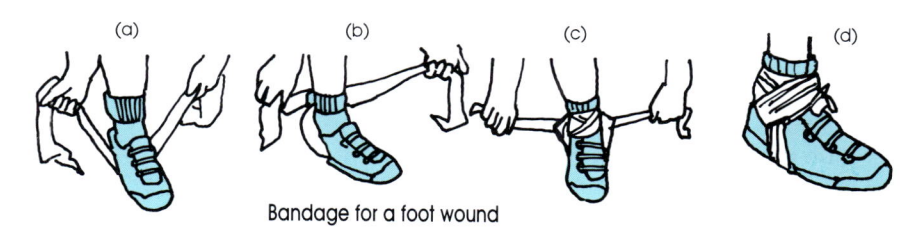

(a) (b) (c) (d)

Bandage for a foot wound

291

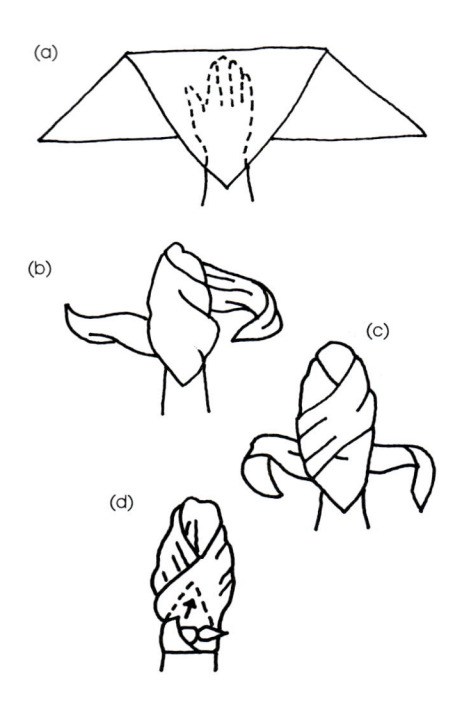

For a hand wound

- Clean wound. Apply dressing.
- Place the injured hand in the centre of the bandage with the injured surface uppermost and the fingers towards the point.
- Draw the point up over the hand, pass the ends around the wrist, and cross them and tie.
- Bring the point over the knot, and fix the bandage over the hand.

Bandage for a hand wound

Fractures

Fractures can be caused by direct action (such as a blow or a fall), indirect action (when the break occurs away from the site of the direct blow) or muscular action (when a kneecap or thigh may break due to a jerk or trip). Fractures will be recognised by pain or discomfort in the region affected; swelling; loss of power of the limb; deformity; irregularity of the bone; unnatural movement, and a bony grating that the injured person may feel. The last two signs should never be sought deliberately.

Fractures are classified as *closed* when the skin surface is not broken; *open* when a wound is present, and *complicated* when a fracture, either closed or open, is associated with an injury to a more important part of the body such as the brain, lungs, and a major blood vessel or nerve. The treatment of complicated fractures always has priority.

If in doubt, treat injury as a fracture, and unless life is endangered by fire, rising water or other hazards, *do not move* the patient before treating the injuries and immobilising any fracture. In all cases of fracture, there is a danger that further injury may be caused if a limb or part is moved before being immobilised.

Immobilising can be achieved by supporting the injured limb or part in as natural a position as possible with bandages, slings and padding.

Emergencies

Fractured collarbone (clavicle)

In the case of a fractured collarbone, the patient will often support the elbow to relieve pain and incline the head towards the injured side.

- Remove and loosen any clothing or straps on the injured side.
- Place padding between the arm and the chest wall.
- Hold the forearm across the chest so the fingertips lie on the opposite shoulder, or as near as possible to this position as the patient will hold the limb in the most comfortable position.
- Support and fix the limb in this position by means of a triangular elevated sling.
- If the patient has to travel some distance or has a rough journey, secure the arm to the chest with a broad or wide bandage.
- Check circulation in the limb. Check comfort of the patient.

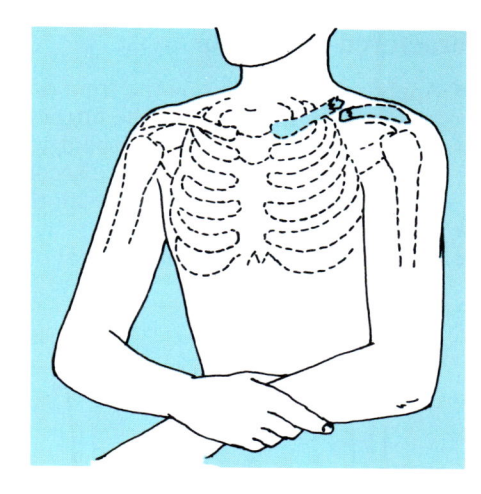

Fractured collarbone

Fractured upper arm (humerus)

- Apply a collar-and-cuff sling.
- Place soft padding between the elbow and the chest.
- Bind the limb firmly to the body, first above the fracture and next below the fracture.
- Check the pulse rate at the wrist to ensure the blood is circulating through the arm. Check comfort of the patient.

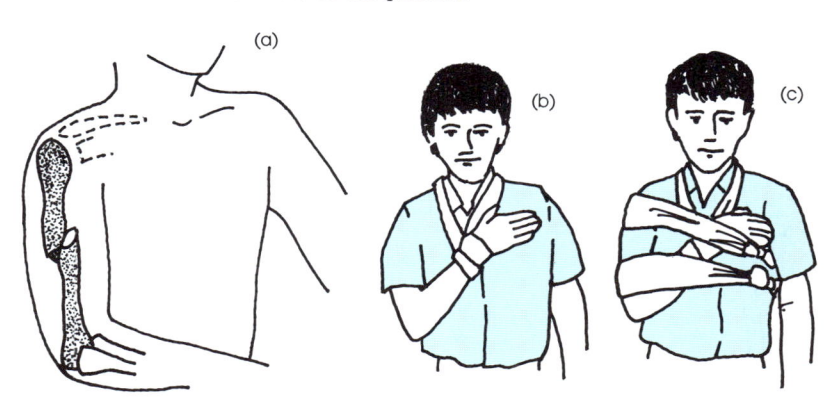

Fractured forearm or wrist

- Apply a padded splint on the front or back of the forearm—the splint must extend from the elbow to the finger tips.
- Bind the limb firmly to the splint with three bandages, the first between the fracture and the elbow, the second between the fracture and the hand, the third supporting the hand with the splint.
- Apply an arm sling.
- Check the circulation and comfort of the patient.

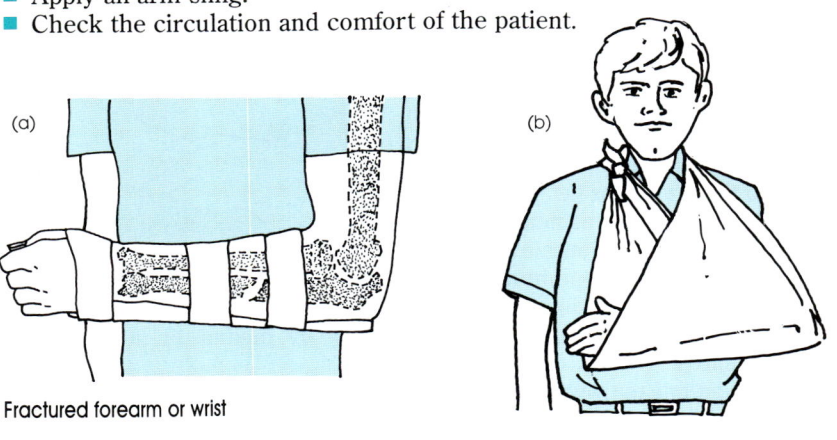

Fractured forearm or wrist

Fractured lower leg

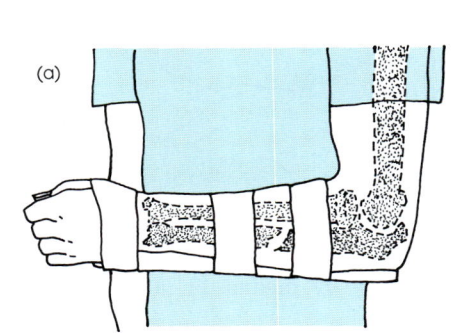

- Draw the limbs together by moving the uninjured limb to the injured limb after placing a well-padded splint between the legs, with extra padding at knees and ankles.
- Place a figure-of-eight bandage around both ankles.
- Bandages have to be placed carefully under the legs.
- Tie bandages as follows: top of thigh; knees above the fracture; below the fracture.
- Tie off on the uninjured side.
- Check the circulation (pulse at ankle) in order to determine that the bandages are not too tight.

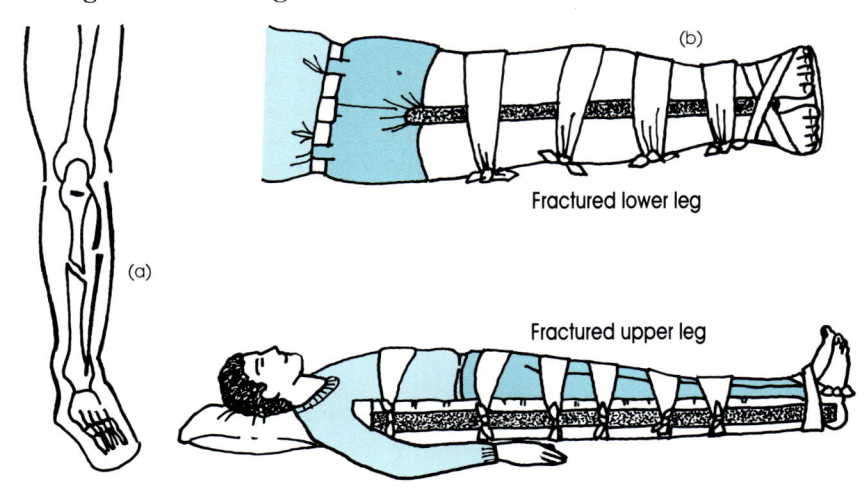

Fractured lower leg

Fractured upper leg

Fractured upper leg

This type of fracture is life-threatening. Medical help is needed urgently.
- Draw the limbs together by moving the uninjured limb to the injured limb after placing a well-padded splint between the legs.
- Bind the ankles together with a figure-of-eight bandage.
- Bandages have to be placed carefully under the patient and a long padded splint placed along the injured side from the armpit to the ankle.
- Tie bandages as follows: around the chest; around the hips; around the ankles; above the fracture; below the fracture; around the knees; around the lower leg.
- Tie off all bandages on the long splint.
- Check the circulation (pulse at the ankle) in order to ensure the bandages are not too tight.

Carrying a patient

Consideration must be given to the following points to help you in selecting the best way of carrying the patient:
- type of injury and the severity
- the emergency nature of the situation
- size of the patient and the carrier
- number of people available to help with the carry
- gear available
- distance to carry the patient and the type of terrain.

Methods of carrying

Cradle carry

This is a very good lift for small children because it holds them close and is thereby reassuring to them.

Human crutch

Use this when the victim can walk with help, for example, sprained ankle.

Piggy-back

Use this for the conscious patient.

Chair carry

This is used to carry a patient who is conscious without serious injury.
   Side by side, or if you have to travel through a narrow passage, you can use fore-and-aft carry.

Cradle carry

Human crutch

Piggy-back

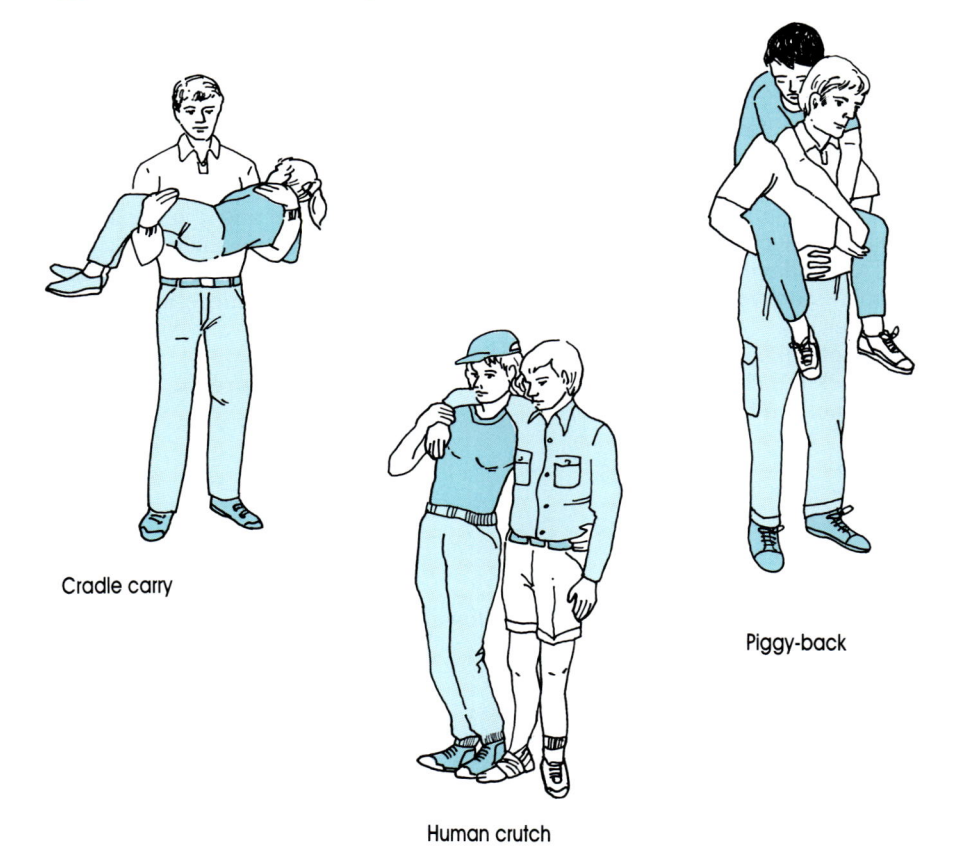

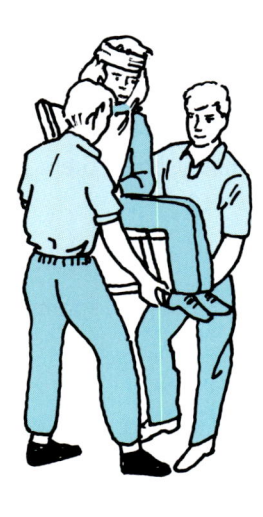

Side-by-side carry with chair

Fore-and-aft carry with chair

Emergencies

Fore-and-aft carry without chair

Two-handed seat

This is used when the patient is unable to use their arms.

(a) Helpers link their hands in the link grip and use padding or grip wrists as in three-handed or four-handed seats.

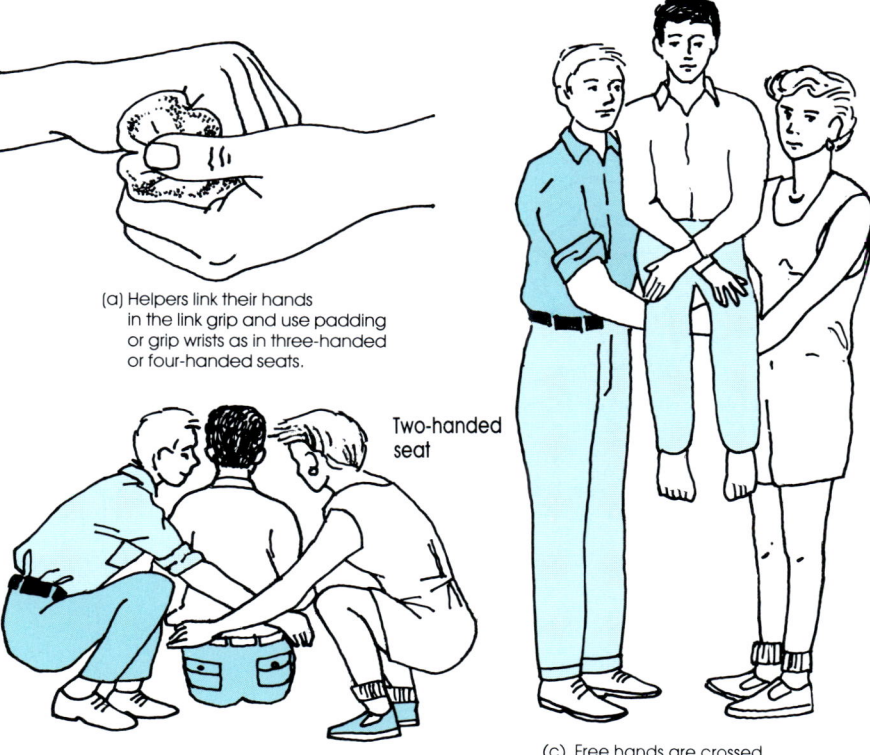

Two-handed seat

(b) Linked hands are placed under the patient's knees

(c) Free hands are crossed behind the patient's back and then grip the waist

Three-handed seat

This is used for supporting either leg when the patient is able to help with one or both arms.

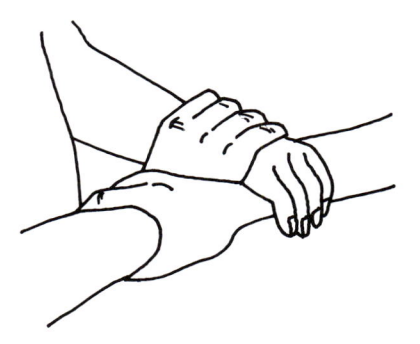

(a) When the left leg is to be supported, helpers grip wrists as shown, with the helper on the left leaving his left hand free

Three-handed seat

(b) Bend down so the patient can sit on helper's hand. The left helper supports the patient's left leg

Four-handed seat

This is used when the patient can help with one or both arms.

(a) Each helper grips his own left wrist with his right hand. Helpers link up

Four-handed seat

(b) Bend down so the patient can sit on helpers' hands as shown

Bites

Snake bites

Venomous snakes are common in Australia. Treatment is more effective if the species is known, because the correct antivenene can be given. Therefore, try to identify the snake if this is possible.

Emergencies

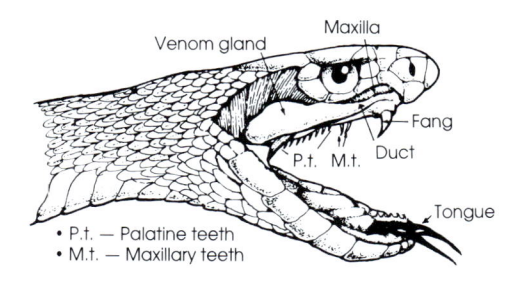

Venom apparatus and dentition of the taipan (O. Scutellatus)

- P.t. — Palatine teeth
- M.t. — Maxillary teeth

Always assume that every bite is by a dangerous snake. Usually two puncture marks about 1 centimetre apart are present. There may be scratching from other fangs, and occasionally there is swelling, reddening or bruising.

First symptoms appear 15 minutes to two hours after the bite: double vision, drowsiness, nausea and vomiting, sweating, faintness, diarrhoea or headache. Pain in the chest and abdomen, and shock, may develop.

Aims of treatment   The treatment aims to:
- prevent absorption of the venom into the general circulation
- reduce the bloodflow through the part and the body as a whole
- place a light dressing on the site of the bite
- obtain an injection of antivenene at the earliest possible moment
- sustain the circulation and respiration

Treatment (pressure immobilisation technique)
- Immediately place a light dressing on the site of the bite then apply a broad, firm bandage around the limb and on the bitten area. It should be as tight as you would bind a sprained ankle. As much of the limb should be bandaged as possible. Crepe bandages are ideal, but any flexible material can be used; for example, tear up clothing or towels into strips.

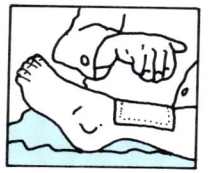

(a) Place a light dressing on the bite site.

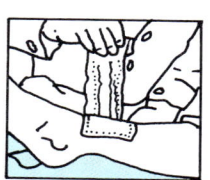

(b) Apply bandage over bite site. Keep 'bitten' limb still.

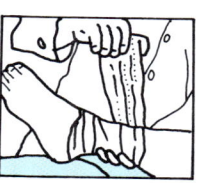

(c) Bind bandage tightly, as for sprained ankle.

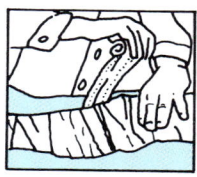

(d) Extend bandage as high as possible, then add splints to futher immobilise limb.

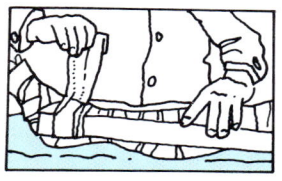

(e) Apply a splint to the limb

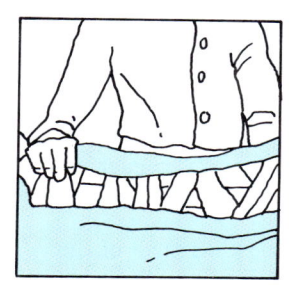

Pressure immobilisation technique

(f) Bind it firmly to as much of the limb as possible

(g) Use bandages, splints and sling for bites on the upper arm

299

- *Do not* wash the bitten area. The snake can often be identified by the detection of venom on the skin (and on the light dressing).
- Keep the limb as still as possible. Bind some kind of splint to the limb, for example, a piece of timber, a spade, any rigid object.
- *Do not* remove jeans and so on — the movement of doing so helps venom to enter the bloodstream.
- Bring transport to the victim when possible, or carry the victim on a stretcher to transport.
- Leave the bandages and splint on until medical help is reached. If the bandages and splint have been applied correctly, they will be comfortable and may be left on for several hours. They should not be taken off until the victim has reached medical help. The doctor will decide when to remove the bandages.
- Reassure the victim, and watch for failing of respiration. Apply necessary treatment.

WARNING: No attempt should be made to cut the wound or suck out the venom.

Spider bites

Only two species of Australian spiders cause fatalities: the redback spider and the funnelweb spider. Treat bites from the redback spider by applying ice to the bite. Seek medical assistance. Watch respiration. Treat bites from the funnelweb spider in the same way as for snake bite.

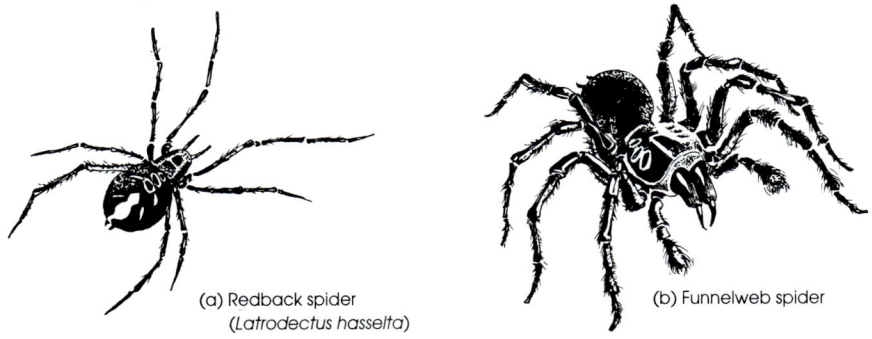

(a) Redback spider (*Latrodectus hasselta*)

(b) Funnelweb spider

Australia's two lethal spiders

Tick bites

Ticks are common sources of annoyance and occasionally of medical problems in the outdoors. They may cause irritation and, occasionally, allergies. Therefore, because *prevention is better than cure*, it is wise to apply repellent to clothing (spray-type repellent on trouser and shirt cuffs, and collars) or to skin (cream-type), bearing in mind that effectiveness usually lasts for only a few hours.

Ticks are often of concern because of their 'stickfast' habits, but treatment is easy and effective and will be dealt with as follows. All three stages, larva (pinpoint size), nymph (pinhead size) and adult female (tealeaf size: 3–4 millimetres) are dealt with similarly.

Emergencies

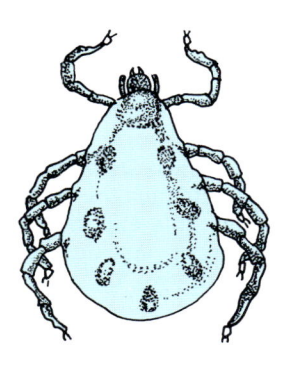

Paralysis (scrub) tick

The Australian paralysis or 'scrub' tick *Ixodes holocyclus* occurs along many parts of the Australian east coast from Cairns in north Queensland to Lakes Entrance in Victoria. Many backyards as well as bush areas are infested. In August each year the adult ticks start to appear in greater numbers, so this is the time to be particularly vigilant after a day in the bush. Children should be checked carefully for attached female ticks by running the fingers through the hair in particular, but other parts of the body such as underarms, groin, ears and other orifices should be examined closely. The following method is based on experience and scientific knowledge.

Recommended (C.S.I.R.O.) method of tick treatment The following steps include explanation and slight modification.

1. To kill the tick as soon as possible is first priority.
2. Although the immediate natural reaction is to try to remove it with fingers or forceps, it may be unwise to do this for a number of reasons. First, you may stimulate further secretion by the tick or tear the skin tissue around the tick's mouthparts thereby releasing more allergens or toxin which will worsen the reaction, whether it is local or truly allergic. Second, you may break off the mouthparts causing a 'foreign body' reaction or granuloma which, although not too serious in itself, is best avoided. Third, you may infect the bite site with fingernails or non-sterile forceps. It should be noted that there have been a number of reports of tick-allergic persons developing a life-threatening 'anaphylactic shock' type reaction immediately following the instinctive physical removal of an attached tick.
3. It is recommended that you treat the tick thoroughly but not excessively with a liquid repellent containing natural pyrethrins or one of the synthetic pyrethroids (some newer batches may not contain pyrethrins but may still be effective; this has to be verified) or similar aerosol spray. Cream repellent will also kill the tick but more slowly, so the spray is preferable. A 'cotton bud' may be soaked in the fluid, or the tick sprayed with repellent, or a kit may be set up consisting of a small, strong dark bottle containing a brush or applicator attached to the cap, for example, a tinea treatment bottle, emptied and thoroughly cleaned and filled with the repellent. Avoid contact with clothing until liquid has been absorbed by the tick or has dried. The old 'bush' remedy of kerosene or turpentine is still fine, particularly for bushwalkers, except those who have sensitive skins.
4. Repeat step 3 a few minutes later if desired, but this should not be necessary.
5. The tick will not detach itself but will die quickly in position, shrivel and drop off with the mouthparts intact. Dropoff may take some hours (up to 24), but there is no risk, because the tick has been killed. Note that none of these treatments will cause the tick to actively detach itself but are designed to kill the tick rapidly and thereby stop secretion. If medicated repellent was used, this should disinfect the bite, but as an added precaution the area may be treated with methylated spirits or other antiseptic, for example, Betadine, say, when you check the tick one hour after the tick has been treated.

6. Check to see that the dead tick has fallen off in 24 hours' time, and in the rare event that it has not, touching the tick will cause it to fall off with the mouthparts intact. It is most important, naturally, to ensure the adult female tick is dead. Disinfect the skin again with, for example, Betadine.
7. Ticks, like other biting pests such as mosquitoes and sandflies, are potentially capable of transmitting diseases, but fortunately in Australia this is a rare event. It is important to kill the tick as soon as possible and avoid crushing an attached tick or stimulating it by finger or instrument manipulation.

Leeches

Leeches can cause a serious loss of blood to a victim. If they are not attached strongly, you may brush them off. If, however, they are too difficult to remove, salt and heat should be applied. A salt solution is the preferred method of removing leeches. Your doctor or chemist will suggest a preparation to prevent leeches attacking you if it is necessary to walk through leech-infested areas.

Bee and wasp stings

Adhere to the following four steps to treat bee and wasp stings.
1. Carefully remove the sting barb left by the bee by scraping sideways. Do not squeeze the barb.
2. Wipe the area clean.
3. Apply a cold compress.
4. Watch for possible allergic reaction. Seek urgent medical help.
5. If shock develops, arrange for medical help.

Mosquito and sandfly bites

For mosquito and sandfly bites, there are two steps as follows.
1. Bathe the area with a weak solution of ammonia or bicarbonate of soda.
2. Apply calamine lotion or zinc cream. Avoid using hot water on the affected area.

Stings caused by marine creatures

Marine creatures may inflict their stings by injection or absorption of venom through the skin or contact with tentacles bearing stinging cells. There are many different types of sea creatures that can inflict a dangerous or fatal sting. You should make it your business to find out which dangerous sea creatures inhabit your swimming area. Snakes, jellyfish, poisonous fish and the blue-ringed octopus can all result in a person requiring Expired Air Resuscitation. *Know the technique.* Find out what treatment is best for stings of different types. Keep up with new discoveries and new methods of treatment.

Emergencies

(a) Blue-ringed octopus

(b) Stonefish

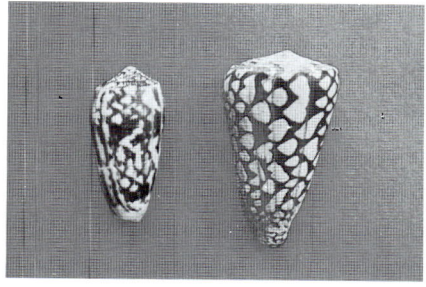

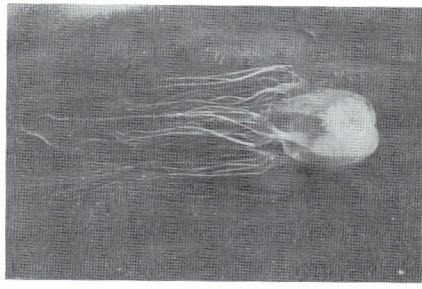

(c) Cone shellfish

(d) Sea wasp

Keep clear of these marine creatures

Blue-ringed octopus

The blue-ringed octopus is quite common in Australian coastal waters and is found in crannies, discarded drink cans, rockpools and underwater caves to a depth of 10 metres. It has a yellowish-brown body and arms, with bluish patterns that glow a deep peacock blue when it is disturbed or angry. It will sting only if picked up and placed on the body, so leave it alone. A bite from its small beak may not even be felt, but it is enough to affect your muscles

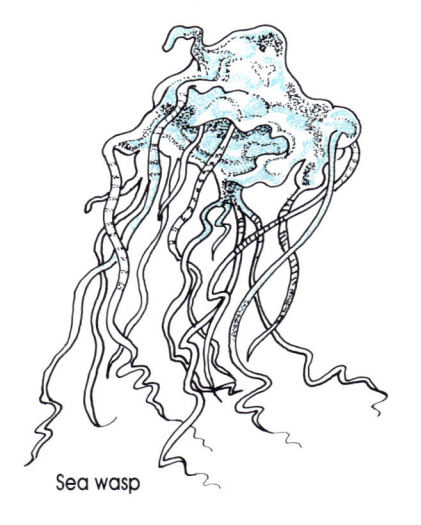

Sea wasp

Blue-ringed octopus

and prevent you from breathing. If somebody has been bitten, get medical help immediately, and if breathing stops, keep the victim alive by Expired Air Resuscitation. Apply pressure immobilisation as for snake bite.

Freshwater stonefish or bullrout (*Notmesus robusta*)

The bullrout or freshwater stonefish is to be found in many freshwater coastal streams of eastern Australia–Queensland and parts of New South Wales. Many injuries caused by the bullrout have been reported in public hospitals.

These fish, because of their colour, are well camouflaged as they lay on the bottom of the creek, either in the weed or debris. The bullrout is a trigger fish; that is, the dorsal spines trigger upwards when touched. Most barb injuries are to the feet, when someone inadvertently jumps or stands on the fish. Pain is *instant* and closely followed by swelling.

Seek immediate medical treatment. Immerse affected part in hot water (43°C). Test first—do not scald the patient's skin. Prevention is better than cure. Wear shoes when swimming or playing in the creek.

Stonefish

Sunburn

The best way to prevent sunburn is to use sun screen and wear a hat. When the skin begins to feel warm and dry, it is a sign that the skin is burning and you had better get out of the sun or put a shirt on. Zinc cream will help to prevent sunburn, particularly on the face and shoulders. If severe sunburn occurs, you must see the doctor as soon as possible. For mild sunburn, the chemist will be able to give you something to relieve pain and prevent infection. Cold water (cold shower) is First Aid management.

(a) Sun-smart

(b) Sun-foolish

Emergencies

Cramps

Cramps are tightening of the muscles and usually occur in the legs, arms or stomach. They are painful but do not have to be fatal. If a cramp hits while you are swimming, take a deep breath and roll into a 'jellyfish' float. Grab your cramped muscle tightly and massage it until it relaxes. When the cramp stops, head for safety using a breaststroke or sidestroke. If other people are present, try floating on your back and signalling for help.

Heat exhaustion

Heat exhaustion is caused by an excess of heat. It usually hits a person in an overheated room, but it may also happen outside in the sun.

The victim's face will be pale, with cold sweat on the forehead. Breathing may be shallow, and the whole body may be clammy from perspiration. Vomiting is common.

Heat exhaustion may be considered shock from heat. First aid therefore consists of aid as used for shock. Move the patient to a shady cool spot. Placed on back, raise feet and loosen clothing. Fan slowly or apply cool, wet cloths. Give the victim sips of salt water: 1 teaspoon of salt to 1 litre of water.

Do not confuse heat exhaustion with heat stroke, which requires a different kind of first aid.

Heat stroke

Heat stroke is usually caused by prolonged exposure to the sun. This is a life-and-death matter: get the doctor right away.

The patient's face is red, hot and dry. Breathing is slow and noisy. The pulse is rapid and strong. The body skin feels dry and hot. The patient may be unconscious.

First-aid treatment is as follows.

- Get the patient into a cool, shaded spot quickly.
- Place the victim in the recovery position.
- Undress immediately down to the person's underwear.
- Begin to cool the victim—especially the head—with water. Cover with dripping wet towels, shirts or cloths and keep them cool by dousing them with water or by wringing them out in cold water from time to time.
- When the patient's body has cooled, stop treatment for a while to see whether it heats up again. If it does, repeat the cooling process over again.
- When the patient regains consciousness, give lots of water to drink.
- This patient must be hospitalised.

Electric shock

After a storm, someone may stumble over a live wire that has fallen down, or someone trying to fix an electrical outlet or electrical appliance may get a shock, or, under certain conditions, faulty house wiring may cause an electric accident. Often the victim receiving the shock is thrown clear of the wire that caused it and can be given first aid right away. If the patient is not breathing, commence Expired Air Respiration and immediately call a doctor. However, if the patient is still grasping the wire, or lying over it, do not touch him/her before switching off the power. Quick thinking and fast action are called for, because if a victim is still in contact with an electrically charged wire it is as dangerous to touch him/her as it is to touch the source of the shock.

Rescuing a person in contact with a live powerline outdoors is extremely dangerous. Do not attempt this type of rescue yourself; call the police or fire brigade and medical help.

How to make a mock emergency

Being able to recognise some of the more common emergencies will enable you to act promptly and take the right course of action with minimum delay when you meet the real thing.

Mocking-up emergencies can be fun and will enable you to test your reactions when called on unexpectedly to rescue a friend or give first aid. When staging a mock emergency, arrange to make clear to passers-by that it is only a mock exercise.

Fractures

Build up a large area of candlewax in the area of the break. Place a short piece of broken chicken-leg bone into the wax so the base of the bone is covered and the short sharp end protrudes from the wax. Add more wax if necessary to cover. Smear the area with a mixture of coldcream and red food colouring for 'blood'.

Cuts

Gradually build up the area where the cut is to be shown by using face putty. Mould the putty to blend into the flesh. Make a cut in the putty with a spatula. Put a mixture of red food colouring and coldcream into the cut and running from the cut to look like blood.

Burns

Superficial burns are shown by lightly blending red lipstick into the flesh and using soft wax or face putty over the reddened area. Deep burns are shown by lightly blending black marking crayon into the area and covering with a light layer of rubber cement. When cement is dry, pick at it with a knife to give the appearance of shredded flesh.

Shock

Shock and fainting have similar symptoms. The victim's face is pale due to the rush of blood from the head. Scouts can learn to identify a shock victim by observing a person made up as follows: Make a mixture of coldcream and blue chalkdust until a pale-blue colour is reached. Rub this on the victim's face.

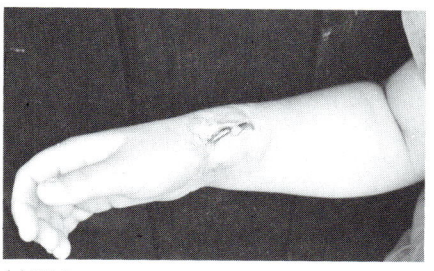

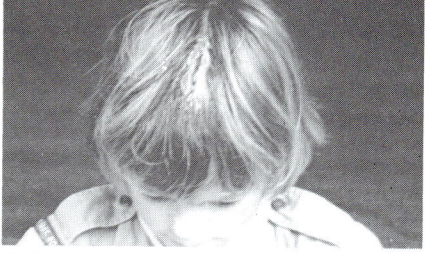

(a) Wrist (b) Scalp

Mock cuts

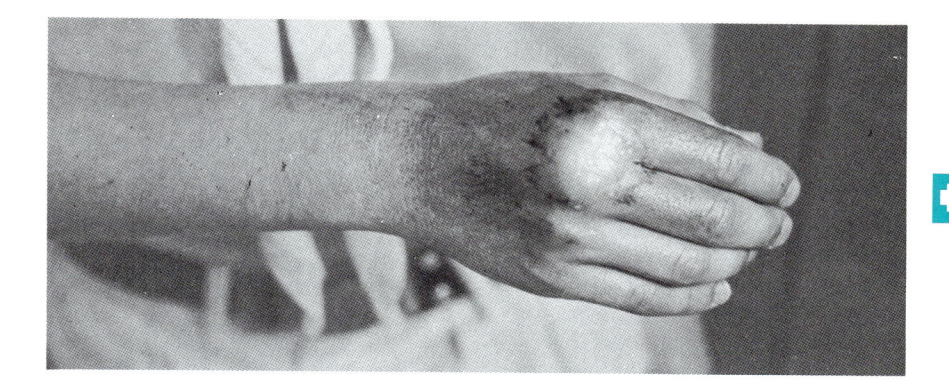

Mock burn

Arterial bleeding

A push-top spray bottle such as one used for window cleaner liquid makes a fine 'heart' for this demonstration. Fill with a mixture of red food colouring and water. Attach a tube, and tape it to the body with the end coming out just at the edge of the shirt sleeve. Cover the end of the tube with melted candle-wax so it blends into flesh. By pushing on the spray bottle, a spurt of 'blood' will appear to come from the wrist artery.

Other accidents

It should not require much imagination to simulate a bicycle accident or someone in difficulties in the water.

For rescue from a smoke-filled room, use suitable materials to fill a room with smoke and provide sack dummies that have to be rescued. Make sure that people taking part cover their mouths and noses with a wet handkerchief and keep as low as possible when moving (the coolest and purest air is near the ground). Practise tying bowlines with rope and dragging an insensible person.

Practise making human chains; passing fire buckets hand-to-hand and linking arms to form a fence; how to hold a canvas groundsheet into which trapped persons may jump, and practise making an improvised stretcher from pieces of wood, Scout belts and shirts or other materials.

Test your knowledge of local emergency numbers and the location of fire hydrants, fire alarms, police stations, fire stations, ambulances and hospitals.

First-aid kit

The minimum first-aid kit for a hike or expedition is listed as follows. Naturally, you can have a lot more in your first-aid kit, but remember you have to carry it.

A copy of a recognised quick reference First Aid book is also a worthwhile item to include in your kit.

Mini first-aid kit

To make a mini first-aid kit, use:

- safety pins: many uses
- scissors (small): cutting
- matches: fire, warmth
- antiseptic cream: cuts, grazes
- adhesive bandage: blisters, cuts
- elastic plaster: large cuts
- first-aid book: small and compact
- triangular bandage
- tablets: headache, pain
- coins: urgent phone call
- tweezers (fine point): splinters
- cottonwool: cleaning
- crepe bandage: sprains, bites.

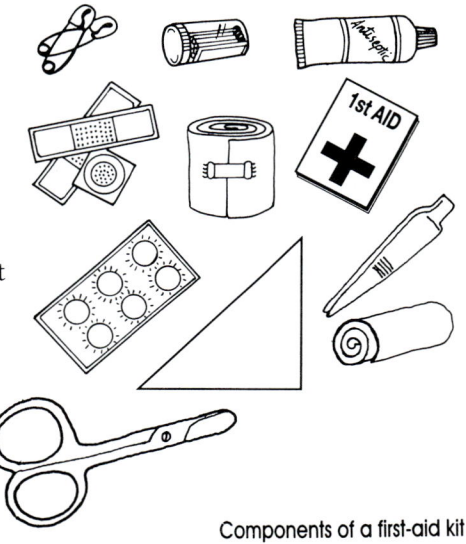

Components of a first-aid kit

Fire

In the case of fire in homes, buildings, factories and institutions, training in evacuation and firefighting procedures is very important.

Everyone has an obligation to gain the necessary knowledge of all emergency procedures including evacuation, correct use of all types of fire extinguishers, the whereabouts of pressurised hose reels and other water supplies, and the quickest method of calling for any type of help.

Delays in calling the fire brigade have caused unnecessary damage to premises, and in some cases loss of life. To help ensure correct action is taken in an emergency, the word 'safe' is used as a memory aid:

S: See that the fire brigade is notified. Telephone '000' in the metropolitan areas or a special number in the country; give the correct location (and a landmark); state the type of fire.

A: Advise others of fire—especially people sleeping on the premises.

F: Fight the fire, only if safe means of escape are known.
E: Evacuate the area—the whole of the building if necessary.

In conjunction with these steps, do the following:

1. Meet the fire brigade at the main entrance or main approaches to the premises and direct the firefighters to the scene of the fire.
2. Close doors and windows where possible to restrict the spread of fire and smoke.
3. Switch off electrical power at the main switchboard.
4. Turn off the gas supply to the premises if a gas appliance is involved in the fire.
5. Do not allow *any* person to re-enter the burning building.

Table 6.1 Fire extinguishers and their effective uses

Type of agent	Water	Foam (AFFF)	Wet chemical	B:(E) Powder	A:B:(E) Powder	Carbon dioxide	Vapourising liquid
Class A fires							
Paper, wood, cloth, and so on where cooling by water or coating by A:B:(E) Powder is effective	yes	yes	yes	Small surface fires only	yes	Small surface fires only	yes
Class B fires							
Petrol, oils, paints Burning liquids where smothering action is required	no	yes	no	yes	yes	yes	yes
Cooking oils, fats, and so on	no	yes	yes	yes	yes*	yes*	no
Category E fires							
Involving energised electrical equipment Fires in motors, switches, appliances, and so on, where a non-conducting extinguishing agent is required	no	no	no	yes	yes	yes	yes

*Limited effectiveness.
Source: Wormald International (Aust.) Pty Limited.

Warning: Follow carefully the instructions on the extinguisher. Do not use the wrong type of extinguisher. For example, if a water-type extinguisher is used on a Class B fire, splashes could cause the fire to spread. If a water extinguisher is used on a Class C fire, there is a possibility that the operator may be electrocuted, because water will conduct electricity.

Principles of fire prevention

- Avoid accumulation of flammable waste matter.
- Do not store quantities of flammable liquids, paint and so on, in the house.
- Keep naked flames, cigarettes and lighted matches well clear of flammable liquids.
- Use electrical equipment only as recommended and provide proper maintenance when necessary.
- Keep matches out of reach of small children.
- Oily cotton polishing mops are a hazard—keep them out of the house.
- Keep chimneys clean.
- Maintain kerosene heaters or refrigerators in proper order.
- Do not move lighted kerosene heaters and keep them out of draughts.
- Use a fire screen. Extinguish hearth fires and inspect the house before going to bed or going out.
- Do not dry clothes close to the fire or stove.
- Store high-pressure gas cylinders in the area provided.
- Strictly adhere to 'No smoking' signs and other safety notices displayed.
- Do not obstruct doorways or passages with chairs or other articles.
- Install proper fire extinguishers.
- Have garden hoses coupled and ready.
- Learn the safe ways to work, and develop safety habits.

Road safety

Australia is a nation in motion. Pedestrians, cyclists and motorcyclists, drivers and passengers of an infinite variety of vehicles, and following many separate routes, all use the one system of roads.

Road safety is a vital part of our daily lives. The education of everyone in the safe use of the streets and highways is one of our most urgent social problems.

Experience has shown that young people who practise correct road-using habits can influence the actions of other young people as well as their parents and other members of the family.

Road safety depends on people

Do you and your parents fully understand and obey all road-traffic rules? Do you:

- keep to the left, particularly when riding in the country?
- keep to the right when walking on roads?
- regulate speed to suit varying traffic or weather conditions?
- keep constantly alert for unexpected actions of other road users?

Emergencies

- give way to other traffic when a dangerous situation is likely to occur, even if the other driver is on your left?
- allow enough space to stop safely in an emergency?
- slow almost to a stop when approaching school crossings and give way to pedestrians using authorised pedestrian crossings?
- insist that children with you sit safely buckled up in the back seat of the car?
- use seatbelts at all times?
- exercise particular care at railway crossings?
- carry your personal-identity details in your pocket?

Changing a tyre

When changing the wheel of a motor vehicle:

- move as far off the road as possible
- see that a chock is placed on both sides of the sound wheel in order to prevent the vehicle running backwards or forwards and so slipping off the jack
- ensure that the jack is on a firm foundation
- keep clear of passing traffic, and if on a corner, put out a warning sign or arrange for someone to warn approaching drivers.

Use wooden or similar blocks

Make sure you use the correct fitting socket

Bicycle safety

- Learn to ride in your yard or on a nearby reserve where riding is permitted. Do not ride on the road until dad or mum says it is okay.
- Avoid busy roads. Use the quieter neighbourhood streets to get where you are going.
- Remember that your bicycle is a vehicle and should not be ridden on the footpath.
- Wear your helmet at all times.
- Stop, look and listen before entering a road.
- Ride on the left-hand side of the road, close to the kerb.
- Obey all traffic signs and signals, as car drivers do.
- Give correct hand signals for turning and stopping.
- Watch for parked cars pulling out or doors opening suddenly.
- Never carry another person on your bicycle.

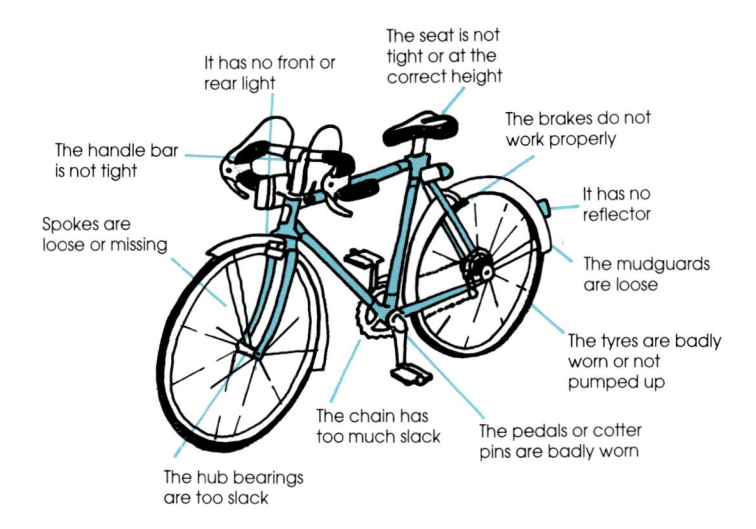

[Diagram of a bicycle with labels pointing to various parts:]
- The seat is not tight or at the correct height
- It has no front or rear light
- The brakes do not work properly
- The handle bar is not tight
- It has no reflector
- Spokes are loose or missing
- The mudguards are loose
- The tyres are badly worn or not pumped up
- The chain has too much slack
- The pedals or cotter pins are badly worn
- The hub bearings are too slack

A bicycle is unroadworthy if it has any of these faults

- You can ride in pairs where there is room, but always allow room on the road for cars to pass.
- Keep your bicycle in good condition. Check that the brakes, tyres and chain are working well.
- Keep your bicycle under control—no stunting on the roads.
- Good lights for night riding and reflectors are essential for your safety. Check they are working well before riding at night.

Explosives

Explosives are useful to mankind and enable work to be done that is often impossible by other means. Their use is strictly controlled in order to permit this class of work to be done with safety.

Carelessness or improper use can result in serious injury or death.

Cartridge type of explosive (dynamite)

These are usually 25 to 30 millimetres in diameter and about 200 millimetres long. The explosive is usually pink and has a stiff-jelly type appearance. This is wrapped in a buff-coloured wax-type paper with the name printed in red.

These explosives deteriorate with age and can become very dangerous to handle. *Do not touch.*

Detonators

These are small explosive charges wrapped in a small-diameter metal tube, approximately 50 millimetres long. They are used for starting an explosion.

Although only a small charge, if handled incorrectly or tampered with in any way, it will explode with enough force to cause serious or even fatal injuries.

Detonator   Dynamite

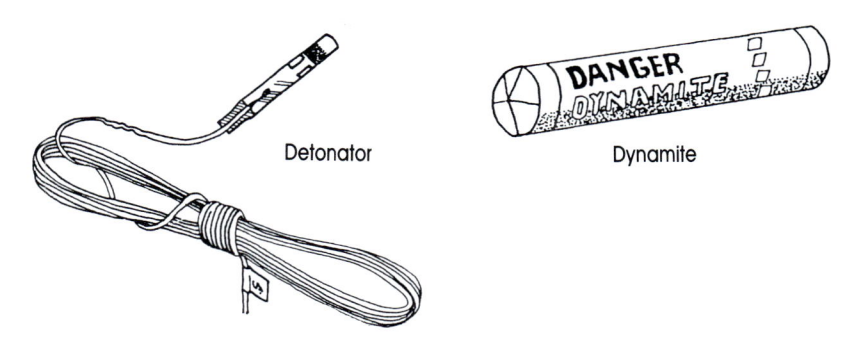

Detonators can be with electric wires of various colours or may be plain without any wires.

If you find any explosives, leave them alone and contact a responsible person, preferably the police or Mines Department or its Explosives Section. These people will see that explosives are disposed of safely.

With any explosive, do not take chances.

Organisations involved in safety and emergencies

Members of the following organisations may be able to help you with talks or demonstrations.

- Road Safety Council
- St John Ambulance Brigade
- Police Department: Rescue Squad, Operation Room, Driving Wing
- Fire Brigade
- Bushfire Brigades
- Lifesaving Clubs
- Sea Rescue Service
- State Emergency Services
- State and Commonwealth Railways
- Department of Aviation
- State Mines Department: Explosives Section, Rescue Section
- Makers of fire extinguishers
- Public hospitals
- Quarantine station
- Meals on wheels
- Lifeline centres

Walking along a road

Always walk in single file on the right-hand side of the road. If you walk this way, facing the traffic, you can see the approaching vehicle, and the driver can see you. You can move over to the right and get off the road without danger to yourself and without interfering with the vehicle. If you are walking on the left-hand side of the road, only the driver can see the danger and avoid an accident. You will not be able to see the car unless you turn around. If you are on a crowded or crooked road, you may not be able to hear or see a car approaching.

If you must walk on the road at night, wear light-coloured or reflective clothing. Tie a white cloth or handkerchief around your neck, right arm or knee. Reflective tape is now available, and running three or four strips across the back and front of your parka or anorak can also help you become more visible.

If you have a torch, shine it down in front of you, not in the eyes of the approaching driver.

Above all, remember where you are, and do not fool around on the road. Besides making you less alert, it will get you out of single file. The roads are built for automobiles, not for pedestrian traffic. You walk the highway at your own risk.

Personal portable stereos

Many people today own a personal portable stereo with earphones. Although they provide much enjoyment to their owners, and cut down on the amount of noise in public (with portable radios/tape machines), these personal stereos may be dangerous if used at very high volumes.

Using earphones, all the owner hears is the music or radio; external sound is minimised. Many people use these while riding bicycles, jogging, or walking to work, play or school. This could be dangerous because the listeners will not be alert to cars, warning shouts or other loud noises. Furthermore, hearing damage may result if they are played on volumes louder than two or three (markings on volume control), over a period of time.

Home safety

Most accidents happen at home, and most of them involve falling. One way to prevent falling accidents is to make sure everything is put away in its proper place after use. Keep stairways and hallways clear of toys, tools, sports equipment and clothing. Keep rugs smooth and furniture in its usual place. Tack down patches smoothly over rips and tears in rugs or carpeting so people will not catch their feet in them and fall. Watch for defective treads on the stairs. Be sure that stairways are kept in good condition, especially when they are carpeted, and the carpeting is held down with brass rods or carpet nails.

Do not lean out of windows, or over bannisters, porches or fire escapes. This is dangerous, even if the railings are secure. If there are young children in the house, particularly toddlers, check that windows are securely fastened, that window screens cannot be pushed out, and that stairs have safety gates with strong catches.

If you have a job that requires use of a step ladder, make sure the one you use is in good condition. If you must use a chair, choose a straight, strong one with a solid seat. Never use a piano stool or a rocking chair or a flimsy chair. When using a ladder, do not lean to the side or reach further than is naturally comfortable. A step ladder should have all four feet on the ground and the braces set. For more complicated work, it is a good idea to enlist the help of a friend.

Another cause of falls is slipping on slippery surfaces. If grease has been spilled on the floor, wipe it up with hot water and soap or baking soda immediately. In winter, make sure melted snow is mopped up and the floor dried. Look out for small rugs on polished floors, especially when they are placed at the foot of stairways, because they can slip out under your feet. Rubber webbing or strips can be used to anchor these rugs and prevent accidents. Also remember that new shoes can slip on shiny or wet floors: rub sandpaper on the bottoms to make them rough.

Keep bottles, flower pots and other objects off the window sills. If they are blown or pushed off, these objects can cause serious injury to people below.

Childproofing

Young children have to be looked after carefully because they are always exploring and getting into things they should not. Childproofing at home does not mean eliminating everything but the basic furniture. It is commonsense and can save the life or prevent serious injury to a small child.

Keep things out of reach of small hands. Never overestimate a child's ability to clamber up shelves or bookcases or to open cupboards. Keep china cabinets, cleaning cupboards and medicine chests securely locked. (*See also* section on 'Poisoning', below.) Keep fragile objects on sturdy shelves or tables in case a toddler bumps into them.

Toys should be kept in a toybox or cupboard in order to prevent falls as well as clutter. Always make sure the toy is suitable for the child's age or size. The local council tests thousands of toys each year and publishes the results in a handy reference booklet. Make sure there are no sharp edges, that small mouth-sized parts are secure, and that the seams on plush toys are well sewn. Repair (or throw away) damaged or broken toys as soon as possible before allowing the child to play with them again.

Poisoning

People are often poisoned by food, such as spoiled meat, fish, fruit, vegetables and canned goods. If a can of food bulges, the contents are spoiled. Discard the can immediately. Do not buy badly dented cans of food. Wash or peel all uncooked fruit and vegetables, because they may have been sprayed with chemical sprays and insecticides that could make you sick.

Be careful with meat, poultry or fish. Cook pork thoroughly, wash poultry carefully before cooking, and keep fish refrigerated or frozen before using. After cooking these foods, wrap well in foil or plastic wrap, and refrigerate immediately. If food is left out on a counter, especially on warm or humid days, it can encourage the growth of harmful bacteria.

People, especially young children or the elderly, are often poisoned by substances found in their own homes. A person may be poisoned by swallowing, inhaling, injecting or absorbing harmful materials. Most poisonings can be prevented with careful handling of poisons.

Always read the labels for instructions when using cleaning supplies or taking medicine. Keep all drugs, cleaning supplies and other potentially harmful products out of reach of children and in a securely locked cupboard. Use containers with childproof caps, and label contents clearly and prominently. Never re-use 'pop' bottles or familiar food containers for storing poisons, because they may be swallowed by mistake for something else.

Always label poisons clearly and make sure the correct label is on the container. There are labels available with the poison symbols if the original ones fall off or wear away. Dispose of empty containers as soon as possible.

Never take or give medicine in the dark. Always check to see you have the right medicine and the correct dosage. Never tell children they are taking 'candy' when it is medicine. Never taste the contents of an unlabelled container. Dispose of old medicines by flushing away or take them to the local poison control centre for safe disposal. Never leave medicines handy in night-table drawers or dresser tops. Many houses have medicine chests filled with old prescriptions—a very dangerous practice. Always clear out the bathroom cabinet on a regular basis and store medicine in use in a locked cupboard or drawer. Never take old medicine, because the chemicals can deteriorate with time, storage environment and contamination.

Poisoning can also occur from eating certain household plants, from using strong chemicals without proper ventilation, or by spilling corrosive liquid on your body. Learn about the plants in the home, and keep the poisonous ones out of reach. Always ensure windows are open and air is circulating when using cleaning fluids. Be alert when pouring liquids for cleaning or stripping.

In case of poisoning . . .

Despite careful precautions, poisoning accidents do happen. *When it does, act quickly and remain calm. Do not panic.* Adhere to the following steps:

1. Try to identify the poison and how it was taken (swallowing, inhaling, injecting or absorbing).
2. Get expert advice by calling a doctor or the Poisons Information Centre. (Keep these numbers by the telephone for easy reference.)
3. Follow their instructions carefully. If help is not available, follow the instructions on the label of the poison container, or these steps, until help becomes available.
4. Give small sips of water or milk or if corrosive just wash the mouth with water or milk. Speed is essential.
5. DO NOT INDUCE THE VICTIM TO VOMIT particularly when corrosive (burning) poisons have been swallowed. These include cleaning compounds with lye, ammonia or bleach; kerosene; lighter fluid; paint thinner, and furniture polish.

   Do not induce vomiting if the victim is unconscious or having convulsions. Keep the victim's head held low in order to allow the stomach contents to run out and not block the air passage. If you are in doubt about the nature of the poison, do not induce vomiting.
6. If the poison is one that has been inhaled, make sure the victim has plenty of fresh air and begin artificial respiration immediately.
7. If the poison is one that has been absorbed, flush the area constantly with running water. In case the poison has affected the eyes, flush them out with slowly running water.

Learn to recognise poison symbols as they appear on consumer products and what to do in case of poisoning. Three degrees of hazard have been determined as follows.
- *Danger:* it could kill you.
- *Warning:* it could make you very sick.
- *Caution:* it could make you sick or hurt you.

Your local poison-control centre has lots of material available for teaching people about the dangers of poisons.

Water safety

Self-rescue

The most important part of any swimming, water-safety or lifesaving program is self-rescue. The most usual term used to describe self-rescue techniques is *survival*. Each of the methods described in this section is essential if you are going to be safe *in*, *on* or *around* water.

The 'HELP' (Heat Escape Lessening Posture) position

The greatest danger to you if you are unexpectedly immersed in water is hypothermia or exposure. Exposure is a drop in body temperature when the body loses more heat than it can generate. Therefore to survive in water, and in particular cold water, you have to reduce the amount of heat lost by the body.

Protective clothing is the most effective way of achieving this. However, if protective clothing is not worn, ordinary clothing will afford some protection and should not be discarded. One way of reducing body-heat loss is to keep as much of the body out of the water as possible. Climb on to a capsized boat or any wreckage floating in the water. If this is not possible, survival time is lengthened by assuming the HELP position if you are wearing a personal flotation device. Draw the knees in towards the chin and press the arms to the sides (similar to the foetal position). This protects the areas of the body that lose the most heat (the head, neck, sides and the groin).

The 'help' position

The 'huddle' position

Based on the same principle as the HELP position, the huddle position is used when there are three or more adults. The sides of the chest are pressed together with the personal flotation devices linked behind. The lower body areas are pressed together. Young persons can then sandwich in the middle. Advantages, other than body-heat-loss control, are the reassurance from members of the group and making the group more clearly visible to rescuers.

The importance of wearing a personal flotation device in cold water conditions cannot be overemphasised. If you are immersed without a flotation device, you may combine various methods of survival such as floating, survival sculling, treading water and survival swimming. All except floating techniques increase the loss of energy and maximise body-heat loss.

The 'huddle' position

Treading water

Treading water

Treading water is a useful survival skill, used in self-rescue, lifesaving and recreational swimming. Its main advantage over other strokes is that it is easy to see where you are because your head is out of the water, with your eyes looking straight ahead.

The most efficient method of treading water is the egg-beater method and this is made more effective when combined with horizontal-arm sculling. The egg-beater kick can provide great vertical lift. The basic action of the kick is an alternating breaststroke kick, with one foot moving clockwise and the other anticlockwise.

The person should 'sit' in the water with a straight back, thighs parallel to the surface and knees apart. The legs drive alternately in a circular motion towards the middle line of the body and rotating from the knees. The action is continuous.

Young children or beginners should learn this skill for two reasons. If a poor swimmer falls into the water, being able to tread water when they bob back to the surface will give them time to see where the edge is and scramble back. It is also helpful for the poor swimmer who swims out of their depth and has to tread water so they can turn around and return to safety.

Slow swimming and floating

Slow swimming sounds easier than fast swimming, until you try it. The slower you swim, the more you sink into the water, therefore it requires practice to control your body position. Try the slow-swimming movements on both front and back, seeing how long you can stay up without getting tired.

Floating is harder than slow swimming, because it means staying up without your arms and legs moving. You should try various floats and survival techniques, such as front, back and vertical floats, in groups and moving from one float to another. This will help you become safer and more confident in the water.

Swimming with a personal flotation device

You will know that it is necessary to wear a personal flotation device at all times while boating or canoeing. It is one thing to be able to stay afloat in a personal flotation device, but it is a different matter when you try to swim. The best stroke to practise is a modified sidestroke or breaststroke. Make sure you practise swimming in your personal flotation device, also putting it on in deep water and removing it. You never know when it could be necessary to take your personal flotation device off; you could be trapped under a boat, or perhaps need it for a rescue aid.

The surface dive and underwater swim

The surface dive and underwater swim are used in search and rescue work, escaping from upturned boats, and just plain fun. There are two main types of surface dive: the duckdive which means you go down head first, and the foot-first dive, which is just as it says. The aim of both methods is to get your body under the water rapidly. Most people swim underwater using a modified breaststroke or sidestroke.

Caution: Do not attempt long underwater swims, and do not take more than three or four deep breaths in succession.

Rescue of others

Rescue

Most water accidents occur close to safety. Do not leap into the water the moment somebody is in difficulty; take a second or two to look around and choose the safest and best method of rescue.

Remember, even a young child can drown you if you allow yourself to be grabbed.

Fieldbook for Australian Scouting

It is the intention of this section not to turn you into a coward but to point out the dangers of contact rescues of violent victims.

If it is too far to reach with a rope, get into a boat and row out to the victim or paddle to him/her in a canoe. If there is no equipment around, the only thing to do is *go*.

Remember: Reach, throw, row, go and tow.

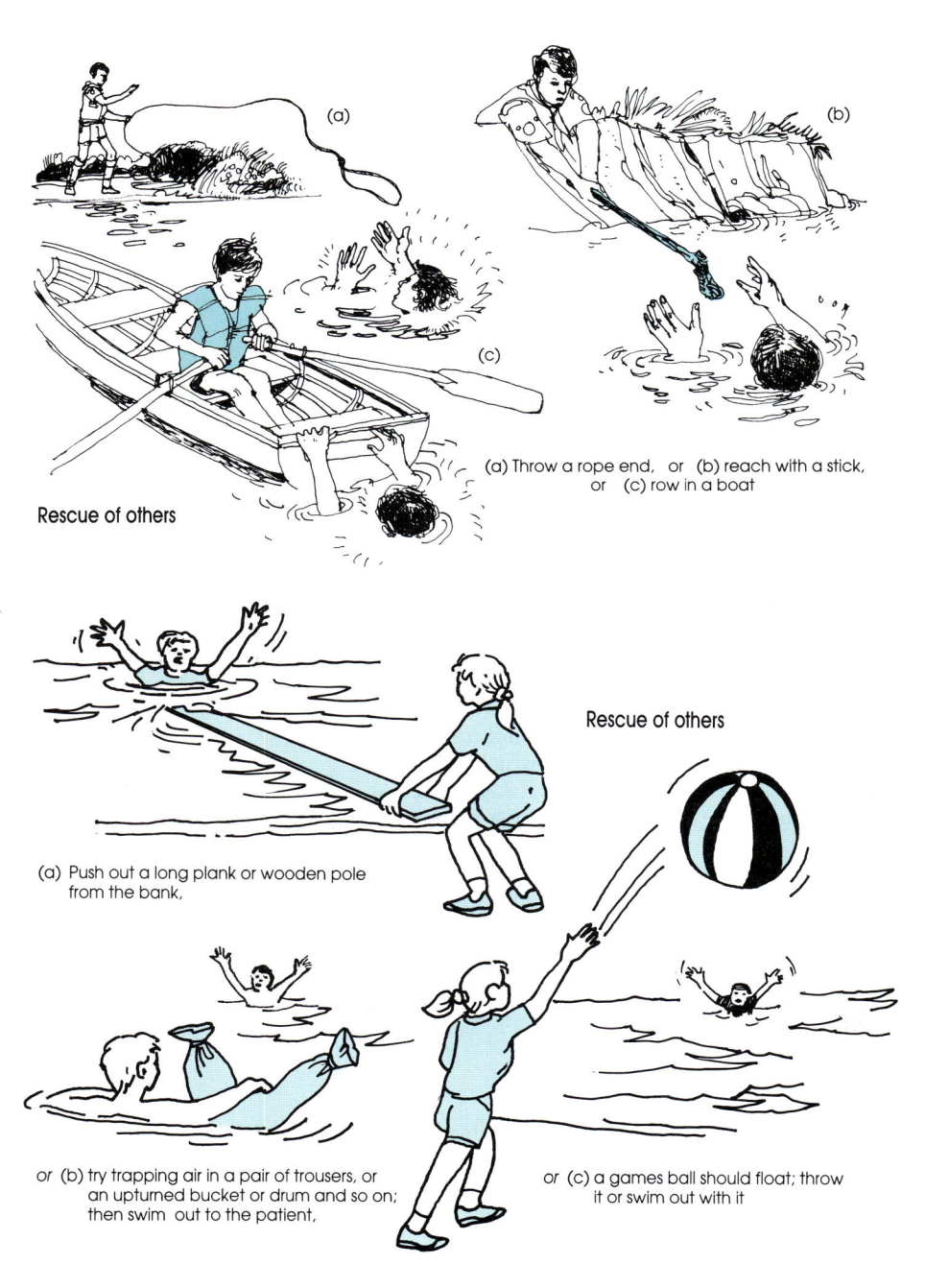

Rescue of others

(a) Throw a rope end, or (b) reach with a stick, or (c) row in a boat

Rescue of others

(a) Push out a long plank or wooden pole from the bank,

or (b) try trapping air in a pair of trousers, or an upturned bucket or drum and so on; then swim out to the patient,

or (c) a games ball should float; throw it or swim out with it

Emergencies

Look around for a buoyant object such as a lifebuoy, lifejacket, large ball, surfboard, child's plastic surfboard, or other inflatable object to throw out.

A good aid to have on hand is a 10 metre-long throwing rope of 8 millimetres diameter. A loop should be spliced on the end to be held, and a monkey fist knot or heaving-line terminal can be tied to the end to be thrown out.

Throwing a rescue line

You have many places to swim—the beach, a river, pool, dam or lake. Make sure your favourite swimming spot is safe. The best place is one that has qualified lifesavers. If there is no supervision, make sure you can swim and always go with a friend—never alone—and never swim in a river or in the sea at night.

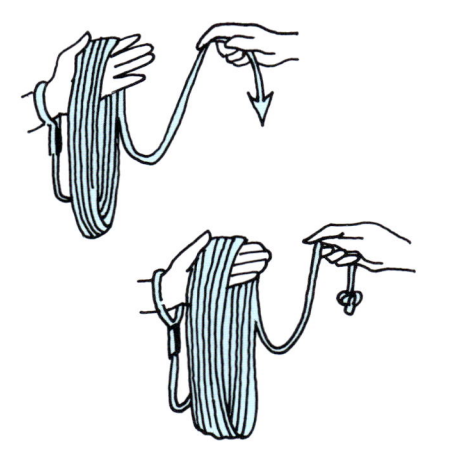

Throwing a rescue line

(a) Everything depends on the care you take in coiling and handling the line before you throw it! Lay the turns alongside each other without crossing, working towards the tips of the fingers and turning it so the free end is nearest the fingertips

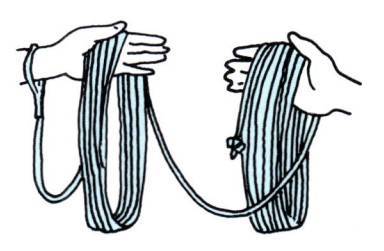

(b) Wrist loop: Without disturbing the arrangement of the turns, transfer two-thirds of the coil to the throwing hand

(c) When ready to throw, stand with the left shoulder towards the target area, swing both arms together across the body (underarm) and throw with a good follow-through. Constant practice and a good follow-through right over the target are the secrets of success

Swim out to help — but only when no other method can be used

Undressing in the water

If you ever fall into the water fully clothed or get thrown out of a boat accidentally, you need to know what to do. Wet clothes get very heavy and will cling to you. This will make it hard to move, and hard to keep your head above water.

Practise in water that is shallow enough to stand up in. Wait until you are good at it before practising in deep water.

Always have a friend with you when you go out on the water.

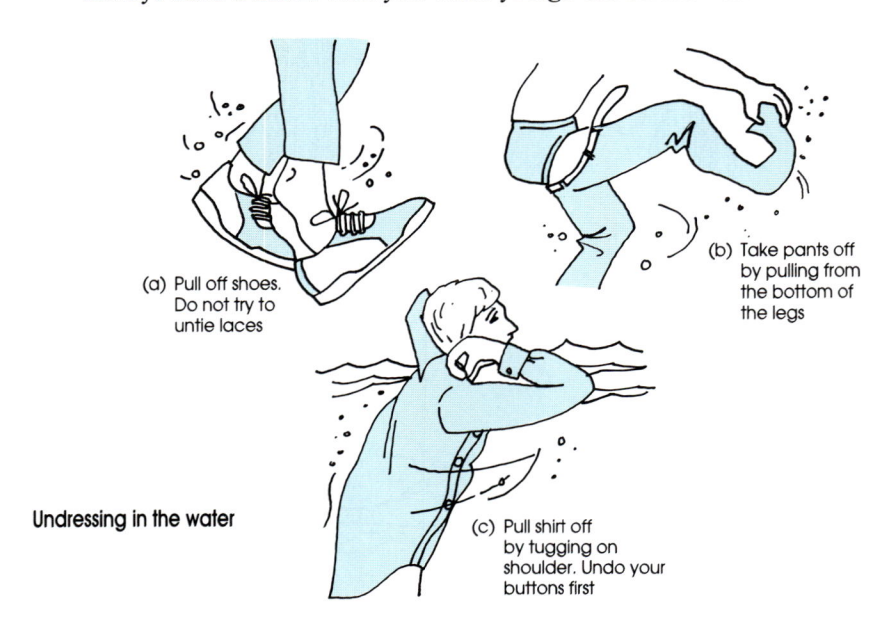

Undressing in the water

(a) Pull off shoes. Do not try to untie laces

(b) Take pants off by pulling from the bottom of the legs

(c) Pull shirt off by tugging on shoulder. Undo your buttons first

Tows

The three tows following are to show you some of the methods used by lifesaving organisations and to help you brush up on your techniques; they are not a substitute for a lifesaving course.

Emergencies

Armpit tow This tow may be used for an unconscious person in calm water. It is a fairly easy tow for a less powerful rescuer, because the victim is in a good towing position and does not hinder the rescuer's sidestroke swimming. This tow is not good for control of an unconscious person's head position.

Cross-chest tow This tow is effective but very demanding on the rescuer. It is a suitable tow for rough water, because it keeps the victim's face clear of the water and the body supported on the rescuer's hip. The rescuer passes his/her arm over the victim's shoulder, across the chest and grips the victim under the armpit. The elbow should be at right angles and pressed on to the victim's chest. The rescuer will use a strong scissor kick and side arm pull.

Armpit tow

Cross-chest tow

Support tow

Support tow This tow is performed by the rescuer holding a flotation object in one hand. The other hand is used to support the victim's chin and the head resting on the rescuer's shoulder. This position helps to keep the victim's airway open and allows the rescuer to apply resuscitation if necessary.

The approach to a panicky swimmer is the most difficult part of the rescue. Unless it is done properly, it could result in double trouble. For this reason, we have not illustrated it. It is best learnt on a lifesaving course.

Fieldbook for Australian Scouting

Methods of landing

If the person is not breathing, getting him/her from the water is not as important as beginning resuscitation. However, if the patient is breathing, then remove him/her from the water as quickly as possible. The most important landing to learn is the *straight-arm lift*. This can be used to get people from deep water on to a boat, jetty or the edge of a pool.

(a) Your weight holds the subject in place while the rescuer mounts the jetty

(b) Your knees flex as the rescuer assumes a firm grasp of the subject's wrists

(c) The subject is lifted from the water and lowered towards the jetty

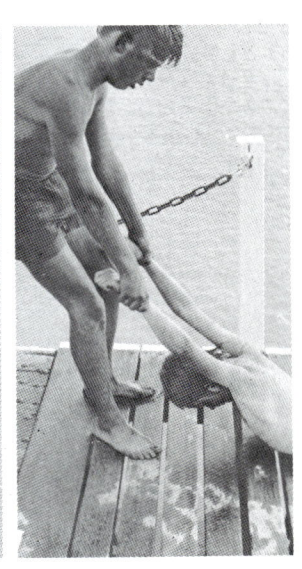

(d) The rescuer protects the subject's head, and guards against slipping by grasp of the wrist

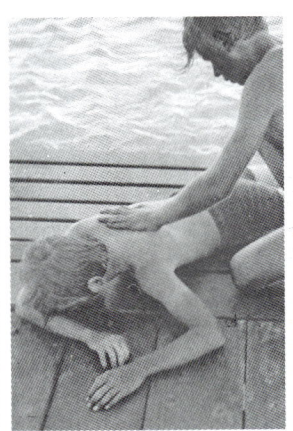

(e) Pressure on the back holds the subject in place as the rescuer grasps near the thigh

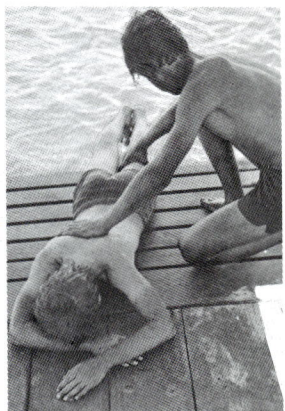

(f) The subject is rotated into a safe position on the jetty

Straight-arm lift

Safety knowledge

At the beach

Where a lifesaving club exists, the safest place to swim is between the flags. At an unpatrolled beach, be wary of bathing away from other people; there is usually a good reason for local people and regular visitors choosing a certain area. If there is surf, choose an area where the waves roll evenly and regularly towards the shore. It is important to keep checking your position with a prominent landmark, in case you gradually drift into a dangerous area. If you are a poor swimmer, do not go far from the shore, and never stand on a sandbar watching your friends surf or swim. When the tide comes in, you might have a long difficult swim to shore. Only strong swimmers should venture out on surfboards or floats. Do not hamper yourself with heavy clothing, particularly jeans, while swimming. Also keep away from jetty pylons, because the swirling water cuts deep holes, which have resulted in a number of drownings.

Swim between the flags

At the river

Many drownings occur each year in our rivers, and many of these could have been avoided had the rules been followed. In the case of organised swimming on hikes or camps, the safe area should be marked out with buoys or sticks, and a responsible swimmer should supervise the group. Throwing and reaching equipment is an essential part of the preparation for a swimming area. Very few rivers are safe for poor swimmers, not only because of strong currents but mainly because of frequent changes to the slope of the bank, the depth of water, and the presence of submerged obstructions. Swimming across a large river is no task for any but the very best swimmers. Even then it is dangerous unless a boat or buoyant aid is taken, because many a good swimmer has suffered cramps, had that unexpected mouthful of water, panicked and drowned. Swim where other people are swimming and you should be much safer. **Remember that the depth and murkiness of most rivers make a quick search and rescue virtually impossible.**

At the pool

All public pools should be safe for swimming, provided they have properly qualified lifesavers supervising continuously. There are still dangers, but most of these can be minimised by proper supervision. The main dangers arise from:

- swimming in the diving area
- poor swimmers venturing into deep water
- running around the edge
- throwing and pushing people into the pool
- diving into the shallow end.

A special warning about home pools: Make it your business to make them safe. No child should be able to wander into a neighbour's backyard pool and drown.

It is not enough to protect the home pool from trespassers, however; it should also be safe for visitors to leave their young children in the backyard, and for any children that live in the house. Many state laws insist that home pools should be covered or fenced. See what you can do to cut down the high number of drownings in home pools.

Dams and lakes

Both these areas can be particularly dangerous unless proper swimming facilities are planned and organised. The biggest danger, as in rivers, is the murky water, and the steep slope. Learners require a gradual slope in order to learn to swim properly, and dams and lakes do not usually have this advantage. If you intend to swim in these places, be prepared. Have the swimming area clearly marked with a rope with floats, and have buoyant aids available in case they are needed.

Expired Air Resuscitation (EAR)

Expired Air Resuscitation saves lives. When breathing stops, life hangs in the balance. If you are there and know how to administer rescue breathing, you may save that life.

Emergencies

In Expired Air Resuscitation you breathe your own breath into the victim's lungs through her nose or mouth or, in the case of a child, gently into both nose and mouth.

Mouth-to-mouth resuscitation

Time is of the utmost importance. Place the victim on their side, and tilt the head back to open the airway. Remove any foreign material from the mouth (dentures should be removed only if broken or loose). Immediately turn the victim onto their back. Tilt the victim's head back, lift the chin forward so the skin is taut over the throat, and start breathing into the mouth. For mouth-to-nose breathing, hold the victim's mouth closed with your hand against the chin and seal your lips around the victim's nose. Then, blow air into the victim until you see the chest rise. Remove your mouth and let the air escape from the victim's lungs while you take a deep breath.

Then blow into his/her lungs again, and again let the air escape; continue blowing about 15 times per minute for an adult, 20 times for a child.

When the victim's breathing starts, time your efforts to fit the victim's efforts to breathe. Keep the victim lying down, and provide warmth with blankets or other covering. Get him/her under a doctor's care during the recovery period.

Naturally, in training for this method it is not necessary for you to do the actual blowing. Learn and demonstrate the correct way of tilting the victim's head back and lifting the jaw up. Explain how you would clean foreign matter out of his/her mouth, place your mouth, and give rescue breathing.

The head of an unconscious person slumps forward, and the base of the sagging tongue blocks the airway. The first job is to open up the airway. This is done by tilting victim's head back and lifting the jaw. When this is done, the base of the tongue is raised off the back of the throat.

It is recommended that you seek training in this skill from registered lecturers—local ambulance, St John, Red Cross, Life Saving Society etc.

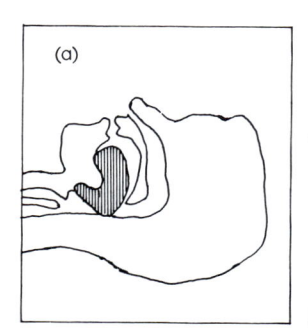

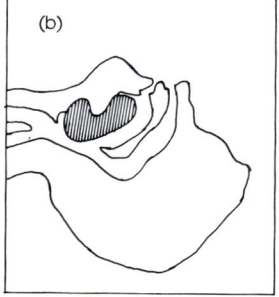

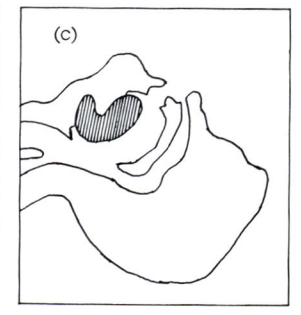

The base of the tongue is raised off the back of the throat

Fieldbook for Australian Scouting

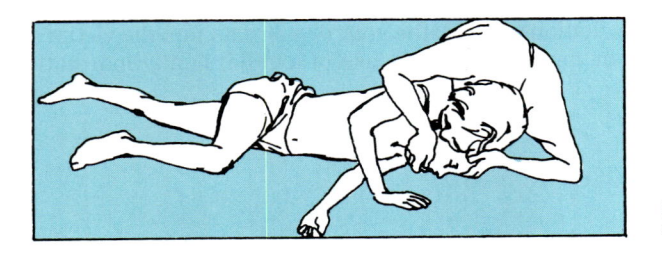

(a) Clear the airway

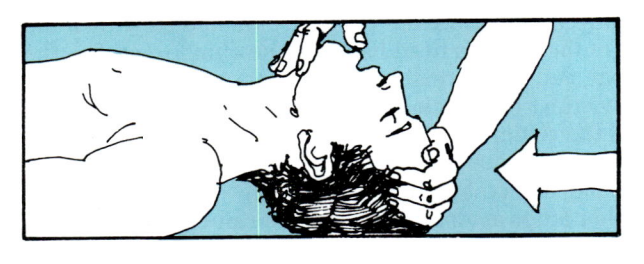

(b) Tilt the head well back

(c)
- Pinch the nostrils (or block the subject's nose with your cheek).
- Place your mouth tightly over the subject's mouth.
- Blow in.

(d)
- Remove your mouth.
- Release the nostrils.
- Listen for air to come out of the subject's lungs.
- Look for the fall of the subject's chest.
- *Blow in again.*

Mouth-to-mouth resuscitation

Survival

Bushfires

It is important for Scouts to know and to apply the fire regulations that are relevant to your area. To prevent bushfires, fire bans and restrictions must be observed.

Whenever you venture into the bush, it is good Scouting to *'Be prepared'* for emergencies such as being trapped by bushfire. Do you have a plan for an emergency of this type? Remember you are in danger of being suffocated by the smoke as well as being severely injured by the heat. Following are some actions that might save your life.

A *flowing* creek would be an ideal shelter from the bushfire. Immerse yourself in the water with only your head above the water, and wait for the fire to pass. Beware of falling trees. Never take refuge in a small body of still water as in a rainwater tank or a small lake—the water might boil! A *large* area of still water would be safer.

If there is no large expanse of water nearby, look for a dry creek bed and cover your face with a wet handkerchief in order to avoid breathing in the smoke. If there is much vegetation along the banks of the creek, you might be able to clear it away or burn it away before the main fire reaches you.

If you have time, it might be possible to get into an area that is already burnt and therefore be able to avoid the flames.

Whatever situation you find yourself in, try to get into a position where there is no fuel for the fire, where you are low to the ground and where you can avoid as much smoke as possible. Naturally, if a high risk of bushfire has been forecast, it might be better if adventures into dry scrub, forest, or large areas of dry grass, were postponed.

Safety and survival in a bushfire area

Though the main emphasis should be on bushfire prevention, you may need to know what to do in case of fire.

In bushfire season, check continuously, by sight and radio, that no fires have started in the area of your activity. It is better to alter your program than to run into danger. It is better to be overdue if it means arriving safely.

Comply with bushfire regulations.

In siting a camp, or hiking through timbered or grassed country, keep in mind the wind and weather conditions, which may change from time to time during the day or night. From these considerations, plan what you would do in the event of a fire approaching from any direction. Always have an escape plan (prepared in your mind) for the most probable paths of a fire; and for the most improbable.

In camp situations, make sure your escape routes are clearly understood by all people present.

If you are in an area where there is a fire:
- keep your party together
- have a strong walker as whipper-in
- be prepared to abandon packs if anyone starts to slow up

- wear clothes to expose as little skin as possible; wool is best
- carry matches
- keep a mental picture of the country.

When the fire is close:

- keep away from dense vegetation
- avoid panic, think out the best plan of escape
- run only when absolutely necessary
- remember that the air nearest to the ground is freshest
- breathe through a wet handkerchief
- remember that even in dense smoke, there are frequent pockets of fresh air.

The fire front is usually narrow (hot deep-burnt to unburnt). Allow it to go past you or, if you go through it, do so as quickly as possible. Radiant heat is the killer. Heat rays travel in straight lines, and are impeded by opaque objects.

How to survive in a bushfire

If your party has the misfortune to be trapped by bushfire, or you find yourself in danger when generously helping to save houses or property, the following expert advice from a CSIRO Bushfire Research Team on how to survive a bushfire could save your life.

On foot

Do not panic   Panic strains nervous and physical energy and clouds judgement. Run only when absolutely necessary. Limit breathing when smoke is dense, and wait for pockets of fresh air before filling the lungs.

The air nearest the ground is freshest and coolest.

Resist the temptation to run from an encircling fire front unless your chances of escape are clearly quite good.

If you decide to flee   Run downhill, because fires move fastest up hill; try to work your way to the flank of the fire and thereby get behind it. Choose a clear path. Do not hesitate in front of flames. If you have to go through for an escape, cover all exposed skin as fast as you can; take some quick, deep breaths, and then move promptly on to the burnt area behind. Do not try to escape through flames more than about 2 metres high or that extend more than 10 metres back, or through dense burning undergrowth.

If you have to stay put   If you are trapped by a high wall of deep flames, light a back-burn at least 7 metres long and stay on the burnt area. Seek every possible shield from radiated heat.

Hide in a running stream or lake, but avoid water tanks above ground level, except as a last resort. (A person almost totally immersed in warm water—say, 46°C—collapses after about three minutes. The fumes will quickly collect in the tank, and may suffocate you.)

If there is no creek or lake at hand, choose the barest patch of ground you can find. Use ruts, logs, rocks or culverts as shelter from radiated heat. Lie flat on the ground, and cover yourself as completely as you can. Best of all, bury yourself in earth. You have a good chance if you do not panic.

Emergencies

(a) Dig a hole and cover yourself

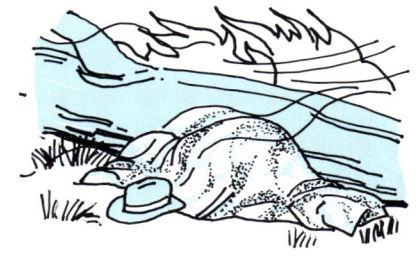

(b) Shelter behind logs or rocks and cover yourself

(c) Hide in a running steam

Bushfire survival methods

In a car

- Stop away from the heaviest vegetation.
- Put headlights on, ignition off.
- Do *not* leave the car.
- Wind up windows; close air vents.
- Get on the floor; cover yourself with rugs if possible.
- *Stay in the car* until the main fire passes.
- *Do not* drive through dense smoke.

In a house

- Close all windows and doors.
- Block crevices beneath doors.
- Stay in a part of house that is away from approaching fire.
- If time, fill the gutters with water, and hose down the walls on the danger side of the house.
- After the main fire passes, inspect the house to see whether any small fires have started.
- If the house is alight and you cannot extinguish the fire, move on to the burnt ground outside.

   Do not be curious unless required to help.

   Avoid bushfires: your curiosity can endanger your own life and the lives of others.

331

If you are lost

Sometimes things go wrong, even with the best made plans, and you may get lost. By following a few simple rules, this does not have to be as serious as it seems.

First, do not panic; sit down and think things out. Try and work out your position, using your map. Work out whether it would be better to go on, go back, or stay put. If you have food and water, it will probably be best to stay put and try to attract attention with a fire — a smoky fire during the day, a blazing fire at night.

If you consider it best to move on, mark the track you take by breaking green twigs, scratching arrows in the dirt, dropping pieces of paper or leaving footprints in the soft earth. Do not move around in bush country at night; make a camp in a sheltered spot and wait until morning. Whenever possible, stick to the ridges, climb a hill or a tree, and look for signs of habitation. Ration out your food supply. Do not exhaust yourself.

The accepted distress signal is three signals together, regularly spaced. These may be given by shouts, whistles, flashing of a mirror or torch, distinctive waving of a cloth, or blanketing a smoky fire. The regularity with which the signals are given is the important thing.

As Scouts sometimes we must be prepared to live off the land. Water is a person's greatest need, followed closely by suitable food. People trained or experienced in bushcraft are capable of surviving in the bush where untrained people will starve — experienced people can live off the land.

You can also train yourself to survive for long periods in the bush after your food supply has run out. There is sure to be food all around, if you know where to look. The food will be different from what you usually eat, and although it may not be to your liking, it will keep you alive.

Trapping or snaring wildlife is a sure way of getting food, but it requires patience and practice. Try setting snares to capture small animals. Fish, yabbies and frogs are a possible source of food around creeks, dams and lakes. Many types of vegetation are edible and nourishing, but it is advisable to cook them before eating them. Avoid berries unless you know they are safe to eat — some types are poisonous. Along the seashore, crabs and shellfish can usually be around the tide mark.

Warning: Do not trap or snare wildlife protected by law in isolated national parks, and use these methods only as a last resort after vegetarian alternatives have been exhausted. Find out which land and water animals are protected before you depart.

Signals

Smoke is one of the best signals you can make: it will be seen for long distances, and if you set your three emergency fires, help will soon be on the way.

A very useful and easy-to-carry piece of signal equipment is a mirror or piece of polished metal. This item has probably been responsible for bringing about more rescues than any other. Carry one in your survival kit. The standard size is about 9×11.5 centimetres. The mirror reflection can be seen for long distances on a clear sunny day.

You can make a signalling mirror from a piece of polished metal by drilling a hole in the exact centre of it for aiming purposes. Even at night, a flashlight or candle directed at the mirror can be very effective.

Table 6.2 Ground–air visual code for use by survivors

Number	Message	Code
1	Require help	V
2	Require medical help	X
3	No or negative	N
4	Yes or affirmative	Y
5	Proceeding in this direction	↑

Note: If in doubt, use international symbol **SOS**.

If the message is received and understood, the aircraft will indicate that ground signals have been seen and understood by —
- day or moonlight
- rocking from side to side

If the message is received and not understood, the aircraft will indicate that ground signals have been seen and not understood by —
- day or moonlight
- making a complete right-hand circle

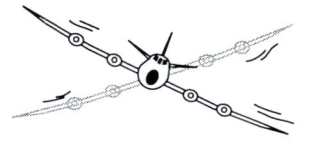

Standard aircraft acknowledgments

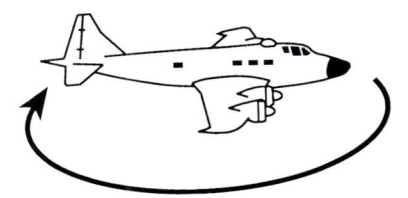

Survival kit

You should carry a survival kit with you on all winter camps and hikes. It can make the difference between being reasonably comfortable and spending some miserable hours or an entire night. Although all the items in the kit are important, the following are a must:

- *matches:* waterproof, or in a waterproof container. A small screwtop film container is good. Do not forget that the striker has to be kept dry too!
- *candle:* just a small piece. It can be used as a firelighter in the wet
- *fishing line:* a small hank. You can use it for fishing or to make snares for small animals
- *fish hooks:* several small ones
- *compass:* a small simple one is enough
- *small sharp knife or razorblade*
- *pencil and paper:* for messages
- *water-purifying tablets:* follow the instructions on the packet
- *whistle:* three evenly spaced signals within half a minute is a recognised distress signal. The signals should be repeated after at least a minute has

elapsed. The acknowledgment is two signals in rapid succession, repeated after two minutes
- *aluminium foil:* two sheets about 300 millimetres square. Use them to make cooking and drinking utensils
- *thin wire* for making snares
- *some form of nutritious food*—sugar cubes, 'beef jerky' (dried meat—*see* next subsection) or chocolate bars.

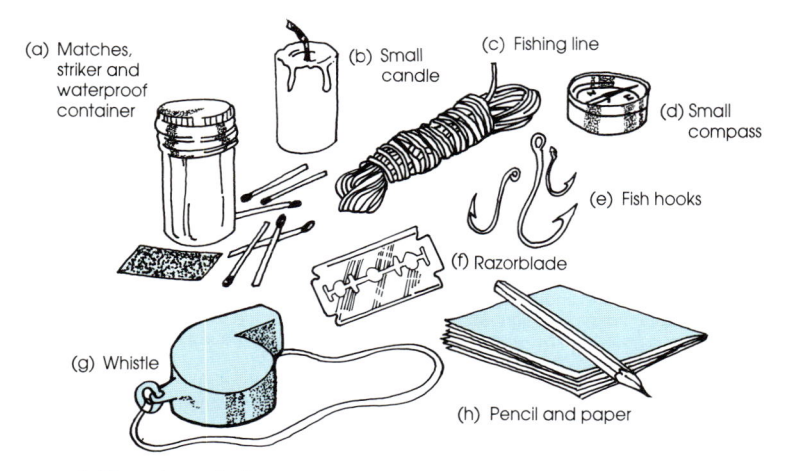

(a) Matches, striker and waterproof container
(b) Small candle
(c) Fishing line
(d) Small compass
(e) Fish hooks
(f) Razorblade
(g) Whistle
(h) Pencil and paper

Some essential items for survival

Beef jerky (dried meat)

To make this useful survival food, you need a billy of boiling, very salty water; meat (with absolutely no fat), and a hot dry wind. The meat should keep indefinitely. When you want to use it, soak it for a time in warm water and then make it into a stew.

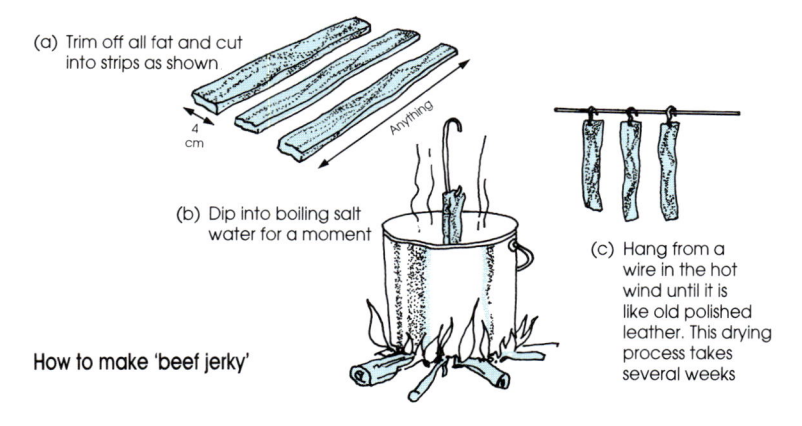

(a) Trim off all fat and cut into strips as shown
4 cm
Anything
(b) Dip into boiling salt water for a moment
(c) Hang from a wire in the hot wind until it is like old polished leather. This drying process takes several weeks

How to make 'beef jerky'

Make utensils from heavy aluminium foil

Diagram (**a**) sets out how to make a billy, diagram (**b**) a cup, from heavy aluminium foil.

Emergencies

(a) BILLY

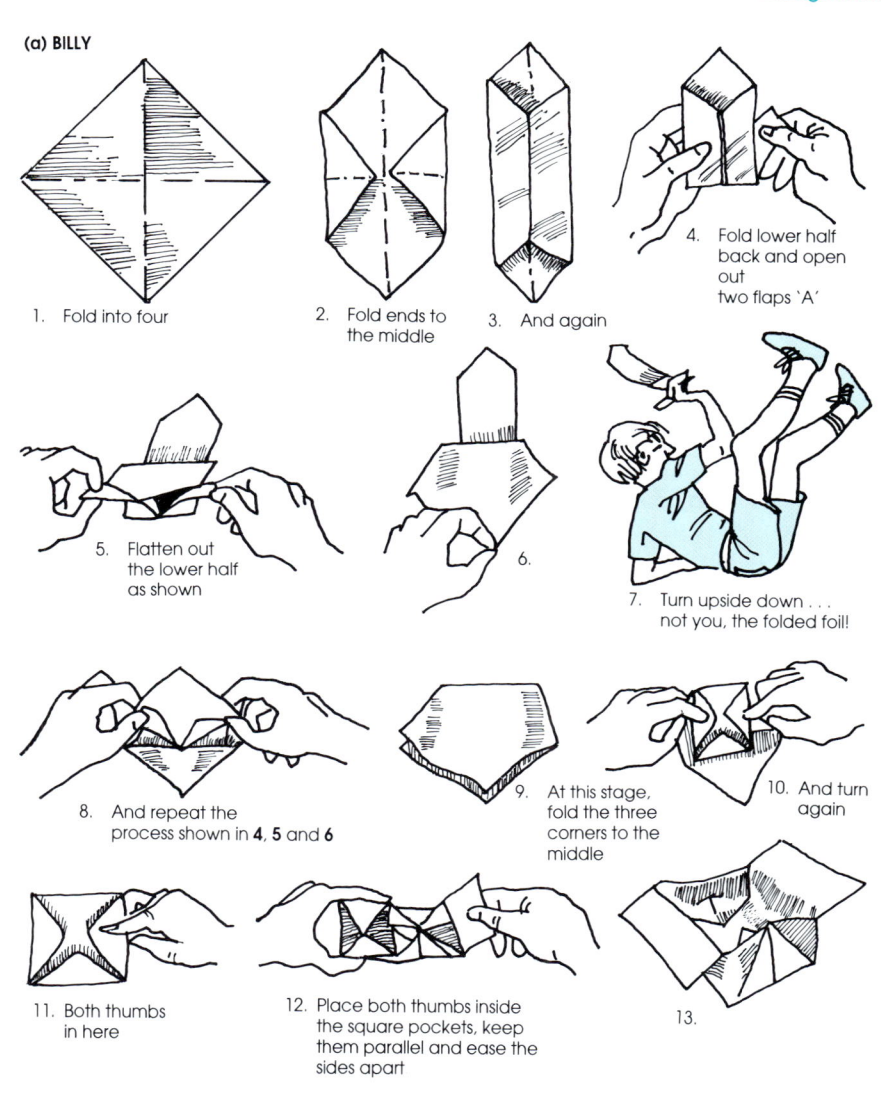

1. Fold into four
2. Fold ends to the middle
3. And again
4. Fold lower half back and open out two flaps 'A'
5. Flatten out the lower half as shown
6.
7. Turn upside down... not you, the folded foil!
8. And repeat the process shown in **4**, **5** and **6**
9. At this stage, fold the three corners to the middle
10. And turn again
11. Both thumbs in here
12. Place both thumbs inside the square pockets, keep them parallel and ease the sides apart
13.

(b) CUP

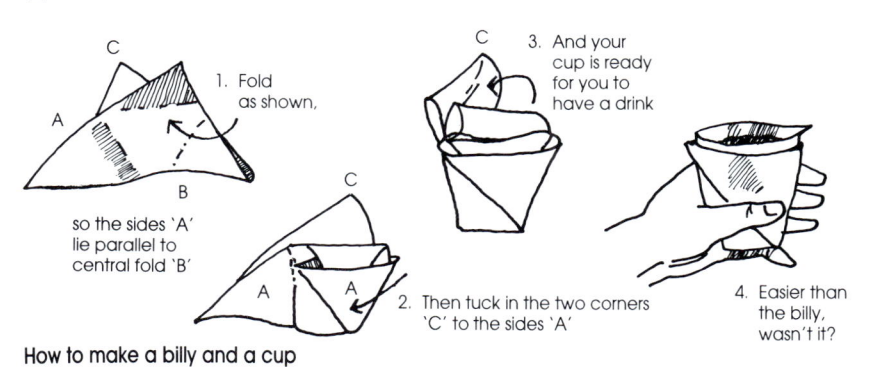

1. Fold as shown, so the sides 'A' lie parallel to central fold 'B'
2. Then tuck in the two corners 'C' to the sides 'A'
3. And your cup is ready for you to have a drink
4. Easier than the billy, wasn't it?

How to make a billy and a cup

335

Winter first aid

People from some parts of Australia need to know this information more than others.

Frostbite and freezing

Sometimes only the surface of the skin is frostbitten; if so, only the skin and the tissue just beneath it are frozen. Sometimes, frostbite may be deep: tissues are badly frozen and may be destroyed.

Surface (superficial) damage usually happens to the ears, nose, cheeks, chin, fingers and toes. It usually comes on slowly and may not be noticed. There is usually no pain, the skin appears waxy and white, and the flesh is firm to the touch but the tissue underneath is soft.

If you are travelling on snowshoes, there is a danger of having your toes frostbitten because your feet cannot move very much. To prevent frostbite, stop once in a while, step out of the harness, and massage your feet gently.

If the temperature is well below zero, or if you are hiking in a very chilly wind, keep making faces rather than allowing the skin of the face to stay in one position. If you keep moving your facial muscles like this, it will help keep your blood circulating. Chewing gum also keeps the face muscles in motion.

Use the 'buddy system' to keep watch on each other. Pair up, and every now and then, stop and check your buddy's face for signs of frostbite.

Only superficial frostbite can be treated on the hike. Treat it by applying the firm, steady pressure of a warm hand, by blowing hot breath on the spot, or by placing frostbitten fingers in the armpit under your clothes.

Frosted toes or heels present the most problems on a hike — particularly because the frostbite may not be noticed. If stinging or numbness develops, find a sheltered spot quickly. Remove your boots and place your foot on the stomach of a trail friend, or cup the foot with warm hands. When it has thawed, change to dry socks and replace your boots, tying the laces loosely to ensure good circulation.

Never rub frostbite with the hand or with snow Deep frostbite or freezing is serious. The part that is frozen will be white, waxy looking and hard to the touch. This condition requires fast medical treatment. Do not try to warm badly frostbitten skin while on the trail. Protect the frozen part from further freezing and from contact with hard objects. Get the victim to a doctor.

Snowblindness

The term *snowblindness* is not quite accurate because actual blindness does not occur. There is first a feeling like grit in the eyes; they become hot and sticky, then begin to water, and the vision becomes blurred. Next comes sharp pain and an impulse to shrink from light.

The sun does not have to be shining to cause snowblindness; the trouble most often develops on days when the sky is slightly overcast and there is little shadow.

Emergencies

Polarised or amber-coloured glasses are good prevention and protection. They must have side ventilation to prevent frosting. If you feel any of the symptoms of snowblindness and do not have sunglasses, keep your eyes fixed on a dark object ahead, such as a dark canvas covering, a loaded toboggan or sled, or the back of a companion mushing ahead of you. A trailbreaker developing eye trouble should fall back to the end of the line.

If you cannot avoid looking at bright snow, you can give your eyes some help by almost closing the lids and looking through your eyelashes.

To cut down on glare, blackening the nose and cheekbones with a mixture of charcoal and grease may be helpful.

Camp treatment for snowblindness consists of applying cold compresses or ice wrapped in gauze and shielding the eyes as effectively as possible. In serious cases, the patient should be kept in a darkened place for as long as necessary.

Emergency snow goggles

These corrugated cardboard snow goggles are easy to make. You will require one square of corrugated cardboard of size 22.5 × 22.5 centimetres, a strong pair of scissors, a bottle of rubber cement, two strong elastic bands, two bread ties, and a sharp knife.

Cut the cardboard into strips about 12 millimetres wide (about 20 strips). Glue them together in a stack. Let the glue dry for about 24 hours, then cut an upside-down 'V'-shaped hole for your nose. With your knife, cut a line down the middle of the cardboard, being careful not to cut the cardboard in half. Do the same about 5 centimetres in from the left and right edges of the cardboard, then bend slightly.

Finally, loop together the two elastic bands and attach to cardboard with ties, as shown in the diagram. You will then have a pair of snow goggles that enable you to see very well between the tiny holes of the corrugated cardboard.

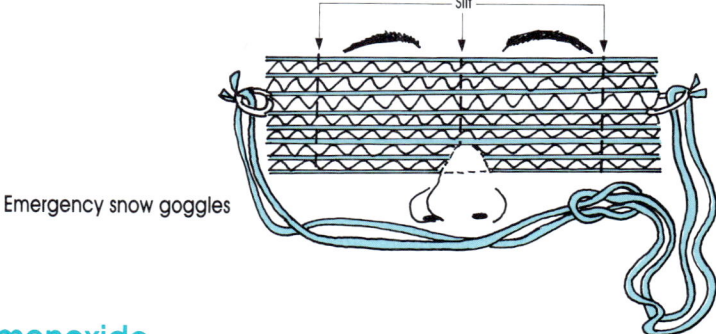

Emergency snow goggles

Carbon monoxide

People camping in winter should understand the danger of carbon-monoxide poisoning in snow houses as well as tents. If you are using gas lamps and stoves for light and heat, your shelter should be well ventilated.

In carbon-monoxide poisoning, there is no smell or other advance warning. A sudden severe headache, dizziness and sickness may be followed quickly by unconsciousness.

To help, remove the patient quickly to fresh air, and if necessary, give Expired Air Resuscitation. Keep the patient warm with blankets and hot drinks.

Hypothermia

Hypothermia is the biggest threat while you are winter camping. Usually people who die from exposure or have 'frozen to death' have died from hypothermia. This occurs when the body loses more heat than it generates. It happens when a person is not dressed warmly enough for the weather. A person could be in danger of hypothermia if exhausted, wet, exposed to wind, or undernourished. Under these conditions, the air does not have to be cold or below freezing—a moderate temperature of 5°C to 10°C can cause death.

To avoid hypothermia, stay dry. Put rain gear on before it starts to rain, and make sure it is waterproof, not only water repellent. Make sure it provides adequate ventilation, otherwise the person will become wet inside from perspiration and the purpose of rain gear will thereby be defeated.

Protect yourself from the wind. Windbreaks and other shelters should be considered before setting out in windy weather.

Make sure you have warm clothing, including a hat. Remember that wool keeps its ability to retain heat even when wet. Put on a spare dry jumper *after* exertion from working or playing, not before.

Avoid exhaustion. Set a reasonable hiking pace that will not leave people ready to drop by mealtime. Do not over-exert yourself in games, because you must keep your energy reserve ready to fight off the chill that indicates the onset of hypothermia.

Finally, make sure you have some high-energy food to nibble on while hiking and that you eat good, nutritious meals at regular times.

Symptoms

Hypothermia can start slowly, as on a hiking trip, or quickly, as in being soaked after falling through ice into freezing water. The symptoms include feeling chilly, tired and irritable. If not helped at this stage, the hypothermia victim begins to shiver uncontrollably. The shivering soon becomes even worse, and the victim may begin to act strangely. Slowing, stumbling, weakness, and repeated falling may happen. If the shivering stops, the person is close to death. Remember, in many cases the victim does not realise what is happening and may deny there is anything wrong.

First aid for hypothermia

If you are on a backpacking trip or winter camping and you realise someone is suffering from hypothermia, *stop immediately*. Put up a shelter. Strip the patient gently and put him/her into a dry, warm sleeping bag; another person sharing the bag with the patient will also help to provide warmth. Do not massage or rub the patient. Light a fire nearby in order to provide heat and to prepare a warm, sweet, nourishing drink.

Remember that the warming process is slow, and it may take six to eight hours to re-warm a person who has been seriously stricken. Even after the victim's body begins to feel warm, the cold blood circulating from the extremities (head, feet and hands) back to the body's core can produce an afterdrop, a continued lowering of the body temperature.

After any serious brush with hypothermia, the outing should be ended. If one person has fallen victim to hypothermia, chances are others may also be in danger. Remember that small people and children who have a smaller body size and less body fat can be more susceptible to the cold.

Winter survival

You will probably never have to survive in the cold without a shelter, fuel and sleeping bags. However, there is always the chance that this emergency may arise, and this section is included for this reason.

Whenever you are in an emergency situation, without the usual protection, do not panic; then, get organised. As a reasonably fit, knowledgeable, thinking person, you should be able to survive if you adhere to the following advice.

- Deal with your immediate problems first. Find water, firewood and shelter. Attend whatever first-aid emergencies come up, and prepare your signal fires.
- Assess your situation. Every emergency has a different set of problems, and every situation provides a set of opportunities. Decide what has to be done and when. Be systematic.
- Establish discipline. This is important if you are alone, and even more so if you are in a group. Do not allow yourself or anyone to waste precious reserves of energy by panicking. It is important that every member of a group works for their survival.
- Marshall your resources. Look at what you have in your pack. Ask how it can be used. Save, conserve, and ration whatever you have.
- Ration your physical and mental resources. Your reserves must be managed carefully. Think about what you are doing, what you can expect to gain, and what you can expect to lose by choosing a certain action. Solve each problem thoroughly and capably.
- Keep your spirits up. This is particularly important within a group. Sing, laugh, play counting games, or whatever, in order to keep good cheer. Highlight your accomplishments and stress the positive.
- Do not surrender to your problems. Keep up appearances by washing when you can, preparing food properly, and keep up good manners and civilised behaviour.
- Handle one problem at a time. Once you have decided you need a shelter, build it. Do not stop halfway through and do something else.
- Once done with food, firewood and shelter, consider your long-term course of action. Assess your situation carefully, and plan alternatives if necessary.
- Take action. When you have decided something, carry through with it. Do what you think is best in light of the conditions.

7
ENVIRONMENT

Natural and human environments

The more travel, hiking trips and camping trips you take, the more you will come to realise nature around you and how vastly nature varies.

The nature of a forest is vastly different from that of a desert, or a paddock, or a seashore, or a city. The nature you find at the top of a mountain is different from what you find near a river.

Not only is nature changing from place to place; it is changing through time. On the farm or in the city, it is easy to see many changes being made around you. New roads are being built; dams are being formed; marshes are being drained and reclaimed. Whenever people change the environment, plant life and wildlife soon change as well.

In addition to changes by people, however, nature goes on changing either quickly or slowly. Soil is forming and moving from place to place; plants and animals are born, growing, dying and decaying. Climate and weather are changing too! Keep these changes in mind as you take imaginary hikes into the environments discussed on the following pages.

Environment

Scouts geared up for hiking in the Australian bush

Heavens — stars and planets

The campfire is over. You and your Patrol are going back to your tents. The trees form a dark wall around you. Above, however, the sky is clear and crowded with thousands of sparkling stars.

Marvel at the universe of stars, and you begin to understand what our environment is all about.

Our Sun is the closest star to our world, the Earth. Apart from the Earth there are eight worlds, the planets, endlessly orbiting the Sun. All are dwarfed by the Sun, the enormous gravity of which keeps the planets in their orbits.

Space is not filled evenly with stars: they cluster in enormous clouds called galaxies, and in between the galaxies there are vast regions of emptiness.

All the stars we see in the sky belong to our own galaxy — it contains 100 billion stars. The hazy band of light called the Milky Way is how our galaxy shows itself.

Stars, including our Sun, are born from huge clouds of hydrogen gas, live for millions or billions of years, and die as tiny 'white dwarfs'; our Sun will do this one day, perhaps in 9 billion years time. The science of astronomy is fascinating, and through it you can learn about exciting things such as supernovas, pulsars, quasars and nebulas . . . even black holes.

Our Sun is a vast hydrogen bomb, 5 billion years old, large enough to contain a thousand Jupiters—the largest planet—or a million Earths. The Sun is 6000°C at its surface and 15 000 000°C at its centre: quite hot, don't you think? Its surface is in constant turmoil with giant streamers of hot gas erupting, and giant explosions sending particles speeding into space. These may be radio waves, X-rays or electrical particles.

Astronomers think that, like our Sun, most stars have planets. Among the 100 billion stars of our galaxy, there may be millions of other solar systems containing planets like Earth. Living things on other worlds would probably not look much like Earth life, but intelligent life in outer space is equally as probable as on Earth.

Planet Earth, our home in space, is a rocky ball 12 756 kilometres in diameter, orbiting around the Sun once each year. Although tiny by comparison with the Sun, Earth's rock weighs 6000 million million million tonnes generating its own gravity pull. The inner core is white-hot iron, and the outer core is red-hot iron, followed by heavy mantle rock and lighter rock crust forming the continents and sea beds.

Held to the Earth by the gravity pull are the great oceans of water and the layer of air called the atmosphere. The air is a mixture of gases, essential to provide and to protect life on Earth. There will be more about these vital parts of our environment later in this chapter.

Two precious life cycles

Let us think of an environment as the home for particular plants and animals that live together and depend for their survival on each other and on the conditions that surround them. Each environment is a complicated system, an *ecosystem*—from the Greek word *oikos*, meaning a home. The study of environments, of the relationship between living things and their surroundings, is called *ecology*—the study of the home.

Oxygen–carbon

In order to understand how living things survive, you must know about two vital life cycles. The most important cycle for all kinds of life is the *oxygen–carbon cycle*, which depends on the sun's energy.

In order to live, you and all other living creatures must breathe. To do this, you draw air into your lungs. The lungs absorb oxygen from the air and use part of it in a process that can be compared with burning. The carbon dioxide that results goes back into the air that you breathe out. Carbon dioxide is also produced by burning all kinds of fuel and when dead plants and animals decay.

Plants require this carbon dioxide in order to grow. By a miraculous process, they combine the carbon in it with water to produce simple sugars.

Environment

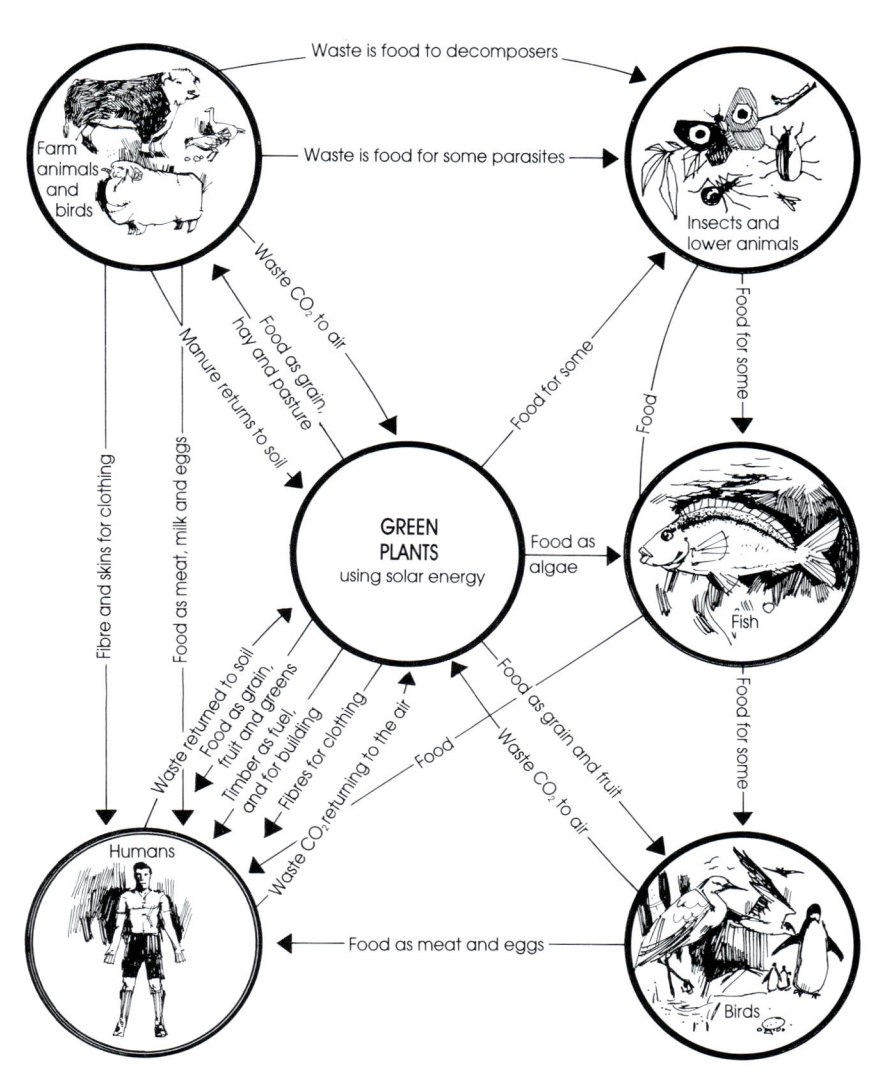

The food chains of life — all forms of life are interdependent

In doing this, they give off oxygen as a byproduct. This process is known as *photosynthesis*—making things with the aid of light. In this process the plants make use of the energy of sunlight and of a green colouring matter in their cells called *chlorophyll*. The plants further combine the sugars with nitrogen and minerals to form many other foods: starches and oils, proteins and vitamins.

All food eaten by you and other animals can be traced to the oxygen–carbon cycle. Bread and cereals, and vegetables and fruits, come directly out of the cycle. Milk, eggs and meat are produced by animals that survive by eating plants.

Fieldbook for Australian Scouting

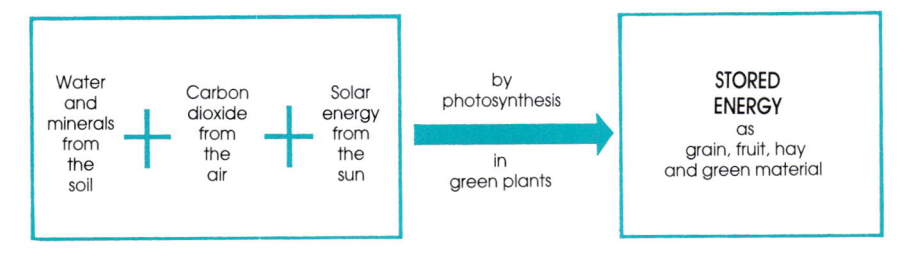

The process of photosynthesis

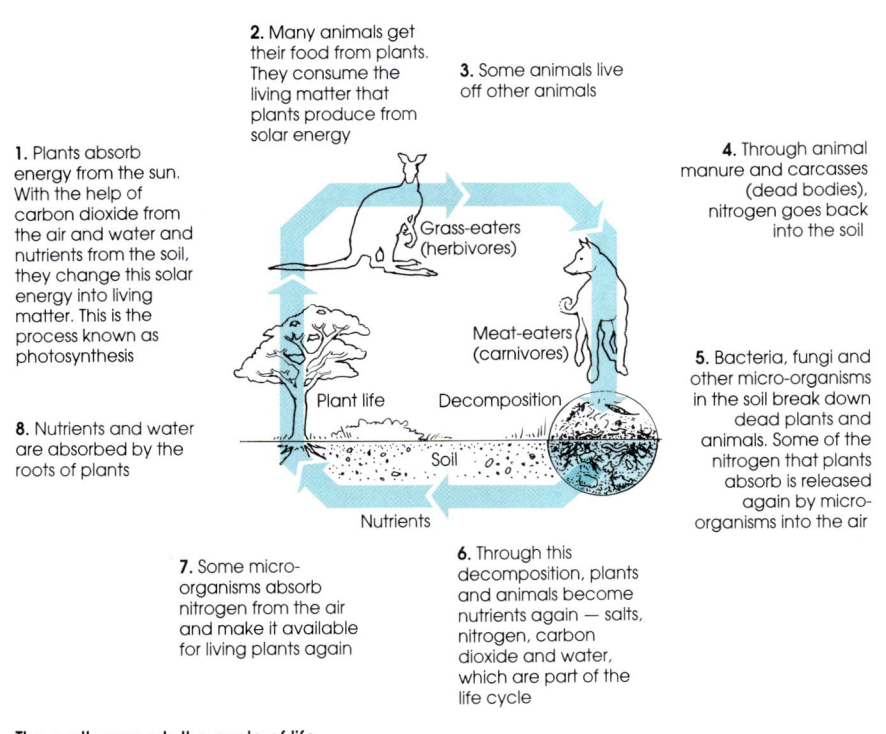

1. Plants absorb energy from the sun. With the help of carbon dioxide from the air and water and nutrients from the soil, they change this solar energy into living matter. This is the process known as photosynthesis

2. Many animals get their food from plants. They consume the living matter that plants produce from solar energy

3. Some animals live off other animals

4. Through animal manure and carcasses (dead bodies), nitrogen goes back into the soil

5. Bacteria, fungi and other micro-organisms in the soil break down dead plants and animals. Some of the nitrogen that plants absorb is released again by micro-organisms into the air

6. Through this decomposition, plants and animals become nutrients again — salts, nitrogen, carbon dioxide and water, which are part of the life cycle

7. Some micro-organisms absorb nitrogen from the air and make it available for living plants again

8. Nutrients and water are absorbed by the roots of plants

The earth supports the cycle of life

Water

The other vital cycle is the *water cycle*. All living things must have fresh water for life and growth. Again, everything depends on the sun's energy. The sun draws fresh water, into the atmosphere, out of the salt water that covers about two-thirds of the earth's surface and out of the lakes and rivers. This water is then redistributed back on earth.

The water cycle involves five stages, outlined as follows.

Environment

The water cycle diagram:

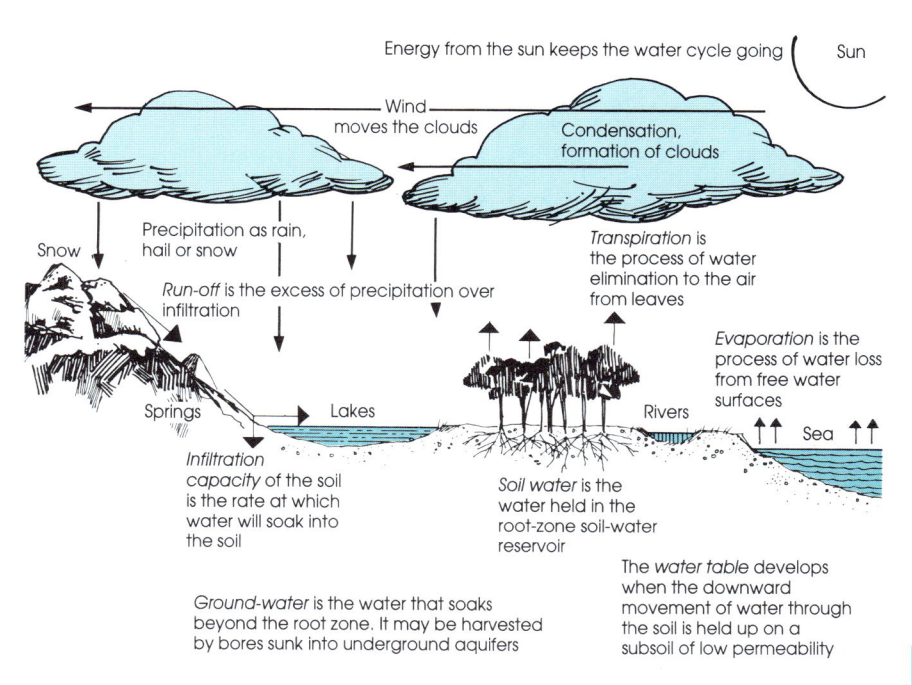

- Energy from the sun keeps the water cycle going — Sun
- Wind moves the clouds
- Condensation, formation of clouds
- Precipitation as rain, hail or snow
- Snow
- *Run-off* is the excess of precipitation over infiltration
- *Transpiration* is the process of water elimination to the air from leaves
- *Evaporation* is the process of water loss from free water surfaces
- Springs, Lakes, Rivers, Sea
- *Infiltration capacity* of the soil is the rate at which water will soak into the soil
- *Soil water* is the water held in the root-zone soil-water reservoir
- *Ground-water* is the water that soaks beyond the root zone. It may be harvested by bores sunk into underground aquifers
- The *water table* develops when the downward movement of water through the soil is held up on a subsoil of low permeability

The water cycle—a continual process of natural purification. Any disturbance of this cycle is a threat to plants, animals and humans

Evaporation This is the process by which water is changed into vapour. It is accelerated by wind and high temperature. When cooled in the upper atmosphere, the water vapour forms clouds.

Transpiration This is the loss of water from plants to the air in the form of vapour. The water entered the plants from the water supply in the soil.

Precipitation This is the way in which water falls from the clouds. This can be as dew, fog, rain, frost, hail, sleet or snow. It happens when the clouds cool so much that the air can no longer hold the water.

Surface runoff This takes place where the droplets fall faster than the soil can soak them up. The excess water runs downhill to streams, rivers and, finally, to lakes and oceans.

Infiltration This is what happens to the droplets that do not run off the land. This water soaks into the soil and is used by plants. It also moves deeper into the soil to become part of the ground-water supply. When all space in the ground is filled, the water flows along cracks or the water table to come up as springs or rivers, returning to the lakes or oceans from which it came.

All living things on earth are interdependent through a series of food chains. Every living thing requires *food + water + energy*. Soil, air, water,

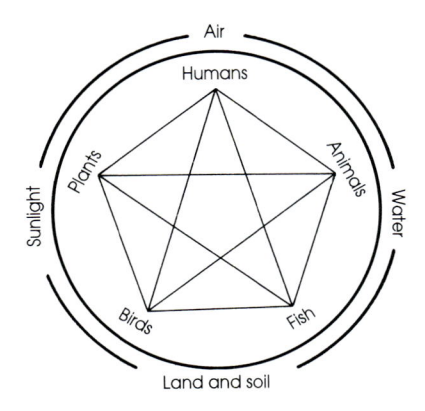

All forms of life are interdependent within the environment

plants, animals, rocks and sunlight are in a web of nature. This makes up the fabric of life on earth as we know it.

The balance of nature is critical. All living things play a part in the huge and complex web of life. If wildlife becomes extinct, the balance will be destroyed.

Pure water

There is as much water on earth today as there ever was or ever will be. The circulation of it in the water cycle is neverending. The glass of water you drink today might have flowed down the Murray River last month; or it could have been some of the Indian Ocean.

It seems as if there is an abundance of water on earth; there is. However, it is mostly salty sea water of no use for drinking, nor for the thousands of other needs we have for water. Only 3% of the world's water is fresh, and a large percentage of it is now so polluted that the cost of purifying it is almost prohibitive.

Australia is the driest continent in the world. Conservation of water and protection of its quality is fundamental to our survival.

Water is scarce and important

The blue planet

When humans saw the world from space for the first time, it looked blue. Now we know that the colour blue is a sign of life. It is the water on earth that gives it the colour blue; water is essential for life.

Although we have plenty of water, we have serious problems with it as a resource.

Environment

The blue planet

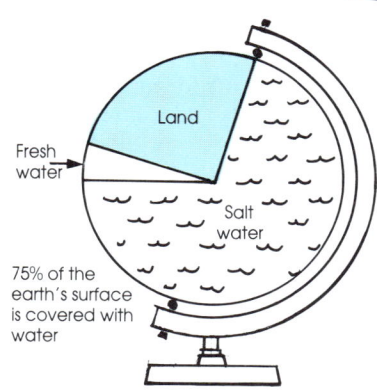

75% of the earth's surface is covered with water
Fresh water
Land
Salt water

Land and water

First, more than 95% of the world's water is salt and can be used neither as drinking water nor for watering fields (irrigation). The remaining 5% is fresh water, but a considerable part of it is ice. This means that less than 3% of the world's water can be used for drinking water or irrigation.

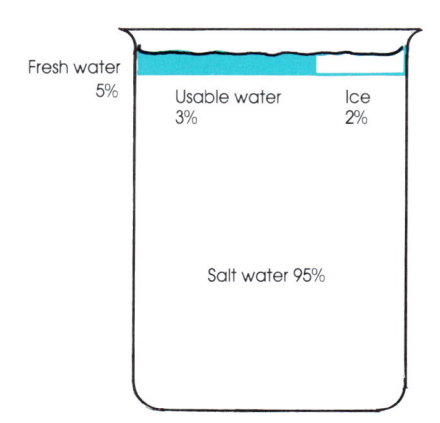

Fresh water 5%
Usable water 3%
Ice 2%
Salt water 95%

Distribution of water

Second, water is unevenly distributed. There are areas where it does not rain at all. Others get so much rain they become flooded.

We can live without food for a month or more. Without water, we can live for only 3 or 4 days.

347

Water makes up 70% to 80% of most living creatures. Water is the principal transport medium for food going into plants and animals, for processing food within them, and then for the removal of waste products.

Plants and animals can take in only water of a high level of purity—low in chemical impurities and free of disease-causing organisms. At the same time, they keep only a small percentage of the water they take in (less than 1%), and the rest is passed out as waste—by plants through transpiration; by animals through perspiration and urine, and during breathing.

Industry uses water as its main cooling agent because of its high specific heat (heat-holding capacity). It is also used as a main solvent carrier of chemicals going into processes and the main carrier for all the waste products of the industrial processes.

Transport systems use waterways. Many recreations use water: swimming, boating, diving and fishing, for example. The vapour form of water (steam) is used for heating and cleaning. The solid form (ice) is used for cooling, and the liquid form is always being used to remove the waste products—heat, solids, chemicals and liquids.

Although people cannot drink sea water it is very important. For example, small plants and animals, called algae and plankton, live in the sea. They are the basic food for other marine life and they also produce about 75% of the oxygen in the air.

Only a few milligrams of DDT per tonnes of water reduces the algae's oxygen-producing ability by half. Anti-fouling paints on yachts moored close to oyster farms have been known to destroy the plant life on which the oysters depend.

The water along our coast, which is so important for animals and bird life and for recreation, must be protected from oil spills and from the dumping of waste and harmful substances.

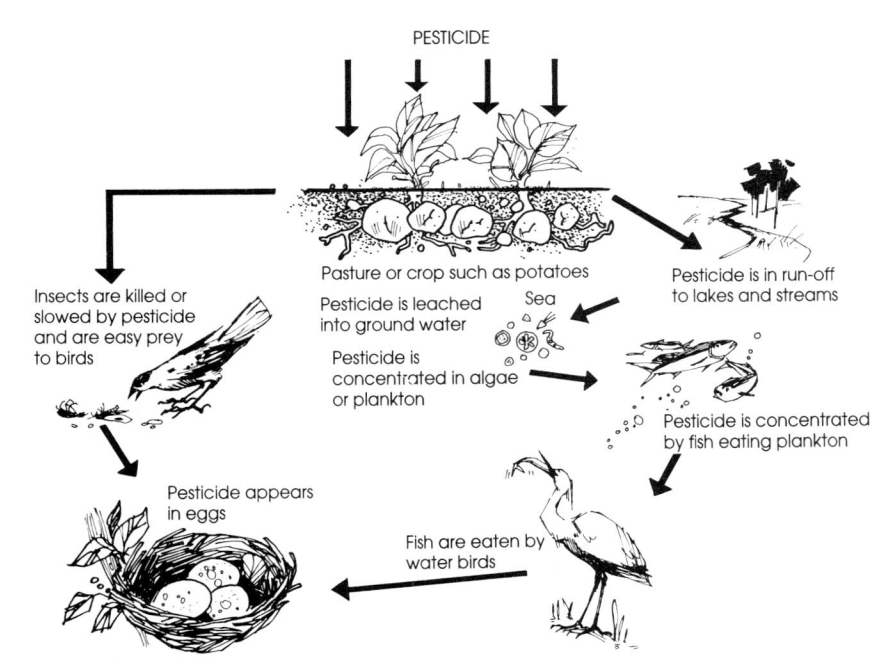

How pesticides affect the food chain

Conservation of water

Some other ideas to protect and conserve water are outlined as follows:

- Fix leaking taps: 10 drips per minute wastes 3000 litres of water per year.
- Rinse plates immediately after eating food off them.
- Use dual-flush toilet cisterns, or reduce the storage by placing a brick in the cistern. A full flush takes 11–12 litres: unnecessary for most uses of the toilet.
- Having a shower generally uses only one-third as much water as a bath—do not stay too long under the shower.
- Turn off the shower while you soap yourself. Install a flow-restricting shower nozzle.
- Turn off the tap when cleaning your teeth—this can save up to 5 litres of water.
- Use timing devices on garden hoses, and use a drip watering system rather than a sprinkler. Water during the cool of the evening, and water less often and more thoroughly.
- Front-loading washing machines use less than top-loading machines.
- Use phosphate-free detergents.
- Wash your car on the lawn, and use a bucket instead of a hose.
- Take waste oil to a recycling point, and never pour it down the drain.

How our waters are fertilised to death

The lakes are fertilised by phosphate-rich sewage water from industries, households, (toilets and detergents) and agriculture. The phosphate is 'food' for the plants in the lake.

An increase in the amount of phosphate increases the plant life (particularly of small plants, and algae).

When these plants eventually die, bacteria act to decompose them. In order to cope with the increasing amount of vegetation, the bacteria require oxygen, which they take from the water.

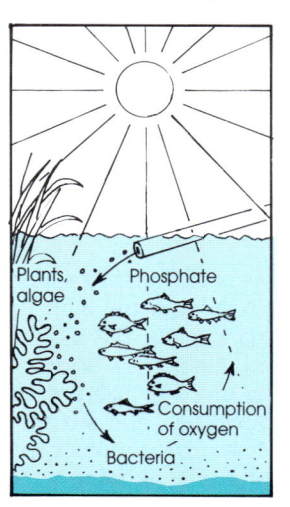

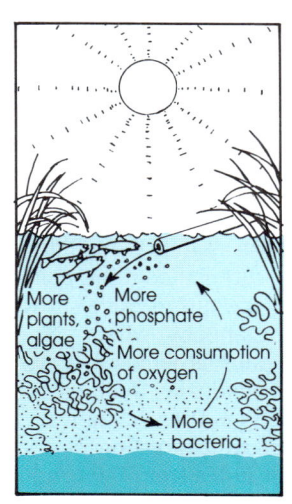

Effects of phosphate fertilisation on a lake

As the water gets dirtier and darker, the sun's rays are prevented from penetrating into the water and helping the plants in the lake to produce fresh oxygen by photosynthesis.

Eventually, the lake reaches the stage at which the bacteria have consumed all the oxygen. The fish then die, and the lake turns into a stinking mudhole.

Water quality

The maintenance of water quality depends on protecting the natural purification cycle: use—disposal—cleansing—re-use.

The purification process is mainly through distillation from the liquid to vapour phase—the *transpiration* of plants; the *evaporation* of perspiration off our bodies; the *evaporation* of water from the soil, lakes and the sea. This is possible only because of the unique property that water has of being able to exist as a solid, a liquid and a 'gas', at normal temperatures and pressure, and the tremendous reserves of water in the biosphere.

Impure water is continually being *filtered* through the soil or purified by evaporation and returning to the earth as *precipitation* in the pure forms of rain, hail or snow. Less than 1% of the world's water is in the usable form of fresh water or water vapour at any one time, while over 99% of it is in storage in the sea and lakes, in the soil, and in ice and snow.

Many of the contaminants in water are of organic origin—plant and animal wastes and industrial wastes. Bacteria and other micro-organisms in the soil and in large bodies of water use these organic substances as food and therefore dispose of them and purify the water in the process. This occurs while water is soaking through the soil or rocks or is 'in store' in rivers, lakes or the sea.

The pollution of water may be by natural organic wastes such as plant litter or animal urine and manure, by human-made organic wastes such as rubbish, waste from industrial processes in factories and processing plants, or by chemicals.

Most organic wastes are broken down by micro-organisms into harmless products if the polluted water is stored long enough. Detergents and petroleum products are not as readily eliminated. Chemical pollution is a special problem in intensive cropping such as in market gardening, for which heavy applications of artificial fertilisers are used, and intensive livestock operations such as poultry or dairy or piggery units, from which urine and manure wastes from many animals is concentrated in a small area.

The problem is greatly intensified if the pollution is occurring in a water-catchment area. Increasing the nitrate level in water results in the build-up of algae and water-living organisms, which can quickly deplete the oxygen level in water, even to the point at which fish are killed.

The use of persistent pesticides such as DDT on crops or pastures in water-catchment areas results in these chemicals reaching the water storages or the sea. The subsequent concentration in a food chain can seriously endanger wildlife thousands of miles from the original point of pollution.

Water harvesting

This is a specialised method of water conservation. The collection and storage of water from a large area in a low-rainfall region, or during periods of excessive rainfall for subsequent use for the watering of stock or irrigation of crops, is called *water harvesting*.

Rainfall is recorded in millimetres (mm), but water for irrigation is measured in megalitres (ML). However, it is easier to visualise the irrigation-water requirements of crops in millimetres, equivalent to rainfall. An orange orchard may use the equivalent of 1250 millimetres of rain in a year to grow its crop of oranges; a vineyard the equivalent of 750 millimetres to grow its crop of grapes; an apple or peach orchard the equivalent of 1000 millimetres.

Table 7.1 Water required to produce food and clothing

Product	Water used (litres)
1 orange	500
1 egg	1 000
1 litre of milk	3 300
1 loaf of bread	2 500
1 kg dried fruit	2 400
1 kg butter	24 000
1 kg meat	112 000
1 woollen suit	1 000 000

The orange tree is an evergreen (it retains its leaves all year round) whereas the apple and peach are deciduous trees (they lose their leaves in winter). The deciduous crops use less water because they are dormant for part of the year. Perennial pastures such as lucerne and phalaris will require more water than annual pastures such as barrel medic and Wimmera ryegrass.

The wheat farmer conserves the whole of the year's rainfall in the soil by fallowing or clean cultivation to keep the soil free of weeds, which would use water. He then plants his wheat crop in the autumn, and it grows and produces its crop of grain in about six months and uses a whole year's rainfall in the process.

In the fruit areas, run-off water from areas of pasture- or timber-land, and off the orchard, may be collected and stored in dams to be used for irrigation to supplement the rainfall on the orchard land.

Dams may be built as a weir across a stream, as a wall across a natural drainage line, or above ground adjacent to a non-perennial stream to be filled by pumping during the winter rainy period. These latter dams are often called 'turkey-nest dams' because of their shape.

A very effective form of water storage is found in nature in underground sandbeds which are porous enough to accept water with a good infiltration rate but sealed below by a layer of rock or soil of low permeability. This type of bed, called an *aquifer*, is then used for an irrigation-water supply by pumping from a well. This method of storage is often possible along non-perennial rivers, and is common in Australia's coastal region of Queensland.

Clean air

What do you get when you mix oxygen and nitrogen and sulphur dioxide and soot and smoke and exhaust fumes? Ordinary city air!

When humans congregate to live in towns and cities, the air begins to lose its purity. First comes the smoke from home fires; then the smoke from mills and factories, in the form of soot and toxic gases. The thousands of cars, trucks and buses burning fuels spew out hydrocarbons, carbon monoxide, nitrogen oxides and sulphur dioxide. By day, the sun's heat cooks the hydrocarbons and nitrogen into troublesome pollutants that sting the eyes and damage the lungs. They cause smog, injure plants and attack cloth and building materials.

The thin layer of air on which all life depends

It is a mistake to believe the air we have is unlimited. The layer of air surrounding the earth is only about 15 kilometres thick. Only the first 5 kilometres of this band contains enough oxygen to support life. If we continue to pollute the air at the current rate, humans will become extinct in the very near future.

The special gas *ozone* is now known to be vitally important. Depletion of ozone is being caused by our pollution of the atmosphere, and there may be dire consequences if this continues.

Ozone is a gas that forms a protective layer high up in the atmosphere (the *stratosphere*). It exists in minute quantities but acts as a vital shield against harmful levels of ultraviolet (UV) radiation from the sun.

Ozone is created from oxygen by the effects of UV radiation in the stratosphere. The ozone layer has been maintained by natural processes for millions of years. Now, in a mere few hundred years since the industrial revolution, the ozone balance has been put at risk.

What damages ozone are the artificial chemicals known as CFCs (chlorofluorocarbons) and *halons*. These pollute the air when they leak from manufactured goods, floating up into the stratosphere. There, the strong sunlight causes the CFCs to break down, producing free chlorine and bromine which have the power to attack and destroy ozone.

The loss of ozone threatens life on earth because it means more harmful UV radiation will reach the earth's surface. Ozone depletion is also likely to alter the world's climate in unpredictable ways.

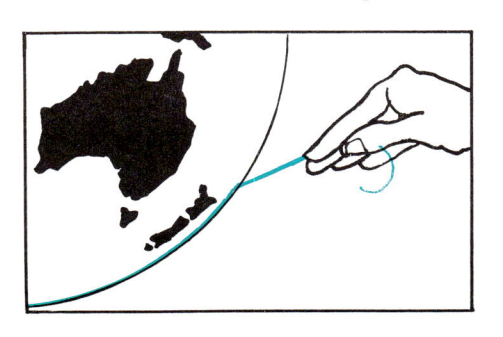

The thickness of the layer of usable air around the earth equals the thickness of a human hair on a globe with a circumference of 45 centimetres

Life hangs by a hair

Environment

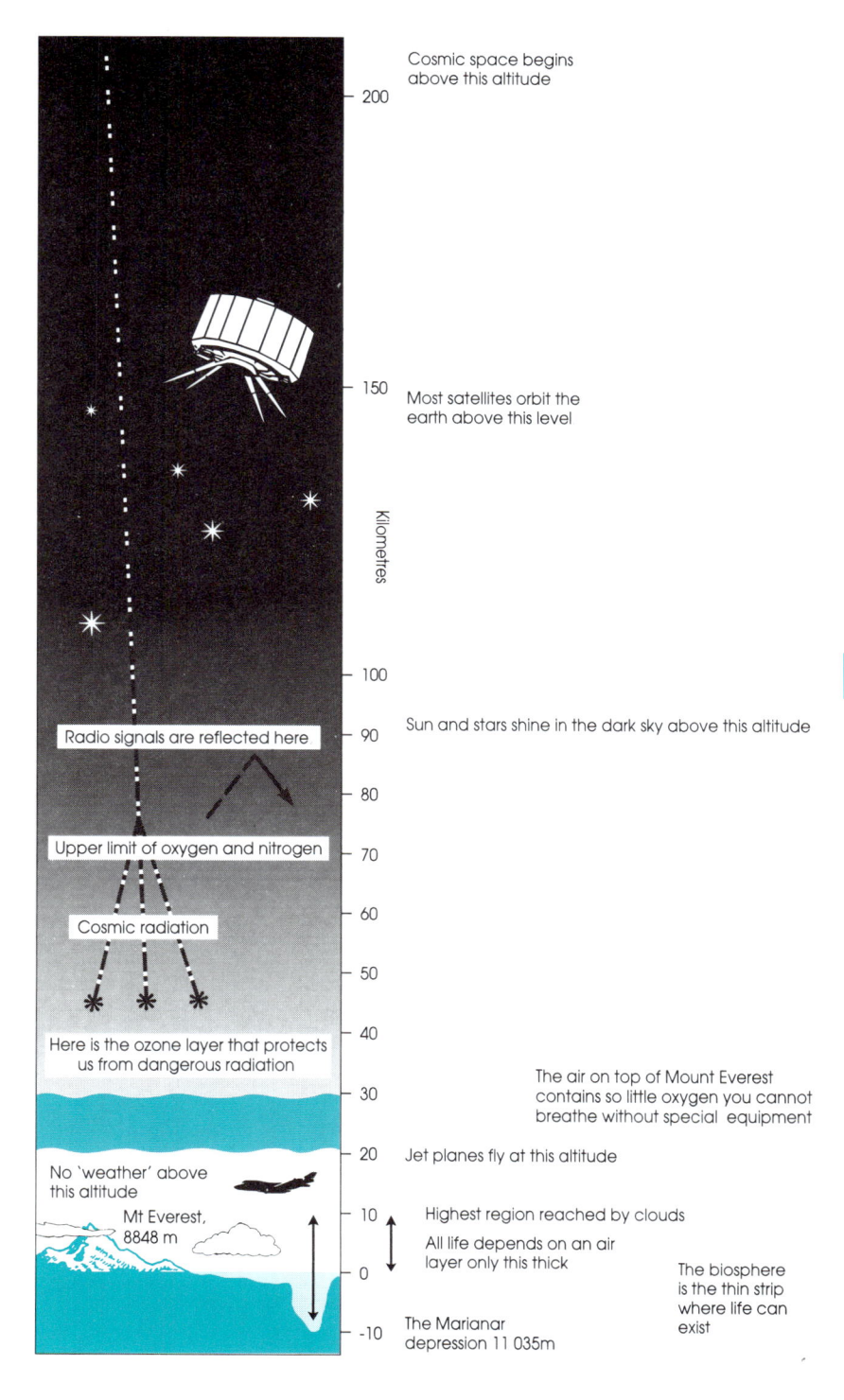

Above and below the earth's surface

Kilometres

- 200 — Cosmic space begins above this altitude
- 150 — Most satellites orbit the earth above this level
- 100
- 90 — Sun and stars shine in the dark sky above this altitude
  - Radio signals are reflected here
- 80
- 70 — Upper limit of oxygen and nitrogen
- 60 — Cosmic radiation
- 50
- 40
  - Here is the ozone layer that protects us from dangerous radiation
- 30 — The air on top of Mount Everest contains so little oxygen you cannot breathe without special equipment
- 20 — Jet planes fly at this altitude
  - No 'weather' above this altitude
- 10 — Highest region reached by clouds
  - Mt Everest, 8848 m
  - All life depends on an air layer only this thick
- 0
  - The biosphere is the thin strip where life can exist
- -10 — The Marianar depression 11 035m

353

Photosynthesis

How vegetation cleans the air

Every leaf acts as an air-purifying filter and as an oxygen factory. When we breathe and when we burn petrol and other kinds of fuel, oxygen is used up and carbon dioxide is released into the air. This process is reversed in the case of plants. Through the process of photosynthesis they absorb carbon dioxide and release oxygen. This is why plants are so important in fighting air pollution. The more plants, the better the air.

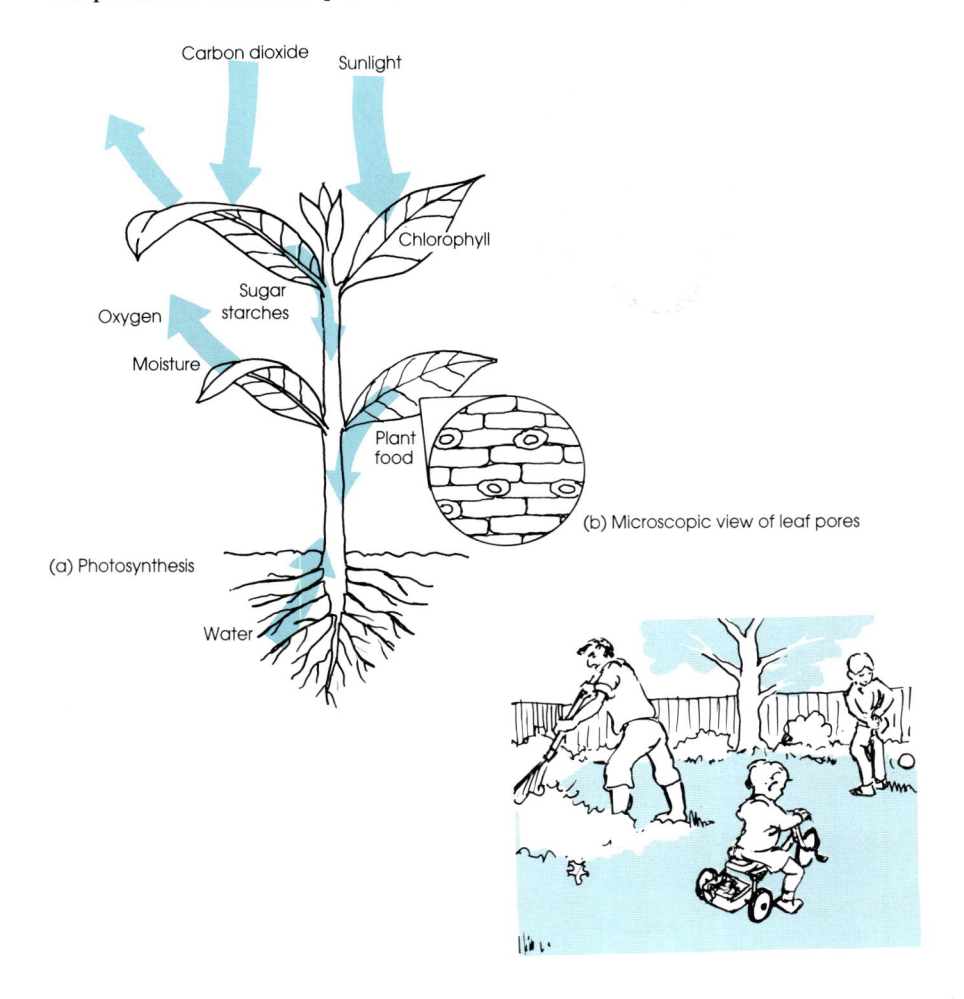

(a) Photosynthesis

(b) Microscopic view of leaf pores

(c) This lawn, 15 x 15 metres, releases enough oxygen for four people

Without plants — no oxygen, and without oxygen — no life. Green plants are our one and only oxygen producer

Conservation of air

Clean air consists almost entirely of oxygen and nitrogen—approximately 21% oxygen and 78% nitrogen. Carbon dioxide makes up less than one-twentieth of 1%. The nitrogen is an inert gas that is an essential constituent of protein foods, but cannot be used directly by most plants and animals. To most living things, the nitrogen is only a 'filler'.

Photosynthesis This is the basic process of all life by which the sun's energy is fixed by green plants in a form that can be used as food or 'fuel' by consumers in the food chain. Photosynthesis in green plants occurs during hours of sunlight, and uses carbon dioxide and water to make carbohydrates and release oxygen. It is nature's air-purification process.

We depend on green plants to maintain our supply of oxygen.

In addition to adequate oxygen, plants and animals require air free from the poisonous pollutants produced by modern-day machines and industries. We depend on the green plants to maintain our supply of oxygen, but they cannot cleanse the air of poisonous pollutants. During the past years, deaths in Australia from respiratory diseases have more than doubled. This is blamed on the effects of smoking and atmospheric pollution.

Most of the energy-producing processes used in the world are basically oxidation processes using a hydrocarbon fuel. Humans and animals oxidise carbohydrates, fires burn (oxidise) wood or coal or fuel oil—all hydrocarbons—and most of our engines use fuel oil or electricity produced from fuel oil.

All these energy-producing processes have carbon dioxide (or carbon monoxide) as a waste product. Humans have so accelerated the consumption rate of stored hydrocarbons, fossil fuels, in the biosphere over the past 100 years that we have significantly altered the composition of the atmosphere we depend on for life.

The motor vehicle is responsible for about 25% of the general air pollution in Australia and it is increasing. The exhaust products from the petrol we use each year add to our air 1 000 000 tonnes of carbon monoxide, 100 000 tonnes of hydrocarbons and 4000 tonnes of other poisonous gases. The lead from the tetraethyl lead accumulates in bone tissue, and the present lead level in bones of city dwellers is up to 100 times that of humans before the advent of motor vehicles.

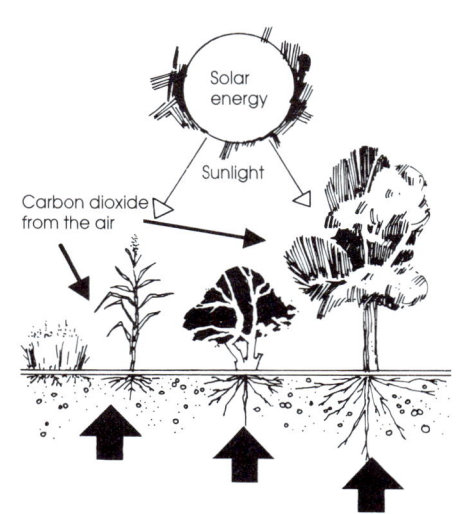

Water and minerals from the soil through the roots

Green plants are the key to all life

Only the green plants can produce oxygen in significant quantities. Conservation of our greenbelts and natural vegetation becomes increasingly important as the human population increases and our use of hydrocarbon fuels increases.

Legislation has been introduced to reduce air pollution by industries and motor vehicles. The internal-combustion engine is a dirty machine and will be replaced by cleaner types of engines powered by fuel cells, gas, electricity or steam.

Fertile soil

Soil and water are inseparable. Without water, soil is unproductive desert. With enough water, soil is able to grow plants on which animals and humans depend for their living.

Without soil and water, all life would perish. And yet, we are careless with soil beyond belief. Millions or even billions of tonnes of soil are carried away by erosion each year, faster than new soil is being formed.

Land and soil care begins at home. It begins with opening your eyes to features that show poor conservation: to the splash erosion on the bare ground below the spilling-over gutter; to the sheet erosion where the rainwater spreads over the sloping lawn; to the rill (tiny stream) erosion as the water speeds downhill in tiny rivulets. By being aware of these erosions, we can begin to take corrective action.

Once the home situation has been taken care of, the next steps could be taken in the schoolgrounds and at the Scout camp; and then, the local watershed and other public lands; and then . . .

How soil is formed

Nature produces soil from many kinds of rocks. It happens as follows.

Changes in temperature During the day, the rock is heated, and at night it cools. Tension occurs and the rock cracks into smaller pieces. This is called *thermal weathering*.

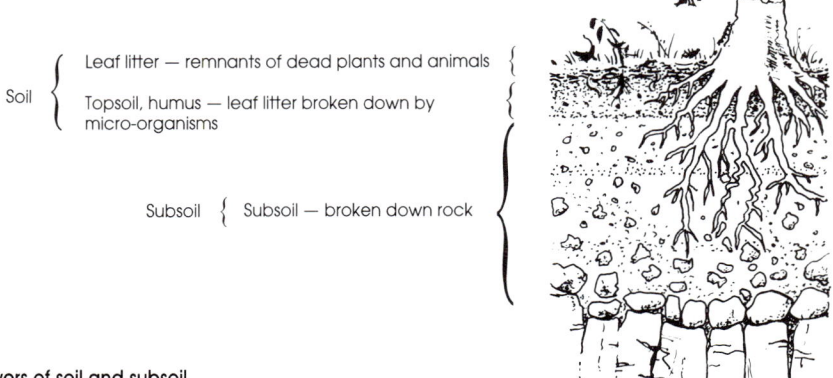

Soil { Leaf litter — remnants of dead plants and animals
       Topsoil, humus — leaf litter broken down by micro-organisms

Subsoil { Subsoil — broken down rock

Layers of soil and subsoil

Plant roots Roots absorb oxygen from the air and from water in the ground and give off carbon dioxide. This gas combines with the moisture of the soil and forms carbonic acid. Carbonic acid helps break down rock particles. This is called *chemical weathering*.

Streams and rivers Stones in running water rub against each other. The fragments are carried away by the water and settle when the strength of the current decreases. New soil is thereby formed.

Glaciers Heavily compressed ice and snow slowly slide downwards, creating friction with the ground and breaking down rock. This debris collects at the end of the glacier, is washed away by streams and rivers, and is eventually deposited as new soil.

(a) Changes in temperature

(b) Plant roots

(c) Streams and rivers

(d) Glaciers

How nature produces soil from rocks

Soil fertility

The fertile soil is one that is physically suitable for the roots of plants to grow in and get their water requirements, and chemically suitable for root growth and for the roots to get the mineral nutrients the plant requires. We therefore refer to *physical fertility* and *chemical fertility*.

Fieldbook for Australian Scouting

Physical fertility

Soil structure

The way in which the particles of sand, silt and clay are bound together in the soil is described as the *soil structure*. The most fertile soil will have a crumbly structure that lets rain or irrigation water and air readily into the soil and does not 'pug' down after rain or cultivation.

Tilth

Because the first roots of germinating seeds are small and have to be kept moist, the soil is cultivated to eliminate weeds and produce a seed bed of fine soil crumbs—called a *tilth*—in which the seeds are sown to germinate.

Soil texture

The physical composition of the soil—that is, the relative proportions of sand (large), silt and clay (small) particles—affects physical and chemical fertility.

The greater proportion of small particles (clay and silt) in the soil, the more water the soil can hold. A clay soil may hold 75 millimetres of *available water* per 30 centimetres of depth compared with only 25 millimetres of available water for 30 centimetres of depth held by a sand. For a sandy loam, the figure is about 50 millimetres.

A soil that will not drain quickly enough to allow roots to get sufficient aeration is said to be *waterlogged*.

Shake well a 200 cc sample of soil in 1 litre of water. As it settles, particles separate in order from the bottom — sand, silt, clay

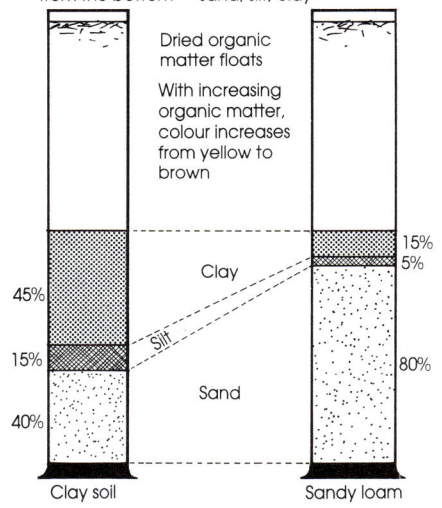

Dried organic matter floats

With increasing organic matter, colour increases from yellow to brown

Clay soil: 45% / 15% / 40%
Sandy loam: 15% / 5% / 80%

Analysis of soil texture

Soil profile The face of a trench cut down 2 metres into undisturbed soil shows a vertical section of the layers in the soil and is called the *soil profile*.

The important layers to identify in the soil profile when assessing fertility are:
1. the surface soil, called the 'A' horizon. This is the *main rooting zone* and may be 15 to 45 centimetres deep
2. the subsoil, called the 'B' horizon. This zone is important in determining how well water will drain out of the surface soil.

Environment

Table 7.2 Particle-size composition of soils

Soil type	Sand (2.0–0.02 mm) %	Silt (0.02–0.002 mm) %	Clay (less than 0.002 mm) %
Sand	90	5	5
Sandy loam	80	5	15
Loam	65	17	18
Clay loam	55	15	30
Clay	40	15	45
Heavy clay	20	20	60

The top few centimetres of the topsoil or 'A' horizon may be darkened with organic matter—the decaying remains of plants. The rest of the 'A' horizon may be much less darkened by organic matter but of the same texture. You can check this by a mechanical analysis.

The organic matter improves soil fertility by improving the soil's structure, by holding the soil particles together in crumbs, and also by improving the soil's water-holding capacity.

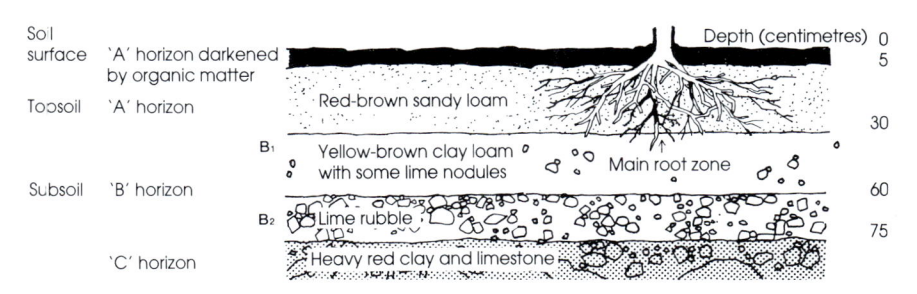

A typical soil profile of southern Australia

Chemical fertility

Plants have to get from the soil all the elements required to build their cell tissues. Large quantities of nitrogen, phosphorus, potassium, sulphur and calcium are required, and these are usually called the *major nutrients*. Magnesium is required in substantial quantities and may also be listed with the 'majors'. Elements required in smaller quantities are manganese, iron, zinc, copper, molybdenum and boron, and these are often called *trace elements*.

A chemically fertile soil is one that can supply all the elements required by plants. A shortage of any one can limit the plant growth, and farmers will therefore apply artificial fertilisers containing the elements that are lacking. Nitrogen fertilisers such as urea, sulphate of ammonia and calcium ammonium nitrate are commonly used. Superphosphate is the main phosphorus

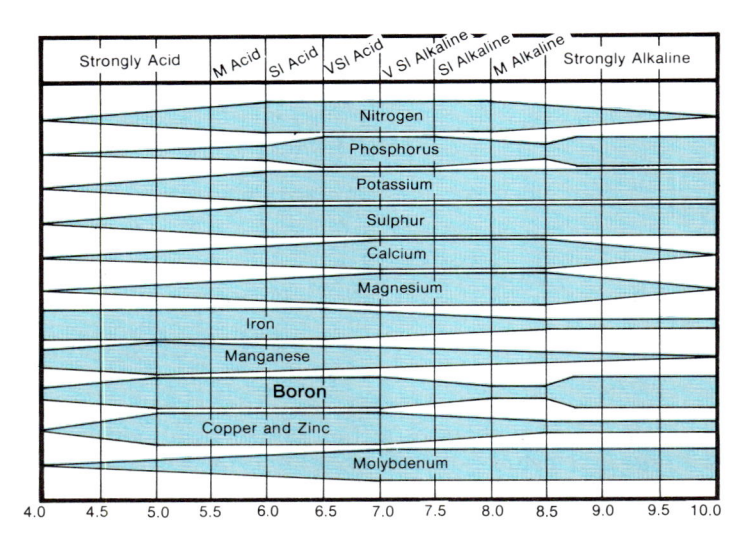

How pH of soil affects the availability of plant nutrients

fertiliser used, whereas potassium sulphate or potassium chloride is used to supply potassium.

Legumes are important in crop rotation in order to build soil fertility, because they have the power to fix nitrogen from the air in the soil by means of the bacteria living in nodules on their roots. Subterranean clover was discovered in South Australia in 1889 by Amos Howard. This legume has revolutionised agriculture, especially pasture improvement, throughout Australia and overseas.

The alkalinity or acidity of a soil is determined mainly by the rainfall conditions under which the soil has developed. It is measured on a pH scale. The pH of the soil affects the availability of nutrients, and may have to be modified by soil treatments such as adding lime or gypsum or sulphur.

Conserving soil fertility

The whole basis of good farming practices is to develop a program of crop rotation and soil management suitable to the area's climate and soil. Soil fertility, both chemical and physical, is maintained and, if possible, improved by application of a suitable program.

Water in soil Roots of plants require *aeration* for healthy growth, so the fertile soil has a mixture of large and small pore spaces between the soil particles and crumbs. After rain or irrigation, the water drains out of the large pores, leaving air pockets.

A soil must be porous enough to allow water in during rain or irrigation. Good structure in the surface soil improves *infiltration*. A sandy soil may have a water intake capacity of over 45 centimetres per hour whereas a clay soil has an infiltration capacity of less than 1 centimetre per hour. The rate at which water will soak in is called the *infiltration* capacity.

Large particles (sand) provide air pockets and large pores to allow water to infiltrate

Small particles (clay) store plant nutrients and hold water around themselves and in the small pores between them for plant roots

Soil pore spaces

Salinity The presence of common salt (sodium chloride) in soil in excessive quantities is harmful to soil fertility. The sodium and chlorine ions are both toxic to plants in excessive quantities, as are most elements if present in excess. Sodium chloride is the common harmful salt in irrigation water and soils of much of Australia's dry country, and is a serious water pollutant.

Reducing soil erosion by wind and water

Wind erosion

Erosion by wind is a problem in the dry-land farming areas of the cereal belt and the pastoral country. The soil can be protected from the wind by windbreaks and soil-surface cover. The methods of preventing wind erosion are to:
- leave scrub along sand ridges and road lines
- plant shelter belts of trees for stock paddocks
- reduce cultivation by having longer rotations and shorter fallows
- reduce stocking rates in order to allow regeneration of soil cover.

Water erosion

Erosion by water is a problem in the cropped areas of the mid–high rainfall country. The soil can be protected from water erosion by reducing runoff and controlling runoff water movement. The methods of preventing water erosion are to:

- improve the soil's water-intake capacity of the soil
- re-plant cleared hilltops with useful timber trees
- contour farm
- grass runoff drainage lines
- stabilise stream banks with trees such as willows.

(a) How soil cover prevents soil loss

(b) Windbreaks — a weapon against erosion

Demonstrations of wind and water erosion and their prevention using seed boxes and household implements

Erosion: how soil is destroyed

A frightening example

About 1000 years ago, vast forests remained in many countries around the Mediterranean Sea. The cultivated soil was fertile and the countries were rich. In their efforts to become even richer, the people cut down the forests to obtain timber and new farmland.

When the forests disappeared, however, the water table dropped. The topsoil dried out and was blown away by the wind. The rain washed the topsoil from the slopes. Soon the slopes could no longer be used to cultivate crops, only for grazing. Sheep and goats nibbled down to the roots, then the wind and rain removed the last remnants of topsoil. Eventually, the once fertile landscape became useless wasteland, and the countries became poorer and poorer.

When rain falls on ground covered by vegetation, the raindrops are cushioned by the plants. The rainwater can then penetrate slowly into the soil.

If the vegetation is removed and the ground is turned into farmland, the rain falls directly on to the soil at certain times of the year. Erosion begins.

With little or no protection by plants, the soil may be washed away during heavy rainfall. The once fertile land is then transformed into grazing land. Sheep and goats feed off the protective plant cover, and the land becomes bare. Erosion continues.

Land covered by forest can absorb four times more water than bare land. When it rains heavily, water that is not absorbed by vegetation descends in torrents and floods the valleys.

Environment

(a) Soil is evenly distributed on the slopes and in the valley

(b) Through erosion, soil is carried down the slopes

(c) Soil has eroded away from the slopes

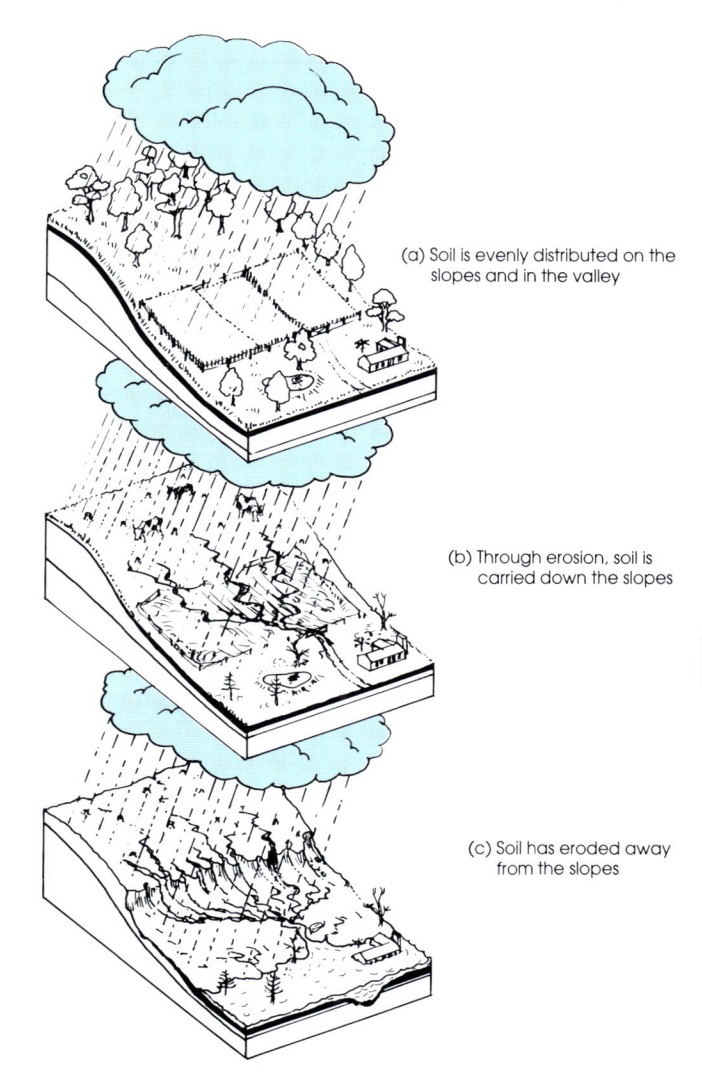

How erosion occurs

The conservation balance sheet

Table 7.3 Water

Causes of pollution	Quality improvers
Animal wastes	Protection of watersheds
Pesticides and fertilisers	Transpiration purifies water
Industrial wastes	Evaporation purifies water
Salt	Controlled use of waterways
Micro-organisms	Filtration and chlorination.

Table 7.4 Soil

Destroyers of soil fertility	Improvers of soil fertility
Salt from poor-quality water	Subclover and other legumes
Excessive cropping	Wider crop rotations
Excessive cultivation	Reduced cultivation
Pesticide residues	Control of pesticide use
Nitrates from intensive stocking	Proper disposal of farm wastes
Wind and water erosion	Contour farming

Table 7.5 Air

Sources of pollution	Purifying processes
Smoke from industries	Control of chimney stacks
Gases from engines	Exhaust filters
Carbon dioxide exhaled	Photosynthesis
Gaseous chemical wastes	Burn cleaner fuels

Conservation of vegetation

We depend on green plants for food, for purifying the air, for timber and for recreational areas—therefore we need more greenbelts and parks. Australia has many unique species of natural flora that must be conserved—therefore we need flora reserves to protect them.

We have some very good natural hardwoods, especially the karri and jarrah of Western Australia and the mountain ash of Tasmania. The radiata pine (or Monterey pine of the United States) is widely planted in Australia in order to provide timber for building and pulping, and to protect watershed areas. The Australian eucalypts are the most widely planted forest trees in the world.

Bushfires

Bushfires present one of the greatest dangers to wildlife and bushland. Wild fires rarely start from lightning—they are sometimes started deliberately, but the common cause of wild bushfires is carelessness.

The campfire or barbecue fire which is not lit with enough attention given to clearing grass and rubbish around the site, or that is built too big, or that is left alight on people's departure—these are frequent causes of fires. The match or cigarette butt that is still alight when it is dropped or thrown away is a common cause. The tractor without a spark arrester, and the car with a hole in the muffler which is driven over dry grass, can both start a fire.

We distinguish between wildfires and controlled burning. The wild fire is the big danger to fauna and flora reserves. The controlled burnoff can eliminate accumulated dry undergrowth, thereby greatly reducing the risk of a high-intensity wild fire. It can be planned to do little damage to fauna and flora.

Environment

Native vegetation

Try to learn to recognise the following key characters of the native vegetation.

- *Eucalypts:* The leaves, when crushed, smell of eucalyptus oil, and the fruit is the typical gumnut. Identify by the shape of the gumnuts and the trunk bark.
- *Acacias:* The wattles have yellow, fluffy-ball or finger-shaped flowers, and the fruit is a pod.
- *Hakeas:* The flowers resemble a round pincushion, and the fruit is shaped like a chicken. The fruit is too hard to be cut with a knife, but if heated, it splits into two halves with a single winged seed inside.
- *Banksias:* The flower cluster is a cylindrical pincushion, and the fruit is characteristically a cylinder shape with 'woody eyes' from which seeds have fallen.
- *Melaleuca:* The paper barks have thick, spongy papery bark, and fruits in clusters.
- *Casuarina:* The she-oaks and bull-oaks have drooping, long needle-like foliage that can be pulled into segments, and small, knobby cones.

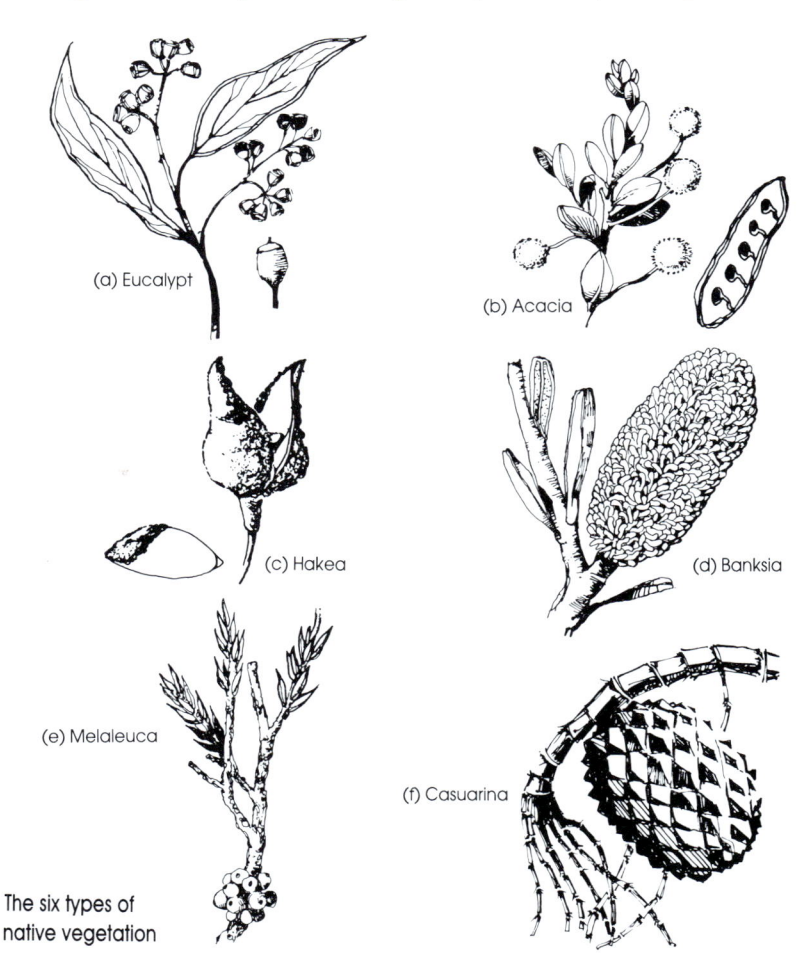

(a) Eucalypt

(b) Acacia

(c) Hakea

(d) Banksia

(e) Melaleuca

(f) Casuarina

The six types of native vegetation

Australian flora conservation

There are more than 12 000 species of Australian flora, and of these, 85% originated in this country. We have a special responsibility to preserve the typically Australian types—the eucalypts and acacias, ti trees, waratahs and kangaroo paws. Many of these are protected and must not be picked.

Many species have already disappeared following clearing, grazing and cultivation, whereas others are threatened with extinction. Figures are known for Victoria, but the situation is similar elsewhere. In Victoria, 48 species are extinct or extremely rare, 201 species are confined to a few small localities, and 22 species are currently threatened with extinction by land developers or bushfires.

The Society of Growing Australian Plants, which has divisions in each state, is especially involved in the preservation of native flora. They have an excellent national journal—*Australian Plants*—as well as local newsletters produced by each state group.

Plant communities

The interaction of an area's plant species with the area's particular soil, climate, topography and fauna has, over a long time, produced unique flora and fauna communities. These can be preserved and protected only by having flora and fauna reserves where they occur.

We therefore need flora reserves in many localities in order to preserve vegetation types, from tropical rainforests to snow-line vegetation, and plant communities in sites, from coastal sand dunes to the inland desert areas.

Parks, gardens and reserves

Australia has more than 1000 parks and reserves over 400 hectares in size, totalling approximately 100 000 square kilometres. In addition, there are thousands of small areas reserved to protect particular plant species or communities.

The state governments are responsible for land and its administration, but many reserves have been called national parks in recognition of their being part of our national heritage. Some of these parks are already well known to Scouts—Lamington Plateau in Queensland, Cradle Mountain–Lake St Clair in Tasmania, Kangaroo Island in South Australia, Pemberton in Western Australia.

Ecologists believe that an area of at least 200 000 hectares must be reserved as a unit in order for an area's flora and fauna to be self-perpetuating. Even then, careful management is essential in order to preserve a balance between access by the general public and adequate protection of plants and food and the animals' shelter.

Some state governments have recognised their responsibility for flora and fauna conservation by passing special Acts of Parliament and appointing ministries or departments to administer parks and reserves.

Fauna conservation

The logical starting point for an interest in conservation is *nature study*. An understanding and familiarity with our birds, animals, plants, insects, beach life and water life is necessary for the genuine conservationist.

Where to start?

The state museums have displays and information on every aspect of our natural heritage. They have information officers who answer particular questions, and displays set up to show flora and fauna that are topical at that time. You can buy informative booklets and reference books on plants, animals, fish, reptiles, seaweeds and many other subjects.

The zoological gardens, wildlife sanctuaries and fauna parks in each state display native birds and animals, and also have information on them.

Become a naturalist

The beginner will learn to identify specimens by comparing them with named collections in the museum or with pictures in reference books. Therefore, visit the museum first in order to see how specimens are named and displayed.

Birds

By visiting the museum, start to practise identifying a group of common birds, and get a picture in your mind of bird sizes, general shapes, head shapes and beaks. Look at them in relation to the 15 reference birds illustrated in our diagrams.

A good pair of binoculars is essential for bird-watching

Fieldbook for Australian Scouting

Next, visit one of the national parks to do some birdwatching. Soon after daybreak is the best time, so an overnight campout would be ideal. A bird list is a good starter, so try to get one for the park you are visiting.

You will require a notebook and pencil—a small sketchbook would be ideal, and a pair of binoculars—'7 × 50' or '8 × 30' or '10 × 50' sizes are good.

(a) Boobook owl (40 cm)

(b) Yellow-tailed black cockatoo (65 cm)

(c) Grey fantail (15 cm)

(d) Starling (21 cm)

(e) White-backed magpie (46 cm)

(f) White-plumed honeyeater (18 cm)

(g) Blackbird (25 cm)

Native birds

Environment

Start to identify the birds you see by comparing them with the illustrations, which will serve as reference sizes.

Note the bird's general size: is it equal to a silvereye, a starling, a magpie or a black cockatoo?

Note its shape and try to sketch it—note especially the body, tail, shape of head and beak; the wings and how they lie; the legs and feet and their

...eral colouring, and note obvious colour patches.
...l. and try to remember its sound and character.
...s habits—How does it perch? Does it flit about? What is ... or bold? Is it in a pair or a flock? Note its flight.
...t identifying birds you should keep a log of the species ...area and the date. The next step is to try recording some

(h) Thornbill (10 cm)

(i) White-winged chough (40 cm)

(j) Indian turtle dove (33 cm)

(k) Silver eye (12 cm)

(l) Red wattle bird (37 cm)

(m) Sparrowhawk (30 cm)

(n) Sparrow (13 cm)

(o) Australian raven (crow) (51 cm)

Native birds

Shells

The beginner should start with dead specimens.

Sort them into the limpet and/or snail-like shells (called *univalves*) and the two-piece shells (called *bivalves*). Try to collect the bivalves with the two pieces still joined together. Next, try sorting the two groups into 'like members', for example, the horn-shaped univalves, the snail-shaped types, the cowrie-shell types, and the limpets, can be easily separated.

The beachcomber will wish to collect the chitons, cuttlefish beaks, sea urchins, sponges and corals found along our beaches in order to complete the collection of coastal life.

Conservation of human history

Each age of history has something to teach us. The preservation of this heritage is the particular responsibility of museums, art galleries and natural-history societies.

Australia has had a relatively short history, but we can help preserve buildings from earlier days, monuments, and records of historical events.

Litter-free land

As you hike with your Patrol, you will feel shocked when you see the beauty of a place desecrated by thoughtless litterbugs. So often their trash is scattered far and wide along our highways, across our countryside, throughout our forests and national parks, and in and on our waters.

The costs of cleaning up litter amount to millions of dollars each year. You, your family and the whole country pay one way or another. Imagine how much good that money could do if we did not have to spend it on cleaning up after thoughtless and careless people.

No littering!

Litter destroys the environment

Litter can be harmful to people and animals and makes the environment most unpleasant. Litter is, to a large extent, wasted resources—resources that could be recycled.

Apart from the ugliness of litter, there can be severe damage to the environment through its effects on birds, animals and other wildlife: some suffer cuts, others get strangled, and others choke. Vermin breeds in refuse and increases the spread of diseases.

The little plague is not only an open-countryside or urban problem. Think of the cinema after a movie show; the football ground, showground or regatta ground after a major event: it is almost as though these functions are places where people learn how to litter. Think about the park or beach or open area a short distance from the schoolground: is it littered by chip packets, drink cartons and drinking straws from the tuck-shop?

Environment

What can you do about litter? Starting with yourself and your Patrol, get going on an anti-litter spree.

- Become an anti-litter 'fiend'. Train yourself to stop littering. Put small rubbish—lolly papers, bus tickets—in your pocket for later disposal at a rubbish bin.
- Make a litter bag for the family car or for a neighbour's car. Take one to camp or on a hike, for taking out your rubbish and someone else's.
- Do not be shy about picking up litter you see in the street. If other people see you doing it, they may follow your example.
- Take part in a litter-cleanup campaign; or organise one of your own, with your Patrol helping.
- Take a two-hour walk around your city. Make one list of things that please you, another of things that should be improved. Set out to arrange some improvement.
- Release your creative urges: turn rubbish into art. Create a masterpiece out of plastic bottles and sell it to the National Gallery, or use cardboard boxes to make a castle for some children.
- Reduce—re-use—recycle waste. Think twice before buying things that generate excessive waste. Try to re-use items—make do and mend! Recycle base materials—paper, cans and glass. The three 'Rs' go hand in hand.
- Get your Troop to get the latest videos on how to improve your local environment, for example, *It's Not All Rubbish*.

Rats thrive among litter; it is a health hazard

Litter destroys rivers and lakes. Even space is becoming a rubbish dump

The beauty of our nature is being spoilt

Litter can be harmful to people . . .

. . . and animals

A litter-free street

Which environment do you prefer?

Fieldbook for Australian Scouting

Recycling has many benefits

Recycling saves energy

It takes
- 66% less energy to recycle paper than to make it from pulp
- 95% less energy to make aluminium from scrap than from ore
- 66% less energy to make steel from scrap than from ore.

The amount of electricity it takes to manufacture one aluminium can would let a person shave daily with an electric razor for three years.

Recycling saves resources and causes less pollution

A return bottle is used on an average of 30 times.
　　Recycled batteries mean nature is saved from harmful substances such as acid, cadmium, nickel and mercury.

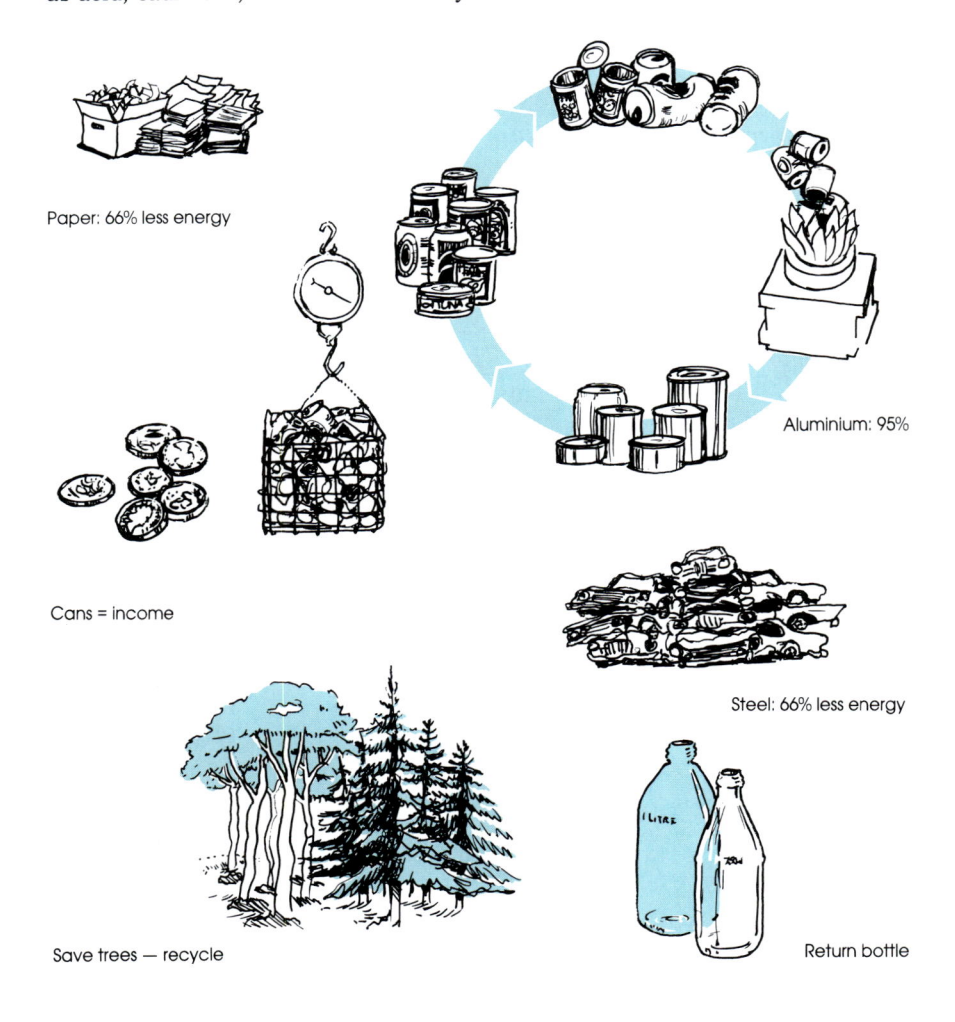

Paper: 66% less energy

Aluminium: 95%

Cans = income

Steel: 66% less energy

Save trees — recycle

Return bottle

Recycling saves valuable forests

One tonne of recycled paper means 16 saved trees plus a lot of saved water and energy.

To print one Sunday issue of the biggest newspaper in the United States takes 48 hectares of forest. This equals an area of 96 football grounds.

Recycling can be a source of income

Collect and sell aluminium cans.

Protect our world

The earth's resources are finite and, with the present pressures of human population, the world is approaching ecological collapse. The earth is only 12 700 kilometres in diameter, and of its surface, 71% is water. Of the small land area, 40% is desert or frozen wilds, and about 30% is marshes, mountains, and forest or land suitable only for grazing.

This leaves barely 10% of the earth's surface suitable for growing crops to feed the world's four billion people. In addition, the world's resources of minerals and fuels are being used up at an increasing rate as the human population increases in number or in material living standard. We have used, wasted or polluted more of our natural resources in the past 100 years than were produced in the previous one million years. This, we now know, is not sustainable.

If we want a future to enjoy, we must:
- *stop* pollution, erosion and waste
- *start* conservation of our natural resources
- *improve* our environment.

We do not have much land to live on

Humans have been cultivating new land throughout their history. Today, most of the arable land around the world is under cultivation. Much of this land has been used for thousands of years.

Through crop rotation, careful fertilisation, and protection of the land from wind and rain (water and wind erosion), the fertility of the soil can be retained.

At the same time there have been other undesirable effects:
- The humus layer has diminished.
- Over-grazing has led to erosion.
- Ground water has been polluted by over-use of artificial fertilisers.
- The building of too many ditches has reduced the ground-water table by drying up the surface of the soil. This in turn causes wind erosion.
- Heavy use of chemicals has led to an accumulation of heavy metals and toxic matter in the soil.

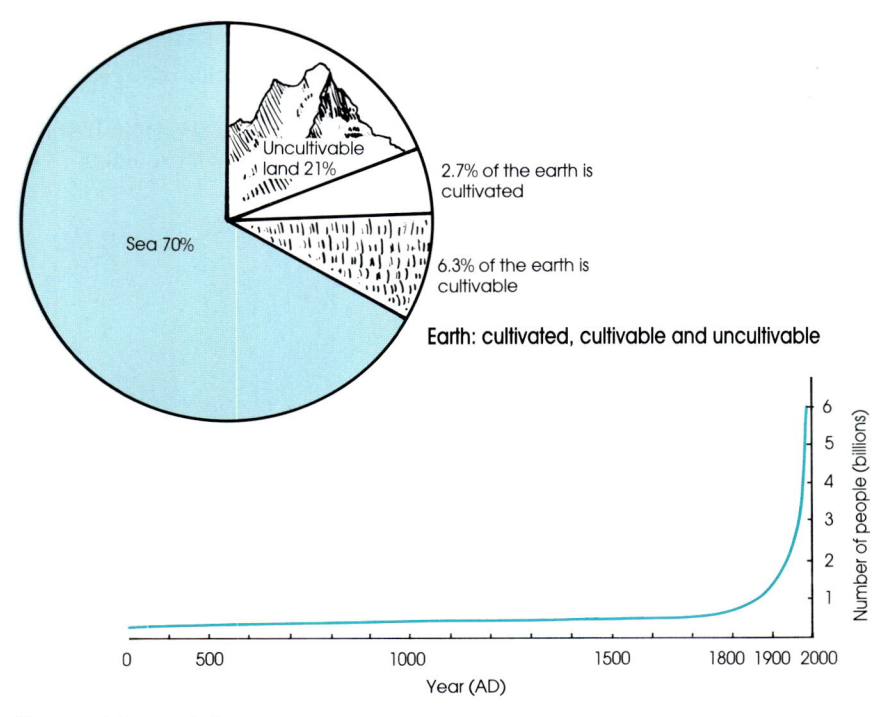

Earth: cultivated, cultivable and uncultivable

- Sea 70%
- Uncultivable land 21%
- 2.7% of the earth is cultivated
- 6.3% of the earth is cultivable

The population-explosion curve

The population explosion

The earth's population is doubling every 30 years at the present rate. Each individual therefore has less and less land from which to live. Starvation in less developed countries, plus ever increasing demands for a higher standard of living in industrialised countries, has resulted in over-intensive use of the best land.

The Australian Scout Environment Charter

A wall chart of the Australian Scout Environment Charter, an adaptation of which is shown in the diagram, is available from your Scout Outdoor Centre. Adopt the Charter as a normal part of your lifestyle.

Conservation

To the world at large, conservation traditionally has meant 'the wise use of natural resources for the greatest good of the most people for the longest time'. We now include the improvement or renewal of these resources.

Environment

All people have their own particular meanings for the word 'conservation'. To some, conservation is an enormous dam for producing electricity. To others, it is a compost heap in the garden for making humus to enrich the soil. To some, it is planting a thousand trees. To others, it is not throwing cigarette butts or litter out of cars. It may mean observing wildlife laws or restoring a dam or stream. On a farm, it may be contour-ploughing a field or preventing dairy effluent from entering a stream. In the city, it may mean using public transport and recycling paper, bottles and cans.

By making conservation part of your everyday thinking and acting, and by working with others in using proper conservation practices, you are helping make a richer and better country. You are helping to protect the world.

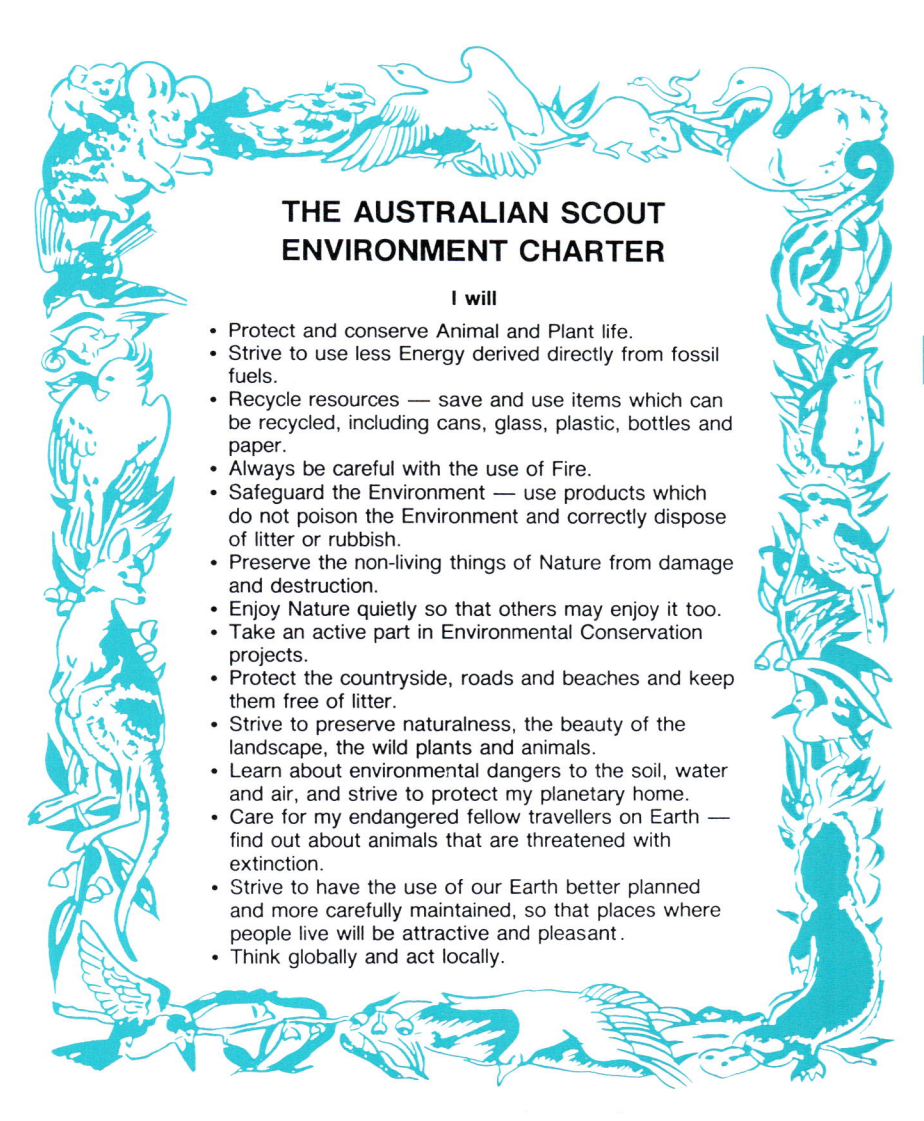

THE AUSTRALIAN SCOUT ENVIRONMENT CHARTER

I will

- Protect and conserve Animal and Plant life.
- Strive to use less Energy derived directly from fossil fuels.
- Recycle resources — save and use items which can be recycled, including cans, glass, plastic, bottles and paper.
- Always be careful with the use of Fire.
- Safeguard the Environment — use products which do not poison the Environment and correctly dispose of litter or rubbish.
- Preserve the non-living things of Nature from damage and destruction.
- Enjoy Nature quietly so that others may enjoy it too.
- Take an active part in Environmental Conservation projects.
- Protect the countryside, roads and beaches and keep them free of litter.
- Strive to preserve naturalness, the beauty of the landscape, the wild plants and animals.
- Learn about environmental dangers to the soil, water and air, and strive to protect my planetary home.
- Care for my endangered fellow travellers on Earth — find out about animals that are threatened with extinction.
- Strive to have the use of our Earth better planned and more carefully maintained, so that places where people live will be attractive and pleasant.
- Think globally and act locally.

8
WATER ACTIVITIES

'... So come Scouts make yourself efficient and if you enjoy Sea Scouting as much as I enjoyed mine you will have a wonderful time.'
—Baden Powell, *Scouting for Boys*

'Nice? It's the *only* thing,' said the Water Rat solemnly, as he leant forward for his stroke. 'Believe me, my young friend, there is *nothing*—absolutely nothing—half so much worth doing as simply messing about in boats.'
—Kenneth Grahame, *The Wind in the Willows*

Like every other sport, hobby or vocation, boating has its own language; each section of boating has its own specialised vocabulary but the general terms are the same. If you understand the words, whichever part of boating you are practising will be more easily understood, and if you understand, your learning is much easier and much more fun.

All the diagrams in this chapter include labels of parts, and a glossary of boating words is featured towards the end of the chapter.

Safety in boats

Every craft you use should be seaworthy for the purpose intended. A canoe suitable for paddling around on a shallow farm dam will probably be completely unsuitable to take out on an open bay; a small open sailing dinghy is unsuitable for the Sydney to Hobart Yacht Race. In other words, pick the right boat for the task ahead. If a suitable craft is not available, do not do that task. The water can provide the best fun you will ever have, but do the wrong thing and it can be the most vicious enemy you will ever meet.

Make sure you are competent to perform your share of running the boat, whether it is a one-person kayak or a crewed yacht: once you are away from your instructor there is no one but you to take responsibility for your actions. If you are incompetent, you are a danger to yourself and to every other user of the waterway. If you *are* competent, you will never do anything as foolish as skylark in the boat; you can have fun without being stupid.

The obvious question, then, is, 'How do I become competent? How do I know whether the boat is right?' The clue to the answer is resource advisers. Most Branches in Australia have a Water Activities Training Centre. Every District where boating is part of the training for Scouts has a Boating Committee. If there are canoeable waters near you, there will probably be a canoe club. If there are sailable waters near you, there is probably a sailing club, and they often require crew members. In every state there is a branch of the Australian Canoe Federation (ACF) and a State Yachting Organisation affiliated with the Australian Yachting Federation (AYF). All these organisations are concerned that exponents of their art are competent, and either run training courses or authorise other people to run courses to acceptable standards. If your Scouting Water Activities Training Centre is affiliated with the ACF and/or the AYF, you can gain not only your Scout qualification but an internationally acceptable ticket.

Weather

In every Scout outdoor activity, weather plays an important role. In water activities, it is the most important outside influence and is completely beyond our control. It therefore follows that every boating enthusiast should be aware of the weather patterns, be able to read and interpret a weather map, and interpret the local weather forecast.

To do this requires an understanding of how the weather pattern is formed. Which way does the wind rotate around a high? Does it rotate the same way around a low? Is this the same in the northern hemisphere? How fast does a cold front move across the Great Australian Bight? Is this important to me when I am crossing a lake with two other canoes? Does it matter if I am taking a Patrol sailing for the day?

You will realise just how important this knowledge is if you ever get caught in a boat by an unexpected weather change.

The labelled weather maps in the diagrams should help you to understand some of the intricacies, but always remember that Australia is a big country that has relatively few weather stations. The best way to teach yourself weather forecasting is probably to keep a log book. On a daily basis, clip the weather map from the newspaper and record the weather in your area. After a few days, study the maps thoroughly, and deduce, from the changes in the first map, what has caused the weather at your home base. You should record temperature, wind direction and force, and, if possible, barometric pressure and humidity. It should not take long before you can see the correlation between the movement of the highs and lows, the warm and cold fronts, and your local weather. You will also see that the highs and lows usually move in the same pattern and at a steady speed.

(a) Sketch 1

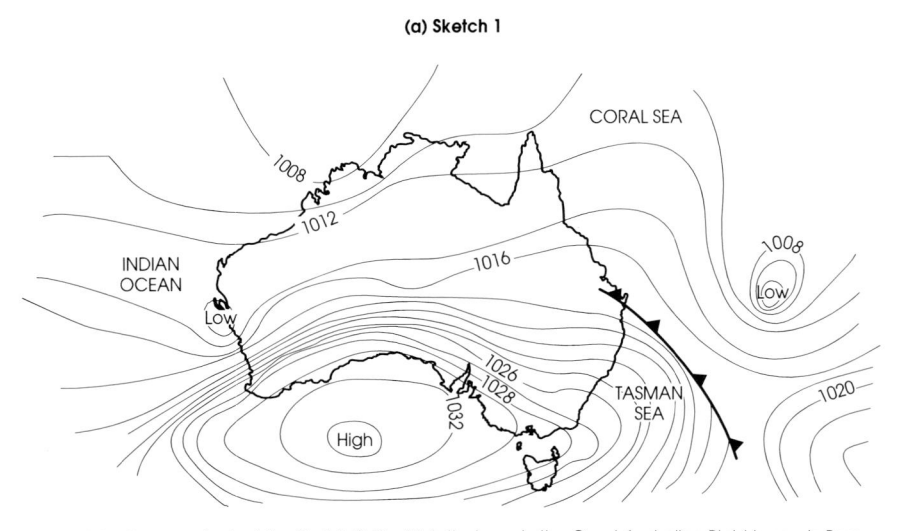

48 hours later the map looked like Sketch 2. The high that was in the Great Australian Bight is now in Bass Strait. The low on the Western Australian coast is now in the Bight. The cold front moved easterly off the map and a new cold front appeared in the south west.

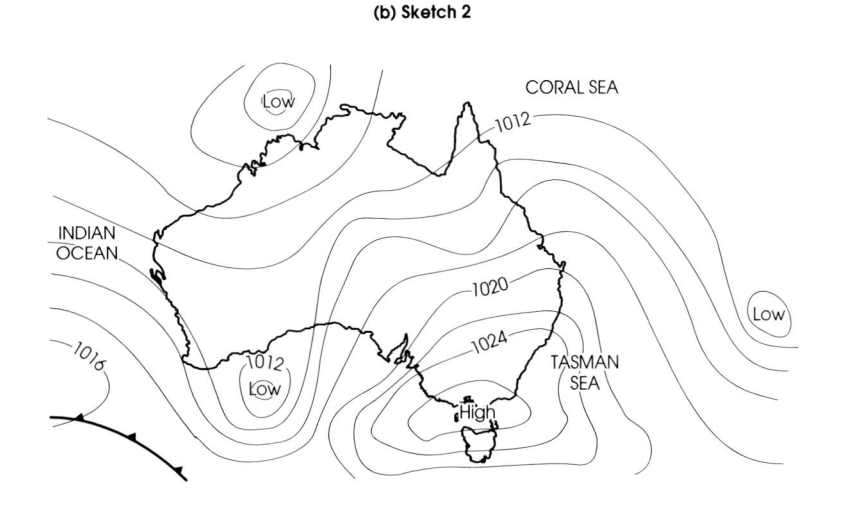

(b) Sketch 2

Weather maps of Australia

Having learnt this, you can look at a weather map and reasonably predict your weather for a day or two ahead.

This will not make you as good a weather forecaster as, for example, Lennox Walker, but it will help you to be a safe boating enthusiast.

Remember that there is no disgrace in calling off a boating activity because the weather is foul or unsafe. Better to be live Scouts than dead heroes.

Water activities

The well-trained Scout has to know what to expect with reference to wind and water, so get into the habit of looking at the sky, studying cloud formations and reading a barometer. Do not be afraid to ask local people such as anglers about their particular stretch of water. The daily newspapers and radio certainly forecast weather and changes as they are expected, but it is valuable to try forecasting for yourself. Remember that, in camp or out on the water, you may not have a radio.

Should there be heavy black rain-bearing or thunder clouds filling the sky, stay ashore, or head for land if you are already on the water. Should a sudden squall come along, a good boating enthusiast makes the crew sit as low as possible in the boat, keeping the centre of gravity low. This also reduces wind resistance. He points the craft into the wind or waves, keeping just enough speed to give headway.

Signs

Learn to recognise the following signs. Note them in your log and you will see how close they are to being right.
- A bright-blue sky almost always means fair weather.
- A vivid-red sky at sunset: fair tomorrow.
- The same sky in the early morning: sailors take warning.
- The sky is dull and greyish at sunset: could be bad weather tomorrow.
- Cloudless sky when the sun sets: fair and cooler tomorrow.
- Check the moon: if there is a ring around it, it means a storm or rain may be on the way.

Weather log

Date	Sunshine			Rain			Wind				Temperature (°C)		
	Most of day	About 1/2 day	Very little	None	Some	A lot	Calm day	Some	A lot	Direction	Cold below 10	Med. 11-20	Warm 21-30	Hot 30
Jan. 4	▓				▨				▓	NE/S	◣		◣	
5														
6														
7														
8														
9														
10														
11														
12														

- A weak washy sun could mean rain.
- Winds: observe type and direction of cloud movement.
- Clouds: the appearance of large heavy banks of increasingly heaped cumulus warns you of the danger of severe squalls and suction winds, thunder, lightning in summer, and hail and snow in winter.

The weather reports on the radio and in the daily newspapers use appropriate terms to cover the winds and waves, but unless you know what they stand for, you could be in trouble; therefore, learn them.

Table 8.1 Types of seas

Type of sea	Wave height (metres)
Slight	0.5–1.0
Moderate (small boats should go home)	1.0–2.0
Rough (Scouts should play games on the beach)	2.0–3.0

Table 8.2 Types of winds

Type of wind	Speed (knots)
Light breeze	4–6
Gentle breeze	7–10
Moderate breeze	11–16
Fresh breeze	17–21
Strong breeze	22–27
Gale (moderate)	28–33

Tides

Ebb and flow

Tides have two main features. First, the regular *rise* and *fall* of the waters of the sea, and second, in conjunction with this, the *flow* and *ebb* of waters in a harbour or along a shore. The rising tide that flows into the shore is the *flood*, and the falling tide that recedes or runs back from the shore is the *ebb*. Between the flood and ebb there is a period of *slack water*.

It is dangerous to generalise, because local conditions vary, but the following is a guide to the way in which tides ebb and flow.

Each day there are two **high tides** with an interval of 12 hours 25 minutes in between.

The tide takes about 6 hours to rise, and it is slow to start, speeds up at about half flood, then slows down again. Should there be a 6 metre rise of tide, the rise each hour would be 0.5 metre, 1.0 metre, 1.5 metres, 1.0 metre, 0.5 metre. The speed of the tidal current approximately corresponds to this, both on ebb and flow.

There are many local variations in tidal conditions and times for ebb and flow. Sometimes the tides lag behind their forecast time because winds hold them up; at other times they are early.

Offshore wind

Onshore wind

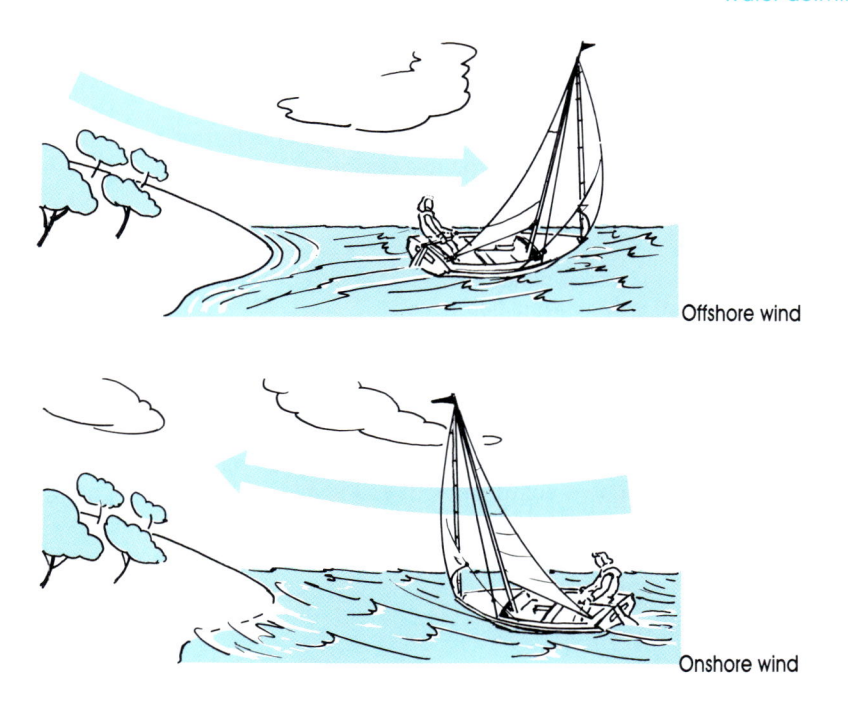

Effect of ebb and flow and the wind on the state of the water

- When the wind is against the tide, the surface of the water becomes broken.
- When the wind and tide are together, the surface of the water is smoother.
- An *onshore* wind, that is, a wind from seaward, will build up bigger seas. This type of wind is less dangerous: although it is harder to get out, you will always have help to get back in.
- If there is an *offshore* wind, that is, a wind blowing from the land, the surface of the water is smoother. Because the landscape on shore is usually sheltered, the weather may appear calmer than it actually is. This type of wind is more dangerous, because it is easy to get out but hard to get back in.

Fetch *Fetch* is the distance that wind has been blowing across water. Long fetch and strong winds create rough water. Short fetch and light winds mean calmer boating conditions.

Lee shore

A *lee* shore is one that has the wind blowing on to it from the sea. If you were sailing past a shore of this type, it would be on the leeward side of your boat.

Advantage The advantage of a lee shore is that you cannot be blown out to sea (but you should watch currents).

Disadvantages The four disadvantages are as follows.
- You must keep well out to sea when sailing past, in order to avoid being blown ashore.
- To increase your offshore distance, you might have to make a series of short tacks while sailing into the wind.

- Putting to sea from a beach is slightly more difficult, because you are sailing into the wind without help from the centre-board until the water is deep enough to lower it.
- If the wind is strong enough, the waves might be choppy and make it more difficult to change course when you are putting to sea.

Weather shore

A *weather* shore is one from which the wind is blowing out to sea, and would lie on the windward side of your boat.

Advantages The two advantages of a weather shore are as follows.
- There is no danger of being blown ashore.
- It is easy to get your boat afloat and sailing without the centre-board until the water is deep enough to lower it.

Disadvantages The disadvantage is that you could be in trouble if you lost your rudder or if the centre-board jambed: you would risk being blown out to sea without control. What would you do in these circumstances?

Tides and currents

Tides are caused by the attraction of the sun and moon on the earth's oceans. Of these, the moon has the greatest effect.

High tides occur twice a day, about 12½ hours apart. *Low tides* occur about 6¼ hours after each high tide.

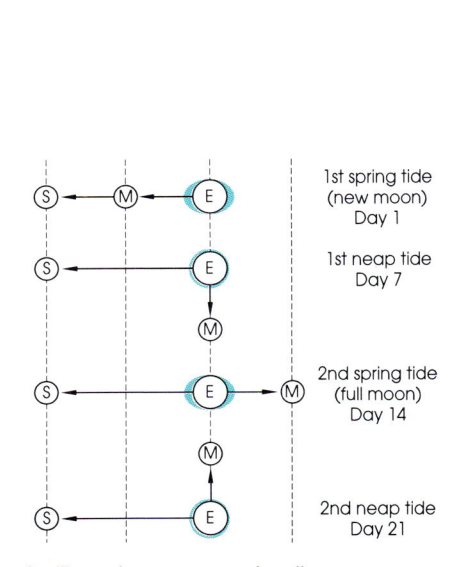

Positions of sun, moon and earth over one month of 28 days

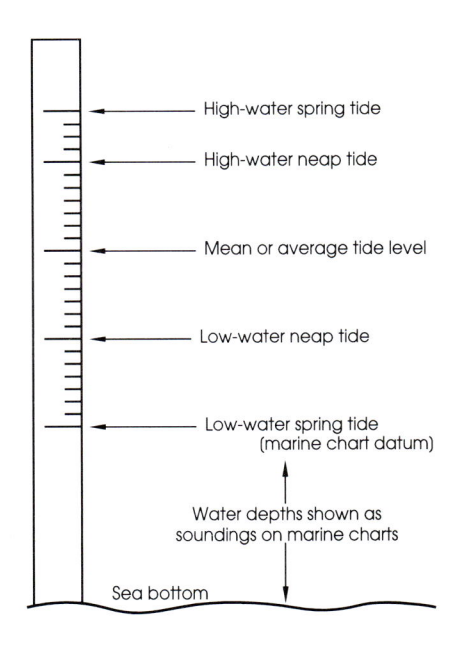

Water-height gauge with tide levels over a 28-day month

Water activities

The height of high and low tides varies from day to day. This is due to the changing position of the moon as it circles the earth each month of 28 days.

At times of a *full moon* and *new moon*, the tide rises higher and falls lower than at other times. This is called a *spring tide*, and has nothing to do with the seasons of the year. It occurs when the sun, moon and earth are in line with one another and pull together on the earth's oceans.

About a week after a spring tide, we have the smallest rise and fall of the water, which is called a *neap tide*. At this time, the sun and moon are not in line with one another and the earth, so that their separate attractions on the oceans do not help one another.

If you were to watch a water-height gauge attached to a jetty over the 28-day month, the various tide levels would look like they do in the next diagram.

Tides do not occur in inland water unless they are connected with the open sea. In these cases, water will flow into and out as the outside ocean level rises and falls.

Tides not only flow up and down river estuaries; they are in motion all around a coastline. Because of shallow water and projecting land, the water flow is disturbed. This forms currents or tidal streams which can extend well into the ocean. These can have a strong effect on the passage of nearby ships.

Personal Flotation Devices (PFDs)

Although most government boating authorities prescribe that private vessels carry PFDs for everyone on board, Scout Regulations insist they be worn at all times afloat. It is too late to put on a vest when your canoe has been capsized by the wash of a ski boat.

The Australian Standards Association has, in recent times, changed the standards in order to avoid the confusion that existed between buoyancy vests, lifejackets and life-preservers.

The standards now list various devices by the type of use they are expected to be put to. The relative standards are Type 1: AS 1512, Type 2: AS 1499, and Type 3: AS 2260; the 'AS' stands for 'Australian Standard'.

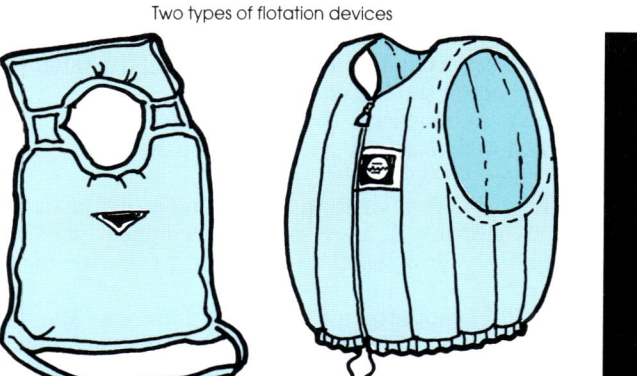

Two types of flotation devices

An approved PFD carries this symbol where it can readily be seen

383

In an emergency, a pair of wet trousers, knotted at the ankles and inflated by swinging through the air, will support a person for a short time. Similarly, the 'bladders' from fruit-juice or wine casks, inflated by blowing through the tap, can be tied together around the chest and will thereby help a person to float. An inflated inner tube will make a lifebuoy, but these are for emergencies only. You should be equipped with the approved PFD and wear it whenever you are afloat.

Correct support: buoyancy placed high on chest

Incorrect support: buoyancy placed too low down

How to wear a PFD

Rescue and resuscitation

Refer to the 'Water safety' section in Chapter 6: Emergencies, page 317. While taking part in water activities, you can seek the help of a member of a lifesaving club to help with the training.

Safety rules and precautions

Prevention is much better than any cure, and a liberal application of commonsense is the best way of accomplishing this. Adhere to the following advice.

- Be able to swim 100 metres after discarding shorts and shirt in the water.
- *Always* wear a suitable lifejacket. See that it is a jacket that gives freedom of movement, will not slide up around your head, and that it is stamped AS 1512; your life may depend on the lastmentioned fact.
- Provide your craft with reserve buoyancy.
- Do not wear any hard-soled footwear in a craft. Keep a pair of gym shoes for use when walking in water.
- Do not wear heavy clothing. Make it light with a sailing jacket over the top. See that it is of a style that will allow it to be removed quickly if necessary in an emergency. A yellow jacket is seen better than one of any other colour.
- Never leave a capsized craft. Do not attempt to right it if you can tow it to a nearby bank or shore. It will float. The only reason for leaving a craft is if it is sinking under you, which means a lack of buoyancy.
- Keep away from weirs and locks, both above and below.
- Keep to your own side of the waterway and out of the way of other craft.

- Before leaving on a trip, tell other people where you are going, and give all information including time of arrival back, so action can be taken if you do not arrive. Boating after dark is *not* recommended, unless under the strict supervision of your Leader.
- Carry a bailer and sponge for removing water from inside your craft.
- Take a first-aid kit. It pays to make this equal to a Patrol one.
- Balance the crew and gear in the craft.
- When boating, look behind as well as in front, so you will know the lay of the land both ways, because you may sometimes travel the same route again but in the opposite direction.
- Take adequate protection against sunburn on legs and face. A large brimmed hat, such as the Scout hat, is ideal headgear. Sunglasses are also helpful for protection of the eyes from reflected glare from the water.
- Because you may not always be within hailing distance, take a whistle: it can be heard further than a voice.
- Always check that the craft are in A1 condition a week or two before the trip starts. Any faults can be more easily fixed at home than at the starting point.
- Always carry a repair kit, and see that items are replaced as soon as possible after use.
- Carry a small emergency supply of food and water even on a one-day trip; include matches in a waterproof container.
- Regular eyeglasses or sunglasses must be protected from accidental loss. A keeper-cord worn around the back of the neck with a light flotation can be attached in order to keep them from sinking if you capsize.

Distress signals

As a Scout, you will be on the road to being a good citizen when you are observant. You can save other people's lives and your own if you are fully familiar with the following distress signals, which are recognised internationally.

- Slowly and repeatedly raise and lower arms outstretched to each side.
- Use a signal consisting of a square flag that has, above or below it, a ball or something resembling a ball.
- Wave a flag. This can be a shirt, singlet or handkerchief tied to a paddle, oar, or a sail batten, held above the head and waved from side to side.
- A foghorn or car-type horn, sounded continually, will attract attention. If you have no horn, what better than a continually repeated blast on a Scout whistle? It is easy to carry and will be heard more easily than a voice. Use the morse-code sign: three short, three long, three short blasts (SOS).
- Hand-held smoke or coloured flares can be purchased from boating stores. Make sure they are dated, and do not buy a flare of any type if it is over three years old. They must be kept in a watertight container.
- The latest Australian-type distress sheet that is recognised by all Sea-Rescue Squadrons is a rectangular sheet of fluorescent orange-red material that bears a letter 'V' in black.
- A mirror or piece of stainless steel will make a good reflector of the sun. Constant flashing will attract attention.
- Waterproof torches are available and will attract attention after sunset.

Fieldbook for Australian Scouting

| Waving your arms | Square flag and a ball | Waving a flag | Whistle and horns |
| Hand-held smoke | Fluoro sheet with 'V' | Flashing a mirror | Waterproof torch |

Distress signals

Reserve buoyancy

Reserve buoyancy does not make a boat float higher in the water or increase its load-carrying capacity. If a boat is swamped, reserve buoyancy makes the boat float higher in the water. This of course, makes it easier to bale out the water and get the boat floating properly again.

Reserve buoyancy can be airtight tanks fitted to the boat, at the bow or stern, or along the sides, under seats or thwarts. In canoes or kayaks, air tanks made from tyre tubes partly pumped up can often do a good job. A more popular method is to use foamed plastic material or empty plastic bottles (properly corked). Kapok sewn into canvas pouches can also be used, but is effective only while it is dry, so the canvas covering must be thoroughly waterproofed before fitting. All these must be fixed so they cannot move about in the craft.

You can test the effectiveness of reserve buoyancy by actually swamping your boat before and after fitting it. You should see quite a large improvement in freeboard (the amount of hull above water) if it is correctly placed.

Canoeing

Hulls

The word 'canoe' covers everything from a hollowed log and a folded piece of bark to the high-tech piece of modern equipment used for flat-water distance races.

Not surprisingly, both basic styles of modern canoes have their origin in or near North America. The *Canadian* is developed from the North American Indian birch-bark canoe, the *kayak* style from the Eskimo single-seat sea-going fishing boat made from seal skins.

The Canadian is basically an open load-carrying craft propelled by single-bladed paddles, whereas the kayak is usually much narrower, is decked, has a cockpit, and is propelled by a two-bladed paddle.

There are many variations on each of these basic types, mostly designed to enable a particular style of boat to be used for a specific type of water. For example, an open traditional Canadian is not very suitable for the rapids and races of white water; it can be used, but you can almost guarantee a boat full of water or a capsize. The *banana-boat* variation, which is more rounded in the bow, decked and cockpitted, is still a Canadian but is designed to meet the requirements mentioned. A *slalom kayak*, such as the KW7, has a small cockpit just big enough to fit your hips and uses a spray sheet secured to the rim of the cockpit and to the paddler's waist to keep unwanted water out. Other kayaks, however, have open cockpits, and sunburnt legs can be an unwelcome result.

Just as there are many *type* variations, many materials are necessary in order to build a canoe. Today, most are fibreglass (more correctly, GRP: glass-reinforced plastic), but good canoes are built from aluminium, wood, plywood, canvas and, more recently, polypropylene. In a Group fleet there could be two of these — expensive but light, lovely to handle, and almost indestructible.

In other words, when you are acquiring a canoe, check it is suitable for the purposes you have in mind. Do not accept the word of the first expert; try many, and do not be biased by the thought of shooting mighty rapids — 90% of Australia's canoeable rivers are classed as flat water. Perhaps the best adage is 'Horses for courses'.

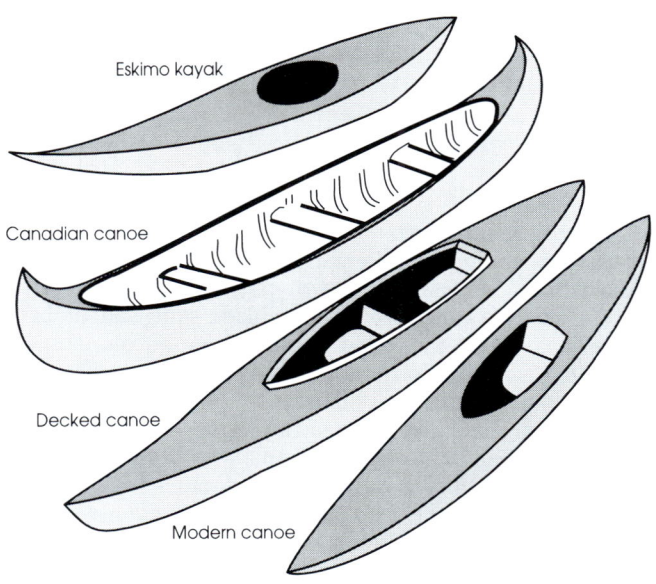

Four types of canoe

(a) Traditional Canadian profiles

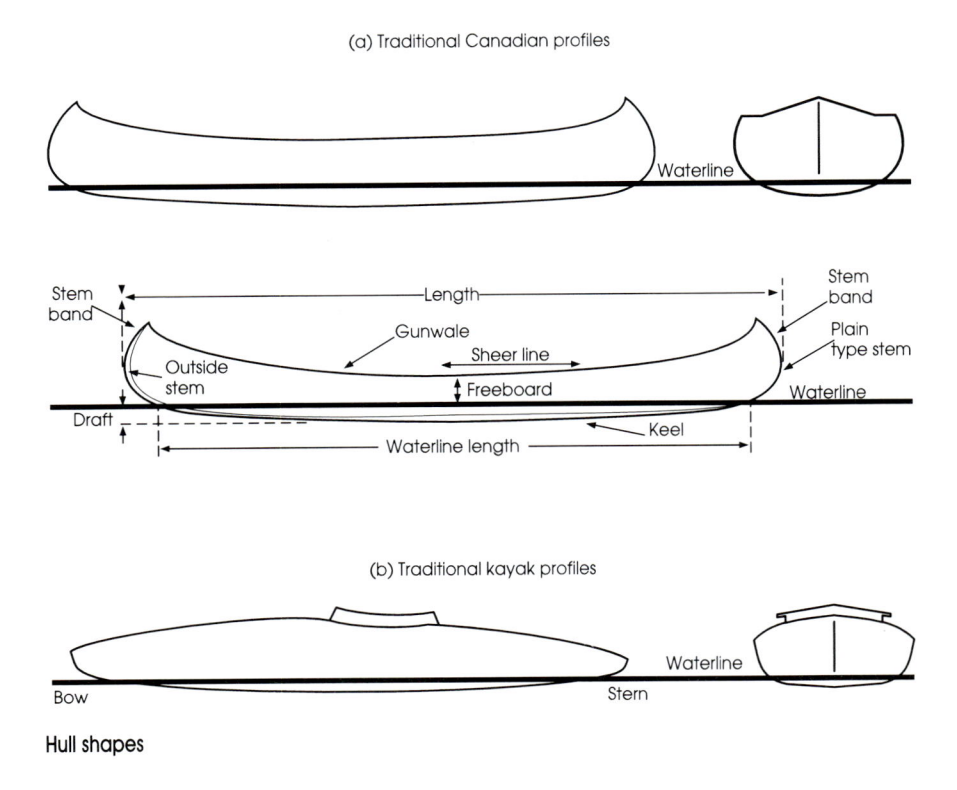

(b) Traditional kayak profiles

Hull shapes

Parts of a canoe

You should try to remember as many parts of the canoe as you can, so you grasp the skill quickly.

Paddles

Like canoes, paddles are made from many types of materials: wood, aluminium, GRP, plastics, and combinations of these.

The paddles could be made with GRP blades, aluminium-tube looms and moulded plastic T-bar handles. If you cannot find the right paddle you can afford, have someone carve a prototype blade from soft timber, make a GRP mould from it, and buy the T-bar handles from an outdoor sports shop and aluminium tube from the local aluminium warehouse. The same mould produces both Canadian and kayak blades.

It is essential that paddles be of the right weight, length and balance for the paddler. You would not expect a Scout who is 140 centimetres tall to use the same paddle as a Rover who is 180 centimetres tall.

Canadian paddles should be about armpit or shoulder height for a stern paddler and about chin height on the bowman. Weight should be comfortable so that after a few hours' paddling it does not feel like it is made of lead. Balance should be well down the shaft, as close to the blade as is practical.

Water activities

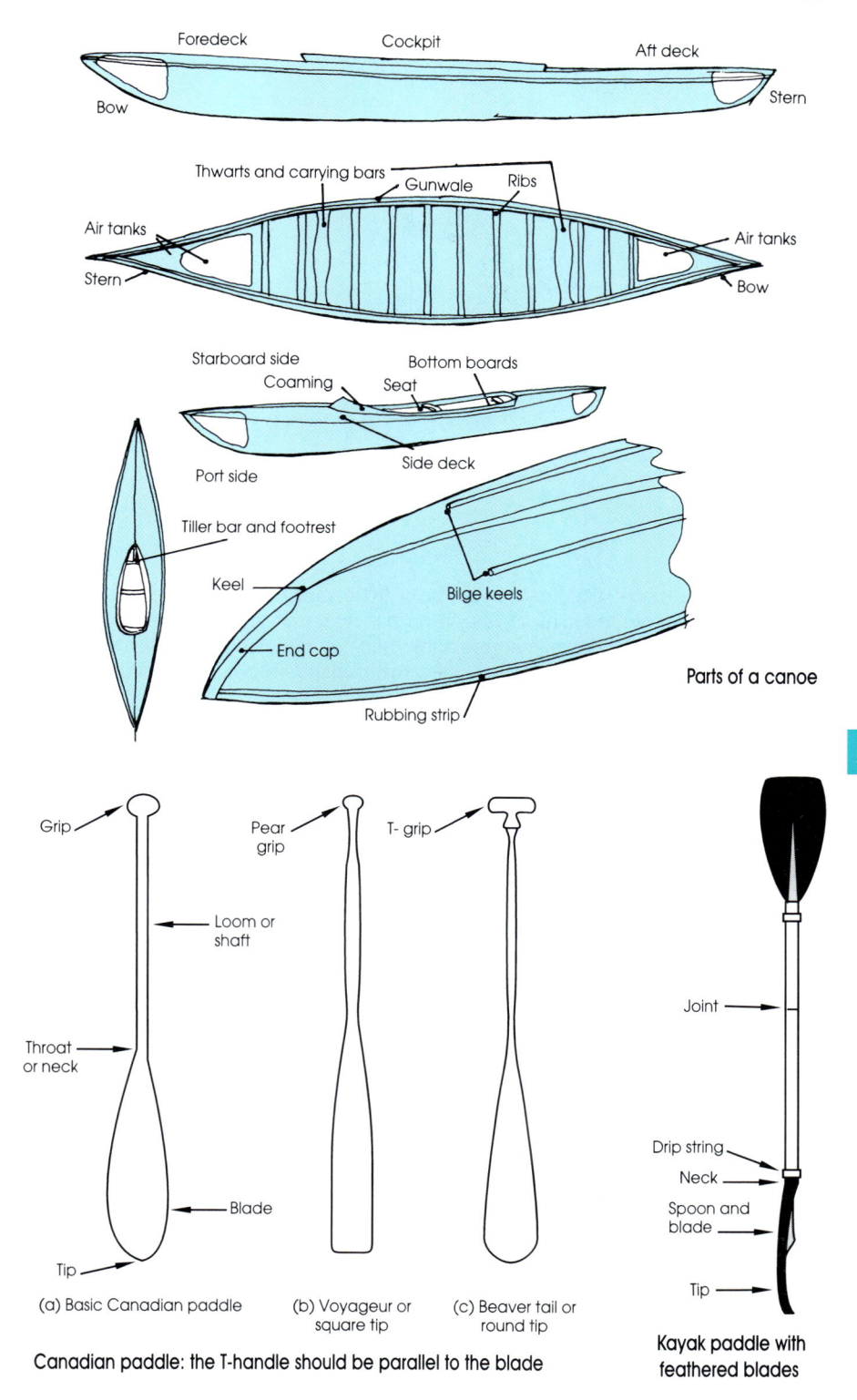

Parts of a canoe

(a) Basic Canadian paddle
(b) Voyageur or square tip
(c) Beaver tail or round tip

Canadian paddle: the T-handle should be parallel to the blade

Kayak paddle with feathered blades

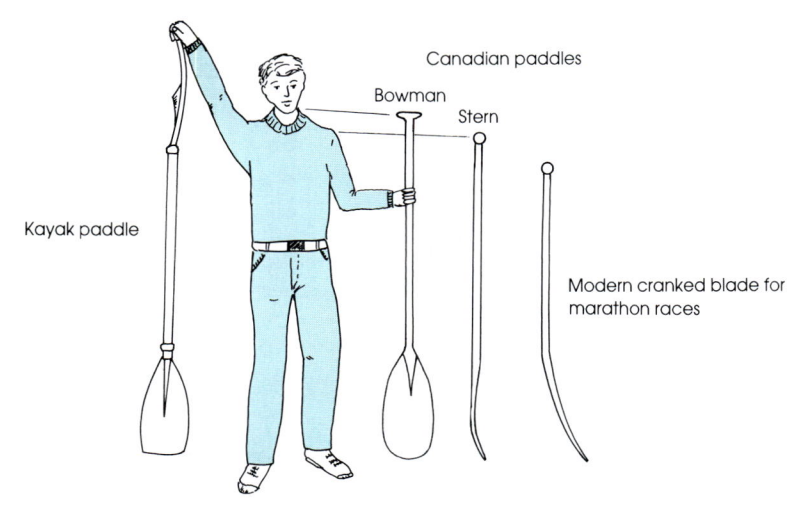

Heights for paddles

Similarly, kayak paddles should be a little more than the height of the palm on an upstretched arm, although on flat water with a foot-pedal rudder, a longer paddle may be more comfortable and the balance dead centre of the shaft. The shaft or loom must be rigid, otherwise the constant whipping of the blades can be very exhausting.

Paddling a canoe

When boarding any canoe or boat, balance is all-important. You should enter a canoe or kayak with one foot on the centreline of the craft; then, holding both gunwales, transfer your weight evenly to your hands, keep your body low, and bring the other foot into the craft. With your weight still on your hands, you can then slide your feet and legs into the correct position to sit or kneel as required by the particular type of craft.

When solo in a Canadian, some people prefer to kneel just aft off its longitudinal balance point, particularly if there is any wind. This allows control of the craft because the wind is affecting bow and stern equally.

You may kneel on both knees or on one, whichever is most comfortable for you, and with knees apart or together. Canoeing is great fun, but it requires skill, especially in use of the paddles.

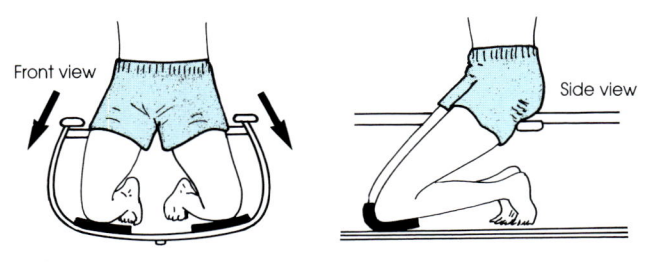

Kneeling in the canoe

Water activities

Strokes

Canadian strokes

Each of the basic strokes in paddling a Canadian is quite simple and can be summarised as follows.

Power or forward stroke The paddle is placed in the water well forward but without straining the person and is then drawn back along and close to the canoe. The blade is to be at right angles to the line of travel. At the end of the stroke the blade is lifted clear, then the stroke is repeated.

Trail or steering stroke The paddle is placed in the water behind or level with the operator, and the blade is at right angles to the line of travel. As the paddle is pulled back along the canoe, the blade is turned to run in line with the line of travel. This helps to correct direction.

Sweep stroke The blade is kept near the surface. Swing wide in an arc and draw quickly inwards. The stroke may be done either forwards or backwards. It is used in order to make a sharp turn. When two paddlers are doing it on opposite sides, a very sharp turn is possible.

Sculling stroke In sculling, the paddle is moved through a small arc of a circle, centred on your sitting position; the blade is facing the canoe at right

Basic Canadian strokes

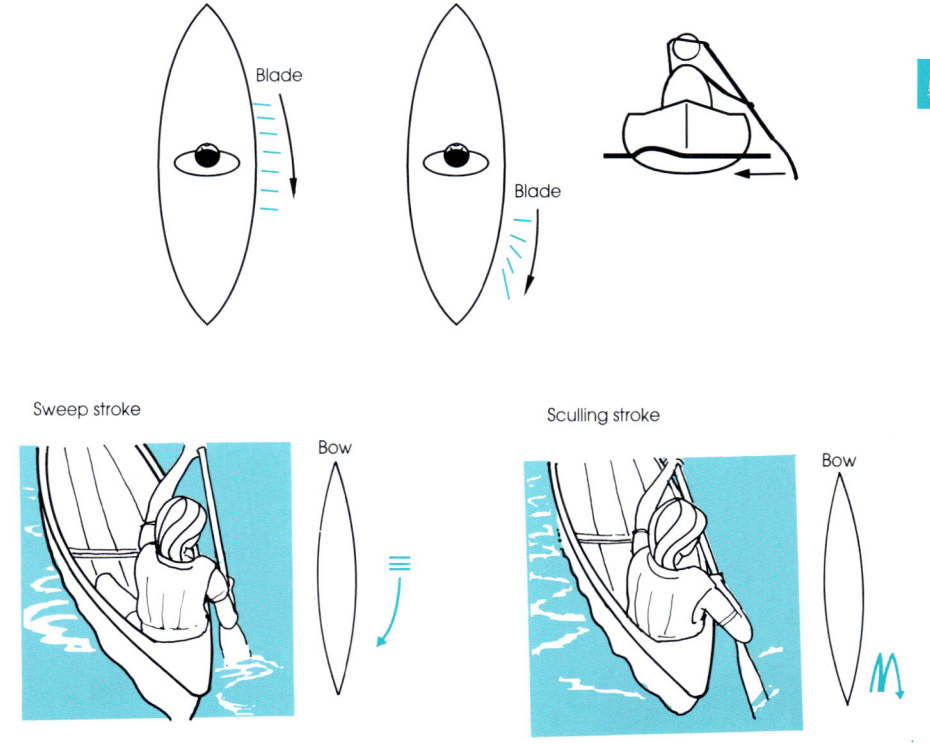

(continued)

angles to centreline, and the shaft is extended sideways. The sculling stroke can be used in order to draw or push the canoe sideways, or it can be used for support. When sculling for support, you use your paddle as an outrigger, and using this movement you can quickly restore your balance when thrown to one side.

Draw stroke The draw stroke is made by reaching straight out to the side and, the blade facing the canoe, you then make a pulling stroke directly to the canoe, thereby pulling it to the side.

Push or pry stroke This stroke is the reverse of the draw.

Back stroke This is made opposite to a forward stroke. Its use is for correcting course, slowing the forward motion of a canoe, quick stopping, or for going astern. When two paddlers are doing it a quick turn can be made by the forward person paddling forward and the after person doing a back stroke on the opposite side.

Underwater stroke The blade is dipped in the water close to the canoe and forward. Draw aft, twist the blade parallel to the canoe, and return the blade to the start again under water. Throughout the whole stroke the blade does not leave the water. Its use is for a silent approach and you have full control over the canoe. It is used principally with a single-bladed paddle only.

Draw stroke

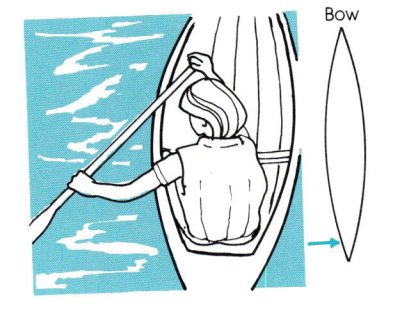

Push or pry stroke

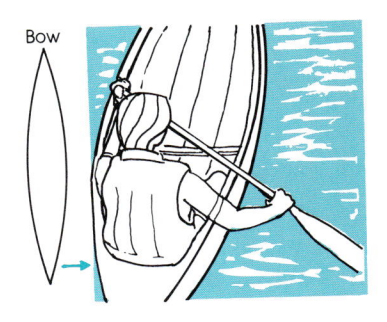

Forward and back stroke

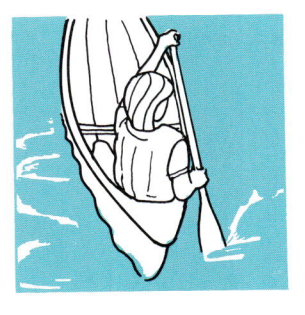

Underwater stroke

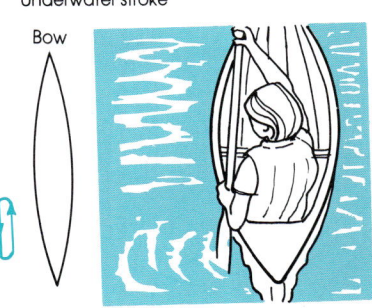

Basic Canadian strokes

Water activities

Combined strokes

Bow rudder **Cross bow rudder** **Bow sweep**

Additional strokes

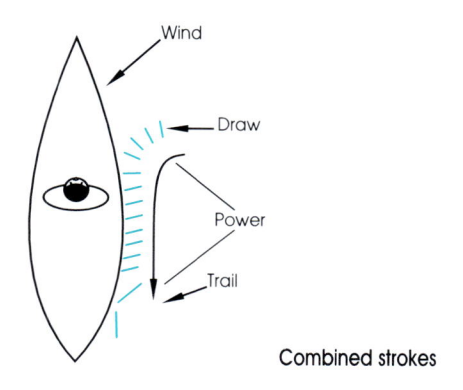

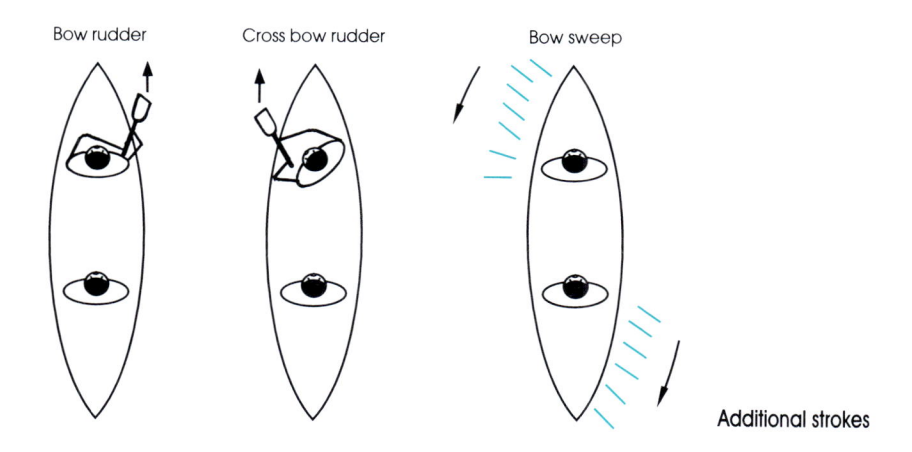

The diagrams show each of these strokes clearly. You should practise them on calm water until you do not have to think about them; then combine them as required to make the canoe do what you want it to do. An example of this is shown in the next diagram.

You should note that if the power stroke is applied mainly under the canoe, the canoe turns less, and less steering is required. If the trail is applied as far to the stern as possible, less steering is again required and therefore less energy wasted.

Additional strokes are used when you are paddling a Canadian two-up (two people aboard): the bow rudder, cross bow rudder and bow sweep, as shown in the diagrams.

Kayak strokes

Use the normal forward stroke using each end of the paddle alternately, the sweep stroke to turn or correct wind drift, and the trail stroke also to correct drift and reverse paddling.

Fieldbook for Australian Scouting

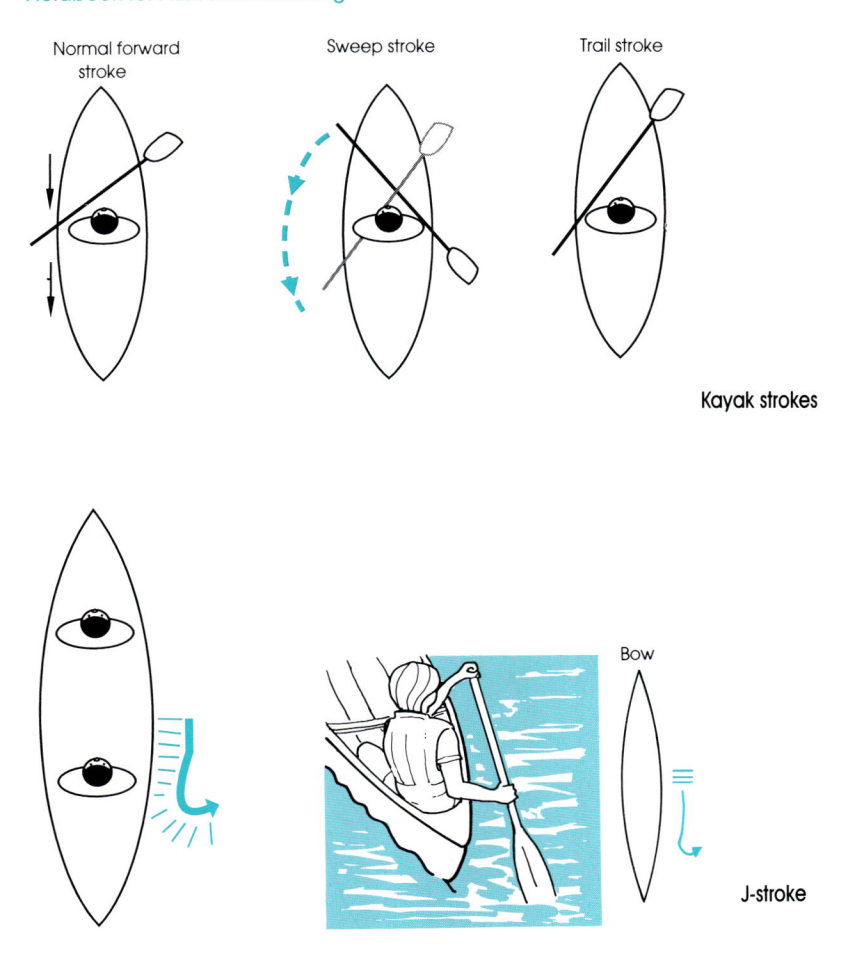

Normal forward stroke

Sweep stroke

Trail stroke

Kayak strokes

Bow

J-stroke

J-stroke The blade is dipped well forward, close to the canoe and drawn back until opposite the hips where the inside edge gradually turns aft and outwards, pressure being exerted continually on the same face of the blade. Cut the blade out of the water and feather back to starting point. Its use is to impart forward motion and guide the direction of the canoe. This stroke is mainly used with a single-bladed paddle.

Ferry glide The ferry glide is a manoeuvre for going to and fro across a river without gaining ground. You must be in a current of about 3 knots minimum to perform this. First of all, you must maintain a steady position by back paddling if the current is with you or forward paddling if the current is against you. From the steady position, you will find that by turning your canoe at a slight angle to the current, the force of the water will move you sideways and cause you to glide over to the side of the river.

If you are with the current, you will turn your canoe's stern to the side you wish to go. If you are heading against the current, your bow must be turned slightly to the side you wish to go.

Water activities

The ferry glide is an essential river technique that enables a canoeist to pick the way carefully around rocks and snags, or to come ashore if a safe course cannot be found.

Refer to the diagram. At point **A** the canoeist judges that if the canoe turns directly across the current after skirting the rocks, it is likely to be swept broadside into the fallen tree at point **B**. Instead, the canoeist back paddles at point **C** in order to hold the canoe against the current, and by tilting the stern to the right, ferry glides through the gap to point **D**, where the canoeist resumes forward paddling. Practise the technique before you need it, on any convenient stretch of moving water.

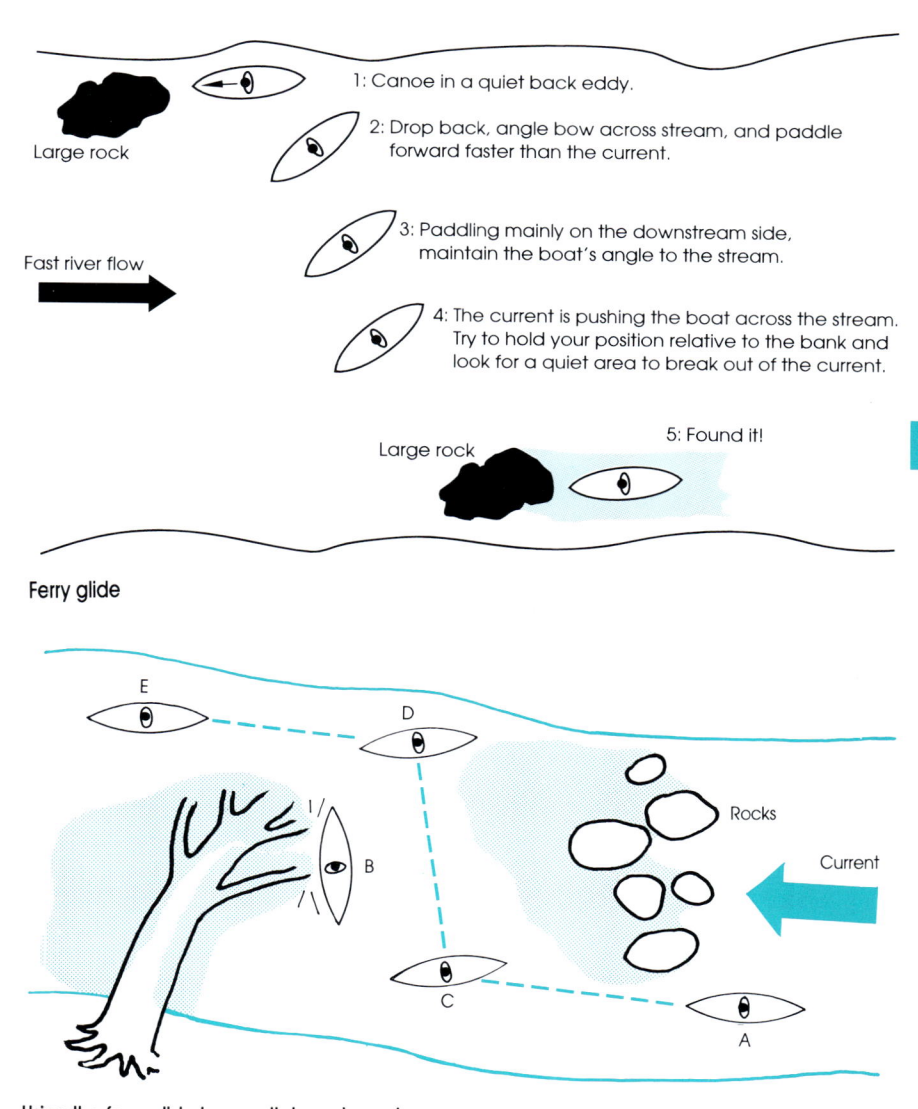

Large rock

1: Canoe in a quiet back eddy.

2: Drop back, angle bow across stream, and paddle forward faster than the current.

Fast river flow

3: Paddling mainly on the downstream side, maintain the boat's angle to the stream.

4: The current is pushing the boat across the stream. Try to hold your position relative to the bank and look for a quiet area to break out of the current.

5: Found it!

Large rock

Ferry glide

E
D
Rocks
B
Current
C
A

Using the ferry glide to negotiate rocks and snags

Types of canoeable waters

There are many classifications of waterways, but for Scout purposes we will look at three basic types.

Flat water

As suggested by the name, flat water is the rivers and creeks, lakes and human-made dams, and human-made watercourses such as canals and ornamental lakes, that present little danger to a canoeist. It is ideal for beginners learning the craft, and for family outings, fishing, and leisure paddling.

White water

This is turbulent water such as a river that has rapids and races. The white 'colour' is caused by bubbles of air, and gives little grip for the paddle blade. The air is trapped by the water rushing over the uneven rocky bottom, and the whiter the water, the more air, the less water and the less grip for the paddle.

This type of canoeing requires a great deal more skill and is not for the beginner. It is essential that you have learnt all the strokes and to have read the water in order to interpret what each ripple, wave and bubble means in relation to its effect on the flow of water, depth of water and formation of the bottom.

Without the skills to do this, you place yourself and your craft at great risk. It is best learnt from a qualified canoe instructor.

Estuary waters

An estuary is by definition a watercourse that was flooded by the sea as the ocean-water levels rose or the land mass sank. Estuaries are therefore tidal and often open to the sea. They can be calm, flat water one moment, covered with choppy or even rolling waves the next. Use of the current weather forecast is very important in order to protect yourself and your crew under these circumstances.

Estuaries are also popular places for other boating enthusiasts. Sailing, sailboarding, power boating and water skiing are common. The best advice, if you are canoeing on popular waters, is to consider every other vessel as skippered by an idiot and give them the widest berth possible. Most 'boaties' are sensible, responsible citizens, but the odd few are larrikins and you cannot tell the difference until they 'hit' you. Saltwater estuaries are often breeding grounds for sharks, and in northern areas of Australia they can be home to saltwater crocodiles.

Shores of estuaries can also be lined with mangroves or, if rocky terrain, covered with oysters: not the best places to try and land an upturned canoe.

The mouth of the estuary also poses another problem: an onshore breeze can change to an offshore in minutes, and an open canadian is not the craft in which to get into an open-ocean swell.

White-water strokes

In white water, a few additional strokes and techniques are useful. The J-stroke is used in place of the power and trail in order to correct course quickly. Reverse paddling is used in order to hold your craft in position or to aid manoeuvring or turning. The ferry glide is used in order to travel across the stream using minimum effort and to break out of the current. For kayaks, the Eskimo roll or screw roll is used; for Canadians, the Canadian roll.

All these are best learnt, as already mentioned, from an experienced instructor.

When you think you are proficient in all these types of situations, try the following practise tests. You could run them as time trials between members of your Patrol or Unit. Use the same course and the same boat for each competitor.

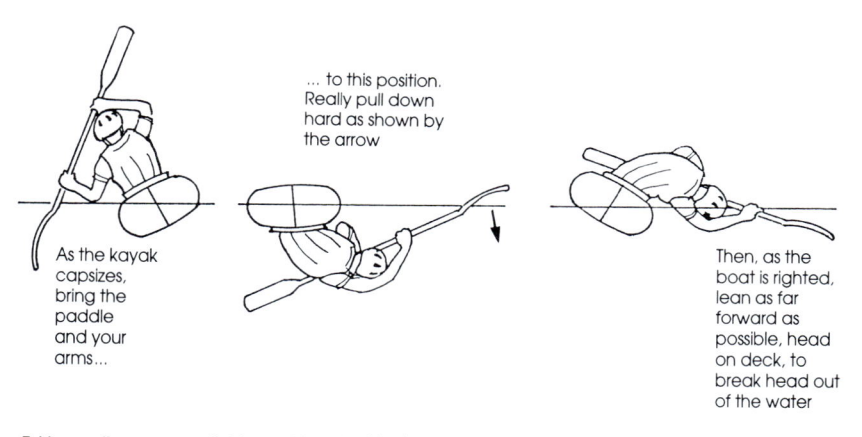

As the kayak capsizes, bring the paddle and your arms...

... to this position. Really pull down hard as shown by the arrow

Then, as the boat is righted, lean as far forward as possible, head on deck, to break head out of the water

Eskimo roll or screw roll (viewed from behind)

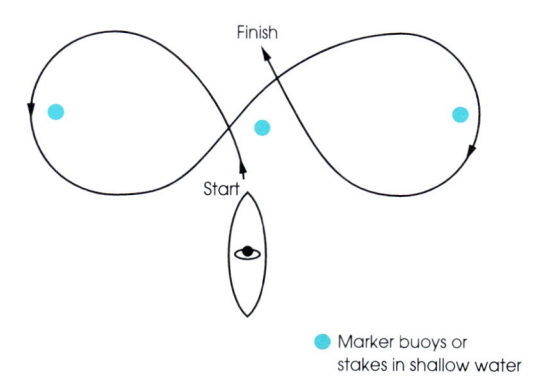

Solo in Canadian figure of eight. Paddle on one side of canoe only

Marker buoys or stakes in shallow water

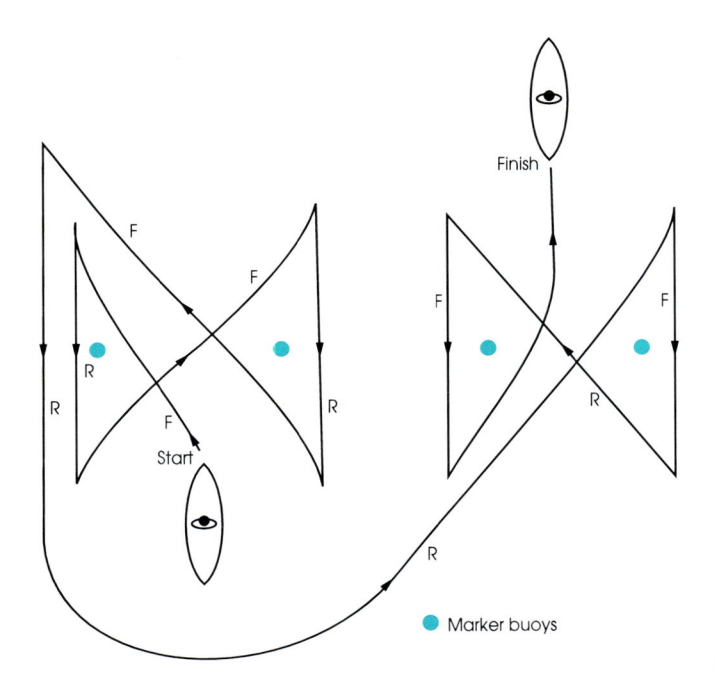

The zig-zag forward paddling (F) and reverse (R)

Balance and paddle support

For proper control, especially in rough water, you must have a secure seating position. In most canoes you can brace your legs comfortably under the middle frame or the underside of the coamings. Otherwise special knee brackets must be fitted, and perhaps footrests as well.

Beginners tend to teeter a good deal, trying to keep their bodies upright so they will not fall out. An experienced canoeist does not depend on the canoe's stability but relies more on the support obtained from the paddle. Like a cyclist, you use body-weight and firm-seating grip in order to control the canoe's balance. For some manoeuvres you will deliberately heel it over.

River hazards should be checked in advance. Major ones such as waterfalls and gorge rapids should be plotted on the trip map, and you should have an assurance from experienced canoeists that you can portage past them if necessary. Lake canoeing should also be planned with care, because conditions on large lakes often approach those on the open sea, and in the event of a capsize you cannot swim ashore as easily as on a river; furthermore, lakes are often dangerously cold. Special group-rescue techniques have been devised for these emergencies. The best safeguard is to have shore support standing by in case your party is overdue. The same precautions should be observed in harbour and estuary canoeing.

The three ways of getting this type of support from the paddle are as follows.

Bracing against ordinary drive strokes   (This is the only support required by racing canoeists, although their canoes are particularly unstable.) Instead of trying to balance your body upright, try leaning towards the blade, and feel it take your weight as you make the stroke. You will soon learn to judge the necessary tilt to give the blade. In rapids you can lean quite hard on to a strong back-paddling half stroke, forcing the blade forwards from behind your hip until it is approximately alongside. This is a powerful braking and manoeuvring stroke as well as a support stroke.

Surface slap This is mainly a beginner's exercise for developing speed and dexterity. Lean over, body and canoe together, holding your paddle loosely well out to the side with the blade flat, until you topple off balance; then, and only then, thrust down hard and fast on the shaft, pushing yourself back on balance before the blade has time to sink. If you dawdle and let it sink, you may find yourself in an irrecoverable position.

Sculling support Skim the blade quickly back and forth across the surface, tilting the leading edge barely upwards at each stroke. When you can judge the wrist action correctly, lean progressively further off balance until eventually, after some practice, you can hold the canoe on its beam ends with your elbow underwater. This is a good exercise, and leads up to the most advanced recovery stroke, the Eskimo roll, in which a canoeist capsizes the kayak, pushes the paddle blade up to the surface on the opposite side of the canoe, makes two firm sculling strokes, and uses the brief support thereby gained in order to lift oneself out of the water.

Capsized canoe

It is advisable to capsize in shallow water when other people are present and practise the drill to follow so you will be prepared in the event of an accidental capsize.

When a canoe capsizes, it usually turns upside down and floats high due to air trapped inside. Whichever way you find it, upside-down or right-way up, leave it that way. If it is on its side, turn it upside-down.

If you are dealing with the canoe on your own, put your paddle in the bottom of the canoe. If you lose it when you capsize, it is better to let it go than leave the canoe to collect it. *Never let go of the canoe.* Move to the bow and swim the canoe to the bank or nearest shallow water. When you are in shallow water, lift one end of the canoe as high as possible and quickly turn it right way up, after which bail out the water left inside.

When with a Group, as you should be, wait for the rest of the Group to come to your help. If the shore is close by, one canoe can tow the capsized craft ashore; the other can tow the canoeists to shallow water where the canoe can be emptied by rocking it to break the air lock. Do not lift the canoe any higher than necessary to let the water flow out. When the insides are almost empty, rock the canoe end-wise to get rid of the water in the ends, then turn the canoe over and lower it into the water right side up.

If the shore is too far away, an alternative method can be used. Lift the bow on to one of the other canoes and allow as much water as possible to drain out, then lift the stern on to the other canoe. When as much water as possible has drained out, turn the canoe over right side up and put it back into the water. Bail out the remainder of the water, then, with the other canoes steadying yours, climb aboard over the stern.

Experienced canoeists seldom fall overboard, because they paddle from a safe, steady, kneeling position. However, beginners who sit high on a seat

Fieldbook for Australian Scouting

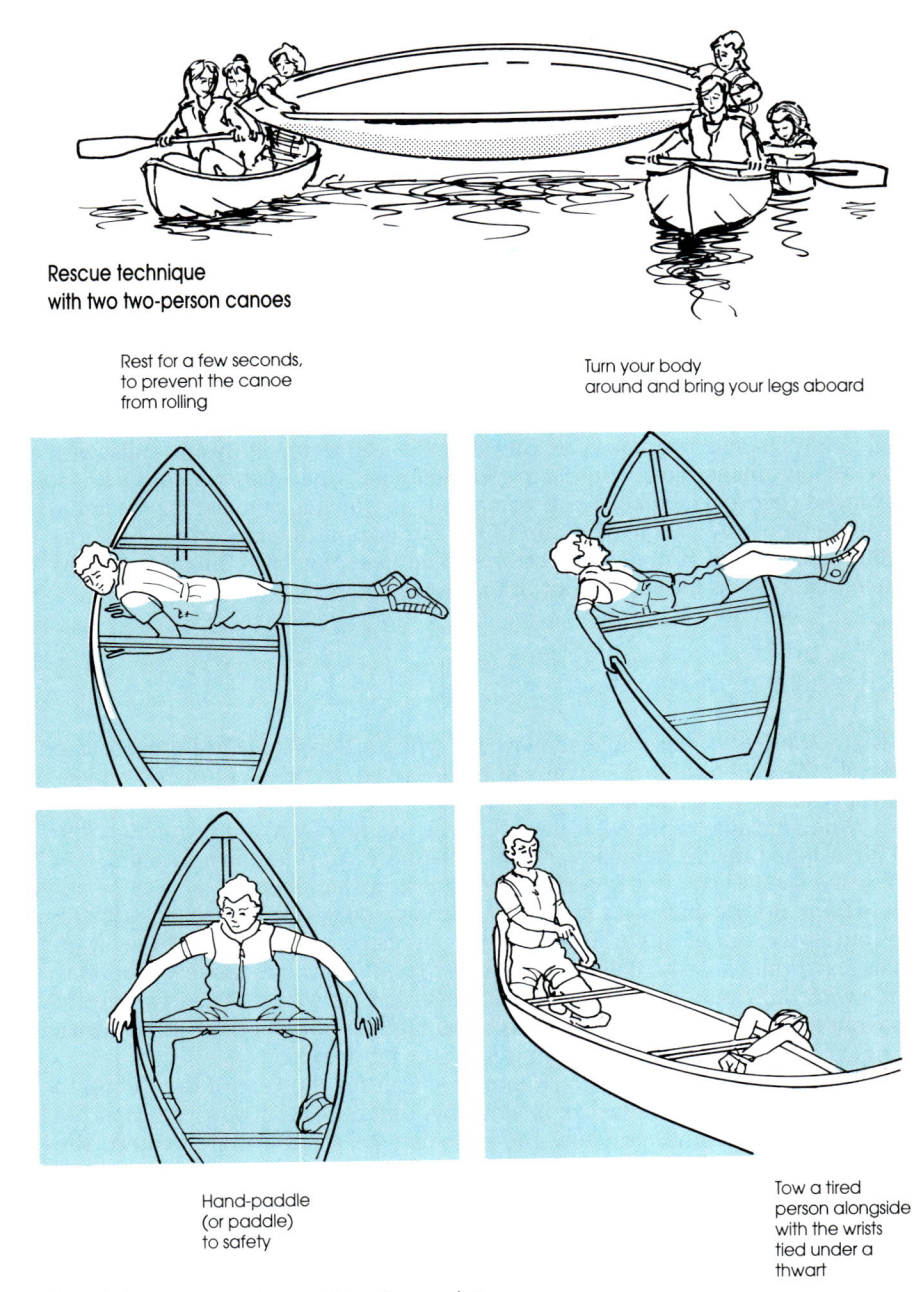

Rescue technique with two two-person canoes

Rest for a few seconds, to prevent the canoe from rolling

Turn your body around and bring your legs aboard

Hand-paddle (or paddle) to safety

Tow a tired person alongside with the wrists tied under a thwart

Re-entering a swamped canoe from deep water

or thwart soon find themselves 'in the drink', soaking wet, with the canoe also full of water.

To be able to re-enter a swamped canoe from deep water is an important safety skill. The easiest method is to reach over the gunwales near amidships, place your hands on the bottom of the canoe, press down, and kick the feet until the canoe is under the hips. Before bringing your legs aboard, rest for a few seconds in order to prevent the canoe from rolling.

Keep your weight low, turn your body around, and bring your legs aboard. From a sitting position, on the bottom of the canoe, paddle or hand-paddle to safety.

A tired or exhausted swimmer who cannot be lifted or helped aboard can hang on to the stern. In bad cases of exhaustion, when a swimmer cannot hold on, tie the wrists together under a thwart and tow the person alongside.

Boarding and alighting from a canoe

There are more mishaps and duckings in boarding a canoe than from any other cause. Learn to board a canoe the correct way right from the start so it becomes a habit and thereby save yourself from embarrassment and wettings.

From the water

1. Face the bow into the current or wind, whichever is the stronger.
2. Face towards the bow and place the paddle across the cockpit.
3. Grasp the paddle, and the farther coaming near the seat, but slightly forward, with the near hand.
4. Grasp the paddle and the other coaming with the other hand.
5. Lift the near foot into the canoe in the centre, in line with the hands.
6. Lift the other foot in.
7. Lower yourself into your seat.

In a double canoe, the stern person boards first; the bow person boards after the stern person is seated.

To disembark into shallow water, reverse the procedure for boarding.

From a bank, pontoon or landing

1. Face forward, the paddle being stored in holders or in the cockpit until you are seated.
2. Reach across and hold a point of the cockpit or far coaming well forward of the seat.
3. Put the near foot in the cockpit over the centreline and far enough forward so you will not have to move it when you sit down.

Grasp the paddle and the coamings with both hands

Lift the near foot in, then the other foot

Lower yourself into your seat

Boarding from the water

Hold a point of the cockpit or far coaming

Put the near foot in the cockpit

Put the other foot in and seat yourself

Boarding from a bank or landing

Grasp both coamings with the hands

Push yourself up

Put the hand nearest the bank on to the bank

Alighting on to a bank or landing

4. Put the other foot in immediately behind the first foot while holding the bank with the other hand, but *do not* lean on it.
5. Seat yourself as soon as possible after putting the second foot in.

To disembark on to a bank

1. Stow the paddles or place them on the bank, then grasp both coamings with the hands and put one foot behind the other over the centreline of the canoe, the foot nearest the bank to be at the rear.
2. Push yourself up and put your weight over your feet, but stay low.
3. Put the hand (farther from the bank) forward on the coaming, the other on to the bank.
4. Stand up and step out. (Do not kick out.)

Putting a canoe or kayak into the water

Always lift a canoe when it is out of the water, otherwise its skin can be damaged by broken glass, tins, jagged stones or timber if it is slid over the ground. When launching single handed, stand at the side of the canoe and grasp the coaming of the cockpit. When the balance is found, lift the canoe up on to your thighs if you wish. Carry it to the edge of the bank with the stern over the water, and lower it to the bank. Move around to the bow and lift, at the same time holding the bow painter. The stern, being in the water, will float and the remainder of the canoe can then be put in the water.

Water activities

When launching two handed, each person, with one on either side of the canoe, picks up the inside of the coaming, lifting the canoe together. They carry it to the bank and position it at right angles so the stern is over the water, lower to the bank. One crew member lifts the bow and puts the remainder of the canoe into the water; the other member holds the painter. Make the painter fast to the shore or landing and leave it so the bow faces into the current.

For heavy or loaded canoes, it may be necessary to handle the canoe at the bow and stern and not by the coaming. If two canoeists must do this and the bank is suitable, the canoe is placed in the water parallel to the shore line.

It is better for loaded canoes to be handled by four people for safety, and in the case of launching or lifting out at steep or difficult banks, four or more people would be essential: one at the bow and the stern, two in the centre.

Loading and trimming a boat

Loading is an art that can be learnt easily, provided the following advice is followed.

The type of container has to be waterproof. It is better to pack your gear into a number of small bags than into a few large ones: small bags are more easily stowed and make for easier trimming of the craft.

Load first the smaller bags of camp gear, food, personal kit and, finally, larger bags of personal gear. In the cockpit on either side of the seats, put wet-weather gear, midday food, water bottle, log book, map and compass. Always make sure everything is fastened in so nothing will be lost in the event of a capsize. Be sure that stowed equipment and lashings do not foul the operation of the boat or impede the crew in a capsize.

Most boats are designed to float almost level when all crew and equipment are loaded aboard. This is most important if the water is rough and waves are likely to wash over the sides. Load your gear and equipment evenly according to weight so the bow and stern are floating at about the same height from the water.

Check that the items you will need or want to use during the day are packed on either side of the seats in the cockpit where they are easily accessible. Keep perishable foods below the waterline where they will keep coolest. See that there is always a little air in waterproof bags, because this will help the buoyancy in the event of a capsize.

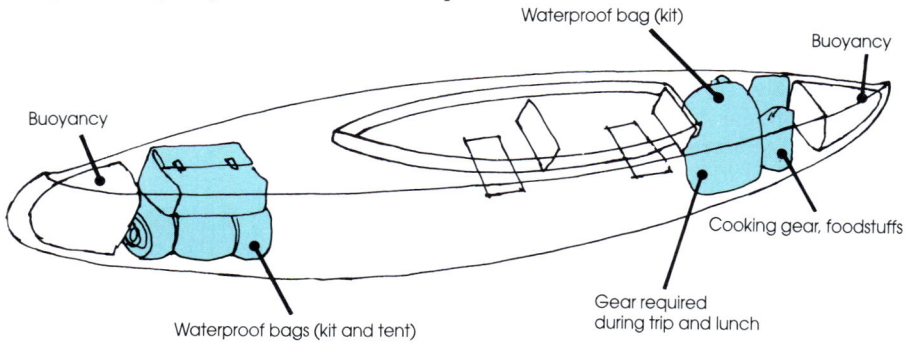

A correctly loaded boat

Trimming a boat means making final adjustments to the loading when all crew members are aboard and all is ready to go afloat. It is usual to trim the load so the bow is floating slightly higher than the stern, but never the other way around if the water is rough.

It is also necessary to trim so the boat does not lean to one side or the other.

Canoe signals

Simple party signals can be developed, using a whistle, and hand or paddle signals. A whistle attracts attention or is good for an emergency; hand signals can then be used to call the group together, indicate a rest stop, or give other instructions. Develop your own signals and make sure everyone is familiar with them.

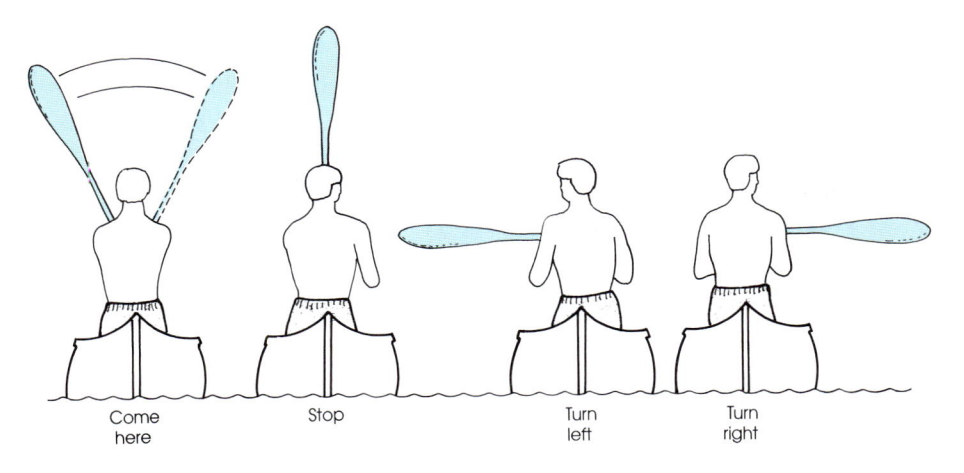

Come here — Stop — Turn left — Turn right

Canoe signals

Portaging

The carry or portage always seems to be waiting at the end of a lake. Sometimes it is a relief after a long paddle, but getting back into the water is also pleasant after a long portage.

The canoe is usually carried upside down on the shoulders. To do this comfortably, rig a carrying yoke using two paddles. Perhaps it will be more convenient for two people to carry the canoe: one person at the bow, the other at the stern. For short portages, the canoe can be carried right side up, two or three people lifting it at the gunwales.

Pulling through rapids

Sometimes you can pull your canoe upstream against a strong current. This is especially a big help when there is no portage trail: you can steer the canoe around rocks, logs and other obstructions. When two people are towing, it's a snap: one person handles each line.

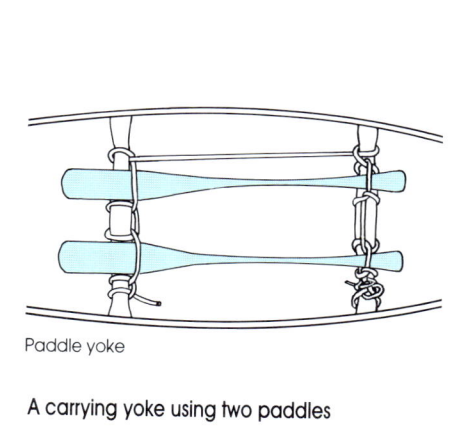

Water activities

Paddle yoke

A carrying yoke using two paddles

One person can carry the yoke upside down on the shoulders

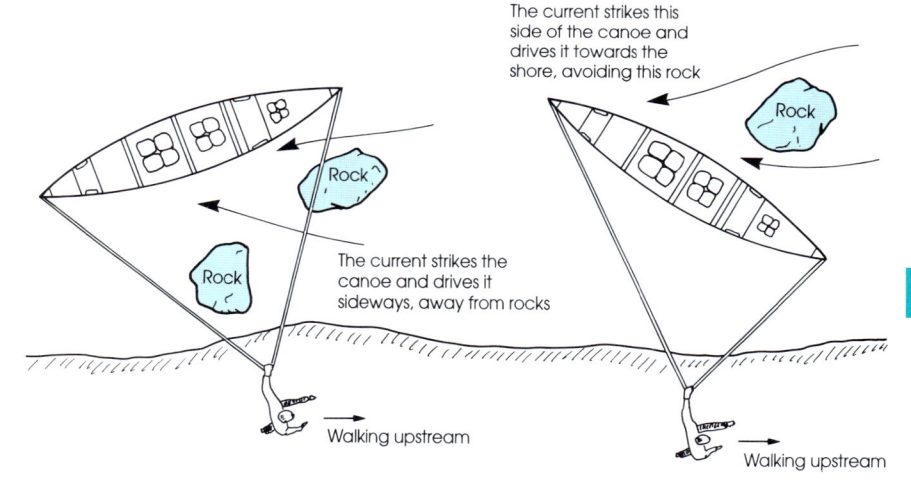

The current strikes this side of the canoe and drives it towards the shore, avoiding this rock

Rock

Rock

The current strikes the canoe and drives it sideways, away from rocks

Rock

Walking upstream

Walking upstream

Towing

One of the main principles of skilled boating requires that you be ready on any and all occasions to render help to other craft that require aid; this may necessitate that you take another boat in tow. A long strong line will be required, especially in rough water.

First method When a boat has *two bits aft instead of a single one amidships*, a bridle is rigged to tow from both, instead of throwing the whole load on one side.

Never stand near a highly strained line in case it breaks, because it will act like a rubber band—many a bad accident has been caused in this way. Always have a sharp cutting instrument ready in case it is necessary to cut the tow cable. Also be ready to drop the anchor if your boat is out of control and you have been cast adrift.

405

First method

Second method

Towing

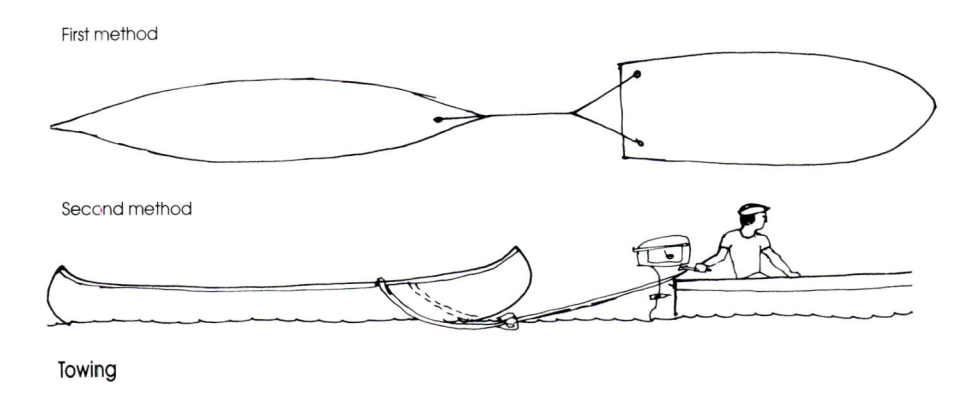

The vessel being towed should always be trimmed so that the stern is set deeper in the water than usual. This lifts the bow of the craft being towed and allows it to track directly behind the towing craft.

It is sometimes preferable for the towing vessel to be tied to the disabled vessel side by side, the mobile vessel one-third of its length behind the disabled one.

Second method   If you have to tow your canoe by a *power boat*, tie the towline to the forward thwart, run the line *under* the canoe, and tie to the other end of the same thwart. This will lift the canoe's bow and will allow it to track directly behind the power boat.

Journey equipment

Make sure you have the following items along with you out on the water:
- a painter at the bow and the stern—the stern painter does not have to be as long as the bow painter
- a light spare line of small circumference—a yellow-coloured nylon, which will float and is easily seen, is recommended
- oars or paddles, as appropriate
- a boat-repair kit
- a rubber waterproof watch
- buoyancy
- a bailer and a sponge or cloth
- spare lifejackets
- a Scout clasp knife
- a water bottle
- a first-aid kit.

Clothing and camp gear

The amount of clothing and gear required for boating is similar to that required for hiking. Take along the items and adhere to the advice set out in the following lists.

Clothing

- a uniform
- a spare long-sleeved shirt—long sleeves for protection against the sun
- shorts
- a jumper for night time
- a waterproof or sailing jacket
- pyjamas
- socks
- gym shoes
- a swimming costume
- sunglasses
- a wide-brimmed hat

Gear

- waterproof bags for holding bedding, clothing and personal gear
- an airtight can—good for cameras, watches and matches
- long narrow bags—better than short fat ones because they stow more easily
- bags preferably made of light rubberised or plastic-coated material. If these are unavailable, ordinary plastic bags will do. To seal the neck or opening, tie and then double back and tie again. Leave air in the bag, because it should float if placed in water
- sleeping bags or blankets—when folded and put in watertight bags, they can be used for seat cushions if required
- a tent
- a gas stove
- a billy
- a frying pan
- a plate and mug
- a Gilwell cooker
- a knife, fork and spoon set
- a waterproof collapsible bucket
- water bottles
- a lamp—fuel or pressure gas
- toilet gear
- food

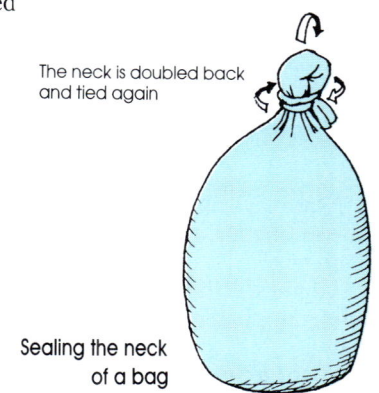

The neck is doubled back and tied again

Sealing the neck of a bag

Making a canoe

Can your team build a canoe? Yes. Seek the help of your Leader or a person who has built a boat. Fabric-covered canoes are extremely simple to construct. The framework consists of widely spaced lengthwise laths on frames, over which is stretched a fabric skin. There are no awkward joints to be cut, and the work can be done with extremely few tools. A plywood canoe requires more skill and tools and may cost a little more. Although plywood has obvious advantages of strength and rigidity, the modern plastic-covered fabrics, which most people use instead of canvas on soft-skinned canoes, are extremely tough. Moulded veneer construction makes a light, fast and attractive hull, but because a mould has to be made first, it is suitable only when several similar canoes are to be made.

Scout Outdoor Centres and/or boat-selling firms in your state will have a number of plans of suitable canoes, which can be made of wood, wood and canvas, vinyl, or fibreglass. Boat stores carry pre-cut packaged boat or canoe kits. Moulds could possibly be borrowed from another Group to make fibreglass canoes; this material makes a very strong canoe, but has no inherent buoyancy.

Repair kit

On any canoe outing of more than a half day, a repair kit for each type of boat should be carried. Fabric-covered boats require pieces of fabric, a waterproof glue, and needle and thread. 'GRP' requires glass fabric or chopped strand mat, resin and catalyst, some wet and dry paper (fairly coarse), and the knowledge to use these materials. Ply and metal boats seem to suffer less damage as easily and usually have only small dings. Repairs can be carried out temporarily with material such as PlastiBond or similar. In all cases, the damaged area must be thoroughly dry. When you think it is dry, swab the area with methylated spirits and leave it for another 10 minutes.

Remember that if you wish to become more than a beginner you must practise and then practise some more, preferably with an instructor correcting your mistakes before they become habits.

Useful reference books to help you learn, and perhaps plan some interesting trips, are available at your Scout Outdoor Centre.

It is a good idea to have short practice trips in order to develop teamwork in paddling and camping assignments before a big trip is undertaken.

Rowboats and rowing

Nowadays, most rowing is done in yacht-tender type dinghies (not to mention the racing shells with sliding seats as used by rowing clubs, and so on).

Gone are the days when most Sea Scouts learnt to row in an ex-navy montague whaler, its five oars of unequal length balancing the effort of the crew.

Also gone, mainly, are the clinker- or carvel-built skiffs usually from about 4 to 6 metres long. Many older Leaders learnt to row in an 18 foot-long six-oared gig of this type. A lovely craft: light enough that four young people could carry it, beamy enough to be stable in the chop of, say, Sydney Harbour, and fitted with a centreboard and fittings to sail as a gaff-rigged sloop.

Again, it is important you understand the names of the parts of the boat. It is surprising how many boating terms have become part of landlubbers' language.

Rowing terms

The terms labelled in the diagrams apply to parts of rowboats regardless of how the boat is constructed or what the materials are.

Water activities

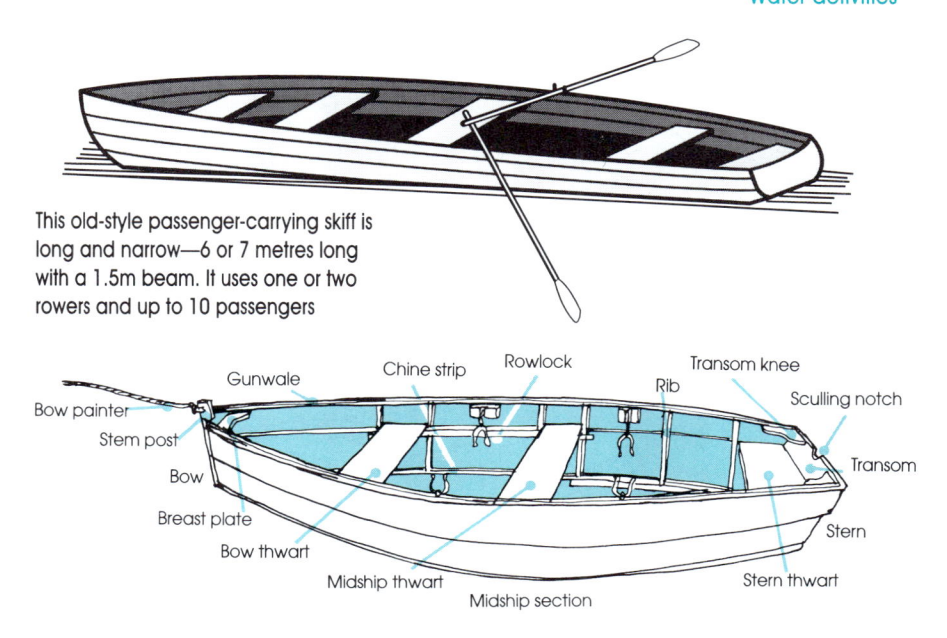

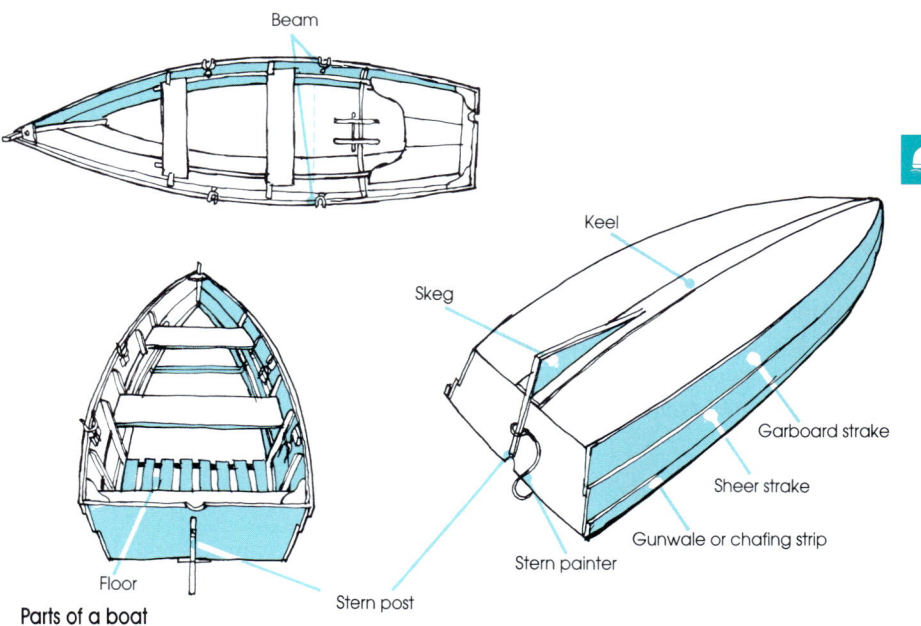

This old-style passenger-carrying skiff is long and narrow—6 or 7 metres long with a 1.5m beam. It uses one or two rowers and up to 10 passengers

Parts of a boat

Types of rowing boats

Aluminium rowboats are light, rugged, and require little maintenance. Flotation units are usually built in. Fibreglass boats also use flotation units. They require little care, but can be heavy to handle.

409

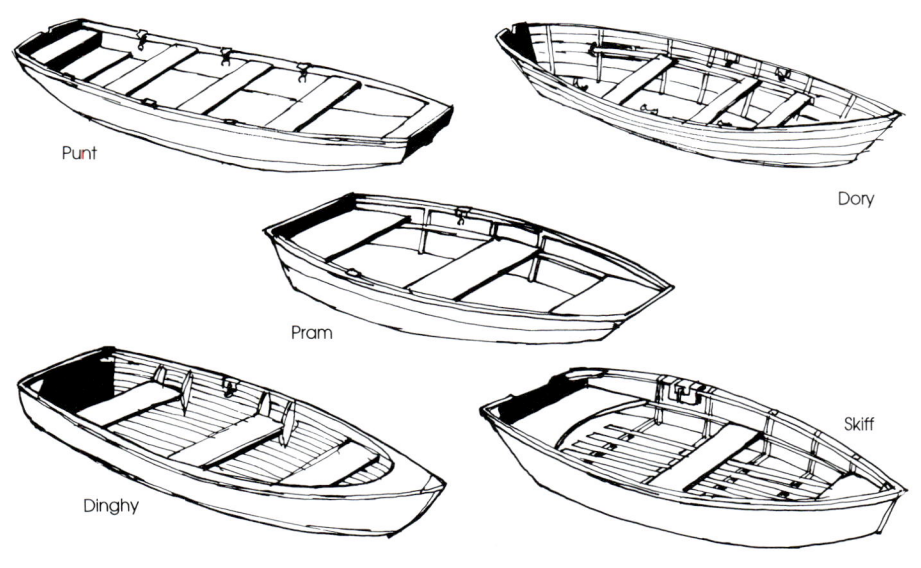

Types of rowing boats

Punt This is a narrow, shallow, flat-bottomed boat with identical square ends that have a sloping overhang.

Dory This is a deep rowboat with a narrow, flat bottom and clinker-built sides that flare out to a relatively wide beam at the level of the gunwales. It has a sharp bow and a narrow 'V'-shaped transom.

Pram This is a short boat with a narrow squared bow and a somewhat wider transom. It is typically 2.5 metres long with a 1.25 metre beam and is usually 'V'-bottomed.

Dinghy This is a small rowboat, usually round-bottomed with a transom stern, and is used as a tender to larger craft.

Skiff This usually refers to a small flat-bottomed rowboat with straight sides, a pointed bow and a transom stern.

Oars and rowlocks

You should also understand the names of the parts of your oar and the pivoting device used.

Oars are made of straight-grained spruce or hardwood. Spruce, although light, wears quickly. Hardwood oars are heavy, but they last longer and can take more hard knocks.

Rowlocks are essential to rowing. There are many types available, but their purpose is the same. They provide a pivot point for rowing, and are the point where the reaction to the stroke is applied to the boat, causing it to move. Rowlocks began as boxes cut into the gunwales. These were replaced by pins mounted on the gunwales. These pins later became the rigid rowlock we know today.

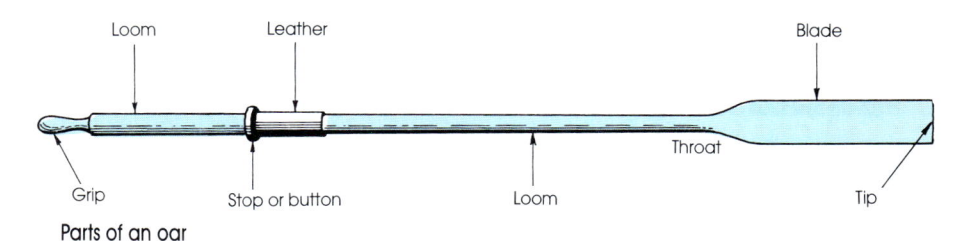

Water activities

Parts of an oar
(Grip, Stop or button, Loom, Leather, Loom, Throat, Blade, Tip)

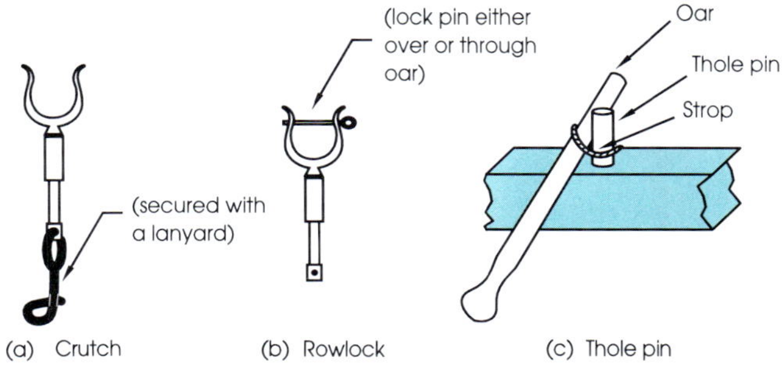

Crutch, rowlock and thole pin
(a) Crutch (secured with a lanyard)
(b) Rowlock (lock pin either over or through oar)
(c) Thole pin (Oar, Thole pin, Strop)

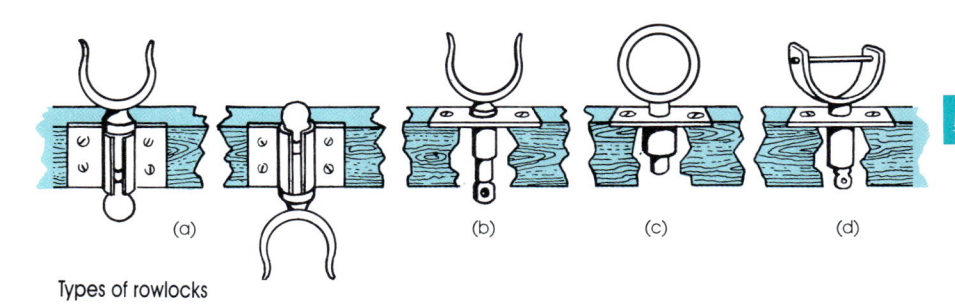

Types of rowlocks
(a) (b) (c) (d)

With reference to the diagrams, rowlock (**a**) is a 'Davis' lock which swings down out of the way when not in use. Rowlock (**c**) is put on the oar before the 'button' or preventer is put on. The pin in rowlock (**d**) goes through the oar and may weaken it. Rowlock (**b**) is a simple swivel rowlock similar to (**a**) except it does not swing down. The oar is simply set into (**a**) and (**b**) when you want to row. In the case of (**c**) and (**d**), the rowlocks are attached to the oars, and must be put into the holes in the gunwales when you are preparing to row.

Entering a boat

Entering a row boat is similar to entering a canoe. If you are on your own, keep as close to the keel line as possible. If you are in a crewed boat, enter in pairs from opposite sides, and sit down facing the stern. If you are boarding from a wharf or bank in deep water, enter one at a time, and maintain the boat's balance or trim as each person enters.

Board a dinghy over the stern

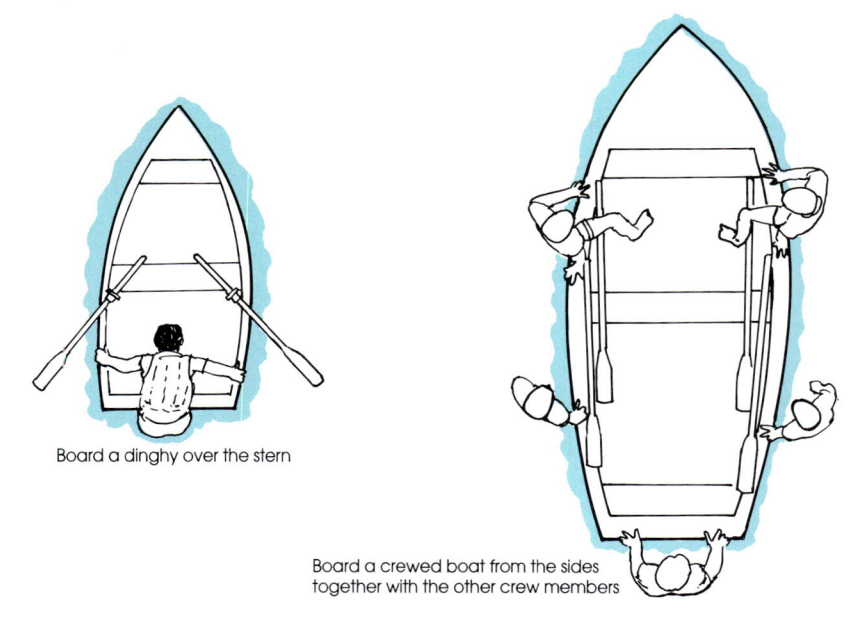

Board a crewed boat from the sides together with the other crew members

How to enter a boat

Rowing

Learning to row is easy. Once you have mastered the four parts of the stroke, you are on your way to getting around quickly and effortlessly on the water.

To row a dinghy or skiff efficiently you use the whole of your body, not only the arms. Your feet have to be braced, preferably against a stretcher so the whole upper body can swing with the oar. When you are seated with the oar at right angles to the keel and parallel with the water, your forearm should also be parallel with the water and your elbows close to your sides.

To start rowing, stretch your arms out and lean forward from the hips, keeping the oar parallel to the water. Then raise your hands to allow only the blade of the oar to enter the water (catch) and lean back with your arms straight. When you are as far back as comfortably possible, continue the pull with your arms (pull), then drop the hands to level with the gunwale, lifting the blade from the water (feather), and recover to the point of arms outstretched in front of you (recovery). Pause, let the boat run for a moment from the power you have exerted, then repeat the stroke.

That pause is important because it allows you time to breathe, and if you are rowing in a crew, it is the space during which the strokes are coordinated. When you are rowing in a crew, your time is always taken from the stroke oar that is that of the rower who is placed in the aftermost starboard-side position.

To row straight course, point the bow to the destination. Pick a landmark on the opposite shore over the centre of the stern and keep it there. Occasionally look over your shoulder to be sure you are not carried sideways by wind or current.

Water activities

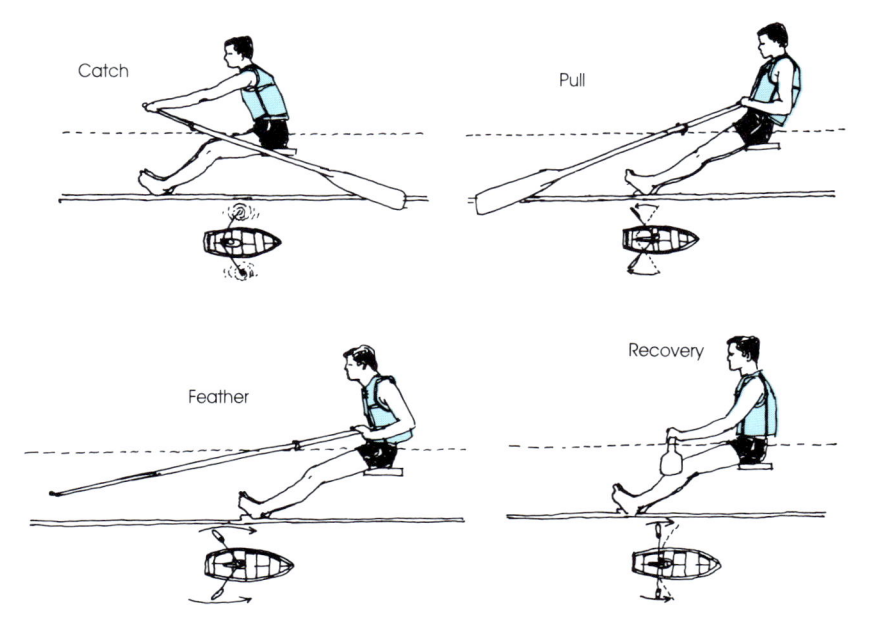

The four parts of the stroke: Catch, Pull, Feather, Recovery

Terms

When you are rowing in a crew, that is, two or more oars each with a separate rower, it is important to work as a team. This is aided if the coxswain gives implicit orders. The traditional orders are as follows.

Out oars The oars are placed in the crutches; the crew members sit at the ready position, oars at right angles to the keel and parallel to the water.

Stand-by The crew members lean forwards and stretch their arms ready to commence the stroke; the oar remains parallel to the water.

Give way together Dip the blades and pull.

Hold water The blades are dipped into the water at right angles to the boat and held (in order to stop the boat quickly).

Hold water port (starboard) Only the nominated side holds water; the other side keeps rowing (in order to turn the boat quickly).

Trail oars The handle end of the oar is passed behind the body, allowing the blade to flow back alongside the boat (this will narrow the boat dramatically).

Back water Literally rowing backwards; done with the arms only. Used to manoeuvre the boat; may be given as backwater port (starboard).

Way enough The order to stop rowing, return to the out-oars position after one more stroke.

Oars Return to the out-oars position.

Boat oars Remove the oar from the crutch and stow it inside the boat, usually between the rower and the gunwale, blade facing aft.

413

Fieldbook for Australian Scouting

Sculling over the stern

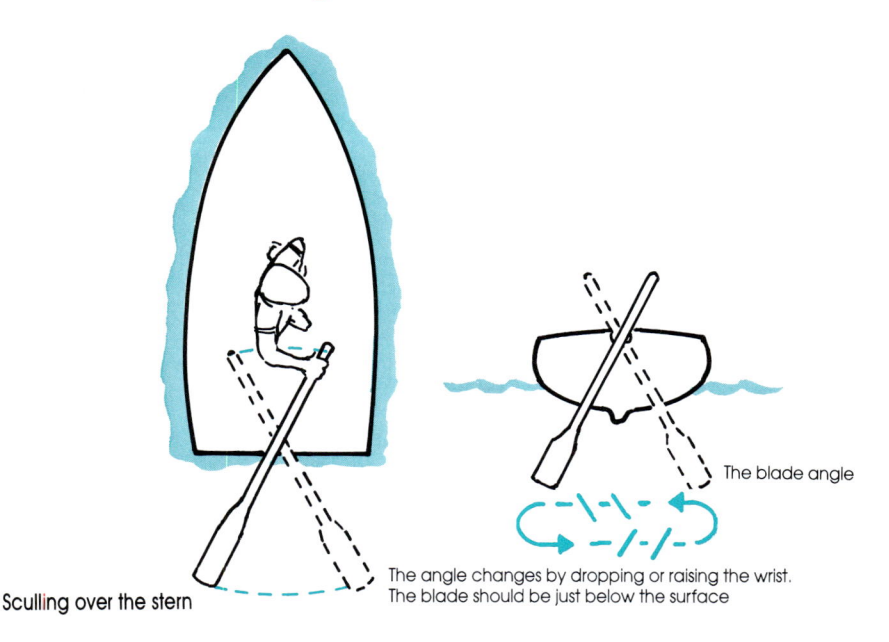

The blade angle

The angle changes by dropping or raising the wrist.
The blade should be just below the surface

Orders are given in mid-stroke and are obeyed after one more stroke, except those marked with an asterisk; they are emergency orders and are obeyed immediately.

Another interesting activity associated with rowing is sculling over the stern, that is, using only one oar over the stern in order to propel the boat forward.

Rowing as part of a crew in a suitable skiff can be very enjoyable in itself and also as a beginning to all other boating. It teaches the essence of balance, trimming and teamwork; in other words, the 'feel' of a boat.

Sailing

Often we are asked, 'Can a boat sail in any direction?'
  The answer: 'Almost.'
  'How can a boat sail against the wind?'
In order to understand this, you have to understand a little of the theory of aerodynamics and hydrodynamics; big words, but relatively simple in the beginning.

What keeps an aircraft in the air? Refer to the aircraft wing diagrams on the facing page.

Let us apply this theory to a sail. Refer to the next diagram.

The boat will therefore crab forwards and sideways. Let us give the boat some lateral resistance: a centreboard or keel and a rudder, as in the next diagram.

The complete theory of sail is reasonably complicated and requires a good knowledge of mathematics and aerodynamics. Following are some simple comments and sketches, however, that will meet the requirements of this test.

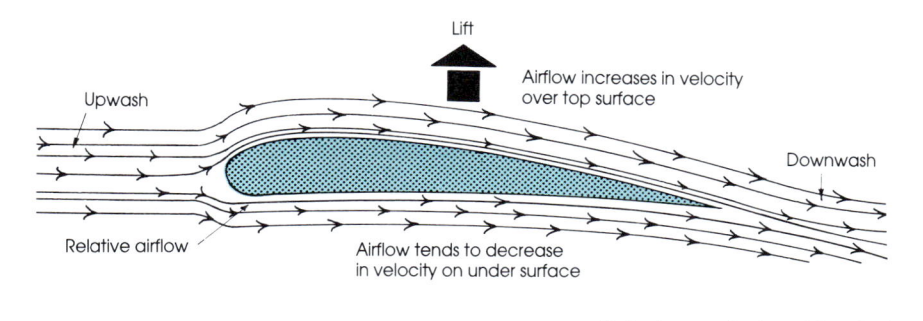

Water activities

Lift

Upwash

Airflow increases in velocity over top surface

Downwash

Relative airflow

Airflow tends to decrease in velocity on under surface

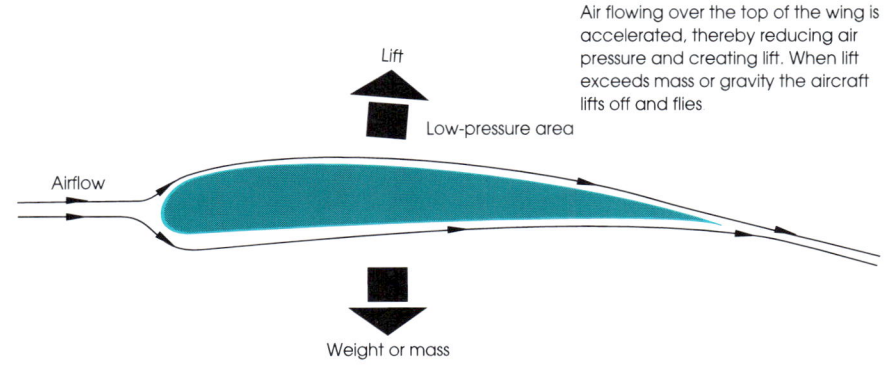

Lift

Low-pressure area

Air flowing over the top of the wing is accelerated, thereby reducing air pressure and creating lift. When lift exceeds mass or gravity the aircraft lifts off and flies

Airflow

Weight or mass

Boat sail

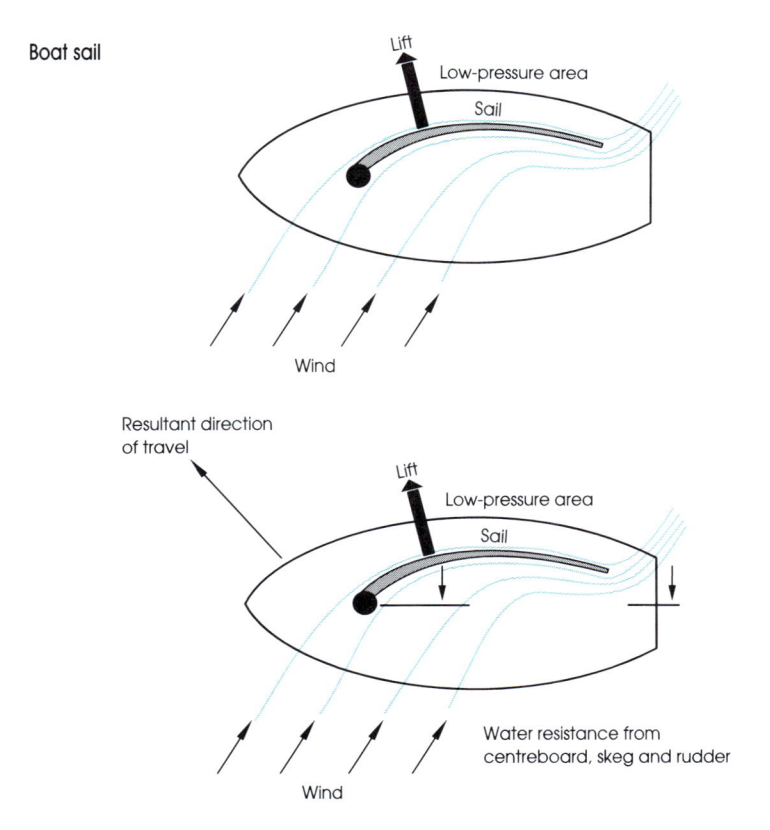

Lift

Low-pressure area

Sail

Wind

Resultant direction of travel

Lift

Low-pressure area

Sail

Water resistance from centreboard, skeg and rudder

Wind

415

In the next diagram, the wind is coming ahead when the boat is close-hauled on a port tack.

The arrow labelled 'A' shows the wind blowing on the mainsail.

This exerts a force shown by line 'B' which is at right angles to the sail.

This force can be considered to be made up of two parts, shown as 'C' and 'D' in the diagram.

If the length of the sides represents the sizes of these forces, we can see that 'D' (headway) is much less than 'C' (leeway). In this situation, the boat will drift sideways at a greater rate than going ahead. The centreboard is used in order to reduce the leeway and help the boat maintain its course.

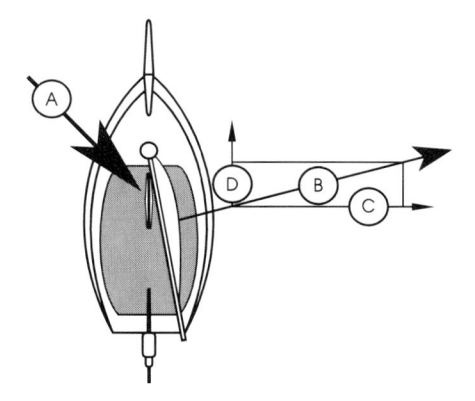

In the next sketch we see what is happening when the wind is blowing from abeam.

The force line 'B' is still at right angles to the sail, and 'C' and 'D' are the leeway and headway components as before.

However, 'C' and 'D' are now more equal in size and there is less tendency to make leeway and more tendency to make headway. Our boat will then be moving faster, and less centreboard will be required in order to reduce sideways drift.

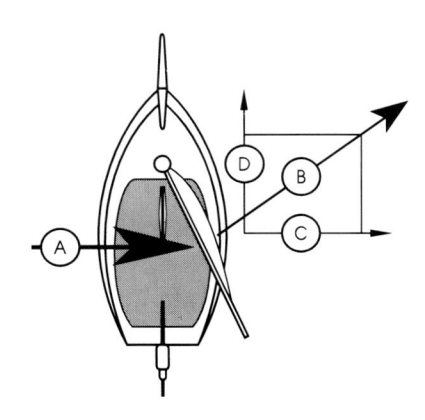

Water activities

In the next and final sketch in this group, the wind is blowing over the port quarter. Headway increases still more in proportion to leeway, and very little use of the centreboard is required.

In these comments we have imagined the force 'B' to be acting on the sail at one point. This point is called the *centre of effort*, and is usually about one-third the way up from the tack of the sail and about one-third the way from luff to leach. This tends to make the boat heel over slightly away from the windward side, and it is part of the coxswain's job to keep this as small as possible by working the rudder.

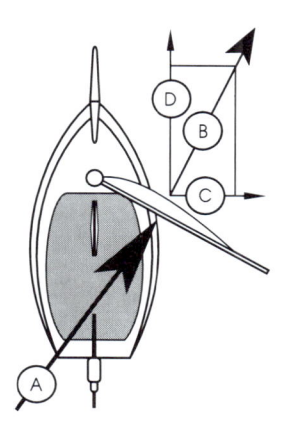

If the wind starts to blow too hard, it becomes much more difficult to keep the boat upright. There is a risk of the leeward gunwale submerging and water flowing into the boat.

When this is likely to happen, the sail area must be reduced by a process know as *reefing*. To do this, the boat must be stopped by bringing its head to wind. The sail is lowered until the reef points can be tied with reef knots, and the reef cringles tied down at the ends. The sail below the reef points is gathered up and one reef point passed under the foot of the sail (not under the boom), and tied to the one on the other side. If eyelets are set into the sail instead of reef points, these are rove to the boom with lacing.

Never leave reefing until the last moment. Always try to anticipate weather conditions, and if possible, be one move ahead of them.

As a small child, did you ever play with the soap in the bath? Squeeze the soap with both hands opposite and nothing happens; but if the squeeze is slightly offset, the soap will shoot off across the room.

If we apply the same logic to our sailboat, you can see the wind pressure trying to force the boat sideways and slightly forwards, and the water pressure on the centreboard and rudder trying to stop the boat moving sideways, so our boat moves forward with some side motion. This is called *leeway*.

Now let us add another sail.

You can see that by adding a jib in front of the mast we have increased the lift to the total sail plan, and this will give us more forward pull.

Not only do we increase the amount of pull; we accelerate the air passing behind the mainsail, which in turn gives more lift further forward on the main, thereby enabling us to point higher into the wind. We can never sail directly into the wind, but if we can average 45° we are doing well.

417

Fieldbook for Australian Scouting

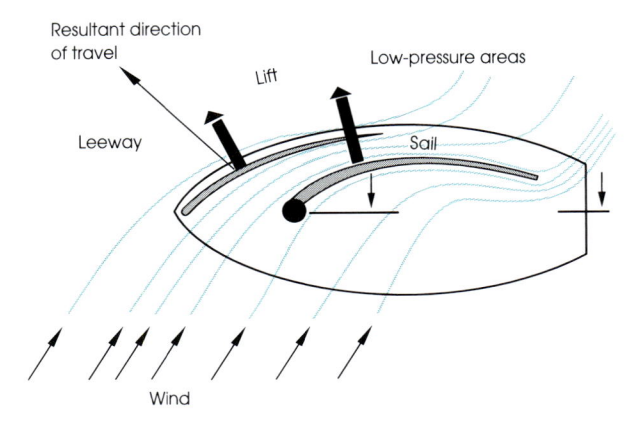

This means that if we wish to sail to a place that is upwind, we will have to sail a zigzag course in order to reach our goal. This is called *tacking*.

Unless the breeze is very light, the crew weight should be on the windward side. You will see as you sit to windward that pulling the tiller toward you causes the boat to swing away from the direction of the wind. Pushing the tiller away from you causes the boat to head into the direction of the wind.

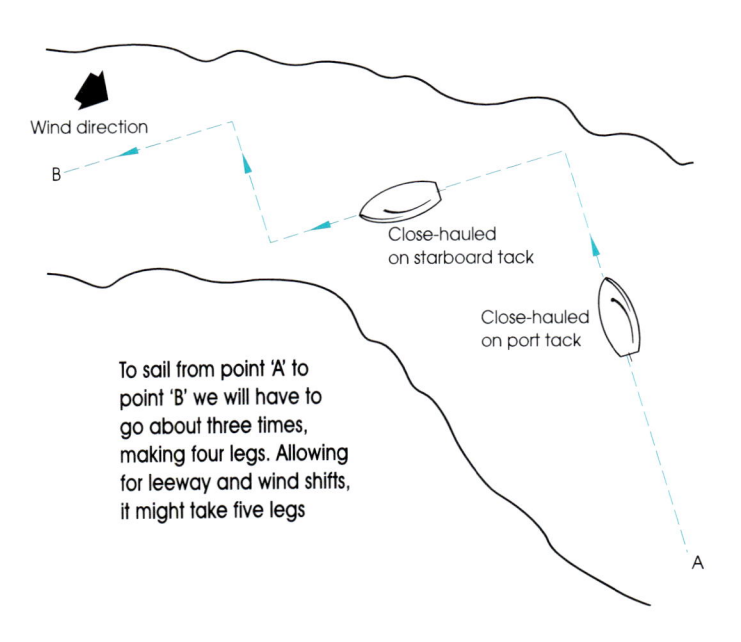

Now look at the sails in the next diagram: they have a graceful curve because of the pressure of the wind. Correct trim of the sails is essential to their effectiveness. It can be learnt only by practice.

Water activities

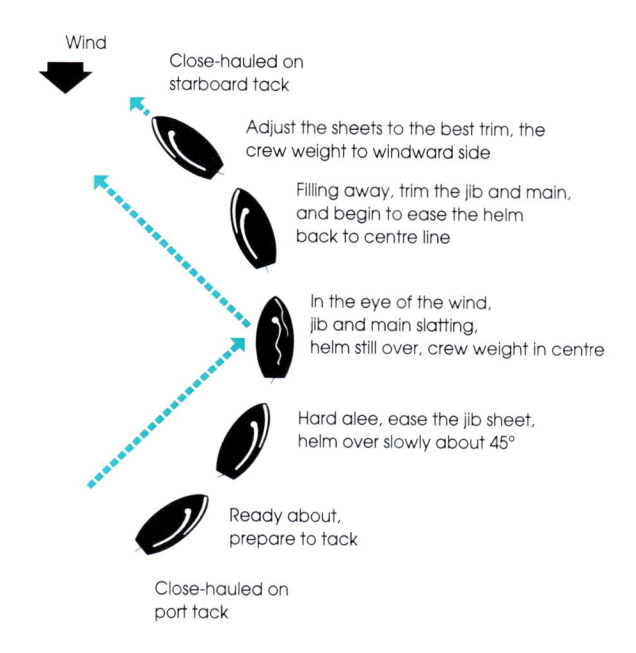

Diagram showing tacking sequence:
- Wind (from top)
- Close-hauled on starboard tack
- Adjust the sheets to the best trim, the crew weight to windward side
- Filling away, trim the jib and main, and begin to ease the helm back to centre line
- In the eye of the wind, jib and main slatting, helm still over, crew weight in centre
- Hard alee, ease the jib sheet, helm over slowly about 45°
- Ready about, prepare to tack
- Close-hauled on port tack

For each leg or tack, the sails will be on alternate sides, and the act of changing direction is called *going about*. In a crewed boat, the skipper usually lets the crew members know when to tack by calling, 'Ready to go about' as a warning, then 'Lee ho' to let them know the tiller or helm has been pushed to the leeside of the boat.

This turns the boat into the wind, the mainsail will be flapping, and if the jib is held hard on, the wind will backwind it and push the boat's bow further around. Once the mainsail is full, the jib is brought across quickly and sheeted home for the new tack.

This process is repeated as often as necessary to reach the mark. In open waters, legs can be quite long. At sea you might remain on the same tack for days, but in enclosed waters, where we mostly sail, a leg of a tack may be only 100 metres or less.

A back-winded jib pushes the bow past the wind. As soon as the mainsail fills, the jib is brought across quickly and sheeted in for the new tack

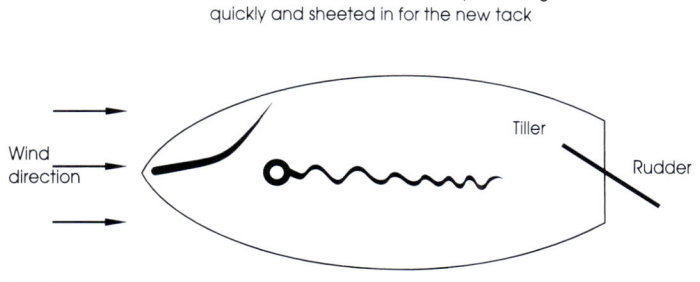

Going about

So far we have discussed sailing against the wind; what about sailing across it? This is easy and is called *reaching*; so easy, in fact, that the old square-rigger sailors called it a 'soldier's breeze' when they could reach.

To reach, we ease the mainsail out to about 45° and the jib similarly so they are both full and drawing. Hold the tiller fairly steady to give the course we want to sail, and away we go.

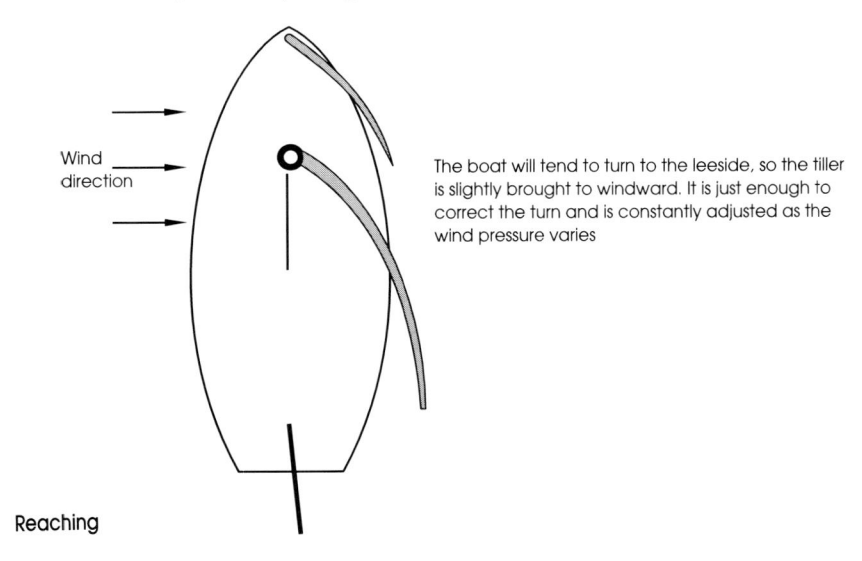

Wind direction

The boat will tend to turn to the leeside, so the tiller is slightly brought to windward. It is just enough to correct the turn and is constantly adjusted as the wind pressure varies

Reaching

Now let us look at sailing downwind. Just ease the sheets as you turn the boat and you are *running*. In a fore- and aft-rigged boat, we should never attempt to sail exactly downwind. Wind is never constant from one direction, and because the shrouds supporting the mast will not allow the mainsail to rotate to square of the boat, we should not let the wind come directly over the stern—always a few degrees to one side.

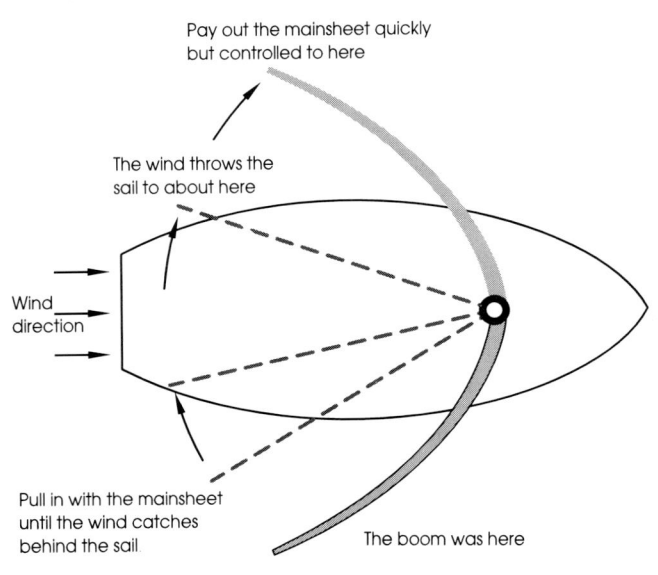

Pay out the mainsheet quickly but controlled to here

The wind throws the sail to about here

Wind direction

Pull in with the mainsheet until the wind catches behind the sail

The boom was here

Gybing

Water activities

This means that to achieve a true downwind course we will have to perform a manoeuvre similar to tacking. This is not difficult, but it requires a little more care and control than going about does. It is called *gybing*.

As the tiller is slowly brought to windward to turn the boat across the wind, the mainsheet is brought in until the wind gets under the sail and lifts the boom across. The tiller is straightened and the mainsheet eased until the main is setting correctly.

Another technique when sailing downwind is called *wing and wing*. Once the main is full and driving on a run, the jib can be brought over and either poled out with a *whisker pole* or, with care, filled by playing the windward jib sheet. You have to be careful with the longitudinal trim (in other words, move the crew weight aft), because you can drive the boat nose first into the water. With a planing hull, however, it is possible to get on to the plane with very little weight change.

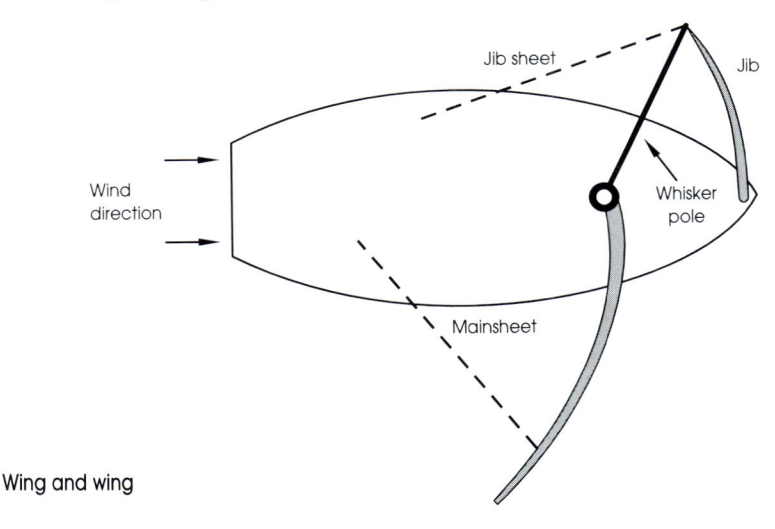

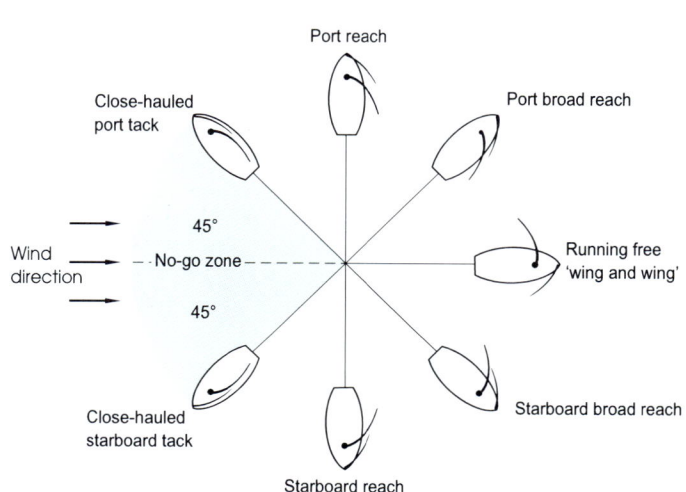

Wing and wing

Points of sail

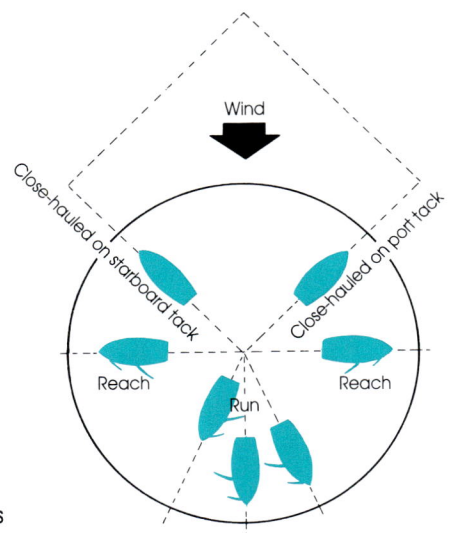

Types of manoeuvres

A boat is on a *starboard tack* when its boom is to port and the wind is coming over the starboard. It is on a *port tack* when the boom is on the starboard and the wind is coming over the port side. Because it is impossible for a sailboat to sail directly into the wind, progress is made to windward in a series of tacks or zigzags, each tack being at about a 45° angle to the wind.

Sailing on a *close beam* or *broad reach* poses no particular problems other than proper trim of the sails and crew-weight distribution. The boom should be at or near a right angle to the direction of the wind.

When *running free* (the most difficult point of sailing), many factors are considered. Carelessness on the helm or a sudden wind shift could cause an accidental jibe with disastrous consequences. Keep a sharp eye on sea and wind conditions, and be ready to meet any changes.

Types of sailboats

We have mentioned various types of craft, and most of you will have read books about the days before steam and diesel propulsion, when big wooden ships were propelled by the wind and carried many types of sail. Most have gone, but large sailboats are still being used for sport.

The sail plan, known as *rig*, usually determines its classification.

Now let us rig our boat. If possible on the rigging ramp or beach, face the boat bow into the wind, check that the bungs are in, that all buoyancy tanks are closed off, and that the mast and spars are all ready to place. Turn now to the section headed 'Stepping the mast' on page 428.

Features of the various types

Cat boat A single triangular sail set on a mast steeped well forward. This is the simplest sail plan of all, and probably the easiest for beginners to handle. It is usually used only on small sailing dinghies.

Water activities

Bermudan This is probably the most popular rig for small craft. Note that there is one headsail (jib) and one triangular mainsail only. Both of these are very easily managed by a two-person crew. The bermudan mainsail is sometimes also known as marconi rig, especially when it is much taller than its breadth.

Sloop This is rather similar to the Bermudan rig, but usually smaller in size. It is ideal for a two-person crew.

Ketch This is a two-masted craft, the after (or mizzenmast) being the shorter of the two, and set forward of the stern of the boat.

Yawl This is another two-masted craft, rather similar to a ketch, but with a shorter after (mizzen) mast set further aft so the sail extends beyond the stern.

Schooner This is another two-masted craft, with the after mast taller than the forward mast.

Cutter This is rather like a sloop but is much larger and usually carrying double headsails.

Cat boat

Bermudan

Sloop

Ketch

Yawl

Cutter

Schooner

Gaff rig This usually employs a four sided sail, and is hoisted on a mast with its head extended aft and upwards by a spar called a gaff. Its foot is extended by a spar called a boom.

Gunter rig This rig uses a gaff which is very long in proportion to the boom and a very short mast. The halyard leads through a sheave (sailor's name for pulley) at the masthead, and is attached to the gaff so that when the gaff is fully hoisted, it extends vertically along and above the mast to form a jib-headed rig.

Lug sail The lug sail is also four sided with the foot longer than the head and the luff much shorter than the leach. It is set on two spars like the boom and gaff of a gaff rig, but in this case the gaff extends forward of the mast, and is secured to it by a lanyard.

Catamaran The twin hulls are joined together with a light deck. This is a very fast-sailing craft. Note also the twin rudders which reach deeply into the water and are connected together with a cross-bar.

Trimaran This is a three-hulled sailing craft, often large in size with cabin accommodation.

Trailer-sailer This is probably the smallest cabin-style sailing craft which can conveniently be transported by a domestic-sized boat trailer.

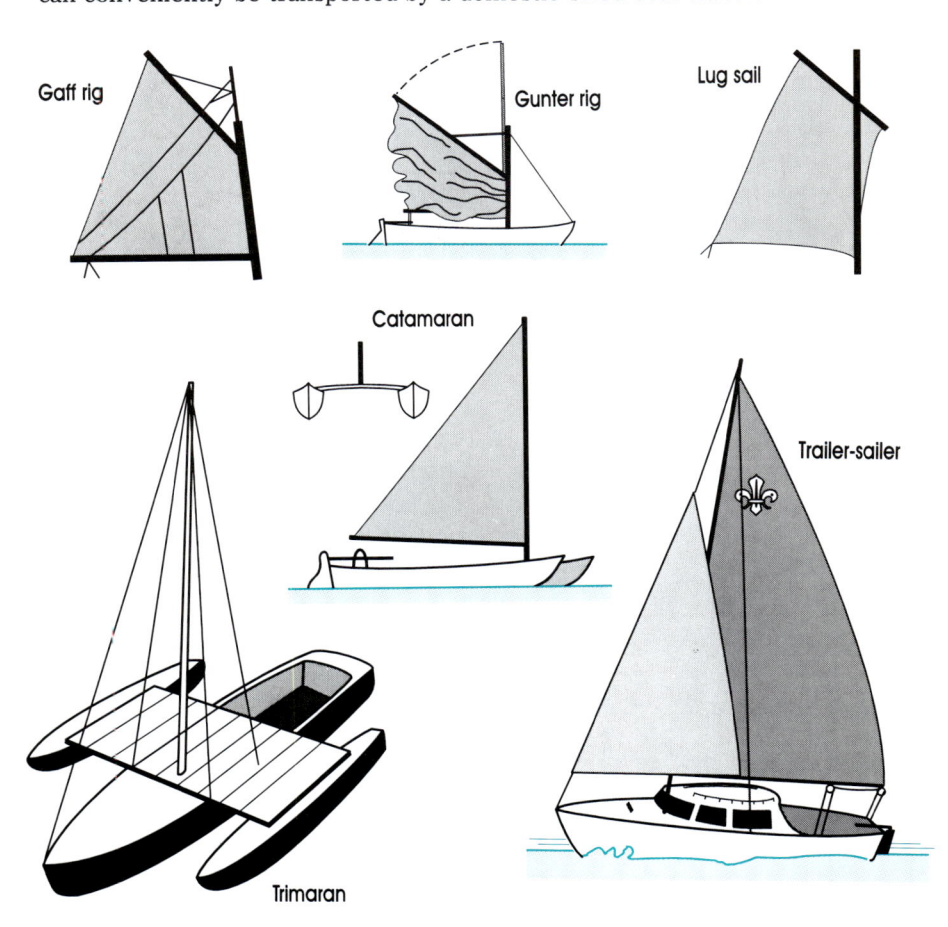

Water activities

Lazy E

Lazy E

Trailer-sailer

From left to right: Vagabond, Heron, NS14, Vagabond.

International Moth

International 505

Fireball

Quickcat

Some of the more popular sailboats

425

Parts of a sailboat

Refer to the next diagram for all the parts of a sailboat.

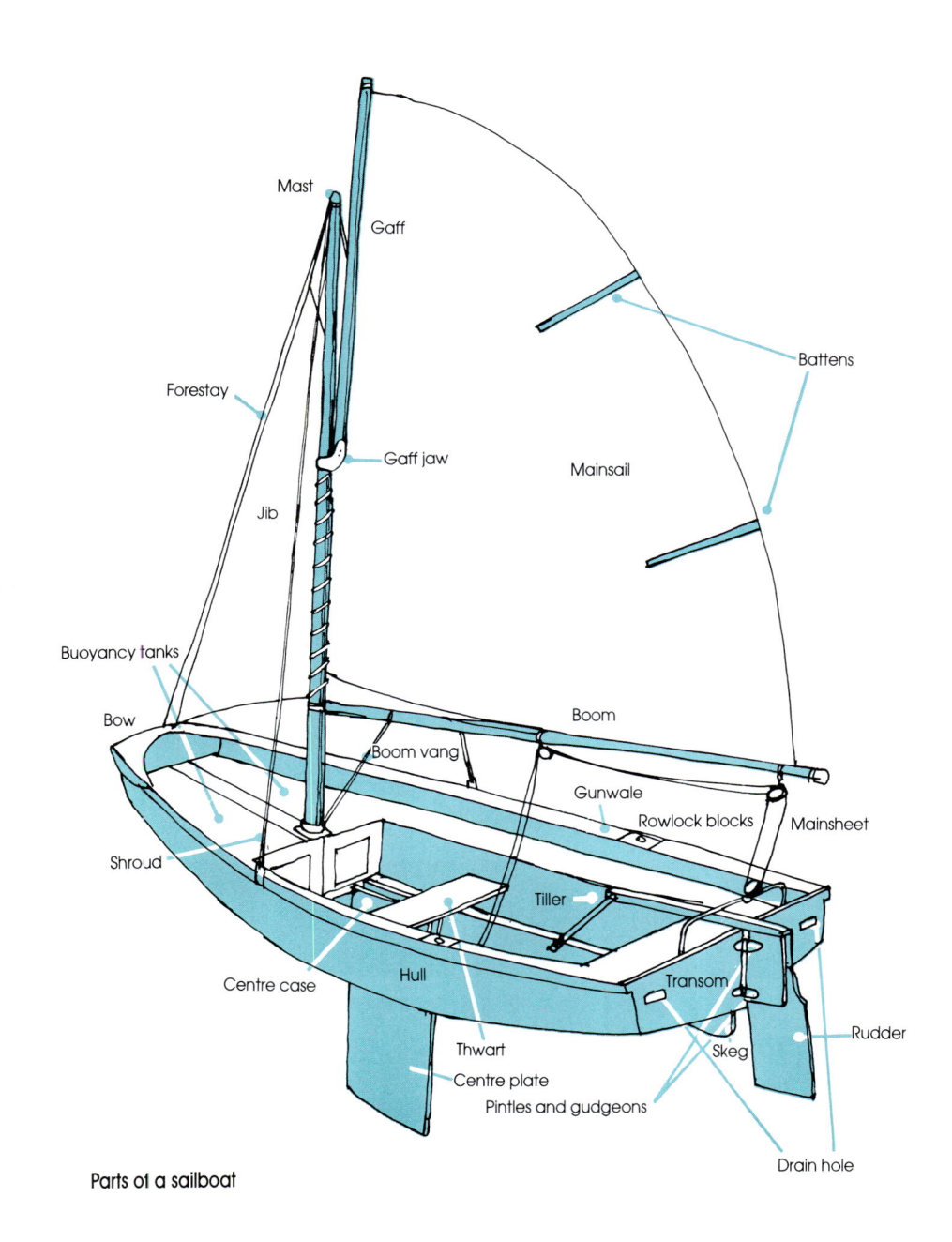

Parts of a sailboat

Water activities

Types of sails

Refer to the next diagrams for all the types of sails.

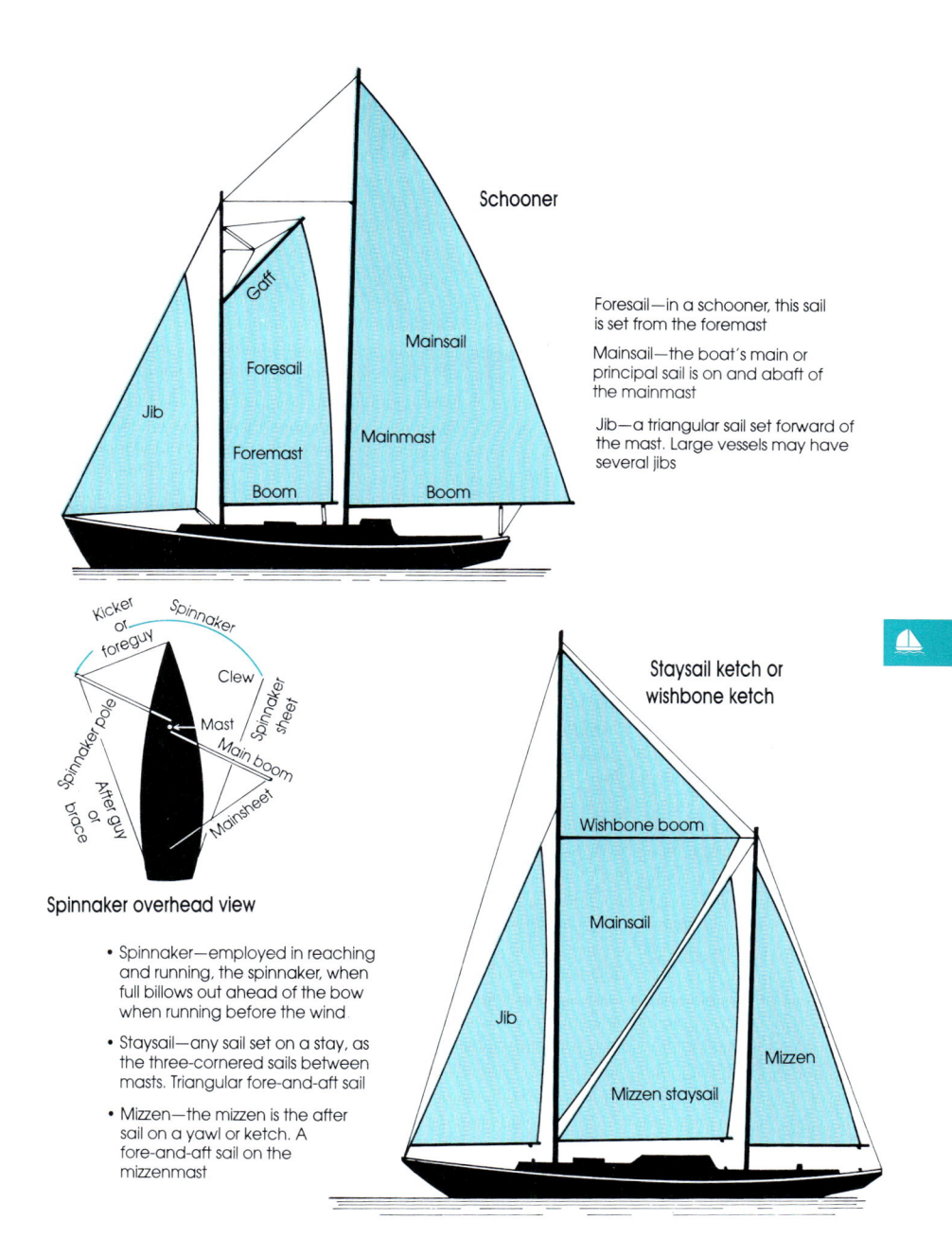

Schooner

Foresail—in a schooner, this sail is set from the foremast

Mainsail—the boat's main or principal sail is on and abaft of the mainmast

Jib—a triangular sail set forward of the mast. Large vessels may have several jibs

Spinnaker overhead view

Staysail ketch or wishbone ketch

- Spinnaker—employed in reaching and running, the spinnaker, when full billows out ahead of the bow when running before the wind.

- Staysail—any sail set on a stay, as the three-cornered sails between masts. Triangular fore-and-aft sail

- Mizzen—the mizzen is the after sail on a yawl or ketch. A fore-and-aft sail on the mizzenmast

427

Gaff and marconi rig

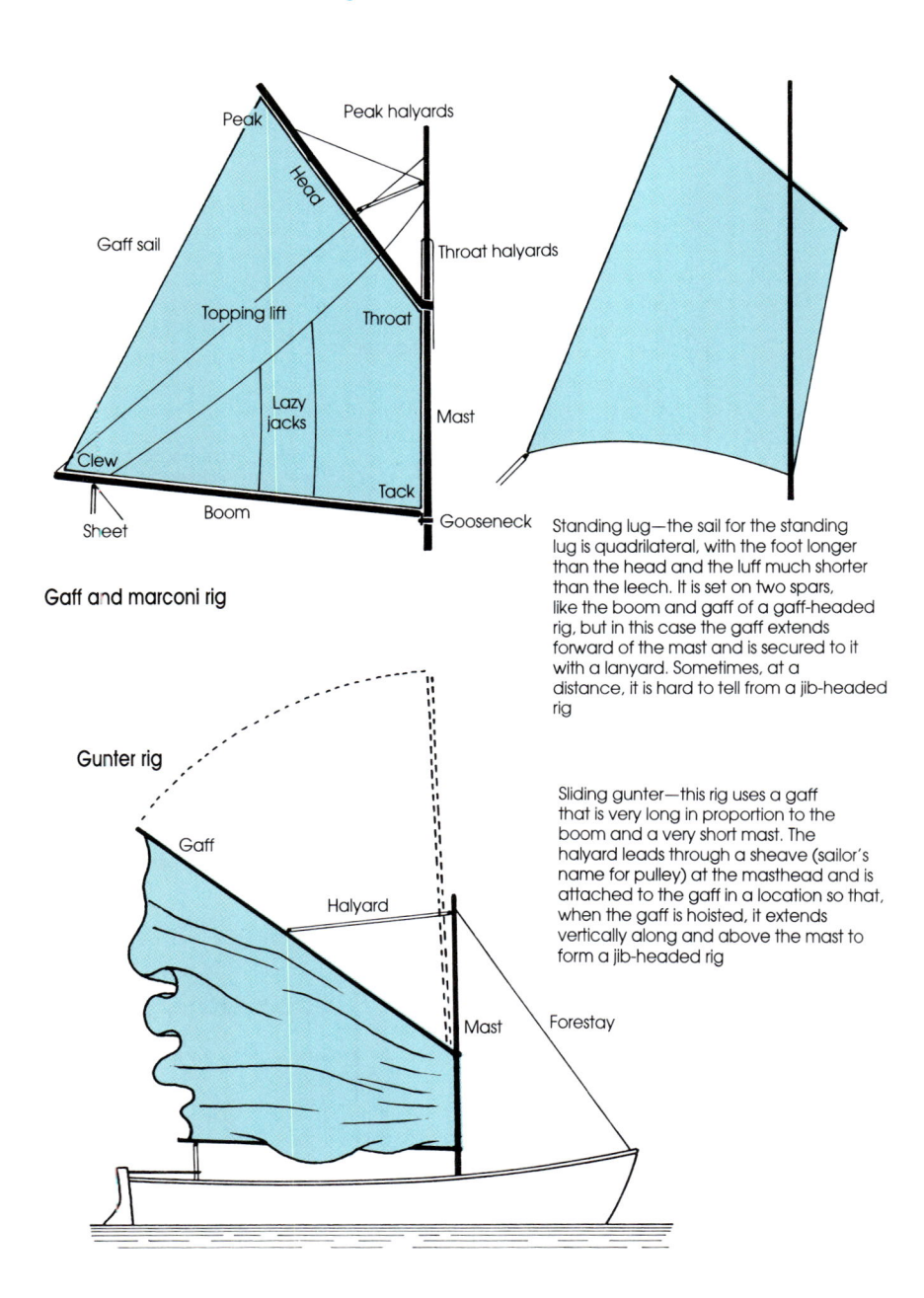

Labels: Peak, Peak halyards, Head, Gaff sail, Topping lift, Throat halyards, Throat, Lazy jacks, Mast, Clew, Tack, Boom, Gooseneck, Sheet

Standing lug—the sail for the standing lug is quadrilateral, with the foot longer than the head and the luff much shorter than the leech. It is set on two spars, like the boom and gaff of a gaff-headed rig, but in this case the gaff extends forward of the mast and is secured to it with a lanyard. Sometimes, at a distance, it is hard to tell from a jib-headed rig

Gunter rig

Labels: Gaff, Halyard, Mast, Forestay

Sliding gunter—this rig uses a gaff that is very long in proportion to the boom and a very short mast. The halyard leads through a sheave (sailor's name for pulley) at the masthead and is attached to the gaff in a location so that, when the gaff is hoisted, it extends vertically along and above the mast to form a jib-headed rig

Stepping the mast

Depending on the type of boat, the mast will pass through a fitting at deck or thwart level into a step or block on the keel of the boat, or will stand on a tabernacle usually mounted at deck level. Carefully place the mast in position, taking care not to tangle any rigging. Then, holding the mast as close as possible to its correct position, attach the shrouds (the side-support wires) to the chain plate on each side of the hull, and take the forestay to its securing point at or near the bow. Shrouds are usually attached with a *shackle* or similar fitting, and the forestay is often attached by lacing; this allows the fore and aft angle of the mast to be varied slightly. Thread the lacing through the eye on the fitting, and back through the eye in the wire several times, then seize the whole together with several half hitches.

At this stage the mast should be self-supporting.

On some small boats, the forestay is built into the leading edge of the jib and requires the jib to be attached to the mast before erecting it. In other small craft, it is easier to set the mast up with the boat on its side. We have seen some very ingeniously made rigging cradles that allow the boat to be rolled on to its side and supported there; these are particularly useful with single-handed craft. Other small-class boats use an unsupported mast, usually fibreglass, which has no shrouds or stays. Others also have a back stay. When acquiring a sailboat, you should always see it rigged and, if possible, have an experienced sailor check out the rigging for you.

Now attach the peak of the mainsail to its halyard, start the bolt rope into the track, and carefully raise the sail, watching at all times the feed into the track. At the same time, feed the battens into their pockets and secure each as you go; these serve to flatten the trailing edge or leech of the sail, which is often curved (called the *roach*). When the sail is all the way up, belay the halyard and fit the boom.

Again, there are multiple variations of attaching the main to the boom. Some rigs are loose footed, that is, the mainsail is attached only at the end of the boom; others use a track similar to the mast; still others lace the main to the boom. Whichever way your boat is rigged, the tension of the sail along the boom should be in a way so that the sail does not pucker. When you have more experience, you should experiment with the tension of the foot, making the sail fuller when the wind is light, flatter when the wind is strong.

Some craft have a down-haul on the boom to tension the leading edge or luff; tighten this so the sail sets smoothly. Most modern boats have a boom vang which helps to prevent the boom rising when running before the wind, mostly attached to the boom at one end and the lower part of the mast at the other. Fit this, usually a small block-and-tackle system, which is also used to adjust the bend of the mast.

Now attach the mainsheet, usually a multi-fall pulley system. Again, there are many variations, but the final pull should come up from the bottom of the boat, not from the boom. If you thread the rope through each time you rig, start with a neat small bowline and finish with a figure-of-eight stopper knot. There is nothing more frustrating than trying to rebuild the mainsheet system in a 20 knot breeze.

Next, attach the jib clew to the bow fitting and its peak to the halyard, hoist and tension until the forestay just starts to slacken, and belay the halyard. All halyards should be fastened simply so they are secure but can be

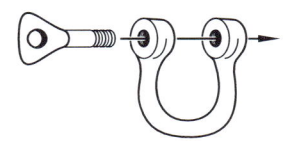

There are many forms of shackles, but all are basically a 'U' shape with a pin either threaded or with some sort of lock

Shackle

Fieldbook for Australian Scouting

undone easily. Multiple turns around a cleat, and knots galore, are a trap if you have to get the sail down in a hurry. Twice do a figure of eight around the cleat; one half hitch on the horn of the cleat is enough. Coil the balance of the halyard neatly, and wedge between the halyard and the mast. Fit the jib sheets, plural. The jib has two sheets, one to each side of the boat. We usually have ours long enough to join the free ends with a sheetbend. That way, when going about the jib, your hand does not have to find the other sheet.

Parts of a sail

Refer to the diagrams for the numbers that correspond to the following definitions and explanations.

1. **Head**   The upper edge of a sail.
2. **Luff**   The foremost edge of a sail.
3. **Leach**   The after edge of a sail.
4. **Foot**   The lower edge of a sail.
5. **Roach**   The curve in the foot and leach of a sail.
6. **Throat**   The upper foremost corner.
7. **Peak**   The upper after corner.
8. **Tack**   The lower foremost corner.
9. **Clew**   The lower after corner.
10. **Cringles**   These are of various sizes and are worked into the corners of the sails, and at each end of each line of reef points.
11. **Eyelet holes**   These are worked into the head of sails, and sometimes the luff and foot for bending the sails to the mast and spars.
12. **Reef points**   These are pieces of line worked into and through the sail for stopping up reefs.
13. **Bolt rope**   This is the roping on the edge of a sail. It is always sewn on the port side of a sail.
14. **Battens**   Battens of wood or cane are fitted into special pockets in the sails for the purpose of stiffening the sail. The pockets always commence at the leach of a sail and are at right angles to the leach.

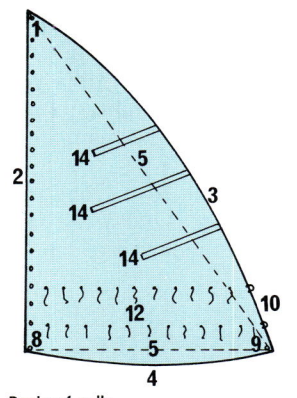

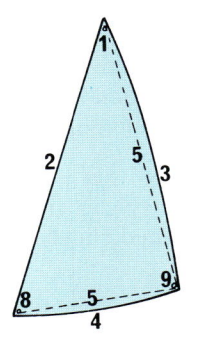

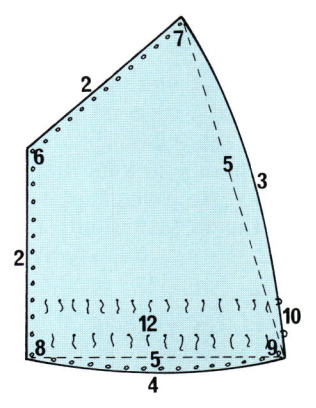

Parts of sails

Water activities

Now we are almost ready to launch and go sailing.

Check: Can you fit the rudder with the boat ashore? Only if it does not protrude below the keel line. A pivoting blade rubber usually can, but a fixed blade has to be done with the boat floating.

Is the centreboard fitted? Pivoting blades are usually permanently in place, but a dagger board has to be inserted while floating.

Are the bungs in? You feel very silly as you fill up with water just a few metres from the launch point.

Have we got a bailer? This should be tied in on a lanyard long enough to allow the bailer to be used.

Have we got a paddle? This is essential if the wind drops, and should also be tied in on a lanyard and stowed out of the way. Under the bow deck or alongside the centreboard case are the usual places.

Okay, let us launch. Carry the boat into the water, then, while one crew member holds the bow and lets the boat stream into the wind, fit the rudder, introduce the daggerboard into the case, and brief the crew members: Who is to do what? When you are satisfied they know their jobs, have them board, one at a time, keeping the boat pointing into the wind, sails flapping. Then, as the sheet hands start to tighten their sheets, allow the boat to pay off to the side you wish to sail, and push off and climb aboard, one hand on the tiller in order to maintain the course you require. As soon as possible, when enough depth of water is under you, get the centreboard and the rudder blade down. Sheets on hard, adjust your course to about 45° off the wind, and you are sailing.

Depending on the waterway and its traffic, this first sail should not be too long. Practise the various points of sail, and come home while you are still fresh. It is when you are tired that you make mistakes, particularly while you are learning.

Rule of the road

Sailing boats traditionally have right of way over all other forms of power. However, in restricted waters such as a harbour, commercial shipping usually has the right of way. Each state has different regulations, so check with the relevant authority before setting out. If a large tanker is trying to travel up a narrow channel, it does not have room to avoid a sailing dinghy, and a commuter ferry trying to keep to timetable cannot avoid you. Therefore keep out of their road.

A boat working into the wind has right of way over a boat reaching, which has right of way over a boat running.

A boat with the wind on the starboard side has right of way over a boat with the wind on the port side on the same point of sail.

We can therefore draw-up a right-of-way chart:

1. working on starboard tack
2. working on port tack
3. reaching on starboard leg
4. reaching on port leg
5. running on starboard leg
6. running on port leg.

431

Returning to shore

As you approach the landing place, all gear should be eased off as follows: centreboard checked ready to raise, or daggerboard partially lifted; rudder ready to lift or unship; then, when in about waist-deep water, let fly all sheets; round the boat up into the wind; one crew member over the side to catch and hold the bow before the boat grounds; everybody out; proceed to unship all the parts that were shipped in this position before sailing. Now carry the boat, still pointing into the wind, to a safe place. If sailing again shortly, and the wind is not too strong, it is probably safe to leave the boat as it is, provided any water inside has been bailed or drained out.

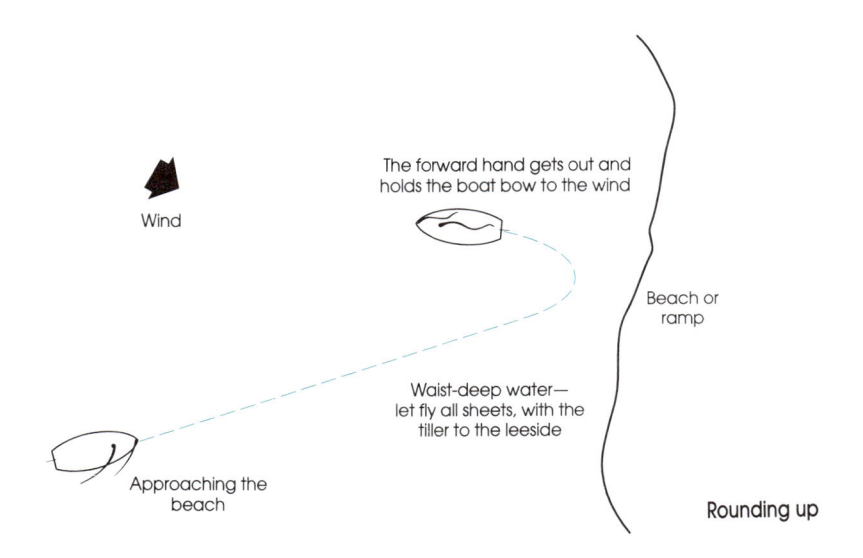

Wind

The forward hand gets out and holds the boat bow to the wind

Beach or ramp

Waist-deep water— let fly all sheets, with the tiller to the leeside

Approaching the beach

Rounding up

Capsize and recovery

Today, most small sailboats are recoverable if capsized, and you *will* capsize. You should practise this recovery when the wind is not too strong, so that when it happens for real, you know exactly how the boat reacts and how to deal with it. As soon as you ditch, have one crew member swim to the bow and hold the boat head into the wind, then to free all sheets so the sails can flap as you right the boat; then to get on to the centreboard and pull on the gunwale to right the boat. Depending on the size of the boat and the size of you, it may take two people on the centreboard to get the necessary leverage. Sometimes extra leverage can be obtained by using the jib sheet to pull instead of the gunwale, letting you get your weight further out along the centreboard. As the boat comes upright, keep its head to the wind, and get the lightest crew member on board to bail while the rest of the crew members help by keeping the boat level. If the water is above the open centreboard case, you will have to stuff a shirt, or something similar, into it in order to stop the water flowing in. If you have venturi bailers, as soon as the boat

Water activities

is stable, climb in, start sailing, and open the venturies; a broad reach is best, giving you speed to suck the water out on an easy point of sail.

A number of small sailboats can be righted in the event of a capsize, but before leaving the land or beach, there are precautions that should be taken, as follows.

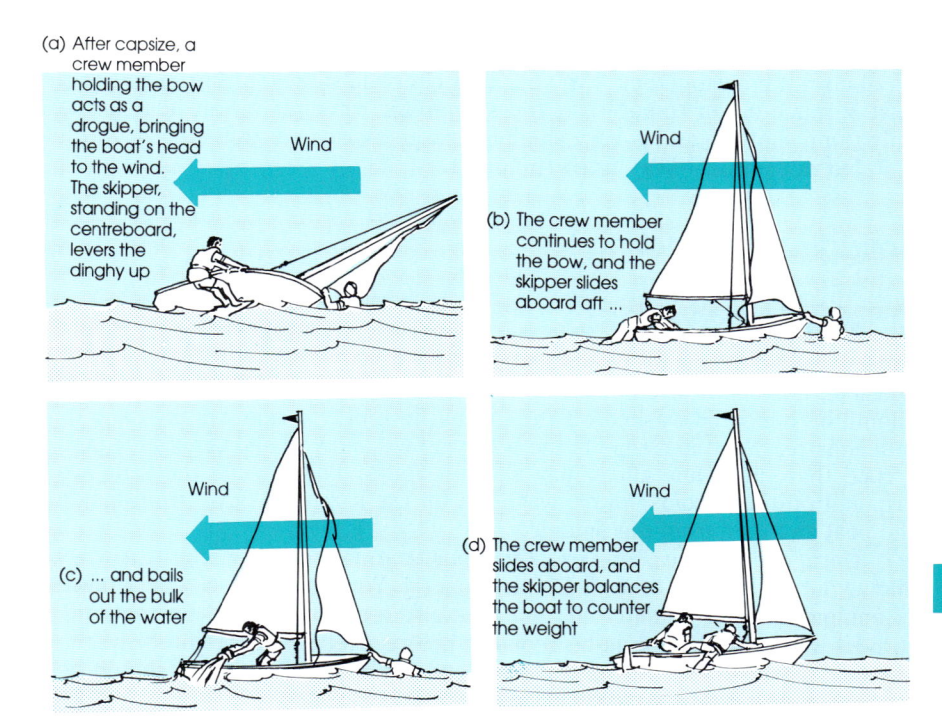

(a) After capsize, a crew member holding the bow acts as a drogue, bringing the boat's head to the wind. The skipper, standing on the centreboard, levers the dinghy up

(b) The crew member continues to hold the bow, and the skipper slides aboard aft ...

(c) ... and bails out the bulk of the water

(d) The crew member slides aboard, and the skipper balances the boat to counter the weight

Capsize and recovery

Recovery

Fieldbook for Australian Scouting

- All personal gear should be well stowed in plastic bags and tied in a suitable out-of-the-way position in the boat.
- All removable gear such as rudder, spare oars, bailer and spare lines should be made fast.
- Be sure your lifejacket is correctly fitted and secure.
- If any of the boat parts or personal gear happen not to be tied down, note the direction in which they float away from you on surfacing after a capsize; then, if the boat is righted, you can pick them up.

Whatever else may happen, stay with the boat if you are unable to right it: a buoyant craft together with your lifejacket will save your life. A capsized boat is much easier to see than you swimming; remember your head is the only thing showing and is very small in a large expanse of water.

Do not panic—stay with the craft.

Unrigging and storing

Our practice has always been to wash the boat, sails and sheets before unrigging. This is not always possible, but a good hose-down of the sails, sheets and hull helps to preserve what is a quite expensive piece of equipment. If possible, hose both sides of the sails while rigged. Sheets and their pulleys should be hosed or washed off the ground in order to remove any sand or other matter. Sand in a rope is the best way we know to shorten its life, and a rope that fails while afloat may shorten yours. Then, while the sails are dripping off the surplus water, wash out all the sand and 'grot' from inside the boat and then from the outside.

Unrig the boat in steps exactly opposite to those of rigging it. Always allow yourself enough time to do this properly. You should check every piece of equipment as it is taken off, and note any repairs that may be required. Frayed wire or rope should be replaced before next use. A splintery batten should be sanded smooth or replaced, and a small tear in a sail should be repaired immediately.

Finally, open all bungs or ports into buoyancy tanks and check them for water. If any, dry them out and find out how it got there as soon as possible. Leave them open during storage in order to allow condensation to dry out.

We prefer to hang our sails up in the boatshed for storage, and they are hung straight off the boat, wet. Sheets are also hung wet in open coils; masts on hooks along the wall; hooks close enough to support the mast so it does not bend, out of the way but easy to reach when required. Booms are usually short enough to store in the boat, along with the centreboard and rudder. The hulls may be racked or stored on the floor, but make sure they are chocked in order to prevent movement. Small sandbags make good chocks for floor storage. Our plywood racing skiff is stored on its trailer, which has been set up to support the hull correctly; although, when it is stored, the tie-down straps are removed or loosened.

Maintenance

'All hands turn to make do and mend' In the days before steam-, petrol-, diesel- or atomic-driven craft, the above saying was heard every day on sailing ships; all it means is that everybody on board had to get busy and do some repairs. It only stands to reason that the better kept boat will perform better than the one that is in a poor condition. Therefore you, together with your Patrol, should spend time during the winter months making and mending.

The amount of work to be done depends on the construction of the craft, the way in which it has been used and stored, and the type of water it has floated on. Regardless of how old the craft is, remember that somebody paid for it and that every Scout is responsible to the Group Committee to help look after it.

To do this, three basic things should be done regularly:
1. painting inside and out, except fibreglass, and making prompt repairs
2. keeping the craft protected when not in use during the off-season
3. handling the craft carefully with responsibility when it is in use.

To carry out maintenance properly, make out a schedule and check each section thoroughly.

The hull Inspect for splits in the planks, broken timbers, soft or rotten patches; if any of these are found make sure your Scouter is advised. Some of these repairs may be done by a Patrol under supervision, but if too bad, an experienced boat builder should be contacted. If anti-fouling paint has been used, it is better to sand the old coating off and repaint.

Hull fittings Do not fail to inspect the copper and brass fittings; replace if required. Scrape the paint from the rudder post, heel, and skeg, and repaint.

Steering controls Examine the steering linkages; replace rusted or weak cables and frayed ropes. Oil pulley blocks if of the older type. Many new-type blocks are being made of plastic and do not require much attention.

Oars and paddles, mast and spars Check carefully for splits or warping. Bind any small cracks, scrape off old varnish, and re-treat. If any of this equipment has any major trouble, it is better to replace it.

Standing and running rigging Frayed or rusted rigging lines should be replaced by new ones of the correct material.

Sails Repair when necessary. Wash sails with a good soap or detergent, hang them out to dry, and when you are sure there is no moisture, fold and pack them away.

Racing

Perhaps you have the competitive spirit. A sailing race may be a thrill from start to finish, and you will never forget the bustling crowd manoeuvring between the buoys on the line.

The sport of racing a sailboat is in the hands of very efficient clubs throughout Australia, and races are conducted within rules of international standard. It is therefore important that you obtain a list of these rules, which must be learnt if you are to be a competitor and succeed. There are keen sailors among Leaders, parents and friends who will help to teach you. If this is not the case, there is always a group of instructors at any yacht club.

All races start with the crossing of a line between two buoys. However, 10 minutes before the start there is a warning gun, and it is in this time that you try to set your craft in a good position to cross the line.

The two types of starting line

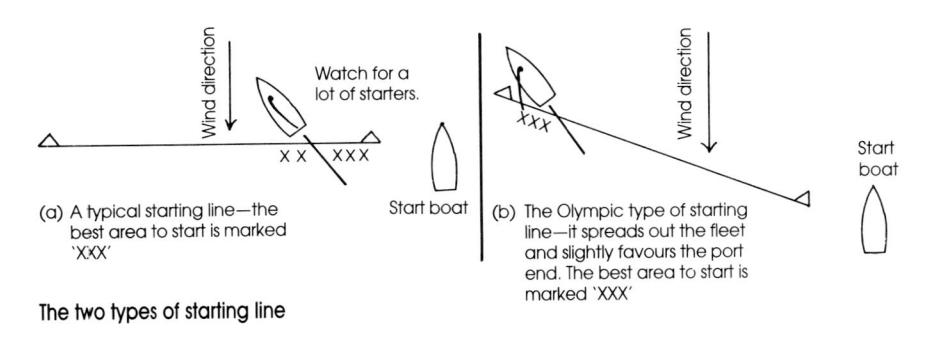

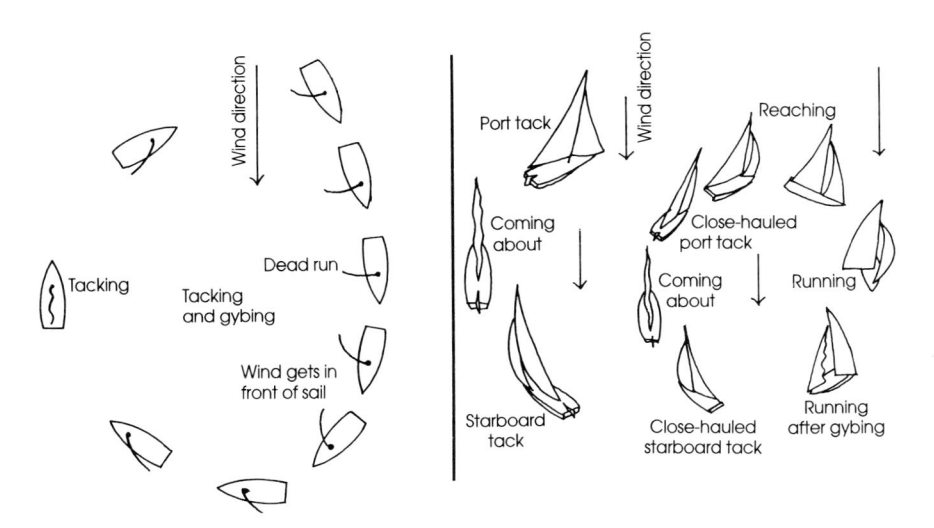

(a) A typical starting line—the best area to start is marked 'XXX'

(b) The Olympic type of starting line—it spreads out the fleet and slightly favours the port end. The best area to start is marked 'XXX'

Racing techniques

When you are a beginner, always watch the skippers who are considered to be among the best sailors of your class. They always manoeuvre themselves so they are not crowded and can get a good start over the line at the starting gun. If you develop a method based on theirs together with the knowledge of your own craft, you will soon see an improvement in your sailing. Having crossed the starting line, put your craft in a position so no other boat is stealing the wind from your sails. Remember that no boat can do its best unless its sails are properly hoisted and set; so always see that the luffs or forward edges are taut, and keep them set at the correct angle to the wind.

There are many techniques to be carried out, such as tacking and gybing and going about. These will come only with practice and training.

Finally, if at all possible, learn to sail with a qualified instructor, at a sailing club or with the Australian Yachting Federation (AYF). The AYF course to start with is the TL1; it will save you much frustration and help you to have many hours of fun afloat.

Sailboarding

In theory, a sailboard obeys the same principles as a sailboat; however, it has no rudder, a rudimentary centreboard, and a skeg or fin at the back.

In practice, the steering is done with the sail. Lean it forward and you will bear away from the wind; lean it back and you will point up into the wind.

Like all other boats, sailboards come in a variety of types and sizes, but there are two basic types: floaters and sinkers.

On a *floater*, you can stand, sit, have a breather, or work out how to make the next point you wish to reach. The *sinker* depends on its speed to plane over the water; it has to be moving to take your weight—not the board to learn on!

Because of the popularity of sailboards the AYF has designed a course to teach the art of sailboarding and we would recommend attending one. If you cannot do so, the basics are set out as follows.

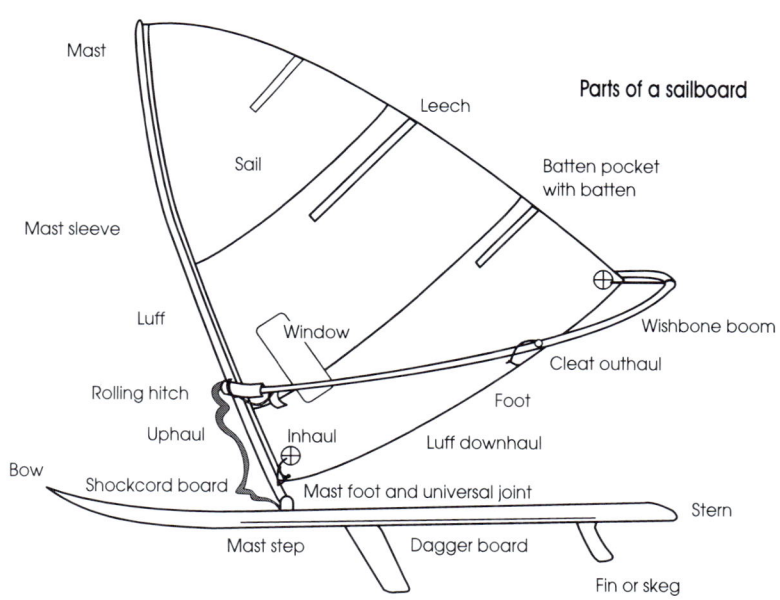

Parts of a sailboard

Labels: Mast, Leech, Sail, Batten pocket with batten, Mast sleeve, Luff, Window, Wishbone boom, Cleat outhaul, Rolling hitch, Foot, Uphaul, Inhaul, Luff downhaul, Bow, Shockcord board, Mast foot and universal joint, Stern, Mast step, Dagger board, Fin or skeg

Basic procedure

- In knee-deep water, face the board into the wind; the sail should be in the water on the side you wish to sail towards.
- From the other side, step up on to the board. Put your feet astride the mast, one foot on the daggerboard slot, facing the sail, and get your balance.
- Grasp the haul rope with your front hand, and haul up the mast hand over hand until you can grab the front of the boom with your front hand.
- Let the sail stream with the wind while you concentrate on balance, then, with the rear hand, grasp the boom a good shoulder's width back and lean the sail slightly forwards as you continue to bring the mast to upright. Surprise: you are sailing!

437

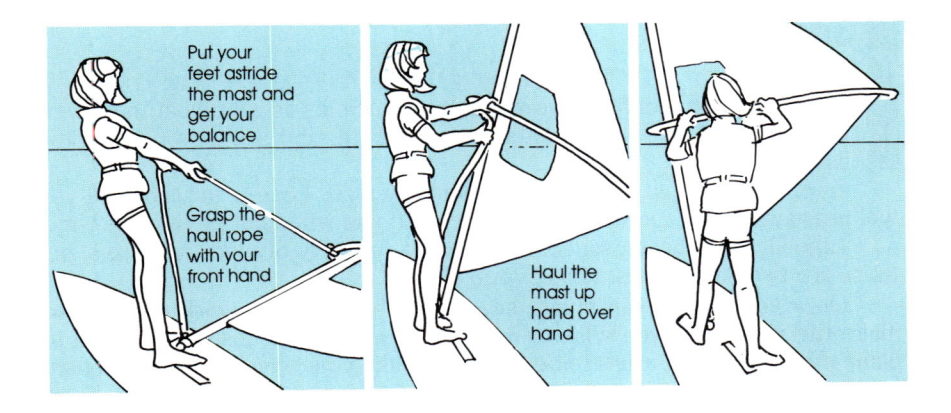

How to start

- As you gain speed, lean the mast slightly backwards to point you closer to the wind or slightly forward to steer away from the wind, paying out the sail as the wind comes behind you, or bringing it in as the wind comes ahead. Remember that an angle of about 45° to the wind is the best you can hope for.
- To *go about*, lean the sail back, and as you come into the wind, step around in front of the mast, lean the sail forward, and as you pay off, bring the sail in again.
- To *gybe*, let the sail spin forwards as you cross behind the mast, and pull it round with the new rear hand.

Easy, isn't it? We guarantee, though, that the first hour with a sailboard on the water will be 15 minutes sailing and 45 in the ditch if you are lucky. Do not give up: concentrate on the basics, and practise. The second hour will be better.

Safety

In all activities, especially water activities, the safety rules are there for your protection and are listed as follows.

- Never windsurf where there are swimmers—you might go over one, causing injury.
- Keep at least 100 metres from the bank or shore.
- Keep clear of rowing boats and canoes.
- Give way to civilian and commercial boats.
- Do not windsurf near port entrances or naval installations.
- Abide by the international 'right of way' rules for sailing craft.
- In an emergency, drop your sail into the water, and you will stop immediately.

Later, when you can sail comfortably, you will look back and laugh at the beginnings; we all do.

With practice comes skill. With skill comes the desire to go further, and this is the time to look at better boards for the type of sailing you want to develop, be it slalom or wave jumping or just plain speed.

Go to it, get wet, but have fun safely.

Power boating

Power boats have two basic forms of propulsion: *inboard* and *outboard*, and two basic hull types: *displacement* and *planing*. Each has its own peculiarities.

In small craft such as Scouts are likely to use, most inboards are on displacement hulls—the older style of open or semi-open or half-cabin timber hulls, and some are on GRP hulls. Hulls designed for outboards are mainly planing hulls.

The fundamental difference in handling an inboard or an outboard is the way they respond to the rudder. An inboard usually has the propeller in front of the rudder so the rudder is using the flow of the water over the hull as well as the prop wash in order to turn the craft. On the other hand, an outboard's propeller is the rudder, so the thrust of the prop is used to turn, and the torque of the propeller can speed the turn in one direction and slow it on the other. A displacement inboard tends to pivot amidships, whereas an outboard tends to pivot on the bow. No two boats handle the same. The variables include the shape of the hull, the size of the prop, the power from the engine, and the load on board.

Unless you are a very experienced boating enthusiast, we would not recommend taking Scouts afloat in a power boat that you have not used before. Spend an hour or two familiarising yourself with the vagaries of the boat and its engine. You should be familiar enough with the motor to be able to adjust and maintain it while afloat. After all, on the water we want to have fun, not put young people into danger.

In most Australian states, a licence is required to drive a power boat if it is capable of reaching certain speeds. This licence is a must for Scouts, as well as the correct Charge Certificate. Because most states do not have a practical examination for their licence, holding a licence does not automatically give you a Charge Certificate.

While you are loading crew and stores, the trim of the boat is important. You might think it looks great to have the bow pointing at the sky, but it is not. The boat has to be loaded so the engine can perform efficiently, and this is usually done by keeping the boat level, both fore and aft and sideways. Always insist that all people on board stay inboard. A youngster sitting with legs dangling over the bow is chewed up by the prop if he/she falls.

Half-cabin type

Runabout type

Fieldbook for Australian Scouting

Safety equipment

Power boats have their own requirements for safety gear. Apart from a bucket or bailer or pump and some paddles, what else do we require? Spare fuel, a fire extinguisher, a first-aid kit, tools to service the motor, spares including, naturally, spark plugs, shear pins for an outboard, and so on. Play it safe and get home.

If you are venturing offshore, a 'V'-sheet and flares, and a radio, are essential. A receiving radio can give you warning of weather changes, and a two-way radio allows you to call for help if needed, or to help someone else in trouble.

Using boats, caution is always the watchword.

Whatever type of boat you use, you should adhere to the following advice.

- Unless your motor can be started in neutral, make sure your boat is headed to open water.
- Be sure motor clamps are tight. Check each time. Use of safety chain or rope is essential.
- Operate your boat at all times with consideration for the boat, the motor, other boating enthusiasts, your passengers and your own safety.
- Never overload a boat.
- Make turns slowly until you are sure of the speed of turn your boat can safely take. Remember that the stern swings out on a turn.
- If your motor turns completely around to reverse, beware underwater obstructions. It is possible to take out a stern this way.
- Know the 'rules of the road'.
- Use Australian Standard approved lifejackets (AS 1512).
- In some Australian states, all craft must be licensed. Check for local regulations with the Commonwealth Department of Shipping and Transport.
- Carry appropriate lights if you are travelling at night.

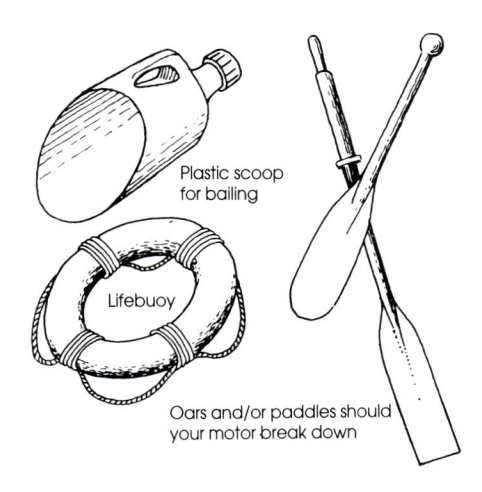

Plastic scoop for bailing

Lifebuoy

Oars and/or paddles should your motor break down

Safety aids

Water activities

(a) Never overload your boat. Carry an approved lifesaving device for everyone aboard

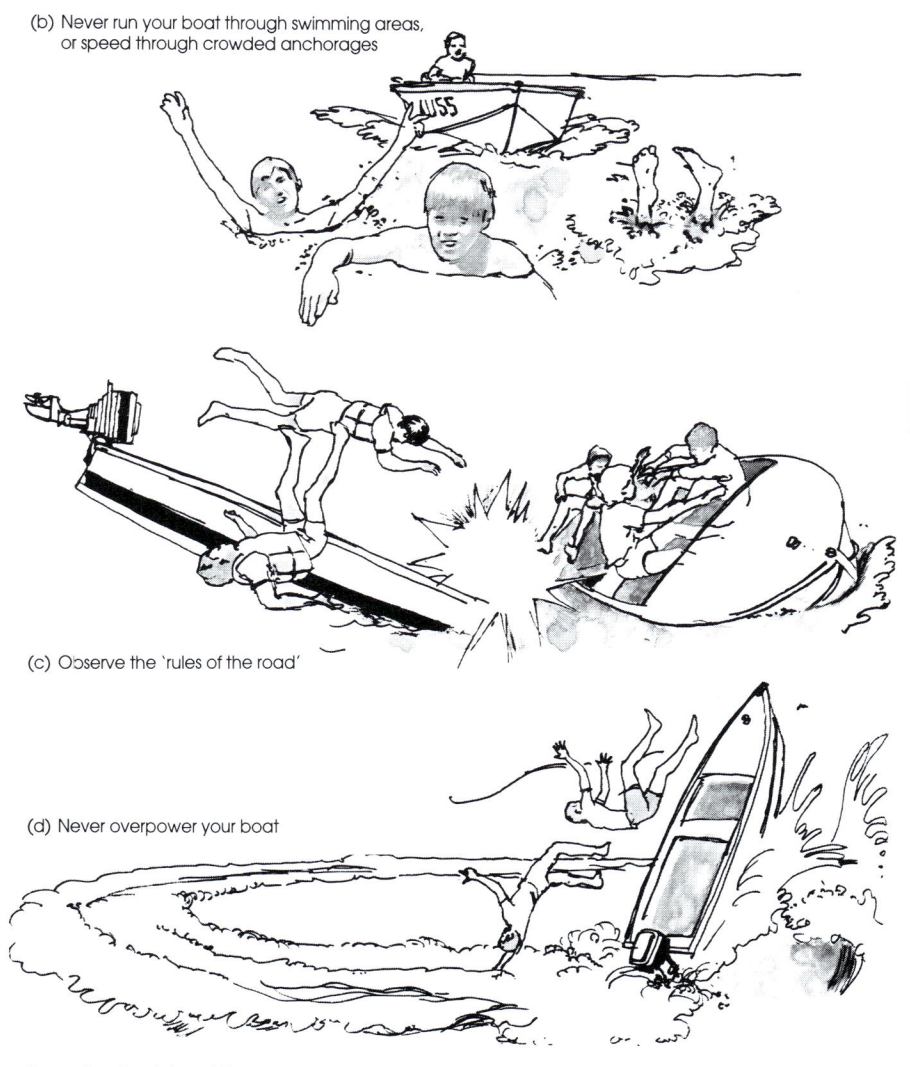

(b) Never run your boat through swimming areas, or speed through crowded anchorages

(c) Observe the 'rules of the road'

(d) Never overpower your boat

Power-boat safety advice

(continued)

441

Fieldbook for Australian Scouting

(e) Keep the cockpit and decks free of loose gear

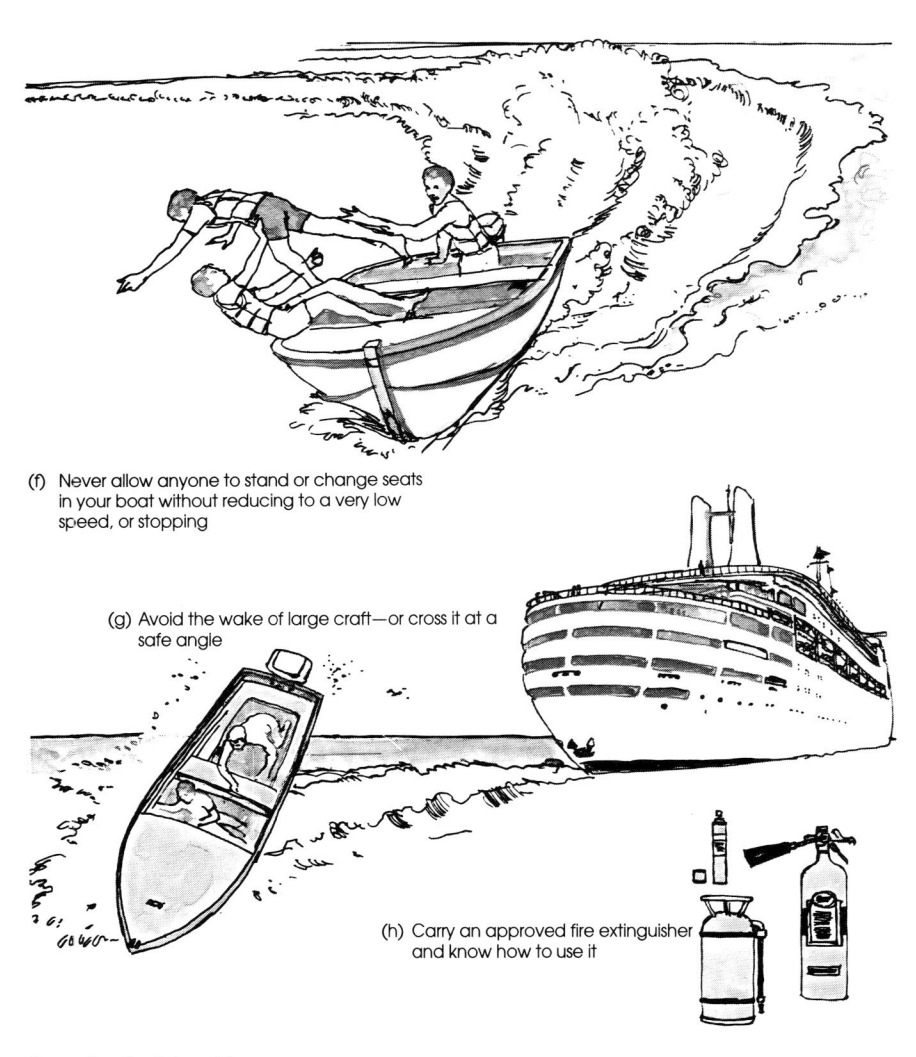

(f) Never allow anyone to stand or change seats in your boat without reducing to a very low speed, or stopping

(g) Avoid the wake of large craft—or cross it at a safe angle

(h) Carry an approved fire extinguisher and know how to use it

Power-boat safety advice

Care of motors

Proper care of an outboard motor will make it last longer and perform better.

Use only proper petrol and oils in your motor and mix in a can, not in your motor's fuel tank. Check the manufacturer's manual for the proper proportions to use.

If your motor is used in salt water, run it in a barrel of fresh water after use in order to remove salt water. If the motor is left on the boat, keep it tilted out of salt water when not in use.

If the motor is not to be used for a long period, store it on a stand. Drain gas from the tank, lines and carburettor; drain water from the motor shaft; refill with grease, and wipe the motor with light oil and cover it.

Keep the clamps holding the motor to the transom tight at all times. If the motor does fall overboard and is retrieved, do not use it until it is put in order by an experienced marine mechanic. You could ruin it if you try to recondition it yourself.

One of the most common repair jobs you will have to do on an outboard motor is replacing the shear pin. This is a piece of metal about 40 millimetres long that locks the propeller to the drive shaft. It is a safety device that breaks (shears off) when the prop hits a rock or other underwater obstruction, thereby saving the drive shaft from damage.

When the pin breaks, your propeller will not turn; however, it is a simple job to replace it:

1. Remove the cotter pin holding the propeller nut.
2. Remove the propeller nut.
3. Remove the propeller.
4. Remove the broken pin and install the new pin.
5. Replace the propeller, nut and cotter pin.

Always carry extra shear pins and cotter pins aboard.
Carry the following items:

- a screwdriver
- an adjustable wrench
- pliers
- a motor manual
- a spark plug.

Submerged motors

There are two situations to consider when you are dealing with a submerged motor: Did it go overboard while running or stopped? If a motor is lost overboard while running, it should always be disassembled before any attempt is made to start it. Internal parts are often sprung, and running the motor under these conditions can result in permanent damage.

A motor lost overboard in salt water for a period longer than two hours should always be disassembled and cleaned before starting is attempted. Some materials used in modern engines are subject to very rapid corrosion in the presence of salt water, and they should be inspected in order to determine whether replacements are required.

Fieldbook for Australian Scouting

A motor lost overboard in fresh water can usually be safely started if recovered within 12 hours, provided no sand or silt is present. Remove the spark plugs and the carburettor orifice screw, and drain all fuel lines and the tank. Pull the starter until all water present has been expelled. Re-assemble and start.

If sand has entered the engine, no attempt at starting should be made. Return it to the dealer for disassembly and cleaning.

If it is possible to have the engine serviced immediately after it has been retrieved after extended submersion, submerge the powerhead in clean fresh water in order to prevent oxidation until it can be serviced.

Anchoring and mooring

Anchoring

When a craft approaches the selected place to anchor, the skipper should head the craft into the wind or current, whichever is the stronger. In a power boat, he should cut the speed of the motor. In a sailing craft, the jib should be taken off. In a rowing boat or canoe, he should cease paddling. As soon as headway is lost, he should drop the anchor over the side until it hits the bottom. He then lets out more line, checking whether the anchor is set in the bottom and not dragging. If the anchor is holding, more line can be paid out to the extent of five to seven times the water depth. In other words, for water 3 metres deep, you pay out a minimum of 15 metres of line.

To *weigh* (pull up) *anchor*, propel the craft towards the anchor until the anchor is immediately below the craft, then continue to pull in the line. Take care as soon as the anchor can be seen, because you do not wish to jag it into the bottom of the hull.

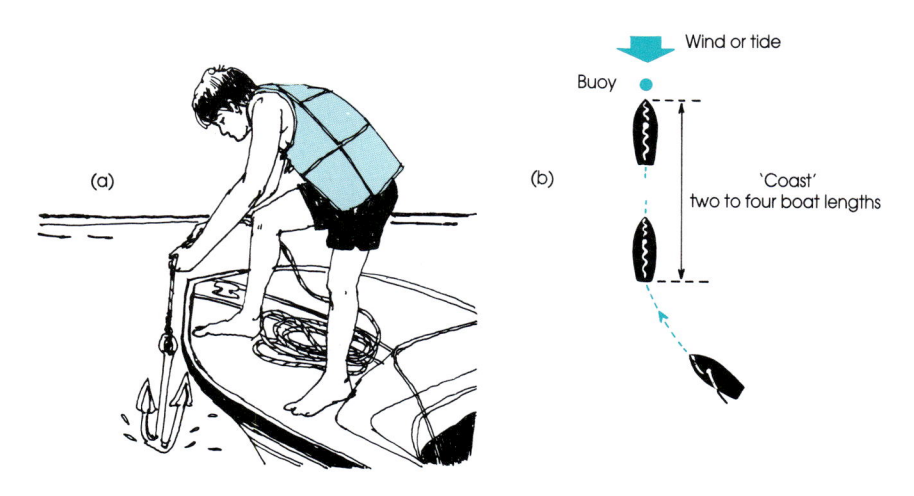

(a)   (b)

Wind or tide
Buoy
'Coast'
two to four boat lengths

Weighing anchor

444

Mooring

Approach the buoy or wharf in a way similar to anchoring with sail, jib off. This leaves the foredeck clear for the bowman to secure a line. To approach a jetty, run in at right angles. When you are a length or two of your craft away, turn to come alongside. Then secure to a bollard or cleat.

The advantages and disadvantages of three types of anchor are outlined as follows.

'Admiralty' pattern or 'yachtsman' anchor

Advantage It will grip in most sea-bottoms, but requires the stock to lie horizontally so the arms and flukes are at right angles to the sea bed. This means it may not get a firm grip on a rocky bottom, and may therefore hold only by the tip or a fluke.

Disadvantage It is very awkward to stow unless the stock is unshipped.

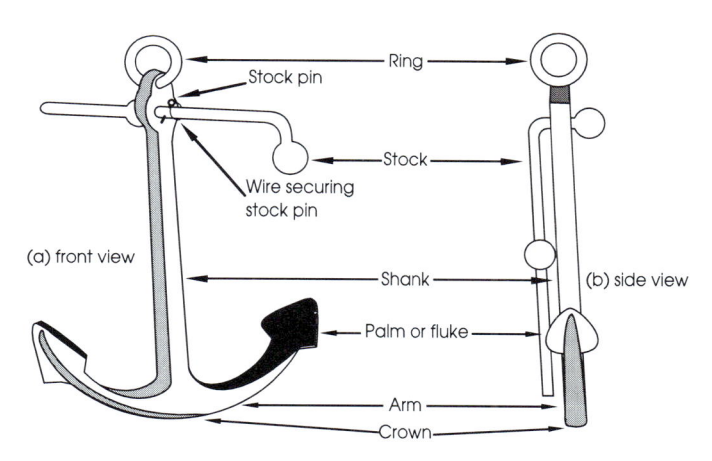

'Admiralty' pattern or 'yachtsman' anchor

'Danforth' pattern anchor

Advantage This is a good general-purpose anchor that is light in weight and easy to stow. Its main use is in clay, mud, and sand sea bottoms. In recent years it has become very popular for small sailing craft.

Disadvantage It is not much use for rocky sea bottoms. Its holding power is probably less than that of the 'Admiralty' pattern.

Grapnel anchor

Advantages This is good only for rocky and weedy sea bottoms. The several flukes can grip an irregular object.

Disadvantages It is bulky to handle and awkward to stow. Its holding power is not as good as that of other types, because the arms can bend and straighten out if there is too much strain.

'Danforth' pattern anchor — Ring, Shank, Palm or fluke, Stock, Crown

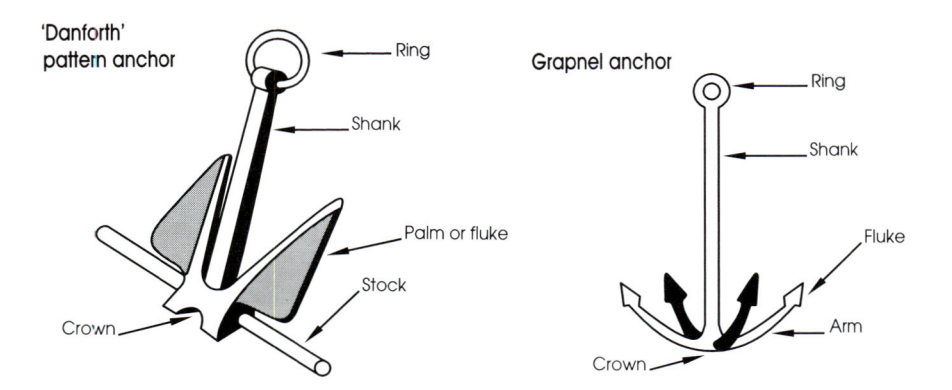

Grapnel anchor — Ring, Shank, Fluke, Arm, Crown

Sea anchor

A sea anchor is a conical- or pyramid-shaped canvas bag (with a small opening in the point of the cone), its mouth held open by a metal hoop or crossbars. When this is streamed on a warp, it acts as a brake on a vessel's speed through the water. A temporary sea anchor can be constructed by lashing two oars together crosswise and fitting a sail over them, or using a hatch cover weighted so as to float vertically.

A sea anchor can be used in order to slow down drift caused by sea and/or wind, to stabilise a yawing boat, and to give better steerage with heavy following seas.

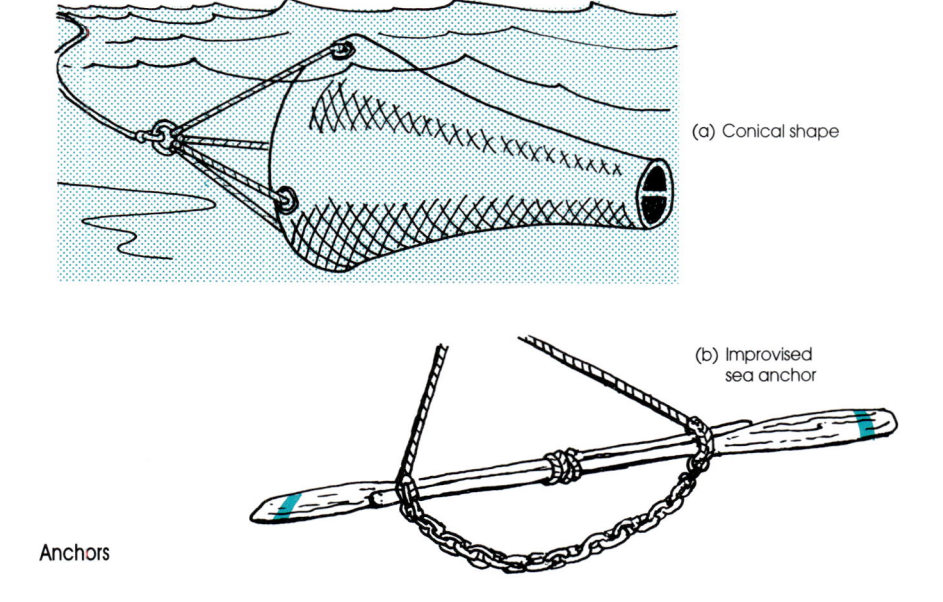

(a) Conical shape

(b) Improvised sea anchor

Anchors

Charts

The symbols used on an 'admiralty chart' or a chart of your local waterways

If you have already used *land maps* while hiking or orienteering, you should have little difficulty in getting to know about *admiralty charts*; although both have some similarities, there are important differences.

An admiralty (marine) chart has two main purposes:
- to show the position of landmarks that can be used to fix the position of your boat by observations
- to show the minimum depth of water you can expect under your boat at any position on the chart and at any time.

They also provide information such as:
- the maximum high tide and minimum low tide (spring tides) on the shoreline. The vertical height between these two is called the *drying height*, and is coloured light olive green. This is handy to know when mooring your boat in order to avoid finding it high and dry when the tide goes out
- the direction and speed of tidal currents during the periods of ebbing and flowing
- the position of hazardous objects such as rocks, wrecks, submarine cables and underwater pipelines
- the nature of the sea bottom as a guide to anchoring
- navigable channels and entrances to ports and the buoys or beacons that mark the safe passage for ships.

Several hundred symbols are used in order to provide all this information, but the following are the most frequently used.

Landmarks These are usually shown by names, such as 'Beacon', 'Church spire', 'Factory chimney', 'Red cliff' and 'Flagmast'. Surrounding hills are usually shown in contour form similar to that of land maps.

Soundings These are shown as numerous small figures scattered over the water area and are usually based on the 'mean low water spring tide' level. This means they show the least amount of water to be expected at the point where the number is placed. In older charts, these figures represent *fathoms*, but in modern charts they represent *metres*.

Lights If mounted on land or on rigid structures, these are always shown as a small five-pointed star, or a black dot, according to their importance. If mounted on a floating buoy, a small sketch of the buoy showing its shape is used. In all cases, these lights have a pear-shaped 'balloon' attachment coloured purple in order to make them readily visible on the chart.

Alongside each of these symbols is lettering to describe the nature of the light: 'F' means a Fixed light, 'Occ' means Occulting, 'Fl' means Flashing, and so on. The colour of the light and the time of its duration is shown by additional lettering such as 'R' (Red), 'G' (Green), 'W' (White) and 'O' (Orange), and times by '4 Sec.', '10 Sec.', and so on. If the light is in a prominent position above sea level, the distance it can be seen under clear weather conditions by a person in a boat is often also *nautical miles*.

Some admiralty-chart signs are as follows.

(a) (i) Position of important light   (ii) Position of minor light

(b) Examples of light description

(i) Gp Occ (2) WR 5 sec 60m 12M   (ii) F.R. 7m 10M

(c) (i) Buoys with top marks only   (ii) Light buoys with top marks   Admiralty – chart signs

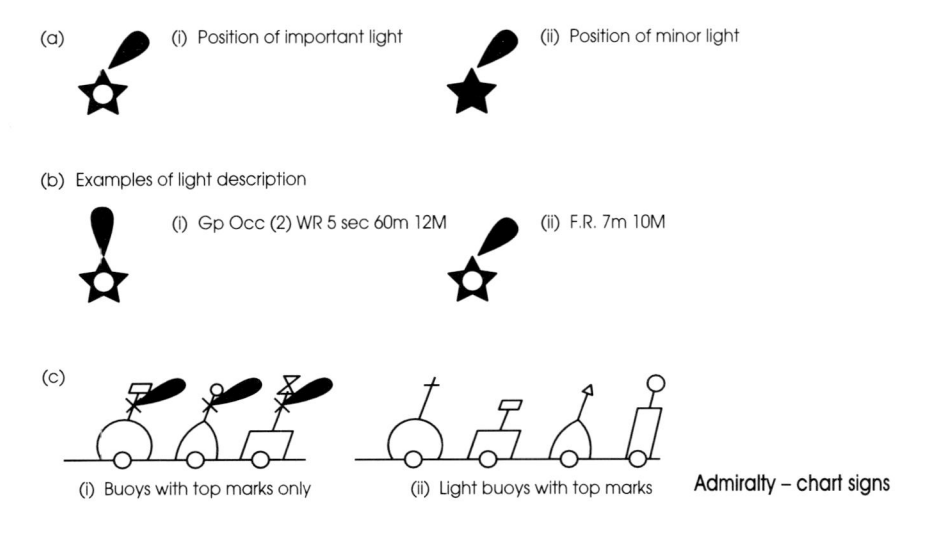

Quality of the sea bottom This is shown by abbreviations such as 'S' (Sand), 'M' (Mud), 'G' (Gravel), 'Cy' (Clay), 'R' (Rock), 'Wd' (Weed). This information is useful in deciding the best position for anchoring.

Tidal currents These are shown by arrows for both rising and falling tides. The arrows show the direction of water flow, and the speed in knots (nautical miles per hour) is shown by a figure above the arrow; for example, '5 Kn'.

Marine charts use geographical latitudes and longitudes, which are printed on all four margins of the chart.

Buoys

Buoys are floating devices, moored to the sea bottom, to mark shipping channels, shoals, banks, rocks or other dangers to navigation. They have coloured tops to indicate their purpose, and sometimes also a light so they can be seen at night. The positions of buoys and the type of light (if any) are shown on marine charts. The four main types of buoy in general use are as follows.

Starboard-hand buoys These are passed on the starboard or right-hand side of a vessel when entering a port from seaward. They are usually conical or beehive in shape, and are painted black all over or in black and white squares. Ships leaving on a voyage should pass these buoys on their port (left-hand) side.

Port-hand buoys These are passed on the port or left-hand side of a vessel entering a port from seaward. They are usually can shaped and painted red all over, or in red and white squares. Ships leaving on a voyage should pass these buoys on their starboard (right-hand) side.

Buoys are usually numbered from the seaward end of a channel, even numbers being given to port-hand buoys and odd numbers to starboard-hand buoys. This helps a skipper know how far he/she has gone up or down a channel.

Middle-ground buoys These are used to mark shoals or other obstructions in a channel. They may be passed on either side with safety. They may also be placed at the junction of two or more channels. They are usually

Water activities

Signs for tidal currents

(a) Steady current — 1 Kn
(b) Flood-tide stream — 5 Kn
(c) Ebb-tide stream — 5 Kn

Marine chart

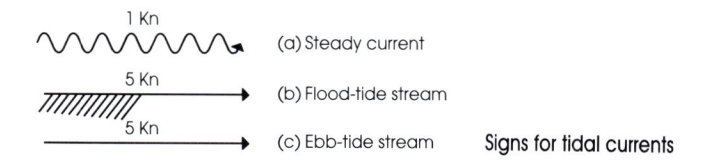

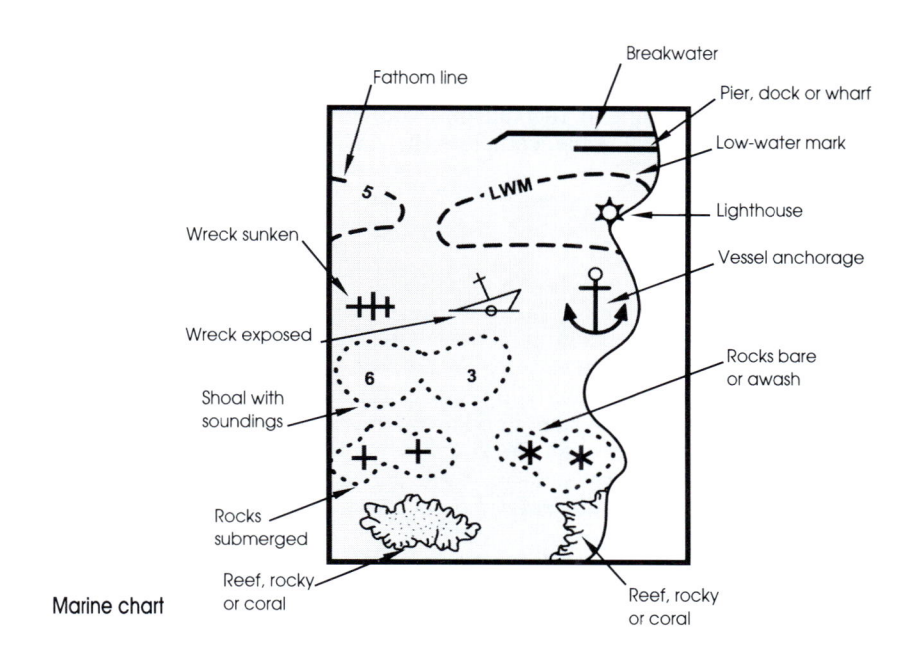

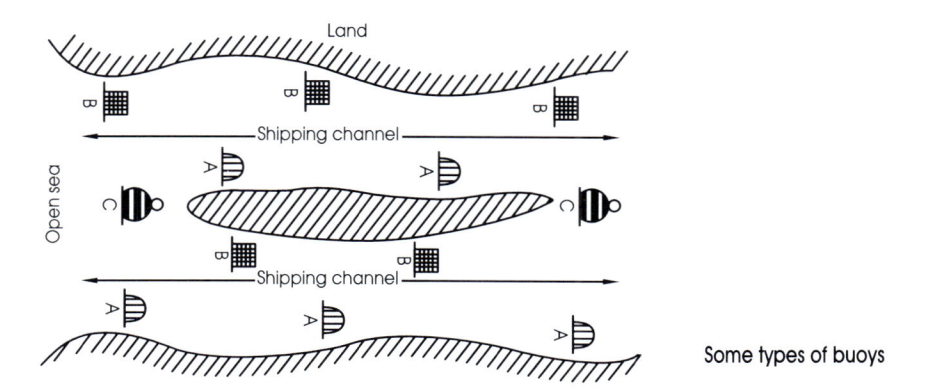

Labels: Fathom line, Breakwater, Pier, dock or wharf, Low-water mark, Lighthouse, Vessel anchorage, Rocks bare or awash, Reef, rocky or coral, Reef, rocky or coral, Rocks submerged, Shoal with soundings, Wreck exposed, Wreck sunken.

Some types of buoys

spherical in shape, and are painted with either red and white, or black and white horizontal stripes.

Special buoys These are used to mark wrecks, danger areas, telegraph or power cables, sewage tunnels, and similar local features, and usually carry

449

some sort of signboard to explain their meaning. They are provided mainly to warn against approaching too close, or to dropping an anchor nearby. If they are reasonably permanent, they are shown on marine charts.

Beacons

Beacons are usually structures placed on land to help a ship's captain find the way into port. They may take the form of lighthouses, factory chimneys, church spires or wooden trellis work set on poles. Sometimes they are simply stakes set in a shallow channel or river to mark the edge of deep water. They are usually shown on a marine chart.

We would recommend that anyone contemplating using power boats with Scouts should, if possible, complete the AYF TL3 training and the Rescue Boat Certificate.

Storing power boats

Modern GRP and aluminium boats are best stored undercover, out of the water. Wooden boats, depending on their size and construction, also benefit from dry storage. If you have to leave the boat on moorings, do not forget that it requires slipping regularly in order to remove growth and to anti-foul. If a reasonable beach is available in tidal waters, de-fouling the boat between tides can be a great exercise for the youngsters. As long as care is taken with supporting the hull properly and safely, and adequate supervision is available, a Troop or Patrol, even a Venturer unit, can have a lot of fun and do a useful job.

Storing motors is another story, however. Outboards require lots of care, particularly if used in salt water. As soon as ashore, the motor should be washed off and flushed through its cooling system with fresh water. Several methods are available to do this. We have used a clamp-on hose attachment which fits over the water intake. Turn on the hose, start the motor, and in five minutes there will be only fresh clean water in the system. Alternatively, set the motor in a 200 litre drum of water and run it for a few minutes. Then spray all over with de-watering material such as RP7 or WD40. Because most outboards have a large aluminium content, corrosion is a constant threat from salt water.

We recently heard of a 6HP being serviced then racked in the boatshed (over salt water) and not used for six months. When the owners went to use it, it was seized solid with internal corrosion. Prevention is always better than cure, and boating gear is not cheap. As the 'old salts' would say, 'Why spoil the ship for a penny's worth of tar?'

As with any form of boating, consult the experts.

Rafting

Rafting can be fun. As with all things on the water, however, safety is paramount. A little knowledge of 'Archimedes' principle' will help in designing a raft.

First, we have to know how big a raft we are building, how heavy it will be, and what load of people and stores it will have to carry. You will notice that weight is the common factor. Why? Because the flotation we use has to support that weight and its own weight.

One litre of water weighs 1 kilogram. If the raft, gear and crew members weigh 600 kilograms, 600 litres of water must be displaced in order to float at water level. Perhaps another 100 litres of displacement would bring the deck to an acceptable height above water.

The usual flotation used by *Scouts* is 20 litre drums or inner tubes. To support 600 kilograms we would require 30 drums just in order to float.

Moral: keep the weight down.

The large 800 litre drums would be very good, but they present another design problem: frontal area. When you try to paddle a raft as against the smooth nose of a canoe, that big area has a lot of water to push aside.

The old 12 gallon drums (about 60 litres) would be very good, if you can find them.

Inner tubes are also very good, because they can be partly inflated and then squashed in order to reduce the frontal area. Large-car or small-truck tubes work best, we have found, but most cars are now tubeless. Big-truck tubes work well, but are heavy. A combination of both—big tubes for main flotation, small tubes to build up the height—will work.

Designing the raft

Experience has shown that a catamaran or trimaran is the most efficient design. The frame must be strong enough to support the load yet light enough not to overload the flotation.

Years ago, when we could cut trees without causing environmental repercussions, we would select a regrowth area some years after a bushfire, then thin out the tall, close-together saplings, perhaps 6 to 7 metres tall and about 70 or 80 millimetres in diameter at the ground. We would trim them, cut them to about 3.5 metres, de-bark them, bundle them together, and hang them from the ridge of the hall by one end of the bundle until thoroughly dry. This process took about two months. The wood was reasonably straight, light and strong and provided the material for our frames.

The frame could be lashed or bolted together. Caution: of you lash, use a cheap twine rather than good ropes. After a couple of days in the water, rope can be very difficult to untie; binder twine or similar can be cut off and discarded. The best twine we ever used was the rayon used in early corded

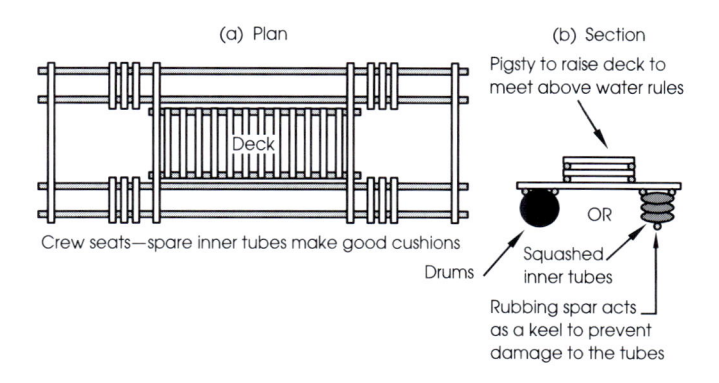

(a) Plan

Deck

Crew seats—spare inner tubes make good cushions

Drums

(b) Section

Pigsty to raise deck to meet above water rules

OR

Squashed inner tubes

Rubbing spar acts as a keel to prevent damage to the tubes

Raft frame

tyres; we managed to score a roll from an old Scout friend who made it. Modern polypropylene-type cord would be satisfactory.

Another suitable material for the frame is plastic conduit (the larger sizes) or plastic water pipe about 50 millimetres in diameter. A plug of polystyrene foam to seal each end and the trapped air will add to the flotation.

Squashed inner tubes or drums are lashed to the underside of the frame and—presto!—you have a raft. To get sufficient tubes on the frame, two, sometimes three, layers are necessary. If the bed of the stream is likely to be rough, an extra spar can be slung under the tubes to act as a rubbing strip.

Another tip to help keep the tubes in place and to reduce drag is to insert the tubes in a woven polypropylene bag and then inflate them. The bags do not weigh much, and the saving in lashing and drag is worth it.

A cone of polystyrene or light tin plate attached to the front and rear drums will help reduce the drag. Polystyrene blocks could also be used as flotation, but purists and traditionalists tend to frown on this practice.

Some Districts have an annual two-day raft race for Venturers, down a well-known river. These are often divided into two divisions: traditional and hi-tech, simply because some of the Units come up with some real technology in building their rafts—even to rowing with oars on sliding seats, and GRP over tube hulls. A traditional inner tube or drummed raft could not hope to match that speed potential. (*See* 'Rafting' section in Chapter 5: Construction, pages 275–8, for other raft ideas.)

Learn the language

As with any sport, boating has its own language, but you do not have to know all the terms in order to enjoy boating. You will feel more at home in boating circles, however, if you understand some of the terms. Listed are a few that will be used with row boats, sail, canoe and power boats, and as you improve your boating skill and work with other people, your knowledge and the use of terms will come naturally.

Two of the most important terms head the following glossary, and it is suggested you know these completely.

Glossary

starboard   the right-hand side of a craft when facing forward to the bow; colour used day and night: green

port   the left-hand side of a craft when facing forward to the bow; colour used day and night: red

amidships   half-way between bow and stern
beam   the greatest width of the craft
belay   to fasten a rope to a cleat or belaying pin

Water activities

blade   the flat or curved part of an oar or paddle used to propel the boat; also describes the flat part of a rudder that actually does the steering

bolt rope   rope sewn into the edge of a sail

boom   a pole or spar to which the foot (lower edge) of a sail is bent (attached)

bow   forward or front end of a craft

break out   to unfurl (as for a flag or sail)

carvel built   a system of planking on wooden boats; each plank is shaped to fit exactly to the adjacent planks, thereby giving a very smooth hull. Gaps between planks were caulked with cotton or hemp soaked in tar or, on small boats, red lead

centreboard   a movable plate of wood or metal that can be raised or lowered through the keel of a boat

chain plate   a fitting, usually on the gunwale to attach the shrouds

chart   marine version of a map showing aids to navigation, shoals, rocks, water depth, dangers, and so on

cleat   a fitting, usually shaped like a 'T' with a short leg and a base, to belay a rope

clinker built   a system of planking wooden boats; each plank overlaps the previous plank. The name is a corruption of the word 'clencher', because each plank was secured by nails clenched over on the inside of the hull. In North America this system of boat building is called 'lap-strake', 'strake' being a plank in the hull

cockpit   open part or well of the boat where the crew members sit

crutch   swivelling 'Y'-shaped fulcrum for an oar

draught   depth of water a boat requires to float in

forestay   the stay to the front or bow of the boat to hold the mast from falling backwards

frames   the transverse members that give the hull its shape

gaff   a spar used at the head of older style mainsails that were four sided

gunwale   originally the top plank of a wooden ship with openings for the cannons to fire; now, the top plank or its equivalent on any hull

helmsman   the person who steers the craft

high   an area of high atmospheric pressure; winds usually rotate anti-clockwise around a high

hull   the main structure of a craft

keel   the main structural framing of a vessel; it runs from the stem to the stern, and the stem and sternposts and ribs or frames are built from this spar. In moulded GRP or plastic boats, it may only be a moulded shape or reinforcing

lanyard   a length of light rope used to secure losable objects

loom   the part of an oar between the blade and the stopper

low   an area of low atmospheric pressure; winds usually rotate clockwise around a low

mast   the upright spar that supports a sail or flags

port   left side of craft when facing the bow

pram flat-bowed boat, usually a dinghy

reaching the point of sail when the wind is coming from the side of the boat

ribs similar to frames used in a planked boat, usually curved by steaming

rowlock similar to a crutch, with a lock pin that prevents the oar from lifting out

rudder movable plate fixed to the stern by which a craft is steered

running the point of sail when the wind is coming from approximately behind the boat; 'abaft the beam'

shackle a 'D'-shaped metal unit used in order to secure a rope to an eye bolt or chain plate

sheet the rope used in order to control a sail

shrouds the wires used in order to support a mast sideways

skeg an external addition to the keel of a boat, intended to help give the boat lateral stability (to help it track straight); on an inboard power boat, it often contains the prop shaft; on sailboards, it is the fin at the back

starboard right side of craft when facing the bow

stays the wires used in order to support a mast fore and aft

stem upright that forms the bow

stern after or back end of a craft

stopper or stop fitting on the loom of an oar in order to prevent the oar from passing too far through the crutch. Traditionally made by wrapping leather around the oar; mostly moulded plastic nowadays; also called the button

strop usually a circle of rope, fibre or wire, made as a grommet, or simply knotted

tacking the act of sailing a zigzag course to sail upwind

thole pin an old method of pivoting an oar; a single wooden pin let into the gunwale with a rope strop around both the oar and the pin

thwart a timber or metal piece that holds the sides of the boat apart; often made wide enough to use as a seat

topsides the sides of the craft from the water line to deck

waterlogged full of water, but still floating (proving adequate buoyancy)

whisker pole a short spar used to pole out the jib when running before the breeze

So there we have it. As the quote from *The Wind in the Willows* goes, there is simply nothing like messing about in boats.

Learning to swim

It is fun to play and swim in the water, but only if you are safe and confident. Learning to swim is a good way to make you confident, but you will find that being able to swim can also put you in danger. Learn all you can about water safety as you learn to swim, and you will be safer and more confident, and more able to enjoy the water.

Water activities

When you are learning to swim, you will progress from an easy stage to a more difficult stage, until you can move through the water, on front or back, with ease.

Some of you will be able to swim already, and most of you will be well adjusted to water. If you are a beginner, study the four main stages set out as follows.

1. Adjustment to the water

If you can hold your breath and duck underneath the water, you have overcome one of the biggest problems in learning to swim. You can learn to control your breathing by bobbing up and down in the water, and when you can do this with your eyes open, you are ready for the next stage. It is fun adjusting to water, because most of the time is taken in playing games.

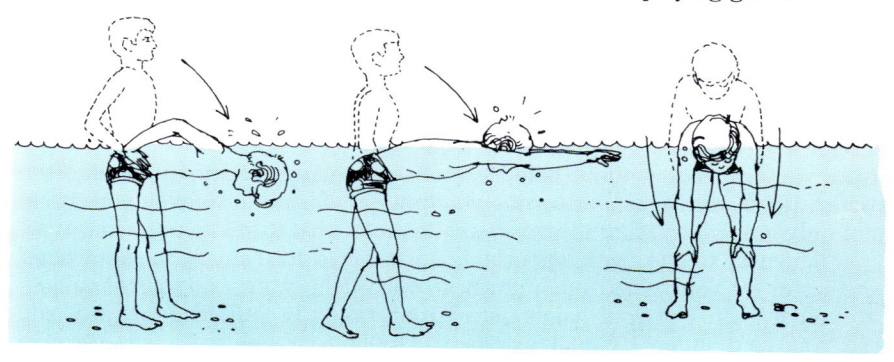

Stage 1: Adjustment to the water

2. Body-buoyancy and safety skills

It has been said that floating is about half of learning to swim. Let us, then, see whether we can get halfway there. The easiest float to learn is the 'jellyfish' float, which means relaxing on top of the water with your arms and legs dangling towards the bottom. This is quite easy to learn, but you must remember to hold your breath and to start the float slowly with your shoulders under the water. To be safe, you should always work with a partner who can help you back on your feet if you require it. Remember: walking in chest-deep water is like walking on the moon—you float and lose your balance. Plenty of games are therefore necessary in order to get you used to this strange feeling. It will not be very long before you can do a 'dead person's' float with arms and legs stretched out so you are streamlined like a torpedo. You can practise pushing one another at targets, as if to blow them up.

It is very important that you learn the 'back' float at this stage. If you cannot do one, now is the time to learn. People who can float and swim on their backs have learnt a safety skill that could save their lives. It is easier to swim on your back if you are tired, because you do not have to worry about controlling your breathing, which you must do if you can swim only on your front. Make sure you learn how to regain your feet from front and back floats before you continue through the skills.

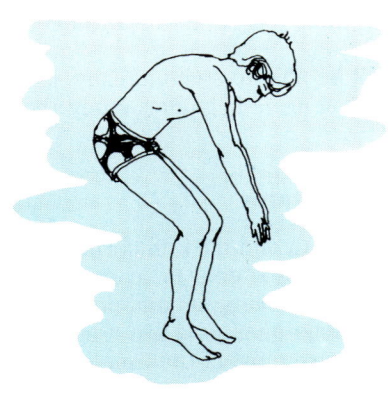

Fieldbook for Australian Scouting

Stage 2: Body-buoyancy and safety skills

3. Movement-through-the-water and safety skills

Now you can float without help, it is an easy matter to move through the water. Begin with a partner towing you first on your front, then on your back: not only is this good fun; it gives you a taste of what it is like to swim.

The next step is a very important one, because you actually move through the water by yourself. Crouch down in waist-deep water so your shoulders are underneath. Put your hands out in front, take a breath, lean forwards and put your face under. By pushing against the bottom, you will move through the water under your own power. Practise with a partner at the beginning, aiming at a few metres first, and gradually increasing the distance until, by pushing against the side of the pool, you find you can move many metres through the water. Again, become confident on both front and back before you worry about the arms or legs.

The kick you learn is the 'flutter' kick, which is efficient only if you have a relaxed leg, a pointed toe and a steady kick. You will find that practice with a kickboard will be less boring than kicking on the side of the pool, and you

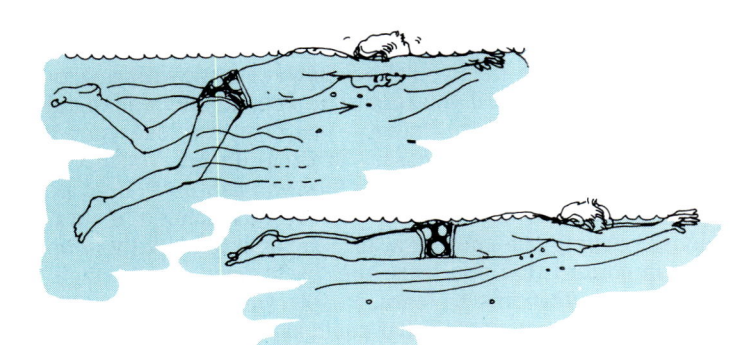

Stage 3: Movement-through-the-water and safety skills

456

can tell whether you are making the movements correctly by observing the speed at which you progress through the water.

There are lots of games you can play now you are confident, can float and can move through the water, but remember: *water-safety knowledge* is your protector—do not leave *it* out of your fun.

4. Combining legs-and-arms and safety skills

One way of moving through the water on your back is by finning with your hands. Your hands act the same as a fish's fins, moving backwards and forwards by your side. Keep your arms straight and make your wrists do most of the work. Again, work with a partner first, until you can combine the flutter kick with the finning well enough to move across the pool.

Coaches have different ideas about teaching 'front crawl', but the easiest way is to experiment with as many different methods as possible. Begin with a front glide and flutter kick, and then add one or two long dog-paddle strokes. Next attempt two or three straight-arm crawl strokes.

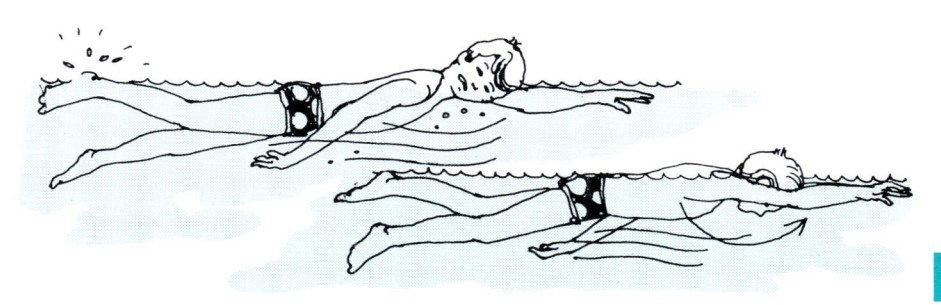

Stage 4: Combining legs-and-arms and safety skills

Gradually build up distance with both strokes, and then, combining the straight-arm action above the water with the bent-arm action of the dog paddle under water, you will have mastered the stroke. Remember to keep your head down, in the same line as when you were practising the front glide. Naturally you cannot travel for very long underwater, therefore you will have to learn how to breathe correctly to the side. If you have been practising your bobbing all this time, the controlled breathing should come more easily, but do not expect to become an expert in one or two lessons.

Some of the safety skills you should learn now are:

- rolling over from front to back, changing strokes, but continuing to swim
- rolling over from back to front
- swimming to the centre of the pool, turning around and returning to the edge
- treading water
- jumping into deep water, levelling off, and swimming back to the edge.

Fieldbook for Australian Scouting

(a) Freestyle stroke: side view

(b) Elementary backstroke: side view

Basic freestyle stroke and backstroke

Water activities

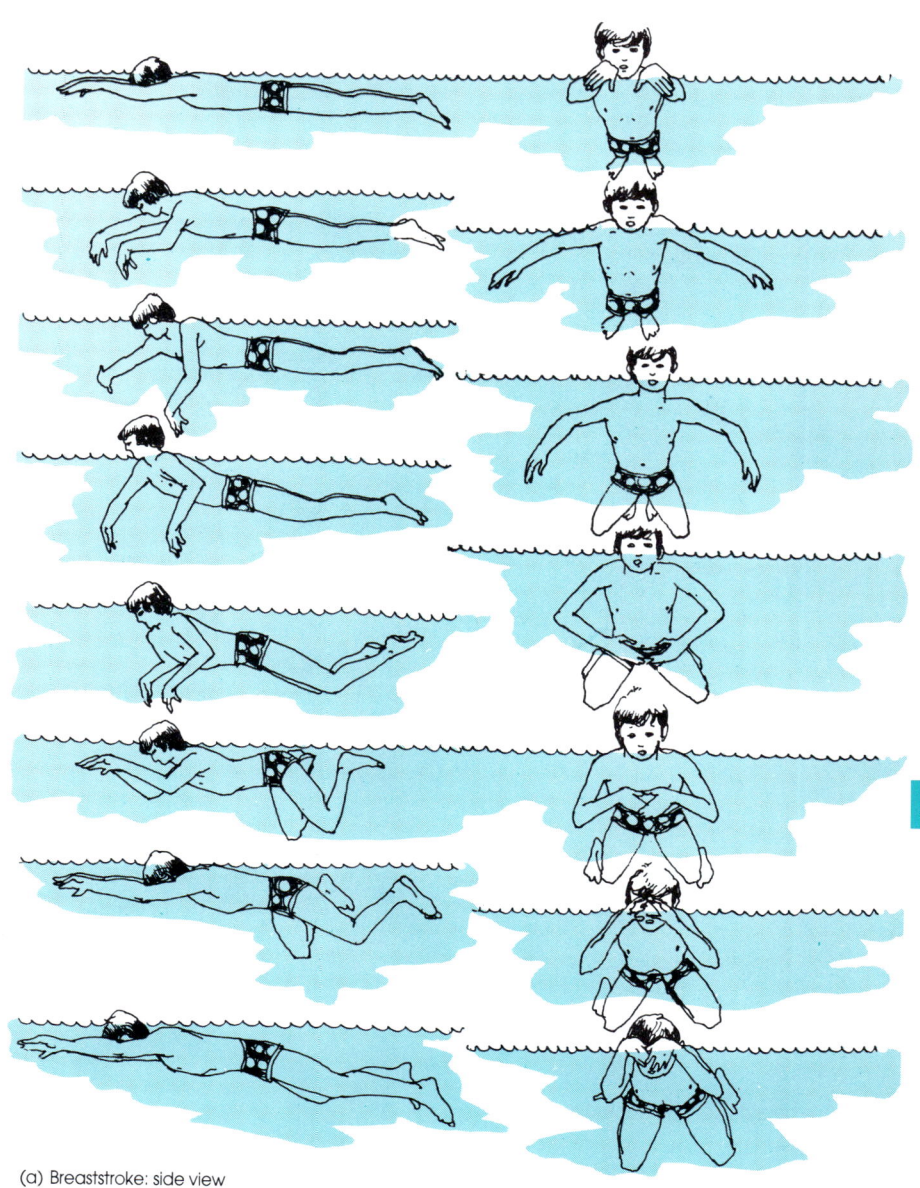

(a) Breaststroke: side view

(b) Breaststroke: front view from below the line of travel

Breaststroke

459

Fieldbook for Australian Scouting

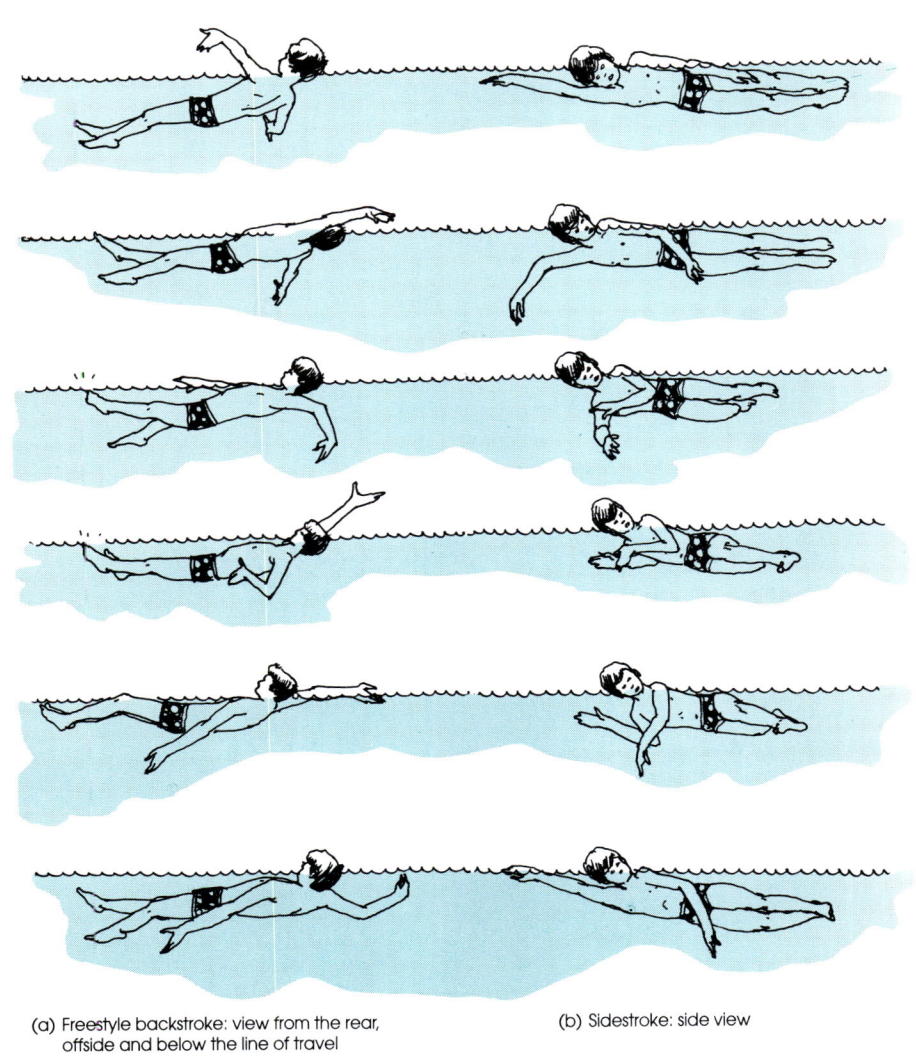

(a) Freestyle backstroke: view from the rear, offside and below the line of travel

(b) Sidestroke: side view

Freestyle backstroke, and sidestroke

Table 8.3 Faults in swimming styles

Minor faults		Major faults	
Front freestyle		**Front freestyle**	
Feet clearing surface on kick	Head buried	Completely irregular breathing or tossing of head to breathe	Legs straight and stiff on kick
Lack of roll	Sway at hips		Kick from knee only
Arms crossing in front of head on recovery	Over-kicking		Overall lack of rhythm
	Tensed forearm on recovery	Legs dropping (poor body position)	Awkward or stiff arm action
	Straight-arm pull		
Back freestyle		**Back freestyle**	
Arms not recovering above shoulder height	Irregular breathing	'Sitting' in water (poor body position)	Water over swimmer's face consistently
	Intermittent kicking	Arms reach behind head	Legs stiff, straight on kick
Hesitation on arm action (not continuous)	Lack of roll	Introduction of sculling action	
	Head buried		
	Straight-arm pull		
Breaststroke		**Breaststroke**	
Prolonged glide	Feet break surface often	Lack of full extension (lack of momentary glide phase)	Arms pull past shoulders
Slight asymmetry of kick			Thrusting on kick (ankles plantar flexed on drive)
Wide-arm pull	Irregular breathing		
Pike at waist on leg recovery	Arm-stroke lifts swimmer out well beyond chin	Straight-arm pull	
Feet break surface often		Use of wedge or scissor kick	
Sidestroke		**Sidestroke**	
'Fishtailing' (legs cross over after kick)	Straight arms on pull	Head held vertically (usually results in poor body position; legs drop)	Not coordinated as an alteration of lower arm pull with paired action of upper arm and legs
Over-reach (beyond chin) or over-pull (beyond side) or upper arm	Prolonged glide		
	Irregular breathing		
	Excessive spread of legs on recovery (*Note:* Regular or inverted scissors may be used)	Swims on front instead of side	Use of rotary or flutter kick
Gradual drop of lower arm on glide			Absence of full extension (momentary glide)
Slight pike position (bent at waist)			
Elementary backstroke		**Elementary backstroke**	
Hips drop on leg recovery	Irregular breathing	Not coordinated as a paired arm and leg action	Use of wedge or scissor kick
Slight sculling on glide	Slight scissoring on kick	Arms recover out of water or directly out to side	'Sitting' position in water
Prolonged glide	Straight-arm pull		Head goes under on each stroke
		Knees rise out of water on recovery	Pronounced sculling or flutter kicking on glide

Warning: Never dive or jump into shallow or unknown water—serious injury can result.

The techniques of rowing and paddling, rigging a sailboat, and packing gear into the craft, are all good Patrol activities. Repairs and maintenance, weather forecasting, and so on, make ideal night programs.

It does not matter how many hours you spend on theory, because the more you know the subject, the better prepared you are; there is no substitute for practical knowledge, however, so practise all you can—it will develop skill and confidence.

In the beginning, all practical work should be carried out in water just deep enough to allow the craft of your choice to float without touching the bottom. Practise capsizing and recovery—then you will not panic if it happens in deep water.

Before going out into the deeper water, be sure you can swim, and always wear your lifejacket.

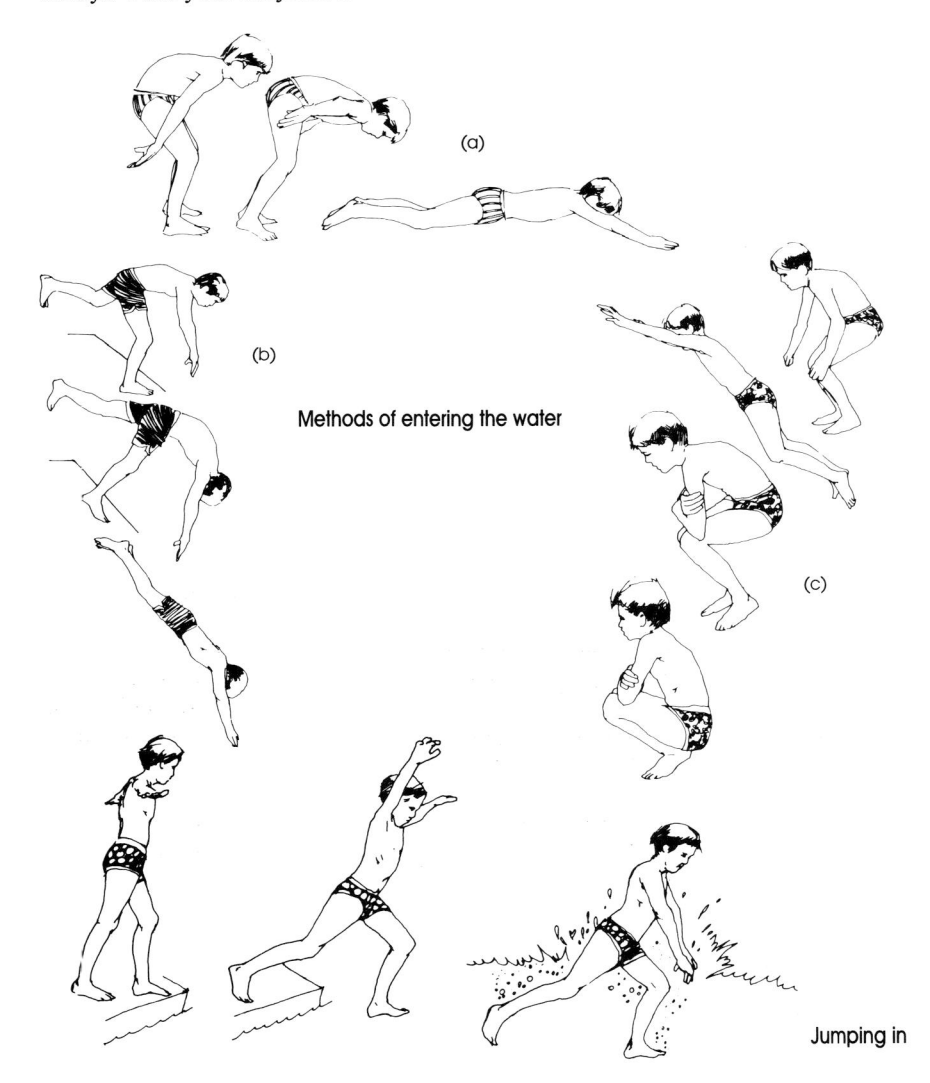

Methods of entering the water

Jumping in

9
WINTER FUN

Winter camping

This knowledge is required for some parts of Australia and if you are touring overseas.

Winter camping has its unique delights that make it an exciting alternative to summer camping. Besides the difference in temperatures, winter camping means coping with new conditions such as adequate shelter and keeping warm and dry. Winter camping means you and your group are more than 'fair-weather' campers: you can live with nature in all its forms, all year round.

Winter camping requires different preparation, and it demands you be much more careful. A mistake made in other seasons may be only an inconvenience, whereas the same error in winter can mean disaster. There are many advantages in winter camping, however, one of them being that you do not need insect repellent. There are many activities to enjoy in winter, including skiing, snowshoeing, sliding and tobogganing.

In this chapter, 'winter camping' means camping at temperatures below freezing and being limited to the tree zone; special winter camping requires special skills, equipment and knowledge and is beyond the scope of this book.

Where to go

If winter camping is a tradition for your Group, you may already have a favourite winter camping spot. You may want to hike to a summer haunt or go to your supper camp. In winter, the scenery changes completely and may feature snow-covered trees and open woods. In some countries the trees will be leafless. The drifting snow gives everything a new shape, and soft new snow makes it easier to track winter birds and animals.

If it is your first winter camp, you should give a lot of thought to selecting a suitable campsite. You must think about how much time you have; how easy it is to get there, whether there is shelter, water and firewood available, and how you will travel.

Weather

Careful attention must be paid to weather reports as part of the preparation for the winter camp. They are usually quite dependable, and for those skiers are useful for snow conditions.

What to wear

In order to truly enjoy winter camping, you must keep warm. The clothing you wear will not make you warm; it will only keep you warm. The warmth is generated from your own body. The clothes you wear will either hold in that heat, thereby keeping you warm, or let it escape and leave you cold.

The secret of keeping warm is to wear layers of loose-fitting clothing, to control perspiration by letting the normal body moisture evaporate, and to keep out the wind. If you wear layers of clothing—two light jumpers instead of one bulky heavy one, two pairs of woollen socks instead of one heavy pair, and so on—the trapped air spaces between the layers will act as insulation almost as much as the clothing itself, and will help keep the heat in.

This space also allows for the normal perspiration to move away from your body. Then, as you perspire from exerting yourself on the trail, setting up the camp, or playing games, you can peel off layers of clothing. Then, as you stop activities, you can add layers to keep warm. If your clothes get damp from perspiration, the insulating property is lost and you will be as cold as if you were wearing light clothing.

In short, winter clothing should achieve three things if you are to be comfortable in winter weather:
1. ventilation
2. insulation
3. wind protection.

A typical winter suit includes long underwear. This could be the fishnet type with 9 mm mesh or larger, and about 5 millimetres in thickness. Smaller holes and 'waffle' construction do not allow enough evaporation. Insulating underwear should not be worn next to the skin because it will absorb perspiration rather than let it evaporate. The exception is woollen underwear, which keeps its insulating properties even when damp.

Winter fun

Next a woollen shirt and pants will make up the first outer layer, followed by a woollen jumper or vest for the second layer. Depending on the cold, you may either cover up with an insulated parka or wear a light jacket, woollen cap, and shoepacks.

There are two ways to cool off while wearing the insulating layers: remove certain layers, or increase the ventilation. Depending, again, on the conditions, whether you are hiking or camping, you may do one or the other. Remember that, on the track, removing layers may be awkward, especially if you have to pack away the removed layer.

Ventilation begins at the points of your body that are the most effective radiators. Remove your parka hood first, keeping your hat on. The opening of your neck and shirt front will allow the heat from your torso to escape. A two-way zipper is very handy in this case. Opening your cuffs has a dual advantage: the wrists and hands are excellent radiators because of the large blood vessels near the skin surface. The air movement up the sleeves will draw warm air away from the arms, especially the underarm area. You can ventilate the lower part of your body by opening your trouser cuffs (a problem in deep-snow conditions) or using high side zippers on your trousers.

Once the ventilation openings are created, airflow should be encouraged by flapping your arms.

Wind protection is important to maintaining the other two conditions. Your parka will take care of this if it is cotton, three-quarter length, and you have nylon wind pants. If these are waterproofed, they can provide rain protection, too. A wind parka and pants may also solve the problem, but they are not waterproof. A nylon poncho may have to be worn, but this will prevent body moisture from escaping, thereby cutting down on your insulation.

Footwear

For hiking without snowshoes or skis, the temperature, weather and the nature of the terrain will suggest the footwear—either moccasins, shoepacks or larrigans, mukluks, laced leather ankleboots or high-cut boots.

(a) Mukluk
(b) Shoepack
(c) Boot
(d) Galosh

Snow footwear

(a) Larrigan

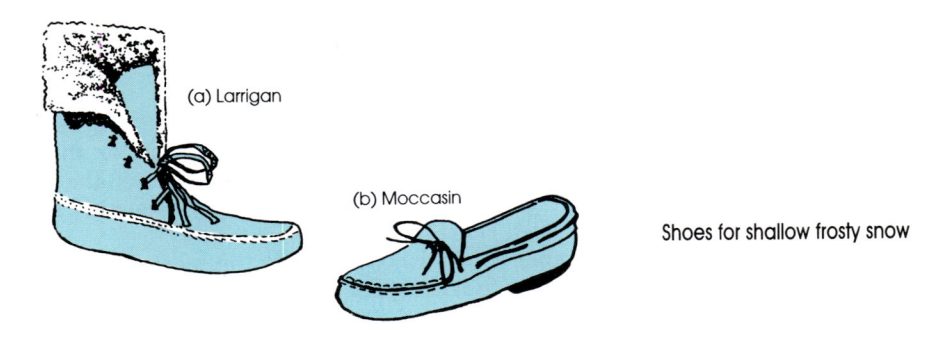

(b) Moccasin

Shoes for shallow frosty snow

For frosty snow that is not too deep, the moccasin is ideal. When you are hiking over bare rough ground, or where you may hit wet snow, as in the middle of a sunny day, the shoepack or larrigan is best. Rubber overshoes worn over moccasins or road shoes also work well in this type of weather. Unless your regular snowboots are lightweight, leave them at home: they are too warm, too heavy, and are likely to cause sweating during long, non-stop hiking.

Footwear should be roomy enough to allow you to wear two pairs of woollen socks plus felt or fleece insoles. These layers inside your boots absorb moisture and keep your feet dry and warm. Tight boots lead to frozen toes or feet, because they cut down on your circulation.

Take along a spare pair of moccasins to change into when the heavy going is over for the day: they will be comfortable and dry and will help prevent frosted toes and cold feet.

Clothing

Socks

Socks should be of soft wool and should be smooth fitting without being too tight. There should be no holes or hard spots where the socks have been mended. Wear two pairs, the second pair a half size larger. Socks should be long enough to roll for dry snow or to pull up well on the calf when you are travelling through damp or melting snow.

Tops

Over your underwear, wear a woollen, flannelette or heavy-cotton shirt, then a jumper or a second woollen shirt. Over all this, a water-repellent and wind-resistant jacket or parka will keep you warm in sub-zero weather. The parka's advantages include roominess for freedom of movement, and inside circulation of air to help eliminate perspiration dampness.

Pants

Woollen pants or wind- and water-repellent ski pants tucked into the tops of your boots will keep your legs warm. Flap or zippered pockets are handy for keeping valuables in and snow out.

Winter fun

(a) Start with 'long johns' and two pairs of socks . . .
(b) Next a flannelette shirt, woollen trousers and heavy boots . . .
(c) Then a woollen turtleneck jumper
(d) In colder weather, add a light jacket, woollen cap or hat, and wear shoepacks
(e) In very severe cold, put a water-repellent jacket over all other clothes, and add mukluks.
(f) Wear woollen mittens with water-repellent mittens over them
(g) Wear two pairs of socks

Wear layers of loose-fitting clothing

Mitts

Knitted woollen mittens or mitten liners inside water-repellent over-mittens are best. Ordinary gloves are not warm enough in sub-zero cold, even with an outer mitten; however, a pair of gloves may be useful around a bivouac (temporary camp) in milder weather.

Light-cotton gloves will give you flexibility to work around the camp. When your hands get cold, slip them back into your mittens to get them warm again. Place your hands under your arms if they get really cold; once warm, you can put on the mittens again. Leather gloves may be useful for working around the fire.

Headwear

Your head is the single best control you have over body temperature. A woollen cap that can be pulled down over the ears should be the first layer, then your insulated parka hood, and finally the hood of your wind parka. The varying use of these three layers will give you a wide range of temperature control.

Points to remember

- All clothing should be loose fitting, not binding, with closures at ankles, wrists and neck.
- Insulating thickness is warmth.

- Ventilate before you sweat. Change damp articles of clothing such as insoles, socks and mittens.
- Use a wind-protection layer.
- Use your head—uncover to cool, cover to warm.
- Increase your metabolism (rate of chemical absorption of food by the human body). Exercise will cause your body furnace to work harder to keep you warm in the cold, so feed it well.

What to take

Following is the basic personal kit for a winter camper. You should use a suitable pack, leaving room for your share of the Patrol gear and food.

To wear

- underwear (flannelette pyjamas or long johns)
- two pairs of woollen socks
- appropriate footwear
- a flannelette or woollen shirt
- pants—wool or ski type
- a woollen jumper
- a parka
- woollen mittens with water-repellent mittens over them
- a woollen cap

To pack

- bedding
- pyjamas or tracksuit
- a winter sleeping bag
- extra bed-socks
- a foam pad
- a plate bag containing a knife, fork, spoon, plate, bowl and cup
- a teatowel

Toiletry

- a towel
- soap and container
- a comb and mirror
- a toothbrush and toothpaste
- talcum powder/deodorant
- personal toiletries

Clothing

- two pairs of extra socks
- extra handkerchiefs
- moccasins
- extra woollen mittens

What to wear

Winter fun

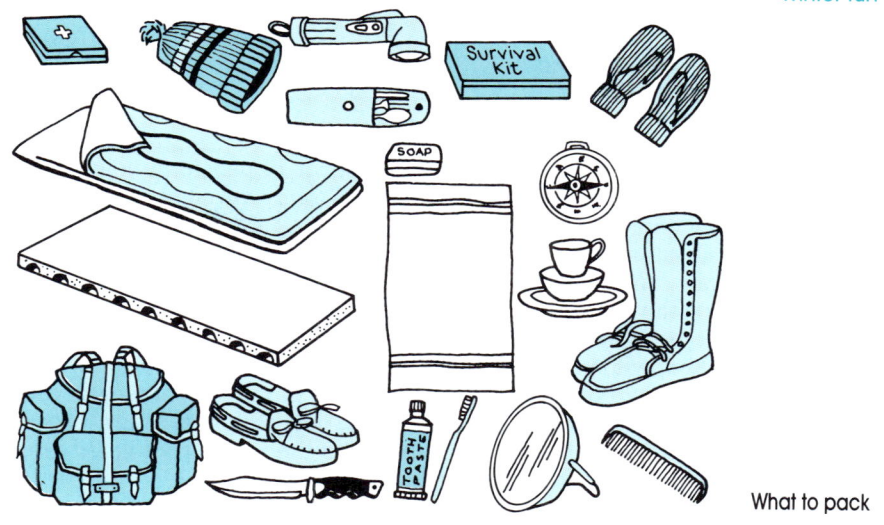

What to pack

Miscellaneous

- notebook and pencil
- an emergency kit (pocket)
- a personal sewing kit
- matches in a waterproof container
- a candle and torch
- a first-aid kit
- a compass
- a whistle
- a pocket knife

Patrol items

Patrol equipment

Following is a sample list of the basic Patrol items you will need for winter camping. Adjust accordingly for longer trips and larger groups:

- tents (as many as required)
- an axe and bow saw
- a kitchen utensil kit
- a dishcloth or mop
- two teatowels
- two canvas buckets
- a wash basin
- a billy with small, medium and large pots with lids
- a frying pan
- a burner stove and fuel container
- a length of soft wire
- 60 metres of cord
- detergent
- a file and sharpening stone
- steel wool
- a clothing and tent-repair kit
- a fire grid (optional)
- oven mitts.

Patrol items

469

How to get there

Travel plans depend on how long you have, where you are going, the weather, the snow conditions, and the number of people in your party. The one-day expedition is easily organised. The overnight or weekend hike will call for more planning of details, including the number of people going, the organisation, food and menus, equipment and programs.

Choose your camp well before dark. It takes longer to make a comfortable camp during the winter than at other times of the year. Remember, also, that darkness comes much earlier in the winter.

Before any expedition sets out, it is a good idea to notify the authorities (police, rangers, and so on), and a member of the group committee, of your intentions—the time of your departure, route, destination, a return checkpoint, and the time limit set for return—so that if the party is not heard from by a certain time, people can start searching for you.

If you are planning to move to your campsite using human power, the use of snowshoes or cross-country skis is a necessity. A toboggan or sled should be used to carry group and individual equipment except for a small pack for each person carrying the necessities: a thermos of hot drink; dried food; a second pair of woollen gloves; a first-aid kit or survival kit.

A well-run party will travel at a speed to match the abilities of the travellers and the severity of the weather. A five-minute stop every half hour is a good rule of thumb. The stop is not intended so much to catch your breath as to cool off in order to prevent sweating, and to have a drink.

During a stop, check for white spots on the cheeks (frostbite) and cold, numb, tingly feet and hands. If eyes are aching, put on polarised sunglasses (on bright days, these should be on all the time), because you do not want to risk snowblindness. Nobody should rest in the snow during a stop, because this can cause snow to melt on clothing. Sit on the toboggan, a log or rocks, if necessary.

Weather precautions should be taken before you travel both to and from the camp. The most important concern is the temperature, including the wind-chill factor. In winter conditions, when temperatures drop too far, you do not travel even if this means staying in the camp for longer than planned. Weather forecasts on radio or television or in the newspapers should be carefully studied, and in camp, the temperature and wind conditions should be checked before you break camp.

Use the chart in Table 9.1 in order to determine your course of action.

- If the result is in the *little danger* area, travel is possible with normal precautions.
- If the result is in the *increasing danger* area, it is best to stay in the camp. Travel should be attempted only in emergency conditions, and frequent checks for frostbite should be made.
- If the result is in the *great danger* area, you must remain in your tents, leaving them only to do essential camp work, and for the shortest time necessary.

Distances travelled should be much shorter than those planned for summer hike or camp. Get some idea of your abilities by doing a full dress rehearsal, using a fully loaded toboggan. Be very careful not to overexert yourself to the point of perspiring.

Table 9.1 Wind chill chart

Wind speed (km/hr)	Temperature (°C)									
Calm—no wind	10	4	−1	−7	−12	−18	−23	−29	−34	−40
8	9	3	−3	−9	−14	−21	−26	−32	−38	−44
17	4	−2	−9	−16	−23	−31	−36	−43	−50	−57
25	2	−6	−13	−21	−28	−36	−43	−50	−58	−65
33	0	−8	−16	−23	−32	−39	−47	−55	−63	−71
42	−1	−9	−18	−26	−34	−42	−51	−59	−67	−76
50	−2	−11	−19	−28	−36	−44	−53	−62	−70	−78
58	−3	−12	−20	−29	−37	−46	−55	−63	−72	−81
67	−3	−12	−21	−29	−38	−47	−56	−65	−73	−82

Note: Wind speeds over 67 km/hr have little additional effect.

Little danger to a properly clad person | *Increasing danger* *Danger of freezing exposed flesh* | *Great danger*

If possible, your route should lead across country. Following travelled roads means losing half the fun, and it also exposes you to any wind. Going across the country, you have the occasional protection of trees and ridges. Frozen streams, rivers and lakes may seem easy and ideal route for part of the way, but travelling on frozen waterways should be done *very carefully*. If possible, you should stay away from frozen water unless you are absolutely sure the ice is sound.

Trail breaking

People with neither skis nor snowshoes will have to break cross-country trails. A good plan is to hike in single file, taking turns as 'lead'. At a given interval or distance, the lead person 'peels off' by stepping aside until the group passes, and then brings up the rear—now going easily in the well-broken trail. The new lead takes a turn at breaking the trail, and so on, until all members share the work of walking through the fresh snow.

Trail breaking

… Fieldbook for Australian Scouting

Transporting gear

For transporting bulkier gear, a toboggan or wide-runner sled is best. Although the ordinary narrow-runner sleigh or bobsled may be fine on a snow-covered road or well-packed trail, on cross-country treks the runners will probably cut through the snow crust. This could cause a pulling problem, thereby upsetting the hike timetable and tiring everyone out.

Toboggan

Loading the toboggan

It is important to know how to load and lash the equipment on the sled or toboggan properly. The following method is a good one.

1. Lay a large piece of canvas on the toboggan. It should be large enough to turn up on all sides and ends and to cover the load completely. You can also use this canvas as a shelter or a windbreak at the campsite.
2. Distribute the load equally so the toboggan will track properly. Make sure the load is packed squarely, nothing sticks out over the edges, and it is not top heavy.
3. When the load is stowed, cover it snugly with the canvas, then start lashing it to the toboggan. Start the lashing rope at the front of the toboggan, crossing over the top, down through the side ropes, back up and over, and so on, to the rear. Bring the lashing rope back up to the front of the toboggan in the same way and secure it with a clove hitch.
4. After you have completed the lashing, you can secure axes, shovels, spare skis and snowshoes on top of the load. Keep these extra items to a minimum.

Time spent in making a neat, secure job before you set out will save time on the trail.

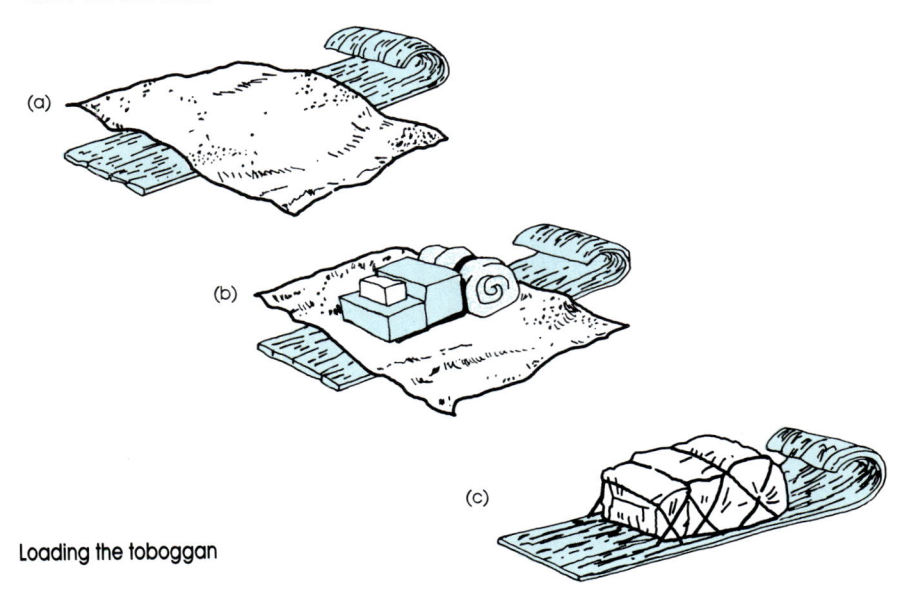

Loading the toboggan

Winter fun

Towing the toboggan

Towing the toboggan

The toboggan is best handled by a crew of three people: two towing, one behind holding the mush rope. The person on the mush rope is in charge, and directs the other two who are pulling. To make the team go slower, the musher calls out 'hi'; to make it move off or go faster, 'mush'. The musher is responsible for holding the toboggan back when going downhill, keeping it straight on the sides of hills, and steering it around holes, trees and other obstacles.

The mush rope is hooked to the stern of the toboggan, and the musher holds the free end by the hand. The musher should not tie the rope around the waist, because this will make it hard on the team if he/she falls or holds back.

The harness rope is passed under the upturned bow of the toboggan or through the towing holes on the bow. The two forward ends are passed over the shoulders of the first person in front of the toboggan, across the chest, and then hooked back into the steel rings by the snap fasteners.

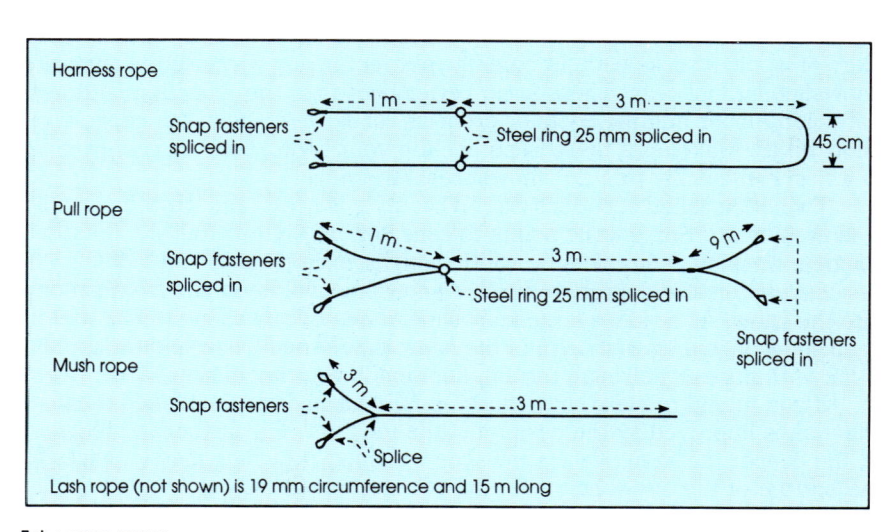

Toboggan ropes

The pull rope is fastened into the steel rings of the harness rope by the snap fasteners, and the forward end is fastened over the shoulders of the second person in the same way that harness rope is fastened to the first.

If the load is heavy, or the going is hard, additional pull ropes and more people may be necessary.

The musher must get all the work possible out of the team and must be constantly on the job, calling to the team, making sure the ropes between the front people are tight, and that each is doing a fair share of the work. Thirty minutes is a good shift for each team, although this will vary depending on how hard the going is.

Toboggan team on skis

If a toboggan team is travelling on cross-country skis, the herringbone technique will usually be used for climbing a hill. If the hill is steep, another team may be harnessed to the team on the toboggan.

Snowshoes

Snowshoes are an important part of winter hiking equipment. You must choose snowshoes carefully; unless you get a good-quality pair of the size and model suited to your weight and size, you will have an unhappy time on the trail. Fragile, poorly made snowshoes can mean broken frames and sagging webbing.

Walking in snowshoes produces much strain on the winter hiker: there is the constant weight of the human body, the wrenches from half-buried stumps, submerged brush, and fallen trees and rocks. The wood of the snowshoe frame must be reasonably light and flexible, but tough and capable of holding its shape.

Soft-soled moccasin boots, large enough to let you wear two or three pairs of woollen socks without binding your feet in any way, are the favourite snowshoeing footwear. There is no better boot than the moccasin, although flat-soled rubber hunting boots or ordinary rubber overshoes can be worn on short hikes. Make sure there is no heel on your boots, because the grinding of a heel can quickly ruin the snowshoes' stringing.

Two often asked questions are, 'What style is best?' and 'How big should a snowshoe be?' Some basic points to consider are styles available, flotation, traction, tracking ability, length, width, weight, front turn-up and binding.

Flotation is the degree to which a snowshoe will keep you from sinking into the snow. As a rule, a large snowshoe of almost any shape works well in deep snow on level ground. When the snow is deep and loose, and the ground is flat with little or no rough terrain, flotation is very important.

If you intend to wear snowshoes on hilly ground, you will need *traction*. Traction is improved by the position of the toe cord. The farther the toe cord is, the deeper the front of the snowshoe will sink. Attaching metal devices to the bottom of the snowshoe will improve traction. It is best to attach them directly beneath the ball of the foot so the full weight of the body will ensure a good grip or bite.

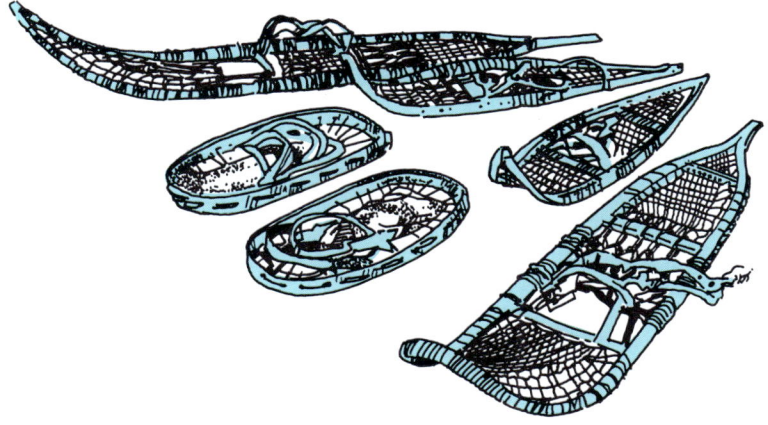

Types of snowshoes

Tracking is simply how well the snowshoe follows the foot. Each time the foot is raised, the toe of the snowshoe should rise up and the tail should drag directly behind. The key to good tracking is the ability of the boot toe to move through the snowshoe toe hole. Snowshoes with a high turned-up toe usually track best because the toe does not catch in the snow. The tail should be heavier than the toe. If you lift a snowshoe by the binding, the tail should drop immediately.

Dimensions are always a compromise. Longer and wider snowshoes naturally have a greater flotation, but the size adds weight. Dimensions also affect a snowshoe's performance, so you must be careful to choose the right size and weight.

- *Length:* Long snowshoes track better but are difficult to handle when making turns.
- *Width:* Unless you are very tall, a shoe more than 25 centimetres wide will tire you because you will be walking with your feet apart.
- *Weight:* Every kilogram on the foot is as tiring as five on the back. Because size adds weight, use as small and light a snowshoe as possible.

Front or toe turn-up on the snowshoe reduces the problem of the snowshoe catching in the snow. If there is too big a turn-up, the snowshoe may crack the wearer on the shins.

The *bindings* used on snowshoes are as important to the snowshoer as the bindings on skis are to skiers. The binding must allow the toe of the boot to move up and down easily through the toe hole in the snowshoe. At the same time, the binding should hold the foot firmly and allow no side play.

The simplest way to bind your foot to a snowshoe is to loop a 2 cm length of lamp wicking over your toes and pass two ends the stringing to either side of the toe hole, then diagonally across the toe, then fasten them above the heel. Unless you know exactly the right way to tie and adjust a homemade harness of this type, however, it is likely to give you trouble. The average snowshoer will find the manufactured harness the best. This is a simple leather pocket or toe cap open at both ends and lashed to the stringing of the shoe. The toe fits into the cap, and the straps from either side run back around the ankle.

Caring for snowshoes

Except for the person who uses snowshoes all through winter, maintenance is easy and can be done once a year.

At the end of the winter season, give the wood and webbing a coat of marine spar varnish. Allow this to dry, then rub lightly with fine steel wool or sandpaper. Then apply a second coat of varnish. (The sandpapering is important in order to ensure the coats hold together well.) A third coat is a good idea but not necessary. The finished job should leave the wood and webbing looking shiny.

Do not varnish your binding harness. If these are leather, treat with a good silicon leather treatment.

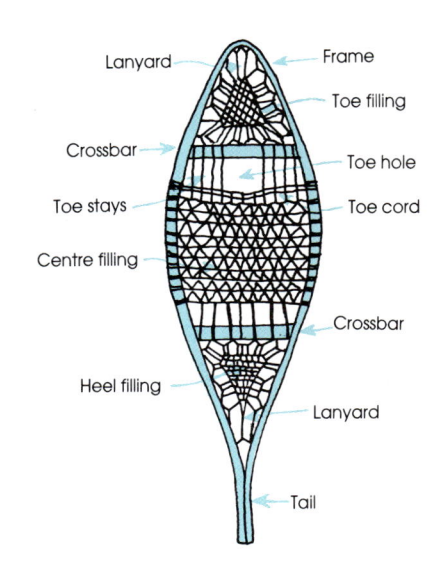

Parts of a snowshoe

Snowshoe materials

Wooden-framed snowshoes remain the ones that most snowshoers choose. The wooden frame is usually white ash, and the lacing is raw untanned cowhide. Although rawhide is tough and will withstand considerable wear, it loses much of its strength when wet. To protect the wood and the rawhide from moisture, they are heavily coated with marine spar varnish.

Some manufacturers use nylon cord for lacing. Both these are waterproof, although nylon tends to wear quickly on breakable crust snow.

Metal frames are also used today, and magnesium and aluminium frames are the most common. Metal frames must be anodised or coated in order to prevent snow from sticking to them.

Plastic snowshoes give problems because of the limitations of the material. They are too flexible, break in cold temperatures, and develop a bowed appearance, the toe and heel pointing up. They do have the advantage of low cost and light weight, however.

Mal de raquette

There is a sort of snowshoe cramp that may slow snowshoers up to disable them for a number of days. This condition was called *mal de raquette* (snowshoes illness) by a French Canadian. People who are new to snowshoeing may at first have cramped muscles and cords from overexertion. Thigh and calf muscles seldom used in ordinary walking will soon react to the unusual gait of snowshoeing. Rest and massages with liniment will usually help lessen the cramps. Begin with short trips, gradually building up to long trips, and you will soon overcome *mal de raquette*.

Skis or snowshoes

Many people today own either skis or snowshoes. If you do not have snowshoes, you can either buy a pair or hunt around for a set of instructions and make your own.

If you want skis you will have to buy them, because they are too difficult to make by yourself.

A combination of these two snow-travel methods may be used, some people using skis, others using snowshoes. If you are planning to travel on snow in a group, the ones using skis should know what they are doing so they do not hold the group back. A novice skier can delay a party, which is something you cannot afford to have happen.

Snowshoeing is fun because it may be a new activity to many people, but do not plan on going too far the first time you wear snowshoes. Most people learn to snowshoe reasonably quickly, but you need the practice in order to handle the exertion of a longer hike in this footwear. Remember, too, that travelling by snowshoe means travelling slowly, because they were not built for speed.

Making camp

When selecting tents for winter camping, you have to keep in mind needs that are different from those considered for summer camping. You have to consider weight, numbers of people, space and warmth. Ventilation is another consideration because it is tempting to zip up tight on a cold night.

Setting up and striking camp should be practised before the camp actually takes place so everyone knows what to do. Standing around while things are getting organised can lead to frostbite.

A warm shelter should be set up as soon as possible after you have had a hot drink and taken a short break to change socks. An area, protected from the wind by a hill, bluff or grove of trees, should be chosen for the campsite.

Camp setup

A suggested drill for a five-member team is as follows.
- Two people unpack the toboggan, light the stove, and get water on for a hot drink. Three people stamp out an area for pitching the tent, first wearing snowshoes, then without snowshoes, until the snow is firmly packed down.
- As soon as the snow is packed down, three people pitch tents.
- By this time the water should be ready for a hot drink. Caution should be taken to ensure clothing does not become wet from perspiration or snow. If clothing is opened up to cool down, it should be secured again in order to retain body heat.
- Once the tents are set up, sleeping gear should be stowed inside to ensure it remains dry and free from snow. Sleeping bags should not be unrolled until ready for use.

Fieldbook for Australian Scouting

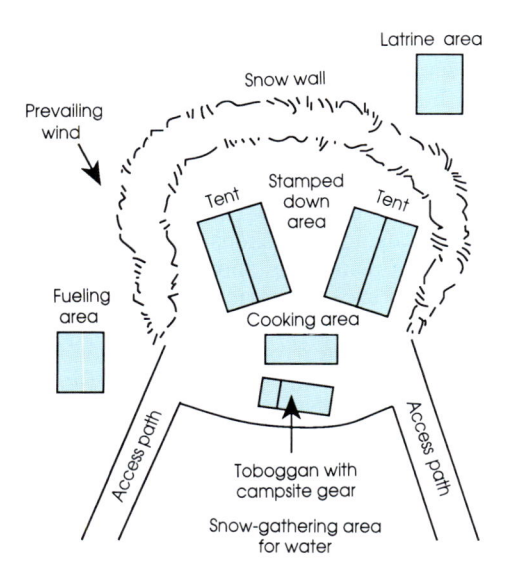

Campsite layout

- The tent should not be used as a gathering place, and, as much as possible, people should remain outside the tents in order to keep snow, from feet and clothing, from accumulating inside the tent. Remember that snow will melt in the tent, from body heat, and that wet equipment is uncomfortable as well as dangerous.

Putting up shelters

When you pitch your tent, it is important to take a careful look at your surroundings. Find out which way the wind blows and from which direction most storms blow up. Then pitch the tent with its back to the wind and bad weather.

To finish campsite development, increase the wind protection by building a snow wall around the edges of the campsite stamped-down area. Equipment should be lined up outside on groundsheets or other waterproof material (except sleeping systems and a change of clothes, which are placed in the tent). Place all group equipment (ice chisel, snowsaw, rope, hatchet, and so on) on the toboggan near the tent.

Remember to keep everyone busy because this will prevent chilling.

Pitching your tent

On hard ground

If you are camping in timbered country, be sure to check for trees growing within 30 metres of your tent: dead branches may fall on you if the wind gets heavy.

(b) The pole may lie on the ground or be lashed higher

(d) If tied rocks are not heavy, pile other rocks against them

Taut-line hitches

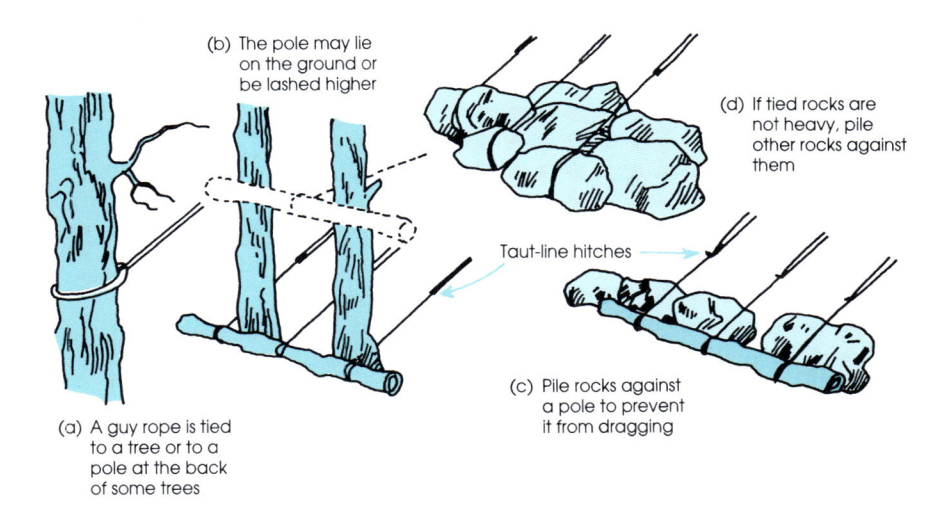

(c) Pile rocks against a pole to prevent it from dragging

(a) A guy rope is tied to a tree or to a pole at the back of some trees

Pitching on hard ground

If the ground is frozen and you cannot drive wooden stakes in, try using metal pegs or long nails. If you feel these are too heavy to carry, or if they are not available, you will require some other method of holding your tent down.

One way is to tie the guy lines to heavy rocks or logs. Another is to cut poles from dead falls (branches) lay them alongside each tent, tie the guy lines to them, and anchor them with heavy rocks or heavy logs or, alternatively, brace them behind trees.

A third method is to sew a valance to your tent. A *valance* is a flap of cloth sewn along the bottom of the wall at the floor line. The flap is usually sewn along the sides but may also be sewn on the ends. After you pitch your tent, pack snow or lay blocks of ice on the valance for a secure setup.

On snow or soft ground

When there is snow on the ground or when you are camping in any place where the ground is not firm enough to hold tent stakes, you can use 'dead men' to hold your tent in place.

'Dead men' are made from short stubby sticks, rocks or short pieces of logs. Bury these objects in a hole after tying the tent guy lines to them.

Crossed sticks work very well. Dig a hole about 30 centimetres deep and 30 centimetres in diameter in the snow or soft earth. In the bottom, place two crossed sticks about 30 centimetres long and 2.5 centimetres in diameter. Then loop a short piece of line under the sticks, and tie a bowline in each end of the line. The two ends of the line should extend to just above ground level. Fill in the hole, and stamp down on the soil or snow. Loop the guy line through the two bow-line loops and use a taut-line hitch exactly as if you were tying the guy line to a tent stake.

(a) Heavy log

(b) Rock buried in snow

(c) 'Dead men' crossed sticks buried

Two bow-line loops

Guy rope taut-line hitched

Pitching on snow or soft ground

Snow shelters

Snow makes the job of building shelters easy. If you do decide to try building a snow shelter during a winter camp, there are two things you must remember:
1. Be sure there is plenty of ventilation, especially when you are heating or lighting the inside by candle or a gas stove. Choose your site so that snow slides or drifting snow will not choke these ventilation holes. You will not need a lot of fresh air, but you will need a steady supply of it.
2. Building a snow shelter can be hot work, so go slowly so you do not soak your inside clothes with sweat. Snow is such a good windbreak and insulator that in any type of snow shelter with a fire inside, overheating will be more of a hazard then freezing.

At the same time your snow shelter is built, have some protective material such as boughs, bark and a plastic or rubber groundsheet, between you and the snow floor.

Tree-base shelter

A tree that has been partly buried by a drift can make an excellent shelter. Dig the snow out from around the tree and down to the base. Make the space large enough so you can sit comfortably. Cover the top with branches and evergreen boughs.

Snow cave

A hole dug into the side of a deep drift makes an excellent emergency shelter. Remember to dig at right angles to the prevailing wind so the entrance will not become blocked with drifting snow. Use a block of snow, or roll a snowball to block off your entrance hole.

Building a fire adds warmth, cheeriness, dries you out, and gives you something to do while waiting for rescue.

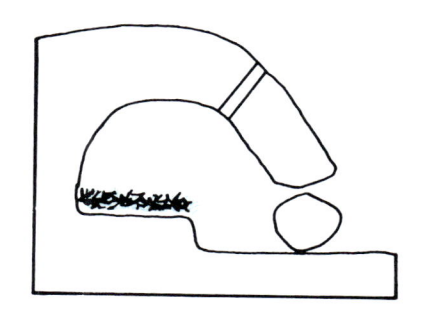

Tree-base shelter

Snow cave

Build your fire on a platform of logs so your shelter floor does not become a soggy mess. You can build this platform with wet logs, and they in turn will be dried out from the heat of the fire for use as fuel later on.

Bedding

When it comes to bedding, you have a choice of sleeping bags or blankets. Which one you choose depends on your personal taste, how cold the nights are, how much weight you can carry, and what you have or can afford to buy or make.

Airspace is the secret of good insulation, whether you are using a sleeping bag or blankets. The thicker the insulation, the warmer you will be. Fluffy loosely woven materials that provide tiny air pockets make the best sleeping gear. For below-zero temperatures, a sleeping bag should have not less than 1.45 kilograms of down filling or 1.9 kilograms of Dacron Fibrefill II.

Whichever type you use, air your bedding every morning as early as possible. During the night, your body gives out a great deal of moisture that is absorbed by your bedding. If the bedding is not thoroughly aired, it will stay damp, and if the nights are cool, you will stay damp too.

Undress and dress inside your sleeping bag. Put on fresh dry underwear at night and sleep in it. Unless you perspire during the night, you can dress over it and wear it all day.

Use a foam pad under your sleeping bag. An air mattress will be too cold unless you put a thick layer of newspaper or spare clothing between it and your bag. Fluff up your sleeping bag to put plenty of air in it, and lay it out on top of the newspapers. If you put the newspapers under your groundsheet, they will become soggy and wet, making it difficult to dispose of them at the end of the camp. If you keep them dry, you can burn them.

If you do not have a sleeping bag, you can make a warm bed of blankets by folding them so there are no side or bottom openings. Use blanket pins to secure them so they will not come apart in the middle of the night.

Tests show that when a person is sleeping, 75% of the heat loss is downward, and only 25% is up through the top of the bedroll. This means that to sleep warmly, you need three layers under you for every layer on top.

Night wear

Suitable sleeping clothes will vary, depending on the temperature and the type of shelter you will be using (cabin, open-front bivouac or tent). In any case, a complete change of clothing from fresh tracksuits to dry socks is a must for comfort and warmth. Change from the skin before turning in for the night. Keep your head out of the sleeping bag, or your breath will condense inside and form a layer of frost. Wear a woollen cap or hooded sweatshirt so you do not lose the heat generated by your body. If you are worried about frostbite on your nose, a piece of gauze stuck across your nose with adhesive tape is a quick and easy safeguard.

Fires for cooking and warmth

Fires have a number of functions: they can provide warmth and light, they provide heat for cooking, and many people find a cheerful fire mentally uplifting.

As a source of warmth, a fire has limited value in winter. Standing around an open campfire in winter, as your would in summer, is next to useless. Cold air, drawn in to feed the fire and as part of the convection current its heat creates, simply places you in a cold draught. It is better to pitch your tent in some sheltered spot, and place your fire in front of the door, where you will receive the heat from the fire but not from the draught.

An alternative to a fire is a tent heater. Operated and handled carefully, a tent heater is safe to use inside. Remember to never fill or ignite a heater inside a tent. Place the heater in a suitable position inside the tent, having tested it unlit beforehand to check for tipping.

You must take two precautions when using a tent heater: remember that the heater uses air in its working, so proper ventilation must be available, and tent flaps should never be sealed shut in the winter, even when the heater is not being used.

The tent must not be allowed to become too warm, especially if it is banked by snow for insulation. If the tent is too hot, the snow becomes like ice, losing the insulating value and beginning to melt. This will cause unwanted dampness in your tent and equipment.

You should also be aware of a condition known as 'tent-eye', an uncomfortable eye irritation caused by the prolonged use of tent heaters. To prevent this, air the tent periodically.

Tent heaters and fuel add weight, so you should consider this carefully before taking them along on a winter camp.

When using a fire for winter cooking, location is very important. As in summer camping, the fire should be well away from the tent and equipment. Build the cooking fire in a sheltered place, because any breeze will cut down its heating ability. Before lighting the fire, dig an area in the snow down to the ground level. If you do not do this first, your fire will melt its way down there.

Lighting a fire in winter may be more difficult, so take some firestarters with you. A supply of dry kindling, wood shavings and dry tinder should be carried in a small plastic bag as an emergency supply. When collecting firewood, look for wood that has not been buried in the snow—these contain ice crystals that must be melted then dried out by the heat of your fire before the logs can be burned as fuel. Remember to keep a billy of water boiling on the fire at all times for emergencies.

An alternative to an open wood fire is the camp stove. A pressurised stove is the best choice because an unpressurised one loses its ability to work well in very cold temperatures. A stove has the advantage of being portable if winds shift, so you can keep it sheltered. Cooking inside tents should be discouraged because of the high risk involved. If the weather is so cold that cooking cannot be done outside, you should first consider breaking camp instead of cooking inside.

As with tent heaters, stoves should be filled and lit well away from the tents.

Using a fire to provide light is usually unnecessary in a winter camp because the light reflected off the snow is enough. Besides, standing around a winter campfire can be very, very cold. The best way to enjoy a fire is from the coziness of your sleeping bag, looking out into the night from your tent.

As a rule, consider using a lantern in winter, because torch batteries have a very short lifespan in the cold.

Food and menus

Winter-camping menus are a little different from those you would prepare for summer outings. Refrigeration is not a worry, but the freezing of some foods can cause a problem. As in summer, the weight of food supplies should be kept to a minimum.

Meal preparation, cooking and cleaning up take longer during winter camping. The cold slows things down, and more time is spent gathering wood, melting snow for water, and setting up the kitchen area. Plan your menus in advance of your trip, making sure a good hot breakfast is ready early every day.

In winter camping, you need high-energy foods because you burn a lot more energy hiking, skiing and working. Following are a few suggestions:

- oatmeal
- bacon
- prepared biscuit and pancake mix
- molasses
- golden syrup
- honey
- dehydrated milk
- vegetable soup
- meats and eggs
- frozen meat
- fish
- Milo
- dried meat
- salt
- butter
- tea
- cocoa
- prunes
- dried apricots
- raisins
- nuts
- chocolate
- egg powder
- sardines
- potatoes
- fruitcake
- biscuits
- cheese
- canned goods
- hard sweets.

A good tip is to prepare food such as baked beans or stews, at home and to freeze them into individual serving sizes; all you have to do is heat one of these servings for a quick, easy meal on the trip.

Hot beverages such as tea, coffee, soups and hot chocolate give energy and heat and are great morale boosters.

Keep the following points in mind when planning your winter menus.

- Weight–food value: when possible, buy dehydrated or freeze-dried foods to save space and cut down on weight. At the same time, remember to include foods of high fat and sugar value.
- Temperature: foods that spoil when they freeze, such as fresh fruits and vegetables, should not be included.
- Do not stick to pot-and-pan cooking. Try cooking food in aluminium foil or a tin can, skewer or spit. You can try broiling using a tennis-racket broiling grill. These cooking utensils are light and do not take up much space. Also, foods cooked using these tools are an interesting change from plain, boiled dishes.
- Remember that the salt content of dehydrated (prepared) foods will be much higher. Salt lightly, if necessary, before serving.

Water for cooking

Take the same precautions for purifying water in the winter as you would in summer camping. See the introduction on water purification in Chapter 3: Campcraft, page 167.

Eating snow to quench your thirst is not a good idea, but using snow water for tea and other hot drinks is fine. Soft snow makes very little water for its bulk, so dig deeper and use the granular snow. Ice is even better if it is available, but chip it first for melting otherwise it will 'burn'.

If you are near water, chop a hole through the ice. Cover your waterhole with loose snow in order to stop it from freezing quickly, and mark it so no one will get a wet foot or leg.

Make your waterhole do 'double duty' by using it as a fishing hole.

Sanitation and hygiene

Garbage and waste-water disposal must be planned carefully. All garbage, including pot and plate scrappings, should be placed in a garbage bag and taken away with you. Burnable garbage should be burned if a fire is used, and tin cans flattened and also taken away. With the heavy use of camping areas, burying garbage is not a good alternative. You should remember this rule: if you carry it in, you carry it out.

Waste water from washing-up or cooking should be poured carefully into a hole dug for the specific meal. The hole should be 150 to 200 millimetres deep into the ground if it can be dug. Otherwise a deep hole in the snow (to ground level if possible) should be used. Because a grease trap will be difficult to set up, strain the water through a dish cloth and shake out the food particles in the garbage bag.

When you are melting snow for water, mark out an area for use, and do not go into it for any other reason.

Washing dishes should be done as soon as possible after the meal is eaten. The cooking pot should be scraped out and put back on the stove filled with soapy water. A second pot of clear water should also be put on. While you are eating, these two pots will heat up.

The first pot is the washing-up pot, the second your rinsing pot. A teaspoon of bleach should be added to the rinsing water. Unless you rinse your dishes a second time in clear hot water, you may have the slight taste of chlorine left on the dishes. You can avoid this by splitting your rinsing water and putting bleach in only one pot.

Personal cleanliness is a must, especially in a winter camp where it is very tempting to forego the morning and nightly rituals because of the cold. Regular washing when you get up, before meals, after certain camp jobs, and after using the latrine, is important for health, sanitation and safety.

Keep a pot of water on the edge of the fire at all times for washing and for when warm water is required (first aid). A basin, soap and towels should be kept handy. (*Note:* use aluminium basins because they are much lighter than stainless steel ones.)

Latrines should be the individual hole variety unless regular toilets are available. Carry a small garden trowel to make your hole (150–200 millimetres deep) if the ground is diggable. If the snow cover is very deep or the ground is frozen, dig a generous hole in the snow to ground level if possible.

A flattened half roll of toilet paper kept in a ziplock or other plastic bag should be part of your personal kit. This paper is also useful as paper towel, or even as tinder if the need arises.

When choosing a site for the latrine, agree on an area away from the campsite, water source and any tracks. After using the latrine, mark it with a deadstick so others will not use the same spot.

Camp hints

Cold metal

Be careful not to touch very cold metal with your bare hands or a cold metal cup with the lips, because you may lose some skin or lip.

If you do touch cold metal and feel yourself sticking to it, stay calm, stay still, and get someone to pour lukewarm water over the 'stuck' area until you can gently pull yourself free.

Night watch

If everyone has proper sleeping equipment, there should be no need for a night fire; it only disturbs other campers and no one gets a proper rest. If your sleeping bag is not designed for extremely cold weather, it is a good idea to keep a warmup fire going and a fire-watch setup to keep the fire going all night.

If you do build a fire, do not bother with a reflector: tests have shown that a reflected fire set in front of a tent only increases the temperature inside the tent by about one degree over that provided by a fire without a reflector.

If the snow is not too deep, scrape it away to bare ground where you plan to build your fire. Place stones or logs on the ground for a base on which to build your fire. Without this, the heat from the fire will thaw the ground under the base, making a muddy mess.

Keeping warm

On hikes, a parka or jacket should be allowed to hang loose. If you become too warm, pump in fresh air by grasping the jacket or parka at the bottom, pulling it outwards and bringing it back several times. When you are resting, the parka cord or sash should be lightly tightened in order to keep in the heat.

To avoid chilling during the regular rest stops, get in a sheltered spot, pair off and sit back to back on packs with a groundsheet around each pair. This back-to-back method gives a good deal of warmth.

If your feet are wet from perspiration or melting snow, change your socks and insoles immediately. You can do this even in severe weather if you get out of the wind.

If you suspect frostbite, set up camp and treat it. Do not try to keep moving if one party member is suffering frostbite. Remember that if frostbite is deep, and footwear is removed, the feet will swell to such an extent that it will be impossible to get the footwear on again.

Winter tools

You have to take extra care when handling an axe in frosty weather: even the sharpest blade may bounce off a solid piece of frozen wood or glance off a knot, and the blade edge may chip and nick.

One of the most useful items for winter camping is the bow saw. It will do twice the work with half the effort, and it cuts easily even if there is frost in the wood.

Axes, saws, knives and shovels can easily be lost when placed on the snow. Have a definite place for tools. If you are working away from the campsite, place your axe or saw where it will not be covered—for example, in a stump or dead tree or on a branch.

Let us make a sleigh

A sleigh is a great way to carry some of the gear to your next winter camp and it makes a great autumn Patrol project.

You require about 12 metres of 1×2 clear pine and 250 grams of 37 millimetre brass screws. Although the diagram shows how you can make your own runners, an old pair of skis will do the trick as well.

When you have finished building the sleigh, you can paint it in Troop or Patrol colours.

Winter fun

(a)

A		80 cm (x 2)
B		67.3 cm (x 2)
C		49.5 cm (x 2)
D		33 cm (x 2)
E		15.2 cm (x 2)
F		162.6 cm (x 2)
G		61 cm (x 6)
H		99.1 cm (x 4)
J		21.6 cm (x 2)
K		175.3 cm or skis (x 2)

- Wood must be soaked in boiling water for at least 2 hours before you try to bend it
- Run a saw cut for 35 cm through the thickness of the ski. Use a piece of veneer or plywood, and glue in place. Form a bend. This method requires no soaking

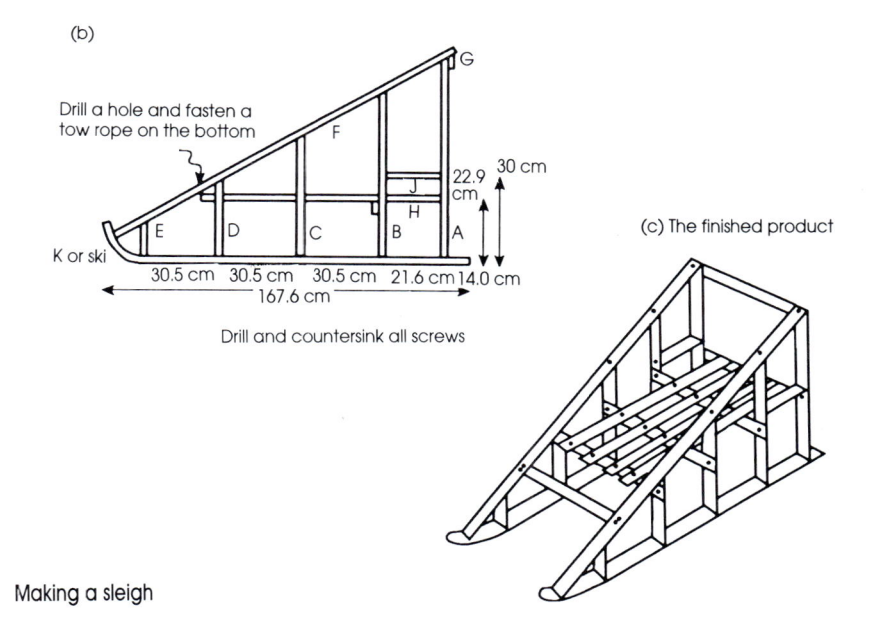

(b)

Drill a hole and fasten a tow rope on the bottom

K or ski

30.5 cm 30.5 cm 30.5 cm 21.6 cm 14.0 cm

167.6 cm

22.9 cm   30 cm

Drill and countersink all screws

(c) The finished product

Making a sleigh

487

Notes